THE
OFFICIAL
HISTORY
OF THE

FIFA
WOMEN'S
WORLD
CUP™

▲ The story of the FIFA Women's World Cup is told in displays at the FIFA Museum. The showcases feature objects from the tournaments as well as original artwork portraying the players who have starred in them.

▶▶ Overleaf: Spain celebrate winning the 2023 FIFA Women's World Cup.

Copyright © FIFA 2025

© FIFA, FIFA's Official Licensed Product Logos, and all brand elements, designs and trade names of FIFA and FIFAe tournaments, events and products are copyrights and / or trademarks of FIFA.

© 2025 International Olympic Committee ("IOC") - All rights reserved. Logos and trademarks of the IOC as well as emblems, mascots and any other Olympic items and properties shown in this publication are copyright protected and/or are trademarks of the IOC.

First published in 2019 by Welbeck

This edition published by Welbeck
An Imprint of HEADLINE PUBLISHING GROUP LIMITED

Created and written by:
FIFA Museum
Seestrasse 27
8002 Zurich
Switzerland

1

Apart from any use permitted under UK copyright law, this publication may only be reproduced, stored, or transmitted, in any form, or by any means, with prior permission in writing of the publishers or, in the case of reprographic production, in accordance with the terms of licences issued by the Copyright Licensing Agency.

Cataloguing in Publication Data is available from the British Library

ISBN: 978-1-03542-189-3

Printed in Dubai

Headline's policy is to use papers that are natural, renewable and recyclable products and made from wood grown in well-managed forests and other controlled sources. The logging and manufacturing processes are expected to conform to the environmental regulations of the country of origin.

HEADLINE PUBLISHING GROUP LIMITED
A Hachette UK Company
Carmelite House
50 Victoria Embankment
London EC4Y 0DZ

The authorised representative in the EEA is Hachette Ireland, 8 Castlecourt Centre, Dublin 15, D15 XTP3, Ireland (email: info@hbgi.ie)

www.headline.co.uk
www.hachette.co.uk

For the avoidance of doubt, all references to the World Cup, and mentions of records gained, be they in relation to attendances, appearances, goalscoring, etc., refer to the women's game. We do not reference men's football unless explicitly stated.

THE
OFFICIAL
HISTORY
OF THE

FIFA WOMEN'S WORLD CUP™

THIRD EDITION

Contents

Foreword	7
Introduction	8
Italy 1970	12
Mexico 1971	16
FIFA takes centre stage	22
China PR 1988	24
China PR 1991	36
Sweden 1995	50
Atlanta 1996	64
USA 1999	74
Sydney 2000	88
USA 2003	98
Athens 2004	112
China PR 2007	124
Beijing 2008	138
Germany 2011	152
London 2012	166
Canada 2015	180
Rio de Janeiro 2016	200
France 2019	214
Tokyo 2020	234
Australia & New Zealand 2023	248
Paris 2024	270
Records	284
FIFA Museum	286

The History of the FIFA Women's World Cup

It is my pleasure to bring you this third edition of the FIFA Museum's history of the FIFA Women's World Cup, updated to include the story of the 2023 tournament in Australia and Aotearoa New Zealand, along with the Tokyo 2020 and Paris 2024 editions of the Women's Olympic Football Tournaments.

Women's football is going through a period of phenomenal growth, and has seen the FIFA Women's World Cup establish itself as one of the pillars of global sport, just three decades after the first edition, in 1991. With every tournament, the number of girls taking up the game grows, as does the number of professional players and teams.

Every FIFA Women's World Cup creates new stories, iconic moments, unforgettable memories and household names who deliver career-defining performances on the greatest stage of all, and the 2023 edition of the tournament was certainly a special one, inspiring any young woman seeking footballing glory.

This book tells the story not just of today's superstars, but also of the trailblazers who paved the way for the current era, and without whom women's football would not be where it is today.

As we look forward to the next edition of the FIFA Women's World Cup, in Brazil, in 2027, let us celebrate the rich history of women's football and dream of its bright future together.

Yours in football,

Gianni Infantino
FIFA President

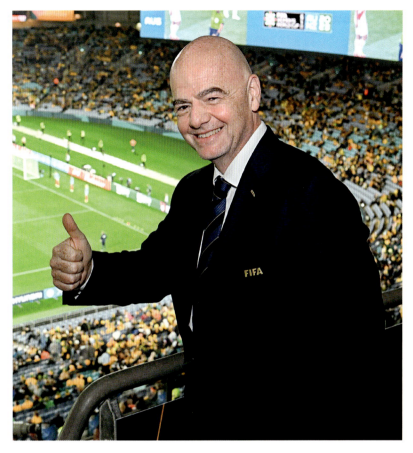

President's foreword

Introduction

Women have been playing ball games for as long as men have. In Homer's *Odyssey*, written nearly 3,000 years ago in the eighth century BC, ball games are referenced twice, most famously when Nausicaa, the princess of the Phaeacians, discovers the shipwrecked Odysseus while singing and playing with a ball at the seaside alongside her maidens:

> When the handmaids and Nausicaa had eaten their fill, they threw off their veils and turned to playing ball, and white-armed Nausicaa was their leader as they sang.

It is not the purpose of this updated edition to retrace the history of ball sports and the women who have played them, but to celebrate those women who, since 1991, have been able to reach the pinnacle of one of those ball games – association football. The FIFA Women's World Cup sits at the top of the footballing pyramid and, in this book, we pay tribute to those players who have achieved the ultimate accolade of being crowned a "world champion". However, this volume is not just about the select few who have achieved that honour. Also included is every single player who has experienced the privilege of taking part in a FIFA Women's World Cup and, to that end, every single game played at the finals is analysed in detail and every last goal, penalty save, team sheet and booking is listed.

Women's football is unique in the sense that the allure of Olympic gold remains a very real aspiration for the elite players, unlike the men's tournament, which is age-restricted. Fixtures in the women's tournament have been full international matches since they were first included in the Olympic programme at the 1996 Games in Atlanta and, as such, they are covered here in the same detail as the FIFA Women's World Cup. Also included are three world tournaments that took place before the launch of the FIFA Women's World Cup. In 1970 and 1971, two unofficial tournaments were held outside of

◀ These two photos are perhaps the first time that women were photographed playing football. The first ten weeks of 1895 were bitterly cold in England, and so the snowy pitch could indicate that these pictures were of the British Ladies' Football Club in training for the Crouch End match.

▲ Illustrations were a popular way of telling the story of football matches and the first game contested by the British Ladies' Football Club was no different. This illustration makes reference to the crowd thinking that one of the players was a boy, whom they christened Tommy!

the confines of established administrative structures, which proved to be important stepping stones towards reviving women's football after 50 years during which it was largely banned and frowned upon. The third pre-World Cup competition covered is the 1988 International Women's Football Tournament held in China, which was to all intents and purposes a trial World Cup ahead of the real thing, which followed three years later, in 1991. But first, let's wind the clock back more than 100 years to 1881 and transport ourselves to the city of Edinburgh, Scotland, and specifically to the ground of Hibernian Football Club…

On 7 May that year, 22 women took to the field for what was likely the first football match played under association rules by women. Billed as a game between England and Scotland, the reality was opaquer, with the teams believed to be made up of actresses hired for a moneymaking tour comprising ten matches, of which the encounter in Edinburgh was the first. At the second game in Glasgow, the *Nottinghamshire Evening Post* reported that "a few roughs broke into the enclosure, and, as these were followed by hundreds soon after, the players were roughly jostled and had prematurely to take refuge in the omnibus which had conveyed them to the ground. Their troubles were not, however, yet ended, for the crowd tore up the stakes and threw them at the departing vehicle, and but for the presence of the police some bodily injury to the females might have occurred". Two further matches were similarly brought to a premature end as the tour moved on to Lancashire, across the border in England. If not exactly the most auspicious start to the women's game, the good ladies of Victorian and Edwardian England were not to be put off. Bound up with the struggles for women's suffrage, Nettie Honeyball (a pseudonym) founded her British Ladies' Football Club in 1894 along with Lady Florence Dixie. The club's first match took place at Crouch End Athletic Ground in north London the following year and drew a crowd of 10,000. The publicity ahead of the match stirred up a good amount of interest and newspaper reporters were dispatched to cover the game. Photos were taken of the two teams before the match and an illustrator was there to sketch impressions. "I founded the association late last year," Honeyball told a journalist at the *Daily Sketch*, "with the fixed resolve of proving to the world that women are not the 'ornamental and useless' creatures men have pictured. I must confess, my convictions on all matters where the sexes are so widely divided are all on the side of emancipation, and I look forward to a time when ladies may sit in Parliament and have a voice in the direction of affairs."

The munitionettes

Needless to say, most men in the football world were not receptive to the idea of women playing "their" game. The Football Association in London (The FA) discussed the growing popularity of matches between men's and women's teams on 25 August 1902 at an FA Council meeting. Afterwards, instructions were issued to all of its affiliated members to refuse permission for their players to play against "lady football teams". This was not the last time that The FA would take action, if not to ban women's football, then to make it very difficult for it to flourish.

A very real challenge to the established order came during the First World War, when women were drafted into the factories in place of the men who had gone to fight at the front. The era of the "munitionettes" who worked in the armaments factories was born. As well as football being played for leisure, it became apparent that fans, deprived of their regular diet of football, would pay to watch

◀ Photo of Dick, Kerr's Ladies Football Club of Preston from 1920. They were one of hundreds of women's teams that sprang up towards the end of the First World War. Dick, Kerr's represented England in a series of matches played against France in 1920, and on their return from Paris they attracted a crowd of 53,000 to a Boxing Day match against St Helens, a world record that stood for half a century.

Introduction

matches involving women. Many of the games during the conflict were therefore played to raise charitable funds for wounded soldiers, or for those suffering from trauma. Matches between women and recovering male soldiers also became very popular. The growth of women's football during the First World War was not just a British phenomenon. The same was happening in France, and in 1916, Alice Milliat established the Fédération des Sociétés Féminines Sportives de France, which organised a national championship for teams from Marseille, Reims, Paris and Toulouse. The female footballers of both nations would forge close relationships after the hostilities ended in 1918.

Banned

New Zealand had been the first country to give women the vote in 1893, followed by Australia in 1902, Finland in 1906 and Norway in 1913. Just ten days after the armistice of 11 November 1918, the United Kingdom extended the franchise to certain women (eight million were initially eligible) and, in 1920, the USA followed suit. Women were finding a voice, and it was in this atmosphere that the famous Dick, Kerr's club invited a French selection comprising the Fémina and En Avant clubs to travel to England to play a match. In the event, it turned into a four-game tour that was billed as England against France. The first of those matches took place on Friday, 30 April 1920, with 25,000 spectators turning up to see the English women beat the French 2-0 in Preston with goals from Florrie Redford and Jennie Harris.

In October 1920, Dick, Kerr's made the return trip to Paris to play four matches, which were again labelled as France against England. In the 20 November 1920 issue of *Le Miroir des Sports*, André Glarner reported in positive terms about the tour. "The match between a French team and an English team was played in front of 10,000 spectators and proved a real success." On Boxing Day 1920, following the team's return from Paris, a record crowd of 53,000 watched Dick, Kerr's play St Helens at Goodison Park in Liverpool, and it was reported in the press that a further 14,000 fans were locked outside. By mid-1921, the first genuine superstar of women's football was emerging – a 16-year-old by the name of Lily Parr. She had scored 43 goals in her first season for Dick, Kerr's and then, on 17 May 1921 at Longton Park in Stoke, she sensationally struck five goals in a match against France. The following day, the *Daily Mirror* newspaper ran a story with two photos of Parr, one showing her scoring her fifth goal and the second of her being chaired off the pitch at the end. Women's football seemed on the cusp of something great. But then, in December 1921, The FA in London passed a resolution that was to leave a stain on football, and the men who ran it, for generations to come.

The minutes of The FA Council's meeting of 5 December 1921 read:

"Complaints having been made as to football being played by women, the Council feel impelled to express their strong opinion that the game of football is quite unsuitable for females and ought not to be encouraged. Complaints have also been made as to the conditions under which some of these matches have been arranged and played, and the appropriation of receipts to other than charitable objects. The Council are further of the opinion that an excessive proportion of the receipts are absorbed in expenses and an inadequate percentage devoted to charitable objects. For these reasons the Council request clubs belonging to the association to refuse the use of their grounds for such matches."

▼ A match in the French Cup from 1923. Football carried on in France and elsewhere after the ban in England, but other countries soon followed suit. Matches became more and more difficult to organise and the women's game gradually disappeared from public view.

Introduction

◀ Lily Parr was perhaps the most famous female footballer until the rebirth of the women's game in the 1970s. Born in St Helens in 1905, she started off as a forward but moved further back down the field as she got older, finishing as a goalkeeper. She finally retired in 1951, and is regarded as a lasting source of inspiration for all women footballers who fought for recognition in the years following the 1921 ban.

While not explicitly banning women's football, only the use of The FA's members' grounds, the effect was to do just that. For 50 years, the women's game all but disappeared, and not just in the United Kingdom. In 1921, The FA was still the most influential football body in the world – and its move had a chilling effect worldwide, with some countries banning women from playing altogether. Socially and culturally, it was frowned upon. However, the flame was never entirely extinguished. There were many examples around the globe of women refusing to accept the status quo, and by the late 1960s, there was sufficient interest for the game to rise again – a reflection, perhaps, of the liberalising of society in that decade.

A new dawn
1969 proved to be a breakthrough year. In November, Piedmont in north-west Italy played host to the Coppa Europa per Nazioni, an unofficial European Championship organised by the newly created Federazione Internazionale Europea Football Femminile (FIEFF). The FIEFF had sent out letters of invitation, one of which landed on the desk of the Danish FA (DBU) in Copenhagen, who forwarded it on to Denmark's most famous club, Femina. They were one of the three teams that travelled to Italy to join the hosts, along with England and France. In the semi-finals, Italy beat France 1-0 in Novara with a goal from Aurora Giubertoni, and Denmark defeated England 4-3 in Aosta, a match in which Sue Lopez scored a hat-trick but still ended up on the losing side.

The Danes went on to play Italy in the Final before a very respectable crowd at the Stadio Comunale, but it was the Italians who established their pre-eminent status with a 3-1 victory. Two of their goals came from 16-year-old forward Maurizia Ciceri and the other was scored by Stefania Medri, another 16-year-old, who liked to copy her hero Omar Sívori by playing with her socks down by her ankles. Earlier, England had beaten France 2-0 in the match for third place, one of the goals being scored by Lopez. It was her fourth of the tournament, which meant she finished as the top scorer. In her book, *Women on the Ball*, she recalled the historic events of November 1969:

"It was a thrill to play foreign opponents on some of the best pitches in Italy. The crowds of 10,000 plus were beyond anything we had experienced. We felt elated to have been part of such an exciting tournament, after the small-scale events in England, and it was remarkable to find everything taken more seriously. It was how we imagined that the professional male players were treated, with nice hotels, beautiful venues and respect, especially from the press."

In the 1960s, Italy was perhaps the most important country for the revival of women's football, certainly within Europe. It had the most sophisticated set-up of any country in the world, and Italian teams and leagues became the first to attract business and commercial sponsors, notably Martini & Rossi. The iconic drinks company was central to the next big development in women's football: two world tournaments that it sponsored and for which it provided the trophy. The first was held in Italy in 1970 and the second in Mexico a year later. Though they cannot be regarded as World Cups in the true sense – as they were both organised by private enterprise and only one of the teams, France in 1971, was run by their national football association – they were both hugely instrumental in changing perceptions of the women's game, which would lead ultimately to the creation of the Women's World Cup in 1991. And so it is with these two tournaments that we start our story…

ITALY 1970

COPPA DEL MONDO
TROFEO MARTINI & ROSSI

In 1970, Italy staged what newspapers of the time referred to as the "Coppa Rimet" of women's football. Although just seven teams took part, six of them from Europe, it was a groundbreaking event. Wearing hastily purchased AC Milan shirts after their usual kit went missing, Denmark won. In the Final, they beat hosts Italy 2-0 before a huge crowd in Turin to win the "Golden Angel" trophy.

Host cities and stadiums

History made in Turin

The Stadio Comunale had seen many great matches playing host to Juventus and Torino in men's football, but it also has a special place in the history of women's football as the venue for the first world championship Final played by women. In all, seven stadiums were used during the nine-day tournament.

▶ The official 1970 tournament poster.

NORTH FIRST ROUND		SOUTH FIRST ROUND	
ENG 5-1 FRG		MEX 9-0 AUT	
DEN 6-1 FRG		ITA 2-1 SUI	

SEMI-FINAL	SEMI-FINAL
DEN 2-0 ENG	ITA 2-1 MEX

MATCH FOR THIRD PLACE
MEX 3-2 ENG

FINAL
ITA 0-2 DEN

Background to Italy 1970

The success of the unofficial 1969 European Championship persuaded the organisers to lay even more ambitious plans for the following year – a world tournament. It was scheduled for July 1970 and nine teams were earmarked to take part: Austria, Czechoslovakia, Denmark, England, France, Italy, Mexico, Switzerland and West Germany. Central to the plans was the sponsorship of drinks company Martini & Rossi, who donated the Trofeo Martini & Rossi for the winners. In the event, two nations dropped out. France withdrew their entry, while the Czechoslovakian team were absent after failing to obtain visas to travel to Italy. The Prague Spring had seen travel restrictions eased and Denmark's BK Femina had even visited Prague, where women's football was well organised, but the subsequent Soviet invasion and clampdown meant that there was to be no Eastern European presence at the tournament.

▲ Denmark played the entire 1970 tournament in the colours of AC Milan after their usual white shirts went missing. Back row (left to right): Jana Mandiková, Maria Ševčíková, Helene Østergaard Hansen, Irene Christensen, Kirsten Evers, Lone Hansen, Inge Kristensen and Lilly Hansen. Front row: Joan Nielsen, Ann Lindh, Jytta Termansen, Birgit Nielsen, Kirsten Schäeffer, Joan Thomsen and Marianne Nielsen.

Northern section

Stadio Luigi Ferraris, Genoa
7.07.1970, **3,000**

ENGLAND 5-1 WEST GERMANY

Briggs (2) 1 9, Stockley 25p, Cross 30, Dolling 61 — Arzdorf 49

Loffi ITA

ENG • Kath **Everitt** - Sue **Knowles**, Valerie **Cheshire** - Not known, Jill **Stockley**, Valerie **Reid** (June **Foulke** 55) - Paula **Rayner**, Angela **King**, Joan **Briggs**, Barbara **Dolling**, Louise **Cross**. *Harry Batt*

FRG • Maria **Nelles** - Anneliese **Probst**, Gaby **Marino** - Helga **Waluga**, Gaby **Wilke** (Christa **Seeliger** 55), Ruth **Rosenberg** - Elisebeth **Schuhmacher**, Margarethe **Holl** (c), Martina **Arzdorf**, Sieglinde **Schmied**, Sieglinde **Justen**. *Heinz Schweden*

Czechoslovakia withdrew, so Denmark played the already eliminated West Germany in an exhibition match.

Stadio Comunale, Bologna
8.07.1970, **5,000**

DENMARK 6-1 WEST GERMANY

Evers (3) 8 35 69, Christensen (2) 9 19, Østergaard Hansen 24 — Arzdorf 15

Acquadro ITA

DEN • Jytta **Termansen** - **Jacobsen**, Birgit **Nielsen** - Ann **Lindh**, Kirsten **Schäeffer** (c), Inge **Kristensen** - Maria **Ševčíková**, Helene **Østergaard Hansen**, Irene **Christensen**, Kirsten **Evers**, Jana **Mandiková**. *Svend Åge Pedersen*

FRG • **Nelles** - Schmid, Marino - Waluga, Wilke, Rosenberg - Schuhmacher, Justen, Arzdorf, Holl, Gisela **Glasmacher**. *Schweden*

Southern section

Stadio della Vittoria, Bari
7.07.1970, **6,000**

MEXICO 9-0 AUSTRIA

Rubio (2) 1 31, Vargas (4) 4 18 47 57, Huerta 8, Hernández (2) 49 61

Turco ITA

MEX • Yolanda **Ramírez** (Elvira **Aracén** 65) - Irma **Chávez**, Elsa **Salgado** - Cristina **García**, Rebeca Lara **Pérez**, Elsa **Huerta** - Alicia **Vargas**, Guadalupe **Tovar** (c) (María Acela **Nila** 56), Silvia **Zaragoza** (Patricia **Hernández** 40), Martha **Coronado**, María Eugenia **Rubio**. *José Morales*

AUT • **Kraus** - **Hackl** (**Zaupmann** 41), **Pinter** - **Svoboda**, **Kunter** (**Holzbauer** 62), **Exeli** - **Kastner**, **Ppai**, **Goldschmidt**, **Wegleiter**, **Zatlokal**

Stadio Donato Vestuti, Salerno
8.07.1970, **10,000**

ITALY 2-1 SWITZERLAND

Mella 15, Avon 70 — Ripamonti 54

Santopietro ITA

ITA • Wilma **Seghetti** - Adriana **Canepa**, Maria **Castelli** - Marisa **Mondo**, Rosanna **Cerutti**, Orietta **Bonanni** - Caterina **Molino** (Alfonsina **Isi** 24) (Emanuela **Pinardi** 45), Claudia **Avon**, Giuliana **Mella**, Enrica **Colla**, Elena **Schiavo**. *Giuseppe Cavicchi*

SUI • Margrit **Schwendimann** - Trudi **Moser**, Elisabeth **Copt**, Yollande **Dieng**, Anneliese **Staudenmann** - Madeleine **Boll**, Kathrin **Moser** - Ursula **Kaiserauer**, Rita **Odermatt** (c), Nadia **Ripamonti**, Nelly **Juillard**. *Jacques Gaillard*

Mexico cause a sensation

The seven teams were divided into two regions, one in the north of Italy and one in the south, with the two winners emerging to meet in the Final. The Czechoslovaks had been drawn in the northern section, but their withdrawal meant that the Danes had a free passage into the semi-finals, although they did play an exhibition match against the West Germans. The England v. West Germany game kicked off the tournament – the first-ever match in a "global" tournament – and Joan Briggs was quick off the mark, scoring in the very first minute. England won 5-1 to set up a semi-final meeting with the Danes. Inge Kristensen remembers that the Danish team only met their coach, Svend Åge Pedersen, on the platform at Copenhagen station before the journey to Italy. "It was a fantastic experience that we will never forget. We were a really good team, which we had supplemented from home with a few guest players from other clubs in the metropolitan area." Italy, meanwhile, won their first match in the southern region after a last-minute goal by Claudia Avon, a teacher by trade, secured a 2-1 victory against Switzerland. They were joined in the semi-finals by Mexico, the only non-Europeans in the tournament, who trounced Austria 9-0 in a remarkable game in Bari. Alicia Vargas, the young star of Mexican football, scored four goals, the first hat-trick at a world tournament. The victory meant that they would face hosts Italy in the semi-final at the Campo Vomero in Naples.

▼ Mexico were the only non-European team at the 1970 tournament. They surprised everyone by beating Austria 9-0 and finishing in third place.

Italy 1970

The Golden Angel

A trophy was commissioned for the 1970 tournament in Italy, and in a strong reference to the Jules Rimet Cup, the Winged Victory of Samothrace was chosen as the central motif. Unlike the Jules Rimet Cup, however, which portrayed an interpretation of the goddess Nike, the Nike figurine on this trophy was a replica of the sculpture in the Louvre. The trophy was also played for in 1971 in Mexico.

> "1970 was an amazing experience for us. We were proud to win the Cup, but also proud that we were pioneers in making women's football popular once again."
>
> BIRGIT NIELSEN, DENMARK

Italy and Denmark set up repeat of 1969 European Championship Final

▶ The Trofeo Martini & Rossi presented to the winners in 1970 and 1971. It is on permanent display at the FIFA Museum in Zurich.

For the second year running, Denmark and England met in a semi-final. One of the curious aspects of this tournament was that Denmark played their matches in the red-and-black stripes of AC Milan. When they arrived at their hotel in Bologna for their first-round match, a Russian football team was checking out and took the Danish kitbag by mistake. It meant a quick visit to a sports shop, where they came away with a set of Milan shirts. The Danes beat England in Milan in the first of the semi-finals with two goals from midfielder Kirsten Evers. The Final would be a repeat of the previous year's unofficial European Championship Final after Italy beat Mexico 2-1 in Naples, with both goals scored by their captain Elena Schiavo. There were some unsightly scenes at the end of the match when a fight broke out between the teams after the Mexicans had tried to claim the match ball as a souvenir. Italy's Enrica Colla was punched in the face and Claudia Avon was approached by another player with a broken bottle. The police had to wade in to stop the mêlée.

Mexico claim third place

The Mexicans made up for the disappointment of their semi-final defeat by securing third place in the tournament with a 3-2 victory over England. A shell-shocked England keeper Kath Everitt was beaten three times in the first 15 minutes. Vargas got the scoring underway in the third minute with her fifth goal of the tournament, which meant she finished as top scorer. The English fought back with two goals of their own, but it wasn't enough.

Denmark on top of the world

FINAL
Stadio Comunale, Turin
15.07.1970, **40,000**

ITALY 🇮🇹 **0-2** 🇩🇰 **DENMARK**

(Schiavo missed penalty 60)   Østergaard Hansen 18, Ševčíková 68

Cosentina ITA

ITA • Seghetti - Canepa, Cerutti, Mondo, Pinardi, Bonanni - Molino, Avon, Mella (Ketty **Rampon** 46), Colla, Schiavo. *Cavicchi*

DEN • Termansen - Joan **Nielsen**, B Nielsen - Lindh, Schäeffer, Evers - Mandiková, Østergaard Hansen, Christensen, Kristensen, Ševčíková. *Pedersen*

A huge crowd of 40,000 filled the Stadio Comunale in Turin with the expectant home fans hoping to see Italy crowned as the first world champions to add to the European title they had won the year before. This was a very high-profile game, with plenty of media attention. The Italian team spent the evening before the Final in the hotel used by Juventus. Meanwhile, there was also the customary complaint about the referee – the Danes were unhappy that the match would be officiated by an Italian. There was huge public interest and the kick-off had to be delayed by 30 minutes to let all of the spectators in. Only 24,000 had paid for their tickets and touts were selling them for double their face value of 1,000 lira before the gates were swamped and the ticketless fans let in. Former Italy and Juventus goalkeeper Giovanni Viola was at the game in his home stadium and was impressed by what he saw. "The level of football was impressive considering the short time women have been playing the game. Of course, there is a lack of experience and that sometimes affects technique, but the football ideas were there and Denmark have shown themselves to be very well organised. In general, they all respect roles and positions." Helene Østergaard Hansen gave Denmark a first-half lead, which they protected until ten minutes from time before giving away a penalty. The normally reliable Elena Schiavo, a track and field athlete with a powerful right foot, fired her effort over the bar, however, and with just two minutes to go the naturalised Czechoslovakian striker Maria Ševčíková secured the win for Denmark. Helene Østergaard Hansen was presented with a trophy representing Nike that had cost the sponsors two million lira and they were feted as world champions on their return to Denmark by the mayor of Copenhagen. There had been plans for a reception at the train station in the Danish capital, but the team arrived three and a half hours before schedule, so there was no one there to greet them. Their triumph had caused quite a stir in the country, and shortly after the team arrived home, a colour broadcast of the whole match was shown on TV with Østergaard Hansen as the co-commentator. As Inge Kristensen recalls, "When we won the Final, there was no limit to the media's coverage of us. We were honoured by all, and there was such a special feeling of stardom throughout that period."

▲ Birgit Nielsen holds the Golden Angel trophy after Denmark's 2-0 win over Italy in the 1970 Final.

▶ The medal won by Birgit Nielsen in 1970. Like the trophy, it features the Winged Victory of Samothrace in the centre.

◀ Denmark are world champions according to *La Stampa* newspaper in Italy amid scary scenes at the Stadio Comunale in Turin, where a huge crowd broke down gates in the crush to get in to see the Final.

MEXICO 1971

CAMPEONATO MUNDIAL DE FÚTBOL FEMENIL
TROFEO MARTINI & ROSSI

For three weeks in 1971, it seemed as if women's football would conquer the world. Over half a million spectators saw six nations compete for the title of world champions. In the group stage, 90,000 fans watched Mexico defeat Argentina – a new world record that was matched at their game against England. The Final against Denmark was watched by 110,000, a figure never since equalled. Fans witnessed a 15-year-old win the title for Denmark as Susanne Augustesen scored a hat-trick to retain the trophy for the Danes.

Host cities and stadiums

Echoes of Mexico 1970

A year on from what was already being regarded as one of the greatest World Cups, the best female players in the world followed in the footsteps of Pelé and co. and they played in the two most iconic stadiums in the country. The Azteca had been the scene of the epic Final between Brazil and Italy, while Guadalajara's Jalisco had witnessed one of the all-time great games between Brazil and England.

▶ Poster from Mexico 1971.

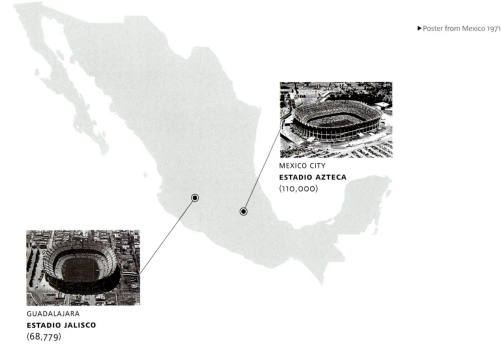

MEXICO CITY
ESTADIO AZTECA
(110,000)

GUADALAJARA
ESTADIO JALISCO
(68,779)

GROUP A			GROUP B		
MEX	3-1	ARG	DEN	3-0	FRA
ARG	4-1	ENG	FRA	0-1	ITA
MEX	4-0	ENG	DEN	1-1	ITA

	W	D	L	+	−	PTS		W	D	L	+	−	PTS
MEX	2	0	0	7	1	4	DEN	1	1	0	4	1	3
ARG	1	0	1	5	4	2	ITA	1	1	0	2	1	3
ENG	0	0	2	1	8	0	FRA	0	0	2	0	4	0

SEMI-FINAL
DEN 5-0 ARG

SEMI-FINAL
MEX 2-1 ITA

MATCH FOR FIFTH PLACE
FRA 3-2 ENG

MATCH FOR THIRD PLACE
ITA 4-0 ARG

FINAL
MEX 0-3 DEN

Story of the qualifiers

After the successful staging of the men's World Cup in June 1970, a two-day conference to discuss who would host the women's edition was held in December 1970 at the Ambassador's Hotel in Turin, Italy, with delegates from Austria, the Netherlands, Italy, England, West Germany, Switzerland, Spain and Mexico, as well as Franco Talanco of Martini & Rossi International. During the discussions, it transpired that Germany, Mexico, Spain and Switzerland were prepared to host the second World Cup, which was planned for 1971. In a second round of voting, Mexico was selected, no doubt inspired by the hugely successful men's World Cup held earlier in the year. Discussions then centred on the effects of altitude. A visit made by the Italy team to Mexico in October 1970 to assess the degree of public interest in women's football helped inform medical opinion; the Italian players showed no clear side effects.

The two friendly games between Italy and Mexico drew crowds of 30,000 and 70,000, proving to the organisers that it would be possible to stage a commercially viable tournament.

After the choice of country, it was agreed that of the six teams at the tournament, four should come from Europe and two from the Americas, one of those being hosts Mexico. A qualifying tournament was needed, as 15 nations were interested in taking part. In the event, only six matches were played, but one of them, the encounter between France and the Netherlands, was historic in its own way as it is the first match that FIFA records as an official international. It took place in Hazebrouck, in the north of France, between Dunkirk and Lille. In 1970, FIFA had sent out a letter to all 135 member associations enquiring as to the position of women's football in their country, and of the 90 that responded, only 12 said that they recognised women's football. One of those was France, but that did not include control of a French national women's team. FIFA's enquiry can now be seen as helping to kick-start the development of the modern game. It prompted the Dutch and French associations to take control of the women's national teams – hence the April 1971 match between the two being recognised as the trailblazing first. More member associations would soon follow suit but none of the other qualifiers for the Mexico tournament is regarded as official. Italy and England saw off Austria to take two of the European places, while Denmark joined the French after a 5-0 win over Sweden in their group. Argentina completed the line-up after beating Costa Rica.

▼ The French team posing for a pre-tournament photo at the Arc de Triomphe before departing for Mexico. Four months earlier, the French had qualified for the finals by beating the Netherlands 4-0 in what is regarded as the first official women's international match. The FFF and KNVB were amongst the first to bring women's football under the control of a national association affiliated to FIFA.

Mexico 1971

Estadio Azteca, Mexico City
15.08.1971, 90,000

MEXICO  3-1 ARGENTINA

Rubio (2) 21 49, Hernández 30   Cardozo 35

Giuseppe Cosentina ITA

MEX • Yolanda **Ramírez** - Irma **Chávez**, Bertha **Orduña**, Martha **Coronado**, Paula **Pérez**, Guadalupe **Tovar** (c), Elsa **Huerta**, Teresa **Aguilar**, Silvia **Zaragoza**, Patricia **Hernández** (Sandra **Tapia** 68), María Eugenia **Rubio**. *Víctor Manuel Meléndez*

ARG • Marta **Soler** - Ofelia **Feito**, Zulma **Gómez**, Teresa **Suárez**, Zunilda **Troncoso**, Angélica **Cardozo** (c), Virginia **Andrada** (Virginia **Cataneo** 69), Eva **Lembesis**, Betty **García**, Elba **Selva**, Blanca **Brúccoli** (María **Cáceres** 50). *Norberto Rozas*

Estadio Azteca, Mexico City
21.08.1971, 25,000

ARGENTINA 4-1 ENGLAND

Selva (4) 6 31 35 63p   Rayner 13

José López Torres MEX

ARG • Soler - Gómez (Feito), Cataneo, Suárez, Troncoso, Cardozo (c) (Cáceres), Andrada, Lembesis, García, Selva, Brúccoli. *Rozas*

ENG • Lillian **Harris** - Jill **Stockley**, Valerie **Cheshire**, Jean **Breckon**, Carol **Wilson** (c), Trudy **McCaffery**, Leah **Caleb**, Louise **Cross**, Janice **Barton** ■ 54, Paula **Rayner** (Gill **Sayell**), Chris **Lockwood**. *Harry Batt*

Estadio Azteca, Mexico City
22.08.1971, 90,000

MEXICO 4-0 ENGLAND

Rangel 5, Aguilar (2) 49 61,
Huerta 63

Stéphane Frère FRA

MEX • Elvira **Aracén** - Lourdes **de la Rosa**, Orduña, Coronado, Pérez, Tovar (c) (María **de la Luz Hernández**), Huerta, Alicia **Vargas**, Zaragoza, Eréndira **Rangel** (Aguilar 36), Rubio. *Meléndez*

ENG • Harris - Stockley (Lockwood), Cheshire, Breckon, Wilson (c), McCaffery (Marlene **Collins**), Caleb, Cross, Barton, Rayner, Yvonne **Farr**. *Batt*

Estadio Jalisco, Guadalajara
18.08.1971, 15,000

DENMARK 3-0 FRANCE

Augustesen 5, LL Nielsen
(2) 27 66

Antonio Salazar MEX

DEN • Birte **Kjems** - Solveig **Hansen**, Lis **Westberg Pedersen** (c), Ann **Andreasen**, Asta **Vig Nielsen**, Annette **Frederiksen**, Marianne **Kamp** (Bente **Jensen** 64), Inger **Pedersen**, Lis Lene **Nielsen**, Helene **Østergaard Hansen**, Susanne **Augustesen**. *Jørgen Andreasen*

FRA • Marie-Louise **Butzig** - Chantal **Serre**, Colette **Guyard**, Nicole **Mangas**, Marie-Bernadette **Thomas**, Betty **Goret** (Régine **Pourveux** 58), Jocelyne **Ratignier**, Claudine **Dié**, Marie-Christine **Tschopp** (c), Jocelyne **Henry**, Ghislaine **Royer** (Armelle **Binard** 55). *Pierre Geoffroy*

Estadio Jalisco, Guadalajara
21.08.1971, 20,000

ITALY 1-0 FRANCE

Schiavo 25

Derrick Caves ENG

ITA • Daniela **Sogliani** - Maria **Fabris**, Anna **Stopar**, Paola **Cardia**, Manuela **Pinardi**, Elena **Schiavo** (c), Aurora **Giubertoni** (Liliana **Mammina** 68), Manola **Conter**, Maurizia **Ciceri**, Claudia **Avon**, Elisabetta **Vignotto** ■ 64. *Giuseppe Cavicchi*

FRA • Butzig - Serre, Thomas, Guyard, Mangas, Goret (Pourveux 64), Binard, Ratignier, Henry, Tschopp (c) (Royer 47), Dié. *Geoffroy*

Estadio Jalisco, Guadalajara
21.08.1971, 13,000

DENMARK 1-1 ITALY

Østergaard Hansen 10   Avon 39

Jean-Pierre Minarich SUI

DEN • Kjems - S Hansen, Westberg Pedersen (c), Andreasen, Vig Nielsen, Frederiksen, Jensen, Pedersen, LL Nielsen, Østergaard Hansen (Lone **Nielsen**), Augustesen. *Andreasen*

ITA • Sogliani - Fabris, Stopar (Rosetta **Cunzolo** 17), Cardia, Maria **Castelli**, Schiavo (c), Carmela **Varone**, Conter, Ciceri, Avon, Vignotto (Mammina 50). *Cavicchi*

Group A

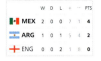

	W	D	L	+	-	PTS
MEX	2	0	0	7	1	4
ARG	1	0	1	5	4	2
ENG	0	0	2	1	8	0

▲ Mexico '71 had a very memorable mascot. Xóchitl was the very public face of the tournament and was described by the organising committee as representing the young female Mexican footballers who played football. The name means "flower" and has its origins in the culture of the Aztecs.

Group B

	W	D	L	+	-	PTS
DEN	1	1	0	4	1	3
ITA	1	1	0	2	1	3
FRA	0	0	2	0	4	0

Touchdown in Mexico

The five travelling teams arrived in Mexico in early August and were given an enthusiastic welcome. The hosts had developed a passion for the game that few elsewhere in the world could match, and the crowds turned up in impressive numbers to watch the 11 games that were played over the course of three weeks. "I don't think we knew what to expect. We had only played in the small qualifying tournament in Sicily, which was played on the park-type pitches we were used to," recalls England's Chris Lockwood. "And suddenly we were in the middle of World Cup fever in this huge glitzy, professionally staged, global tournament." The teams were certainly well taken care of, with all the airfares, hotels, playing kits and other expenses paid for by the sponsors. There was money to be made in women's football.

Records tumble

Mexico kicked off the World Cup with a 3-1 win over Argentina at the Azteca, which had witnessed Pelé and Brazil winning one of the all-time great Finals in the men's World Cup just over a year before. That opener was watched by a new world-record crowd for women's football of 90,000, beating the record set by the match between Dick, Kerr's and St Helens at Goodison Park on Boxing Day 1920. They followed this a week later with a convincing 4-0 win over England in front of another crowd of 90,000 to top the group. For a nation that had only been introduced to the game the previous decade, Mexico's progress was impressive, and it built upon the 9-0 victory over Austria in the previous year's tournament. Their star player, Alicia Vargas, failed to find the net, but she was still the face of the tournament and even featured on the cover of *Balón* magazine.

Joining Mexico in the semi-finals from Group A were Argentina, who comfortably beat England 4-1 in the other match in the group. Elba Selva scored all four goals for the Argentines against an England team that had caused controversy back home when the women selected to travel to Mexico had nothing to do with the newly formed Women's Football Association. Instead, the team was based on the Chiltern Valley club created by Harry Batt and his wife, June. A 13-year-old Leah Caleb, compared in the British press to George Best, was part of the England team. "We were banned for taking part in the unofficial World Cup. But they realised very quickly that they were being ridiculous and our bans were lifted." With such a young and inexperienced team, England finished bottom of their group and were left with a play-off for fifth place.

Lost in the desert

The second group, which was based in Guadalajara, saw all three games played at another iconic stadium – the Jalisco, scene of the epic Brazil-England match in the 1970 men's World Cup. The group featured the two best teams in the world at the time, Denmark and Italy. Having been represented by their famous club side Femina at both the 1969 European Championship and the 1970 World Cup, the newly formed Danish Women's Football Union preferred to pick a more representative team. Training camps were set up and trial matches played to determine the squad that would travel to Mexico. Helene Østergaard Hansen was the only player from the Femina club selected and as a result was the sole player to appear in all three tournaments, in 1969, 1970 and 1971. Her career went back to 1959 and the founding of Femina, when she and a group of other handball players were persuaded by the eponymous newspaper to switch to football. Inge Kristensen was appointed captain. The Danes saw the Italians as their fiercest rivals for the title and they were aware that they were up against a better-prepared team. On arrival in Mexico, the Danes were given a bus that broke down in the middle of the countryside on the way to their base in Guadalajara. As they faced the prospect of a long wait before being rescued, they were surprised to see the Italian team pass them in a fully modern coach. The suspicion was that the Italian sponsors of the tournament were laying on special services for the Italian team, but the Danes were picked up by their rivals. On the coach that day was a 15-year-old striker called Susanne Augustesen. The incident did not faze her and she scored the opening goal of the Danes' 3-0 win over France. Having missed out on the 1970 title, the Italians were determined to go one better this time around. Captain Elena Schiavo gave them a 1-0 victory over France, setting up a match with the Danes to determine who would finish top of the group and avoid the hosts in the semi-final. A 1-1 draw meant that the Danes would face the less-feared Argentines and the Italians would be up against hosts Mexico.

A noisy reception in Mexico City

SEMI-FINAL
Estadio Azteca, Mexico City
28.08.1971, **30,000**
DENMARK 🇩🇰 **5-0** 🇦🇷 ARGENTINA
LL Nielsen (3) 35 48 69, Østergaard Hansen 52, Frederiksen 64

Antonio Salazar MEX

DEN • Kjems - S Hansen, Westberg Pedersen (c), Andreasen, Vig Nielsen, Frederiksen, Pedersen, Kamp, Østergaard Hansen, LL Nielsen, Augustesen. *Andreasen*
ARG • Soler - Cataneo (Gómez), Feito, Suárez, Cardozo (c), Troncoso, Andrada, Lembesis, García, Selva, Brúccoli. *Rozas*

SEMI-FINAL
Estadio Azteca, Mexico City
28.08.1971, **80,000**
MEXICO 🇲🇽 **2-1** 🇮🇹 ITALY
Hernández (2) 7p 24p   Varone 6

Stéphane Frère FRA

MEX • Aracén - Chávez, Orduña, Pérez, Coronado, Vargas, Huerta (Tapia), Aguilar, Zaragoza, Hernández, Rubio (De la Rosa 65). *Meléndez*
ITA • Sogliani - Castelli, Stopar (Fabris 53), Cardia, Pinardi, Schiavo (c), Varone, Conter, Ciceri, Avon, Giubertoni (Mammina 43). *Cavicchi*

▲ A crowd of 80,000 watched Mexico's 2-1 victory over Italy in the semi-final at the Estadio Azteca. Note the pink-and-white goalposts!

The ill feeling between the Mexicans and the Italians that had marred the end of the 1970 semi-final flared up again in this final-four encounter. After moving to Mexico City from Guadalajara, the Italian team found their hotel surrounded by noisy Mexican fans on the eve of the semi-final, and they were kept awake all night. In the passionate atmosphere of the Azteca the following day, the Italians managed to silence the crowd with an early goal from Carmen Varone, but the Mexican response was superb. A minute later they were level. Patricia Hernández scored her second goal of the competition and her fifth over the two tournaments, and she added a second before half-time. No one had scored more in the first two World Cups. Try as they might, there was nothing the Italians could do to break down the Mexican defence, who had become masters at preserving a first-half lead. The hosts were in the Final and the Italians had fallen just short again. The other semi-final, played on the same day, had been a much more straightforward affair, with Denmark easily beating Argentina 5-0. There was a hat-trick for Lis Lene Nielsen and goals for Helene Østergaard Hansen and Annette Frederiksen as the Danes set up a tricky Final against the hosts.

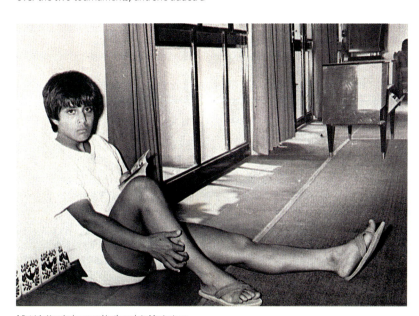

▲ Patricia Hernández scored both goals in Mexico's 2-1 victory over Italy in the semi-final. Following on from her strike in the first round against Argentina, this brace took her total to three, matching the number she had scored in the 1970 tournament. Over the two tournaments, no one managed to score more.

Hard lessons for England and Argentina

MATCH FOR FIFTH PLACE
Estadio Jalisco, Guadalajara
28.08.1971, **25,000**
FRANCE 🇫🇷 **3-2** 🏴󠁧󠁢󠁥󠁮󠁧󠁿 ENGLAND
Binard 12, Henry 22, Tschopp 32   Barton 10, Cross 17

Grecia del Ángel MEX

FRA • Butzig, Serre, Guyard, Mangas, Thomas, Goret, Binard, Ratignier, Henry (Royer 25), Tschopp (c), Dié. *Geoffroy*
ENG • Harris - Cheshire, Elsa **Salgado**, Teresa **Viguera** (Lockwood 36), Collins, Breckon, Cecilia **Gallegos**, Sayell, Rayner, Barton, Cross. *Batt*
Due to injuries, England fielded three Mexican players: Salgado, Viguera and Gallegos.

MATCH FOR THIRD PLACE
Estadio Jalisco, Guadalajara
4.09.1971, **50,000**
ITALY 🇮🇹 **4-0** 🇦🇷 ARGENTINA
Vignotto (3) 4 32 67, Schiavo 63

Antonio Salazar MEX

ITA • Sogliani - Fabris, Pinardi, Cardia, Cunzolo, Schiavo (c), Conter, Avon, Varone, Ciceri (Mammina 46), Vignotto. *Cavicchi*
ARG • Soler - Susana **Lopreito** (Cataneo), Andrada, Feito, Cardozo (c), Troncoso, Lembesis, Suárez, García, Selva, Brúccoli (Cáceres). *Rozas*

One unique aspect of the tournament was that each team played three matches regardless of the outcome of their games, and so the two teams placed bottom of their first-round groups – England and France – played off for fifth place. There were five goals in the first half, with France fighting back from 2-1 down to beat England 3-2 in Guadalajara. It was a disappointing end for England, but it did prompt major changes back home. The WFA (with the tacit approval of The FA) gained control of the women's team and 15 months later, they played their first official international, in a match against Scotland. Just as significantly, the infamous ban was consigned to history. Just how outclassed the England team had been was illustrated when Argentina, who had beaten the English 4-1, were then thrashed by Italy in the match for third place on the back of their 5-0 defeat at the hands of Denmark. The Italians won 4-0, with Elisabetta Vignotto scoring a hat-trick and the other goal coming from Schiavo.

Mexico 1971

15-year-old Augustesen wins the world crown for Denmark

FINAL
Estadio Azteca, Mexico City
5.09.1971, **110,000**
MEXICO 0-3 DENMARK
Augustesen (3) 28 42 51

Jean-Pierre Minarich SUI

MEX • Elvira Aracén - Irma Chávez (Lourdes de la Rosa), Martha Coronado, Bertha Orduña, Paula Pérez, Alicia Vargas, Elsa Huerta, Silvia Zaragoza, Teresa Aguilar, Patricia Hernández, María Eugenia Rubio (Eréndira Rangel 56). *Víctor Manuel Meléndez*

DEN • Birte Kjems - Solveig Hansen, Lis Westberg Pedersen (c), Ann Andreasen, Asta Vig Nielsen (Mona Lisa **Jensen** 65), Annette Frederiksen, Marianne Kamp (Bente Jensen), Inger Pedersen, Helene Østergaard Hansen, Lis Lene Nielsen, Susanne Augustesen. *Jørgen Andreasen*

There had never been a match like it in women's football before. The exact crowd figure may never be known. The tournament organisers put it at around 80,000, but the suspicion was that this was actually much lower than the real figure in order to maximise profits. What is beyond doubt is that this was the biggest crowd ever to watch a women's football match – bigger than the 1999 World Cup Final at the Rose Bowl or the 2012 Olympic Final at Wembley. And the star of the show was a 15-year-old. For Susanne Augustesen, the Final had the aura of an American spy movie. Aware of the distractions that the Italians had suffered on the eve of the semi-final, the Danes were taking no chances. For the night before the game, the Danish embassy surreptitiously arranged for the team to be dispersed to the private homes of embassy staff so as to get a good night's rest. And it worked. "We all slept well that night, and I wasn't really nervous before the game," remembers Augustesen. "We were excited because it was the Final. We went out into the stadium, over the athletics track and we looked up and saw all the people. It seemed to go on forever. But I quickly looked down and focused on the match. There were 110,000 spectators, but once the game started, I thought no more about it."

The pink-and-white goals were still there, an ever-present feature of the tournament, and after 28 minutes the Mexicans were picking the ball out of theirs after Augustesen gave Denmark the lead, much to the delight of the 300 Danes in the crowd. Augustesen had picked up a pass on the left from Lis Lene Nielsen and dribbled into the penalty area. "I shot straight at the goal and then she fumbled it. It really wasn't a very strong shot!" Augustesen remembers. There was panic among the Danes as the half drew to a close, as goalkeeper Birte Kjems recalls. "During half-time there was to be a parade of horses in the stadium. In the minutes before the break, the horses lined up behind my goal, ready for the show. But I have an allergy to horses and I immediately started sneezing and couldn't stop!" Half-time could not come soon enough.

In the second half, Mexico pressed but fell further behind after another defensive mistake. Goalkeeper Elvira Aracén played the ball out to a defender who had not noticed that Augustesen was lurking nearby. The Danish forward dispossessed her near the goal line, and with the goalkeeper off her line, scored from a tight angle. "During the match the Mexican team was very much focused on keeping an eye on Lis Lene, who was the tournament top scorer," Kjems remembers. "Susanne used this, and filled the space. She also had that special something that is so hard to describe. With her fantastic technique and speed, she settled the match."

Augustesen's third goal was the best of the lot. After being picked out in the box by a team-mate, Augustesen dribbled past a defender before unleashing a powerful left-foot shot which gave Aracén no chance. Denmark had retained their title. Mexico's key strength during the tournament had been the passion of their fans, but by the end they were applauding the Danes. But there was disappointment too. As Denmark were presented with the trophy, the stadium emptied, though there was a huge crowd to greet them on their arrival back at Copenhagen airport, sombreros and all, and for days they were fully in the media spotlight, especially their 15-year-old heroine.

◄▼ Denmark's Lis Lene Nielsen shoots as team-mate Susanne Augustesen looks on before a packed Estadio Azteca.

▼ Danish striker Susanne Augustesen beats the Mexican keeper but doesn't add to her tally of three goals in the Final.

Mexico 1971

▶ Ticket from the 1971 Final.
FIFA Museum Collection

◀ Youth and experience. Susanne Augustesen with the trophy, alongside Helene Østergaard Hansen. Østergaard Hansen was the only player to appear in all three Finals. She played in 1969, 1970 and 1971, and was the only player to win the titles in both 1970 and 1971.

An enduring record

The record attendance for a women's football match was broken three times within the space of ten months – all of them in Mexico. In late 1970, Mexico played the touring Italian team before 70,000 at the Azteca, breaking the record set 50 years earlier at Goodison Park, Liverpool, in the match between Dick, Kerr's and St Helens. Then, in the group stage, 90,000 saw Mexico's games against Argentina and England, a figure that was beaten a week later in the Final between Mexico and Denmark. No other women's match has ever been watched by so many people.

◀ Denmark captain Lis Pedersen lifts the Golden Angel as Denmark are crowned world champions for the second time. It would be another 20 years before the FIFA Women's World Cup took centre stage as the pinnacle of the world game.

> *I'm sure we won the championship in 1971 because we were the most cohesive team. Yes, of course the team also had stars but we were fighting for each other.*
>
> INGER TULLE PEDERSEN

▶ Lis Lene Nielsen, Birte Kjems, Susanne Augustesen and Annette Frederiksen proudly show off their medals.

◀ Denmark arrive back at Copenhagen airport. Back row (left to right): Annette Frederiksen, Lone Nielsen, Lis Pedersen (holding the trophy), Lena Schelke and Inger Tulle Pedersen. Front row: Solveig Hansen and Birte Kjems.

▶ Lis Pedersen with the Golden Angel trophy. Inger Tulle Pedersen looks on.

FIFA takes centre stage

FIFA takes centre stage

1970 FIFA circular no. 142 establishes the status of women's football in the member associations

1971 First official international recognised by FIFA between France and the Netherlands

1974 FIFA approves the staging of the Nordic Championship in Finland

1978 FIFA approves the staging of the Women's World Invitational Tournament in Chinese Taipei

1982 Germany becomes the 25th nation to play an international match

1983 FIFA approves the staging of the Guangzhou International Football Tournament

1986 The FIFA Congress in Mexico City puts the development of women's football more firmly on the agenda

1988 FIFA stages a trial World Cup – the International Women's Football Tournament in Guangzhou

1989 FIFA stages the first instruction course for women's referees

1990 Moldova and Romania become the 50th and 51st nations to play an international match when they meet in Bucharest

1991 FIFA organises the first FIFA Women's World Cup in China PR

1994 FIFA publishes its first official list of women's referees and lineswomen

1995 Ecuador becomes the 75th nation to play an international match

1995 Sweden hosts the second FIFA Women's World Cup

1996 FIFA organises the first Women's Olympic Football Tournament, at the Atlanta Games

1998 Uganda becomes the 100th nation to play an international match

1999 The USA hosts the third FIFA Women's World Cup

2000 The second Women's Olympic Football Tournament, at the Sydney Games

2001 Mia Hamm wins the first FIFA Women's World Player of the Year Award

It all began with the innocuous-sounding FIFA circular no. 142. Until then, FIFA's involvement in women's football had been merely to refer questions to the national association of the person enquiring. That changed on 3 March 1970. Under the presidency of Sir Stanley Rous, but driven by René Courte, the assistant secretary, FIFA dipped its toes in the water by sending out the circular to all its member associations asking as to the status of the women's game in the country. There were eight questions, the first of which asked simply "Does your federation officially recognise Football for women?" Ninety of the 135 associations answered and of those, 12 replied that they did – Algeria, South Africa and Upper Volta from Africa; Chinese Taipei, Singapore and Thailand from Asia; Guatemala and Jamaica from the Americas; and France, West Germany, Sweden and Wales from Europe. For the 78 who ticked the box indicating that they didn't recognise women's football, FIFA proposed the following in the circular. "If women's teams exist in your country, would it not be better to put them under the control of your federation than to allow national and international 'managers' to profit by them?"

The results of the survey were published in *FIFA News* no. 88 of September 1970 and the responses were varied. West Germany's DFB replied that on 21 March, just over two weeks after having received the circular, "a decision was taken to terminate the negative attitude towards women's football. At the next congress, regulations will be discussed to allow regular organisation of football competitions for women." France also indicated that it had created a Committee of Study to look into the question, but many of the responses were not positive, including one from an Asian association saying simply "May God have mercy on us." *FIFA News* stated that the association in question had better remain nameless!

Officially recognised international matches under the control of national associations affiliated to FIFA began in April 1971. The first, between France and the Netherlands in Hazebrouck, was played just three weeks shy of the 90th anniversary of the first unofficial match between Scotland and England in 1881. Italy played their first game in November that year, with Switzerland, Yugoslavia, Scotland and England joining the ranks in 1972. 1973 saw debuts for Finland, Sweden, Northern Ireland and the Republic of Ireland, while July 1974 witnessed the launch of the first officially sanctioned tournament under the auspices of FIFA – the Nordic Championship played in Finland. But progress was slow. By the end of 1975, just 36 internationals had been played, increasing to 125 by the end of the decade.

The number of official international matches didn't tell the whole story, however. Many more matches were being played unofficially, often between national teams and representative or club sides. And then there were matches played by national teams not recognised by their national associations. This was particularly the case in Asia, where the Asian Ladies Football Confederation staged championships in 1975, 1977, 1979, 1981 and 1983. None of these matches are recorded as official and it illustrated the need for formal control of women's football at every level. That came from a combination of initiatives from FIFA and the continental confederations.

In 1982, UEFA launched the first official European Competition for Women's Football, culminating in the Final between Sweden and England in 1984. The OFC followed with a small three-team tournament in New Caledonia in 1983, while the AFC celebrated merging with the Asian Ladies Football Confederation by staging the first official Asian Women's Championship in Hong Kong in 1986. It was at this time that Norway's Ellen Wille made her now famous speech to the 1986 FIFA Congress in Mexico City. The momentum in women's football had reached a tipping point.

▶ The number of official international matches played each year since the first in 1971.

Year	–	Count	Year	–	Count	Year	–	Count	Year	–	Count	Year	–	Count
1971	–	2	1982	–	37	1993	–	98	2004	–	280	2015	–	482
1972	–	5	1983	–	40	1994	–	146	2005	–	257	2016	–	437
1973	–	7	1984	–	35	1995	–	219	2006	–	430	2017	–	423
1974	–	12	1985	–	43	1996	–	188	2007	–	449	2018	–	614
1975	–	10	1986	–	65	1997	–	196	2008	–	367	2019	–	587
1976	–	14	1987	–	61	1998	–	262	2009	–	307	2020	–	207
1977	–	15	1988	–	81	1999	–	236	2010	–	514	2021	–	487
1978	–	26	1989	–	62	2000	–	265	2011	–	501	2022	–	681
1979	–	34	1990	–	99	2001	–	245	2012	–	405	2023	–	761
1980	–	20	1991	–	162	2002	–	289	2013	–	377			
1981	–	40	1992	–	68	2003	–	366	2014	–	554			

A framework for women's competitions

For the 30 years following the 1986 Congress, FIFA and the confederations created the organisational framework for international women's football. Of immediate concern was the establishment of a World Cup. In 1987, FIFA lent organisational support and know-how to the Women's World Invitational Tournament, staged in Chinese Taipei, a competition that had its origins nine years previously and was played with a mixture of national, representative and club teams. The following year, Hong Kong businessman and FIFA Executive Committee member Henry Fok persuaded the Chinese FA and the AFC to stage what was in effect a trial run for a World Cup. With the full backing of FIFA – it was even referred to as the FIFA International Women's Football Tournament in internal FIFA publications – the province of Guangdong played host to 12 national teams from all six confederations. With FIFA partners ISL marketing and promoting the tournament, it was considered a resounding success and gave FIFA the green light to stage the first World Cup. 1991 was an historic year for the women's game. Three new continental championships were created – in Africa, South America and in the Concacaf region – in order for teams to qualify for the inaugural World Cup later in the year. A calendar was now in place to structure international fixtures. It was expanded in 1996 when, at FIFA's request, the IOC accepted women's football as part of the programme for the Atlanta Olympic Games. It had been suggested at first that the tournament should be an age-restricted event like the men's, but that was dropped in favour of a competition for full national teams. Since then, FIFA has had the responsibility of organising both the FIFA Women's World Cup and the Women's Olympic Football Tournament – the twin pillars of the global game.

◂ Along with establishing a structure for women's competitions, FIFA has invested heavily in developing the game on the pitch, helping to raise standards among coaches and players. Goalkeeping is one of the areas where the improvements have been most notable.

Developing women's football

In 2002, FIFA launched the first of its women's youth competitions, the FIFA U-19 Women's World Championship (now the FIFA U-20 Women's World Cup), and the FIFA U-17 Women's World Cup was added in 2008. If the first quarter of a century after the Mexico City Congress can be described as FIFA developing the competition framework for women's football, the focus in recent years has been on developing the game itself, and a major landmark was reached in 2016 with the creation of the FIFA Women's Football Division. In 2018, FIFA launched its Women's Football Strategy with five key goals – to develop and grow the game on and off the pitch; to showcase the game by improving and adding further competitions, especially at club level; to communicate and commercialise the game by broadening the exposure it gets as well as its commercial value; to govern and lead by institutionalising women's football with the aim of striving for a fair gender balance throughout the game; and finally to educate and empower women and girls through football. From the first tentative steps with the 1988 International Women's Football Tournament and the 1991 World Cup, women's football has come a long way. But this is just the start of the story. The time has arrived where the women's and men's games are now moving forward in tandem, just as they do in so many other sports such as tennis, athletics and swimming, something few would have believed possible just a couple of decades ago.

FIFA takes centre stage

2002 FIFA launches the FIFA U-20 Women's World Cup

2003 The USA hosts the fourth FIFA Women's World Cup

2004 The third Women's Olympic Football Tournament, at the Athens Games

2006 Djibouti becomes the 150th nation to play an international match

2007 China PR hosts the fifth FIFA Women's World Cup

2008 FIFA launches the FIFA U-17 Women's World Cup

2008 The fourth Women's Olympic Football Tournament, at the Beijing Games

2010 Qatar becomes the 175th nation to play an international match

2010 Silvia Neid wins the first FIFA Women's World Coach of the Year Award

2011 Germany hosts the sixth FIFA Women's World Cup

2012 The fifth Women's Olympic Football Tournament, at the London Games

2014 FIFA's survey shows 88,262 registered female coaches, 76,458 registered female referees and 4,801,360 registered female players

2015 Canada hosts the seventh FIFA Women's World Cup

2016 Creation of the FIFA Women's Football Division

2016 The sixth Women's Olympic Football Tournament, at the Rio Games

2018 Launch of the FIFA Women's Football Strategy

2019 France hosts the eighth FIFA Women's World Cup

2019 FIFA's worldwide survey reveals 13.36 million girls and women playing organised football

2022 Saudi Arabia becomes the 205th nation to play an international match

2023 Australia and Aotearoa New Zealand co-host the ninth World Cup, the first to feature 32 teams

2027 The World Cup heads to South America for the first time in its tenth edition, with Brazil as the host

1988

Following a plea at the 1986 FIFA Congress in Mexico City from Norway's Ellen Wille that FIFA pay more attention to women's football, FIFA took up China's offer to host an international tournament two years later. Twelve teams, representing all six confederations, gathered in the Southern Chinese province of Guangdong for what, in effect, was a trial World Cup. Won by Norway, it was declared a success and three years later the FIFA Women's World Cup was launched.

Trailblazers

◄ Norway with the International Women's Football Tournament trophy after beating Sweden 1-0 in the Final in Guangzhou.

▼ Celebrations at the stadium in Jiangmen before the first match of the tournament between Australia and Brazil.

"We knew that we were representing our country, but we also thought we were representing women's football, because a good showing at that tournament would mean there would be a World Cup. That was our understanding and that's how we viewed it."

Joan McEachern, Canada

"We were all acutely aware that this was the big time and we really wanted to do well, not just for ourselves and our own team and country, but also for the sport. We'd been waiting and hoping for FIFA to organise a global international tournament and it was finally happening, so we were beyond excited."

Moya Dodd, Australia

1988 Overview

CHINA PR 1988

INTERNATIONAL WOMEN'S FOOTBALL TOURNAMENT

Background to the tournament

Setting the stage for a World Cup

The stakes could not have been higher. A good trial event and FIFA would act to create a Women's World Cup. A disaster… and the profile of the women's game might not recover for years. And so, 107 years after the historic game between Scotland and England in Edinburgh, 12 nations gathered in the plush White Swan Hotel in Guangzhou on the banks of the Pearl River to get ready to not only fight for a trophy, but also to shape the future of women's football. There had been misgivings. The traditional sponsors of the men's game did not seem to be interested in backing a women's tournament, and there hadn't been a flurry of applications to host a tournament either. The answer was to be found in Hong Kong, which had for more than a decade been the epicentre of the women's game in Asia. The Asian Ladies Football Confederation had organised an Asian championship there in 1975 and, aware of the possibilities, Dr Henry Fok, a wealthy Hong Kong tycoon and a member of the FIFA Executive Committee, persuaded the AFC and the Chinese Football Association to back the tournament.

Regulations

FIFA's stamp of approval

Just as in the World Cups that would follow this tournament, FIFA awarded winners medals and runners-up medals to the two Finalists. They also gave medals to the two defeated semi-finalists even though a match for third place was played.

▲ ▶ Winners, runners-up and third-place medals from the 1988 International Women's Football Tournament.
FIFA Museum Collection

Regulations

A tournament for national teams

In 1987, FIFA had given advice to the organisers of the Women's World Invitational Tournament in Chinese Taipei, but the 1988 tournament went a stage further. The teams had to be genuine national teams and not club sides or regional selections masquerading as national teams. In effect, it was to be a World Cup in everything but name.

Overview 1988

Host cities and stadiums
Guangzhou hosts the world

All five stadiums used in the tournament were located in the greater Guangzhou metropolis in Guangdong province. Tianhe Stadium and the People's Stadium were located in Guangzhou itself, while Panyu, Foshan and Jiangmen were located a short drive to the south.

GUANGZHOU
TIANHE STADIUM
(60,000)

PANYU
YINGDONG STADIUM
(18,000)

JIANGMEN
JIANGMEN STADIUM
(13,000)

FOSHAN
FOSHAN STADIUM
(14,000)

GUANGZHOU
GUANGDONG PROVINCIAL PEOPLE'S STADIUM
(25,000)

Regulations
80-minute matches

It may have been deeply unpopular with most players and coaches, but the matches at China 1988 and at the first World Cup in 1991 were only 80 minutes in duration "in order to protect the players". The size of the ball was not stipulated in the regulations, only that it should be "in accordance with the provisions of the Laws of the Game". The regular size 5 ball was chosen, but the discussions over whether the smaller size 4 should be used had been another point of contention for players and coaches. The system used to determine group placings was the total number of points, followed by goal difference, the number of goals scored, the score of the head-to-head, the number of wins, and finally the drawing of lots – in that order. The same system was used to determine the two third-placed teams to qualify for the quarter-finals, without, obviously, the head-to-head criterion.

1988 Group stage

Group A

	W	D	L	+–	PTS
CHN	3	0	0	11	6
CAN	1	1	1	7	3
NED	1	1	1	4	3
CIV	0	0	3	1 17	0

Hosts China through with ease

It was a clear night in Guangzhou as 45,000 spectators took their seats in the high-banked Tianhe Stadium stands to witness history in the making. An immense dragon-lion had danced and twirled its way around the pitch, and troupes of football-kitted women, carrying the 12 competing teams' national flags, had stepped in time to a marching band. Then it was time for China and Canada to get the FIFA-backed International Women's Football Tournament underway – a trial run for a promised World Cup. With her bare shins and jinking runs, winger Wu Weiying did so in some style, rifling in a shot for the opener before unleashing another fierce drive that was blocked by Canada keeper Janice Cossar into the path of the onrushing Sun Qingmei, who tapped in to seal a 2-0 win. In Foshan, the Netherlands overcame international newcomers Côte d'Ivoire 3-0, debutant Regina Miltenburg and midfielder Daniëlle de Winter on target alongside Ria Vestjens, a national team player for almost a decade, who scored from the spot. Keeper Els van den Hoek showed her mettle against China, denying Sun Qingmei and Li Xiufu, but a skilful Dutch team were ultimately undone by Sun, who pounced on a defensive mistake to score the only goal. Canada stayed in contention with a 6-0 win over Côte d'Ivoire, Annie Caron scoring twice and Fabienne Gareau, Cathy Ross and Joan McEachern all bagging their first international goals. Paula Mostert threw Canada a late lifeline when her own goal cancelled out Vestjens' opener for the Netherlands, and both sides would reach the knockouts. Meanwhile, Monique Djagane Odio grabbed a consolation for Côte d'Ivoire as they fell 8-1 to the reigning Asian champions, Liu Ailing and Zhang Honghong scoring braces as table-topping China became the only team with a perfect group campaign.

Tianhe Stadium, Guangzhou
1.06.1988, 20:20, **45,000**

CHINA PR 2-0 CANADA

Wu Weiying 23
Sun Qingmei 71

Richard Lorenc AUS
Karl-Erik Davidsen SWE & Romualdo Arppi Filho BRA

CHN • 1 Zhong Honglian - 2 Chen Xia (12 Wang Hong 52), 3 Cao Ping (c), 5 Shui Qingxia, 6 Li Xiufu, 15 Wen Lirong, 11 Sun Qingmei, 10 Liu Ailing, 14 Wang Fei, 7 Wu Weiying, 13 Niu Lijie (17 Zhang Honghong 65). *Shang Ruihua*

CAN • 1 Janice Cossar - 14 Sue Brandt, 4 Michelle Ring ■44, 12 Cathy Ross ■58, 6 Geraldine Donnelly (c), 15 Jodie Biggan, 8 Joan McEachern, 13 Connie Cant, 16 Silvana Burtini (3 Shelly Vernon 70), 11 Annie Caron, 17 Fabienne Gareau. *Neil Turnbull*

Foshan Stadium, Foshan
1.06.1988, 20:20, **12,000**

CÔTE D'IVOIRE 0-3 NETHERLANDS

Miltenburg 17
Vestjens 28p, de Winter 52

Zdeněk Havlíček TCH
Yoshisato Okaya JPN & Egil Nervik NOR

CIV • 1 Marie-Chantal Sery - 5 Dorothée Behi ■5, 2 Agnès Koua ■45, 3 Viviane Dalli, 4 Rose Obre, 6 Mireille Dao (14 Mariam Dao 33), 8 Gladys Adou (c), 9 Elisabeth Landet, 10 Adèle Tchetche, 11 Monique Djagane Odio, 12 Eugénie Vallin Diblete (13 Marthe Obite 48). *Désiré Sikely*

NED • 1 Els van den Hoek - 2 Jacqueline Zwarts, 3 Ria Vestjens (c), 4 Anja van Rooijen-Bonte (13 Jolanda Leemans 60), 6 Janny Timisela, 7 Fien Timisela, 8 Daniëlle de Winter, 9 Marjoke de Bakker (15 Tsjitske Schuil 51), 10 Sarina Wiegman, 12 Paula Mostert, 16 Regina Miltenburg. *Piet Buter*

Guangdong Provincial People's Stadium, Guangzhou
3.06.1988, 19:45, **18,000**

CHINA PR 1-0 NETHERLANDS

Sun Qingmei 59

Romualdo Arppi Filho BRA
Egil Nervik NOR & Zdeněk Havlíček TCH

CHN • Zhong Honglian - Chen Xia, Cao Ping (c), Shui Qingxia, 4 Liu Qingwen, Li Xiufu, Wu Weiying, Liu Ailing, Sun Qingmei, Niu Lijie, Wang Fei. *Shang Ruihua*

NED • van den Hoek - Zwarts, Vestjens (c), ■12, van Rooijen-Bonte, J Timisela, F Timisela, de Winter (11 Angelique Bovee 66), de Bakker, Wiegman, Mostert, Miltenburg. *Buter*

Foshan Stadium, Foshan
3.06.1988, 19:45, **8,480**

CÔTE D'IVOIRE 0-6 CANADA

Caron (2) 11 21, Gareau 24, Ross 35, McEachern 61, Cant 72

Yoshisato Okaya JPN
Karl-Erik Davidsen SWE & Richard Lorenc AUS

CIV • 21 Marcelline Kouame Adjo - Dao, Dalli, Obre, Koua, Obite, 7 Solange Goli Ahipeau, Adou (c), Vallin Diblete (Tchetche 48), 15 Marie-France N'Goran Koffi ■15 (Landet 33), Djagane Odio. *Sikely*

CAN • 18 Carla Chin - 7 Jenny Hafting, Ross, Ring, Brandt, McEachern, Cant, Donnelly (c), Burtini (2 Cathy Klein 50), Gareau ■31 (10 Carrie Serwetnyk 50), Caron. *Turnbull*

Guangdong Provincial People's Stadium, Guangzhou
5.06.1988, 19:45, **8,000**

CHINA PR 8-1 CÔTE D'IVOIRE

Liu Ailing (2) 10 19   Djagane Odio 58
Zhang Honghong (2) 18 41
Li Xiufu 24
Feng Jianhong 42
Shi Guihong 50
Wu Weiying 75

Karl-Erik Davidsen SWE
Zdeněk Havlíček TCH & Romualdo Arppi Filho BRA

CHN • Zhong Honglian - Cao Ping (c), Liu Qingwen, Shui Qingxia, Li Xiufu (8 Feng Jianhong 31), Wu Weiying, Liu Ailing, Sun Qingmei (16 Shi Guihong 31), Wang Fei, Wen Lirong, Zhang Honghong. *Shang Ruihua*

CIV • Sery - 16 Petronille N'Guessan (Koua 23 ■28 ■35 ■35), Djagane Odio ■29, Obre, Behi, Obite, Goli Ahipeau (Dao 63), 17 Korotoumou Konate, Landet, Adou (c), Tchetche. *Sikely*

Foshan Stadium, Foshan
5.06.1988, 19:45, **10,300**

CANADA 1-1 NETHERLANDS

Mostert OG 68   Vestjens 9

Egil Nervik NOR
Richard Lorenc AUS & Yoshisato Okaya JPN

CAN • Cossar - Brandt, Ross, Ring, Biggan (Klein 54), Hafting, McEachern, Cant, Donnelly (c), Caron ■71, Gareau (Vernon 54). *Turnbull*

NED • van den Hoek (c) - Zwarts, Vestjens, van Rooijen-Bonte, J Timisela, F Timisela, de Winter, de Bakker, Wiegman, Mostert, Miltenburg. *Buter*

31

The number of years separating Sarina Wiegman's appearance in this tournament and the 2019 World Cup, where as coach she led the Netherlands to the Final. She would go on to reach the Final again in 2023, as head coach of England.

▶ China welcomes the world. The flags of the 12 competing nations are paraded before the China v Canada match. The Canadians had warmed up outside Tianhe Stadium in semi-darkness with bats flying overhead. "We were very nervous," recalls Joan McEachern. "Prior to that night we had played in front of no more than 200 people. But that crowd was huge."

Three-way tie at the top as Thais miss out

More than 15,000 spectators turned out to watch Brazil face Australia on a hot afternoon in Jiangmen. The Brazil national team, formed just two years earlier, handed a debut to future legend Sissi, but it was Australia's Janine Riddington and Anissa Tann who really impressed, Riddington after chipping keeper Lica for the only goal of the game and the first of this tournament, and debutant Tann for heading off the line while nursing a broken wrist. Thailand were undone by Norway's star in the making, Linda Medalen, whose first two international goals helped secure a 4-0 victory. Two days later, Thailand fell 3-0 to Australia, with Julie Dolan, who had captained the Aussies in their first official match in 1979 while still a teenager, breaking the deadlock after 54 minutes, and with 18-year-old Julie Murray and Carol Vinson also weighing in with goals. Roseli and Mariléia dos Santos, aka Michael Jackson, were on target as Brazil pulled off a stunning 2-1 victory over European champions Norway. The South American rookies then thumped Thailand 9-0, Cebola scoring four and Sissi notching her first international goal. Thailand were out, but Norway were back on track as captain Heidi Støre scored twice in a 3-0 win over Australia, the two teams joining Brazil in the knockouts.

◂ Illustration of the Brazil team. Until nine years earlier it had been illegal for women to play football in Brazil.

Group B

	W	D	L	+	-	PTS
BRA	2	0	1	11	2	4
NOR	2	0	1	8	2	4
AUS	2	0	1	4	3	4
THA	0	0	3	0	16	0

1

Janine Riddington's goal was the first scored in a FIFA women's competition. However, she was denied the opportunity to try and be the first to score in a World Cup after Australia failed to qualify for the finals in 1991.

2

The number of bizarre sending-offs in this group. And both were men! Eurico Lyra, the head of the Brazilian delegation, was dismissed after running onto the pitch to celebrate the winning goal in Brazil's 2-1 victory over Norway, while Australia's coach John Doyle was sent off during the match against Thailand for "coaching with a loud voice" after being told to stop.

◂ Norway needed to beat Australia to guarantee their place in the quarter-finals, which they did with a 3-0 victory. Australia's Anissa Tann (tenth person from the left), who had been instrumental in their two previous victories, played with a huge plaster cast after breaking her wrist in the win over Brazil.

Jiangmen Stadium, Jiangmen
1.06.1988, 15:30, 15,000
BRAZIL 0-1 AUSTRALIA
Riddington 21

Chen Shengcai CHN
Wang Xuezhi CHN & Li Shaofeng CHN

BRA • 1 **Lica** - 8 **Marisa**, 4 **Michael Jackson**, 9 **Cebola**, 10 **Elane**, 13 **Roseli**, 14 **Sissi**, 15 **Fanta**, 16 **Flordelis** (5 **Marcinha** 40), 18 **Lúcia**, 2 **Pelézinha**. *João Varella*

AUS • 1 Toni **McMahon** - 6 Julie **Dolan** (c), 2 Mandi **Langlar**, 5 Debbie **Nichols**, 7 Jane **Oakley** (4 Julie **Murray** 62), 9 Joanne **Millman**, 10 Carol **Vinson**, 12 Kerry **Millman** (11 Moya **Dodd** 78), 14 Kim **Lembryk** ■ 25, 15 Janine **Riddington**, 17 Anissa **Tann**. *John Doyle*

Jiangmen Stadium, Jiangmen
1.06.1988, 17:30, 15,000
NORWAY 4-0 THAILAND
Scheel 29,
Medalen (2) 30 51
Hegstad 59

Alfred Kleinaitis USA
John Meachin CAN & Zhang Jicheng CHN

NOR • 1 Reidun **Seth** - 8 Heidi **Støre** (c), 16 Cathrine **Zaborowski**, 6 Liv **Strædet**, 4 Bjørg **Storhaug**, 5 Gunn **Nyborg**, 2 Toril **Hoch-Nielsen** (10 Turid **Storhaug** 61), 7 Tone **Haugen** (3 Lisbeth **Bakken** 56), 9 Birthe **Hegstad**, 11 Linda **Medalen**, 14 Ellen **Scheel**. *Erling Hokstad*

THA • 1 Jumroon **Sungthong** (18 Niramol **Reamrat** 50) - 4 Nongyao **Wongkasemsak**, 3 Bussara **Rungsawai**, 2 Manee **Anuntadechochai**, 6 Prapa **Bouthong** ■ 18, 12 Tiw **Medfai**, 16 Jaroon **Gulteon**, 10 Sunee **Krissanachandee**, 9 Jongdee **Krissana**, 7 Pantipa **Mingkwan** ■ 24, 11 Thongdum **Unjai** (8 Apiwan **Ownsoennearn** 56). *Feongvit Thongpramool*

Jiangmen Stadium, Jiangmen
3.06.1988, 15:30, 12,000
AUSTRALIA 3-0 THAILAND
Dolan 54
Murray 61
Vinson 73

John Meachin CAN
Wang Xuezhi CHN & Lin Haiwei CHN

AUS • McMahon - Dolan (c), Langlar, Nichols, Oakley (Murray 22) (3 Leanne **Priestley** 76), J Millman, Vinson, K Millman, Lembryk, Riddington, Tann. *Doyle*

THA • Reamrat - Wongkasemsak, Rungsawai, Anuntadechochai, Medfai, Gulteon, Bouthong ■ 57, Krissanachandee, Krissana, Mingkwan, Unjai. *Thongpramool*

Jiangmen Stadium, Jiangmen
3.06.1988, 17:30, 12,000
BRAZIL 2-1 NORWAY
Roseli 18   Scheel 77
Michael Jackson 55

Alfred Kleinaitis USA
Chen Shengcai CHN & Zhang Jicheng CHN

BRA • Lica ■ 36 - Marisa, Pelézinha (3 **Russa** 79), Michael Jackson, Marcinha, 7 **Fia**, Sissi, Elane ■ 38, Roseli, Fanta, Lúcia. *Varella*

NOR • Seth - Støre (c), Zaborowski (13 Agnete **Carlsen** 57), Strædet, B Storhaug, Nyborg, Haugen (T Storhaug 57), Hoch-Nielsen, Medalen, Hegstad, Scheel. *Hokstad*

Jiangmen Stadium, Jiangmen
5.06.1988, 15:30, 16,000
BRAZIL 9-0 THAILAND
Sissi 2
Cebola (4) 17 41 63 71
Roseli (2) 34 67
Lúcia 39
Michael Jackson 76

Chen Shengcai CHN
Zhang Jicheng CHN & Li Shaofeng CHN

BRA • Lica - Marisa, Pelézinha (Fia 40), Michael Jackson, Marcinha, Cebola, Elane, Roseli, Sissi, Fanta, Lúcia. *Varella*

THA • Sungthong - Wongkasemsak, Anuntadechochai, Rungsawai, Medfai, Gulteon, Krissanachandee (5 Maneath **Maneewong** 57), Mingkwan, Ownsoennearn (13 Jessarin **Cheotklang** 69), Krissana, Unjai. *Thongpramool*

Jiangmen Stadium, Jiangmen
5.06.1988, 17:30, 16,000
AUSTRALIA 0-3 NORWAY
Støre (2) 11 65
Medalen 61

John Meachin CAN
Wang Xuezhi CHN & Alfred Kleinaitis USA

AUS • McMahon (18 Theresa **Jones** 73) - Dolan (c), Langlar, J Millman, Vinson, K Millman, Lembryk, Riddington, Tann, Nichols (Priestley 56), Murray. *Doyle*

NOR • 12 Hege **Ludvigsen** - Støre (c) ■ 49, Zaborowski, Strædet, B Storhaug, Nyborg, Haugen (Bakken 73), Hoch-Nielsen (T Storhaug 70), Hegstad, Scheel, Medalen. *Hokstad*

1988 Group stage

Yingdong Stadium, Panyu
1.06.1988, 19:30, **15,000**
JAPAN 2-5 USA
Tezuka 20   Jennings (3) 13 29 51
Nagamine 76   Bates 21, Henry 35
Celestin N'Cho CIV
Yu Jingyin CHN & Sun Baojie CHN

JPN • 1 Masae **Suzuki** - 3 Midori **Honda**, 4 Mayumi **Kaji**, 16 Yumi **Watanabe** (13 Tomoko **Matsunaga** 71), 6 Chiaki **Yamada**, 7 Michiko **Matsuda**, 15 Takako **Tezuka**, 10 Futaba **Kioka** (8 Asako **Takakura** 72), 9 Kaori **Nagamine**, 11 Etsuko **Handa**, 5 Akemi **Noda**. *Ryohei Suzuki*

USA • 1 Amy **Allmann** - 5 Lori **Henry** (c), 8 Linda **Hamilton**, 16 Debbie **Belkin**, 14 Joy **Biefeld**, 3 Shannon **Higgins**, 10 Michelle **Akers**, 7 Tracey **Bates**, 9 Mia **Hamm** (11 Brandi **Chastain** 40), 12 Carin **Jennings**, 13 Kristine **Lilly** (15 Wendy **Gebauer** 55). *Anson Dorrance*

Yingdong Stadium, Panyu
1.06.1988, 21:15, **15,000**
SWEDEN 1-0 CZECHOSLOVAKIA
H Johansson 76
Chris van der Laar NED
Sukho Vuddhijoti THA & Liu Jingli CHN

SWE • 1 Elisabeth **Leidinge** - 2 Anette **Hansson**, 18 Anette **Winnow**, 4 Pia **Syrén** (15 Helen **Johansson** 58), 17 Anette **Palm** (13 Anneli **Andelén** 40), 9 Pärnilla **Larsson**, 6 Ingrid **Johansson**, 8 Camilla **Andersson** (c), 5 Eva **Zeikfalvy**, 10 Lena **Videkull**, 16 Gunilla **Axén**. *Gunilla Paijkull*

TCH • 1 Milada **Novotna** - 2 Marie **Tlachová**, 3 Jaroslava **Farmackova**, 4 Dagmar **Prochazkova**, 5 Eva **Haniaková**, 14 Milena **Reifova** (13 Jana **Kostilkova** 62), 7 Jana **Paolettiová**, 8 Jana **Bělíková**, 9 Alena **Chmelova**, 10 Helena **Petrmichlova**, 11 Alena **Nováková**. *Pavel Genzer*

Yingdong Stadium, Panyu
3.06.1988, 19:30, **13,000**
JAPAN 1-2 CZECHOSLOVAKIA
Handa 16   Nováková (2) 17 35
Sukho Vuddhijoti THA
Chris van der Laar NED & Sun Baojie CHN

JPN • Suzuki - Honda, Kaji, Noda, Watanabe (17 Taeko **Kawasumi** 75), Matsuda, Yamada (Takakura 70), Tezuka, Kioka, Nagamine, Handa. *Suzuki*

TCH • Novotna - Tlachová (Reifova 75), Farmackova, Haniaková, Prochazkova, 15 Milena **Valesova**, 6 Zdenka **Chalúpková**, Bělíková, Chmelova (Paolettiová 56), Petrmichlova, Nováková. *Genzer*

Yingdong Stadium, Panyu
3.06.1988, 21:15, **15,000**
SWEDEN 1-1 USA
Andelén 17   Belkin 15
Celestin N'Cho CIV
Liu Jingli CHN & Li Yingming CHN

SWE • Leidinge - Hansson, Zeikfalvy, I Johansson, 7 Pia **Sundhage**, Andersson (c) (3 Marie **Karlsson** 51), Larsson, Videkull, Andelén (11 Anneli **Gustafsson** 51), H Johansson, Winnow. *Paijkull*

USA • Allmann - Henry (c), 17 Megan **McCarthy**, Hamilton, Bates (Chastain 23) (Gebauer 56), Higgins, Akers, Belkin, Hamm, Jennings, Lilly. *Dorrance*

Yingdong Stadium, Panyu
5.06.1988, 19:30, **14,000**
SWEDEN 3-0 JAPAN
Videkull 4
H Johansson 11
Gustafsson 62
Sukho Vuddhijoti THA
Liu Jingli CHN & Zhang Yiduan CHN

SWE • 12 Ing-Marie **Olsson** - Winnow (Larsson 21), 14 Tina **Nilsson**, Palm, I Johansson (Axén 40), Gustafsson, Sundhage, Andersson (c), H Johansson, Andelén, Videkull. *Paijkull*

JPN • Suzuki - Honda ▇ 34, Kaji, Noda, Matsunaga, Kioka, 12 Akiko **Hayakawa** (Kawasumi 72), Takakura, Tezuka (Matsuda 52), Handa, Nagamine. *Suzuki*

Yingdong Stadium, Panyu
5.06.1988, 21:15, **15,000**
CZECHOSLOVAKIA 0-0 USA
Chris van der Laar NED
Celestin N'Cho CIV & Yu Jingyin CHN

TCH • Novotna - Tlachová ▇ 38, Farmackova, Prochazkova, Haniaková, Chalúpková, Paolettiová, Bělíková, Chmelova (Kostilkova 62), Petrmichlova, Nováková. *Genzer*

USA • Allmann - Henry (c), McCarthy, Hamilton, Belkin, Bates, Higgins, Biefeld, Gebauer (2 Carla **Werden** 30), Lilly, Hamm. *Dorrance*

Group C

	W	D	L	+	-	PTS
SWE	2	1	0	5	1	5
USA	1	2	0	6	3	4
TCH	1	1	1	2	2	3
JPN	0	0	3	3	10	0

▶ The first USA squad to take part in an official competition. Back row (left to right): Megan McCarthy, Joy Biefeld, Brandi Chastain, Michelle Akers, Linda Hamilton, Debbie Belkin, Julie Foudy, Lori Henry. Front row: Wendy Gebauer, Kristine Lilly, Mia Hamm, Carin Jennings, Tracey Bates, Shannon Higgins. Seated: Amy Allmann, Kim Maslin.

Swedes march on as USA edge Czechoslovaks

Seven goals flew in as a USA side featuring 16-year-olds Mia Hamm and Kristine Lilly faced Japan in Panyu. Japan's leading scorer Kaori Nagamine hit the target two days before her 20th birthday, but Anson Dorrance's side spoiled the party with a 5-2 win, Carin Jennings hitting the tournament's first hat-trick. It took a rather fortunate cross-cum-shot from Helen Johansson for former European champions Sweden to beat Czechoslovakia. Two days later, Japan fell 2-1 to the Czechoslovaks, Alena Nováková's brace cancelling out a 16th-minute opener from Etsuko Handa, who had made history as a 16-year-old in 1981 when she scored Japan's first official goal. Anneli Andelén secured a draw for Sweden when she cancelled out Debbie Belkin's first goal for the USA in a 1-1 draw, and an emphatic 3-0 win over Japan would see Gunilla Paijkull's side top the group, star striker Lena Videkull and Johansson on target, with Anneli Gustafsson also bagging her first international goal. USA striker Michelle Akers missed the game against Czechoslovakia with a head injury, but a goalless draw would see the Americans through, Pavel Genzer's side missing out on the chance to progress because of goal difference.

2 The number of hat-tricks in this tournament. America's Carin Jennings scored the first, on the opening day of matches. Brazil's Cebola bettered that with four against Thailand in the last round of group games.

▶ A punishing schedule of a game every other day meant that players had limited time off. Here, the USA team visit the Lotus Mountain near Panyu.

Quarter-finals 1988

◂ Moya Dodd's shirt from the 1988 tournament in Guangzhou. She appeared as a substitute in Australia's opening match against Brazil. After an injury ended her career at the age of 29, she qualified as a lawyer and became a sports administrator, serving on the FIFA Executive Committee.
FIFA Museum Collection

Sundhage sends Canada home

Tianhe Stadium, Guangzhou
8.06.1988, 21:00, **15,000**

CANADA 🇨🇦 **0-1** 🇸🇪 **SWEDEN**

Sundhage 5

Egil Nervik NOR
Wang Xuezhi CHN & Zhang Jicheng CHN

CAN • Chin - Hafting, Ross, Ring, Brandt, McEachern, Cant (9 Linda **Petrasch** 55), Klein, Donnelly (c), Gareau (Burtini 25), Caron. *Turnbull*

SWE • Leidinge - Andersson (c), Hansson, Karlsson, Zeikfalvy, I Johansson, Larsson, Sundhage, Gustafsson (Syrén 60 ■ 79), Videkull, Axén (Andelén 25). *Paijkull*

Straight after China's seven-goal thriller came a match that was settled by one, but only after an end-to-end finish. These two sides had met once before, Sweden winning 2-0 in the USA in 1987, a year after Canada's national team had been created. A powerful header from former Lazio professional Pia Sundhage a mere five minutes into the match would see her side emerge victorious here too. But Canada made a game of it and in a tit-for-tat second-half exchange, Anneli Gustafsson came close for the 1987 European silver medallists, while first-half substitute Silvana Burtini and Joan McEachern almost pulled goals back for Neil Turnbull's team. "The comments afterwards from the Swedish side were very complimentary," said midfielder McEachern. "I'm not sure they expected us to play as well as we did. The feeling that we had progressed so much in that one year was very rewarding."

7

All seven goals in China's 7-0 quarter-final victory over Australia were scored by different players – a record that was only equalled at a global tournament by the USA at the 2019 World Cup during their 13–0 win over Thailand.

China overwhelm Australia

Tianhe Stadium, Guangzhou
8.06.1988, 19:00, **30,000**

CHINA PR 🇨🇳 **7-0** 🇦🇺 **AUSTRALIA**

Li Xiufu 4, Niu Lijie 12
Liu Ailing 41
Zhang Honghong 55
Chen Xia 60
Sun Qingmei 61
Wu Weiying 75p

Chris van der Laar NED
Alfred Kleinaitis USA & John Meachin CAN

CHN • Zhong Honglian - Chen Xia, Cao Ping (c), Shui Qingxia, Li Xiufu (Feng Jianhong 52), Wu Weiying, Liu Ailing (Zhang Honghong 52), Sun Qingmei, Niu Lijie, Wang Fei, Wen Lirong. *Shang Ruihua*

AUS • Jones - Langlar (8 Leigh **Wardell** 67), Murray, Nichols (16 Sharon **Dewar** 41), Dolan (c), J Millman, Vinson, K Millman, Lembryk, Riddington, Tann. *Doyle*

A wall of noise greeted China and Australia at Tianhe Stadium as they contested the first quarter-final of the tournament and their fourth match in eight days. Keeper Toni McMahon, who had played in Australia's first official match in 1979, was not fit and in her place came Theresa Jones. But John Doyle's green-and-gold-shirted Australia side could not get close to the fast, fluid and technically excellent hosts, who scored seven goals without reply. "Although we were beaten by China, we were proud as a team with what we had achieved," says striker Anissa Tann, who played with her broken wrist wrapped in a foam covering and remembers a stream of Chinese spectators asking for players' autographs as they watched Canada face Sweden in the game that followed. The Australians took a memento of the tournament home too – they were allowed to keep their jerseys, although not their shorts!

▸ Receipts given to Moya Dodd by the Australian Women's Soccer Association. Dodd and her team-mates each paid AUS $850 to take part in the tournament. This covered internal airfares to attend a training camp in Australia beforehand, tracksuits and other equipment. "This was the equivalent to three weeks pay," Dodd recalls. "I paid it in two instalments!"

◂ Pia Sundhage scores the only goal of the game in Sweden's quarter-final victory over Canada in Guangzhou.

31

Brazil come from behind to beat Dutch

Foshan Stadium, Foshan
8.06.1988, 20:00, **12,000**
NETHERLANDS 1-2 BRAZIL
de Bakker 10   Cebola 11, Sissi 62

Richard Lorenc AUS
Li Yingming CHN & Yu Jingyin CHN

NED • 17 Lies **Kols** - Miltenburg, Mostert, van Rooijen-Bonte, (Leemans 64), J Timisela, F Timisela, Vestjens (c), Wiegman, de Winter, Zwarts, de Bakker. *Buter*

BRA • Lica, Marisa, Pelézinha, Michael Jackson, Marcinha, Fia (11 **Sandra** 67), Cebola (Russa 77), Elane, Roseli, Sissi, Fanta. *Varella*

Having only debuted in 1986, Brazil were short on experience compared to the Netherlands, whose national side had played 60 international matches since their first official game in 1971, but João Varella's talented players had still turned heads in China by topping their group ahead of Norway. They would overcome the odds again in Foshan against a team that featured future European Championship-winning manager Sarina Wiegman in midfield and top striker Marjoke de Bakker leading the line. De Bakker, who had made a scoring debut in 1979 against Wales, delivered a dream start with a goal after ten minutes. However, Piet Buter's side were forced to regroup a minute later when Cebola levelled with her fifth goal of the tournament, and the Dutch squad were soon heading home after Sissi, who had celebrated her 21st birthday six days earlier, scored what would prove to be the winner in the 62nd minute.

▶ Action from the quarter-final between the Netherlands and Brazil in Foshan. The Brazilians won the match 2-1, their third consecutive victory after losing their opener. Australia's Moya Dodd had assumed that the women's team would be a reflection of the men's team. "We were staggered that we'd been able to beat Brazil. What we didn't appreciate was how little support and structure they had been able to enjoy." It was to be a familiar story for the Brazilian women in the years to come.

Strike one to Norway as USA stumble

Yingdong Stadium, Panyu
8.06.1988, 20:00, **15,000**
NORWAY 1-0 USA
Henry OG 43

Romualdo Arppi Filho BRA
Zhong Bohong CHN & Liu Jingli CHN

NOR • Ludvigsen - Støre (c), Zaborowski, Strædet, B Storhaug, Nyborg, Haugen, Hoch-Nielsen, Hegstad, Scheel, Medalen (17 Sissel **Grude** 71). *Hokstad*

USA • Allmann - Henry (c), McCarthy (4 Marcia **McDermott** 67), Hamilton, Belkin, Bates, Higgins, Biefeld, Lilly, Jennings, Hamm. *Dorrance*

4

There were four sets of sisters playing at this tournament. Sweden had twins Helen and Ingrid Johansson; Australia were represented by Joanne and Kerry Millman, while Bjørg Storhaug was joined by her sister Turid in the Norwegian squad. The Dutch duo of Janny and Fien Timisela made up the quartet.

It was almost three years since the USA had made their international bow, and in that time they had faced Norway twice. In the first of those two games, a brace from striker April Heinrichs and a goal from Shannon Higgins had shocked the newly crowned European champions, but in the second game six days later, Tone Haugen scored the winner for Norway. This first competitive match between the two nations marked the start of one the great rivalries in the early years of international competition. The Norwegians won here thanks to an own goal from stalwart Lori Henry, the defender who had taken the armband when captain Heinrichs had returned home from China after hearing that her father was ill. Henry, the only player to have appeared in every USA international since their debut sent the ball into her own net and Norway into the last four. The USA were out, but Heinrichs, Henry and co. would be back with a vengeance in Guangzhou three years later.

◀ The Norway team took time out to visit Guangzhou Zoo during the tournament.

> " It was extremely hot and humid. That was quite unusual for us – coming from cold Norway to warm China. "
>
> HEIDI STØRE, NORWAY

Semi-finals 1988

Sweden end hosts' dreams

Tianhe Stadium, Guangzhou
10.06.1988, 20:00, **20,000**

CHINA PR 🇨🇳 **1-2** 🇸🇪 **SWEDEN**

Niu Lijie 10   Gustafsson 37, H Johansson 51

Alfred Kleinaitis USA · Romualdo Arppi Filho BRA & Richard Lorenc AUS

CHN • Zhong Honglian - Cao Ping (c), Chen Xia, Shui Qingxia (Shi Guihong 73), Li Xiufu, Wu Weiying, Liu Ailing (Zhang Honghong 58), Sun Qingmei, Niu Lijie, Wang Fei, Wen Lirong. *Shang Ruihua*

SWE • Leidinge - Hansson, Karlsson, Zeikfalvy, Sundhage, Andersson (c), Syrén 31), Larsson, Gustafsson, Andelén, Nilsson, H Johansson ■ 34 (Videkull 60). *Paijkull*

The year 1984 had been a momentous one for these two sides. Back then, six of Sweden's current squad had tasted success as the winners of the first European Championship, while China's top female players came together for their first national team training camp. China played their first official match two years later, a 2-1 loss to the USA at the 1986 Mundialito in Italy, but they would end the year on top by winning the Asian Women's Championship. Li Xiufu and Cao Ping had been part of the set up since the beginning, but the core of this squad had been together for two years and the hosts had wowed crowds with their ability. Playing in front of 20,000 supporters, Niu Lijie gave her team every chance of reaching a showcase home Final when she scored her second goal of the tournament, this one after just ten minutes. However, an experienced Sweden side would not be easily overcome and after Anneli Gustafsson levelled with her second in three matches, 22-year-old striker Helen Johansson, twin sister of Ingrid and a teenage member of the 1984 European title-winning side, hit her third of the competition to see the Scandinavians through.

◀ The official report filed by referee John Meachin after the Brazil–Norway match. Right from their first game in 1986, the Brazilian women shortened their names to a popular name. For instance, number 4 Michael Jackson's real name was Mariléia dos Santos, which was what was recorded in the report.

Scheel double seals Final place for Norway

Yingdong Stadium, Panyu
10.06.1988, 20:00, **18,000**

BRAZIL 🇧🇷 **1-2** 🇳🇴 **NORWAY**

Sissi 55   Scheel (2) 7 76

John Meachin CAN · Chris van der Laar NED & Chen Shengcai CHN

BRA • Lica - Pelézinha ■ 39 (Russa 59), Michael Jackson, Marcinha, Elane, Sandra, Cebola, Roseli, Sissi, Fanta, Lúcia (c). *Varella*

NOR • Ludvigsen - Zaborowski, Strædet, B Storhaug, Nyborg, Haugen, Støre (c), Hoch-Nielsen (T Storhaug 56), Hegstad, Medalen (Grude 61), Scheel. *Hokstad*

Norway striker Ellen Scheel had scored on her debut in 1985 aged just 16, and had found the back of the net again two years later, but she was still seeking her third international goal when she arrived in China. The 19-year-old promptly delivered it in her side's victory over Thailand, but her second, against Brazil in the group stage, had proved to be a mere consolation as Erling Hokstad's team fell to a shock 2-1 defeat. In the semi-final, Scheel was on fire against the same opposition in Panyu, scoring after seven minutes, and with Brazil yet to settle their nerves as half-time approached, the Scandinavians looked on course for a fairly routine win. Sissi changed all that 15 minutes after the re-start, unleashing a superb long-range free kick in the style of dead-ball specialist Zico, and the game burst into life. Sissi threatened to score again, but with four minutes remaining Scheel broke the deadlock with a shot that rolled under keeper Lica and into the net. Norway had reached their second major Final in under a year after winning the 1987 European Championship, while Brazil, who were gracious in defeat, could look forward to a battle for third place with the hosts in Guangzhou.

◀ Elisabeth Leidinge was a solid last line of defence as an experienced Sweden team ended the run of hosts China. China had played their first international just two years earlier while the Swedes had 15 years of experience behind them.

1988 Match for Third Place

Tianhe Stadium, Guangzhou
12.06.1988, 18:00, **35,000**

CHINA PR 🇨🇳 **0-0** 🇧🇷 **BRAZIL**
3-4 PSO

Roseli ⚽ Wu Weiying ✖ (saved) Fanta ✖ (saved) Liu Ailing ⚽ Marisa ⚽ Chen Xia ⚽ Sandra ⚽ Wang Fei ⚽ Cebola ✖ (missed) Li Xiufu ✖ (saved) Michael Jackson ⚽ Zhang Honghong ✖ (missed)

⚽ Egil Nervik NOR
🚩 Alfred Kleinaitis USA & Chris van der Laar NED

CHN • Zhong Honglian - Cao Ping (c), Chen Xia, Shui Qingxia, Li Xiufu, Wu Weiying, Liu Ailing, Sun Qingmei, Niu Lijie (Zhang Honghong 44), Wang Fei, Wen Lirong. *Shang Ruihua*

BRA • 12 **Simone** - Marisa, Lúcia (Russa 56 🟥 60), Pelézinha (Sandra 40), Michael Jackson, Marcinha, Cebola, Elane, Roseli, Sissi, Fanta. *Varella*

Penalties seal third place for Brazil

Met by searing heat, high humidity and 35,000 expectant spectators, China and Brazil came out all guns blazing in their bid for bronze and would bow out having delivered a goalless but gripping 80 minutes and the ultimate nail-biter – a penalty shoot-out decider. China could have put the game to bed in normal time, fans' favourite Wu Weiying setting up Niu Lijie only for her powerful strike to fly past the post. Wu herself rounded keeper Simone but blasted her shot into the side netting, and Liu Ailing skipped past three defenders only to see her effort smothered by the Brazilian shot-stopper, who was making her first appearance of the tournament. Brazil had opportunities too, Lúcia going agonisingly close with a looping left-foot shot only for keeper Zhong Honglian to punch clear, and Cebola spurning a chance in front of an open goal. With neither side able to find that killer winner in their sixth game in 12 days, it came down to penalties. The contest turned in Brazil's favour when Simone saved a tame effort from Wu, who had played every minute of every match, scoring three times along the way. Michael Jackson duly buried her penalty kick, leaving Zhang Honghong knowing that she had to deliver too. It was not to be, the substitute sending her shot wide and Brazil into raptures. João Varella's rookies had won and as goalkeeper Simone fell to her knees with arms aloft, an ecstatic squad descended on her in celebration.

▲ Brazil's Simone celebrates winning the penalty shoot-out to secure third place after China's Zhang Honghong fired her penalty past the post.

A one-off trophy

Martini & Rossi had commissioned a trophy for the two tournaments they had sponsored in 1970 and 1971, so the trophy made for the 1988 International Women's Football Tournament was the second of four different trophies awarded to women for what can be regarded as global tournaments. This trophy, which is on display at the Norwegian Football Association, was only used for this tournament, with a new trophy created for the first World Cup three years later. A fourth – the current FIFA Women's World Cup Trophy – would follow in 1999.

28

Pia Sundhage made her international debut aged 15 in 1975 and also scored the winning penalty as Sweden beat England in the 1984 European Championship Final. This was her first appearance in a global tournament. Twenty-eight years later, she was the Sweden coach at the 2016 Olympics, the only person from the 1988 tournament to make it to Rio. In between, she captained Sweden to bronze in the 1991 World Cup and played in Sweden's home World Cup in 1995 as well as the Olympics in 1996. Sundhage then embarked on a successful coaching career as assistant with China at the 2007 World Cup and then as head coach with the USA in 2011, Sweden in 2015 and Brazil in 2023. She won Olympic gold twice with the USA, at the 2008 and 2012 Olympics, and led Sweden to silver in 2016. She was crowned FIFA Women's World Coach of the Year in 2012.

1988 Final

Tianhe Stadium, Guangzhou
12.06.1988, 20:00, **35,000**

SWEDEN 0-1 NORWAY

Medalen 58

Romualdo Arppi Filho BRA
John Meachin CAN & Chen Shengcai CHN

Sweden: 1 Leidinge; 3 Karlsson, 4 Syrén, 5 Zeikfalvy (Nilsson 70), 6 I Johansson (c); 7 Sundhage, 9 Larsson, 11 Gustafsson; 15 H Johansson (Andersson 41), 13 Andelén, 16 Axén. Coach: Paijkull

Norway: 12 Ludvigsen; 2 Hoch-Nielsen (T Storhaug 41), 5 Nyborg, 6 Strædet, 16 Zaborowski; 8 Støre (c), 7 Haugen, 4 B Storhaug; 14 Scheel (Grude 65), 11 Medalen, 9 Hegstad. Coach: Hokstad

▲ The Norway team line up before the Final against Sweden. This was the 12th meeting of the two nations and the Swedes went into the match as favourites, holding the upper hand with seven victories and three draws. Norway's win in Guangzhou was only their second over their neighbours, and it followed on from their 2-1 victory over Sweden in the 1987 European Championship Final.

Medalen wins it for Norway

When it came to bragging rights, Sweden had held the upper hand over neighbours Norway, having been beaten just once in ten meetings until 1986 – but then came two Finals in quick succession, both of which the Swedes lost. Trude Stendal helped settle the first of them, scoring twice in 1987 as Norway wrestled Sweden's European crown from their grasp. Almost a year to the day later, the two Scandinavian rivals met in Guangzhou with a world title at stake, although this time it would take a neat goal and the miss of the century to see Norway prevail.

Before the game, the two sides had enjoyed some downtime, the Swedes making the most of the warm weather by the pool, Norway being mobbed by schoolchildren as they visited Guangzhou Zoo. But this trip to China was all about footballing glory and it had been played out in front of some of the biggest crowds these players had ever known. "It was very hard to hear," recalls talismanic captain Heidi Støre. "It was not normal for someone from Norway to play in front of that kind of audience, so many… it was amazing."

There were 35,000 spectators at Tianhe Stadium for this Final, and although the tactical and direct game that followed would not have them all on the edge of their seats as the match for third place had beforehand, there was plenty of goalmouth action. Norway's Ellen Scheel almost gave the neutrals something to cheer when she connected with the ball from six yards out, only for her header to fly over the crossbar. Sweden keeper Elisabeth Leidinge then stopped Linda Medalen from pouncing on a good cross from Turid Storhaug. But Medalen would get the better of the Swedish defence in the 58th minute, outmuscling defender Pia Syrén and dinking the ball past Marie Karlsson before slotting it under Leidinge.

Gunilla Paijkull's side were galvanised and this time Norway keeper Hege Ludvigsen needed to be alert as the Swedes piled on the pressure. Their best chance came right at the death, though, Ludvigsen diving to save Anneli Andelén's powerful shot only to see it rebound off the post into the path of Anneli Gustafsson. The striker only needed to guide the ball into the net, but ended up skying her shot over the bar and Norway held on to be crowned champions. "The relief!" said Støre, looking back. "I was so tired after so many games in a short time and when she missed, you couldn't believe it was possible. We were lucky."

▼ Norway celebrate winning the 1988 International Women's Football Tournament at Tianhe Stadium in Guangzhou.

1991

In 1991, China staged the first Women's World Cup. Matches lasted 80 minutes, and the first goal was scored by the hosts' Ma Li. In the semi-finals, the USA beat Germany 5-2 – the start of a rivalry between the two most successful women's teams. In the Final in Guangzhou, 63,000 fans watched the USA become the first world champions, Michelle Akers-Stahl scoring twice in a 2-1 win over Norway.

A whole new ball game

The 1991 World Cup gave women's football a huge boost in profile, especially in America where the first world champions were given a reception at the White House by President George Bush on their return home. The tournament also encouraged more football associations around the world to bring women's football under their control and to create women's national teams. Most importantly, there was now a regular pattern to the international fixture list, allowing associations to plan ahead and create programmes for players, coaches and referees. Prior to the landmark 1986 FIFA Congress, just 30 nations had played an official international, 22 from Europe, three from Oceania, four from Asia, and one from the Americas. By 1991 that figure had grown to 62 and by the year 2000 it had reached 108.

▼ The USA team with President Bush at a White House reception.

1991 **Overview**

CHINA 1991

FIFA WORLD CHAMPIONSHIP FOR WOMEN'S FOOTBALL

Story of the qualifiers

Continental championships as qualifiers

▼ Pennant from the first World Cup.
FIFA Museum Collection

Six of the 12 teams that took part in the 1988 International Women's Football Tournament didn't make it to the first Women's World Cup. Australia, Canada, Côte d'Ivoire, Czechoslovakia, the Netherlands and Thailand were all missing. Côte d'Ivoire didn't even enter the first Women's African Football Championship, a tournament created for the purpose of qualifying for the Women's World Cup and won by Nigeria, who convincingly beat Cameroon 6-0 on aggregate in the Final. Concacaf also created a new women's championship to serve a dual purpose of World Cup qualifying and continental championship. From this, only the USA qualified after beating Canada 5-0 in the Final in a tournament played in Port-au-Prince in Haiti. In South America, Brazil hosted and won the first South American Women's Football Championship, a tournament consisting of just three teams, now known as the *Copa América Femenina*. The OFC Nations Cup had been running since 1983 in Oceania, but the 1991 tournament doubled up as a World Cup qualifying campaign, New Zealand finishing above Australia thanks to more emphatic wins over Papua New Guinea – the only other entrants – after the two had both beaten each other 1-0 at home. In Asia, Japan hosted the 1991 AFC Women's Championship, a tournament that could trace its heritage back to 1975 with the creation of the Asian Ladies' Football Confederation. In the Final they lost 5-0 to China PR, but they still qualified for the finals, as did Chinese Taipei, winners of the match for third place against North Korea. In Europe, the top five teams at the 1991 UEFA European Women's Championship qualified. The 18 entrants had been divided into five groups from which eight qualified for the quarter-finals. The winners of those ties qualified for both the Women's World Cup and the European Championship (a tournament won by Germany) while Sweden filled the remaining spot in China as the losing quarter-finalist with the best record.

Golden Ball
Carin Jennings USA

Silver Ball: Michelle Akers-Stahl USA
Bronze Ball: Linda Medalen NOR

Group stage

GROUP A			GROUP B			GROUP C		
CHN	4-0	NOR	JPN	0-1	BRA	TPE	0-5	ITA
DEN	3-0	NZL	SWE	2-3	USA	GER	4-0	NGA
CHN	2-2	DEN	JPN	0-8	SWE	TPE	0-3	GER
NOR	4-0	NZL	BRA	0-5	USA	ITA	1-0	NGA
NOR	2-1	DEN	JPN	0-3	USA	TPE	2-0	NGA
CHN	4-1	NZL	BRA	0-2	SWE	ITA	0-2	GER

	W	D	L	+	−	PTS		W	D	L	+	−	PTS		W	D	L	+	−	PTS
CHN	2	1	0	10	3	5	USA	3	0	0	11	2	6	GER	3	0	0	9	0	6
NOR	2	0	1	6	5	4	SWE	2	0	1	12	3	4	ITA	2	0	1	6	2	4
DEN	1	1	1	6	4	3	BRA	1	0	2	1	7	2	TPE	1	0	2	2	8	2
NZL	0	0	3	1	11	0	JPN	0	0	3	0	12	0	NGA	0	0	3	0	7	0

Knockout stages

QUARTER-FINAL	QUARTER-FINAL	QUARTER-FINAL	QUARTER-FINAL
CHN 0-1 SWE	NOR 3-2 AET ITA	DEN 1-2 AET GER	USA 7-0 TPE

SEMI-FINAL	SEMI-FINAL
SWE 1-4 NOR	GER 2-5 USA

MATCH FOR THIRD PLACE
SWE 4-0 GER

FINAL
NOR 1-2 USA

Overview 1991

12 TEAMS

USA WINNERS

NOR SECOND SWE THIRD

LING LING
OFFICIAL MASCOT

OFFICIAL LOGO

26 MATCHES PLAYED

32 YELLOW CARDS

1 RED CARDS

99 GOALS

3.8 AVERAGE GOALS PER MATCH

ETRUSCO UNICO
OFFICIAL MATCH BALL

510 000 SPECTATORS

19 615 AVERAGE PER MATCH

Host cities and stadiums
A sense of déjà vu

As in the 1988 International Women's Football Tournament, all the stadiums used in 1991 were located in the greater Guangzhou metropolis in Guangdong province. From the five cities involved, four stadiums remained from 1988. Foshan's New Plaza was opened for the finals while Zhongshan was added to the list. The distances involved were small. Panyu, the venue furthest from Guangzhou, was only a short 30-minute drive away.

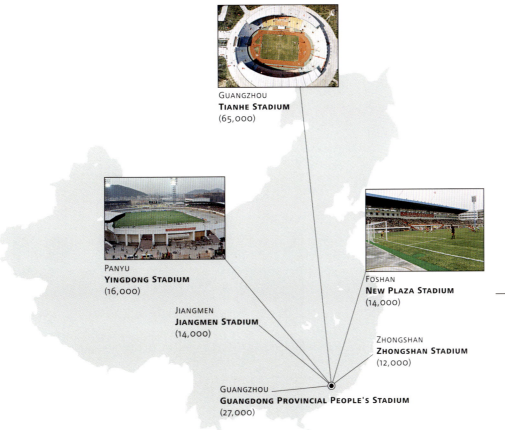

GUANGZHOU
TIANHE STADIUM
(65,000)

PANYU
YINGDONG STADIUM
(16,000)

JIANGMEN
JIANGMEN STADIUM
(14,000)

FOSHAN
NEW PLAZA STADIUM
(14,000)

ZHONGSHAN
ZHONGSHAN STADIUM
(12,000)

GUANGZHOU
GUANGDONG PROVINCIAL PEOPLE'S STADIUM
(27,000)

×10

Golden Boot
Michelle Akers-Stahl USA

Silver Boot: Heidi Mohr GER ×7
Bronze Boot: Carin Jennings USA ×6
Linda Medalen NOR ×6

1991 The opening ceremony

▲ A giant phoenix takes centre stage at the opening ceremony of the 1991 World Cup in Guangzhou.

A phoenix from the ashes

The Chinese hosts chose the phoenix as the central motif of the opening ceremony, symbolising the rebirth of women's football after the long years of neglect. Tianhe Stadium in Guangzhou was full to its 65,000 capacity to watch the ceremony as well as China's 4-0 victory over pre-tournament favourites Norway.

◄ Tickets for the opening ceremony and the China versus Norway match.

Group A

◀ Liu Ailing (10) scored two goals in the opening match of the finals against Norway. She celebrates with Sun Wen.

Hosts China off to a spectacular start

Only a special game of football could match the spectacle of the elegant opening ceremony in Guangzhou, and China's clash with Norway duly delivered. With a fourth-minute penalty save by Zhong Honglian, a mesmerising run and pinpoint 25-yard strike from Liu Ailing, and a shock 4-0 win, the hosts were on top. Bank clerk Helle Jensen's two goals in a 3-0 win over a spirited New Zealand team put Denmark into the mix, but Norway were too, bouncing back with a 4-0 win over the haka-dancing Kiwis, whose midfielder Julia Campbell agonisingly netted the first-ever Women's World Cup own goal. Later, 27,000 spectators roared as China twice came back against Denmark in a 2-2 thriller described by Danish coach Keld Gantzhorn as their "best-ever match". China finished top with a 4-1 win over New Zealand, who joyously celebrated when postwoman and bus driver Kim Nye bagged their only goal. Meanwhile Norway, who had beaten Denmark in the semi-finals of the European Championship earlier that year, skipped around Yingdong Stadium in their stockinged feet having beaten them again to reach the quarters, although the Danes would still go through as one of the two best third-placed teams.

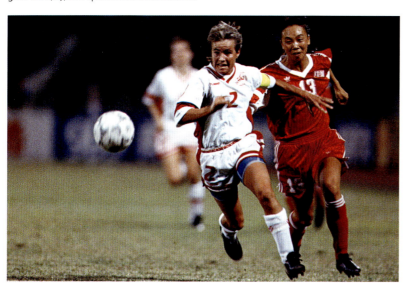

◀ Denmark captain Karina Sefron (2) in action with China's Niu Lijie. The Danes drew 2-2 with the hosts and qualified for the quarter-finals as one of the two best third-placed teams.

	W	D	L			PTS
CHN	2	1	0	10	3	5
NOR	2	0	1	6	5	4
DEN	1	1	1	6	4	3
NZL	0	0	3	1	11	0

62 countries had played an official international match by the time the 1991 World Cup kicked off.

Tianhe Stadium, Guangzhou
16.11.1991, 20:45, **65,000**

CHINA PR 4-0 **NORWAY**

Ma Li 22 (Haugen penalty saved 4)
Liu Ailing (2) 45 50
Sun Qingmei 75

Salvador Imperatore CHI
Maria Herrera Garcia MEX & Cláudia Vasconcelos BRA

CHN • 1 Zhong Honglian - 5 Zhou Yang - 8 Zhou Hua, 3 Ma Li, 12 Wen Lirong - 10 Liu Ailing, 9 Sun Wen (17 Zhu Tao 70), 4 Li Xiufu (c) - 7 Wu Weiying (6 Shui Qingxia 47), 13 Niu Lijie, 11 Sun Qingmei. *Shang Ruihua*

NOR • 1 Reidun Seth - 8 Heidi Støre (c) - 2 Cathrine Zaborowski, 16 Tina Svensson, 5 Gunn Nyborg - 6 Agnete Carlsen, 9 Hege Riise, 7 Tone Haugen, 4 Gro Espeseth (15 Anette Igland 62) - 10 Linda Medalen, 11 Birthe Hegstad (17 Ellen Scheel 59). *Even Pellerud*

Tianhe Stadium, Guangzhou
17.11.1991, 19:45, **14,000**

DENMARK 3-0 **NEW ZEALAND**

H Jensen (2) 15 40
Mackensie 42

Omer Yengo CGO
Vassilios Nikakis GRE & Li Haiseng CHN

DEN • 1 Helle Bjerregaard - 4 Bonny Madsen - 2 Karina Sefron (c), 3 Jannie Hansen - 12 Irene Stelling, 7 Susan Mackensie, 9 Annie Gam-Pedersen, 8 Lisbet Kolding (17 Lotte Bagge 64), 14 Marianne Jensen - 11 Hanne Nissen (13 Annette Thychosen 54), 10 Helle Jensen. *Keld Gantzhorn*

NZL • 1 Leslie King (c) - 3 Cinnamon Chaney (15 Terry McCahill 41) - 10 Donna Baker (6 Lorraine Taylor 54), 2 Jocelyn Parr, 12 Julia Campbell - 13 Kim Nye, 5 Deborah Pullen, 7 Maureen Jacobson, 8 Monique van de Elzen - 9 Wendi Henderson, 11 Amanda Crawford. *Dave Boardman*

Guangdong Provincial People's Stadium, Guangzhou
19.11.1991, 19:45, **27,000**

CHINA PR 2-2 **DENMARK**

Sun Wen 37, Wei Haiying 76   Kolding 24, Nissen 55

Vassilios Nikakis GRE
Cláudia Vasconcelos BRA & Omer Yengo CGO

CHN • Zhong Honglian - Zhou Yang - Zhou Hua, Ma Li, Wen Lirong - Sun Wen, Liu Ailing, Li Xiufu (c) ■ 50, Sun Qingmei - Wu Weiying (14 Zhang Yan 59), Niu Lijie (15 Wei Haiying 71). *Shang Ruihua*

DEN • Bjerregaard - Madsen - Sefron (c), J Hansen, 6 Mette Nielsen - Stelling, Gam-Pedersen, Mackensie, Kolding - Nissen (Bagge 71), H Jensen. *Gantzhorn*

Guangdong Provincial People's Stadium, Guangzhou
19.11.1991, 15:30, **12,000**

NORWAY 4-0 **NEW ZEALAND**

Campbell OG 30
Medalen (2) 32 38, Riise 49

Salvador Imperatore CHI
Maria Herrera Garcia MEX & Li Haiseng CHN

NOR • Seth - Støre (c) - Svensson, Zaborowski, Nyborg - 13 Liv Strædet, Haugen (14 Margunn Humlestøl 76), Carlsen, Riise, Medalen ■ 34, Hegstad (Scheel 59). *Pellerud*

NZL • King (c) - McCahill - Nye, Campbell, Chaney (4 Lynley Pedruco 28) - Taylor, Pullen, Jacobson, Baker - Crawford (Van de Elzen 45), Henderson. *Boardman*

Yingdong Stadium, Panyu
21.11.1991, 19:45, **15,500**

NORWAY 2-1 **DENMARK**

Svensson 14p   Thychosen 54p
Medalen 56

Vadim Zhuk BLR
Dai Yuguang CHN & Yu Jingyin CHN

NOR • Seth - Støre (c) - Svensson, Nyborg ■ 33 - Strædet (Espeseth 29), Carlsen, Zaborowski, Haugen, Hegstad - Medalen ■ 30 (Scheel 62), Riise. *Pellerud*

DEN • Bjerregaard - Madsen - Sefron (c), J Hansen - Stelling, Kolding, Gam-Pedersen, Mackensie, Nielsen (M Jensen 50) - Nissen (Thychosen 41), H Jensen. *Gantzhorn*

New Plaza Stadium, Foshan
21.11.1991, 19:45, **14,000**

CHINA PR 4-1 **NEW ZEALAND**

Zhou Yang 20,   Nye 65
Liu Ailing (2) 22 60
Wu Weiying 24

Gyanu Shrestha NEP
Gertrud Regus GER & John Toro Rendon COL

CHN • Zhong Honglian - Zhou Yang - Zhou Hua, Ma Li, Wen Lirong - Li Xiufu (c) (Shui Qingxia 28), Sun Wen, Liu Ailing - Wu Weiying (Wei Haiying 63), Niu Lijie, Sun Qingmei. *Shang Ruihua*

NZL • King (c) - McCahill - Taylor, Pedruco, Baker (Crawford 26) - Jacobson, 17 Lynne Warring (Campbell 65), Nye, Pullen - Henderson, Van de Elzen. *Boardman*

1991 Group stage

New Plaza Stadium, Foshan
17.11.1991, 19:45, **14,000**

JAPAN 0-1 BRAZIL
Elane 4

Jun Lu CHN
Zuo Xiudi CHN & Gertrud Regus GER

JPN • 1 Masae **Suzuki** - 5 Sayuri **Yamaguchi** - 2 Midori **Honda**, 4 Mayumi **Kaji**, 13 Kyoko **Kuroda** - 8 Michiko **Matsuda**, 11 Futaba **Kioka**, 10 Asako **Takakura** (17 Yuriko **Mizuma** 52), 16 Takako **Tezuka** - 15 Kaori **Nagamine**, 9 Akemi **Noda** (c). *Tamotsu Suzuki*

BRA • 1 **Meg** - 4 **Elane** 67 - 3 **Marisa** (c) (16 **Doralice** 15), 8 **Solange** - 17 Rosangela **Rocha** 79, 5 Marcia **Silva**, 2 Rosa **Lima**, 6 **Fanta**, 18 Maria Lucia **Lima** 58 - 10 **Roseli**, 9 **Adriana** (11 **Cenira** 70). *Fernando*

Yingdong Stadium, Panyu
17.11.1991, 19:45, **14,000**

SWEDEN 2-3 USA
Videkull 67, I Johansson 73 — Jennings (2) 40+2 52, (Hansson penalty missed 66) — Hamm 63

John Toro Rendon COL
Dai Yuguang CHN & Yu Jingyin CHN

SWE • 1 Elisabeth **Leidinge** - 3 Anette **Hansson** - 2 Malin **Lundgren**, 4 Camilla **Fors** (16 Ingrid **Johansson** 54), 5 Eva **Zeikfalvy** - 6 Malin **Swedberg**, 7 Pia **Sundhage** (c), 17 Marie **Karlsson** (15 Helen **Nilsson** 64), 9 Helen **Johansson** 64 - 10 Lena **Videkull**, 11 Anneli **Andelén**. *Gunilla Paijkull*

USA • 1 Mary **Harvey** - 4 Carla **Werden** - 9 Mia **Hamm** 25, 14 Joy **Biefeld**, 16 Debbie **Belkin** - 3 Shannon **Higgins**, 11 Julie **Foudy**, 13 Kristine **Lilly** (8 Linda **Hamilton** 33) - 2 April **Heinrichs** (c), 10 Michelle **Akers-Stahl**, 12 Carin **Jennings**. *Anson Dorrance*

New Plaza Stadium, Foshan
19.11.1991, 19:45, **14,000**

JAPAN 0-8 SWEDEN
Videkull (2) 1 (30 secs) 11
Andelén (2) 15 60
Lundgren 25, Nilsson 27,
Sundhage 34
Kaji OG 74

Gyanu Shrestha NEP
Gertrud Regus GER & Dai Yuguang CHN

JPN • Suzuki - Yamaguchi 55 - Honda, Kaji, Kuroda - Tezuka, Matsuda, Kioka, Takakura - Noda (c), Nagamine (Mizuma 67). *Suzuki*

SWE • Leidinge - Hansson - Lundgren, Karlsson, Zeikfalvy - I Johansson, Sundhage (c), Videkull (8 Susanne **Hedberg** 41), H Johansson (14 Camilla **Gustafsson** 35) - Andelén, Nilsson. *Paijkull*

Yingdong Stadium, Panyu
19.11.1991, 19:45, **15,500**

BRAZIL 0-5 USA
Heinrichs (2) 23 35
Jennings 38, Akers-Stahl 39
Hamm 63

Vadim Zhuk BLR
Zuo Xiudi CHN & Yu Jingyin CHN

BRA • Meg - Marisa (c) - Elane, Rosa Lima, Solange (Doralice 39) - 14 **Nalvinha**, Marcia Silva, 7 Marilza **Silva** (15 **Pretinha** 57), Fanta - Roseli 70, Cenira. *Fernando*

USA • Harvey - Werden - Biefeld, Hamilton - Hamm, Higgins, Foudy, Lilly (Belkin 67) - Heinrichs (c) (6 Brandi **Chastain** 41), Akers-Stahl, Jennings. *Dorrance*

Yingdong Stadium, Panyu
21.11.1991, 15:30, **12,000**

BRAZIL 0-2 SWEDEN
Sundhage 42p, Hedberg 56

Jun Lu CHN
Yu Jingyin CHN & Dai Yuguang CHN

BRA • Meg - Marisa (c) - Elane, Doralice - Rosa Lima, Marcia Silva (Pretinha 60), Cenira, 13 Marcia **Taffarel**, Fanta - Adriana (Nalvinha 62), Roseli. *Fernando*

SWE • 12 Ing-Marie **Olsson** - 13 Marie **Ewrelius** - Fors, Karlsson (I Johansson 41) - 18 Pärnilla **Larsson**, Hedberg, Sundhage (c), Gustafsson, Swedberg, Andelén, Nilsson. *Paijkull*

New Plaza Stadium, Foshan
21.11.1991, 15:30, **14,000**

JAPAN 0-3 USA
Akers-Stahl (2) 20 37,
Gebauer 39
(Hamm penalty missed 51)

John Toro Rendon COL
Zuo Xiudi CHN & Gertrud Regus GER

JPN • Suzuki - Yamaguchi - Honda, Kaji, Kuroda - Kioka, Matsuda, Takakura (14 Etsuko **Handa** 60), Nagamine - Tezuka, Noda (c). *Suzuki*

USA • Harvey - Werden (c) 31 - Hamilton, 5 Lori **Henry** - 7 Tracey **Bates**, Foudy, Chastain, Belkin - Gebauer, Akers-Stahl (Hamm 41), Jennings (Lilly 41). *Dorrance*

Group B

	W	D	L	+	-	PTS
USA	3	0	0	11	2	6
SWE	2	0	1	12	3	4
BRA	1	0	2	1	7	2
JPN	0	0	3	0	12	0

▶ The USA team before their group B match against Sweden in Panyu. Back row (left to right) Joy Biefeld, Carla Werden, Debbie Belkin, Michelle Akers-Stahl, Mary Harvey, April Heinrichs. Front row: Julie Foudy, Mia Hamm, Kristine Lilly, Shannon Higgins, Carin Jennings.

USA and Sweden outclass Brazil and Japan

30
Lena Videkull's goal after 30 seconds against Japan is still the quickest in World Cup history.

Reformed six months earlier after a three-year hiatus and missing playmaker Sissi, who was not released by her club, Brazil got off to a flyer with a victory over Japan. Having missed chance after chance, Japan ultimately lost to a fourth-minute goal that the Asian Championship runners-up struggled to accept had crossed the line. Despite their individual flair, it would be Brazil's only highlight and Japan's most effective display as Sweden, led by Gunilla Paijkull, the only female head coach in the competition, and the USA, with their own chef in tow, sizzled. Against one another, they served up what Anson Dorrance called "a credit to women's football" – a sumptuous five-goal classic that the 1991 Concacaf champions almost let slip when Sweden hit two goals, one a 30-yard thunderbolt from Ingrid Johansson, in a whirlwind final 14 minutes. The USA's "triple-edged sword" of Carin Jennings, Michelle Akers-Stahl and April Heinrichs went on to scythe through both Brazil and Japan to finish unbeaten. In Foshan, Lena Videkull bagged what is still the fastest goal in Women's World Cup history as Sweden battered Japan 8-0, the tournament's most emphatic victory, before a 2-0 win over Brazil saw the former European champions into the quarters.

Takakura

Japan midfielder Asako Takakura would go on to become national team coach in 2016, the first woman to hold the post.

▶ Carin Jennings (12) scored two goals against Sweden, although her second looked to have been scored by April Heinrichs. Jennings' shot had come back across the goal after hitting the crossbar and post, and was put away by Heinrichs.

Morace and Mohr take Italy and Germany through

With their own supply of pasta and seemingly limitless energy, Italy kicked off with a bang, putting five goals past Chinese Taipei, with captain Carolina Morace bagging the first Women's World Cup hat-trick in a blistering 30-minute spell. Germany's skipper and most-capped player Silvia Neid also made a scoring start in a 4-0 rout of African champions Nigeria, although her delight turned to despair when the recurrence of an old injury ended her World Cup 36 minutes in. The European champions regrouped to beat Chinese Taipei 3-0 as Bettina Wiegmann converted the first Women's World Cup penalty and the skilful Heidi Mohr hit her second brace in two games. Italy, in contrast, were reliant on Morace, and they needed her late goal to beat a defensively efficient Nigeria, who were not only the youngest but one of the newest sides in the tournament having been formed in January 1991. 'La Tigre' Morace could not prevent a subsequent 2-0 loss to Germany, but both the European sides were through. As were Chinese Taipei, whose own star skipper Chou Tai Ying helped secure victory over Nigeria despite the loss of 18-year-old keeper Lin Hui Fang after six minutes to the first Women's World Cup red card.

◀ Heidi Mohr scored twice in Germany's opening match against Nigeria. She followed that with three more in the group stage and one in both the quarter and semi-finals.

Group C

	W	D	L	+	-	PTS
GER	3	0	0	9	0	6
ITA	2	0	1	6	2	4
TPE	1	0	2	2	8	2
NGA	0	0	3	0	7	0

◀ Italy's Silvia Fiorini in action against Chinese Taipei. Carolina Morace scored the first-ever World Cup hat-trick in this match.

18 The average age of the Nigeria squad was 18 years and eight months, the youngest at any World Cup or Olympic Games.

Jiangmen Stadium, Jiangmen
17.11.1991, 19:45, 11,00
CHINESE TAIPEI 0-5 **ITALY**
Ferraguzzi 15, Marsiletti 29
Morace (3) 37 52 66

Fathi Boucetta TUN
Linda May Black NZL & Ingrid Jonsson SWE

TPE • 1 **Hong** Li Chyn - 4 **Lo** Chu Yin - 12 **Lan** Lan Fen, 3 **Chen** Shwu Ju - 11 **Hsu** Chia Cheng, 17 **Lin** Meei Jih (15 **Wu** Min Hsun 49), 6 **Chou** Tai Ying (c), 8 **Shieh** Su Jean, 9 **Wu** Su Ching - 14 **Ko** Chiao Lin, 10 **Huang** Yu Chuan (7 **Lin** Meei Chun 62). *Chong Tsu Pin*

ITA • 1 Stefania **Antonini** - 6 Maura **Furlotti** (13 Emma **Iozzelli** 48), 5 Raffaella **Salmaso**, 3 Marina **Cordenons** - 16 Fabiana **Correra** (17 Nausica **Pedersoli** 59), 8 Federica **D'Astolfo**, 4 Maria **Mariotti**, 10 Feriana **Ferraguzzi**, 11 Adele **Marsiletti** - 7 Silvia **Fiorini** 59, 9 Carolina **Morace** (c). *Sergio Guenza*

Jiangmen Stadium, Jiangmen
17.11.1991, 15:30, 14,000
GERMANY 4-0 **NIGERIA**
Neid 16, Mohr (2) 32 34
Gottschlich 57

Rafael Rodriguez SLV
James McCluskey SCO & Wang Xuezhi CHN

GER • 1 Marion **Isbert** (c) - 5 Doris **Fitschen** - 4 Jutta **Nardenbach**, 3 Birgitt **Austermühl** - 14 Petra **Damm**, 8 Bettina **Wiegmann**, 2 Britta **Unsleber** (6 Frauke **Kuhlmann** 35), 10 Silvia **Neid** (c) (13 Roswitha **Bindl** 36), 16 Gudrun **Gottschlich** - 7 Martina **Voss**, 9 Heidi **Mohr**. *Gero Bisanz*

NGA • 1 Ann **Agumanu** - 10 Mavis **Ogun** - 4 Adaku **Okoroafor** (11 Gift **Igunbor** 34), 5 Omo-Love **Branch**, 14 Phoebe **Ebimiekumo** - 2 Diana **Nwaiwu**, 12 Florence **Omagbemi**, 13 Nkiru **Okosieme** (c), 15 Ann **Mukoro** - 9 Ngozi **Uche** (7 Chioma **Ajunwa** 41), 8 Rita **Nwadike**. *Jo Bonfrere NED*

Zhongshan Stadium, Zhongshan
19.11.1991, 19:45, 10,000
CHINESE TAIPEI 0-3 **GERMANY**
Wiegmann 10p
Mohr (2) 21 50

Fathi Boucetta TUN
Linda Black NZL & Rafael Rodriguez SLV

TPE • 18 **Lin** Hui Fang - **Lo** Chu Yin - **Hsu** Chia Cheng, **Wu** Min Hsun, **Lan** Lan Fen, **Chen** Shwu Ju - **Chou** Tai Ying (c), **Wu** Su Ching, **Huang** Yu Chuan (2 **Liu** Hsiu Mei 66), **Shieh** Su Jean - **Ko** Chiao Lin (**Lin** Meei Chun 46). *Chong Tsu Pin*

GER • **Isbert** (c) - **Fitschen** - 15 Christine **Paul**, **Nardenbach** (**Kuhlmann** 41) - **Bindl**, **Damm**, **Wiegmann**, **Austermühl** (11 Beate **Wendt** 61), **Gottschlich** - **Voss**, **Mohr**. *Bisanz*

Zhongshan Stadium, Zhongshan
19.11.1991, 15:30, 12,000
ITALY 1-0 **NIGERIA**
Morace 68

James McCluskey SCO
Ingrid Jonsson SWE & Wang Xuezhi CHN

ITA • **Antonini** - **Furlotti** - **Cordenons**, 2 Paola **Bonato** (15 Anna **Mega** 63) - **Correra**, **D'Astolfo**, **Ferraguzzi**, **Marsiletti**, 14 Elisabetta **Bavagnoli** (**Mariotti** 36) - **Fiorini**, **Morace** (c). *Guenza*

NGA • **Agumanu** - **Ogun** - **Nwaiwu** (6 Nkechi **Mbilitam** 78), **Branch**, 17 Edith **Eluma** 75, 3 Ngozi **Ezeocha** - **Ajunwa**, **Omagbemi**, **Okosieme** (c) - **Nwadike**, **Uche** (18 Rachael **Yamala** 73). *Bonfrere NED*

Jiangmen Stadium, Jiangmen
21.11.1991, 19:45, 14,000
CHINESE TAIPEI 2-0 **NIGERIA**
Lin Meei Chun 38
Chou Tai Ying 55

Rafael Rodriguez SLV
Linda Black NZL & Fathi Boucetta TUN

TPE • **Lin** Hui Fang 5 - **Lo** Chu Yin, **Hsu** Chia Cheng, **Wu** Min Hsun, **Lan** Lan Fen - **Liu** Hsiu Mei (**Hong** Li Chyn 6), **Wu** Su Ching (**Lin** Meei Jih 78), **Chou** Tai Ying (c), **Chen** Shwu Ju - **Lin** Meei Chun, **Shieh** Su Jean. *Chong Tsu Pin*

NGA • **Agumanu** - **Ogun** - **Nwaiwu**, **Branch**, **Eluma**, **Ezeocha** (**Yamala** 41) - **Ajunwa**, **Okosieme** (c), **Omagbemi** (**Mukoro** 60) - **Uche** 48, **Nwadike**. *Bonfrere NED*

Zhongshan Stadium, Zhongshan
21.11.1991, 19:45, 12,000
ITALY 0-2 **GERMANY**
Mohr 67, Unsleber 79

James McCluskey SCO
Ingrid Jonsson SWE & Wang Xuezhi CHN

ITA • **Antonini** - **Iozzelli** - **Salmaso**, **Cordenons**, **Bavagnoli** - **Ferraguzzi** 50, **Mariotti**, **D'Astolfo**, **Marsiletti** - **Fiorini** (**Mega** 34) (**Correra** 65), **Morace** (c). *Guenza*

GER • **Isbert** (c) - **Fitschen** - **Paul**, **Austermühl** - **Unsleber** 50, 17 Sandra **Hengst** (**Kuhlmann** 41), **Bindl**, **Wiegmann**, **Gottschlich** (**Wendt** 68) - **Voss**, **Mohr**. *Bisanz*

1991 Quarter-finals

◀ Heidi Mohr scored an extra time winner in the quarter-final against Denmark.

Hosts fall to early Sundhage goal

Tianhe Stadium, Guangzhou
24.11.1991, 19:45, **55,000**

CHINA PR 0-1 SWEDEN

Sundhage 3
(Sundhage penalty saved 35)

John Toro Rendon COL
Cláudia Vasconcelos BRA & Maria Herrera Garcia MEX

CHN • Zhong Honglian - Zhou Yang - Wen Lirong, Ma Li ■ 66 - Zhou Hua, Liu Ailing, Li Xiufu (c), Sun Wen, Zhang Yan (Wei Haiying 45) - Wu Weiying (Niu Lijie 75), Sun Qingmei. *Shang Ruihua*

SWE • Leidinge - Hansson - Lundgren ■ 39, Karlsson, Zeikfalvy - Nilsson (Hedberg 67), I Johansson, Sundhage (c), H Johansson ■ 57 (Ewrelius 65) - Videkull, Andelén ■ 58. *Paijkull*

A Liu Ailing bullet ricocheted off the post, Chinese keeper Zhong Honglian saved a Pia Sundhage penalty and her opposite number Elisabeth Leidinge steadfastly repelled a constant bombardment. In the end, though, this third-ever meeting between the two sides was settled by a pinpoint third-minute header from Sweden skipper Sundhage, her third goal of the tournament. 55,000 spectators watched the drama unfold at Tianhe Stadium in Guangzhou but this was not the result they had hoped for. Even so, head coach Shang Ruihua's relatively inexperienced and youthful side had inspired a nation on their way to the knockout stage and as Sweden's centurion Sundhage fell to her knees at the final whistle, she must have thanked her lucky stars for 34-year-old shot-stopper Leidinge. "We had the best player in Elisabeth," she admitted later. "She saved us big time."

◀ Bettina Wiegmann in action against Denmark. 12 years later she would lift the World Cup for Germany.

Mohr to the rescue

Denmark's official World Cup song, "Going for Goals", may have been penned by midfielder Lotte Bagge, but it was Germany's prolific striker Heidi Mohr who popped up with a 98th-minute winner in Zhongshan to keep her side on track and into the semi-finals. It was the 24-year-old's sixth goal of the tournament and perhaps her most important for the two-time European champions in China. It had certainly been a battle to the finish after laboratory worker Susan Mackensie's 25th-minute penalty had cancelled out 20-year-old Bettina Wiegmann's, and neither side could find the decisive winner in normal time. Gero Bisanz's team may have won it with a last-gasp header, but their talented opponents departed China knowing they had held their own in the first Women's World Cup match to go to extra time.

Zhongshan Stadium, Zhongshan
24.11.1991, 15:30, **12,000**

DENMARK 1-2 GERMANY
AET

Mackensie 25p   Wiegmann 17p, Mohr 98

Vassilios Nikakis GRE
Zuo Xiudi CHN & Vadim Zhuk BLR

DEN • Bjerregaard - Madsen - Stelling, Sefron (c) ■ 17, Nielsen - Thychosen, Kolding, Gam-Pedersen ■ 70, Mackensie - H Jensen (18 Janne **Rasmussen** 73), Nissen (Bagge 47). *Gantzhorn*

GER • Isbert (c) - Fitschen - Austermühl ■ 37, Paul - Damm, Wiegmann, Kuhlmann, Gottschlich (Unsleber 51), Bindl (Wendt 89) - Voss, Mohr. *Bisanz*

◀ Norway's Tone Haugen and Italy's Silvia Fiorini in their quarter-final match.

Thriller in Jiangmen

Jiangmen Stadium, Jiangmen
24.11.1991, 19:45, **13,000**

NORWAY 3-2 ITALY
AET

Hegstad 22, Carlsen 67, Svensson 96p Salmaso 31, Guarino 80

Rafael Rodriguez SLV
Linda Black NZL & James McCluskey SCO

NOR • Seth - Støre (c) - Svensson, Zaborowski, Nyborg - Humlestøl (Igland 79), Haugen, Carlsen - Riise ▮ 97, Scheel, Hegstad. *Pellerud*

ITA • Antonini - Iozzelli - Salmaso (Bonato 36), Cordenons ▮ 20 - D'Astolfo, Ferraguzzi, Mariotti (18 Rita **Guarino** 68), Marsiletti, Bavagnoli - Fiorini, Morace (c). *Guenza*

With a last-minute equaliser, a penalty decider and 100 minutes of action, Norway's battle for superiority over Italy was a thriller. Twice Norway took the lead, but twice Italy replied, the first time when Raffaella Salmaso's lucky bounce on the wet pitch deceived keeper Reidun Seth and cancelled out Birthe Hegstad's 22nd-minute opener. Then, just as midfielder Agnete Carlsen looked to have won it for Norway, super-sub Rita Guarino scored at the death to force extra time. The match was finally settled by a steely 96th-minute spot kick from 25-year-old student Tina Svensson, the defender's second converted penalty in successive matches. Italy had finished fourth in European qualifying and had arrived in China eager to make similar inroads on the world stage. Sergio Guenza's side had battled valiantly in Jiangmen, but it was Even Pellerud's 1991 European Championship silver medallists who would live to fight another day.

▼ Mia Hamm is brought down by Chinese Taipei keeper Hong Li Chyn. Michelle Akers-Stahl scored from the resulting penalty.

5

The five goals scored by Michelle Akers-Stahl in the USA's quarter-final victory over Chinese Taipei is a World Cup record that was matched by compatriat Alex Morgan in 2019.

The Akers-Stahl show

New Plaza Stadium, Foshan
24.11.1991, 19:45, **12,000**

USA 7-0 CHINESE TAIPEI

Akers-Stahl (5) 8 29 33 44p 48, Foudy 38, Biefeld 79

Omer Yengo CGO Gertrud Regus GER & Ingrid Jonsson SWE

USA • Harvey - Werden (Henry 57) - Hamilton, Biefeld, Higgins, Hamm, Foudy, Lilly - Heinrichs (c) (Belkin 41), Akers-Stahl, Jennings. *Dorrance*

TPE • Hong Li Chyn - Lo Chu Yin - Lan Lan Fen, 16 **Chen** Shu Chin, Wu Min Hsun - Hsu Chia Cheng, Wu Su Ching (Liu Hsiu Mei 74), Chen Shwu Ju ▮ 23, Chou Tai Ying (c) - Lin Meei Chun, Shieh Su Jean. *Chong Tsu Pin*

Before the USA ran out against underdogs Chinese Taipei in Foshan, no player had ever hit five goals in a single match in any FIFA World Cup. By the time the Americans left the pitch having crushed their opponents 7-0, their striker Michelle Akers-Stahl had. "It was like wow, wow, wow, good, oh my gosh," she would later recall. "It was sort of mind-blowing." It was also a typically ruthless display by the 25-year-old, who had scored 11 goals in five qualifying matches and was described by head coach Anson Dorrance ahead of the tournament as a "personality player" with an "insatiable scoring mentality". It was a humbling defeat, but with an average age of 20, Chinese Taipei's squad had surpassed expectations. Trickier tests lay ahead for the USA, but with powerful no. 10 Akers-Stahl spearheading their charge, they were starting to look untouchable.

1991 **Semi-finals**

▲ Norway's Anette Igland (15) evades tackles from Pia Sundhage and Marie Ewrelius.

Norway fight back to reach the Final

Yingdong Stadium, Panyu
27.11.1991, 15:30, **16,000**

SWEDEN 🇸🇪 **1-4** 🇳🇴 **NORWAY**

Videkull 6   Svensson 39p, Medalen (2) 41 77, Carlsen 67

James McCluskey SCO / Fathi Boucetta TUN & Rafael Rodriguez SLV

SWE • Leidinge - Hansson (Nilsson 51) - Lundgren, Karlsson, Zeikfalvy - Hedberg (Swedberg 63), Sundhage (c), I Johansson, Ewrelius - Videkull, Andelén. *Paijkull*

NOR • Seth - Støre (c) - Espeseth, Svensson (Igland 61) - Carlsen, Haugen, Zaborowski, Nyborg - Riise, Medalen, Hegstad. *Pellerud*

When it comes to football rivalries, Sweden versus Norway is among the fiercest. The Swedes, first-ever champions of Europe in 1984, had lost not only that crown to Norway in 1987, but the final of the FIFA International Women's Football Tournament the following year as well. Little wonder then that Sweden's two-time player of the year Lena Videkull was mobbed by almost every team-mate on the pitch six minutes into the match in Panyu after planting the ball beyond Norway custodian Reidun Seth, who also happened to be on the books of Swedish club GAIS. As half-time approached, Sweden were ahead, but then Hege Riise was felled in the penalty area, spot-kick specialist Tina Svensson stepped up, slotted home and the game was wide open. By full time, Norway had four goals to Sweden's one. Bagging two of them, one a mere 30 seconds into the second half, was policewoman and Norwegian club football's top scorer Linda Medalen. Used as a central defender in the European Championship in July, she made her mark as a striker in China. Sweden would go on to battle Germany for third place, but Norway were set for the first-ever Women's World Cup Final.

50

Carin Jennings became the first American player to reach 50 caps when she took the field for the semi-final against Germany. The hat-trick she scored took her goals to 27 in those 50 games.

"Crazy Legs" kicks Germans into touch

Guangdong Provincial People's Stadium, Guangzhou
27.11.1991, 19:45, **15,000**

GERMANY 🇩🇪 **2-5** 🇺🇸 **USA**

Mohr 34, Wiegmann 63   Jennings (3) 10 22 33, Heinrichs (2) 54 75

Salvador Imperatore CHI / Gyanu Shrestha NEP & Jun Lu CHN

GER • Isbert (c) - Fitschen ▮ 59 - Paul, Nardenbach, Austermühl (Unsleber 60) - Kuhlmann, Bindl, Wiegmann, Gottschlich (Wendt 50) - Voss, Mohr. *Bisanz*

USA • Harvey - Werden - Biefeld, Hamilton - Hamm, Higgins, Foudy, Lilly - Heinrichs (c), Akers-Stahl ▮ 67, Jennings. *Dorrance*

Germany had in-form striker Heidi Mohr, the USA had their piercing "triple-edged sword" of Carin Jennings, Michelle Akers-Stahl and April Heinrichs. The question was, would any of them find the time and space to make a difference in this knockout match between two of the tournament's most clinical sides? The answer was, of course, a resounding yes, and the 15,000 spectators, who included the legendary Pelé, were treated not just to a Jennings hat-trick, but a back-flicked Mohr goal and a Heinrichs double. Only Akers-Stahl missed out, although the 5'10" forward certainly played her part and hit a 17th-minute rocket from 25 yards out that rattled not only the post but the two-time European champions too. Without their injured captain Silvia Neid at the helm and with less than three days' grace since their extra-time exertions against Denmark, Germany were unable to match the athleticism and firepower of the USA. The inspirational Mohr and rising talent Bettina Wiegmann got on the scoresheet, beating keeper Mary Harvey, an FSV Frankfurt player at the time, with two fine goals. By then though, "Crazy Legs" Jennings had done the damage and USA skipper Heinrichs coolly finished the job off.

▼ Carin Jennings (12) opens the scoring for the USA in their 5-2 semi-final victory over Germany. She scored a first-half hat-trick.

1991 Match for Third Place

Guangdong Provincial People's Stadium, Guangzhou
29.11.1991, 19:45, **20,000**

SWEDEN 🇸🇪 **4-0** 🇩🇪 GERMANY

Andelén 7, Sundhage 11, Videkull 29, Nilsson 43

Cláudia Vasconcelos BRA
Linda Black NZL & Zuo Xiudi CHN

```
                    1
                 Leidinge

                   13
                 Ewrelius

         2          17           5
      Lundgren    Karlsson    Zeikfalvy

      6         7          10          9
   Swedberg  Sundhage(c) Videkull  H Johansson
P
a
i                  11          15
j              Andelén ▪60  Nilsson ▪53
k
u
l
l                  9          7
                  Mohr       Voss
B
i      11        13         8         14        16
s    Wendt     Bindl    Wiegmann    Damm    Gottschlich
a             (18 Michaela
n               Kubat 38)
z
                   2          4
                Unsleber   Nardenbach
                        5
                     Fitschen

                        1
                     Isbert (c)
                  (12 Elke Walther 60)
```

▲ Sweden celebrate their third-place finish.

Sweden's first-half barrage stuns Germany

It took just seven minutes for Gunilla Paijkull's Sweden to stake their claim in the battle for bronze against the top-ranked side in Europe. Their opening goal was simple enough, unmarked Anneli Andelén letting fly with a speculative shot that beat Marion Isbert, one of the two best keepers in the competition. The other was her opposite number Elisabeth Leidinge, but it would be the Germany keeper who would be the busier of the two on this particular night as the Germans conceded three goals in less than half an hour, with Pia Sundhage and then Lena Videkull netting to end their tournament with four and five goals respectively. Helen Nilsson finished the Germans off and made it four on the night with a smart shot after a mistake by the defence. Having shrugged off a poor showing in the European Championship earlier that year, the World Cup bronze medal was Sweden's to wear. Germany, under Gero Bisanz and his assistant Tina Theune-Meyer, had enjoyed a faultless start but an exhausting knockout campaign and left with the Fair Play Trophy. Overseen by Cláudia Vasconcelos, the first woman to referee in a FIFA competition, and featuring the only side in the tournament to be managed by a female head coach, the match for third place set a new benchmark for women in football. Remarkably, it brought these two opponents face to face for the first time in their histories too. They would do battle over medals again in 2003, but that is another story.

The history maker

Brazilian referee Cláudia Vasconcelos became the first woman to referee a match at the World Cup when she took charge of the match for third place between Sweden and Germany. She was joined by two other women – Linda Black and Zuo Xiudi – who ran the line. There were six female officials at the tournament. "The decision to appoint women as match officials showed how far the 'ladies in black' have come in making a career in football," stated the World Cup technical report.

▶ Cláudia Vasconcelos makes history by becoming the first woman to referee a World Cup match.

1991 Final

▲ Norway captain Heidi Støre and USA skipper April Heinrichs shake hands before the kick-off of the first World Cup Final.

1991 World Cup Final

Tianhe Stadium, Guangzhou
30.11.1991, 19:45, **63,000**

NORWAY 🇳🇴 **1-2** 🇺🇸 **USA**

Medalen 29   Akers-Stahl (2) 20 78

Vadim Zhuk BLR
Ingrid Jonsson SWE & Gertrud Regus GER

Champions of the world!

When it came down to it, they were the two best teams in the tournament. Both operated with three strikers, both boasted an array of technically brilliant players, and both had seen off some of the newest and oldest teams in the women's game to reach the Final. With so much riding on the result, neither would play with the panache that had brought them to this moment, but both were confident they could win.

"I was like, of course we're going to win," Michelle Akers-Stahl would say later. "It wasn't even a question." With a full complement of stars at his disposal, USA manager Anson Dorrance knew they had a chance. As did Norway forward Hege Riise, who gave a cheeky smile when the television cameras passed her in the line-up. "When we stood there ready for the Final, thinking about everything we had accomplished, we felt confident that we could perform against the USA as well," she said.

With goalkeeper Reidun Seth passing a late fitness test, coach Even Pellerud was able to send his best XI out for what was also Norway's 100th international match. Having featured in every Norway game since their debut in 1978, defender Gunn Nyborg was a centurion too and was later handed the match ball by three-time FIFA World Cup winner Pelé.

There was no time for sentiment out on the pitch though, as Akers-Stahl showed when she stormed into the penalty area to power home a header with deadly accuracy against the run of play for 1-0. Anything Akers-Stahl could do, Norway's Linda Medalen could too and with keeper Mary Harvey struggling to reach a looping free kick in the box, the 26-year-old rose to head backwards into the net for her sixth goal of the tournament.

With extra time looming, USA coach Dorrance could feel the pressure building. "I felt like I was creating diamonds in my lower intestines from the pressure," he would later admit. Then up popped cool-as-a-cucumber Akers-Stahl, who pounced on Tina Svensson's rushed backpass, dinked the ball beyond the outstretched hand of Seth with her left foot and slotted it home with her right.

It was the USA's 25th goal of the tournament, the 99th of one of the highest-scoring FIFA competitions ever, and it confirmed the Americans as worthy winners of the inaugural Women's World Cup.

▼ Michelle Akers-Stahl (10) in action during the 1991 World Cup Final. She scored twice to take her tally to 10 – a record for any World Cup.

Final 1991

April the first

An inaugural World Cup will by its very nature produce a number of firsts. But the most prized of these is the honour of being the first World Cup-winning captain. In 1930 it was José Nasazzi in the men's World Cup, a name that resonates down through history. In 1991, it was April Heinrichs who had the honour of being the first to lift the Women's World Cup.

▶ A giant replica World Cup trophy is displayed as part of the closing ceremony after the Final.

▶ April Heinrichs lifts the World Cup after the Americans beat Norway 2-1 in Guangzhou.

◀ The kit worn by April Heinrichs during the first World Cup Final, along with the winners medal she received.
FIFA Museum Collection

100

The World Cup Final was Norway's 100th international match. Incredibly, defender Gunn Nyborg had played in every single one of them. She was presented with the match ball as a tribute. The USA's Michelle Akers-Stahl celebrated her 50th cap by scoring both goals for her team.

◀ The first world champions.

1995

Sweden, one of the pioneers of women's football, hosted the second World Cup finals, a small-scale tournament in mainly provincial towns. Neighbours Norway won all their six matches, beating defending champions USA 1-0 in the semi-finals and Germany 2-0 in the Final in Stockholm. In an echo of the Jules Rimet Cup, the trophy was stolen from the headquarters of the Norwegian FA in 1997.

Soccer Moms in Sweden

Sweden hosted their second World Cup, 37 years after the first. It was the first time Europe had hosted the women's event and the only time until Germany 16 years later. Played in midsummer when Swedish towns enjoy their outdoor civic festivals, the World Cup became the focus for the celebrations in the venues where it was being played, with even the players joining in. But there was criticism that even in stadiums with low capacities, it was still hard to tempt the festivalgoers to come and watch the games as well. The tournament also witnessed the birth of the real Soccer Moms, with Joy Fawcett the first mother to have played for the USA national team. Her husband Walter and daughter Katelyn Rose were in Sweden to watch all her games.

▼ Joy Fawcett's husband Walter and their daughter Katelyn Rose.

▼ Joy Fawcett with her daughter.

1995 Overview

SWEDEN 1995

FIFA WORLD CHAMPIONSHIP FOR WOMEN'S FOOTBALL

Story of the qualifiers

Arrivederci Italia, Hello England

Once again, continental championships doubled up as World Cup qualifiers for Sweden '95, with the exception of Asia where the Asian Games were used, and the final line-up bore a striking resemblance to that of four years previously in China with nine of the 12 teams qualifying again. Indeed, in a sign of the overwhelming prowess of the leading nations in women's football, five of the six continental champions in 1991 retained their title four years later. The only exception was in Oceania where Australia secured their spot on goal difference over New Zealand. The Kiwis needed to beat Papua New Guinea 10-0 in their final match but could only score six and missed out. From Europe, Italy, those great pioneers of the European game, were absent with England securing a first qualification in their place. Concacaf were given an extra berth, which meant that Canada accompanied the USA on the trip to Sweden.

▶ Sweden 1995 pennant.
FIFA Museum Collection

Golden Ball

Hege Riise NOR

Silver Ball: Gro Espeseth NOR
Bronze Ball: Ann Kristin Aarønes NOR

Group stage

GROUP A	GROUP B	GROUP C
SWE 0-1 BRA	NOR 8-0 NGA	USA 3-3 CHN
GER 1-0 JPN	ENG 3-2 CAN	DEN 5-0 AUS
SWE 3-2 GER	NOR 2-0 ENG	USA 2-0 DEN
BRA 1-2 JPN	NGA 3-3 CAN	CHN 4-2 AUS
SWE 2-0 JPN	NOR 7-0 CAN	USA 4-1 AUS
BRA 1-6 GER	NGA 2-3 ENG	CHN 3-1 DEN

	W	D	L	+	−	PTS
GER	2	0	1	9	4	6
SWE	2	0	1	5	3	6
JPN	1	0	2	2	4	3
BRA	1	0	2	3	8	3

	W	D	L	+	−	PTS
NOR	3	0	0	17	0	9
ENG	2	0	1	6	6	6
CAN	0	1	2	5	13	1
NGA	0	1	2	5	14	1

	W	D	L	+	−	PTS
USA	2	1	0	9	4	7
CHN	2	1	0	10	6	7
DEN	1	0	2	6	5	3
AUS	0	0	3	3	13	0

Knockout stages

QUARTER-FINAL	QUARTER-FINAL	QUARTER-FINAL	QUARTER-FINAL
GER 3-0 ENG	SWE 1-1 (3-4) CHN	JPN 0-4 USA	NOR 3-1 DEN

SEMI-FINAL	SEMI-FINAL
GER 1-0 CHN	USA 0-1 NOR

MATCH FOR THIRD PLACE

CHN 0-2 USA

FINAL

GER 0-2 NOR

Overview 1995

12 TEAMS

NORWAY WINNERS

GER SECOND — USA THIRD

FIFFI OFFICIAL MASCOT

WOMEN'S WORLD CUP '95 SWEDEN OFFICIAL LOGO

26 MATCHES PLAYED

66 YELLOW CARDS

4 RED CARDS

99 GOALS

3.81 AVERAGE GOALS PER MATCH

QUESTRA OFFICIAL MATCH BALL

112 213 SPECTATORS

4 316 AVERAGE PER MATCH

Host cities and stadiums

Echoes of 1958

Sweden became the first nation to host both the men's and the women's World Cups, with three of the 12 stadiums used in 1958 selected for the 1995 tournament. They were the Olympia Stadion in Helsingborg, which staged the opening match, the Arosvallen in Västeras, and the Råsunda in Solna, venue for both the 1958 and 1995 Finals.

Regulations

The golden goal

As in 1991, with only three groups of four, it meant that the two best third-placed teams joined the top two from each group in qualifying for the quarter-finals. In the knockout rounds, matches would go to extra time if tied after 90 minutes, and for the first time there was provision for a golden goal should a team score in extra time.

GÄVLE
STRÖMVALLEN
(6,700)

SOLNA, STOCKHOLM
RÅSUNDA
(36,800)

VÄSTERÅS
AROSVALLEN
(10,000)

KARLSTAD
TINGVALLA
(5,500)

HELSINGBORG
OLYMPIA STADION
(14,500)

×6

Golden Boot

Ann Kristin Aarønes NOR

Silver Boot: Hege Riise NOR ×5
Bronze Boot: Shi Guihong CHN ×3

The pioneers

Brazil's Cláudia Vasconcelos may have made history in 1991 by becoming the first woman to referee a match at the World Cup finals, but it was in 1995 that the practice became mainstream. Of the 12 referees appointed, seven were female, while there were seven lineswomen to five linesmen. Half of the 26 matches were refereed by women, including all-female teams at the opening match in Helsingborg and the Final in Stockholm. The curtain raiser at the Olympia Stadion was taken by Canada's Sonia Denoncourt with Corinne Lagrange from France and Veronika Schluchter of Switzerland running the line. Sweden's Ingrid Jonsson took charge of the Final along with Denmark's Gitte Holm and Mexico's María Rodríguez, and the Scandinavian presence was no surprise. In 1985, the international friendly between Sweden and Norway was the first official international match controlled by a trio of female officials, the result of a coordinated ten-year plan within Scandinavia to get women involved with taking charge of the increasing number of matches being played by female teams. One of the lineswomen that historic day was Ingrid Jonsson.

Yet another Scandinavian initiative was the creation of refereeing courses designed specifically for women and run by female instructors. In order to gain experience, women were integrated into mixed trios first for women's matches, but also later for men's games. In the wake of the successful 1988 International Women's Football Tournament, FIFA organised an instructors course in Norway the following year for female referees, which opened the door for women to take control of more international matches, and by the 1995 World Cup the results were beginning to show. The first official list of women referees and lineswomen was drawn up by FIFA in November 1994 with 26 referees and 31 lineswomen.

The 1995 technical report for the World Cup noted that, in the Cooper Test to assess the fitness of the officials, "the women referees generally obtained better results than their male colleagues" and it went on to say that "although the performances of the women referees as compared with the male referees did not differ greatly, the women were more nervous due to lack of international experience". The report also said that "their confidence palpably grew in the course of the tournament and they achieved excellent results". In terms of legacy, Sweden 1995 provided a springboard for the future development of female officials to the point that it would be inconceivable to host a World Cup without every official being female. And that step was taken just four years later at the 1999 World Cup in the USA.

Lineswomen make a brief appearance

It was not a term that stood the test of time, but "lineswomen" finally gained official recognition with badges of their own for the 1995 World Cup, even though the official regulations of the tournament continued to refer to them as linesmen! Any uncertainty or confusion was removed the following year when the gender-neutral term "assistant referee" was introduced after the 1996 IFAB meeting in Rio de Janeiro.

▶ Canada's Sonia Denoncourt (centre-left) and her all-female team of officials before the 1995 World Cup opening match in Helsingborg.

▶ Lineswoman badge. *FIFA Museum Collection*

Jonsson sets the standard

Ingrid Jonsson was the first woman to take charge of a World Cup Final and she was a pioneer in her field. After many years as a player, she took up refereeing in 1983. In 1986 she started officiating matches in the Swedish women's league and was part of the historic 1989 FIFA referees course in Norway. As a leading instructor for female referees in Sweden, it was in no small measure thanks to her work that the country had more than 1,000 female referees by the time of the 1995 World Cup. The 1995 Final actually wasn't her first. She had been a lineswoman for the 1991 World Cup Final in Guangzhou.

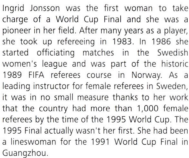

◀ Sweden's Ingrid Jonsson books Norway's Linda Medalen during the 1995 World Cup Final.

▼ Sweden's Ingrid Jonsson shakes hands with USA captain Carla Overbeck. She is flanked by Brazil's Ana Bia Batista on the left and Christine Frai of Germany on the right.

Group stage 1995

Group A

◀ Anneli Andelén (10) in action against Japan. She scored Sweden's second goal to ensure they qualified for the quarter-finals.

	W	D	L	+	−	PTS
GER	2	0	1	9	4	6
SWE	2	0	1	5	3	6
JPN	1	0	2	2	4	3
BRA	1	0	2	3	8	3

Sweden through after scare

After the glamour of the opening ceremony in China four years previously, came the flag-flying quad bikes, traditional guitar song and sashaying dancers of Sweden. It was midsummer in Helsingborg, and an Olympia Stadion – packed with youngsters in face paint, supporters of all ages in Sweden shirts and a smattering of grown men in Viking helmets – was ready for the official opening of the second Women's World Cup. Just as in 1991, Sweden were drawn to meet Brazil in the group stage and as the two sides stepped on to the pitch, they were greeted by a carnival atmosphere. Earlier, in Karlstad, Germany had overcome Japan 1-0 to set the ball rolling, with skipper Silvia Neid scoring the 100th goal of the Women's World Cup. Sweden, runners-up to Germany in the European Championship final, were expected to emerge victorious in their opener against a Brazil side prepared by several training camps but only 13 international matches since 1986. The South Americans had not read the script, though, and took a first-half lead through Roseli that they refused to relinquish. Japan, bolstered by a professional domestic league, stopped Brazil in their tracks when they avenged their controversial loss of four years earlier with a 2-1 victory inspired by captain Akemi Noda. Sweden finally had Helsingborg rocking after Malin Andersson and most-capped player Pia Sundhage scored in a remarkable fight-back from 2-0 down to beat Germany 3-2, each goal marked by a joyous sit-down celebration. Germany finished on top, however, after bettering Sweden's modest 2-0 win over Japan, beaten 8-0 by the Swedes in 1991, with a 6-1 blitz of Brazil that saw teenager Birgit Prinz score the 150th Women's World Cup goal. Third-placed Japan were also into the knockouts; Brazil's consolation would be an Olympic berth.

Michael Jackson in Sweden

Well, not the real one anyway. Mariléia dos Santos was given the nickname by her team-mates and was part of the Brazil squad in the 1988 International Women's Football Tournament, here in Sweden, and at the 1996 Olympics.

Olympia Stadion, Helsingborg
5.06.1995, 18:00, **14,500**

SWEDEN 🇸🇪 **0-1** 🇧🇷 **BRAZIL**

Roseli 37

Sonia Denoncourt CAN
Corinne Lagrange FRA & Veronika Schluchter SUI

SWE • 1 Elisabeth **Leidinge** ■ 75 - 3 Åsa **Jakobsson** (20 Sofia Johansson 83) - 2 Malin **Lundgren** (6 Anna **Pohjanen** 43), 4 Pia **Sundhage**, 5 Kristin **Bengtsson** - 7 Lena **Videkull** (c), 9 Malin **Andersson**, 16 Eva **Zeikfalvy** - 15 Anneli **Olsson** (8 Susanne **Hedberg** 61), 11 Ulrika **Kalte**, 10 Anneli **Andelén**. *Bengt Simonson*

BRA • 1 **Meg** - 8 **Cenira** - 3 **Elane**, 19 **Suzy** - 6 **Fanta**, 10 **Sissi** (c), 5 **Leda Maria** (4 **Solange** 16) (20 **Tânia** 83), 2 **Valeria** - 7 **Pretinha** ■ 21, 11 **Roseli**, 9 **Michael Jackson** ■ 57. *Ademar Fonseca*

Tingvalla, Karlstad
5.06.1995, 14:00, **3,824**

GERMANY 🇩🇪 **1-0** 🇯🇵 **JAPAN**

Neid 23

Petros Mathabela RSA
Peter Kelly TRI & María Rodríguez MEX

GER • 1 Manuela **Goller** - 5 Ursula **Lohn** - 3 Birgitt **Austermühl**, 2 Anouschka **Bernhard** - 7 Martina **Voss** (16 Birgit **Prinz** 65), 23 Silvia **Neid** (c), 8 Bettina **Wiegmann**, 6 Maren **Meinert**, 4 Dagmar **Pohlmann** - 11 Patricia **Brocker** (13 Melanie **Hoffmann** 82), 9 Heidi **Mohr**. *Gero Bisanz*

JPN • 1 Junko **Ozawa** - 2 Yumi **Tomei**, 3 Rie **Yamaki**, 4 Maki **Haneta**, 6 Kae **Nishina** - 9 Futaba **Kioka** (11 Etsuko **Handa** 80), 12 Yumi **Obe**, 8 Asako **Takakura**, 7 Homare **Sawa** - 17 Tamaki **Uchiyama** (13 Kaori **Nagamine** 73), 10 Akemi **Noda** (c). *Tamotsu Suzuki*

Olympia Stadion, Helsingborg
7.06.1995, 19:00, **5,855**

SWEDEN 🇸🇪 **3-2** 🇩🇪 **GERMANY**

Andersson (2) 65p 86   Wiegmann 9p
Sundhage 80   Lohn 42

Linda Black
Veronika Schluchter SUI & Corinne Lagrange FRA

SWE • Leidinge - Sundhage, Jakobsson, Bengtsson (14 Åsa **Lönnqvist** 35) - Kalte, Videkull (c), Zeikfalvy (Olsson 84), Pohjanen (17 Malin **Flink** 51), Andersson, 18 Helen **Nilsson**, Andelén. *Simonson*

GER • Goller - Austermühl ■ 61, Lohn, Bernhard, Pohlmann - Meinert, Neid (c) ■ 14, Wiegmann, Voss (14 Sandra **Minnert** 84) - Brocker (Prinz 57), Mohr. *Bisanz*

Tingvalla, Karlstad
7.06.1995, 19:00, **2,286**

BRAZIL 🇧🇷 **1-2** 🇯🇵 **JAPAN**

Pretinha 7   Noda (2) 13 45

Catherine Hepburn USA
María Rodríguez MEX & Peter Kelly TRI

BRA • Meg - Cenira - Solange (16 **Formiga** 72), Suzy - Fanta, Elane ■ 26, Sissi (c), Valeria - Pretinha, Roseli, Michael Jackson ■ 10 (15 **Nalvinha** 83). *Ademar*

JPN • Ozawa - Obe ■ 48, Yamaki, Haneta, Nishina - Takakura, 16 Nami **Otake**, Kioka, Sawa - Uchiyama, Noda (c). *Suzuki*

Arosvallen, Västerås
9.06.1995, 19:00, **7,811**

SWEDEN 🇸🇪 **2-0** 🇯🇵 **JAPAN**

Videkull 66
Andelén 88

Petros Mathabela RSA
Mohammed Osman SDN & Mamadou Touré MLI

SWE • Leidinge - Sundhage, Jakobsson (Olsson 46), Bengtsson - Andersson, Zeikfalvy (Lönnqvist 58), Videkull (c), Pohjanen (Flink 90) - Kalte, Andelén, H Nilsson. *Simonson*

JPN • Ozawa - Nishina, Yamaki ■ 15, Haneta, Obe - Sawa (Handa 76), Takakura, Kioka, Otake (Nagamine 46) - Uchiyama, Noda (c). *Suzuki*

Tingvalla, Karlstad
9.06.1995, 19:00, **3,203**

BRAZIL 🇧🇷 **1-6** 🇩🇪 **GERMANY**

Roseli 19   Prinz 5
                               Meinert 22
                               Wiegmann 42p
                               Mohr (2) 78 89
                               Bernhard 90

Alain Hamer LUX
Peter Kelly TRI & María Rodríguez MEX

BRA • Meg - Elane, Solange ■ 30, Suzy ■ 7 ■ 63 ■ 63, Cenira ■ 25 - Valeria (Formiga 80), Sissi (c), Leda Maria ■ 62 (14 **Márcia Taffarel** 90), Fanta - Pretinha (Tânia 66), Roseli. *Ademar*

GER • Goller - Lohn - Austermühl ■ 35 (17 Tina **Wunderlich** 46 ■ 65), Bernhard, Wiegmann, Neid (18 Pia **Wunderlich** 83) - Mohr, Neid (c), Voss, Pohlmann - Meinert (Brocker 74), Prinz ■ 59. *Bisanz*

1995 Group stage

Group B

Unstoppable Norway

Norway had beaten some men's teams before arriving in Sweden, and Nigeria were the first side in the group to experience their sheer class. It was a baptism of fire for the African champions and they were blown away 8-0, Kristin Sandberg scoring with both feet and her head for a perfect hat-trick. Canada's late two-goal surge gave fellow debutants England a scare, but Gillian Coultard's brace either side of a Marieanne Spacey penalty secured the win. After an overnight journey by sleeper train, an England team that included future boss Hope Powell faced Norway in Karlstad. Both were European Championship losing semi-finalists, but Norway's athleticism and goals from Tone Haugen and Hege Riise proved to be the difference. Canada, quarter-finalists in the 1988 International Women's Football Tournament, dropped valuable points when Nigeria pulled back from 3-1 down to draw, and they were homeward bound after a 7-0 loss to Norway, Ann Kristin Aarønes with a hat-trick this time. With a knockout berth at stake, England and Nigeria was a feisty five-goal affair, with Hammarby IF striker Karen Farley scoring twice and setting up Karen Walker to see Ted Copeland's side safely into the quarters.

	W	D	L	+	−	PTS
NOR	3	0	0	17	0	9
ENG	2	0	1	6	6	6
CAN	0	1	2	5	13	1
NGA	0	1	2	5	14	1

Tingvalla, Karlstad
6.06.1995, 19:00, 4,344

NORWAY 8-0 NIGERIA

Sandberg (3) 30 44 82
Riise 49, Aarønes (2) 60 90
Medalen 67, Svensson 76p

Referee: Alain Hamer LUX
Assistants: Hisae Yoshizawa JPN & Gitte Holm DEN

NOR • 1 Bente **Nordby** - 2 Tina **Svensson**, 3 Gro **Espeseth**, 4 Anne Nymark **Andersen** 5 Nina Nymark Andersen 77, 13 Merete **Myklebust** - 6 Hege **Riise** (18 Tone Gunn **Frustøl** 69), 8 Heidi **Støre** (c) (16 Marianne **Pettersen** 55), 7 Tone **Haugen** - 9 Kristin **Sandberg**, 10 Linda **Medalen**, 11 Ann Kristin **Aarønes**. *Even Pellerud*

NGA • 1 Ann **Agumanu** - 10 Mavis **Ogun** - 14 Phoebe **Ebimiekumo**, 5 Omo-Love **Branch** (7 Nkechi **Mbilitam** 73 ■ 86), 3 Ngozi **Ezeocha** ■ 69 (11 Prisca **Emeafu** 71) - 2 Florence **Omagbemi** (c), 13 Nkiru **Okosieme**, 20 Ann **Mukoro** - 12 Mercy **Akide** (18 Patience **Avre** 46), 8 Rita **Nwadike**, 4 Adaku **Okoroafor**. *Paul Hamilton*

Olympia Stadion, Helsingborg
6.06.1995, 19:00, 655

ENGLAND 3-2 CANADA

Coultard (2) 51p 85   Stoumbos 87
Spacey 76p   Donnelly 90+1

Referee: Eva Ödlund SWE
Assistants: Jeon Young Hyun KOR & Manuel Yupanqui Souza PER

ENG • 1 Pauline **Cope** - 3 Tina **Mapes** (2 Hope **Powell** 70), 4 Samantha **Britton**, 11 Brenda **Sempare**, 5 Clare **Taylor** - 8 Deborah **Bampton** (c), 10 Karen **Burke**, 6 Gillian **Coultard**, 7 Marieanne **Spacey** - 14 Karen **Walker** (12 Kerry **Davis** 75), 9 Karen **Farley** ■ 77. *Ted Copeland*

CAN • 18 Carla **Chin** - 4 Michelle **Ring**, 10 Veronica **O'Brien**, 9 Janine **Wood**, 5 Andrea **Neil** - 13 Angela **Kelly**, 14 Cathy **Ross** (15 Suzanne **Muir** 78), 6 Geraldine **Donnelly** (c) ■ 44, 3 Charmaine **Hooper** - 2 Helen **Stoumbos** ■ 17, 17 Silvana **Burtini**. *Sylvie Béliveau*

Tingvalla, Karlstad
8.06.1995, 19:00, 5,520

NORWAY 2-0 ENGLAND

Haugen 7
Riise 37

Referee: Eduardo Gamboa Martinez CHI
Assistants: Gitte Holm DEN & Hisae Yoshizawa JPN

NOR • **Nordby** - **Svensson**, N Nymark **Andersen** ■ 34, **Espeseth** (c), **Myklebust** - **Riise** (14 Hege **Gunnerød** 85), **Haugen**, A Nymark **Andersen** - **Sandberg** (**Pettersen** 66), **Medalen** (15 Randi **Leinan** 73), **Aarønes**. *Pellerud*

ENG • **Cope** - **Sempare** ■ 54, **Mapes**, **Taylor**, **Britton** (**Davis** 65) - **Burke**, **Bampton** (c), **Coultard** (20 Rebecca **Easton** 82), **Spacey** (**Powell** 36) - **Farley**, **Walker**. *Copeland*

Olympia Stadion, Helsingborg
8.06.1995, 19:00, 250

NIGERIA 3-3 CANADA

Nwadike 26, Avre 60   Burtini (2) 12 55
Okoroafor 77   Donnelly 20

Referee: Pirom Un-Prasert THA
Assistants: Manuel Yupanqui Souza PER & Eva Ödlund SWE

NGA • **Agumanu** - **Ogun**, **Omagbemi** (c), **Branch** (**Mbilitam** 41 ■ 83), **Emeafu** - **Ebimiekumo**, **Avre** ■ 14, 6 Yinka **Kudaisi**, **Nwadike** - 15 Maureen **Mmadu** (**Mukoro** 60), **Okoroafor**. *Hamilton*

CAN • **Chin** - 16 Luce **Mongrain** ■ 44, **Wood**, **Neil**, **O'Brien** (19 Suzanne **Gerrior** 61) - **Kelly**, **Donnelly** (c), **Hooper** - 11 Annie **Caron** (**Stoumbos** 77), **Burtini**, **Ring**. *Béliveau*

Strömvallen, Gävle
10.06.1995, 16:00, 2,715

NORWAY 7-0 CANADA

Aarønes (3) 4 21 90+3
Riise 12, Pettersen (2) 71 89
Leinan 84

Referee: Maria Siqueira BRA
Assistants: Gitte Holm DEN & Christine Frai GER

NOR • **Nordby** - **Svensson**, **Espeseth**, A Nymark **Andersen**, **Myklebust** - **Pettersen**, **Haugen** (19 Agnete **Carlsen** 69), **Støre** (c), **Riise** (**Leinan** 46), **Medalen** (**Sandberg** 46), **Aarønes**. *Pellerud*

CAN • **Chin** - **Ross**, **Ring** ■ 88, **Wood**, **Muir** (**Neil** 85) - **Hooper** ■ 36, **Donnelly** (c) ■ 80, **Kelly**, **Caron** ■ 26 - **Stoumbos**, **Burtini**. *Béliveau*

Tingvalla, Karlstad
10.06.1995, 16:00, 1,843

NIGERIA 2-3 ENGLAND

Okoroafor 13   Farley (2) 10 38
Nwadike 74   Walker 27

Referee: Ingrid Jonsson SWE
Assistants: Hisae Yoshizawa JPN & Maria Rodríguez MEX

NGA • **Agumanu** - **Ogun** - **Omagbemi** (c), **Kudaisi** ■ 68 - **Ezeocha** (**Mmadu** 44 ■ 90), **Emeafu**, **Mukoro**, **Ebimiekumo** ■ 5 - **Avre** (**Okosieme** 47), **Nwadike**, **Okoroafor** (9 Ngozi **Uche** 53). *Hamilton*

ENG • 13 Lesley **Higgs** - **Mapes**, **Taylor** (**Britton** 81), **Sempare** (**Easton** 58), **Davis** - **Burke**, **Bampton** (c), **Coultard**, **Spacey** (**Powell** 70) - **Farley**, **Walker**. *Copeland*

▶ The one that got away, but Ann Agumanu had eight goals put past her in Nigeria's opening match against Norway.

17

Norway scored 17 goals without reply – a record for any World Cup or Olympic group that stood for 24 years until it was broken by the USA at France 2019.

▶ Action from England against Canada. Three of the five goals came in the last five minutes.

Group C

The holders march on

With Michelle Akers, Julie Foudy, Mary Harvey and Kristine Lilly having all played for Tyresö FF, there was a familiarity about the USA for Swedish fans. There was a new look to the champions though, with Tony DiCicco as head coach, retired skipper April Heinrichs his assistant, Mia Hamm in attack and Briana Scurry in at No.1. Akers was still key, but her part in the group stage was ended by injury against China, now led by Ma Yuanan. Rallying after the loss of their talisman to lead 3-1, the USA were hit by an equaliser from Sun Wen. After losing Sonia Gegenhuber to a red card, an Australia side featuring Fortuna Hjørring's Alison Forman were overcome 5-0 by a Danish line-up that included four of her club mates. Denmark had already beaten the USA that year, but World Cup bragging rights went to the Americans after they beat the Danes, even though Hamm had to step in for the red-carded Scurry. "It was my first, and hopefully last, time in goal," Hamm declared. Tied on points after China's win over debutants Australia, the USA beat the same opponents 4-1 to finish top on goal difference, Debbie Keller's late goal topping China's 3-1 tally over Denmark.

Time-out!

FIFA first experimented with time-outs at the 1995 World Cup.

Each team was allowed to call one two-minute break per half. The rules were tightened mid-tournament to enable the teams to call for a time-out only at throw-ins, goal kicks or after a goal had been scored, but they weren't universally popular. Australia were the only team to take advantage of every opportunity, while the Germans refused to take any at all.

	W	D	L	+	-	PTS
USA	2	1	0	9	4	7
CHN	2	1	0	10	6	7
DEN	1	0	2	6	5	3
AUS	0	0	3	3	13	0

◀ Mia Hamm celebrates her goal against China. In the match against Denmark she replaced Briana Scurry in goal meaning that in 1991 and 1995 she had played in every position – as a goalkeeper, defender, midfielder and forward.

Strömvallen, Gävle
6.06.1995, 19:00, **4,635**

USA 3-3 **CHINA PR**

Venturini 22 — Wang Liping 38
Milbrett 34, Hamm 51 — Wei Haiying 74, Sun Wen 79

Ingrid Jonsson SWE
Christine Frai GER & Ana Bia Batista BRA

USA • 1 Briana **Scurry** - 4 Carla **Overbeck** (c), 8 Linda **Hamilton**, 14 Joy **Fawcett**, 11 Julie **Foudy** - 5 Tiffany **Roberts**, 15 Tisha **Venturini**, 13 Kristine **Lilly** - 12 Carin **Gabarra**, 10 Michelle **Akers** (16 Tiffeny **Milbrett** 18) (3 Holly **Manthei** 76), 9 Mia **Hamm**. *Tony DiCicco*

CHN • 1 **Zhong** Honglian - 5 **Zhou** Yang - 3 **Fan** Yunjie, 13 **Niu** Lijie - 12 **Wen** Lirong, 2 **Wang** Liping ■ 3, 16 **Chen** Yufeng (10 **Liu** Ailing 47), 17 **Zhao** Lihong - 15 **Shi** Guihong (7 **Wei** Haiying 35), 9 **Sun** Wen, 11 **Sun** Qingmei (c) (8 **Shui** Qingxia 84). *Ma Yuanan*

Arosvallen, Västerås
6.06.1995, 19:00, **1,500**

DENMARK 5-0 **AUSTRALIA**

Krogh (2) 12 48, Nielsen 25
Jensen 37, C Hansen 86

Bente Skogvang NOR
Mohammed Osman SDN & Mamadou Touré MLI

DEN • 1 Dorthe **Larsen** - 3 Kamma **Flæng** - 5 Katrine **Pedersen** (19 Jeanne **Axelsen** 78), 4 Lene **Terp**, 6 Rikke **Holm** - 12 Anne **Nielsen**, 7 Annette **Laursen** ■ 28 (15 Christina **Bonde** 65), 10 Birgit **Christensen**, 9 Helle **Jensen** (c) - 11 Gitte **Krogh**, 14 Lene **Madsen** (13 Christina **Hansen** 63). *Keld Gantzhorn*

AUS • 1 Tracey **Wheeler** - 6 Anissa **Tann-Darby** - 7 Alison **Forman** ■ 25, 8 Sonia **Gegenhuber** ■ 30 - 2 Sarah **Cooper**, 12 Michelle **Watson** ■ 45, 5 Cheryl **Salisbury** ■ 37 (9 Angela **Iannotta** 57), 4 Julie **Murray** (c), 3 Jane **Oakley** - 16 Lisa **Casagrande** (19 Lizzy **Claydon** 79), 10 Sunni **Hughes** (15 Kim **Lembryk** 57). *Tom Sermanni SCO*

Strömvallen, Gävle
8.06.1995, 19:00, **2,704**

USA 2-0 **DENMARK**

Lilly 9
Milbrett 49

Mamadouba Camara GUI
Ana Bia Batista BRA & Christine Frai GER

USA • **Scurry** ■ 88 - **Overbeck** (c), **Hamilton** (2 Thori **Staples** 53), **Fawcett** - **Roberts**, **Venturini**, **Foudy** ■ 38, **Lilly** - **Hamm** ■ 29, **Milbrett** (6 Debbie **Keller** 61), **Gabarra** (7 Sarah **Rafanelli** 85). *DiCicco*

DEN • **Larsen** ■ 55 - **Flæng** - **Pedersen**, **Terp**, **Holm** - **Nielsen**, **Christensen**, **Laursen** (**Axelsen** 46), **Jensen** (c) - **Madsen** (20 Christina **Petersen** 61 ■ 89), **Krogh** (C **Hansen** 53). *Gantzhorn*

Arosvallen, Västerås
8.06.1995, 19:00, **1,500**

CHINA PR 4-2 **AUSTRALIA**

Zhou Yang 23 — Iannotta 25
Shi Guihong (2) 54 78 — Hughes 89
Liu Ailing 90+3

Maria Siqueira BRA
Mamadou Touré MLI & Mohammed Osman SDN

CHN • **Zhong** Honglian - **Wang** Liping, **Fan** Yunjie, **Zhou** Yang (c) ■ 79, 14 **Xie** Huilin - **Chen** Yufeng (**Wen** Lirong 69), **Liu** Ailing, **Zhao** Lihong - **Shi** Guihong, **Sun** Wen, **Shui** Qingxia (**Wei** Haiying 27). *Ma Yuanan*

AUS • **Wheeler** - **Cooper**, **Forman**, **Salisbury** ■ 73 (**Claydon** 77), **Oakley** - **Watson** ■ 83, **Murray** (c) (14 Denie **Pentecost** 81), **Tann-Darby**, **Lembryk** ■ 62 (**Casagrande** 62) - **Iannotta**, **Hughes**. *Sermanni SCO*

Olympia Stadion, Helsingborg
10.06.1995, 16:00, **1,105**

USA 4-1 **AUSTRALIA**

Foudy 69, Fawcett 72 — Casagrande 54
Overbeck 90+2p
Keller 90+4

Pirom Un-Prasert THA
Corinne Lagrange FRA & Jeon Young Hyun KOR

USA • 18 Saskia **Webber** - **Overbeck** (c) - **Hamilton**, **Staples** - **Manthei** (**Gabarra** 46), **Venturini** ■ 53, **Lilly**, **Fawcett** - **Milbrett** (**Keller** 78), **Hamm**, 19 Amanda **Cromwell** (**Foudy** 61). *DiCicco*

AUS • **Wheeler** - **Cooper**, **Forman** ■ 42, **Tann-Darby**, **Gegenhuber** - **Oakley** (17 Sacha **Wainwright** 75), **Murray** (c) ■ 88, **Iannotta** ■ 82 - **Hughes**, **Lembryk** (11 Kaylene **Janssen** 82), **Casagrande** (**Claydon** 67). *Sermanni SCO*

Arosvallen, Västerås
10.06.1995, 16:00, **1,619**

CHINA PR 3-1 **DENMARK**

Shi Guihong 21, Sun Wen 76 — Bonde 44
Wei Haiying 90

Eduardo Gamboa Martínez CHI
Mamadou Touré MLI & Mohammed Osman SDN

CHN • 20 **Gao** Hong - **Zhou** Yang (c) - **Fan** Yunjie, **Wen** Lirong, **Xie** Huilin - **Wang** Liping, **Liu** Ailing, **Sun** Wen, **Zhao** Lihong - **Wei** Haiying, **Shi** Guihong (**Shui** Qingxia 73). *Ma Yuanan*

DEN • **Larsen** - C **Hansen**, **Pedersen** (18 Bettina **Allentoft** 43), **Terp**, **Holm** - **Nielsen** ■ 56, 2 Louise **Hansen**, **Jensen** (c) (**Bonde** 26), **Christensen** - **Madsen** (**Petersen** 79), **Krogh**. *Gantzhorn*

1995 Quarter-finals

Easy for Germany

Arosvallen, Västerås
13.06.1995, 20:15, **2,317**

GERMANY 🇩🇪 **3-0** 🏴󠁧󠁢󠁥󠁮󠁧󠁿 **ENGLAND**

Voss 41, Meinert 55
Mohr 82

Bente Skogvang NOR
Gitte Holm DEN & Jeon Young Hyun KOR

GER • Goller - Lohn - Bernhard, Wiegmann, Minnert - Neid (c), Voss, Pohlmann - Mohr, Prinz (Brocker 67), Meinert (P Wunderlich 85). *Bisanz*

ENG • Cope - Mapes (17 Louise **Waller** 79), Sempare ▪70, Taylor (Britton 87), Davis - Burke, Coultard (Easton 46 ▪57), Spacey, Bampton (c) - Walker, Farley. *Copeland*

Only two years into their backing by The Football Association, England were still playing catch-up with the world's best in terms of investment, youth development and fitness. Reaching the knockouts in Sweden was therefore something of an achievement in itself and after six defeats in six meetings with Germany, the most recent in the European Championship semi-finals, there was only an outside chance they would progress. Nevertheless, an England squad boasting raw talent and a lively camaraderie beamed in their oversized men's shirts before facing a youthful German team blessed with technique, power and experience. England stood firm for 41 minutes before Martina Voss broke their resistance, and Maren Meinert and Heidi Mohr finished them off. "We held our own," striker Karen Farley would later recall. "The crushing thing was that we couldn't go to the Olympics." Only a non-existent Great Britain side could do that, so ninth-placed Brazil went instead.

▶ Action from Germany against England. The Germans were the only team to fly between venues. The other teams took the train.

Gao Hong saves the day

Olympia Stadion, Helsingborg
13.06.1995, 20:15, **7,537**

SWEDEN 🇸🇪 **1-1** 🇨🇳 **CHINA PR**
AET
3-4 PSO

Kalte 90+3   Sun Qingmei 29

Sun Wen ⊕ Andersson ✖ Xie Huilin ⊕ Videkull ⊕ Chen Yufeng ⊕ Pohjanen ⊕ Shui Qingxia ⊕ Sundhage ⊕ Liu Ailing ✖ Nessvold ✖

Sonia Denoncourt CAN
Manuel Yupanqui Souza PER & Corinne Lagrange FRA

SWE • Leidinge - Bengtsson (13 Annika **Nessvold** 65), Hedberg, Sundhage, Zeikfalvy (Lönnqvist 46) - H Nilsson, Videkull (c), Pohjanen, Andersson - Kalte, Andelén (Flink 71). *Simonson*

CHN • Gao Hong - Wang Liping (Shui Qingxia 103), Fan Yunjie, Zhou Yang (c), Xie Huilin ▪22 - Wen Lirong, Sun Qingmei, Zhao Lihong (Chen Yufeng 119) - Sun Wen, Liu Ailing ▪77, Shi Guihong (Wei Haiying 51). *Ma Yuanan*

If home fans had experienced a rollercoaster of emotions during Sweden's dramatic group campaign, they were in for another rocky ride as the hosts and China served up an historic Women's World Cup first — a penalty shoot-out. The two sides had, of course, met at this stage in 1991 when Sweden ended China's tournament on their home soil. Both sides fielded a handful of players from that match here, and one of them, China's Sun Qingmei, looked to have settled old scores with a first-half header in an electrifying match packed with chances. Then, with seconds remaining, Ulrika Kalte planted Malin Andersson's cross into the net, the crowd were in raptures, the game into extra time. After extra time failed to separate the sides, Sweden's World Cup was ended by two penalty saves from a woman who kicked off her career in a factory team, China's commanding presence between the sticks, Gao Hong.

▼ The agony of a penalty shoot-out defeat. Sweden's Anna Pohjanen (6) scored hers, but it wasn't enough.

▼ China's Gao Hong saves Annika Nessvold's penalty to send the hosts crashing out.

No Akers? No problem

Strömvallen, Gävle
13.06.1995, 17:15, **3,756**

JAPAN ● 0-4 ▇ **USA**

Lilly (2) 8 42
Milbrett 45
Venturini 80

Eduardo Gamboa Martínez CHI
Mohammed Osman SDN & Mamadou Touré MLI

JPN • Ozawa - Tomei, Yamaki ■ 72, Haneta, Nishina - Kioka, Takakura, Obe, Handa (Otake 46) - Uchiyama, Noda (c). *Suzuki*

USA • Scurry - Hamilton, Overbeck (c), Fawcett - Roberts ■ 47, Venturini (Cromwell 80), Foudy, Lilly (Staples 68) - Hamm (Keller 61), Milbrett, Gabarra. *DiCicco*

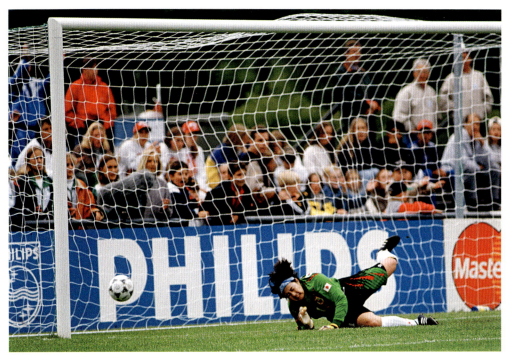

▲ Japan's Junko Ozawa fails to stop Kristine Lilly's opening goal for the USA.

While all-time leading striker Michelle Akers continued her recovery, the USA had shared the scoring load between eight players and were now two games away from the winner-takes-all final. Japan stood in their way first, but even with their improved organisation, mental strength, tireless running and 16-year-old prodigy Homare Sawa, they only had two goals to their name in Sweden. Despite the return of USA keeper Briana Scurry, Japan believed they had a chance to add to their tally. The USA were imperious from front to back though, and the quality of Kristine Lilly's eighth-minute 30-yard piledriver and 22-year-old Tiffeny Milbrett's searing volley and neat forward roll celebration were breathtaking. It was a formative experience for Japan, who would rise again many years later, doing so against the USA no less, but this day belonged to the reigning champions.

▲ Denmark's Dorthe Larsen saves a shot by Norway's Hege Riise.

Norway win Scandinavian derby

Tingvalla, Karlstad
13.06.1995, 17:15, **4,655**

NORWAY ▇ 3-1 ▇ **DENMARK**

Espeseth 21 — Krogh 86
Medalen 64
Riise 85

Pirom Un-Prasert THA
Peter Kelly TRI & María Rodríguez MEX

NOR • Nordby - Svensson, Espeseth, A Nymark Andersen, Myklebust - Riise, Støre (c), Haugen, Aarønes (Carlsen 76) - Pettersen (Leinan 84), Medalen ■ 23. *Pellerud*

DEN • Larsen - Flæng - Pedersen, Terp, Holm ■ 90 - Jensen (c) - Nielsen, L Hansen (Laursen 63), Christensen - Madsen (Bonde 86), Axelsen (Krogh 46). *Gantzhorn*

Bente Nordby was a teenage benchwarmer in 1991 but she arrived in Sweden as Norway's first-choice keeper and was unbeaten in the World Cup ahead of this clash of Scandinavian rivals. Having conceded 25 goals to Norway in their previous six meetings, Denmark knew they had to put Nordby to the test in Karlstad if their campaign was to continue. Keld Gantzhorn's side had come on in leaps and bounds since they met in the 1991 finals, but Norway's will to win proved too strong and they shuffled along on their hands and knees in celebration as goals from Gro Espeseth, Linda Medalen and Hege Riise beat Denmark's own excellent keeper Dorthe Larsen. The Danes were out, but not without halting 20-year-old Nordby's run first, substitute Gitte Krogh slotting in a late consolation to stop the keeper's unbeaten clock on 356 minutes and finish the tournament as Denmark's top scorer in the process.

1995 **Semi-finals**

Ecstasy for Norway, agony for Støre

Arosvallen, Västerås
15.06.1995, 17:15, **2,893**
USA 🇺🇸 **0-1** 🇳🇴 NORWAY
Aarønes 10

Alain Hamer LUX Manuel Yupanqui Souza PER & Jeon Young Hyun KOR
USA • Scurry - Overbeck (c) - Hamilton, Fawcett - Roberts (Milbrett 53), Foudy, Venturini, Gabarra, Lilly - Hamm, Akers. *DiCicco*
NOR • Nordby - Svensson ■ 6, N Nymark Andersen, Espeseth, Myklebust - Riise, Haugen (Pettersen 69), Støre (c) ■ 22 ■ 76 ■ 76, A Nymark Andersen - Aarønes, Medalen. *Pellerud*

When it came to World Cup grudge matches, the USA versus Norway is one of the great rivalries in the women's game. Crushed by a late goal in the 1991 final, Norway were rigorously prepared for Sweden, as were the champions, in camp together since February. A penalty shoot-out had seen Norway win the teams' most recent battle, for third place at the Algarve Cup. The stakes were higher this time though, and while Norway had on-fire striker Ann Kristin Aarønes to lead their line, two parts of the USA's 1991 "triple-edged sword" were back in business as Michelle Akers returned from injury to take her place alongside Carin (Jennings) Gabarra. With five goals in four games, Aarønes was the sharper though, and she rose to head beyond Briana Scurry after just ten minutes. Norway were flying and with the champions behind for only the second time in a World Cup match, head coach Tony DiCicco issued a rallying cry. "I told my players not to panic, to keep working hard and get hold of the game," he said. They almost did in a desperate late push after Norway's most-capped player Heidi Støre was red-carded, but Even Pellerud's ten remaining players – and the woodwork – held firm to see Norway through.

▶ Norway captain Heidi Støre is sent off after a second yellow card in the semi-final against the USA. It meant she missed the Final and the opportunity to lift the World Cup.

Wiegmann knocks China out

Olympia Stadion, Helsingborg
15.06.1995, 20:15, **3,693**
GERMANY 🇩🇪 **1-0** 🇨🇳 CHINA PR
Wiegmann 79

Petros Mathabela RSA Peter Kelly TRI & María Rodríguez MEX
GER • Goller - Lohn - Bernhard, Austermühl - Neid (c), Wiegmann, Meinert, Pohlmann - Mohr, Prinz (P Wunderlich 83), Voss. *Bisanz*
CHN • Gao Hong - Wen Lirong ■ 52, Wang Liping, Zhou Yang (c), Fan Yunjie (Chen Yufeng 86) - Sun Wen, Liu Ailing, Shi Guihong ■ 65, Zhao Lihong - Sun Qingmei, Xie Huilin. *Ma Yuanan*

An hour after Norway and the USA had delivered a gripping finish in Västerås, two continental champions were ready to face off in Helsingborg. After seeing off all-comers with the exception of hosts Sweden, Germany were the favourites to reach the final. China, having survived a draining extra-time battle and penalty shoot-out with the Swedes, had already made history as the first Asian team to reach the last four. The real prize was agonisingly close, and the match was as well, both keepers and defences busily repelling attacks at either end. Midway through the second half, Sun Wen looked to have broken the deadlock only to wallop the post, and moments later Germany captain Silvia Neid, in her 100th international, combined to brilliant effect with teenager Birgit Prinz, jinked into the box but skied her shot with only Gao Hong to beat. In the end, it all came down to a poor clearance from defence and a late goal from Bettina Wiegmann, the midfielder's third of the tournament. China now faced a battle for third, Germany were vying for the title and as they bobbed and hugged in a circle at the final whistle, their relief seemed heartfelt.

▲ Maren Meinert (6) was one of the six German players in the 1995 squad who were part of the World Cup-winning squad of 2003.

1995 Match for Third Place

Strömvallen, Gävle
17.06.1995, 16:00, **4,335**
CHINA PR 0-2 USA
Venturini 24, Hamm 55

Sonia Denoncourt CAN · Manuel Yupanqui Souza PER & Hisae Yoshizawa JPN

20 Gao Hong

2 Wang Liping
3 Fan Yunjie (Chen Yufeng 72)
13 Niu Lijie
14 Xie Huilin ▪ 90+2

12 Wen Lirong
10 Liu Ailing
9 Sun Wen (Wei Haiying 59)
17 Zhao Lihong

15 Shi Guihong
11 Sun Qingmei (c)

Ma Yuanan

DiCicco

12 Gabarra (Rafanelli 80)
16 Milbrett (Keller 68)
9 Hamm

13 Lilly
15 Venturini
11 Foudy

14 Fawcett
4 Overbeck (c)
8 Hamilton (Roberts 54)
2 Staples

1 Scurry

27

China's Liu Ailing played in every match for China from the 1988 International Women's Football Tournament to the Sydney Olympics in 2000. In those 27 matches she started 26 and was a half-time substitute in the other.

Medals all round

After their hard-fought 3-3 draw in their opening match of the campaign, the USA and China were pitched together again and while it was not the longed-for final that both teams had surely dreamed of, there was a medal at stake nevertheless. At the same Strömvallen Stadium 11 days previously, four-time Asian champions China had staged a rousing revival to level the scores against a USA side stung by the loss of inspirational striker Michelle Akers to knee and head injuries after just seven minutes. Tisha Venturini had taken on the mantle of hotshot in Akers' absence, and the 22-year-old joined Kristine Lilly and Tiffeny Milbrett on three goals for the USA when she broke the deadlock of an evenly contested match with a header on 24 minutes. After Briana Scurry had kept the USA in the lead just before the break with full-stretch saves from China's top goalscoring talents Shi Guihong and Sun Wen, a moment of class from Mia Hamm in the second half wrapped it up. Deployed in midfield and defence at the first World Cup, Hamm had stepped into April Heinrichs' striking boots after the captain's retirement and was already their top scorer for the year when she finished a driving run from her own half with a supergoal. The USA had won bronze but Akers was already eyeing another shot at gold. "I am very proud of my team in the way they came back and played with pride," she said. "We're looking forward to the World Cup in 1999."

▼ The Chinese and American teams after the match for third place. From the first World Cup in 1991 until the 2003 finals, it was customary for both the winners and losers of this match to receive medals.

1995 Final

17

At 17, Birgit Prinz remains the youngest player to appear in a World Cup Final. She was also younger than another famous 17-year-old in the men's World Cup – Pelé – who played in the 1958 Final in the same stadium.

Norway back at the summit

The stage was set for an intriguing battle between two of Europe's top teams in the pouring rain at the Råsunda. Brazil's men had laid the ghosts of their 1950 World Cup defeat to rest by winning the World Cup in this stadium 37 years earlier, so could Norway put the disappointment of four years ago to bed here too? They were the only unbeaten team in the competition, but they were up against a side that had defeated them in two European Championship finals. Both teams were strong and talented though, and each fielded players who could turn a match in the blink of an eye. Whatever happened, a new name was set to be carved into the trophy and Women's World Cup history.

Five of the stars from the 1991 final lined up for Norway, including the youngest player on the pitch that day in China, Gro Espeseth, who took the armband in place of suspended captain Heidi Støre. Veterans Heidi Mohr and Silvia Neid led Germany's charge, and the skipper was determined to enjoy every second after missing all but 37 minutes of the inaugural tournament through injury.

"I had prepared really well," Neid would later recall. "It was clear that it was my last World Cup." Neid might have left Sweden with the match ball from Germany's semi-final as a memento of her 100th cap, but she would not claim a gold medal – Norway's winning mentality was too finely tuned for that. So was player of the tournament Hege Riise, who grabbed the game by the scruff of the neck in the first half with a world-class solo run and goal, which was swiftly followed by Norway's second from Marianne Pettersen.

"We didn't think about what was at the end of the tournament," Riise would say later. "But a lot about every match, what's the next step, the next step, and that way an energy is built up which makes it almost impossible to lose." Germany attempted to buck the trend and Neid came closest with a powerful late header, but Even Pellerud's side held firm to become the first European team to hold the Women's World Cup aloft. Influential captain Støre summed up the mood when she said: "We stood up for each other and found the winning recipe that summer."

1995 World Cup Final

Råsunda, Solna, Stockholm
18.06.1995, 18:00, **17,158**

GERMANY 🇩🇪 **0-2** 🇳🇴 **NORWAY**
Riise 37, Pettersen 40

Ingrid Jonsson SWE · Gitte Holm DEN & María Rodríguez MEX

▼ Action from the 1995 World Cup Final. Two goals scored late in the first half won it for Norway.

Final 1995

2

The number of sisters who have been crowned world champions. The 1995 World Cup Final saw Norway's Anne and Nina Nymark Andersen appear in the 2-0 victory over Germany... Nina in defence and Anne in midfield. They are also the only twins to win either the women's or men's World Cup. The following year they would both win a bronze medal at the Atlanta Olympics.

▶ Norway with the World Cup trophy. It was later stolen from the headquarters of the Norwegian FA during renovation work.

◀ Heidi Støre's gold medal.
FIFA Museum Collection

The snake

It was the iconic celebration of the 1995 World Cup, as Norway captain Heidi Støre recalls. "It was actually something Hege Riise and I, who were room-mates, invented one night in Sweden during pre-camp and introduced to the girls. We were watching a basketball game from the USA on TV, they had a special celebration – I don't remember what – and we agreed that we needed something ourselves. That's how we came up with 'the snake'."

▶ Norway's goal celebrations became an iconic feature of the tournament. It helped that they scored an incredible 23 in total.

◀ Norway's Gro Espeseth had the honour of lifting the World Cup. At the 1988 International Women's Football Tournament Heidi Støre had lifted the trophy for the Norwegians, but was absent from the 1995 Final after being sent off in the semi-final.

1996

Women's football was accepted as an official Olympic sport for the first time at the Centennial Games in Atlanta in 1996. Eight teams played a total of 16 games in two groups, followed by the semi-finals, a bronze medal match and a Final. The USA claimed the first Olympic title in women's football when they beat China 2-1 in the Final. Tiffeny Milbrett scored a second-half winner in front of a huge crowd of 76,489 at the Sanford Stadium in Athens, Georgia.

Recognition at last

▼ Michael Johnson sets a new world record in the 200m at the Olympic Stadium.

Football had first been recognised as an official sport for men at the 1908 Olympic Games in London. Eighty-eight years later, women were at last given the same recognition – five years after the first Women's World Cup and largely as a consequence of it. Thousands of enthusiastic spectators witnessed the historic triumph of America's women footballers as well as a first Olympic title for an African country, after Nigeria claimed gold in the men's tournament. This was the Olympics of Michael Johnson, the first man to win both the 200m and 400m, but the Games were marred by accusations of over-commercialisation and the Olympic Park bombing of 27 July in which two people died and 111 were injured. After the Games, the Olympic Stadium was converted into a baseball ground for the Atlanta Braves and renamed Turner Field, and in 2017 it began another phase of redevelopment when it was bought by Georgia State University.

1996 **Overview**

ATLANTA 1996

WOMEN'S OLYMPIC FOOTBALL TOURNAMENT

Story of the qualifiers

England miss out

There was not enough time to organise a qualifying tournament for the 1996 Atlanta Olympics so FIFA decided that the top eight finishers at the 1995 World Cup would qualify automatically. However, the quarter-finalists in Sweden included England, a footballing nation not recognised by the IOC. The reluctance of the Welsh, Northern Irish and Scots to undermine their historical status as independent footballing nations, despite the political unity of a United Kingdom comprising all four, meant that a Great Britain football team was simply not a fixture at the Olympics. And that was not about to change for these Games. The FA in London, whose team had qualified, simply did not have the authority to select a Great Britain team, even if it wanted to. Brazil replaced England as the team with the best record from the group stage and they joined the USA from North America, China and Japan from Asia, and four teams from Europe – world champions Norway, World Cup runners-up Germany along with quarter-finalists Sweden and Denmark.

Regulations

Squads of 16

Despite a schedule of three group games in five days, each of the eight teams was restricted to a squad of just 16 players. There was, however, a provision to call up replacements in the event of injury from a reserve list of four players.

▲ After winning the play-off for third place at the 1995 World Cup in Sweden, the USA team held up a banner looking forward to the first Women's Olympic Football Tournament the following year.

Group stage

*The groups in the Women's Olympic Football Tournament were designated E and F because groups A, B, C and D were used in the men's tournament.

GROUP E			GROUP F		
USA	3-0	DEN	NOR	2-2	BRA
SWE	0-2	CHN	GER	3-2	JPN
USA	2-1	SWE	NOR	3-2	GER
DEN	1-5	CHN	BRA	2-0	JPN
USA	0-0	CHN	NOR	4-0	JPN
DEN	1-3	SWE	BRA	1-1	GER

	W	D	L	+	−	PTS		W	D	L	+	−	PTS
CHN	2	1	0	7	1	7	NOR	2	1	0	9	4	7
USA	2	1	0	5	1	7	BRA	1	2	0	5	3	5
SWE	1	0	2	4	5	3	GER	1	1	1	6	6	4
DEN	0	0	3	2	11	0	JPN	0	0	3	2	9	0

Knockout stages

SEMI-FINAL			SEMI-FINAL		
CHN	3-2	BRA	NOR	1-2	USA

BRONZE MEDAL MATCH

BRA	0-2	NOR

GOLD MEDAL MATCH

CHN	1-2	USA

Overview 1996

8 TEAMS

USA WINNERS
CHN SECOND
NOR THIRD

691 762 SPECTATORS
43 235 AVERAGE PER MATCH

TOP OF THE MEDAL TABLE
UNITED STATES 44 32 25
RUSSIA 26 21 16
GERMANY 20 18 27
CHINA PR 16 22 12
FRANCE 15 7 15
ITALY 13 10 12

16 MATCHES PLAYED
31 YELLOW CARDS
4 RED CARDS

53 GOALS
3.31 AVERAGE GOALS PER MATCH

QUESTRA OLYMPIA
OFFICIAL MATCH BALL

Host cities and stadiums

Destination USA Part 1

There was criticism from within FIFA at the IOC's decision to take both the women's and the men's Olympic Football Tournaments away from host city Atlanta – not even the Finals were played in the main Olympic Stadium. In fact, the group matches were not even played in Georgia. Group E was based in Miami and Orlando in Florida, while Group F took place in Washington DC and Birmingham, Alabama. The knock-out stage was played in Georgia in the city of Athens, 115 kilometres to the east of Atlanta.

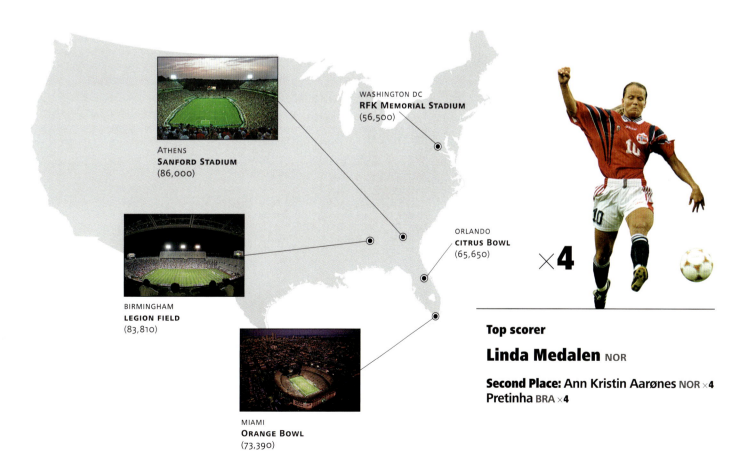

ATHENS
Sanford Stadium
(86,000)

WASHINGTON DC
RFK Memorial Stadium
(56,500)

ORLANDO
Citrus Bowl
(65,650)

BIRMINGHAM
Legion Field
(83,810)

MIAMI
Orange Bowl
(73,390)

×4

Top scorer

Linda Medalen NOR

Second Place: Ann Kristin Aarønes NOR ×4
Pretinha BRA ×4

1996 Group stage

Group E

Citrus Bowl, Orlando
21.07.1996, 16:00, **25,303**

USA 🇺🇸 **3-0** 🇩🇰 **DENMARK**

Venturini 37, Hamm 41
Milbrett 49

👁 Cláudia Vasconcelos BRA
🚩 Maria Rodriguez MEX & Nelly Viennot FRA

USA • 1 Briana **Scurry** - 14 Joy **Fawcett**, 4 Carla **Overbeck** (c), 6 Brandi **Chastain** - 8 Shannon **MacMillan**, 11 Julie **Foudy**, 10 Michelle **Akers** (3 Cindy **Parlow** 62), 15 Tisha **Venturini**, 13 Kristine **Lilly** - 9 Mia **Hamm** (12 Carin **Gabarra** 75), 16 Tiffeny **Milbrett** (5 Tiffany **Roberts** 66 ■ 85), *Tony DiCicco*

DEN • 1 Dorthe **Larsen** - 12 Lene **Terp**, 4 Kamma **Flæng** ■ 78, 3 Bonny **Madsen**, 5 Rikke **Holm** ■ 85 - 6 Christina **Petersen**, 7 Birgit **Christensen**, 8 Lisbet **Kolding** (c) (2 Annette **Laursen** 68), 13 Anne Dot **Eggers Nielsen** - 10 Gitte **Krogh** (15 Christina **Bonde** 80), 11 Lene **Madsen** (9 Helle **Jensen** 46). *Keld Gantzhorn*

Orange Bowl, Miami
21.07.1996, 16:00, **46,727**

SWEDEN 🇸🇪 **0-2** **CHINA PR**

Shi Guihong 31
Zhao Lihong 32

👁 Gamal El Ghandour EGY
🚩 Jeon Young Hyun KOR & Carlos Velazquez URU

SWE • 1 Annelie **Nilsson** - 4 Annika **Nessvold** - 2 Cecilia **Sandell**, 3 Åsa **Jakobsson** (13 Camilla **Svensson** 46), 5 Kristin **Bengtsson** - 6 Anna **Pohjanen** ■ 57 ■ 60, 7 Pia **Sundhage** (c), 10 Ulrika **Kalte** (16 Hanna **Ljungberg** 71), 8 Malin **Swedberg** ■ 88 - 14 Maria **Kun** (9 Malin **Andersson** 64), 11 Lena **Videkull**. *Bengt Simonson*

CHN • 16 Gao **Hong** - 12 Wen **Lirong**, 2 Wang **Liping** (13 Liu **Ying** 65), 5 Xie **Huilin**, 8 Shui **Qingxia** (4 Yu **Hongji** 60 ■ 68) - 3 Fan **Yunjie**, 9 Sun **Wen**, 10 Liu **Ailing**, 6 Zhao **Lihong** - 15 Shi **Guihong** (7 Wei **Haiyong** 60), 11 Sun **Qingmei** (c). *Ma Yuanan*

Citrus Bowl, Orlando
23.07.1996, 18:00, **28,000**

USA 🇺🇸 **2-1** 🇸🇪 **SWEDEN**

Venturini 59, MacMillan 62   Overbeck OG 64

👁 Bente Skogvang NOR
🚩 Dramane Dante MLI & Maria Rodriguez MEX

USA • Scurry - Fawcett, Overbeck (c), Chastain - MacMillan (7 Staci **Wilson** 89), Venturini, Akers, Foudy, Lilly - Hamm (Gabarra 85), Milbrett (Roberts 58). *DiCicco*

SWE • Nilsson - Nessvold ■ 87 - Sandell ■ 59 (Jakobsson 67), Svensson, Bengtsson - 15 Julia **Carlsson** (Ljungberg 56), Andersson, Sundhage (c), Swedberg - Kalte (Kun 85), Videkull. *Simonson*

Orange Bowl, Miami
23.07.1996, 18:00, **34,871**

DENMARK 🇩🇰 **1-5** **CHINA PR**

L Madsen 55   Shi Guihong 10, Liu Ailing 15
                 Sun Qingmei (2) 29 59
                 Fan Yunjie 36

👁 Benito Archundia MEX
🚩 Peter Kelly TRI & Mohammed Osman SDN

DEN • Larsen - B Madsen - Petersen (Laursen 84), Flæng, Holm - Jensen (Eggers Nielsen 45), Christensen, Terp, Kolding (c) - Krogh, Bonde (L Madsen 42). *Gantzhorn*

CHN • Gao Hong - Wen Lirong, Fan Yunjie, Xie Huilin, Wang Liping - Shui Qingxia, Liu Ailing (Yu Hongji 84), Sun Wen (14 **Chen Yufeng** 43), Zhao Lihong - Sun Qingmei (Liu Ying 61), Shi Guihong. *Ma Yuanan*

Orange Bowl, Miami
25.07.1996, 18:30, **55,650**

USA 🇺🇸 **0-0** **CHINA PR**

👁 Pierluigi Collina ITA
🚩 Mohammed Osman SDN & Carlos Velazquez URU

USA • Scurry - Fawcett, Overbeck (c), Chastain - Roberts, Foudy, Akers, Venturini (Parlow 63), Lilly ■ 34 - MacMillan, Milbrett (Gabarra 30). *DiCicco*

CHN • Gao Hong ■ 89 - Wen Lirong, Fan Yunjie, Xie Huilin, Wang Liping - Shui Qingxia (Chen Yufeng 53), Liu Ailing ■ 49, Sun Wen, Zhao Lihong ■ 68 - Sun Qingmei (c), Shi Guihong (Wei Haiyong 88). *Ma Yuanan*

Citrus Bowl, Orlando
25.07.1996, 18:30, **17,020**

DENMARK 🇩🇰 **1-3** 🇸🇪 **SWEDEN**

Jensen 90   Swedberg (2) 62 68
               Videkull 76

👁 Cláudia Vasconcelos BRA
🚩 Nelly Viennot FRA & Maria Rodriguez MEX

DEN • Larsen - B Madsen, Terp, Flæng, Holm (c) - Petersen (14 Merete **Pedersen** 69), Christensen, Eggers Nielsen, Laursen (Jensen 46) - Krogh ■ 36, L Madsen. *Gantzhorn*

SWE • Nilsson (12 Ulrika **Karlsson** 31) - Nessvold - Svensson, Sandell (Jakobsson 27), Bengtsson - Swedberg, Andersson, Sundhage (c), Pohjanen - Kalte (Kun 84), Videkull. *Simonson*

	W	D	L	+	-	PTS
CHN	2	1	0	7	1	7
USA	2	1	0	5	1	7
SWE	1	0	2	4	5	3
DEN	0	0	3	2	11	0

▶ Kristine Lilly (13) in action against Denmark's Christina Petersen in the opening match.

China pip the USA to top spot

High heat and humidity couldn't wilt China's *Steel Roses* as they vied with tournament favourites USA to win the group. The Americans kicked off the short five-day group phase with an electrifying 3-0 win against Denmark at Orlando's Citrus Bowl – part of a double-header with Hungary against Nigeria in the men's tournament. Both the USA and China won their first two matches, sealing qualification for the semi-finals before the final round of group matches. China's victory over Denmark, the tournament's youngest team with an average age of 23, was the competition's highest-scoring game. The youthful Danes were on the back foot as experienced striker Helle Jensen could only manage 45 minutes a game due to an injured knee. Sweden captain Pia Sundhage led her side from midfield but was unable to prevent defeats against either the Chinese or the Americans. They did, however, manage a 3-1 consolation win against the Danes in the final group game, despite the early substitution of goalkeeper Annelie Nilsson following an elbow in the face. A short-lived Olympic record crowd of 55,650 turned up to see the 0-0 draw between China and the USA as the Chinese won the group and ended the hosts' 15-game winning run.

▶ Joy Fawcett is honoured before winning her 100th cap in the group match against Sweden. Captain Carla Overbeck won her 100th in the following match against China. The other centurions were Kristine Lilly, Mia Hamm, Carin Gabarra and Michelle Akers.

Brazil knock out Germany

Canadian Sonia Denoncourt became the first woman to referee an Olympic match, taking charge of the Germany – Japan fixture in the group's opening game. Despite the sticky conditions, reigning world champions Norway proved their superiority in a tightly contested group that illustrated the rapid improvements being made by women's sides worldwide. There were also some new stars and outstanding performances by established names. Defender Nina Nymark Andersen, who trained with men's team Tromsø when not working as a chef, impressed with her distribution of the ball, though the Norwegians were upset by underdogs Brazil, conceding an 89th-minute Pretinha goal in their 2-2 draw. Brazil had qualified for Atlanta as the team with the best record of those knocked out at the group stage in Sweden, and seven of the squad were veterans of the first World Cup. Roseli and Pretinha in particular were an effective force upfront and in the final group game against Germany – the World Cup runners-up in Sweden – they sealed a semi-final place at their opponents' expense, despite conceding an early goal to Pia Wunderlich after just four minutes. This time it was Sissi, a veteran of the 1988 tournament, who secured the point to take Brazil through. They were joined by the Norwegians, who beat Japan 4-0 in Washington.

Group F

	W	D	L	+	−	PTS
NOR	2	1	0	9	4	7
BRA	1	2	0	5	3	5
GER	1	1	1	6	6	4
JPN	0	0	3	2	9	0

◀ Norway's Hege Riise and Germany's Bettina Wiegmann battle it out in midfield.

◀ Brazil's Formiga (8) tackles Japan's Homare Sawa. Both played in the 2015 World Cup 19 years later!

RFK Stadium, Washington DC
21.07.1996, 15:00, **45,946**

NORWAY 2-2 BRAZIL

Medalen 32   Pretinha (2) 57 89
Aarønes 68

José Maria García-Aranda ESP
Lencie Fred VAN & Mohamed Al Mossawi OMA

NOR • 1 Bente **Nordby** ▪44 - 2 Agnete **Carlsen**, 3 Gro **Espeseth** (c), ▪67, 4 Nina **Nymark Andersen**, 5 Merete **Myklebust** - 6 Hege **Riise**, 8 Heidi **Støre** (11 Brit **Sandaune** 31), 14 Tone **Haugen** (13 Tina **Svensson** 76), 7 Anne **Nymark Andersen** - 16 Ann Kristin **Aarønes**, 10 Linda **Medalen** ▪72. *Even Pellerud*

BRA • 1 **Meg** - 6 **Elane** - 2 **Nenê** (13 **Marisa** 85), 14 **Tânia**, 4 **Fanta** - 8 **Formiga**, 10 **Sissi** (c), 5 **Márcia Taffarel**, 16 **Sônia** (19 **Kátia** 83) - 11 **Roseli**, 7 **Pretinha** (9 Michael **Jackson** 86). *José Duarte*

Legion Field, Birmingham
21.07.1996, 13:30, **44,211**

GERMANY 3-2 JAPAN

Wiegmann 5   Kioka 18
Tomei OG 29, Mohr 52   Noda 33

Sonia Denoncourt CAN
Gitte Holm DEN & Janice Gettemeyer USA

GER • 1 Manuela **Goller** - 5 Doris **Fitschen** - 3 Birgitt **Austermühl**, 13 Sandra **Minnert** - 7 Martina **Voss**, 2 Jutta **Nardenbach**, 10 Silvia **Neid** (c), 8 Bettina **Wiegmann**, 14 Pia **Wunderlich** (4 Kerstin **Stegemann** 65) - 9 Heidi **Mohr**, 11 Patricia **Brocker** (15 Birgit **Prinz** 53 ▪87). *Gero Bisanz*

JPN • 1 Junko **Ozawa** - 3 Rie **Yamaki** - 5 Yumi **Obe**, 2 Yumi **Tomei**, 4 Maki **Haneta** ▪12, 6 Kae **Nishina** ▪71 - 9 Futaba **Kioka**, 8 Asako **Takakura**, 7 Homare **Sawa** - 12 Tamaki **Uchiyama** (11 Etsuko **Handa** 73), 10 Akemi **Noda** (c). *Tamotsu Suzuki*

RFK Stadium, Washington DC
23.07.1996, 18:30, **28,000**

NORWAY 3-2 GERMANY

Aarønes 5, Medalen 34   Wiegmann 32
Riise 65   Prinz 62

Edward Lennie AUS
Jorge Luis Arango COL & Yuri Dupanov BLR

NOR • Nordby - Svensson (Haugen 76), N Nymark Andersen, Espeseth (c), Myklebust - 9 Marianne **Pettersen** (15 Trine **Tangeraas** 65), Riise, Carlsen, A Nymark Andersen - Aarønes ▪47, Medalen. *Pellerud*

GER • Goller - Fitschen - Nardenbach, Austermühl, Minnert - Wunderlich (Stegemann 54), Neid (c) (16 Renate **Lingor** 76), Wiegmann, Voss - Brocker (Prinz 52), Mohr. *Bisanz*

Legion Field, Birmingham
23.07.1996, 16:30, **26,111**

BRAZIL 2-0 JAPAN

Kátia 68
Pretinha 78

Ingrid Jonsson SWE
Janice Gettemeyer USA & Gitte Holm DEN

BRA • 12 **Didi** - Elane - Nenê, Márcia Taffarel, Tânia, Fanta - Formiga, Sissi (c), Sônia ▪25 (Kátia 36) - Roseli, Pretinha. *Duarte*

JPN • Ozawa - Yamaki - Obe, Tomei, Haneta, Nishina - Kioka, Takakura (13 Nami **Otake** 72), Sawa - Uchiyama, Noda (c). *Suzuki*

RFK Stadium, Washington DC
25.07.1996, 18:30, **30,237**

NORWAY 4-0 JAPAN

Pettersen (2) 25 86
Medalen 60
Tangeraas 74

Omar Al Muhanna KSA
Mohamed Al Mossawi OMA & Lencie Fred VAN

NOR • Nordby - Svensson, N Nymark Andersen, Espeseth (c) (Haugen 77), Myklebust - Riise (Sandaune 70), Carlsen, A Nymark Andersen - Pettersen, Medalen (Tangeraas 61), Aarønes. *Pellerud*

JPN • 16 Shiho **Onodera** - Yamaki - Obe (14 Kaoru **Kadohara** 78), Tomei, Haneta, Nishina - Kioka, Takakura, Sawa - Uchiyama (15 Miyuki **Izumi** 81), Noda (c). *Suzuki*

Legion Field, Birmingham
25.07.1996, 18:30, **28,319**

BRAZIL 1-1 GERMANY

Sissi 53   P Wunderlich 4

Sonia Denoncourt CAN
Gitte Holm DEN & Janice Gettemeyer USA

BRA • Meg - Elane - Nenê, Márcia Taffarel, Tânia ▪70, Fanta ▪90 - Formiga, Sissi (c), Kátia (16 Sônia 85) - Roseli, Pretinha. *Duarte*

GER • Goller - Fitschen - Austermühl ▪58, Minnert - Voss, Nardenbach (Stegemann 46), Neid (c) (6 Dagmar **Pohlmann** 68), Wiegmann, Wunderlich - Mohr, Brocker (Prinz 42). *Bisanz*

1996 Semi-finals

▲ China's Wen Lirong tackles Brazil's Roseli. In 11 matches between the two nations from 1986 to 2017, this was the only one in which the Chinese emerged triumphant.

> **These Olympics demonstrated just how good some players and countries are.**
>
> MICHELLE AKERS, USA

China's late show stuns Brazil

Sanford Stadium, Athens
28.07.1996, 15:00, **64,196**
CHINA PR 3-2 **BRAZIL**
Sun Qingmei 5, Wei Haiying (2) 83 90   Roseli 67, Pretinha 72

Ingrid Jonsson SWE • Nelly Viennot FRA & Maria Rodriguez MEX

CHN • Gao Hong - Wen Lirong ■ 61 - Fan Yunjie, Xie Huilin, Shui Qingxia (Yu Honggi 70) - Wang Liping, Liu Ailing, Sun Wen, Zhao Lihong - Shi Guihong (Wei Haiying 55), Sun Qingmei (c). *Ma Yuanan*
BRA • Meg - Elane - Nenê, Tânia ■ 36 ■ 43 ■ 43, Fanta - Formiga, Márcia Taffarel, Sissi (c), Kátia (3 **Suzy** 46) - Pretinha, Roseli. *Duarte*

A goal by Wei Haiying in the game's final minute, an eight-yard drive following a pass from Sun Qingmei, won an exhilarating game of football for China. The match was part of a double-header with the USA v Norway semi-final as the tournament moved to Sanford Stadium in Athens. Blistering heat – coaches tried to cool their players down with spray bottles from the touchline – set the scene for the hotly contested match in which tempers frayed at times. In the first half, China dominated possession and took an early lead through a stunning Sun Qingmei goal. They frustrated Brazil's strikers with tight marking, and Tânia's reckless defending earned her a pair of yellow cards and she was sent off two minutes before the break. Fifteen minutes after half-time, Wen Lirong joined her following a tackle on Pretinha. This galvanised Brazil, Roseli equalising in the 67th minute and Pretinha notching a second five minutes later by shooting from the edge of the area past Gao Hong. A mad scramble followed as the Chinese tried to rescue the game. They piled on the pressure and with just seven minutes remaining, substitute Wei Haiying levelled the scores following a cross from skipper Sun Qingmei. Then came Wei's last-minute winner.

USA win with a golden goal

Sanford Stadium, Athens
28.07.1996, 17:30, **64,196**
NORWAY 1-2 AET **USA**
Medalen 18   Akers 76p, MacMillan 100 GG

Sonia Denoncourt CAN • Jorge Luis Arango COL & Gitte Holm DEN

NOR • Nordby - Svensson (Tangeraas 71), N Nymark Andersen, Espeseth (c) ■ 77, Myklebust - Riise, Carlsen ■ 54 ■ 86, A Nymark Andersen - Pettersen, Medalen, Aarønes. *Pellerud*
USA • Scurry - Fawcett, Overbeck (c), Chastain - Foudy, Venturini, Akers, Roberts, Lilly - Milbrett (MacMillan 96), Hamm. *DiCicco*

Shannon MacMillan, who had worked her way back into the team for the first time since March 1994, scored a golden goal from a Julie Foudy pass to win this semi-final and spark wild celebrations at Sanford Stadium. This was a rematch of the 1995 World Cup semi-final between two of the great rivals of the era, and it was a fiercely contested match from the start. Veteran Norway striker Linda Medalen opened the scoring with an 18th-minute goal past Briana Scurry. It was her fourth goal and it proved to be enough for her to finish the tournament as joint top scorer. The two sides went toe to toe in an evenly contested game that was marked by stamina and physicality in challenges. The game turned on a controversial penalty given for handball against Norway's skipper Gro Espeseth. A long throw into the box by Brandi Chastain was judged to have brushed Espeseth's arm by referee Sonia Denoncourt, although even the Americans didn't appeal. Michelle Akers sent her penalty in the opposite direction to the diving Bente Nordby. With the score tied at the end of normal time, MacMillan came on for Tiffeny Milbrett and the rest, as they say, is history.

▼ Down and out. Norway can't believe it while the USA celebrate Shannon MacMillan's extra-time golden goal that took them through to the first Olympic Final.

1996 Bronze Medal Match

Sanford Stadium, Athens
1.08.1996, 18:00, **76,489**

BRAZIL 0-2 NORWAY

Aarønes (2) 21 25

Ingrid Jonsson SWE | Gitte Holm DEN & Carlos Velazquez URU

		1 Meg		
		6 Elane		
	3 Suzy		4 Fanta	
13 Marisa	8 Formiga	5 Márcia Taffarel (Kátia 46)	10 Sissi (c) (Nenê 86)	16 Sônia (Michael Jackson 70)
	7 Pretinha		11 Roseli	
	10 Medalen		16 Aarønes	
9 Pettersen (Haugen 89)	7 A Nymark Andersen	15 Tangeraas (17 Tone Gunn **Frustøl** 89)		6 Riise
5 Myklebust	3 Espeseth (c) ■ 67		4 N Nymark Andersen (Svensson 46)	11 Sandaune
		1 Nordby		

Duarte | Pellerud

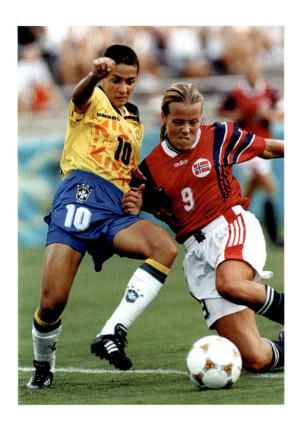

◂ Brazil captain Sissi takes on Norway's Marianne Pettersen in the bronze medal match.

Aarønes at the double

Norway began this bronze medal match still smarting from their gut-wrenching extra-time semi-final loss to the USA. Yet they managed to secure a win over Brazil thanks to a brace of goals by Ann Kristin Aarønes. That took the Golden Boot winner from the 1995 World Cup to four goals alongside team-mate Linda Medalen, but without the assists that earned Medalen the accolade of top scorer here. Aarønes, the 23-year-old six-foot-one forward, wearing her iconic white headband, delivered the first blow to Brazil's hopes of a medal 21 minutes into the game with a volley that evaded goalkeeper Meg. Four minutes later, Aarønes stole through the defence and scored with a soaring shot past Meg's reaching arm for the second. For Brazil, Pretinha, looking for her fifth goal of the tournament, was always dangerous but was frustrated time and again by Bente Nordby in the Norwegian goal. In the second half, Pretinha again asked questions of the Norwegian defenders, while Roseli had a goal disallowed for handball. Brazil's veteran stalwart Michael Jackson came on for her final international game – three days later her namesake was part of the Centennial Games' closing ceremony – but the Norwegians remained steadfast to hold on for the medal. That meant that in the four international tournaments played since 1988, they had claimed medals in all of them – gold in 1988 and 1995, silver in 1991 and now a bronze. Despite losing, Brazil proved they had the ability to compete with the best – as they were to show over the coming decade.

> **" Our generation carried a pressure to get results in order to plant the seeds for future generations to harvest. "**
>
> MÁRCIA TAFFAREL, BRAZIL

▸ Brazil's Meg stops a Norwegian attack, but the South Americans missed out on bronze after two first-half goals in four minutes by Ann Kristin Aarønes.

1996 Gold medal match

▲ Julie Foudy (11) in action with Sun Wen. Foudy won her 98th cap in the Final.

1996 Gold Medal Match

Sanford Stadium, Athens
1.08.1996, 20:30, **76,489**

CHINA PR 1-2 **USA**

Sun Wen 32 MacMillan 19, Milbrett 68

Bente Skogvang NOR / Nelly Viennot FRA & Maria Rodriguez MEX

China PR
- 16 Gao Hong
- 3 Fan Yunjie
- 2 Wang Liping (Yu Honggi 86)
- 5 Xie Huilin ■7
- 8 Shui Qingxia
- 13 Liu Ying
- 9 Sun Wen
- 10 Liu Ailing
- 6 Zhao Lihong
- 15 Shi Guihong (Wei Haiying 69)
- 11 Sun Qingmei (c)

Ma Yuanan

USA
- 8 MacMillan
- 16 Milbrett ■33 (Roberts 71)
- 9 Hamm (Gabarra 89)
- 13 Lilly ■15
- 10 Akers
- 15 Venturini
- 11 Foudy
- 6 Chastain
- 4 Overbeck (c)
- 14 Fawcett
- 1 Scurry ■40

DiCicco

The golden girls

While the USA's competitive rivalry with Norway was more long-standing, dating back to their quarter-final in the 1988 International Women's Football Tournament, the competition between the USA and China was equally compelling. The two teams were regular opponents and increasingly knew each other's strengths and weaknesses. USA goalkeeper Mary Harvey, a veteran of the 1991 team, recalled: "It was a little disquieting to play someone who you knew really well," she said. "We really had to prepare very differently to play China than to play Norway." The focus was on remaining calm when China gained possession of the ball. "They were so good technically, so fit and fast, that if you lost possession, you wouldn't get it back for a while." The game itself was physical and exhausting with no fewer than four yellow cards shown in the first half. The heat pushed both sides to their limits. Shannon MacMillan, having earnt back a starting position thanks to her semi-final golden goal, scored first. Kristine Lilly made a superb run down the left and sent a dangerous cross into the box. Mia Hamm's powerful shot was touched brilliantly onto the post by Gao Hong, but MacMillan was there to prod the rebound home. In the 32nd minute, China were back in the game. Sun Wen, one of the world's best players and an astute attacker, ran on to a long ball forward and took advantage of the fact that USA keeper Briana Scurry's had come off her line, with a lob that sailed over the American's head. Brandi Chastain tried to stop the ball going over the line with a desperate lunge but only succeeded in helping it on its way. The game was won by Tiffeny Milbrett in the 68th minute. Mia Hamm laid the ball off for Joy Fawcett whose run took her into the box before laying on a perfect pass for Milbrett to side-foot the ball home. Star playmaker Hamm was stretchered off with an injury in the last minute but the USA hung on to claim their historic gold medal. "It's a feeling of immense joy and incredible satisfaction," Michelle Akers later said of the intense emotions that day. It was a special win for the Americans, the first time they had been victorious in a major tournament on home soil. It also set high expectations for the squad to win again three years later when the United States would host the World Cup.

▶ Tisha Venturini (15) and Liu Ailing during the Final.

Gold medal match 1996

▶ The USA team celebrate winning gold at the final whistle.

1090

The number of combined caps of the USA team that beat China in the 1996 Olympic Final. Few teams could match the Americans for experience and it told in the end. The total number of caps for each player was: Lilly 123, Hamm 121, Gabarra 119, Akers 111, Fawcett 103, Overbeck 102, Foudy 98, Venturini 73, Milbrett 67, Roberts 58, Scurry 46, Chastain 40, and MacMillan 29.

A watershed

The Atlanta Games were a watershed for women's football thanks in part to the record-breaking crowds. The gold medal match attracted 76,489 people, at the time the largest crowd to attend a women's match in the USA. Mary Harvey recalled how, on the day of the gold medal match, she and her team-mates watched the television news broadcasts of the immense traffic jams filling the roads en route to Sanford Stadium. "It was pretty amazing because we're realising: that's our game traffic – all those people, that snarl, was because they're coming to watch our Final," she said. "It was just nuts!" That summer was a breakthrough both for women's football and for women and sport in the United States. While the Title IX legislation encouraged greater girls' participation – nearly one third of American footballers were female and Olympic gold medals could inspire the next generation of elite players – the USA's win in 1996 also changed attitudes globally by demonstrating the potential mass public spectatorship and fandom for elite women's football.

▲ Briana Scurry and Carin Gabarra celebrate at the end of the 1996 Olympic Final.

▼ Back row: Roberts, Parlow, Wilson, MacMillan, Hamm, Akers, Foudy, Lilly, Venturini
Front row: Harvey, Chastain, Scurry, Overbeck, Gabarra, Fawcett, Milbrett.

1999

The 1999 finals in America were a landmark in the women's game. A much wider audience was attracted by live broadcasts of all the matches – and the Final, at the Rose Bowl in Pasadena, attracted a crowd of 90,185, the biggest in the history of the FIFA Women's World Cup. The USA won a second title by beating China on penalties. Brandi Chastain's celebration of her winning kick is one of the iconic football images.

The 99er effect

They are known simply as the 99ers... The names of the USA team that won the 1999 World Cup will echo down through the ages, but the 99ers are more than just World Cup winners. This team represented so much more. They won the coveted Sports Illustrated Sportsperson of the Year award, an honour won more often than not by men from the traditional "Made in America" sports, and not only did the 99ers take women's football into the mainstream of American sporting life, their influence was undeniably global. They demonstrated the skill and ability to convince an often sceptical world that women's football deserved to be taken seriously and that this was a sport that was here to stay. It was the start of the professionalisation of the game as national associations began to realise that they had an obligation to the growing number of girls and women who wanted to play the game and that they should be encouraging even more to take up the sport. That's quite a legacy for 20 players, and of course it was not all down to them, but women's football needed poster girls to announce its arrival and the 99ers certainly fitted the bill.

◀ Brandi Chastain celebrates her winning penalty in the 1999 World Cup Final.

▼ USA team captain Carla Overbeck presents President Bill Clinton with a commemorative shirt at a White House reception.

1999 Overview

USA 1999

FIFA WOMEN'S WORLD CUP USA 1999

Story of the qualifiers

A 16-team tournament

The qualifying stakes were raised by the introduction of four more places in the final tournament, but results in the qualifiers served to highlight the disparity in standards between the top nations and those just starting out, most notably with Japan's 21-0 victory over Guam, a scoreline matched by Canada in their win over Puerto Rico, as well as by New Zealand and Australia with their respective wins over Samoa and American Samoa. Once again, continental championships were used to determine the finalists, with the exception of Europe. In Asia, that meant the 1997 AFC Women's Championship, which was played in Guangdong, China. The hosts beat North Korea 2-0 in the Final with both goals by Liu Ailing, and it was another double, by Homare Sawa, that saw Japan clinch the third available place for Asia with a 2-0 play-off win over Chinese Taipei. The semi-finals of the 1998 Women's African Football Championship saw the decisive matches in Africa, with Nigeria's win over Cameroon and Ghana's victory over Congo DR enough to see both qualify for the USA. In the Americas, Brazil beat Argentina in the Final of the 1998 South American Championship, which meant that the Argentines met the 1998 Concacaf Women's Championship runners-up Mexico for a place in the World Cup, a tie ultimately won by the Mexicans. They were joined by champions Canada, winning the title in the absence of the USA, who had already qualified as hosts. In Europe, the top 16 teams were drawn into four groups of four with the winners of each – Sweden, Italy, Norway and Denmark – joined by the winners of the two second-place play-offs – Germany and Russia. Australia, winners of the 1998 OFC Women's Championship, completed the line-up of finalists.

▶ Pennant from the World Cup draw.
FIFA Museum Collection

Golden Ball
Sun Wen CHN

Silver Ball: Sissi BRA
Bronze Ball: Michelle Akers GER

Group stage

	GROUP A	GROUP B	GROUP C	GROUP D
	USA 3-0 DEN	BRA 7-1 MEX	JPN 1-1 CAN	CHN 2-1 SWE
	PRK 1-2 NGA	GER 1-1 ITA	NOR 2-1 RUS	AUS 1-1 GHA
	USA 7-1 NGA	BRA 2-0 ITA	JPN 0-5 RUS	CHN 7-0 GHA
	PRK 3-1 DEN	GER 6-0 MEX	NOR 7-1 CAN	AUS 1-3 SWE
	USA 3-0 PRK	MEX 0-2 ITA	NOR 4-0 JPN	GHA 0-2 SWE
	NGA 2-0 DEN	GER 3-3 BRA	CAN 1-4 RUS	CHN 3-1 AUS

	W D L + − PTS	W D L + − PTS	W D L + − PTS	W D L + − PTS
	USA 3 0 0 13 1 9	BRA 2 1 0 12 4 7	NOR 3 0 0 13 2 9	CHN 3 0 0 12 2 9
	NGA 2 0 1 5 8 6	GER 1 2 0 10 4 5	RUS 2 0 1 10 3 6	SWE 2 0 1 6 3 6
	PRK 1 0 2 4 6 3	ITA 1 1 1 3 3 4	CAN 0 1 2 3 12 1	AUS 0 1 2 3 7 1
	DEN 0 0 3 1 8 0	MEX 0 0 3 1 15 0	JPN 0 1 2 1 10 1	GHA 0 1 2 1 10 1

Knockout stages

QUARTER-FINAL	QUARTER-FINAL	QUARTER-FINAL	QUARTER-FINAL
CHN 2-0 RUS	NOR 3-1 SWE	USA 3-2 GER	BRA 4-3 AET NGA

	SEMI-FINAL		SEMI-FINAL
	NOR 0-5 CHN		USA 2-0 BRA

MATCH FOR THIRD PLACE
BRA 0-0 (5-4) NOR

FINAL
USA 0-0 (5-4) CHN

Overview 1999

16 TEAMS

USA WINNERS

CHN SECOND   BRA THIRD

NUTMEG
OFFICIAL MASCOT

32 MATCHES PLAYED

78 YELLOW CARDS

5 RED CARDS

123 GOALS

3.84 AVERAGE GOALS PER MATCH

1 214 221 SPECTATORS   **37 944** AVERAGE PER MATCH

OFFICIAL LOGO

ICON
OFFICIAL MATCH BALL

▶ USA '99 attracted record crowds for games in the United States.

Host cities and stadiums

Destination USA Part 2

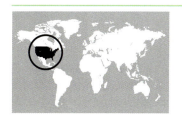

Five of the eight stadiums used at USA'94 were in action again at USA'99, including the Rose Bowl in Pasadena, Los Angeles, which hosted the Final at both tournaments. The three extra stadiums were the Civic Stadium in Portland, the Spartan Stadium in San Jose and the Jack Kent Cooke Stadium in Washington DC. In 1994, and at the 1996 Olympics, Washington DC had played host to games, but at the RFK Stadium, and not at the more recently built Jack Kent Cooke Stadium.

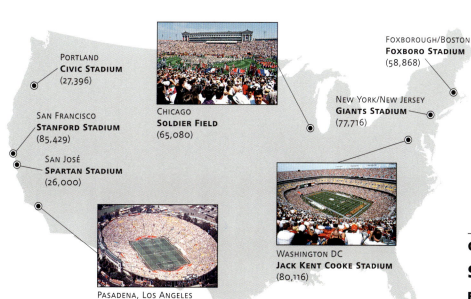

PORTLAND
CIVIC STADIUM
(27,396)

SAN FRANCISCO
STANFORD STADIUM
(85,429)

SAN JOSÉ
SPARTAN STADIUM
(26,000)

CHICAGO
SOLDIER FIELD
(65,080)

FOXBOROUGH/BOSTON
FOXBORO STADIUM
(58,868)

NEW YORK/NEW JERSEY
GIANTS STADIUM
(77,716)

WASHINGTON DC
JACK KENT COOKE STADIUM
(80,116)

PASADENA, LOS ANGELES
ROSE BOWL
(95,542)

×**7**

Golden Boot

Sissi BRA **& Sun Wen** CHN

Bronze Boot: Ann Kristin Aarønes NOR ×4

1999 Group stage

Group A

Giants Stadium, New York/New Jersey
19.06.1999, 15:00, **78,972**

USA 🇺🇸	**3-0**	🇩🇰 DENMARK

Hamm 17, Foudy 73, Lilly 89

Sonia Denoncourt CAN
Ana Perez PER & Hisae Yoshizawa JPN

USA • 1 Briana Scurry - 14 Joy Fawcett, 20 Kate Sobrero, 4 Carla Overbeck (c), 6 Brandi Chastain - 11 Julie Foudy, 10 Michelle Akers, 13 Kristine Lilly - 9 Mia Hamm (2 Lorrie Fair 88), 12 Cindy Parlow, 16 Tiffeny Milbrett (8 Shannon MacMillan 82). Tony DiCicco

DEN • 1 Dorthe Larsen - 6 Jeanne Axelsen, 4 Lene Terp (c), 3 Karina Christensen, 14 Katrine Pedersen - 10 Gitte Krogh, 9 Christina Petersen (18 Lise Søndergaard 83), 8 Janne Rasmussen - 11, 15 Mikka Hansen (19 Janni Johansen 63) - 11 Merete Pedersen, 12 Lene Jensen Revsbeck (7 Louise Hansen 78). Jørgen Hvidemose

Rose Bowl, Los Angeles
20.06.1999, 18:30, **17,100**

KOREA DPR	**1-2**	🇳🇬 NIGERIA

Jo Song Ok 74 | | Akide 50, Nwadike 79

Katriina Elovirta FIN
Comfort Cofie GHA & Maria Rodriguez MEX

PRK • 18 Kye Yong Sun - 13 Ri Ae Gyong - 12 Kim Hye Ran, 2 Yun In Sil, 7 Ri Hyang Ok - 1, 4 Kim Sun Hui (11 Jo Jong Ran 61) - 10 Kim Kum Sil (c) (14 Pak Jong Ae 29), 6 Sol Yong Suk (9 Ri Kyong Ae 55), 16 Ri Kum Suk - 5 - 15 Jin Pyol Hui - 88, 3 Jo Song Ok. Myong Tong Chan

NGA • 1 Ann Chiejine - 2 Yinka Kudasii (4 Adanna Nwaneri 86 - 88), 5 Eberechi Opara - 81, 11 Prisca Emeafu, 6 Kikelomo Ajayi - 14 Florence Omagbemi (c), 13 Nkiru Okosieme - 18 Patience Avre, 19 Mercy Akide - 90+3, 8 Rita Nwadike, 20 Ifeanyichukwu Chiejine (17 Nkechi Egbe 70). Ismaila Mabo

Soldier Field, Chicago
24.06.1999, 19:00, **65,080**

USA 🇺🇸	**7-1**	🇳🇬 NIGERIA

I Chiejine OG 19, Hamm 20, Milbrett 21 23 83, Lilly 32, Akers 39, Parlow 41 | | Okosieme 2

Nicole Petignat SUI
Susanne Borg SWE & Ghislaine Labbé FRA

USA • Scurry - Fawcett, Overbeck (c), Sobrero (9 Sara Whalen 46) - Lilly, Akers (Fair 46), Hamm (MacMillan 51), Foudy, Chastain - Parlow, Milbrett. DiCicco

NGA • A Chiejine - Kudasii, Opara, Emeafu (9 Gloria Usieta 84), Ajayi - 45+1 - Omagbemi (c), Okosieme - Avre - 31 (7 Stella Mbachu 53), Akide, Nwadike, I Chiejine (Egbe 43). Mabo

Civic Stadium, Portland
24.06.1999, 18:00, **20,129**

KOREA DPR	**3-1**	🇩🇰 DENMARK

Jin Pyol Hui 15, Jo Song Ok 39, Kim Kum Sil 73 | | Johansen 74

Martha Toro COL
Maria Rodriguez MEX & Ana Bia Batista BRA

PRK • Kye Yong Sun - Ri Ae Gyong - Yun In Sil, Ri Hyang Ok, Kim Sun Hui - 34 (Kim Hye Ran 46) - Jin Pyol Hui, Kim Kum Sil (c), Sol Yong Suk, Pak Jong Ae - 49 - 86 - Ri Kum Suk - 81, Jo Song Ok - 83. Myong Tong Chan

DEN • Larsen - Axelsen, Terp (c) - 36, K Pedersen, 5 Marlene Kristensen (2 Hanne Sand Christensen 9) - Krogh, Petersen, Rasmussen, L Hansen - Jensen Revsbeck (Johansen 46), M Pedersen (M Hansen 63). Hvidemose

Foxboro Stadium, Boston
27.06.1999, 19:00, **50,484**

USA 🇺🇸	**3-0**	KOREA DPR

MacMillan 56, Venturini (2) 68 76

Katriina Elovirta FIN
Maria Rodriguez MEX & Cleidy Ribeiro BRA

USA • Scurry - 5 Tiffany Roberts (3 Christie Pearce 73), Overbeck (c), Fawcett, Whalen - 15 Tisha Venturini, Chastain, Lilly - Hamm (Foudy 46), Parlow (Milbrett 46), MacMillan. DiCicco

PRK • Kye Yong Sun - Yun In Sil, Ri Ae Gyong (17 Yang Kyong Hui 71), 5 Kim Sun Hye - 8, Kim Sun Hui - Kim Hye Ran, Kim Kum Sil (c) - 74, Ri Hyang Ok, Sol Yong Suk, Jin Pyol Hui (Jo Jong Ran 61) - Jo Song Ok - 24. Myong Tong Chan

Jack Kent Cooke Stadium, Washington DC
27.06.1999, 16:00, **22,109**

NIGERIA 🇳🇬	**2-0**	🇩🇰 DENMARK

Akide 25, Okosieme 81

Maria Siqueira BRA
Hisae Yoshizawa JPN & Ana Perez PER

NGA • A Chiejine - Kudasii, Opara, Emeafu - 90+1, I Chiejine (Nwaneri 81) - Omagbemi (c), Akide, Okosieme - Avre, Egbe (Mbachu 54 - 88), Nwadike. Mabo

DEN • Larsen - Axelsen, Terp (c), K Pedersen, Sand Christensen - 17 Hanne Nørregaard (Jensen Revsbeck 32), Petersen, Rasmussen, M Hansen (M Pedersen 58) - Krogh - 50 (L Hansen 66), Johansen. Hvidemose

	W	D	L	+	-	PTS
🇺🇸 USA	3	0	0	13	1	9
🇳🇬 NGA	2	0	1	5	8	6
PRK	1	0	2	4	6	3
🇩🇰 DEN	0	0	3	1	8	0

▶ Mia Hamm scores the USA's second goal in the 7-1 victory over Nigeria.

Nigeria hit for seven but qualify

1348

That's how many seconds it took the USA to score six goals against Nigeria – one every 224 seconds. The seven first-half goals in the match is a record half-time score. Remarkably, when the USA went 4-1 up, they were trailing 6-3 on corners!

"Watch Me Play" was a key message of USA 99 and with tickets selling like hot cakes, "soccer" fans looked ready to answer the call. A sold-out opening day double-header at the Giants Stadium in New Jersey was a taste of things to come and with 78,972 in attendance, a record for a women's sporting event in the USA was set. The atmosphere was electric and after pop stars B*Witched, Billie and NSYNC had added a musical spark to the opening ceremony, it was down to the players to set the tournament alight. Fittingly, the world's leading striker Mia Hamm bagged the first goal of USA 99 in a vibrant, attacking match with Denmark. The American No.9 also set up Julie Foudy for the 200th goal in the history of the World Cup and New York-born Kristine Lilly, the most-capped player in the world, rounded off the scoring on home turf. Meanwhile, Mercy Akide inspired Nigeria's first Women's World Cup win, a 2-1 defeat of North Korea. "We are not afraid of the United States, they are ladies just like us," declared 'Marvellous' Mercy before facing the Olympic champions. A goal from Nkiru Okosieme after 73 seconds was an early scare for the USA and although the game ended 7-1, Nigeria never gave up. There was also no way back for Denmark after debutants North Korea beat them for their first win on the world stage and Janni Johansen's crowd-pleasing back-heeled goal was scant consolation. The Danes had won every game in qualifying, but they returned home pointless after being denied by the woodwork and keeper Ann Chiejine in a 2-0 loss to African champions Nigeria, who secured a historic quarter-final berth. That same evening in Boston, more than 50,000 fans witnessed two-goal Tisha Venturini backflip in celebration as the table-topping hosts beat a compact, feisty, but homebound North Korea.

▶ Michelle Akers (10) and Christina Petersen (9) during the opening match of the tournament. The crowd of 78,972 was a record for a match in the USA.

▶▶ America's Kristine Lilly (centre) in action against North Korea.

Sissi double knocks out Italy

Group B

Labelled the "group of death", the combination of most improved nation, Brazil, alongside 1997 European champions Germany and runners-up Italy was a heady mix. Mexico, featuring a number of US-based college students, endured a testing debut, falling behind within 130 seconds to South American champions Brazil. Maribel Domínguez scored ten goals in qualifying and equalised here, but Pretinha and Sissi were on fire with a hat-trick apiece. For Italy, talismanic captain Carolina Morace had retired but attacking midfielder Antonella Carta and goal-getter Patrizia Panico had since emerged, while Germany were now overseen by Tina Theune-Meyer with retired skipper Silvia Neid as her assistant. They had beaten Italy to the European crown two years earlier, but it took a penalty from Bettina Wiegmann to cancel out Panico's opener and ensure a share of the spoils. Sissi's two goals were enough to see off Italy as Maravilha saved a Carta penalty, and Germany, inspired by finals debutant Inka Grings, thrashed Mexico to set up a dramatic battle for top spot. Six goals flew in, with Wiegmann scoring on her 100th appearance for Germany, but Maycon's equaliser at the death won the group for Brazil. Meanwhile, Italy finally tasted victory, beating Mexico in front of more than 50,000 in Boston.

	W	D	L	+	–	PTS
BRA	2	1	0	12	4	7
GER	1	2	0	10	4	5
ITA	1	1	1	3	4	4
MEX	0	0	3	1	15	0

◀ Brazil's Kátia celebrates her equaliser against Germany.

◀ Italy's Patrizia Panico (9) in action against Mexico. She scored a goal in the 2-0 victory but the win wasn't enough to see the Italians through to the next stage.

Group stage 1999

Giants Stadium, New York/New Jersey
19.06.1999, 17:30, **78,972**

BRAZIL 7-1 MEXICO

Pretinha (3) 3 12 90+1, Dominguez 10
Sissi (3) 29 42 50,
Kátia 35p

Nicole Petignat SUI
Corrie Kruithof NED & Susanne Borg SWE

BRA • 1 Maravilha - 3 Elane (c) - 16 Marisa, 5 Cidinha (7 Maycon 46), 13 Fanta (6 Juliana 82), 2 Nenê - 15 Raquel, 10 Sissi, 11 Suzana - 17 Pretinha, 9 Kátia (8 Formiga 72). Wilsinho

MEX • 1 Linnea Quiñones - 3 Martha Moore (5 Paty Perez 73), 4 Gina Oceguera (c), 9 Lisa Nañez ■ 53, 2 Susy Mora - 8 Andrea Rodebaugh, 20 Denise Ireta ■ 4, 11 Monica Gerardo (14 Iris Mora 78 ■ 89), 6 Fatima Leyva (15 Laurie Hill 46), 13 Mónica González - 10 Maribel Dominguez ■ 74. Leonardo Cuéllar

---

Rose Bowl, Los Angeles
20.06.1999, 16:00, **17,100**

GERMANY 1-1 ITALY

Wiegmann 61p   Panico 36

Bola Abidoye NGA
Adeola Adeyemi NGA & Jackeline Saez PAN

GER • 1 Silke Rottenberg - 2 Kerstin Stegemann, 5 Doris Fitschen (c), 4 Steffi Jones, 3 Ariane Hingst - 8 Sandra Smisek (16 Renate Lingor 86), 10 Bettina Wiegmann, 11 Maren Meinert (20 Monika Meyer 82), 17 Pia Wunderlich - 18 Inka Grings, 9 Birgit Prinz. Tina Theune-Meyer

ITA • 1 Giorgia Brenzan - 4 Luisa Marchio, 20 Roberta Stefanelli, 5 Daniela Tavalazzi - 8 Manuela Tesse (2 Damiana Deiana 68), 15 Adele Frollani (3 Paola Zanni 71), 14 Federica D'Astolfo ■ 32, 10 Antonella Carta (c), 13 Anna Duó - 7 Rita Guarino (18 Silvia Fiorini 89), 9 Patrizia Panico. Carlo Facchin

---

Soldier Field, Chicago
24.06.1999, 17:00, **65,080**

BRAZIL 2-0 ITALY

Sissi (2) 3 63   (Carta penalty saved 33)

Gitte Nielsen DEN
Corrie Kruithof NED & Ann Wenche Kleven NOR

BRA • Maravilha - Marisa, Elane (c), 4 Tânia ■ 74, Nenê ■ 4 (Juliana 89) - Cidinha, Suzana ■ 35, Sissi, Raquel (Formiga 46) - Pretinha, Kátia (Maycon 75). Wilsinho

ITA • Brenzan - Marchio, Stefanelli, Tavalazzi - Frollani (Deiana 55), Tesse, D'Astolfo ■ 21, Carta (c) (Fiorini 58), Duó ■ 13 - Panico, Guarino ■ 71 (17 Silvia Tagliacarne 74). Facchin

---

Civic Stadium, Portland
24.06.1999, 20:30, **20,129**

GERMANY 6-0 MEXICO

Grings (3) 10 57 90+2,
Smisek 45+1, Hingst 49,
Lingor 89

Im Eun Ju KOR
Boni Bishop TRI & Jackeline Saez PAN

GER • Rottenberg - 13 Sandra Minnert, Fitschen (c), Jones, Hingst - Smisek, Wiegmann (6 Melanie Hoffmann 69), Meinert ■ 21 (Lingor 64), P Wunderlich - Prinz (12 Claudia Müller 75), Grings. Theune-Meyer

MEX • Quiñones - Oceguera (c) - 7 Mónica Vergara (Gerardo 62), Nañez, Perez - Leyva, Ireta, Hill, S Mora, Rodebaugh (González 57) - Dominguez. Cuéllar

---

Foxboro Stadium, Boston
27.06.1999, 16:30, **50,484**

MEXICO 0-2 ITALY

Panico 37
Zanni 51

Bola Abidoye NGA
Jackeline Saez PAN & Comfort Cofie GHA

MEX • Quiñones - S Mora, Oceguera (c), Perez - Leyva (Ireta 66), Vergara (Hill 55), Rodebaugh (c) ■ 74, Nañez, Moore (González 42) - Dominguez (c), Gerardo. Cuéllar

ITA • Brenzan - Tavalazzi, Marchio, Zanni - Deiana, 16 Tatiana Zorri, Frollani, 19 Alessandra Pallotti, Duó (Stefanelli 46) - Panico, Guarino (Tagliacarne 46). Facchin

---

Jack Kent Cooke Stadium, Washington DC
27.06.1999, 13:30, **22,109**

GERMANY 3-3 BRAZIL

Prinz 8   Kátia 15
Wiegmann 46p Sissi 20
Jones 58   Maycon 90+4

Im Eun Ju KOR
Boni Bishop TRI & Adeola Adeyemi NGA

GER • Rottenberg - Hingst, Fitschen (c), Jones, Minnert ■ 68 - 7 Martina Voss (Smisek 29), Meinert, Wiegmann, P Wunderlich (14 Tina Wunderlich 46 ■ 85) - Prinz, Grings (Meyer 89). Theune-Meyer

BRA • Maravilha - Marisa (Fanta 33 ■ 85), Elane (c), Tânia, Nenê - Raquel (Formiga 60 ■ 79), Suzana (Maycon 65), Cidinha, Sissi - Pretinha, Kátia. Wilsinho

1999 Group stage

Group C

Spartan Stadium, San José
19.06.1999, 19:00, **23,298**

JAPAN 1-1 **CANADA**
Otake 64 Burtini 32

🏁 Maria Siqueira BRA
🚩 Comfort Cofie GHA & Cleidy Ribeiro BRA

JPN • 18 Nozomi **Yamago** - 7 Yumi **Tomei**, 12 Hiromi **Isozaki**, 5 Tomoe **Sakai**, 6 Kae **Nishina** - 9 Tamaki **Uchiyama**, 8 Ayumi **Hara**, 10 Homare **Sawa** (c), 14 Tomomi **Mitsui**, 15 Mito **Isaka** (16 Yayoi **Kobayashi** 52) - 11 Nami **Otake**. *Satoshi Miyauchi*

CAN • 1 Nicci **Wright** - 3 Sharolta **Nonen**, 9 Janine **Helland**, 7 Isabelle **Morneau** - 4 Tanya **Franck**, 13 Amy **Walsh**, 10 Charmaine **Hooper** 🟨 5, 6 Geraldine **Donnelly**, 12 Isabelle **Harvey** - 17 Silvana **Burtini** (c) (5 Andrea **Neil** 55), 11 Shannon **Rosenow**. *Neil Turnbull*

Foxboro Stadium, Boston
20.06.1999, 16:00, **14,873**

NORWAY 2-1 **RUSSIA**
Sandaune 28 Komarova 78
Pettersen 68

🏁 Zuo Xiudi CHN
🚩 Ghislaine Labbé FRA & Lu Lijuan CHN

NOR • 1 Bente **Nordby** - 4 Silje **Jørgensen**, 3 Gøril **Kringen**, 10 Linda **Medalen** (c), 14 Anne Nymark **Andersen** - 20 Unni **Lehn** (7 Tone Gunn **Frustøl** 61), 6 Hege **Riise**, 8 Monica **Knudsen** (17 Anita **Rapp** 86), 2 Brit **Sandaune** - 13 Ragnhild **Gulbrandsen** (15 Dagny **Mellgren** 74), 11 Marianne **Pettersen**. *Per-Mathias Høgmo*

RUS • 1 Svetlana **Petko** - 3 Marina **Burakova** - 5 Tatiana **Cheverda**, 16 Natalia **Filippova**, 4 Natalia **Karasseva** - 14 Olga **Karasseva** (6 Galina **Komarova** 46), 7 Tatiana **Egorova**, 8 Irina **Grigorieva** (c), 9 Alexandra **Svetlitskaya** (13 Elena **Fomina** 84) - 10 Natalia **Barbashina**, 11 Olga **Letyushova** (15 Larissa **Savina** 73). *Yuri Bystritskiy*

Civic Stadium, Portland
23.06.1999, 18:00, **17,668**

JAPAN 0-5 **RUSSIA**
 Savina 29,
 Letyushova (52 90,
 N Karasseva 58, Barbashina 80

🏁 Sandra Hunt USA
🚩 Ana Bia Batista BRA & Boni Bishop TRI

JPN • Yamago - Sakai (2 Rie **Yamaki** 69) - Tomei, Isozaki, Nishina - Mitsui, Sawa (c) 🟨 72, Hara, Isaka (Kobayashi 64) - Uchiyama, Otake (13 Miyuki **Yanagita** 57). *Miyauchi*

RUS • Petko - Burakova - Cheverda, Filippova, N Karasseva - Komarova, Egorova (Fomina 79), Grigorieva (c), Svetlitskaya (O Karasseva 46) - Savina (Barbashina 72), Letyushova. *Bystritskiy*

Jack Kent Cooke Stadium, Washington DC
23.06.1999, 18:00, **16,448**

NORWAY 7-1 **CANADA**
Aarønes (2) 8 36, Lehn 49, Hooper 31
Riise 54, Medalen 62,
Pettersen 76
S Gulbrandsen 87

🏁 Tammy Ogston AUS
🚩 Ri Song Ok PRK & Lu Lijuan CHN

NOR • Nordby - Jørgensen, Kringen 🟨 45+1, Medalen (c), Nymark Andersen (Frustøl 46) - Lehn (16 Solveig **Gulbrandsen** 70), Riise, Knudsen (19 Linda **Ørmen** 62), Sandaune - 9 Ann Kristin **Aarønes**, Pettersen. *Høgmo*

CAN • Wright - Nonen, Helland, Morneau - Franck, Walsh, Donnelly, Harvey - Rosenow (18 Mary Beth **Bowie** 70), Hooper, 16 Jeanette **Haas** (Neil 16). *Turnbull*

Soldier Field, Chicago
26.06.1999, 18:30, **34,256**

NORWAY 4-0 **JAPAN**
Riise 8p, Isozaki OG 26,
Aarønes 36, Mellgren 61

🏁 Marisela Contreras VEN
🚩 Ghislaine Labbé FRA & Susanne Borg SWE

NOR • Nordby - Jørgensen 🟨 73, 18 Anne **Tønnessen** 🟨 83, Medalen (c) (Kringen 11) 2 Henriette **Viker** 57), Sandaune - Lehn, Riise, Knudsen, Frustøl - Mellgren, Aarønes (R Gulbrandsen 38). *Høgmo*

JPN • Yamago - Tomei, Yamaki, Isozaki, Nishina - Isaka (Kobayashi 60), Hara (19 Kozue **Ando** 86), Mitsui, Uchiyama (Yanagita 78) - Otake, Sawa (c) 🟨 65. *Miyauchi*

Giants Stadium, New York/New Jersey
26.06.1999, 12:00, **29,401**

CANADA 1-4 **RUSSIA**
Hooper 76 Grigorieva 54
 Fomina (2) 66 86
 O Karasseva 90+1

🏁 Zuo Xiudi CHN
🚩 Lu Lijuan CHN & Ri Song Ok PRK

CAN • Wright - Nonen, Helland (c), Morneau - Franck 🟨 32, Donnelly, Walsh, Harvey 🟨 49 - Rosenow (8 Sarah **Maglio** 80), Hooper, Bowie (Burtini 55). *Turnbull*

RUS • Petko - Cheverda (2 Yulia **Yushekivitch** 72), Burakova, Filippova, N Karasseva 🟨 77 - Komarova, Egorova (Fomina 61), Grigorieva (c), O Karasseva - Barbashina (Savina 56), Letyushova. *Bystritskiy*

	W	D	L	+	-	PTS
NOR	3	0	0	13	2	9
RUS	2	0	1	10	3	6
CAN	0	1	2	3	12	1
JPN	0	1	2	1	10	1

▶ Russia's Natalia Barbashina (10) tackles Japan's Kae Nishina during her team's 5-0 victory over the Japanese in Portland.

▶ Marianne Pettersen (11) was one of six goalscorers in Norway's 7-1 victory over Canada in Washington DC. Her teammate Ann Kristin Aarønes scored twice.

Norwegian clean sweep

Canada skipper Silvana Burtini, a FIFA record-holder after hitting eight past Puerto Rico in qualifying, got the highest-scoring group off the mark with an early goal in San José. Then, within the space of nine minutes, Canada lost Burtini to an old hamstring injury and their lead to Japan through a Nami Otake equaliser. Norway, now led by Per-Mathias Høgmo, were flying after 1995 Final scorer Marianne Pettersen netted the decider against Russia, who then belied their debutant status by walloping Japan, skippered by 20-year-old Homare Sawa. Worse was to come for Canada, hit for seven by Norway for a second successive finals, with Charmaine Hooper's maiden World Cup goal merely a consolation. Hooper, the most eye-catching player of the 1999 FIFA World Stars match, netted for the Concacaf champions against Russia too, but they lost 4-1 and the team whose main warm-up had been a low-key Varna Cup win in April were into the quarter-finals. With their later kick-off, Norway and Japan knew their fates but still slugged it out on a waterlogged pitch in Chicago, the Norwegians losing Linda Medalen then Ann Kristin Aarønes to injury, but winning the game and the group.

Group stage 1999

Group D

	W	D	L	+	−	PTS
CHN	3	0	0	12	2	9
SWE	2	0	1	6	3	6
AUS	0	1	2	3	7	1
GHA	0	1	2	1	10	1

◀ Hanna Ljungberg scored twice in Sweden's 3-1 victory over Australia.

◀◀ Ghana earned a draw in their World Cup debut against Australia. Defender Patience Sackey (2) thwarts an attack by Dianne Alagich.

China power through

Sweden and China brought 15 World Cup finals debutants to USA 99 between them, but all knew the historical importance of their group curtain-raiser – the two sides had previously ended each other's home Women's World Cups. Kristin Bengtsson wowed the crowd of 23,298 with her second-minute opener, but goalscorers Jin Yan and Liu Ailing delivered for China on the big stage. Buoyed by government funding, Australia had lived and trained together for almost a year, while captain Julie Murray, dropped in 1996, had become their star striker under new coach Greg Brown. Murray delivered against newcomers Ghana, down to ten after an early red card, but the Oceania champions failed to take advantage after Nana Gyamfuah hit an immediate leveller. China were clinical when the Black Queens saw red for a second successive match, Sun Wen hitting a hat-trick in a decisive win. Hanna Ljungberg's brace helped Sweden avenge their 1999 Algarve Cup loss to Australia and the Matildas, whose teenage forward Alicia Ferguson collected the fastest red card in Women's World Cup history, were knocked out by top-of-the-table China. Sweden took second, Victoria Svensson beating Ghana's courageous keeper Memunatu Sulemana twice in a vital victory.

102

It took just 102 seconds from the start of the match for Australia's Alicia Ferguson to see red, the quickest sending-off in World Cup history.

◀ After losing their opening match against China, Sweden needed to beat Australia. Here they celebrate going 3-1 up.

Spartan Stadium, San José
19.06.1999, 17:00, **23,298**

CHINA PR 2-1 SWEDEN

Jin Yan 17, Liu Ailing 69 — Bengtsson 2

Virginia Tovar MEX
Maria Rodriguez MEX & Jackeline Saez PAN

CHN • 18 **Gao Hong** - 5 **Xie** Huilin (7 **Zhang** Ouying 59), 3 **Fan** Yunjie, 12 **Wen** Lirong, 14 **Bai** Jie - 2 **Wang** Liping, 13 **Liu** Ying, 10 **Liu** Ailing, 6 **Zhao** Lihong - 8 **Jin** Yan, 9 **Sun** Wen (c) (11 **Pu** Wei 74). *Ma Yuanan*

SWE • 1 Ulrika **Karlsson** - 2 Karolina **Westberg**, 7 Cecilia **Sandell**, 3 Jane **Törnqvist**, 4 Åsa **Lönnqvist** - 6 Malin **Moström** (17 Linda **Fagerström** 77), 9 Malin **Andersson** (c), 10 Hanna **Ljungberg**, 5 Kristin **Bengtsson** (20 Tina **Nordlund** 88) - 18 Therese **Lundin** (8 Malin **Gustafsson** 46), 11 Victoria **Svensson**. *Marika Domanski Lyfors*

Foxboro Stadium, Boston
20.06.1999, 19:30, **14,873**

AUSTRALIA 1-1 GHANA

Murray 74 — Gyamfuah 76

Kari Seitz USA
Ann Wenche Kleven NOR & Ri Song Ok PRK

AUS • 20 Tracey **Wheeler** - 4 Sarah **Cooper**, 19 Dianne **Alagich**, 5 Traci **Bartlett** ■ 89, 3 Bridgette **Starr** - 10 Angela **Iannotta** (7 Lisa **Casagrande** 59 ■ 65), 18 Alison **Forman**, 14 Joanne **Peters** (17 Kelly **Golebiowski** 89), 11 Sharon **Black** - 9 Julie **Murray** (c), 8 Cheryl **Salisbury**. *Greg Brown*

GHA • 1 Memunatu **Sulemana** - 2 Patience **Sackey**, 4 Regina **Ansah** ■ 4, 5 Elizabeth **Baidu**, 3 Rita **Yeboah** ■ 11 - 8 Barikisu **Tettey-Quao** ■ 26, 20 Genevive **Clottey** ■ 80 - 7 Mavis **Dgajmah** (17 Sheila **Okai** 32) (15 Nana **Gyamfuah** 65), 9 Alberta **Sackey** (c) ■ 15, 10 Vivian **Mensah**, 11 Adjoa **Bayor** (19 Stella **Quartey** 79). *Emmanuel Afranie*

Civic Stadium, Portland
23.06.1999, 20:30, **17,668**

CHINA PR 7-0 GHANA

Sun Wen (3) 9 21 54,
Jin Yan 16,
Zhang Ouying (2) 82 90+1,
Zhao Lihong 90+2

Elke Günthner GER
Cleidy Ribeiro BRA & Adeola Adeyemi NGA

CHN • Gao Hong - Wang Liping, Fan Yunjie, Wen Lirong, Bai Jie - Pu Wei (Xie Huilin 73), Liu Ying, Liu Ailing (15 Qiu Haiyan 58), Zhao Lihong - Jin Yan (Zhang Ouying 51), Sun Wen (c). *Ma Yuanan*

GHA • Sulemana - P Sackey ■ 28, Ansah ■ 53, Baidu, Yeboah ■ 16 - Gyamfuah (Dgajmah 74 ■ 89), Quartey, Clottey, Bayor (13 Lydia **Ankrah** 56) - Mensah, A Sackey (c). *Afranie*

Jack Kent Cooke Stadium, Washington DC
23.06.1999, 20:30, **16,448**

AUSTRALIA 1-3 SWEDEN

Murray 32 — Törnqvist 8
Ljungberg (2) 21 69

Fatou Gaye SEN
Hisae Yoshizawa JPN & Ana Perez PER

AUS • 1 Belinda **Kitching** - Cooper (Iannotta 76), Alagich ■ 79, Bartlett, Starr (6 Anissa **Tann-Darby** 87) - Casagrande, Forman ■ 85, Peters, Black (Golebiowski 58) - Murray (c), Salisbury. *Brown*

SWE • Karlsson - Westberg, Sandell, Törnqvist (14 Jessika **Sundh** 75), Lönnqvist - Moström, Andersson (c), 15 Linda **Gren** (Gustafsson 46), Bengtsson ■ 53 (Lundin 57) - Svensson, Ljungberg. *Domanski Lyfors*

Soldier Field, Chicago
26.06.1999, 16:00, **34,256**

GHANA 0-2 SWEDEN

— Svensson (2) 58 86
(Andersson penalty saved 62)

Sonia Denoncourt CAN
Ann Wenche Kleven NOR & Corrie Kruithof NED

GHA • Sulemana - Clottey, Baidu, A Sackey (c), P Sackey - Tettey-Quao, Quartey - Ankrah (Okai 65 ■ 81), Mensah, Gyamfuah ■ 10 (14 Mercy **Tagoe** 84), Bayor. *Afranie*

SWE • Karlsson - Westberg, Sandell, Törnqvist, Lönnqvist - Moström, Andersson (c), Gustafsson (Fagerström 87), Bengtsson (Nordlund 60) - Svensson, Ljungberg (Lundin 57). *Domanski Lyfors*

Giants Stadium, New York/New Jersey
26.06.1999, 14:30, **29,401**

CHINA PR 3-1 AUSTRALIA

Sun Wen (2) 39 51 — Salisbury 66
Liu Ying 73

Sandra Hunt USA
Ana Perez PER & Hisae Yoshizawa JPN

CHN • Gao Hong - Wang Liping, Fan Yunjie ■ 4, Wen Lirong ■ 70, Bai Jie - Pu Wei, Liu Ying, Liu Ailing, Zhao Lihong (Xie Huilin 75) - Jin Yan (Zhang Ouying 46), Sun Wen (c) (Qiu Haiyan 63). *Ma Yuanan*

AUS • Kitching - Alagich, Tann-Darby, Bartlett, Starr - Casagrande (Iannotta 72), Salisbury (15 Peita-Claire **Hepperlin** 86), Forman (16 Amy **Wilson** 79), Golebiowski - 13 Alicia **Ferguson** ■ 2, Murray (c). *Brown*

1999 Quarter-finals

Russia miss out on semis and Olympic qualification

Spartan Stadium, San José
30.06.1999, 17:00, **21,411**

CHINA PR 2-0 RUSSIA

Pu Wei 37, Jin Yan 56

Nicole Petignat SUI • Boni Bishop TRI & Comfort Cofie GHA

CHN • Gao Hong - Wang Liping, Fan Yunjie, Wen Lirong, Bai Jie - Pu Wei (Qiu Haiyan 80 ▮ 90+2), Liu Ying, Liu Ailing, Zhao Lihong - Jin Yan (Zhang Ouying 89), Sun Wen (c). *Ma Yuanan*

RUS • Petko - Cheverda ▮ 35, Burakova, Filippova, N Karasseva - Komarova (Svetlitskaya 88), Egorova (Fomina 46), Barbashina (Savina 68), Grigorieva (c), O Karasseva - Letyushova. *Bystritskiy*

Russia were revelling in their chance to impress on the world stage and their stock had risen after emphatic wins over Japan and Canada. With ten goals from eight different players and star skipper Irina Grigorieva, dependable defender Marina Burakova and top forward Natalia Barbashina in their squad, Yuri Bystritskiy's side were no lightweights. Ma Yuanan's reigning Olympic silver medallists were blessed with experience though, and they led the way in San José.

Russia's 29-year-old shot-stopper Svetlana Petko oversaw their determined resistance against China's all-out attack, but was hit by a sucker punch when teenage midfielder Pu Wei took a shot from distance that bounced under her body and over the line. Striker Jin Yan added insult to injury, stabbing home captain Sun Wen's left-footed free kick as it rebounded off the post to book her first and China's second successive semi-final berth.

▶▲ Sun Wen (centre) was the joint top scorer at the World Cup, but the goals in China's 2-0 quarter-final win over Russia in San José were scored by Pu Wei and Jin Yan.

◀ China goalkeeper Gao Hong conceded just two goals in six matches at USA '99, and none in this quarter-final against Russia.

▲ China celebrate qualifying for the World Cup semi-final after their victory over Russia.

Ten up for Norway

Spartan Stadium, San José
30.06.1999, 19:30, **21,411**

NORWAY 3-1 SWEDEN

Aarønes 51, Pettersen 58, Riise 72p   Moström 90+1

Im Eun Ju KOR • Hisae Yoshizawa JPN & Ghislaine Labbé FRA

NOR • Nordby - Jørgensen, Kringen, Medalen (c), Sandaune - Lehn (Mellgren 77), Riise, Knudsen, Frustøl (S Gulbrandsen 46 ▮ 55) - Pettersen, Aarønes (Rapp 81). *Høgmo*

SWE • Karlsson - Westberg, Sandell, Törnqvist, Lönnqvist - Nordlund (19 Minna **Heponiemi** 81), Moström, Andersson (c), Bengtsson (Lundin 46) - Gustafsson (Sundh 72), Svensson. *Domanski Lyfors*

10

Norway's 3-1 win over Sweden was their tenth successive World Cup victory, a record that stood until it was beaten by the USA in 2019.

With a place at Sydney 2000, a semi-final berth and the small matter of a World Cup title defence at stake, there was everything to play for in Norway and Sweden's 30th encounter. Having lost Pia Sundhage, Lena Videkull and several other stalwarts to retirement, Sweden's former assistant, and now head coach, Marika Domanski Lyfors had revamped the squad. So while eight of her starting XI were World Cup debutants, nine were European Championship semi-finalists. Norway had flopped in that competition, but they were winners on this stage, securing a then-record tenth successive World Cup victory. Sweden started brightly enough but missed the injured Hanna Ljungberg, and in a 21-minute second-half blitz, Norway's lethal 1995 goal-getters Ann Kristin Aarønes, Marianne Pettersen and Hege Riise killed their Scandinavian rivals off. Malin Moström's 91st-minute goal would, however, see Sweden squeeze past Russia to an Olympic spot.

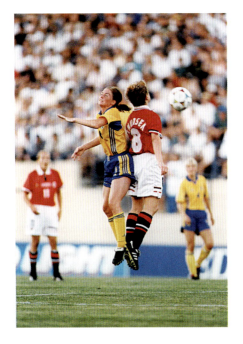

◀ Sweden's Malin Moström and Norway's Monica Knudsen (8) during their quarter-final in San José.

Germans push hosts to the limit

Jack Kent Cooke Stadium, Washington DC
1.07.1999, 19:00, **54,642**

USA 🇺🇸 **3-2** 🇩🇪 GERMANY

Milbrett 16, Chastain 49, Fawcett 66   Chastain OG 5, Wiegmann 45+1

Martha Toro COL ◆ Ana Perez PER & Corrie Kruithof NED

USA • Scurry - Fawcett, Overbeck (c), Sobrero, Chastain (Fair 73) - Foudy (MacMillan 65), Akers, Lilly - Hamm, Milbrett, Parlow (Roberts 85). *DiCicco*
GER • Rottenberg - Hingst, Fitschen (c) ■ 53, Jones, Minnert - Smisek (Lingor 84), Wiegmann, Meinert, P Wunderlich (Meyer 53) - Prinz, Grings (Hoffmann 90+2). *Theune-Meyer*

▶ Action during the quarter-final between the USA and Germany in Washington DC.

World Cup legend Pelé had witnessed the USA's seven-goal thriller of a win over Germany in 1991, but this time President Bill Clinton joined a lively 54,642 spectators to watch this five-goal rollercoaster. Defender Brandi Chastain scored two of the goals, one for each team, starting with a fifth-minute backpass into her own net. It was a head-in-hands moment, but Tiffeny Milbrett, whose goal had clinched Olympic gold for the USA in 1996, swiftly restored parity. Only three 1991 veterans were in Tina Theune-Meyer's talented line-up in America and one of them was Bettina Wiegmann, a scorer against the USA on the world stage then and again here with an impressive ninth World Cup goal. The four-time European champions would not avenge that defeat on their opponents' home soil though, as 30-year-old Chastain delivered a redemptive equaliser and Joy Fawcett headed home a stylish winner.

◀ Goalkeeper Judith Chime came on as a first-half substitute after Nigeria found themselves 3-0 down. They fought back to 3-3 but then lost to a golden goal.

16

Nigeria's Ifeanyichukwu Chiejine turned 16 just before the World Cup. When she made her debut against North Korea in the group stage, she was 16 years and 34 days old – the youngest player to take part in the World Cup or Olympics until South Korea's Casey Phair, who was eight days younger when she took to the field at the 2023 World Cup.

Sissi seals thriller with golden goal

Jack Kent Cooke Stadium, Washington DC
1.07.1999, 21:30, **54,642**

BRAZIL 🇧🇷 **4-3** 🇳🇬 NIGERIA
AET

Cidinha (2) 4 22, Nene 35, Sissi 104 GG   Emeafu 63, Okosieme 72, Egbe 85

Virginia Tovar MEX ◆ Maria Rodriguez MEX & Jackeline Saez PAN

BRA • Maravilha - Nenê, Tânia, Elane (c), Suzana ■ 81 - Cidinha, Formiga, Sissi, Raquel (Maycon 66) - Pretinha, Kátia. *Wilsinho*
NGA • A Chiejine (12 Judith **Chime** 40) - Kudaisi (Nwaneri 77 ■ 102), Opara, Emeafu, I Chiejine (Ajayi 26) - Avre ■ 41 ■ 87 ■ 87, Omagbemi (c) ■ 28, Akide, Okosieme, Nwadike ■ 12 - Egbe. *Mabo*

◀ Brazil's Sissi celebrates her extra-time golden goal winner against Nigeria.

It took the first-ever Women's World Cup golden goal to settle the first quarter-final to feature an African or South American side and what a winner it was. Unleashed by the left foot of playmaker Sissi, it flew over the Nigerian wall, bounced off the upright and into the net. It was the 32-year-old's seventh goal in four games. "I'd never been so prolific," the free-kick specialist would later admit. It was an agonising finish for Nigeria after a magnificent comeback from 3-0 down. Defender Prisca Emeafu, their top scorer Nkiru Okosieme and striker Nkechi Egbe had fired their recovery in a blistering 22-minute spell. Nigeria's adventure was over, but they had recorded two Women's World Cup wins, impressed in the knockout stage and would write their name in the history books as the first African women's team to qualify for the Olympics.

1999 Semi-finals

Chinese reach near-perfection

Foxboro Stadium, Boston
4.07.1999, 19:30, **28,986**

NORWAY 🇳🇴 **0-5** 🇨🇳 **CHINA PR**

Sun Wen (2) 3 72p, Liu Ailing (2) 14 51, Fan Yunjie 65

Sonia Denoncourt CAN • Maria Rodriguez MEX & Ana Perez PER

NOR • Nordby - Jørgensen, Kringen, Medalen (c), Sandaune - Lehn (Mellgren 46), Riise, Knudsen (Frustøl 76), S Gulbrandsen - Aarønes (R Gulbrandsen 46), Pettersen. *Høgmo*
CHN • Gao Hong - Wang Liping, Fan Yunjie, Wen Lirong, Bai Jie - Pu Wei (Zhang Ouying 76), Liu Ying, Liu Ailing, Zhao Lihong (Qiu Haiyan 78) - Jin Yan, Sun Wen (c). *Ma Yuanan*

Two truly unstoppable goals and a total team performance brought the 4th of July action and Norway's Women's World Cup record ten-match winning run to a dramatic close on a humid evening in Boston. The reigning world champions had not lost in the World Cup since the USA had edged them to the title in the 1991 Final and had only conceded four goals, but China smashed that achievement in the space of 69 minutes at Foxboro Stadium, kicking off with a fine goal from captain Sun Wen in the third minute and concluding with her nerveless penalty kick in the 72nd. In between, midfielder Liu Ailing, who had scored twice against Norway in the 1991 finals, almost broke the net with two ferocious volleys, one with each foot. Norway's usually devastating direct style had proved ineffective against the speed and skill of China and although Per-Mathias Høgmo's side ramped up their tempo midway through the second period, shot-stopper Gao Hong was equal to anything Dagny Mellgren, Hege Riise and Marianne Pettersen threw at her. The world champions would now contest third place with Brazil, while China had their eyes on the ultimate prize.

▲▲ The Chinese players huddle before their semi-final against Norway. They ended Norway's run of 10 consecutive wins.

▲ Sun Wen (2) gave China a third-minute lead in their 5-0 semi-final victory over Norway in Boston.

▼▼ The USA team celebrate qualifying for the Final after their 2-0 win over Brazil in San Francisco.

▼ Michelle Akers (10) was a huge influence at the 1999 World Cup despite suffering from the Epstein-Barr virus which causes chronic fatigue. She sealed victory over Brazil with a penalty.

Perfect 4th of July for the USA

Stanford Stadium, Palo Alto, San Francisco
4.07.1999, 13:30, **73,123**

USA 🇺🇸 **2-0** 🇧🇷 **BRAZIL**

Parlow 5, Akers 80p

Katriina Elovirta FIN • Hisae Yoshizawa JPN & Ghislaine Labbé FRA

USA • Scurry - Fawcett, Chastain, Sobrero, Overbeck (c) - Lilly, Akers 90, Foudy - Milbrett (17 Danielle **Fotopoulos** 88), Parlow (MacMillan 62), Hamm (Fair 85). *DiCicco*
BRA • Maravilha - Nenê, Juliana, Elane (c), Tânia 13 - Cidinha, Formiga, Sissi 41, Suzana (Maycon 70) - Kátia 90+2, Pretinha. *Wilsinho*

At USA 94, Brazil's men had ended the home team's World Cup dreams at Stanford Stadium. Would Brazil's women follow in their footsteps at the same venue exactly five years to the day after? They might well have done were it not for a string of saves from Briana Scurry after an early goal from 21-year-old Cindy Parlow and a late Michelle Akers' penalty. Brazil never stopped pressing their claim for a place in the Final though. Nene went agonisingly close to an equaliser in the second half, but her cross-cum-shot was acrobatically saved by Scurry. Maravilha had saved a penalty in the group stage, but she was beaten by a perfect spot kick from Akers ten minutes from time and so were Brazil in front of 73,123 spectators. In qualifying, Brazil had scored 66 goals and conceded three. They and maestro Sissi had delivered some moments of magic on their way to a historic semi-final berth, but this day belonged to the hosts and if there had been a roof on the bowl-like stadium, the thousands who cheered and hollered when the whistle blew on this gripping Samba-style Independence Day clash would surely have raised it.

Third place 1999

Brazil claim bronze after first World Cup goalless draw

Rose Bowl, Los Angeles
10.07.1999, 10:15, **90,185**

BRAZIL 0-0 **NORWAY**
5-4 PSO

Riise ⚽ Pretinha ✖ Medalen ⚽ Cidinha ⚽ Jørgensen ✖ Kátia ⚽ Sandaune ⚽ Maycon ⚽ S Gulbrandsen ⚽ Nenê ⚽ Aarønes ✖ Formiga ⚽

Im Eun Ju KOR • Hisae Yoshizawa JPN & Maria Rodriguez MEX

▲ Action from the match for third place between Norway and Brazil.

1999 Match for Third Place

They had scored 16 apiece on their way to the semi-finals but when it came to the match for third place, neither Brazil nor Norway could find that decisive goal. Yet this prelude to the prestigious Final was no bore draw and it got the inflatable orange clackers of thousands of fans at the Rose Bowl banging. Norway had beaten Brazil in the bronze medal match at the 1996 Olympics and the scorer of their winning goals then, Ann Kristin Aarønes, had chances here, as did 1995 Final scorers Marianne Pettersen and Hege Riise. But Brazil made inroads against a packed Norwegian midfield and keeper Bente Nordby needed to be on her mettle to twice deny Pretinha, while Sissi, who played football with rolled-up socks and dolls' heads in her youth, only had to slot the ball into a gaping goal after giving Norway the slip, but the angle was too acute even for a player of her dynamism. So, the first-ever Women's World Cup match to finish goalless was decided in the most dramatic way possible, by a penalty shoot-out. The Rose Bowl had seen it all before, of course, when Brazil's men had beaten Italy on penalties to win the 1994 World Cup. Their female counterparts held their nerve here too. Sissi knelt in the centre circle hardly able to watch, but the tournament's Silver Ball and Golden Boot winner joined the pile-on as the team descended on Formiga to celebrate her decisive spot kick.

◀▲ Brazil celebrate Formiga's penalty that sealed third place at the 1999 World Cup.

◀ The Brazilian squad proudly display their medals after beating Norway on penalties at the Rose Bowl.

1999 **Final**

Chastain seals it for the 99ers

Rose Bowl, Los Angeles
10.07.1999, 12:50, **90,185**

USA 🇺🇸 **0-0** 🇨🇳 CHINA PR
AET
5-4 PSO

Xie Huilin ⚽ Overbeck ⚽ Qiu Haiyang ⚽ Fawcett ⚽ Liu Ying ✖ Lilly ⚽ Zhang Ouying ⚽ Hamm ⚽ Sun Wen ⚽ Chastain ⚽

Nicole Petignat SUI — Ghislaine Labbé FRA & Ana Perez PER

They were the best teams in the tournament and had historic scores to settle, China having lifted the 1999 Algarve Cup at the Americans' expense, and the USA having edged their arch-rivals to Olympic gold at Atlanta 1996. After 120 minutes of high-tempo, skilful football, some late chances and a dramatic goal-line clearance, it would take a nerve-jangling penalty shoot-out to separate them in Pasadena, but what a defining moment in the history of the women's game it would turn out to be.

A record 90,185 spectators had poured into the Rose Bowl to witness the third Women's World Cup Final and the atmosphere was simply extraordinary. Ramped up by a vivid performance from pop queen Jennifer Lopez and a four-jet fly-past during a goosebump rendition of the Star-Spangled Banner from Hanson, it was at fever pitch by the time the teams kicked off.

Ten US and eight Chinese Olympians were in the starting line-up, among them stalwarts Liu Ailing and Wen Lirong, who had played in every World Cup match for China since 1991, and the USA's two "moms" Carla Overbeck and Joy Fawcett, who had not missed a minute of World Cup action since starting in the 1991 semi-final.

With Mia Hamm, Tiffeny Milbrett and Cindy Parlow operating in front of Michelle Akers, and the tournament's joint top scorer and eventual Golden Ball winner Sun Wen spearheading China's potent strikeforce, the game had goals written all over it. But after a speedy start from the USA, it settled into an even contest in the boiling heat, the best chance falling to Fan Yunjie in extra time, but her potential golden goal winner was cleared off the line by Kristine Lilly.

So, it fell to penalty kicks and with Briana Scurry leaping off her line to deny Liu Ying, the decisive fifth fell to left-back Brandi Chastain. She had missed from the spot against China in the Algarve Cup Final and was asked by coach Tony DiCicco to strike with her left foot despite never having done so before. Nevertheless, Chastain strolled up to the spot and coolly dispatched the winner before sinking to her knees, pulling off her shirt and pumping her fists in celebration. The USA were Women's World Cup champions for a second time and Chastain and her teammates instant icons of the game for generations to come.

4

The USA team made history as the only subjects to have graced the covers in the same week of all four of *Time* magazine, *Newsweek* (below), *People* and *Sports Illustrated*.

▲ *FIFA Museum Collection*

▼ Champions of the world for a second time. The USA celebrate their 1999 world title.

Final 1999

▲ Carla Overbeck lifts the new World Cup trophy.

▶ Shirt and gloves worn by Briana Scurry during the 1999 World Cup Final.
FIFA Museum Collection

1999 World Cup Final

▶ The crucial moment of the 1999 Final penalty shoot-out. Briana Scurry saves from Liu Ying.

▶ Eight members of the 1991 USA World Cup-winning squad join in the celebrations after the 1999 Final, including captain April Heinrichs (2).

82

82 games in World Cup history and not a single 0-0 draw, and then two come along on the same day. The third-place and Final double-header may have attracted the biggest crowd for a game in the USA, but the 90,185 fans didn't get to see a goal in four hours of open play.

2000

A thrilling Final between Norway and the USA saw an injury-time equaliser for the Americans and then a Dagny Mellgren golden goal in extra time for Norway who took gold. It was an epic clash between the best two teams of the previous decade. In the six world tournaments played in the 12 years from 1988, these two sides had won all of them, winning three titles apiece.

Aussie Rules!

In 1996, IOC President Juan Antonio Samaranch had damned the Atlanta Games with faint praise... "most exceptional" he said. Sydney 2000 received the usual accolade of "best ever" and with over one million spectators watching the two Olympic Football Tournaments, football played its part in making these Games an outstanding festival fit for the new millennium. In the men's tournament, Cameroon took gold after trailing in the semis and in the Final where they beat Spain on penalties. The USA, Russia and China headed the medal table with Australia the best of the rest. The Aussies won 16 gold, three of which were won by swimming sensation Ian Thorpe. He was the star of the games along with compatriot Cathy Freeman who had lit the Olympic Flame before going on to win the 400m. But for sheer Olympic spirit, Equatorial Guinea's Eric Moussambani – Eric the Eel – captured the hearts of all those in the Sydney Aquatic Centre. He had never seen an Olympic size pool before and swam the 100m freestyle in a leisurely 1:52.72, one of the slowest times in Olympic history.

▼ Cathy Freeman striding in for gold.

2000 Overview

SYDNEY 2000

WOMEN'S OLYMPIC FOOTBALL TOURNAMENT

Story of the qualifiers

Olympic debuts for Africa and Oceania

For the second Women's Olympic Football Tournament in a row, the seven best teams at the previous FIFA Women's World Cup secured a berth at the Games, along with the hosts. That meant that all six confederations were represented, unlike in Atlanta four years previously. Nigeria's exploits at USA'99 ensured that they became the first African nation to take part while Australia were the first nation from the Oceania Football Confederation. The unlucky quarter-finalists from the World Cup who did not make the cut were Russia. They missed out on goals scored, having lost 2-0 to China, whereas Sweden had lost 3-1 to Norway. It was the closest that Russia, a traditional Olympic powerhouse, had come to fielding a women's football team at the Olympics.

▶ All six confederations were represented in the women's football tournament at Sydney despite qualification being based on results at USA '99.

▼ Brazilian fans enjoying the atmosphere at the Sydney Olympics.

Group stage

GROUP E		
AUS	0-3	GER
SWE	0-2	BRA
AUS	1-1	SWE
GER	2-1	BRA
AUS	1-2	BRA
GER	1-0	SWE

	W	D	L	+	−	PTS
GER	3	0	0	6	1	9
BRA	2	0	1	5	3	6
SWE	0	1	2	1	4	1
AUS	0	1	2	2	6	1

GROUP F		
USA	2-0	NOR
CHN	3-1	NGA
USA	1-1	CHN
NOR	3-1	NGA
USA	3-1	NGA
NOR	2-1	CHN

	W	D	L	+	−	PTS
USA	2	1	0	6	2	7
NOR	2	0	1	5	4	6
CHN	1	1	1	5	4	4
NGA	0	0	3	3	9	0

Knockout stages

SEMI-FINAL
GER 0-1 NOR

SEMI-FINAL
USA 1-0 BRA

BRONZE MEDAL MATCH
GER 2-0 BRA

GOLD MEDAL MATCH
NOR 3-2 AET USA

Overview 2000

8 TEAMS	NORWAY WINNERS				16 MATCHES PLAYED	42 GOALS
	USA SECOND	GER THIRD			47 YELLOW CARDS	2.63 AVERAGE GOALS PER MATCH
326 215 SPECTATORS	**20 388** AVERAGE PER MATCH				0 RED CARDS	GAMARADA OFFICIAL MATCH BALL

UNITED STATES	37	24	32	
RUSSIA	32	28	29	
CHINA PR	28	16	14	
AUSTRALIA	16	25	17	
GERMANY	13	17	26	
FRANCE	13	14	11	

TOP OF THE MEDAL TABLE

Host cities and stadiums

MCG welcomes back the Olympics 44 years on

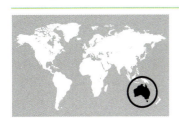

The Melbourne Cricket Ground had hosted the Final of the football tournament at the 1956 Olympics and staged matches in both the women's and men's tournaments 44 years later. Just three stadiums were used in the women's event, the fewest at either the Women's Olympic Football Tournament or at the FIFA Women's World Cup. The Final was held at the Sydney Football Stadium, built in 1986 next to the Sydney Cricket Ground. Its replacement on the same site was a venue for the 2023 World Cup.

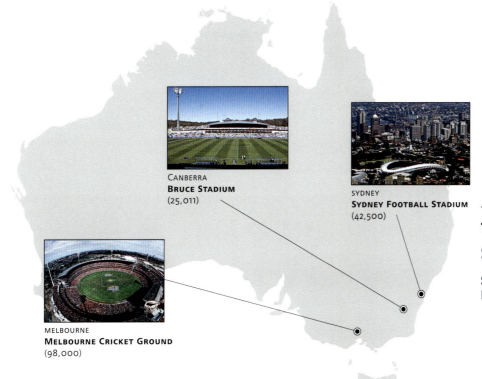

CANBERRA
Bruce Stadium
(25,011)

SYDNEY
Sydney Football Stadium
(42,500)

MELBOURNE
Melbourne Cricket Ground
(98,000)

×4

Top scorer

Sun Wen CHN

Second Place: Tiffeny Milbrett USA × 3
Birgit Prinz GER × 3

2000 Group stage

Bruce Stadium, Canberra
13.09.2000, 17:00, **24,800**

AUSTRALIA 🇦🇺 **0-3** 🇩🇪 **GERMANY**

Grings 35
Wiegmann 70
Lingor 90+1

🟨 Bola Abidoye NGA
🚩 Ana Perez PER & Cleidy Ribeiro BRA

AUS • 1 Tracey **Wheeler** - 6 Anissa **Tann-Darby**, 5 Dianne **Alagich**, 8 Cheryl **Salisbury**, 14 Sacha **Wainwright**, 12 Bryony **Duus** (4 Heather **Garriock** 72), 7 Alison **Forman** (c), 2 Kate **McShea** 🟨 57, 16 Amy **Wilson** - 10 Sunni **Hughes** (13 Alicia **Ferguson** 46), 9 Julie **Murray** (17 Kelly **Golebiowski** 62). *Chris Tanzey*

GER • 1 Silke **Rottenberg** - 2 Kerstin **Stegemann**, 4 Steffi **Jones**, 5 Doris **Fitschen** (c), 13 Sandra **Minnert** - 15 Ariane **Hingst** 🟨 43, 16 Renate **Lingor**, 10 Bettina **Wiegmann**, 9 Birgit **Prinz** - 6 Maren **Meinert**, 11 Inka **Grings**. *Tina Theune-Meyer*

Melbourne Cricket Ground, Melbourne
13.09.2000, 17:00, **58,432**

SWEDEN 🇸🇪 **0-2** 🇧🇷 **BRAZIL**

Pretinha 21
Kátia 70

🟨 Sandra Hunt USA
🚩 Lynn Fox NZL & Comfort Cofie GHA

SWE • 1 Caroline **Jönsson** - 4 Sara **Larsson**, 7 Cecilia **Sandell**, 2 Karolina **Westberg**, 5 Kristin **Bengtsson** - 6 Malin **Moström**, 10 Hanna **Ljungberg**, 3 Jane **Törnqvist** (15 Linda **Fagerström** 85), 11 Victoria **Svensson** (17 Therese **Sjögran** 76) - 9 Malin **Andersson** (c), 8 Tina **Nordlund**. *Marika Domanski Lyfors*

BRA • 1 **Andréia** - 15 **Simone**, 3 **Juliana**, 6 **Tânia** (4 **Mônica** 78), 16 **Rosana** - 8 **Cidinha**, 5 **Daniela** - 7 **Formiga**, 10 **Sissi** (c) - 12 **Pretinha** (13 **Maycon** 82), 9 **Kátia** (11 **Roseli** 82). *José Duarte*

Sydney Football Stadium, Sydney
16.09.2000, 17:30, **33,600**

AUSTRALIA 🇦🇺 **1-1** 🇸🇪 **SWEDEN**

Salisbury 57   Andersson 66p

🟨 Sonia Denoncourt CAN
🚩 Jackeline Saez PAN & Hisae Yoshizawa JPN

AUS • Wheeler - Tann-Darby, Alagich 🟨 65, Salisbury, Wainwright - Duus (Garriock 77), Forman (c), McShea, Wilson (11 Sharon **Black** 45) - Ferguson (Golebiowski 78), Hughes 🟨 57. *Tanzey*

SWE • Jönsson - Larsson, Sandell, Westberg, Bengtsson - Nordlund (Fagerström 76), Moström, Törnqvist, Andersson (c), - Ljungberg, Svensson (Sjögran 54). *Domanski Lyfors*

Bruce Stadium, Canberra
16.09.2000, 17:30, **17,000**

GERMANY 🇩🇪 **2-1** 🇧🇷 **BRAZIL**

Prinz (2) 33 41   Raquel 72

🟨 Martha Toro COL
🚩 Comfort Cofie GHA & Sanna Luhtanen FIN

GER • Rottenberg - Stegemann 🟨 32, Jones, Fitschen (c) 🟨 22, Minnert - Hingst, Lingor 🟨 83, Wiegmann, Prinz - Meinert, Grings. *Theune-Meyer*

BRA • Andréia - Simone (Roseli 46), Juliana, Mônica 🟨 90, Cidinha (14 **Raquel** 69 🟨 73), Rosana - Sissi (c), Daniela 🟨 33, Formiga (2 **Nenê** 46) - Kátia, Pretinha. *Duarte*

Sydney Football Stadium, Sydney
19.09.2000, 17:30, **29,400**

AUSTRALIA 🇦🇺 **1-2** 🇧🇷 **BRAZIL**

Hughes 33   Raquel 56
                     Kátia 64

🟨 Vibeke Karlsen NOR
🚩 Sanna Luhtanen FIN & Marie-Louise Svanström SWE

AUS • Wheeler - Tann-Darby, Alagich 🟨 69, Salisbury, 3 Bridgette **Starr** - Duus 🟨 48 (Wilson 62), Forman (c), McShea (Golebiowski 74), Black (Garriock 70) - Ferguson, Hughes. *Tanzey*

BRA • Andréia - Simone, Juliana, Tânia, Rosana (Maycon 46) - Cidinha, Sissi, Daniela, Raquel (Formiga 57) - Kátia 🟨 68, Pretinha (Roseli 74). *Duarte*

Melbourne Cricket Ground, Melbourne
19.09.2000, 17:30, **7,000**

GERMANY 🇩🇪 **1-0** 🇸🇪 **SWEDEN**

Hingst 88

🟨 Wendy Toms ENG
🚩 Lynn Fox NZL & Comfort Cofie GHA

GER • Rottenberg - 14 Tina **Wunderlich**, Jones, Fitschen (c), Minnert - Hingst, Wiegmann, 17 Melanie **Hoffmann** (Lingor 46 🟨 66), Prinz - Grings (7 Claudia **Müller** 46), Meinert (8 Nicole **Brandebusemeyer** 87). *Theune-Meyer*

SWE • Jönsson - 12 Hanna **Marklund** (14 Sara **Johansson** 82), Sandell, Westberg, Larsson 🟨 79 - Moström, 16 Malin **Swedberg** (Svensson 59), Törnqvist 🟨 27, Andersson (c), Nordlund (Sjögran 46) - Ljungberg. *Domanski Lyfors*

Group E

	W	D	L	+	-	PTS
GER	3	0	0	6	1	9
BRA	2	0	1	5	3	6
SWE	0	1	2	1	4	1
AUS	0	1	2	2	6	1

▶ Alicia Ferguson and Sissi during Australia's 2-1 defeat at the hands of Brazil.

Australia fail to make the most of home advantage

3
Australia are one of just three host nations to have failed to get past the group stage in either the Olympics or the World Cup. The others were Greece four years later and New Zealand in 2023.

Hosts Australia kicked off the tournament at Bruce Stadium in Canberra, but their debut appearance at the Olympics was not a happy one as they crashed 3-0 to Germany. New head coach Chris Tanzey had hoped that a pre-tournament training camp in which his squad were based together full-time for several months would pay dividends, but a draw in their second match, against Sweden, followed by defeat at the hands of Brazil saw his team knocked out at the first hurdle. European champions Germany were favourites to top the group as they aimed to turn their dominance in Europe into success on the world stage.

Having beaten Australia, two goals from Birgit Prinz were enough to beat Brazil in their next match, a win that saw them through to the semis as group winners. The Brazilians had signalled their intent by beating Sweden in their opening match, Pretinha and Kátia scoring the goals that put them on course to finishing second in the group ahead of the Swedes. Sweden were curiously underwhelming at these Olympics but coach Marika Domanski Lyfors was moulding a team around the talents of Hanna Ljungberg and Victoria Svensson that would shine at the World Cup in three years' time.

▶ Bettina Wiegmann, Tina Wunderlich, Steffi Jones, Doris Fitschen and Claudia Müller celebrate Germany's late victory over Sweden which saw their team finish with maximum points.

Group stage 2000

USA and Norway through the "group of death"

Group F

Group F was called the "group of death", and there could be little argument given the strength of the teams involved. Between them, the USA and Norway had won every title available since the launch of world tournaments 12 years earlier in 1988, while China were beaten finalists in both the 1996 Olympics and in the 1999 World Cup. The Americans – world and Olympic champions – beat the Norwegians 2-0 in the opening match of the group with goals from Tiffeny Milbrett and Mia Hamm. It was the seventh time they had faced each other in 2000 and this victory evened up the results at three wins each. With African champions Nigeria struggling, the final group game between China and Norway would decide who would join the Americans in the semi-finals. Chinese captain Sun Wen, soon to be named as the joint FIFA Female Player of the Century, was a literature student who had penned a song encouraging girls to pursue their football dreams. She scored her fourth goal of the tournament to equalise against Norway, but just three minutes later Margunn Haugenes restored the Scandinavians' lead with a beautiful curling shot into the top-right corner which left Gao Hong flailing in the Chinese goal. Norway were into the semis.

	W	D	L	+	–	PTS
USA	2	1	0	6	2	7
NOR	2	0	1	5	4	6
CHN	1	1	1	5	4	4
NGA	0	0	3	3	9	0

◀ Norway celebrate their decisive victory over China which saw them qualify for the semi-finals.

◀ China's Liu Ying and Nigeria's Nkiru Okosieme in action during their Group F match in Canberra.

Melbourne Cricket Ground, Melbourne
14.09.2000, 17:30, **16,043**

USA 🇺🇸 **2-0** 🇳🇴 **NORWAY**

Milbrett 18
Hamm 24

Im Eun Ju KOR
Hisae Yoshizawa JPN & Jackeline Saez PAN

USA • 18 Siri **Mullinix** - 3 Christie **Pearce**, 14 Joy **Fawcett**, 15 Kate **Sobrero**, 6 Brandi **Chastain** - 8 Shannon **MacMillan**, 11 Julie **Foudy** (c), 2 Lorrie **Fair**, 13 Kristine **Lilly** - 9 Mia **Hamm** (12 Cindy **Parlow** 70), 16 Tiffeny **Milbrett**. *April Heinrichs*

NOR • 1 Bente **Nordby** - 5 Gro **Espeseth** 🟨 75, 3 Gøril **Kringen** (c) 🟨 52, 4 Anne **Tønnessen**, 2 Brit **Sandaune** - 10 Unni **Lehn**, 6 Hege **Riise**, 8 Monica **Knudsen** (7 Solveig **Gulbrandsen** 46), 9 Anita **Rapp** (16 Ragnhild **Gulbrandsen** 71) - 14 Dagny **Mellgren**, 11 Marianne **Pettersen** (17 Christine **Bøe Jensen** 55). *Per-Mathias Høgmo*

Bruce Stadium, Canberra
14.09.2000, 17:30, **16,000**

CHINA PR 🇨🇳 **3-1** 🇳🇬 **NIGERIA**

Zhao Lihong 12   Nkwocha 85p
Sun Wen (2) 57 83

Martha Toro COL
Sanna Luhtanen FIN & Marie-Louise Svanström SWE

CHN • 18 **Gao Hong** - 11 **Pu Wei** (5 **Xie Huilin** 82), 2 **Wang Liping**, 3 **Fan Yunjie**, 12 **Wen Lirong**, 4 **Bai Jie** - 10 **Liu Ying**, 10 **Liu Ailing**, 6 **Zhao Lihong** - 9 **Sun Wen** (c), 8 **Jin Yan** (17 **Zhang Ouying** 71). *Ma Yuanan*

NGA • 1 Ann **Chiejine** (18 Judith **Chime** 87) - 2 Yinka **Kudaisi**, 4 Perpetua **Nkwocha**, 5 Eberechi **Opara** 🟨 84, 6 Kikelomo **Ajayi** - 14 Florence **Omagbemi** (c), 10 Mercy **Akide** (7 Stella **Mbachu** 58), 13 Nkiru **Okosieme** - 12 Patience **Avre** 🟨 77 (11 Ifeanyichukwu **Chiejine** 81), 9 Gloria **Usieta**, 8 Rita **Nwadike**. *Ismaila Mabo*

Melbourne Cricket Ground, Melbourne
17.09.2000, 17:30, **32,500**

USA 🇺🇸 **1-1** 🇨🇳 **CHINA PR**

Foudy 38   Sun Wen 67
(Lilly penalty saved 75)

Nicole Petignat SUI
Marie-Louise Svanström SWE & Lynn Fox NZL

USA • Mullinix - Pearce, Fawcett, Sobrero, Chastain (Parlow 62) - MacMillan (5 Nikki **Serlenga** 80), Fair, Foudy (c), Lilly - Milbrett, Hamm 🟨 67. *Heinrichs*

CHN • Gao Hong - Wang Liping, Fan Yunjie 🟨 73, Wen Lirong, Bai Jie - Pu Wei, Liu Ying, Liu Ailing, Zhao Lihong - Sun Wen (c), Jin Yan (Zhang Ouying 61). *Ma Yuanan*

Bruce Stadium, Canberra
17.09.2000, 17:30, **9,150**

NORWAY 🇳🇴 **3-1** 🇳🇬 **NIGERIA**

Mellgren 22, Riise 62p,   Akide 78
Pettersen 90+3

Tammy Ogston AUS
Cleidy Ribeiro BRA & Ana Perez PER

NOR • Nordby - Espeseth, Kringen (c), Tønnessen (13 Kristin **Bekkevold** 4), 12 Silje **Jørgensen** (Sandaune 80) - Mellgren, S Gulbrandsen 🟨 55 (Knudsen 59), Riise, Lehn, Pettersen - R Gulbrandsen 🟨 12. *Høgmo*

NGA • Chime - Opara - Kudaisi, Nkwocha, Ajayi - Omagbemi (c), 1 5 Maureen **Mmadu** 🟨 29 (Akide 54), Okosieme - Avre (I Chiejine 57), Mbachu, Nwadike. *Mabo*

Melbourne Cricket Ground, Melbourne
20.09.2000, 17:30, **9,000**

USA 🇺🇸 **3-1** 🇳🇬 **NIGERIA**

Chastain 26, Lilly 35   Akide 48
MacMillan 56

Im Eun Ju KOR
Jackeline Saez PAN & Hisae Yoshizawa JPN

USA • Mullinix - Pearce, Fawcett, Sobrero, Chastain - MacMillan, Foudy (c), Fair, Lilly (Serlenga 46 🟨 49) - Hamm (Parlow 70), Milbrett. *Heinrichs*

NGA • A Chiejine 🟨 54 (Chime 64) - Omagbemi (c) (Mmadu 72), Opara, Nkwocha - Kudaisi, Okosieme, Akide 🟨 55, Ajayi (Avre 20 🟥 90) - Mbachu, Nwadike, I Chiejine. *Mabo*

Bruce Stadium, Canberra
20.09.2000, 17:30, **11,532**

NORWAY 🇳🇴 **2-1** 🇨🇳 **CHINA PR**

Pettersen 55   Sun Wen 75p
Haugenes 78

Sonia Denoncourt CAN
Ana Perez PER & Cleidy Ribeiro BRA

NOR • Nordby - Espeseth 🟨 45, Bekkevold, Kringen (c), Jørgensen (Sandaune 84) - S Gulbrandsen, Riise, Lehn (Knudsen 51) - Mellgren (15 Margunn **Haugenes** 61), R Gulbrandsen, Pettersen. *Høgmo*

CHN • Gao Hong - Wang Liping, Fan Yunjie, Wen Lirong, Bai Jie - Pu Wei, Liu Ying 🟨 45+1 (Xie Huilin 66), Liu Ailing, Zhao Lihong - Sun Wen (c), Jin Yan (Zhang Ouying 46). *Ma Yuanan*

2000 Semi-finals

▲ Kristin Bekkevold and Inka Grings during the semi-final between Norway and Germany. Norway won thanks to a Tina Wunderlich own goal just before the end.

Agony for Wunderlich

Sydney Football Stadium, Sydney
24.09.2000, 17:30, **16,710**

GERMANY 🇩🇪 **0-1** 🇮🇸 **NORWAY**

T Wunderlich OG 80

Im Eun Ju KOR / Jackeline Saez PAN & Ana Perez PER

GER • Rottenberg - T Wunderlich, Jones, Fitschen (c), Minnert - Hingst, Meinert, Wiegmann, Prinz - Stegemann, Grings. *Theune-Meyer*

NOR • Nordby - Sandaune ■16, Bekkevold, Kringen (c), Jørgensen - S Gulbrandsen, Riise, Bøe Jensen (Knudsen 33), Mellgren (Haugenes 55) - Pettersen (Lehn 86), R Gulbrandsen. *Høgmo*

These European rivals fought to the bitter end at Sydney Football Stadium for the right to contest the gold medal match, a showdown that was settled in the end thanks to an own goal by Germany's Tina Wunderlich ten minutes before the end. Norway certainly rode their luck in this tournament and they were put under pressure by the Germans for much of the game. Chances, however, were few and far between. A Sandra Minnert free kick midway through the first half forced a great save from Bente Nordby and then a long clearance by goalkeeper Silke Rottenberg was not dealt with by Kristin Bekkevold, giving Inka Grings a great opportunity to give Germany the lead just before half-time – but her shot went just wide. The Norwegians pressed more in the second half but this was a game crying out for a goal. When it came, it was from a mistake. Hege Riise lofted a long ball forward from just outside the centre circle and, under no pressure at all, Tina Wunderlich headed the ball back towards her goalkeeper. Rottenberg, however, had come off her line and the ball sailed over her head and into the net. Bettina Wiegmann had a chance to level soon after but Norway were in the Final.

> "Being in the Olympic Village, surrounded by greatness… world-class athletes…an experience I will never forget."
>
> SISSI, BRAZIL

Hamm makes it two in a row for USA

Bruce Stadium, Canberra
24.09.2000, 17:30, **11,000**

USA 🇺🇸 **1-0** 🇧🇷 **BRAZIL**

Hamm 60

Nicole Petignat SUI / Lynn Fox NZL & Comfort Cofie GHA

USA • Mullinix - Pearce, Fawcett, Sobrero, Chastain - MacMillan (Parlow 79 ■90+1), Foudy (c), Fair ■44, Lilly ■63 - Milbrett ■68, Hamm. *Heinrichs*

BRA • Andréia - Juliana ■49, Tânia, Daniela - Simone ■31, Cidinha, Maycon - Formiga ■59, Sissi (c) (Raquel 83) - Kátia ■47 (Roseli 58), Pretinha. *Duarte*

A controversial Mia Hamm goal in the 60th minute ignited this match between the two best teams in the Americas. Until then, it had not been a particularly great advert for the talent in the two sides. The game was a repeat of the World Cup semi-final 14 months earlier, but although the USA put Brazil under spells of pressure, they were vulnerable to the counter and in the first half the Brazilians had eight corners to just one for their opponents. There were no clear-cut chances in the first half, the flow of the game disrupted by a number of strong tackles. There was more of the same in the second half when, on the hour, Formiga took Mia Hamm's legs from under her. Brandi Chastain's resulting free kick from just inside the Brazil half was lofted deep into the area where it was headed back across goal by Lorrie Fair to the unmarked Hamm who coolly shot home from an acute angle. The Brazilians claimed that Tiffeny Milbrett had impeded their keeper Andréia, an incident that was not seen by the referee. The fouls continued – there were eight bookings – and there was a great save by Siri Mullinix to deny Roseli, but the Brazilians were unable to get back into the match.

▼ Captains Julie Foudy of the USA and Sissi of Brazil before the semi-final in Canberra.

▲ American fans celebrate their team qualifying for a second successive Olympic Final.

2000 Bronze Medal Match

Sydney Football Stadium, Sydney
28.09.2000, 17:00, **11,200**

GERMANY 2-0 **BRAZIL**

Lingor 64, Prinz 79

Im Eun Ju KOR — Lynn Fox NZL & Jackeline Saez PAN

▶ Germany's Birgit Prinz (9) beats Brazil's Simone in the bronze medal match. Prinz scored the second goal in their 2-0 win.

Lingor and Prinz seal bronze for Germany

Birgit Prinz was becoming something of a thorn in the side of the Brazilians. Her two goals had secured victory for the Germans in the group game between the two, and in this match she scored again to secure the bronze medal. Brazil dominated in the first half but were missing their influential forward Kátia, who was out with a hamstring injury. Germany's solid defence, marshalled by skipper Doris Fitschen, were in control and when Brazil did break through, as Formiga did early on, Silke Rottenberg was proving her credentials as one of the best keepers in the world. For their part, the Germans were restricted to long-range shots – both Sandra Minnert and Maren Meinert went close from distance – but it was not until the second half that the deadlock was broken. After 64 minutes, the ever-dangerous Inka Grings was brought down just outside the box and from the resulting free kick Renate Lingor scored with a stunning 20-yard strike which gave Andréia in the Brazil goal no chance. The tempo of the match increased as the Brazilians sought to level the scores but as they pressed they began to leave space at the back and Grings could have had a hat-trick. Both sides went close as the game moved from end to end. But for a miskick by Pretinha, Brazil could have equalised when she was left with just the keeper to beat. Then with 11 minutes remaining Prinz ran on to a long ball by Lingor and coolly placed her shot between Andréia and Juliana.

The start of a revolution

Tina Theune-Meyer wasn't the first female coach to win a World Cup or Olympic medal – Sweden's Gunilla Paijkull had done so in 1991 – but by leading Germany to third place in Sydney, she ushered in a new era. Of the 12 tournaments that followed in both competitions, the winning coach in ten of them was female.

▶ Goalkeeper Andréia consoles Juliana after Brazil missed out on bronze.

2000 Gold medal match

▲▼ Norwegian fans (above) and American fans (below) were fortunate to be witness to one of the all-time great women's matches.

2000 Gold Medal Match

Sydney Football Stadium, Sydney
28.09.2000, 20:00, **22,848**

NORWAY 3-2 USA
AET

Espeseth 44, R Gulbrandsen 78, Mellgren 102 GG Milbrett (2) 5 90+2
Norway win on the golden goal

Sonia Denoncourt CAN | Hisae Yoshizawa JPN & Ana Perez PER

The game of the century?

This was a Final worthy of any competition – a classic that had it all and which is still regarded as one of the greatest women's games ever played, between the two standout teams of the era. The clash had a history stretching back to the first World Cup Final nine years earlier, via two semi-finals – at the 1995 World Cup and the epic match at the 1996 Olympics in Atlanta when Shannon MacMillan's golden goal sent the USA into the Final. The 102 sweat-stained minutes of this game marked the pinnacle of the intense rivalry between these two nations, culminating in Dagny Mellgren's stunning finale. For USA coach April Heinrichs, who was only months into the job, the familiarity bred by the two sides' frequent showdowns was a problem. "If you're the more dominant team then the other starts to learn more about you," she said. "At the same time, they helped us get better, they were our training partners in a way."

The match started off at an intense pace and just five minutes in, Tiffeny Milbrett gave the Americans the lead. Julie Foudy fed Mia Hamm whose run to the goal line and turn beat Gøril Kringen before she pulled the ball back to Milbrett. It had been a breathtaking start. The USA looked sharp and were quicker to the ball, but the Norwegian defence was well organised, repeatedly catching Hamm offside. Then, as the tempo dipped temporarily before the break, Hege Riise's corner was met superbly by Gro Espeseth and Norway were back in the game.

The Norwegians started the second half the stronger and could have had a penalty for handball within a minute of the restart, but it was the Americans who had chance after chance. Had it not been for Bente Nordby in goal, the Norwegians could have been three or four behind. Her save from Hamm on 71 minutes was the save of this and perhaps any other tournament. By then, Kringen had also headed brilliantly off the line after a superb American move involving the livewire Kristine Lilly and the indefatigable Milbrett. Then, on 78 minutes, Norway's midfield dynamo Riise found Unni Lehn on the right wing, who launched a deep cross which Ragnhild Gulbrandsen headed home after Joy Fawcett and Siri Mullinix had collided with each other.

Two minutes before the end, Kringen made another saving tackle but this game still had plenty to give. With just a minute of injury time left, Cindy Parlow found Hamm on the right wing and her cross into a crowded box was headed home by Milbrett, who at 157 centimetres was the shortest player in the American team. There were some tired legs going into extra time but the threat of a golden goal did not dim the intensity. Norway were now the more threatening with Riise in the thick of it, and it was her long ball forward from the centre circle into the box which created the winner. Joy Fawcett's clearing header hit substitute Mellgren's arm and dropped perfectly for her to fire home a controversial winner and bring this sensational game to an end. "It's most brutal when a team can be dominant and still lose the game," Heinrichs reflected.

▲ Norway captain Gøril Kringen is forced into desperate measures to try to stop the USA's Mia Hamm moments before the American crossed for Tiffeny Milbrett's injury-time equaliser in the Olympic Final in Sydney.

Bridging the gap: a global professional league

An attempt to convert the enthusiasm that fans demonstrated at the 1996 Olympics and 1999 World Cup to attend live women's football matches was made in spring 2001 when the Women's United Soccer Association (WUSA) was launched. Franchises across eight American cities featured many international stars who participated in the Sydney Games, including Sun Wen, Gao Hong, Birgit Prinz, Hege Riise, Dagny Mellgren, and Pretinha – effectively making it a global championship. For the USA players, the WUSA bridged a gap, according to April Heinrichs. "The WUSA was first-class: the goals, ambition and investment," she said of the league's attempt to create sustainable opportunities for high-level women's football. "We wanted to put women's football on the map." It was quality, exciting, and quick-paced football but unfortunately, due to funding problems, the league was suspended in 2003 after just three seasons.

▲ Norway's starting line-up for the Final. Back row (left to right): Ragnhild Gulbrandsen, Marianne Pettersen, Margunn Haugenes, Hege Riise, Solveig Gulbrandsen. Front row: Monica Knudsen, Bente Nordby, Brit Sandaune, Gro Espeseth, Silje Jørgensen and Gøril Kringen. Match winner Dagny Mellgren came on as a substitute.

▶ Ragnhild Gulbrandsen (16) leads the celebrations after Dagny Mellgren's golden goal for Norway.

The Gulbrandsens

Both Ragnhild and Solveig Gulbrandsen, two of Norway's gold medal-winning team in Sydney, came from footballing families. Ragnhild's father Odd Gulbrandsen played for Rosenborg BK in the early 1970s, while Solveig's father Terje represented Norway twice in 1969. Her mother, Inger Elise Johansen, was a rhythmic gymnast.

3X3

Before 2016, only three women had won a World Cup, Olympic gold and a European championship: Gro Espeseth, Bente Nordby and Hege Riise. They completed the remarkable hat-trick in Sydney having won the Euros in 1993 and the World Cup in 1995.

▼ The Norwegian team about to receive their gold medals.

2003

The 2003 finals were scheduled to take place in China again, but the SARS epidemic forced a relocation to the USA. The hosts were tipped to win a third World Cup, but they lost 3-0 in the semi-finals to Germany, who went on to beat Sweden 2-1 in the Final in Carson. Nia Künzer's golden goal made Tina Theune-Meyer the first female coach to win the World Cup.

SARS disrupts the World Cup

On 26 May 2003, FIFA announced that due to an outbreak of the SARS virus in China, it was relocating the World Cup to the USA. At the same time, it awarded the 2007 finals to the Chinese and allowed them to keep their automatic qualification slot for 2003 that came with being the original hosts. The USA were best placed to step in at short notice for what was the third major women's football tournament in the country in seven years following the Olympics in 1996 and the World Cup in 1999. In comparison to four years earlier, however, this tournament was relatively low key. There was insufficient time to draw in big numbers to the stadiums, as had been the case in 1999. The Final was staged in Los Angeles once again, but instead of a potential 90,000 crowd in the Rose Bowl, the 27,500-capacity Home Depot Center in Carson was chosen.

▼ Preparations for the World Cup in China were far advanced before it was relocated to the USA.

2003 **Overview**

USA 2003

FIFA WOMEN'S WORLD CUP USA 2003

Story of the qualifiers

Debuts for Argentina, France and South Korea

In Europe, the top 16 ranked teams were divided into four groups of four, with the winners – Norway, Sweden, Russia and Germany – qualifying directly. Play-offs for the runners-up saw France beat Denmark, and England overcome Iceland. France then continued an unbeaten record against the English which stretched back to 1977, with goals by Marinette Pichon in the first leg of the Final and Corinne Diacre in the second. Unlike Europe, the five other confederations relied on their continental championships for qualifiers. Brazil and Argentina topped the final South American standings – a first qualification for the Argentines. In Africa, Nigeria beat Ghana 2-0 in the Final, with both making it through to the World Cup after beating South Africa and Cameroon in the semi-finals. Normal service was resumed in Concacaf with the USA and Canada qualifying from the Women's Gold Cup, a Final won by the Americans thanks to a Mia Hamm golden goal. Third-placed Mexico then lost a play-off to Japan after goals from Homare Sawa and Karina Maruyama. North Korea won the 2003 Asian Women's Championship and were joined at the Finals by their neighbours from the south, the third of the trio of debutants, who qualified by beating Japan in the third-place play-off, runners-up China having already qualified automatically as the original hosts. The final place went to Australia, who beat New Zealand 2-0 in the deciding match in the 2003 OFC Championship in Canberra.

◀ The FIFA Fair Play medal for the 2003 World Cup. It was won by China PR.
FIFA Museum Collection

▶ Official pennant for the 2003 World Cup.
FIFA Museum Collection

Golden Ball

Birgit Prinz GER

Silver Ball: Victoria Svensson SWE
Bronze Ball: Maren Meinert GER

Group stage

GROUP A	GROUP B	GROUP C	GROUP D
NGA 0-3 PRK	NOR 2-0 FRA	GER 4-1 CAN	AUS 1-2 RUS
USA 3-1 SWE	BRA 3-0 KOR	JPN 6-0 ARG	CHN 1-0 GHA
SWE 1-0 PRK	NOR 1-4 BRA	GER 3-0 JPN	GHA 0-3 RUS
USA 5-0 NGA	FRA 1-0 KOR	CAN 3-0 ARG	CHN 1-1 AUS
SWE 3-0 NGA	KOR 1-7 NOR	CAN 3-1 JPN	GHA 2-1 AUS
PRK 0-3 USA	FRA 1-1 BRA	ARG 1-6 GER	CHN 1-0 RUS

	W D L + − PTS		W D L + − PTS		W D L + − PTS		W D L + − PTS
USA	3 0 0 11 1 9	BRA	2 1 0 8 2 7	GER	3 0 0 13 2 9	CHN	2 1 0 3 1 7
SWE	2 0 1 5 3 6	NOR	2 0 1 10 5 6	CAN	2 0 1 7 5 6	RUS	2 0 1 5 2 6
PRK	1 0 2 3 4 3	FRA	1 1 1 2 3 4	JPN	1 0 2 7 6 3	GHA	1 0 2 2 5 3
NGA	0 0 3 0 11 0	KOR	0 0 3 1 11 0	ARG	0 0 3 1 15 0	AUS	0 1 2 3 5 1

Knockout stages

QUARTER-FINAL	QUARTER-FINAL	QUARTER-FINAL	QUARTER-FINAL
BRA 1-2 SWE	USA 1-0 NOR	GER 7-1 RUS	CHN 0-1 CAN

SEMI-FINAL	SEMI-FINAL
USA 0-3 GER	SWE 2-1 CAN

MATCH FOR THIRD PLACE
USA 3-1 CAN

FINAL
GER 2-1 AET SWE

Overview 2003

16 TEAMS

GERMANY WINNERS

SWE SECOND **USA** THIRD

679 664 SPECTATORS   **21 240** AVERAGE PER MATCH

NO OFFICIAL MASCOT WAS CREATED FOR THE 2003 WORLD CUP DUE TO THE CHANGE OF HOST NATION

OFFICIAL LOGO

32 MATCHES PLAYED

65 YELLOW CARDS

1 RED CARDS

107 GOALS

3.34 AVERAGE GOALS PER MATCH

FEVERNOVA OFFICIAL MATCH BALL

Host cities and stadiums

Destination USA Part 3

When the World Cup unexpectedly returned to America in 2003, just one stadium used in 1999 was put into action again – PGE Park in Portland. Boston was a host city again, but the old venue in Foxboro had been replaced by the new Gillette Stadium on the same site. Los Angeles and Washington also had matches in both tournaments, but different stadiums were selected: the Home Depot Center in Carson, LA and the RFK in Washington DC.

PORTLAND
PGE PARK
(28,359)

PHILADELPHIA
LINCOLN FINANCIAL FIELD
(70,000)

FOXBOROUGH/BOSTON
GILLETTE STADIUM
(68,000)

WASHINGTON DC
RFK MEMORIAL STADIUM
(53,000)

COLUMBUS
COLUMBUS CREW STADIUM
(22,555)

CARSON/LOS ANGELES
HOME DEPOT CENTER
(27,500)

×7

Golden Boot

Birgit Prinz GER

Silver Boot: Maren Meinert GER ×4
Bronze Boot: Kátia BRA ×4

2003 Group stage

Group A

Lincoln Financial Field, Philadelphia
20.09.2003, 14:45, **24,346**

NIGERIA 🇳🇬 **0-3** 🇰🇵 **KOREA DPR**

Jin Pyol Hui (2) 13 88
Ri Un Gyong 73

Nicole Petignat SUI
Elke Lüthi SUI & Nelly Viennot FRA

NGA • 12 Precious **Dede** - 16 Florence **Iweta**, 3 Bunmi **Kayode**, 6 Kikelomo **Ajayi** 🟨 28, 14 Ifeanyichukwu **Chiejine** (5 Onome **Ebi** 85) - 7 Stella **Mbachu**, 17 Florence **Omagbemi** (c) (15 Maureen **Mmadu** 44), 2 Efioanwan **Ekpo**, 11 Nkechi **Egbe** (18 Patience **Avre** 46) - 10 Mercy **Akide** 🟨 22, 4 Perpetua **Nkwocha**. *Sam Okpodu*

PRK • 1 **Ri** Jong Hui (c) - 6 **Ra** Mi Ae, 2 **Yun** In Sil, 17 **Jon** Hye Yong 🟨 71, 12 **Jang** Ok Gyong - 14 **O** Kum Ran, 15 **Ri** Un Gyong, 19 **Ri** Hyang Ok 🟨 25, 11 **Yun** Yong Hui (16 **Pak** Kyong Sun 57) - 10 **Jin** Pyol Hui, 7 **Ri** Kum Suk (9 **Ho** Sun Hui 81). *Ri Song Gun*

RFK Memorial Stadium, Washington DC
21.09.2003, 12:30, **34,144**

🇺🇸 **USA 3-1 SWEDEN** 🇸🇪

Lilly 27, Parlow 36   Svensson 58
Boxx 78

Zhang Dongqing CHN
Liu Hsiu Mei TPE & Hisae Yoshizawa JPN

USA • 1 Briana **Scurry** 🟨 13 - 3 Christie **Pearce**, 14 Joy **Fawcett**, 6 Brandi **Chastain** (4 Cat **Reddick** 45), 15 Kate **Sobrero** - 11 Julie **Foudy** (c), 7 Shannon **Boxx**, 13 Kristine **Lilly** - 9 Mia **Hamm**, 20 Abby **Wambach** (16 Tiffeny **Milbrett** 56), 12 Cindy **Parlow** (10 Aly **Wagner** 70 🟨 72). *April Heinrichs*

SWE • 1 Caroline **Jönsson** - 4 Hanna **Marklund**, 2 Karolina **Westberg**, 3 Jane **Törnqvist**, 7 Sara **Larsson** - 9 Malin **Andersson** (c) (17 Anna **Sjöström** 77 🟨 90+3), 6 Malin **Moström**, 14 Linda **Fagerström**, 15 Therese **Sjögran** (18 Frida **Östberg** 46) - 10 Hanna **Ljungberg** (20 Josefine **Öqvist** 83), 11 Victoria **Svensson**. *Marika Domanski Lyfors*

Lincoln Financial Field, Philadelphia
25.09.2003, 16:45, **31,553**

SWEDEN 🇸🇪 **1-0** 🇰🇵 **KOREA DPR**

Svensson 7

Tammy Ogston AUS
Airlie Keen AUS & Jacqueline Leleu AUS

SWE • **Jönsson** - **Marklund**, **Westberg** 🟨 52, **Törnqvist**, **Larsson** - **Andersson** (5 Kristin **Bengtsson** 65), **Moström** (c), **Östberg**, **Fagerström** (**Sjöström** 56) - **Ljungberg** (**Öqvist** 86), **Svensson**. *Domanski Lyfors*

PRK • **Ri** Jong Hui (c) - **Ra** Mi Ae (13 **Song** Jong Sun 62), **Jon** Hye Yong, 5 **Sin** Kum Ok (**Yun** In Sil 55), **Jang** Ok Gyong 🟨 56 - **O** Kum Ran, **Ri** Un Gyong, **Ri** Hyang Ok, **Yun** Yong Hui (**Ho** Sun Hui 36) - **Jin** Pyol Hui, **Ri** Kum Suk. *Ri Song Gun*

Lincoln Financial Field, Philadelphia
25.09.2003, 19:30, **31,553**

🇺🇸 **USA 5-0** 🇳🇬 **NIGERIA**

Hamm (2) 6p 12, Parlow 47
Wambach 65, Foudy 89p

Florencia Romano ARG
Sabrina Lois ARG & Alejandra Cercato ARG

USA • **Scurry** - 2 Kylie **Bivens**, **Fawcett**, **Reddick**, **Sobrero** - **Foudy** (c), **Boxx** (5 Tiffany **Roberts** 71), **Wagner** (**Wambach** 46), **Lilly** - **Hamm**, **Parlow** (**Milbrett** 57). *Heinrichs*

NGA • **Dede** - **Kayode**, **Omagbemi** (c) 🟨 76, **Ajayi**, **Chiejine** - **Avre**, 13 Nkiru **Okosieme**, **Mmadu**, **Mbachu** - **Akide**, **Nkwocha**. *Okpodu*

Columbus Crew Stadium, Columbus
28.09.2003, 13:00, **22,828**

SWEDEN 🇸🇪 **3-0** 🇳🇬 **NIGERIA**

Ljungberg (2) 56 79
Moström 81

Sonia Denoncourt CAN
Denise Robinson CAN & Lynda Bramble TRI

SWE • **Jönsson** - **Marklund**, **Westberg**, **Bengtsson** (**Sjöström** 46), **Larsson** - **Andersson** (c) (**Sjögran** 66), **Moström**, **Östberg**, 19 Sara **Call** - **Ljungberg**, **Svensson** (**Öqvist** 85). *Domanski Lyfors*

NGA • **Dede** - **Iweta** (**Ebi** 83), **Ajayi**, **Omagbemi** (c), **Chiejine** - **Avre** (8 Olaitan **Yusuf** 89), **Okosieme** (**Ekpo** 65), **Mmadu**, **Mbachu** - **Akide**, **Nkwocha**. *Okpodu*

Columbus Crew Stadium, Columbus
28.09.2003, 15:45, **22,828**

🇰🇵 **KOREA DPR 0-3** 🇺🇸 **USA**

Wambach 17p
Reddick (2) 48 66

Sueli Tortura BRA
Cleidy Ribeiro BRA & Marlei Silva BRA

PRK • **Ri** Jong Hui (c) - **Ra** Mi Ae, **Yun** In Sil, **Sin** Kum Ok (**Jon** Hye Yong 26), **Jang** Ok Gyong - **O** Kum Ran 🟨 16 (**Song** Jong Sun 53), **Ri** Un Gyong, **Ri** Hyang Ok, **Yun** Yong Hui 74 🟨 90+1 - **Jin** Pyol Hui, **Ri** Kum Suk. *Ri Song Gun*

USA • **Scurry** - **Pearce**, **Fawcett** (c), **Reddick**, **Sobrero** (17 Danielle **Slaton** 73) - **Roberts**, **Bivens**, **Wagner**, **Lilly** (**Foudy** 46) - **Milbrett** 🟨 40, **Wambach** 🟨 22 (8 Shannon **MacMillan** 56). *Heinrichs*

	W	D	L	+	-	PTS
🇺🇸 USA	3	0	0	11	1	9
🇸🇪 SWE	2	0	1	5	3	6
🇰🇵 PRK	1	0	2	3	4	3
🇳🇬 NGA	0	0	3	0	11	0

Holders and hosts off to a perfect start

Preceded by 300 flag-waving children and "American Idol" star Justin Guarini, there was less razzamatazz to the hosts' opener than in 1999, but as the USA's former World Cup-winning captain Carla Overbeck paraded the trophy around the RFK Memorial Stadium centre circle, the stage was set for yet another world-class football showcase on US soil. Poignantly, after the shock collapse of the WUSA professional league days earlier, Washington Freedom striker Mia Hamm got the USA off to a winning start in her home stadium, setting up Kristine Lilly, Cindy Parlow and Shannon Boxx, who was making only her third appearance. North Korea were still relative World Cup rookies, but they had taken China's Asian crown, and European Championship silver medallists Sweden needed all their defensive strength and an early goal from Victoria Svensson to secure a crucial win in Philadelphia. That evening, the reigning champions, now coached by 1991 World Cup-winning captain April Heinrichs, were rampant against Nigeria, Hamm scoring twice and 23-year-old Abby Wambach bagging her first World Cup goal in a 5-0 rout. China-based Perpetua Nkwocha and W-League star Mercy Akide went close for the African champions against Sweden, but despite the heroics of keeper Precious Dede, Hanna Ljungberg scored twice in a 3-0 win and Nigeria finished pointless and goalless. Sweden's progression was finally assured as the USA, with Hamm on the bench, overcame North Korea, with college star Cat Reddick scoring twice as the hosts advanced unbeaten.

▶ Nigeria's Precious Dede repels a USA attack in the third meeting in four years between the two nations in the World Cup and Olympics.

45

The number of minutes played by Brandi Chastain in the 2003 finals before she broke her foot in the USA's opening match against Sweden.

▶ Sweden's Victoria Svensson (11) scored an early goal in a 1-0 victory over North Korea in Philadelphia ensuring the Swedes qualified for the quarter-finals at the expense of the Koreans.

Group B

Debutants France foiled by Norway

In Boston Breakers star Dagny Mellgren and Philadelphia Charge goal-getter Marinette Pichon, Norway and France boasted WUSA's joint top scorers for 2003. And it was Mellgren's Norway who emerged victorious on Pichon's home ground in the opening match of the tournament. With several crucial saves, it was Norway's "un-retired" goalkeeper Bente Nordby who took the plaudits. "She was the difference today," said coach Åge Steen. South Korea's own hotshot, 16-year-old student Park Eun Sun, had scored seven in qualifying, but it was Brazilian teenager Marta who made a mark in their encounter, nervelessly scoring her 11th goal in nine games, with a Kátia brace making it 3-0. Brazil's 1999 stars Sissi and Pretinha were missing through injury, but coach Paulo Gonçalves had a blend of youth and experience at his disposal and a nervous Norway were dispatched 4-1. France were still in the mix thanks to a late Pichon goal in an end-to-end match with South Korea that brought out the best in keeper Céline Marty. Pichon left it late against Brazil too, but Kátia's opener was enough to seal top spot for the South American champions, while Norway took second after beating South Korea 7-1, their third seven-goal salvo in three World Cups.

◀ Norway's Linda Ørmen shoots under pressure from Brazil's Simone. Both sides qualified for the quarter-finals.

	W	D	L	+	-	PTS
BRA	2	1	0	8	2	7
NOR	2	0	1	10	5	6
FRA	1	1	1	2	4	4
KOR	0	0	3	1	11	0

◀ French forward Hoda Lattaf (18) comes close to beating Bente Nordby. The French lost the game 2-0 and the result proved to be the difference between the two teams in the final standings.

Group stage 2003

Lincoln Financial Field, Philadelphia
20.09.2003, 12:00, **24,346**

NORWAY 2-0 FRANCE

Rapp 47, Mellgren 66

Kari Seitz USA
Karalee Sutton USA & Sharon Wheeler USA

NOR • 1 Bente **Nordby** - 16 Gunhild **Følstad**, 4 Monica **Knudsen**, 3 Ane **Stangeland**, 2 Brit **Sandaune** - 8 Solveig **Gulbrandsen** (7 Trine **Rønning** 80), 20 Lise **Klaveness** ■ 90+1, 10 Unni **Lehn** (6 Hege **Riise** 89), 9 Anita **Rapp** ■ 86 - 14 Dagny **Mellgren** (c), 11 Marianne **Pettersen** (17 Linda **Ørmen** 90+1). *Åge Steen*

FRA • 1 Céline **Marty** - 2 Sabrina **Viguier**, 5 Corinne **Diacre** (c), 4 Laura **Georges**, 3 Peggy **Provost** - 18 Hoda **Lattaf** (15 Laëtitia **Tonazzi** 72), 10 Élodie **Woock**, 6 Sandrine **Soubeyrand**, 8 Sonia **Bompastor** - 7 Stéphanie **Mugneret-Béghé** (17 Marie-Ange **Kramo** 82), 9 Marinette **Pichon**. *Élisabeth Loisel*

RFK Memorial Stadium, Washington DC
21.09.2003, 15:15, **34,144**

BRAZIL 3-0 KOREA REPUBLIC

Marta 14p, Kátia (2) 55 62

Tammy Ogston AUS
Irina Mirt ROU & Katarzyna Nadolska POL

BRA • 1 **Andréia** - 3 **Juliana** (c), 4 **Tânia**, 2 **Simone**, 14 **Rosana** - 7 **Formiga** ■ 2 (19 **Priscila** 89), 5 **Renata Costa**, 18 **Daniela** - 10 **Marta** - 16 **Maycon** (11 **Cristiane** 78), 17 **Kátia**. *Paulo Gonçalves*

KOR • 12 **Kim** Jung Mi - 4 **Kim** Yu Jin, 18 **Kim** Yoo Mi ■ 22 (6 **Jin** Suk Hee ■ 46 71), 20 **Yoo** Young Sil (c), 9 **Song** Ju Hee - 16 **Shin** Sun Nam, 14 **Han** Jin Sook, 15 **Kim** Kyul Sil (8 **Hwang** In Sun 65), 10 **Kim** Jin Hee (17 **Sung** Hyun Ah 49) - 7 **Park** Eun Sun, 11 **Lee** Ji Eun. *An Jong Goan*

RFK Memorial Stadium, Washington DC
24.09.2003, 17:00, **16,316**

NORWAY 1-4 BRAZIL

Pettersen 45   Daniela 26, Rosana 37
                       Marta 59, Kátia 68

Xonam Agboyi TOG
Perpétué Krebe CIV & Florence Biagui SEN

NOR • Nordby - Følstad, Knudsen, Stangeland, Sandaune - S Gulbrandsen (Klaveness 74), Rønning ■ 77, Lehn (Riise 74), Rapp (Ørmen 46) - Mellgren (c), Pettersen. *Steen*

BRA • Andréia - Juliana (c), Simone, Tânia, Rosana - Formiga (8 **Rafaela** 88), Renata Costa ■ 51, Daniela (Priscila 90) - Marta - Maycon (Cristiane 80), Kátia. *Gonçalves*

RFK Memorial Stadium, Washington DC
24.09.2003, 19:45, **16,316**

FRANCE 1-0 KOREA REPUBLIC

Pichon 84

Zhang Dongqing CHN
Liu Hsiu Mei TPE & Hisae Yoshizawa JPN

FRA • Marty - 13 Anne-Laure **Casseleux** (20 Emmanuelle **Sykora** 81), Diacre (c) ■ 65, Georges, Provost - Kramo, Woock ■ 37 (14 Virginie **Dessalle** 89), Soubeyrand, Bompastor - Mugneret-Béghé (Tonazzi 68), Pichon. *Loisel*

KOR • Kim Jung Mi - Kim Yu Jin, Kim Yoo Mi, Yoo Young Sil (c) ■ 45 (Jin Suk Hee 83), Song Ju Hee - Shin Sun Nam (2 **Kim** Joo Hee 83), Han Jin Sook, Kim Kyul Sil (19 **Lee** Myung Hwa 75 ■ 83), Kim Jin Hee - Park Eun Sun, Lee Ji Eun. *An Jong Goan*

Gilette Stadium, Foxborough, Boston
27.09.2003, 12:45, **14,356**

KOREA REPUBLIC 1-7 NORWAY

Kim Jin Hee 75   S Gulbrandsen 5
                      Mellgren (2) 24 31
                      Pettersen 40, Sandaune 52
                      Ørmen (2) 80 90

Tammy Ogston AUS
Airlie Keen AUS & Jacqueline Leleu AUS

KOR • Kim Jung Mi - Kim Yu Jin (Jin Suk Hee 55), Kim Yoo Mi, Yoo Young Sil (c), Song Ju Hee - Kim Joo Hee, Han Jin Sook (13 **Kim** Yoo Jin 30), Kim Kyul Sil, Kim Jin Hee - Park Eun Sun (3 **Hong** Kyung Suk 59), Lee Ji Eun. *An Jong Goan*

NOR • Nordby - 15 Marit **Fiane Christensen**, Knudsen, Stangeland, Sandaune - S Gulbrandsen (18 Ingrid **Fosse** 73), Rønning (Ørmen 69), Klaveness (Riise 81), Lehn - Mellgren (c), Pettersen. *Steen*

RFK Memorial Stadium, Washington DC
27.09.2003, 12:45, **17,618**

FRANCE 1-1 BRAZIL

Pichon 90+2   Kátia 58

Cristina Ionescu ROU
Irina Mirt ROU & Katarzyna Nadolska POL

FRA • Marty - Viguier (Lattaf 85), Diacre (c), Georges, Provost ■ 72 - Kramo, Woock (11 Amelie **Coquet** 73), Soubeyrand, Bompastor - Mugneret-Béghé (Tonazzi 46), Pichon. *Loisel*

BRA • Andréia - Juliana (c), Simone, Tânia (13 **Mônica** 88), Rosana - Rafaela, Priscila (Cristiane 46), Daniela ■ 51 - Marta - Maycon, Kátia. *Gonçalves*

2003 Group stage

Columbus Crew Stadium, Columbus
20.09.2003, 17:45, **16,409**

GERMANY 🇩🇪 **4-1** 🇨🇦 **CANADA**

Wiegmann 39p   Sinclair 4
Gottschlich 47, Prinz 75,
Garefrekes 90+2

Im Eun Ju KOR
Choi Soo Jin KOR & Hong Kum Nyo PRK

GER • 1 Silke **Rottenberg** - 2 Kerstin **Stegemann**, 5 Steffi **Jones**, 17 Ariane **Hingst** (4 Nia **Künzer** 65), 3 Linda **Bresonik** ▮ 45+1 - 10 Bettina **Wiegmann** (c), 6 Renate **Lingor** (18 Kerstin **Garefrekes** 73) - 13 Sandra **Minnert**, 14 Maren **Meinert** ▮ 78, 19 Stefanie **Gottschlich** - 9 Birgit **Prinz**. *Tina Theune-Meyer*

CAN • 1 Karina **LeBlanc** ▮ 21 - 18 Tanya **Dennis**, 6 Sharolta **Nonen**, 10 Charmaine **Hooper** (c) ▮ 38, 16 Brittany **Timko** - 8 Kara **Lang** (9 Rhian **Wilkinson** 46), 8 Kristina **Kiss**, 13 Diana **Matheson**, 5 Andrea **Neil** - 2 Christine **Latham**, 12 Christine **Sinclair**. *Even Pellerud NOR*

Columbus Crew Stadium, Columbus
20.09.2003, 20:30, **16,409**

JAPAN 🇯🇵 **6-0** 🇦🇷 **ARGENTINA**

Sawa (2) 13 38
Yamamoto 64
Otani (3) 72 75 80

Katriina Elovirta FIN
Emilia Parviainen FIN & Andi Regan NIR

JPN • 1 Nozomi **Yamago** - 4 Yasuyo **Yamagishi** (3 Hiromi **Isozaki** 73), 2 Yumi **Obe** (c), 14 Kyoko **Yano** - 7 Naoko **Kawakami**, 5 Tomoe **Sakai**, 8 Tomomi **Miyamoto**, 16 Emi **Yamamoto** - 10 Homare **Sawa** (18 Karina **Maruyama** 80) - 6 Yayoi **Kobayashi** (9 Eriko **Arakawa** 57), 11 Mio **Otani**. *Eiji Ueda*

ARG • 1 Romina **Ferro** - 2 Clarisa **Huber** - 4 Andrea **Gonsebate**, 19 Celeste **Barbitta** ▮ 59, 3 Mariela **Ricotti** (6 Noelia **López** 76) - 14 Fabiana **Vallejos**, 9 Marisa **Gerez** (c), 18 Mariela **Coronel**, 10 Rosana **Gómez** ▮ 18 (17 Valeria **Cotelo** 46) - 8 Natalia **Gatti** ▮ 39, 20 María **Villanueva** ▮ 16 (7 Karina **Alvariza** 46). *Carlos Borrello*

Columbus Crew Stadium, Columbus
24.09.2003, 17:45, **15,529**

GERMANY 🇩🇪 **3-0** 🇯🇵 **JAPAN**

Minnert 23
Prinz (2) 36 66

Sueli Tortura BRA
Cleidy Ribeiro BRA & Marlei Silva BRA

GER • Rottenberg - Stegemann, Jones, Hingst (Bresonik 72), Minnert - Wiegmann (c) (Künzer 78 ▮ 80), Lingor - Garefrekes, Meinert, Gottschlich (8 Sandra **Smisek** 64) - Prinz. *Theune-Meyer*

JPN • Yamago - Yamagishi, Obe (c), Yano (Isozaki 60) - Kawakami, Sakai (17 Miyuki **Yanagita** 56), Miyamoto, Yamamoto - Sawa - Kobayashi (Arakawa 56), Otani. *Ueda*

Columbus Crew Stadium, Columbus
24.09.2003, 20:30, **15,529**

CANADA 🇨🇦 **3-0** 🇦🇷 **ARGENTINA**

Hooper 19p
Latham (2) 79 82

Nicole Petignat SUI
Elke Lüthi SUI & Nelly Viennot FRA

CAN • 20 Taryn **Swiatek** - Dennis, Nonen, Hooper (c), Timko - Lang, Kiss, Matheson ▮ 41 - Wilkinson ▮ 62 (17 Silvana **Burtini** 75), Latham (4 Sasha **Andrews** 83 ▮ 86), Sinclair. *Pellerud NOR*

ARG • Ferro - Huber - Gonsebate, Barbitta, Ricotti ▮ 29 (López 78) - Vallejos, Gerez (c), Coronel (15 Yanina **Gaitán** 84), Gómez - 11 Marisol **Medina**, Villanueva (Alvariza 75). *Borrello*

Gilette Stadium, Foxborough, Boston
27.09.2003, 15:30, **14,356**

CANADA 🇨🇦 **3-1** 🇯🇵 **JAPAN**

Latham 36, Sinclair 49   Sawa 20
Lang 72

Im Eun Ju KOR
Choi Soo Jin KOR & Hong Kum Nyo PRK

CAN • Swiatek - Dennis, Nonen, Hooper (c), 7 Isabelle **Morneau** ▮ 45+1 - Lang (Wilkinson 85), Timko, Matheson, Neil (Kiss 77) - Latham (Burtini 60), Sinclair. *Pellerud NOR*

JPN • Yamago - Yamagishi, Obe, Isozaki - Kawakami, Sakai (Yanagita 62), Miyamoto, Yamamoto (20 Aya **Miyama** 89) - Sawa - Kobayashi (Arakawa 54), Otani. *Ueda*

RFK Memorial Stadium, Washington DC
27.09.2003, 15:30, **17,618**

ARGENTINA 🇦🇷 **1-6** 🇩🇪 **GERMANY**

Gaitán 71   Meinert (2) 3 43
             Wiegmann 24p, Prinz 32
             Pohlers 89, Müller 90+2

Bola Abidoye NGA
Elke Lüthi SUI & Liu Hsiu Mei TPE

ARG • Ferro - Huber - Gonsebate, Barbitta, López - Vallejos, Gerez (c), Coronel, Gómez (Gaitán 56) - M Medina, Villanueva (Alvariza 85). *Borrello*

GER • Rottenberg - Stegemann, Jones (12 Sonja **Fuss** 62), Hingst, Minnert - Wiegmann (c), Lingor - Garefrekes (11 Martina **Müller** 46), Meinert, Gottschlich (20 Conny **Pohlers** 46) - Prinz. *Theune-Meyer*

Group C

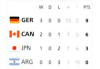

	W	D	L	+	–	PTS
GER	3	0	0	13	2	9
CAN	2	0	1	7	5	6
JPN	1	0	2	7	6	3
ARG	0	0	3	1	15	0

50/150

Bettina Wiegmann scored her 50th international goal against Canada and made her 150th appearance in the following game against Japan.

▶ Canada captain Charmaine Hooper (10) first played for Canada in 1986. The 2003 World Cup was her third finals and the first time that she and her country made it past the group stage.

Germany power through

Canada were yet to win a Women's World Cup game and Christine Sinclair's fourth-minute header had certainly shocked Germany in their opener, but they were still left chasing that elusive first victory after the European champions came back to win 4-1, Bettina Wiegmann notching up her 50th international goal in the process. That same evening, Japan doubled their World Cup win tally, Homare Sawa hitting a breathtaking volley and Mio Otani scoring the competition's fastest hat-trick in an emphatic 6-0 victory over attack-minded but defensively inexperienced Argentina, who lost Natalia Gatti to a 39th-minute red card. Germany boss Tina Theune-Meyer was impressed by Japan's "tricks and flicks" but they could not live with her strong and speedy team, who marched into the quarters with a 3-0 win. Goals from WUSA stars Charmaine Hooper and Christine Latham against debutants Argentina broke Canada's World Cup duck and their own knockout berth was assured when 16-year-old Kara Lang settled an edgy 3-1 win over Japan, who had a goal ruled out for offside. Argentina bowed out with another heavy loss, this time to a Birgit Prinz-inspired Germany, but they finally got off the scoring mark through Yanina Gaitán.

▲ Germany's Nia Künzer outjumps Rhian Wilkinson (9) and Charmaine Hooper in her country's 4-1 win over Canada in Columbus.

▼ Japan's Mio Otani (11) scored the only hat-trick of the tournament in the 6-0 victory over debutants Argentina in Columbus.

1, 2, 3

A clean sweep of medals – that's what four of the Germany side completed in 2003. Bettina Wiegmann, Birgit Prinz, Maren Meinert and Sandra Minnert were all runners-up at the 1995 World Cup, won bronze at the 2000 Sydney Olympics and winners medals in these finals.

Group stage 2003

Group D

	W	D	L	+	-	PTS
CHN	2	1	0	3	1	7
RUS	2	0	1	5	2	6
GHA	1	0	2	5	2	3
AUS	0	1	2	3	5	1

◂◂▴ Australia's Rhian Davies outjumps Russia's Anastasia Pustovoitova (18) and Elena Fomina. Fomina missed a penalty but scored a last-minute winner for the Russians.

◂ Ghana captain Alberta Sackey made her 44th consecutive start for her country in the match against China.

Russia at the double

A crushing last-minute goal that came out of the blue saw Russia edge out Australia in a match that either side could have won. Elena Fomina, who had earlier missed a penalty, won it for Russia, but having seen Kelly Golebiowski's opener cancelled out a minute later by an own goal, it was a heart-breaking start for the Oceania champions. Ghana, the tournament's lowest-ranked team, were determined not to repeat the 7-0 loss they suffered at China's hands in 1999. Coach Oko Aryee would have been satisfied then, when only Player of the Century Sun Wen managed to squeeze a goal past keeper Memunatu Sulemana. Russia proved more clinical, overcoming Ghana's dominant opening display with a 3-0 victory that secured their knockout spot. China and Australia's draw in the later kick-off left their World Cup fates hanging in the balance. The 2002 African women's player of the year Alberta Sackey ended Australia's hopes though, the second of her two goals securing Ghana's first finals win while also going down in history as the 400th of the competition. That result saw China through, and with the shackles off they beat Russia to top the group, Bai Jie scoring the winner in a lively display.

16

At 16 years and 107 days, Elena Danilova didn't feature for Russia in the group stage, but in the quarter-finals, on her international debut, she became the youngest scorer in World Cup history despite her side's 7-1 defeat to eventual champions Germany.

Home Depot Center, Carson, Los Angeles
21.09.2003, 17:30, **15,239**

AUSTRALIA 1-2 **RUSSIA**

Golebiowski 38   Alagich OG 39, Fomina 89
(Fomina penalty missed 72)

Bola Abidoye NGA
Perpétué Krebe CIV & Florence Biagui SEN

AUS • 1 Cassandra **Kell** - 4 Dianne **Alagich**, 3 Sacha **Wainwright** (8 Bryony **Duus** 45+1), 5 Cheryl **Salisbury** (c) - 6 Rhian **Davies**, 15 Tal **Karp** (9 April **Mann** 90+1), 10 Joanne **Peters**, 2 Gillian **Foster** - 11 Heather **Garriock**, 7 Kelly **Golebiowski**, 17 Danielle **Small**. Adrian Santrac

RUS • 12 Alla **Volkova** - 18 Anastasia **Pustovoitova** (5 Vera **Stroukova** 67), 2 Tatiana **Zaytseva**, 3 Marina **Burakova** (c), 4 Marina **Saenko** - 6 Galina **Komarova**, 13 Elena **Fomina** ■ 83, 7 Tatiana **Egorova** (15 Tatiana **Skotnikova** 68), 14 Oxana **Shmachkova** - 10 Natalia **Barbashina**, 11 Olga **Letyushova** ■ 87. Yuri Bystritskiy

Home Depot Center, Carson, Los Angeles
21.09.2003, 20:15, **15,239**

CHINA PR 1-0 **GHANA**

Sun Wen 29

Sonia Denoncourt CAN
Denise Robinson CAN & Lynda Bramble TRI

CHN • 18 **Zhao** Yan - 20 **Wang** Liping, 3 **Li** Jie, 5 **Fan** Yunjie, 19 **Han** Duan (16 **Liu** Yali 59) - 11 **Pu** Wei, 10 **Liu** Ying, 17 **Pan** Lina (12 **Qu** Feifei 36), 6 **Zhao** Lihong (15 **Ren** Liping 88) - 7 **Bai** Jie, 9 **Sun** Wen (c). Ma Liangxing

GHA • 1 Memunatu **Sulemana** - 7 Genevive **Clottey**, 14 Elizabeth **Baidu**, 16 Lydia **Ankrah**, 3 Mavis **Danso** - 18 Mavis **Dgajmah** ■ 90 (9 Akua **Anokyewaa** 90+2), 10 Adjoa **Bayor**, 6 Florence **Okoe**, 4 Patience **Sackey** - 13 Yaa **Avoe** (17 Belinda **Kanda** 58), 15 Alberta **Sackey** (c) (8 Myralyn **Osei Agyemang** 83). Oko Aryee

Home Depot Center, Carson, Los Angeles
25.09.2003, 16:15, **13,929**

GHANA 0-3 **RUSSIA**

Saenko 36, Barbashina 54
Letyushova 80

Kari Seitz USA
Karalee Sutton USA & Sharon Wheeler USA

GHA • Sulemana (c) - Clottey, Baidu, Ankrah, Danso - Dgajmah, Bayor, Okoe, P Sackey (Kanda 78) - Osei Agyemang (Anokyewaa 52), Avoe (A Sackey 58). Aryee

RUS • Volkova - Stroukova, Zaytseva, Burakova (c), Saenko - (Pustovoitova 74) - Komarova, Fomina, Egorova (Skotnikova 59), 19 Elena **Denchtchik** (8 Alexandra **Svetlitskaya** 46) - Barbashina, Letyushova. Bystritskiy

Home Depot Center, Carson, Los Angeles
25.09.2003, 19:00, **13,929**

CHINA PR 1-1 **AUSTRALIA**

Bai Jie 46   Garriock 28

Katriina Elovirta FIN
Emilia Parviainen FIN & Andi Regan NIR

CHN • Zhao Yan - Wang Liping, Li Jie, Fan Yunjie, Liu Yali - 8 **Zhang** Ouying (Ren Liping 74), Pu Wei, Liu Ying ■ 55, Zhao Lihong (Qu Feifei 85) - Bai Jie (13 **Teng** Wei 90), Sun Wen (c). Ma Liangxing

AUS • Kell - Alagich ■ 89, Salisbury (c), 13 Karla **Reuter** - Davies, Karp, Peters, Foster - Garriock, Golebiowski ■ 90+1, Small (Duus 76). Santrac

PGE Park, Portland
28.09.2003, 17:15, **19,132**

GHANA 2-1 **AUSTRALIA**

A Sackey (2) 34 39   Garriock 61

Xonam Agboyi TOG
Perpétué Krebe CIV & Florence Biagui SEN

GHA • Sulemana - Clottey, Baidu, Ankrah ■ 58, Danso (Avoe 75) - Dgajmah, Bayor, Okoe, P Sackey - 11 Gloria **Foriwa** (Osei Agyemang 67) (Anokyewaa 90+1), A Sackey (c). Aryee

AUS • 12 Melissa **Barbieri** - Alagich, Salisbury (c), Reuter (14 Pamela **Grant** 90) - Davies, Karp (Duus 33), Peters, Foster (Mann 43) - Garriock ■ 52, Golebiowski, Small. Santrac

PGE Park, Portland
28.09.2003, 20:00, **19,132**

CHINA PR 1-0 **RUSSIA**

Bai Jie 16
(Liu Ying penalty missed 21)

Florencia Romano ARG
Sabrina Lois ARG & Alejandra Cercato ARG

CHN • 1 **Han** Wenxia - Wang Liping, Li Jie, Fan Yunjie, Liu Yali - Pu Wei, Liu Ying, 14 **Bi** Yan (Qu Feifei 55), Zhao Lihong (Ren Liping 62) - Bai Jie, Sun Wen (c). Ma Liangxing

RUS • Volkova - Stroukova, Zaytseva, Burakova (c), Saenko - Komarova, Fomina ■ 90, Egorova, Svetlitskaya - Barbashina, Letyushova (Skotnikova 66). Bystritskiy

◂ China's Sun Wen (9) celebrates her goal against Ghana. The Chinese won 1-0 and finished top of the group.

2003 Quarter-finals

Youthful Brazil fall to Sweden

Gilette Stadium, Foxborough, Boston
1.10.2003, 16:30, **25,103**

BRAZIL 🇧🇷 **1-2** 🇸🇪 **SWEDEN**

Marta 44p   Svensson 23, Andersson 53

Zhang Dongqing CHN
Liu Hsiu Mei TPE & Hisae Yoshizawa JPN

BRA • Andréia - Juliana (c) ■ 52, Simone (Cristiane 58), Tânia, Rosana - Formiga (9 **Kelly** 81), Renata Costa, Daniela ■ 37 - Marta - Maycon, Kátia. *Gonçalves*

SWE • 12 Sofia **Lundgren** ■ 43 - Marklund, Westberg, Törnqvist, Larsson (Call 90) - Andersson (Sjögran 72), Moström (c), Östberg, Sjöström ■ 15 - Ljungberg, Svensson. *Domanski Lyfors*

▶ Sweden's Victoria Svensson (11) formed an effective striking partnership with Hanna Ljungberg. Here she gets the better of Brazil's Daniela to open the scoring.

With a squad that featured only a handful of their 1999 bronze medallists, seven under-19 starlets and with an average age of just 22, Brazil were a team in transition. Nevertheless, they had breezed into the knockouts, WUSA star Kátia and teenager Marta combining to brilliant effect with six of the side's eight goals. Marta scored again here, winning and converting a penalty to cancel out Victoria Svensson's headed opener. Malin Andersson's stunning 20-yard free kick restored Sweden's lead and an intense battle ensued, with keepers Andréia and Sofia Lundgren both tested. Brazil had beaten Sweden in the 1995 World Cup and 2000 Olympics, but Marika Domanski Lyfors' side were determined to break that spell and after defender Anna Sjöström cleared a late Marta corner off the line and Kátia had a penalty shout denied at the death, they had done so. Their bogey team were out and Sweden were marching on.

USA win the clash of the champions

Gilette Stadium, Foxborough, Boston
1.10.2003, 19:30, **25,103**

USA 🇺🇸 **1-0** 🇳🇴 **NORWAY**

Wambach 24, (Hamm penalty saved 67)

Nicole Petignat SUI   Elke Lüthi SUI & Nelly Viennot FRA

USA • Scurry - Pearce, Fawcett, Reddick, Sobrero - Foudy (c) (Bivens 81), Boxx, Lilly - Hamm, Wambach, Parlow (Milbrett 72). *Heinrichs*

NOR • Nordby ■ 66 - Fiane Christensen (Ørmen 77), Knudsen, Stangeland, Sandaune - S Gulbrandsen, Rønning (Rapp 24), Klaveness ■ 75, Lehn ■ 80 (Riise 84 ■ 86) - Mellgren (c), Pettersen. *Steen*

Norway's head coach Åge Steen had tempted 1995 World Cup winners Marianne Pettersen and Bente Nordby out of retirement ahead of USA 2003, and with talismanic midfielder Hege Riise only half-fit and Ingrid Hjelmseth injured, it had proved a wise move. On the way to their quarter-final date with old foes the USA, Pettersen had scored twice, while Nordby had made some crucial saves. Norway's veteran shot-stopper would go on to be crowned player of the match after repelling Mia Hamm's 67th-minute penalty kick, Cindy Parlow's goal-bound header and generally bossing her defence in front of just over 25,000 fans on a cold night in Boston. Norway had beaten the USA at the World Cup and Olympics and had reached the final four in every edition of this competition, but their run would end here, striker Abby Wambach's powerful first-half header sealing it for the hosts.

▼ Kristine Lilly (13) had played for the USA at the 1988 International Women's Football Tournament, and in every tournament since.

▶ America's Abby Wambach (20) scored the only goal of the game in the quarter-final against Norway at Gillette Stadium in Boston.

Russia brought down to earth with a bump

PGE Park, Portland
2.10.2003, 16:30, **20,012**

GERMANY 7-1 RUSSIA

Müller 25, Minnert 57
P Wunderlich 60, Garefrekes (2) 62 85
Prinz (2) 80 89

Danilova 70

Im Eun Ju KOR
Choi Soo Jin KOR & Irina Mirt ROU

GER • Rottenberg - Stegemann, Minnert, Hingst, Gottschlich - Wiegmann (c) (Künzer 66), Lingor (16 Viola **Odebrecht** 82) - Garefrekes, Meinert, Müller (7 Pia **Wunderlich** 57 ■ 66) - Prinz. *Theune-Meyer*
RUS • Volkova - Stroukova, Zaytseva, Burakova (c), Saenko - Komarova, Skotnikova, Egorova (16 Marina **Kolomiets** 75), Svetlitskaya (Denchtchik 34) - Barbashina, Letyushova (17 Elena **Danilova** 46). *Bystritskiy*

Russia boss Yuri Bystritsky had said it did not matter who his side faced after their loss to China pitched them against Germany. The 11th-ranked side in the world would, however, need to buck a staggering trend if they were to progress. In their ten previous meetings, Germany had won eight times, drawn twice, scored 29 and conceded just two. Led by 37-year-old captain Marina Burakova, the oldest player in the tournament, Russia restricted Germany to just one goal in the first half, Martina Müller scoring after 25 minutes. But they were hit for six in the second period, Sandra Minnert and Pia Wunderlich scoring before Kerstin Garefrekes and Birgit Prinz hit a brace apiece. Germany's defence would be beaten by Russia though, 16-year-old Elena Danilova jinking round Minnert before coolly slotting past keeper Silke Rottenberg to become the youngest goalscorer in Women's World Cup history.

▲ Players from both Germany and Russia acknowledge the crowd after the quarter-final at Portland between the two.

Canada find the winning formula

PGE Park, Portland,
2.10.2003, 19:30, **20,012**

CHINA PR 0-1 CANADA

Hooper 7

Kari Seitz USA
Karalee Sutton USA & Sharon Wheeler USA

CHN • Han Wenxia - Wang Liping, Li Jie, Fan Yunjie, Liu Yali (Teng Wei 82 ■ 90+2) - Pu Wei, Liu Ying (Zhang Ouying 65), Bi Yan, Zhao Lihong (Ren Liping 58) - Bai Jie, Sun Wen (c). *Ma Liangxing*
CAN • Swiatek - Dennis, Nonen, Hooper (c) ■ 76, Morneau (Burtini 12) - Lang ■ 42 (Kiss 90), Timko, Matheson, Neil ■ 53 - Latham (Wilkinson 73), Sinclair. *Pellerud NOR*

▲ Boots worn at the 2003 World Cup by China's Sun Wen
FIFA Museum Collection

▶ Charmaine Hooper (10) celebrates her game-winning goal for Canada against China.

28 and out

China's quarter-final defeat at the hands of Canada brought the career of China's Sun Wen to an end after 28 matches and 16 goals in the World Cup and Olympics. She also captained her side in 13 of those matches.

▶▶ China after their defeat to Canada. Sun Wen is number 9.

With just one more piece of the quarter-final jigsaw remaining, all eyes at PGE Park were on University of Portland superstar Christine Sinclair and Canada as they took on 1999 Finalists China. Ma Liangxing's side had been overhauled since the 2000 Olympics and although their blend of old heads and youngsters had yet to hit the heights, China's record of 10 wins in 12 meetings hung over Canada ahead of this tie. Yet Canada had improved under coach Even Pellerud, a World Cup winner with Norway, and Sinclair and Christine Latham both went close in a gripping match that saw China lay siege to Taryn Swiatek's goal and captain Sun Wen rattle the crossbar. Remarkably, one goal settled the game, and that was scored in the seventh minute by Charmaine Hooper. "It's bigger than anything we've done before," Hooper declared afterwards, as Canada prepared to step into the unknown.

2003 Semi-finals

▼ Action from the semi-final between Germany (white) and the USA (red) in Portland.

Germany stun the hosts and holders

PGE Park, Portland
5.10.2003, 16:30, **27,623**

USA 0-3 **GERMANY**

Garefrekes 15, Meinert 90+1, Prinz 90+3

Sonia Denoncourt CAN — Denise Robinson CAN & Lynda Bramble TRI

USA • Scurry - Bivens (Milbrett 70), Fawcett, Reddick, Sobrero - Foudy (c), Boxx, Lilly - Hamm, Wambach, Parlow (Wagner 52). *Heinrichs*
GER • Rottenberg - Stegemann, Minnert, Hingst, Gottschlich - Wiegmann (c), Lingor - Garefrekes, Meinert, P Wunderlich - Prinz. *Theune-Meyer*

With a slew of chances, two goals at the death and tears after the final whistle, the USA's match-up with Germany in Portland would go down as one of the most exciting games in Women's World Cup history. It was always going to be tight, Germany having let in just three goals in four games to the USA's one, but after a frenetic start, Kerstin Garefrekes found a way past Briana Scurry, heading in off the crossbar. Keeper Silke Rottenberg stood firm, repelling Kristine Lilly and Mia Hamm, while her opposite number Scurry athletically denied Birgit Prinz and captain Bettina Wiegmann.

With her side chasing an equaliser, USA coach April Heinrichs threw on a third striker and Tiffeny Milbrett, playing in front of her home crowd, looked to have won a penalty after a clash with Rottenberg, but her appeal was waved away. Then, with the USA surging forward, they were punished, Maren Meinert and tournament top scorer Prinz both netting breakaway goals in injury time. It had been a classic and the players received a standing ovation from a raucous crowd of almost 28,000, but a first Women's World Cup defeat on home soil was still a bitter pill for the USA to swallow.

◄ Germany's defence holds firm against an American onslaught. Ariane Hingst (17) thwarts another attack under pressure from Abby Wambach (20).

Sweden's late show

PGE Park, Portland
5.10.2003, 19:30, **27,623**

SWEDEN 2-1 **CANADA**

Mostrom 79, Öqvist 86   Lang 64

Katriina Elovirta FIN — Emilia Parviainen FIN & Andi Regan NIR

SWE • Jönsson - Marklund, Westberg, Törnqvist, Bengtsson (13 Sara **Johansson** 75) - Andersson (Sjögran 70), Moström (c), Östberg, Sjöström (Öqvist 70) - Ljungberg, Svensson. *Domanski Lyfors*
CAN • Swiatek - Dennis, Nonen, Hooper (c), Burtini (Kiss 55) - Lang, Timko, Matheson, Neil - Latham (Wilkinson 74), Sinclair. *Pellerud NOR*

Victoria "Vickan" Svensson had scored important goals as Sweden advanced to the semi-finals, and her contribution to their victory over Canada in Portland was key. Ranked 12th in the world, Even Pellerud's side had already given women's football in Canada a shot in the arm by reaching the final four. They came out all guns blazing against fifth-ranked Sweden, Charmaine Hooper and Christine Latham both testing keeper Caroline Jönsson. But Sweden cranked up the pressure and Pellerud switched to 5-3-2 to nullify their attacking threat. It was goalless for over an hour until teenage free-kick specialist Kara Lang broke the deadlock to give Canada the lead, unleashing a powerful shot that stung Jönsson's hands on its way into the net. Jönsson kicked the post, Marika Domanski Lyfors made a double substitution ... out went Anna Sjöström and captain Malin Andersson, and in came Josefine Öqvist and Therese Sjögran. Up stepped "Vickan", first laying a quick free kick on a plate for Malin Moström to belt home, then marauding into the box and squaring to Öqvist, who side-footed in off the post and into the net. Öqvist wept, Svensson was crowned player of the match and Sweden were in the Final.

▼ Sweden captain Malin Moström (6) celebrates her equaliser in the semi-final against Canada in Portland.

2003 Match for Third Place

Home Depot Center, Carson, Los Angeles
11.10.2003, 12:30, 25,253

USA 3-1 **CANADA**

Lilly 22, Boxx 51, Milbrett 80 — Sinclair 38

Tammy Ogston AUS — Airlie Keen AUS & Jacqueline Leleu AUS

▼ Canada's Sasha Andrews (4) challenges Mia Hamm (9) during the match for third place at Carson, Los Angeles.

Consolation for the USA

The oldest team in the tournament were set to play their sixth game in their sixth different city when they faced Canada in the match for third place in front of more than 25,000 spectators in California. Yet as April Heinrichs' side went on a lap of honour at full time, Mia Hamm, Joy Fawcett and Julie Foudy also knew they had played their last World Cup match. Canada's own legend, 35-year-old captain Charmaine Hooper, bowed out too and did so knowing her team had played their part in the tournament's success, going from no wins on the world stage to a battle for bronze in the space of three weeks. They were underdogs here, having won just three times in 31 meetings with their North American neighbours and with a golden goal defeat to the USA in the 2002 Concacaf Women's Gold Cup Final still fresh in their minds. After falling behind to a fine opening goal from the boot of Kristine Lilly, Canada rallied, Christine Sinclair pulling them back into it with an equaliser just before the break. But World Cup debutant Shannon Boxx restored the hosts' lead with a header that was also the USA's 1000th goal in international football before Tiffeny Milbrett scored to keep the USA's impressive record of a medal finish at every Women's World Cup intact. "It's not where we wanted to be," said 31-year-old Hamm afterwards. "But you have to regroup and have to play with pride and that's what you saw here."

▶ The USA team with their medals.

2003 World Cup Final

Germany on top of the world

Home Depot Center, Carson, Los Angeles
12.10.2003, 10:00, 26,137

GERMANY 2-1 SWEDEN
AET

Meinert 46, Künzer 98 GG — Ljungberg 41

Cristina Ionescu ROU — Irina Mirt ROU & Katarzyna Nadolska POL

Theune-Meyer
- 1 Rottenberg
- 2 Stegemann, 13 Minnert, 17 Hingst, 19 Gottschlich
- 10 Wiegmann (c), 6 Lingor
- 18 Garefrekes (Müller 76), 14 Meinert, 7 P Wunderlich (Künzer 88)
- 9 Prinz

Domanski Lyfors
- 11 Svensson, 10 Ljungberg
- 17 Sjöström (Fagerström 53), 18 Östberg, 6 Moström (c), 9 Andersson (Sjögran 53)
- 7 Larsson (Bengtsson 76), 3 Törnqvist, 2 Westberg, 4 Marklund
- 1 Jönsson

With their impressive run to the Final, Germany had already done enough to overtake the Americans as the number-one team in the world in the forthcoming FIFA ranking. Could they take their world title as well? First they would have to beat a pacy Sweden side that had improved with every World Cup match.

Germany had been here before, of course, assistant coach Silvia Neid and four of the starting XI having played their part in their 1995 Final loss to Norway. Sweden had the edge when it came to World Cup wins over the Germans though, beating them in the 1991 match for third place and the 1995 group stage. Germany's rain-sodden golden-goal victory over Sweden in the European Championship Final in 2001 was more relevant though, and head coach Tina Theune-Meyer had shown her charges recordings of that match in preparation for this tie. For their part, Sweden wanted revenge. "It'd be great to get our own back," said forward Hanna Ljungberg.

Between them, Sweden's female player of 2002 Ljungberg and her strike partner Victoria Svensson had scored more than 80 goals for their country, bagging five at this World Cup alone. They would combine to devastating effect here too, 24-year-old Ljungberg collecting Svensson's knock-on, storming into the box and smartly beating Silke Rottenberg to give Marika Domanski Lyfors' side a deserved lead with four minutes of the first half remaining.

Sweden had dominated the first period but Germany were level within a minute of the second, talismanic veteran Maren Meinert calmly side-footing home the equaliser after collecting a canny pass from Birgit Prinz, who had been the youngest player to appear in a Women's World Cup Final in 1995. A fight to the finish followed, with Prinz, captain Bettina Wiegmann, Ariane Hingst and Pia Wunderlich all coming close, and Svensson and Ljungberg almost scoring at the opposite end.

Then, two minutes from time, Theune-Meyer threw on defender Nia Künzer, telling her: "Try to stop them scoring, but get up front and try to score yourself." When the match went to sudden death in extra time, Künzer did exactly as her manager had requested, rising to head home a free kick from 1. FFC Frankfurt team-mate Renate Lingor to win the Final for Germany. A golden goal had undone Sweden again, but both sides had played their part in a world-class tournament.

◀ Action from the 2003 World Cup Final. Sweden led 1-0 at half-time but lost 2-1.

▶ Kerstin Garefrekes was a constant threat for Germany down the right wing.

Final 2003

▲ Germany celebrate winning the World Cup for the first time. Their 2-1 victory over debut Finalists Sweden came courtesy of a Nia Künzer (4) golden goal. Captain Bettina Wiegmann lifts the trophy.

The first!

In the fourth World Cup, Tina Theune-Meyer became the first female coach to win it. Her opposite number Marika Domanski Lyfors made it an all-female Final. Indeed, the top three teams were all coached by women, with the USA's April Heinrichs completing the trio.

▶ Sweden coach Marika Domanski Lyfors (left) and her opposite number, Germany's Tina Theune-Meyer.

2004

As the Olympics returned to Greece for the first time since 1896, Norway were the first reigning champions not to be present to defend an Olympic or world title. Instead the USA made it to their third Olympic Final in succession, beating world champions Germany in the semi-finals and Brazil in the Final to win gold for a second time. Coach April Heinrichs became the first to win a title as a player and coach having captained the USA to their World Cup triumph 13 years earlier.

The Olympics returns to its roots

It was to general surprise that Athens was overlooked to stage the Centennial Games in 1996, but sentiment demanded that the Olympics return to its Greek roots eight years later. Preparations were fraught right up to the opening ceremony, but ticket sales exceeded those of Seoul and Barcelona, despite Greece having a fraction of the population of either South Korea or Spain. The enthusiasm of the local crowds was helped in no small measure by the extraordinary and unexpected success of the Greek football team at Euro 2004 just over a month before the opening ceremony. An embarrassing doping incident involving two Greek athletes at the start of the Games failed to detract from the sporting excellence on show. German Kayaker Birgit Fischer became only the second athlete after Hungary's Aladár Gerevich to win gold at six different Olympics, having won her first in 1980, while the American Michael Phelps launched his glittering Olympic career with eight medals in the pool. In the men's football tournament, Argentina matched the achievement of neighbours Uruguay 80 years earlier by winning gold for the first time, Carlos Tevez scoring the only goal of the Final in a 1-0 victory over Paraguay.

▼ Michael Phelps was one of the stars of the Athens Olympics. He won six gold and two bronze medals in the pool.

2004 Overview

ATHENS 2004

WOMEN'S OLYMPIC FOOTBALL TOURNAMENT

Story of the qualifiers

Norway miss out

The intention was to stage qualifying tournaments specifically for the 2004 Women's Olympic Football Tournament, but that only happened in four of the six continental confederations. Europe and South America were the two exceptions. UEFA decided that the two top-placed European teams at the 2003 World Cup would qualify along with hosts Greece. That meant no place for the Olympic title holders Norway, who had been knocked out by the USA in the World Cup quarter-finals. Instead it was Finalists Sweden and Germany who took their place amongst the ten nations. In South America, Brazil were chosen after having won the 2003 South American title, a success that had also seen them qualify for the World Cup that year. The remaining six places were split between the other four confederations and in each a qualifying tournament was held. China and Japan claimed the two places for Asia following a tournament staged in Hiroshima and Tokyo, with the two Koreas the beaten semi-finalists. Australia claimed the single place up for grabs in Oceania, while Nigeria beat South Africa for the one place allocated to Africa. That left the two slots for Concacaf which were claimed by the USA and Mexico, with Canada surprisingly losing to the Mexicans in the semi-finals.

▲ USA supporters have always been a colourful and vocal presence at the Women's Olympic Football Tournament.

Overview 2004

UNITED STATES	36	39	26
CHINA PR	32	17	14
RUSSIA	28	26	36
AUSTRALIA	17	16	17
JAPAN	16	9	12
GERMANY	13	16	20

TOP OF THE MEDAL TABLE

10 TEAMS · USA WINNERS · BRA SECOND · GER THIRD

208 637 SPECTATORS   **10 432** AVERAGE PER MATCH

20 MATCHES PLAYED · **37** YELLOW CARDS · **1** RED CARDS

55 GOALS · **2.75** AVERAGE GOALS PER MATCH · **PELIAS** OFFICIAL MATCH BALL

Host cities and stadiums

Football in the home of the Olympics

The group games in the women's tournament were played as double-headers with matches in the men's tournament for which there was an average of 12,544 fans for each game.

But the Greek fans deserted the women from the quarter-finals onwards when the tournaments separated. The average fell to just 4,860 per match.

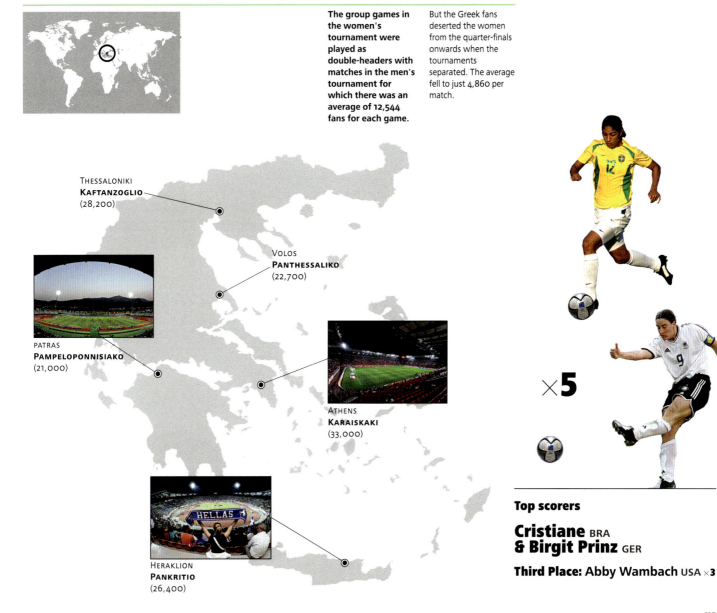

Thessaloniki **Kaftanzoglio** (28,200)
Volos **Panthessaliko** (22,700)
Patras **Pampeloponnisiako** (21,000)
Athens **Karaiskaki** (33,000)
Heraklion **Pankritio** (26,400)

×5

Top scorers

Cristiane BRA
& Birgit Prinz GER

Third Place: Abby Wambach USA ×3

2004 Group stage

Group E

Panthessaliko, Volos
11.08.2004, 18:00, **10,104**

SWEDEN 0-1 **JAPAN**
Arakawa 24

Fatou Gaye SEN
Mariette Bantsimba CGO & Tempa Ndah BEN

SWE • 1 Caroline **Jönsson** - 2 Karolina **Westberg**, 4 Hanna **Marklund**, 3 Jane **Törnqvist**, 5 Kristin **Bengtsson** - 6 Malin **Moström**, 8 Frida **Östberg**, 9 Malin **Andersson** (c) (17 Anna **Sjöström** 57), 15 Therese **Sjögran** (16 Salina **Olsson** 84) - 10 Hanna **Ljungberg** (12 Josefine **Öqvist** 68), 11 Victoria **Svensson**. *Marika Domanski Lyfors*

JPN • 1 Nozomi **Yamago** - 5 Naoko **Kawakami**, 3 Hiromi **Isozaki** (c), 13 Aya **Shimokozuru**, 12 Yasuyo **Yamagishi** - 6 Tomoe **Sakai**, 8 Tomomi **Miyamoto**, 15 Yayoi **Kobayashi** (17 Kozue **Ando** 56) (15 Miyuki **Yanagita** 85) - 11 Mio **Otani**, 10 Homare **Sawa**, 9 Eriko **Arakawa** (14 Karina **Maruyama** 66). *Eiji Ueda*

Karaiskaki, Athens
14.08.2004, 18:00, **14,126**

JAPAN 0-1 **NIGERIA**
Okolo 55

Dianne Ferreira-James GUY
Jackeline Saez PAN & María Isabel Tovar MEX

JPN • Yamago - Kawakami, Isozaki (c), Shimokozuru, Yamagishi (7 Emi **Yamamoto** 84) - Sakai, Miyamoto (Yanagita 20), Kobayashi (Maruyama 60) - Otani, Sawa, Arakawa. *Ueda*

NGA • 1 Precious **Dede** - 2 Efioanwan **Ekpo**, 13 Yinka **Kudaisi** (c), 17 Chima **Nwosu** - 3 Felicia **Eze**, 15 Maureen **Mmadu** ■ 31, 10 Mercy **Akide** (5 Ajuma **Ameh** 76), 6 Faith **Ikidi** (14 Akudo **Sabi** 81) - 11 Vera **Okolo**, 4 Perpetua **Nkwocha**, 7 Stella **Mbachu**. *Ismaila Mabo*

Panthessaliko, Volos
17.08.2004, 18:00, **21,597**

SWEDEN 2-1 **NIGERIA**
Marklund 68, Moström 73   Akide 25

Silvia De Oliveira BRA
Ana Da Silva Oliveira BRA & Aracely Castro BOL

SWE • Jönsson - 7 Sara **Larsson**, Westberg, Marklund, Bengtsson - Sjöström (Öqvist 63), Moström (c), Östberg, Sjögran (13 Lotta **Schelin** 46) - Ljungberg ■ 37 (14 Linda **Fagerström** 80), Svensson. *Domanski Lyfors*

NGA • Dede - Ekpo, Kudaisi (c), Nwosu (Sabi 83) - Eze, Mmadu, Akide ■ 45+1 (Ameh 70), Ikidi - Okolo, Nkwocha, Mbachu (16 Nkechi **Egbe** 78). *Mabo*

	W	D	L	+	-	PTS
SWE	1	0	1	2	2	3
NGA	1	0	1	2	2	3
JPN	1	0	1	1	1	3

Japan finish bottom but still qualify

Sweden, World Cup Finalists the previous year, were expected to win the group with ease, but they suffered an upset at the hands of Japan in their opening match. A goal in the 24th minute by Olympic debutant Eriko Arakawa, who led the attack, sealed the win for the Japanese. Coach Eiji Ueda's joy was short-lived, however, as Nigeria, in their second consecutive Olympic tournament, defeated Japan three days later at the Karaiskaki Stadium, a venue originally used as a cycling track at the 1896 Olympic Games. Striker Vera Okolo, whose goal against South Africa in the qualifiers had secured the Super Falcons' place in Athens, gave Nigeria the lead which they then clung on to. In the final game, Sweden recovered from their surprise loss against Japan to beat Nigeria. The Nigerians dominated the first half and went in to the break 1-0 up thanks to a goal by veteran Mercy Akide, but the Swedes came alive in the second half to score twice within the space of five minutes thanks to goals from defender Hanna Marklund and Malin Moström. That left all three teams equal on points, and with eight of the ten entrants qualifying for the quarter-finals, all three teams from this group progressed.

▲ With ten teams vying for the eight quarter-final places, Sweden's win over Nigeria meant all three teams in Group E qualified for the next round, each having won a match.

▼ Germany's Birgit Prinz scored four goals against China in their extraordinary 8-0 victory in Patras.

Group F

Pampeloponnisiako, Patras
11.08.2004, 18:00, **14,657**

GERMANY 8-0 **CHINA PR**
Prinz (4) 13 21 73 88
P Wunderlich 65
Lingor 76p
Pohlers 81
Müller 90

Kari Seitz USA
Denise Robinson CAN & Jackeline Saez PAN

GER • 1 Silke **Rottenberg** - 2 Kerstin **Stegemann**, 17 Ariane **Hingst**, 4 Steffi **Jones**, 15 Sonja **Fuss** (5 Sarah **Günther** 58) - 3 Kerstin **Garefrekes**, 10 Renate **Lingor**, 6 Viola **Odebrecht**, 7 Pia **Wunderlich** (16 Conny **Pohlers** 74) - 9 Birgit **Prinz** (c), 8 Petra **Wimbersky** (11 Martina **Müller** 80). *Tina Theune-Meyer*

CHN • 1 Xiao **Zhen** - 2 Jin **Xiaomei** (4 Wang **Liping** 66), 3 Li **Jie**, 5 Fan **Yunjie** (c), 15 Ren **Liping** - 12 Qu **Feifei** ■ 74, 6 Pu **Wei**, 8 Bi **Yan** (16 Zhang **Ying** 68), 17 Ji **Ting** - 10 Teng **Wei**, 9 Han **Duan** (11 Bai **Lili** 60). *Zhang Haitao*

Pampeloponnisiako, Patras
14.08.2004, 18:00, **5,112**

CHINA PR 1-1 **MEXICO**
Ji Ting 34   Domínguez 11

Cristina Ionescu ROU
Katarzyna Nadolska POL & María Luisa Villa Gutiérrez ESP

CHN • Xiao Zhen - Wang Liping (Jin Xiaomei 67), Li Jie, Fan Yunjie (c), Ren Liping ■ 18 - Qu Feifei, Pu Wei, Bi Yan (Han Duan 62), Ji Ting - Teng Wei, Zhang **Ouying** (Bai Lili 77). *Zhang Haitao*

MEX • 18 Pamela **Tajonar** - 2 Elizabeth **Gómez**, 3 Rubí **Sandoval**, 4 Mónica **González** (c), 5 María de Jesús **Castillo** - 15 Dioselina **Valderrama** (14 Nancy **Gutiérrez** 46), 6 Mónica **Vergara**, 8 Fatima **Leyva** (7 Juana **López** 74) - 10 Iris **Mora** ■ 71, 9 Maribel **Domínguez**, 11 Patricia **Pérez** (13 Luz del Rosario **Saucedo** 36). *Leonardo Cuéllar*

Karaiskaki, Athens
17.08.2004, 18:00, **26,338**

GERMANY 2-0 **MEXICO**
Wimbersky 20, Prinz 79

Krystyna Szokolai AUS
Airlie Keen AUS & Jacqueline Leleu AUS

GER • Rottenberg - Stegemann, Hingst, Jones, Günther - Garefrekes (Pohlers 64), Navina **Omilade**, Lingor (Odebrecht 46), 14 Isabell **Bachor** - Prinz (c), Wimbersky (Müller 46). *Theune-Meyer*

MEX • 1 Jennifer **Molina** - Gómez, Sandoval, González (c), 16 Alma **Martínez** - Valderrama, Vergara ■ 48 (Gutiérrez 80), Leyva - Mora (López 76), Domínguez, 17 Guadalupe **Worbis** (Castillo 67). *Cuéllar*

	W	D	L	+	-	PTS
GER	2	0	0	10	0	6
MEX	0	1	1	1	3	1
CHN	0	1	1	1	9	1

Germany score eight against inexperienced Chinese

World champions Germany got their campaign off to an extraordinary start with an 8-0 win over China, an Olympic record that still stands. Birgit Prinz, 2003 FIFA Women's World Player of the Year, started the avalanche in the 13th minute and scored a second eight minutes later, aided by Kerstin Stegemann. Germany maintained pressure on China's disorganised defence, with a Pia Wunderlich goal in the 65th minute before a five-goal spree in the 17 minutes before the end. Prinz, who scored four goals, claimed the first hat-trick in a women's match at the Olympics. China's shaky performance was attributed to them fielding a team that lacked experience at major international tournaments; only four players had participated in the 2000 Sydney Games, the result of rebuilding following the retirement of legendary star attacker Sun Wen, as well as Liu Ailing and Bai Jie, players central to the *Steel Roses'* dominance in the 1990s. China drew with Olympic debutants Mexico three days later thanks to 21-year-old striker Ji Ting, which meant that if Mexico could avoid a drubbing against Germany in their final game, they would send the Chinese home. They managed that by restricting the Germans to a 2-0 victory.

Hosts Greece outclassed

The United States, out to win gold for retiring playmaker Mia Hamm, prevailed over the hosts and first-time Olympic participants Greece in the group's opening match. There were first-half goals for Shannon Boxx and Abby Wambach, who had both been part of the USA squad for the 2003 World Cup, as well as an 82nd-minute strike from Hamm which seemed to illustrate a seamless generational on-pitch transition. Similarly, Brazil's win over Australia owed much to their young striker Marta, scorer of the game-winning goal, who linked up brilliantly with experienced forwards Pretinha and Formiga. Australia claimed their first Olympic win in their next match, a first-half goal by Heather Garriock consigning coach Xanthi Konstantinidou's Greece team to a second defeat. In the match to decide who would finish top of the group, Brazil dominated the first half against the USA, but they succumbed to second-half goals from Hamm and Wambach, the win securing April Heinrichs' players a place in the quarter-finals. Brazil's 7-0 victory over Greece featured a hat-trick by 19-year-old Cristiane in her Olympic debut and ensured their spot in the next round, as did Australia's draw with the USA. The Matildas came from behind with a late equaliser, a header by Joanne Peters, after Kristine Lilly had given the Americans a first-half lead.

Group G

	W	D	L	+	–	PTS
USA	2	1	0	6	1	7
BRA	2	0	1	8	2	6
AUS	1	1	1	2	2	4
GRE	0	0	3	0	11	0

◀ Brazil's Roseli (17) is watched by Greek defender Sophia Smith. Despite recruiting players from the USA who had Greek heritage, the hosts were badly outclassed and lost this match 7-0.

◀ Australia's Joanne Peters (10) receives close attention from Kate Markgraf (15). Peters scored a late equaliser for the Australians.

Pankritio, Heraklion
11.08.2004, 18:00, **15,757**

GREECE 🇬🇷 **0-3** 🇺🇸 **USA**

Boxx 14
Wambach 30
Hamm 82

Jenny Palmqvist SWE
Emilia Parviainen FIN & Andi Regan NIR

GRE • 1 Maria **Giatrakis** - 2 Angeliki **Lagoumtzi**, 4 Kalliopi **Stratakis**, 8 Konstantina **Katsaiti**, 3 Sophia **Smith** - 12 Amalia **Loseno**, 16 Eleni **Benson**, 6 Eftichia **Michailidou** (c), 13 Alexandra **Kavvada** (14 Anastasia Papadopoulou 59) - 15 Tanya **Kalyvas** (10 Natalia Chatzigiannidou 46) - 11 Dimitra **Panteleiadou** (7 Vasiliki **Soupiadou** 76). Xanthi Konstantinidou

USA • 1 Briana **Scurry** - 3 Christie **Rampone**, 14 Joy **Fawcett**, 4 Cat **Reddick**, 15 Kate **Markgraf** - 11 Julie **Foudy** (c) (8 Angela **Hucles** 71), 7 Shannon **Boxx**, 10 Aly **Wagner** (5 Lindsay **Tarpley** 61), 13 Kristine **Lilly** - 9 Mia **Hamm**, 16 Abby **Wambach** 🟨 49 (12 Cindy **Parlow** 79). April Heinrichs

---

Kaftanzoglio, Thessaloniki
11.08.2004, 18:00, **25,152**

BRAZIL 🇧🇷 **1-0** 🇦🇺 **AUSTRALIA**

Marta 36

Christine Frai GER
Nelly Viennot FRA & María Luisa Villa Gutiérrez ESP

BRA • 18 **Andréia** - 3 **Mônica** 🟨 64, 5 **Juliana** (c), 6 **Renata Costa** (2 **Grazielle** 13) (12 **Cristiane** 83), 4 **Tânia** - 14 **Elaine**, 8 **Daniela**, 7 **Formiga**, 11 **Rosana** (15 **Maycon** 76) - 9 **Pretinha**, 10 **Marta**. René Simões

AUS • 1 Cassandra **Kell** - 2 Rhian **Davies**, 4 Dianne **Alagich**, 5 Cheryl **Salisbury** (c), 3 Sacha **Wainwright** - 6 Sally **Shipard** (9 Kylie **Ledbrook** 83) - 14 Gillian **Foster** (11 Lisa **De Vanna** 57), 17 Danielle **Small**, 10 Joanne **Peters** 🟨 15, 8 Heather **Garriock** - 7 Sarah **Walsh** (16 Selin **Kuralay** 71). Adrian Santrac

---

Pankritio, Heraklion
14.08.2004, 18:00, **8,857**

GREECE 🇬🇷 **0-1** 🇦🇺 **AUSTRALIA**

Garriock 27

Bentla D'Coth IND
Shiho Ayukai JPN & Liu Hongjuan CHN

GRE • Giatrakis - Lagoumtzi (9 Angeliki **Tefani** 73), Stratakis, Katsaiti, Smith - Loseno, Benson, Chatzigiannidou (17 Maria **Lazarou** 46), Michailidou (c), Papadopoulou 🟨 77 - Panteleiadou (Soupiadou 46). Konstantinidou

AUS • Kell - Davies (De Vanna 46), Alagich 🟨 43, Salisbury (c), Wainwright - Shipard - Foster (12 Karla **Reuter** 74), Small, Peters, Garriock - Walsh (Kuralay 58). Santrac

---

Kaftanzoglio, Thessaloniki
14.08.2004, 18:00, **17,123**

USA 🇺🇸 **2-0** 🇧🇷 **BRAZIL**

Hamm 58p
Wambach 77

Dagmar Damkova CZE
Emilia Parviainen FIN & Nelly Viennot FRA

BRA • Andréia - Mônica 🟨 58, Juliana (c), Tânia - Elaine, Daniela, Formiga, Rosana (16 **Kelly** 72) (Grazielle 84) - Pretinha, Cristiane (Maycon 65), Marta. Simões

USA • Scurry - Rampone 🟨 88, Fawcett, Reddick (2 Heather **Mitts** 81), Markgraf - Foudy (c), Boxx, Wagner (Tarpley 58), Lilly (17 Heather **O'Reilly** 69) - Hamm, Wambach 🟨 49. Heinrichs

---

Pampeloponnisiako, Patras
17.08.2004, 18:00, **7,214**

GREECE 🇬🇷 **0-7** 🇧🇷 **BRAZIL**

Pretinha 21
Cristiane (3) 45+1 55 77
Grazielle 49, Marta 70
Daniela 72

Christine Frai GER
Emilia Parviainen FIN & María Luisa Villa Gutiérrez ESP

GRE • Giatrakis (18 Ileana **Moschos** 80) - Lagoumtzi, Stratakis 🟨 38, Katsaiti, Smith - Loseno, Benson, Michailidou (c) 🟨 31, Papadopoulou (Soupiadou 46) - Kalyvas - Panteleiadou (5 Athanasia **Pouridou** 69 🟨 87). Konstantinidou

BRA • Andréia - 13 **Aline**, Juliana (c), Tânia (Grazielle 25) - Elaine, Daniela, Formiga 🟨 43 (17 **Roseli** 54), Rosana 🟨 41 (Maycon 58) - Pretinha, Cristiane, Marta. Simões

---

Kaftanzoglio, Thessaloniki
17.08.2004, 18:00, **3,320**

USA 🇺🇸 **1-1** 🇦🇺 **AUSTRALIA**

Lilly 19   Peters 82

Cristina Ionescu ROU
Katarzyna Nadolska POL & Nelly Viennot FRA

USA • Scurry - Mitts, Fawcett, Reddick, Markgraf - Foudy (c), Boxx (Tarpley 67), Wagner (Hucles 74), Lilly - Hamm (O'Reilly 67), Parlow 🟨 72. Heinrichs

AUS • Kell - Davies, Alagich (De Vanna 62), Salisbury (c), Wainwright - Shipard - 13 Thea **Slatyer** (Reuter 43), Small (Foster 67), Peters, Garriock - Walsh. Santrac

2004 Quarter-finals

◀ The USA's Kristine Lilly (13) opens the scoring in the quarter-final against Japan.

Japan fall to controversial winner

Kaftanzoglio, Thessaloniki
20.08.2004, 18:00, 1,418

USA 2-1 JAPAN

Lilly 43   Yamamoto 48
Wambach 59

Silvia De Oliveira BRA
Ana Da Silva Oliveira BRA & Aracely Castro BOL

USA • Scurry - Rampone, Fawcett, 6 Brandi **Chastain**, Markgraf - Foudy (c), Boxx, Tarpley, Lilly 45+1 - Hamm 86, Wambach. *Heinrichs*

JPN • Yamago - Kawakami (Maruyama 77), Isozaki (c), Shimokozuru, 2 Kyoko **Yano** (Yamagishi 46) - Sakai, Miyamoto, Yamamoto (Yanagita 68) - Otani, Sawa, Arakawa. *Ueda*

Experience eventually told for April Heinrichs' side but for much of the match, played under the sweltering Greek sun, the Japanese held their own. They enjoyed a good spell of first-half pressure, but just before half-time, the Americans made the breakthrough. Kristine Lilly's persistence down the left led to confusion in the Japanese defence, and Lilly was there to flick the loose ball past goalie Nozomi Yamago. Minutes into the second half, Emi Yamamoto opened up the game when she scored direct from a free kick past Briana Scurry to equalise. Nadeshiko fans pounded on their drums, filling the stadium with noise to encourage their team, but Eiji Ueda's side were level for just 11 minutes. Abby Wambach's winner had a touch of controversy about it though. Japan's backline pushed forward at a free kick, but Shannon Boxx timed her run perfectly. However, Wambach looked offside when the free kick was taken, but was on hand to score from Boxx's pass across the keeper.

▲ All eyes on Mia Hamm (9). The American striker is the centre of attention for her Japanese opponents.

▶ Abby Wambach (in red) scored the winner for the USA against Japan, her third goal of the tournament.

So close for Nigeria

Pampeloponnisiako, Patras
20.08.2004, 18:00, 2,531

GERMANY 2-1 NIGERIA

Jones 76   Akide 49
Pohlers 81

Bentla D'Coth IND
Liu Hongjuan CHN & Shiho Ayukai JPN

GER • Rottenberg - Stegemann, Hingst, Jones, 13 Sandra **Minnert** (Fuss 79) - Garefrekes, Lingor, Odebrecht, P Wunderlich (Bachor 55) - Prinz (c), Wimbersky (Pohlers 46). *Theune-Meyer*

NGA • Dede - Ekpo 21, Kudaisi, Sabi - Eze (Nwosu 79), Mmadu 90+1, Akide, Ikidi - Okolo, Nkwocha (Mbachu 87), 8 Rita **Nwadike** (c) (9 Blessing **Igbojionu** 68). *Mabo*

Germany came from behind, scoring two goals within five minutes late in the second half to secure a hard-fought win over Nigeria and a place in the semi-finals. Ismaila Mabo's players pushed Germany all the way in a tightly contested, physical match. Germany had two early shots on goal but could not find a way past goalkeeper Precious Dede. Nigeria ramped up the pressure, and went close just before half-time, and they carried that momentum into the second half. Showing grace under fire, striker Mercy Akide proved why she had been named in the 2004 FIFA Women's World Stars when she drove the ball through the legs of Silke Rottenberg in the 49th minute after a perfectly weighted pass from Perpetua Nkwocha. But 27 minutes later Germany equalised with a Steffi Jones header from a corner before second-half substitute Conny Pohlers dispossessed Dede with her head before prodding the ball home to seal the win in the 81st minute.

Brazil stroll through to third consecutive Olympic semi-final

Mexico's Olympic campaign was over within an hour as Brazil's dangerous attack overwhelmed their opponents. The South American champions dominated from the very first whistle, although Mexico's 19-year-old goalkeeper Pamela Tajonar kept them at bay for 25 minutes. It could not last, however, as Cristiane continued her scoring spree and opened Brazil's account with a header, followed four minutes later by a goal from Formiga. Try as they might, Mexico just could not get going, and by the hour mark the Brazilians were 5-0 up thanks to a further three goals in 11 minutes, with Cristiane and Formiga each adding their second and Marta rounding off the scoring. With five goals, Cristiane was the tournament's top scorer, a title she shared with Germany's Birgit Prinz. A second yellow card just before the end earned Mexico's Maribel Domínguez the only red card of the tournament.

Pankritio, Heraklion
20.08.2004, 21:00, 3,012
MEXICO 0-5 BRAZIL
Cristiane (2) 25 49
Formiga (2) 29 54
Marta 60

Fatou Gaye SEN
Mariette Bantsimba CGO & Tempa Ndah BEN

MEX • Tajonar - Gómez, Sandoval, González (c), Castillo (Worbis 65) - Valderrama ■ 88, Vergara (López 46), Leyva - Mora, Domínguez ■ 16 ■ 85 ■ 85, Martínez (Gutiérrez 46). *Cuéllar*

BRA • Andréia - Mônica, Juliana (c), Tânia ■ 19 (Aline 56 ■ 67) - Elaine, Daniela, Formiga (Roseli 77), Rosana - Pretinha (Renata Costa 63), Cristiane, Marta. *Simões*

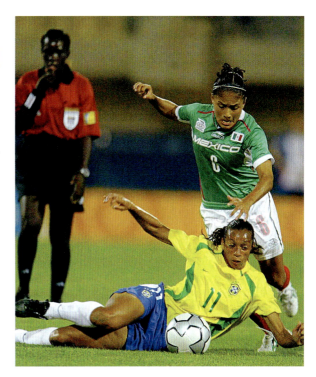

▶ Brazil's Rosana (11) and Mexico's Mónica Vergara during the quarter-final in Heraklion.

▶ Sweden's Karolina Westberg (yellow) and Australia's Sarah Walsh during the quarter-final clash between the two nations in Volos.

▲ Action from the quarter-final between Mexico and Brazil.

2943

Just over 11,000 fans turned up for the four quarter-final matches, at 2,943 per game. With the women no longer part of double-headers with the men, Greek fans seemed unwilling to watch top-class female athletes at work.

Too little too late for Australia

Panthessaliko, Volos
20.08.2004, 21:00, 4,811
SWEDEN 2-1 AUSTRALIA
Ljungberg 25   De Vanna 79
Larsson 30

Dagmar Damkova CZE
María Luisa Villa Gutiérrez ESP & Katarzyna Nadolska POL

SWE • Jönsson - Larsson, Westberg, Marklund, Bengtsson - Sjöström (Olsson 87), Moström (c), Östberg, Sjögran (Öqvist 71) - Ljungberg (Fagerström 77), Svensson. *Domanski Lyfors*

AUS • Kell - Davies, Alagich, Salisbury (c), Wainwright - Shipard - Foster (Kuralay 61), Small (De Vanna 36), Peters, Garriock - Walsh. *Santrac*

Two first-half goals by Sweden reminded the world that the 2003 World Cup runners-up were still a force to be reckoned with as they dashed Australia's hopes – despite a late rally by the Matildas. Marika Domanski Lyfors' side dominated the first half-hour of play. After 25 minutes, Malin Moström won possession in midfield and fed Hanna Ljungberg, who evaded two defenders before shooting across goal to open the scoring. Five minutes later, a Kristin Bengtsson corner kick was nodded back towards the goal by Victoria Svensson to defender Sara Larsson, who headed past Cassandra Kell. Australia picked up when the 19-year-old Lisa De Vanna came on as a substitute in the first half and pulled a goal back. A long ball forward was headed on and De Vanna's pace took her beyond two defenders before she slid the ball past Caroline Jönsson in the Swedish goal. But it proved to be too little, too late to change the outcome.

2004 Semi-finals

O'Reilly to the rescue for the USA

Pankritio, Heraklion
23.08.2004, 18:00, **5,165**

USA	2-1 AET	GERMANY
Lilly 33, O'Reilly 99		Bachor 90+2

Krystyna Szokolai AUS · Airlie Keen AUS & Jacqueline Leleu AUS

USA • Scurry ■ 86 - Rampone, Fawcett, Chastain (Reddick 51), Markgraf ■ 34 - Foudy (c) ■ 21 (Wagner 65 ■ 77), Boxx, Tarpley (O'Reilly 75), Lilly - Hamm, Wambach. *Heinrichs*
GER • Rottenberg - Stegemann, Hingst, Jones, Minnert - Garefrekes, Lingor, Odebrecht (Fuss 71), Pohlers (Müller 58) - Prinz (c), P Wunderlich (Bachor 39 ■ 41). *Theune-Meyer*

▲ Heather O'Reilly (17) scores an extra-time winner for the USA in the semi-final against Germany.

An extra-time winner by Heather O'Reilly, a late substitute, kept the USA's quest for a gold medal alive in a close match against Germany. The duel between the world's top two teams was a rematch of the World Cup semi-final from the year before, which Germany had won 3-0. In the following months, both teams looked to bring in fresh blood as key players retired. Yet this contest exposed the reigning world champions as they searched for that elusive Olympic crown to match their world and European titles. A Kristine Lilly goal in the first half seemed to have won it for the Americans, her left-foot shot finishing off a superb eight-pass move that left the Germans mesmerised. Germany pressed in the second half but they left it very late to send the game into extra time. Two minutes into five minutes of injury time, their 21-year-old substitute Isabell Bachor turned brilliantly in the box to beat Christie Rampone before firing past the diving Briana Scurry. In extra time, Wambach and Mia Hamm combined well before Hamm sent a dangerous cross into a packed box where O'Reilly got to it first to score the winner.

▲ The USA celebrate qualifying for a third consecutive Olympic Final.

Third time lucky for Brazil

Pampeloponnisiako, Patras
23.08.2004, 21:00, **1,511**

SWEDEN	0-1	BRAZIL
		Pretinha 64

Dianne Ferreira-James GUY · Jackeline Saez PAN & María Isabel Tovar MEX

SWE • Jönsson - Larsson, Westberg, Marklund, Bengtsson (Öqvist 86) - Sjöström (Andersson 78), Moström (c), Östberg, Sjögran (Schelin 72) - Ljungberg, Svensson. *Domanski Lyfors*
BRA • Andréia - Mônica, Juliana (c), Tânia - Elaine, Daniela, Formiga ■ 61, Rosana (Maycon 79) - Pretinha (Renata Costa 87), Cristiane, Marta. *Simões*

Veteran striker Pretinha scored in the second half to send Brazil into their first Olympic Final, dispatching the Swedish team that had knocked them out in the quarter-finals of the previous year's World Cup. Brazil began strongly but were kept at bay by Caroline Jönsson. The Swedes fought their way back into the game, relying on counter-attacks, and went close through midfielder Anna Sjöström. But Marika Domanski Lyfors' players could not live with Brazil's rhythm or the technical prowess and speed of young forwards Cristiane and Marta, the former who announced her arrival on the world stage at this tournament. The deadlock was broken just past the hour mark. A sensational through ball from Marta unlocked the Swedish defence and was matched by a great finish from an acute angle by Pretinha. It was the Rio de Janeiro native's second goal of the tournament and one she later recalled as among her fondest memories. The Swedes pressed for an equaliser but Brazil were not to be denied a place in their first world Final. Consolation for Sweden came later in the shape of the FIFA Fair Play Award which they shared with Japan.

▼▼ Brazil and Sweden take the field before their semi-final in Patras.

▼▼ Pretinha (17) scored a second-half goal against Sweden which secured a first-ever Final appearance for the Brazilians.

2004 Bronze Medal Match

Karaiskaki, Athens
26.08.2004, 18:00, **10,416**

GERMANY 🇩🇪 **1-0** 🇸🇪 **SWEDEN**

Lingor 17

Kari Seitz USA
Denise Robinson CAN & María Isabel Tovar MEX

Theune-Meyer

1 Rottenberg
2 Stegemann
17 Hingst
4 Jones
13 Minnert (Günther 56)
3 Garefrekes
10 Lingor
6 Odebrecht (Omilade 56)
16 Pohlers
9 Prinz (c)
8 Wimbersky (Fuss 83)

Domanski Lyfors

11 Svensson (Sjögran 43)
10 Ljungberg ■ 68
8 Östberg
9 Andersson (c)
6 Moström
17 Sjöström (Fagerström 46)
5 Bengtsson (Schelin 76)
10 Törnqvist
4 Marklund
7 Larsson
1 Jönsson

▶ Germany's Birgit Prinz (9) takes on Sweden's Sara Larsson (7). The match was a rerun of the previous year's World Cup Final.

Bronze part two for Germany

A goal by Renate Lingor early in the first half clinched bronze for Germany, ending Sweden's hopes of a medal to add to the silver won at the 2003 World Cup. The two countries had been evenly matched during the 1990s, but the Germans were now beginning to steal a march. Their previous encounter had been the 2003 World Cup Final, won by Tina Theune-Meyer's side in Carson, California. This match, played at the Karaiskaki as part of a double-header with the Final, made it six competitive wins in a row. The game's only goal came early on and it was elegant in its simplicity. Ariane Hingst played a crossfield ball out of defence to Sandra Minnert, whose precise 40-metre ball forward picked out Conny Pohlers on the left wing. Her pull-back found Lingor, whose first-time shot beat Caroline Jönsson – but only just as the Swedish keeper got an arm to it but only succeeded in helping the ball into the net. The Swedes were always dangerous. A few minutes later, Frida Östberg saw her header from a free kick brilliantly tipped over the bar by Silke Rottenberg in the German goal. Marika Domanski Lyfors brought Therese Sjögran off the bench just before half-time, and then Linda Fagerström and Lotta Schelin in the second half to try and break their opponents down, but Germany stood firm to win bronze for the second Olympics in succession.

▶ Germany celebrate winning bronze for the second Olympics running.

2004 Gold medal match

▲ Abby Wambach (16) celebrates scoring the winning goal in the 2004 Olympic Final.

Wambach seals gold for America

Going into the match, history certainly favoured the USA. In the 20 meetings prior to the Final, they had beaten Brazil 17 times and lost just once – in 1997. But Brazil's young squad were not intimidated as they had scored 14 goals in their five games leading up to the Final. The Americans, on the other hand, had experience on their side and were determined to send the USA's "Fab Five" golden generation of Brandi Chastain, Joy Fawcett, Julie Foudy, Mia Hamm and Kristine Lilly home with one last gold medal. "We were shouldering the burden of losing in 2003," coach April Heinrichs recalled of how the USA entered the Olympics as a changed team after the World Cup – a little more committed and more motivated than before. Four years on from their extra-time golden-goal loss to Norway, the Americans were driven in Athens. "They were never content to be the best in the world," Heinrichs said. "They wanted to prove it again." From the start Brazil pressed – a Rosana shot went just over the bar – keeping the more experienced, albeit slower, USA scrambling to gain possession. The Americans, however, went into the break ahead. A rasping shot from 25 metres out saw Lindsay Tarpley break the deadlock after 39 minutes, having been set up by Chastain – a goal worthy of any Final. The Brazilians refused to let their heads drop and almost equalised before half-time, Cristiane forcing a fantastic save from Briana Scurry after a goalmouth scramble following a free kick. Brazil kept the pressure up in the second half as Mônica earned a caution for a cynical challenge on Hamm, and their persistence was rewarded 17 minutes before the end when Cristiane beat Fawcett to Formiga's long ball forward and her cross was prodded home by Pretinha after Scurry could only knock it into her path. Brazil twice went agonisingly close to clinching the game, with Cristiane and Pretinha both hitting the post, but the game went into extra time. There was a replacement referee for extra time, with fourth official Dianne Ferreira-James on for the injured Jenny Palmqvist, and for the second Olympic Final in a row, Heinrichs had to gear up her team for one last push. This time it worked. Although Brazil continued to dominate the game, Abby Wambach had the best chance of the first additional period. And then in the second, a clearing header from Mônica following a free kick went out for a corner. Lilly found Wambach deep in the area, and the striker headed home to give the "Fab Five" their golden send-off.

2004 Gold Medal Match

Karaiskaki, Athens
26.08.2004, 21:00, 10,416

USA 2-1 BRAZIL
AET

Tarpley 39, Wambach 112   Pretinha 73

Jenny Palmqvist SWE (Dianne Ferreira-James GUY 90)
Emilia Parviainen FIN & Nelly Viennot FRA

▼ The Brazil team before the Final. Back row (left to right): Elaine, Daniela, Formiga, Tânia, Mônica and Andréia. Front row: Rosana, Cristiane, Marta, Pretinha and Juliana.

Gold medal match 2004

▲ Cristiane (12) was joint top scorer at the 2004 Olympics but in the Final she could not add to her five goals.

▲ Mia Hamm (red shirt) played her final tournament match for the USA in the 2004 Olympic Final. Despite being only six years her junior, Formiga (7) was still playing 17 years later at the Tokyo Olympics.

The end of an era

Athens 2004 was a final hurrah for a number of players from the early years of world competition. The gold medal match was an emotional farewell for Brandi Chastain, Joy Fawcett, Julie Foudy and Mia Hamm, all of whom had been in the 1988 team that had travelled to China for the International Women's Football Tournament. True pioneers. Among their legacies was building a dominant USA team that had won hearts and minds back home. But the USA were not the only team that experienced a changing of the guard. Other teams saw their pioneers of the 1990s hang up their boots to make way for the younger generation, chief among them Brazil's Pretinha. There was a farewell too for Nigeria's star playmaker Mercy Akide, who had ushered the Super Falcons through their first two Olympic campaigns. With other superstars like China's Sun Wen also having retired and with Norway having failed to qualify, a new page had been turned in the history of women's football.

2

April Heinrichs (left) had been the first captain to lift the World Cup back in 1991 and here she became the first female coach to lead her side to Olympic gold – a unique double.

◀ The USA team celebrate winning gold in Athens. Seven of the team had also won gold in Atlanta.

2007

Four years later than planned, China hosted the finals again. But as in 1991, they lost 1-0 in the quarter-finals. In this decade, Germany won every World Cup and European Championship. They retained the global title by beating Brazil 2-0 in Shanghai, Birgit Prinz scoring a record 14th finals goal. Nadine Angerer, who didn't concede a goal in the tournament, saved a penalty from Marta, the World Player of the Year.

China suffers the blues

▼ Chinese girls looking forward to the World Cup.

This was the third major tournament to be played in China following on from the 1988 International Women's Football Tournament and the first World Cup in 1991. The hosts had hoped that hosting the finals in 2003 would culminate in the team finally winning the trophy, but the SARS outbreak had ended those dreams and by the time the 2007 finals came along, the pioneers like Sun Wen who had come so close in 1996 and 1999 were gone. The landscape for women's football was changing rapidly. Just before the finals kicked off, Laos became the 168th country to play an official international, a big increase on the 138 who had played a match before the 2003 finals. FIFA member associations were finding that investing in women's football quickly produced dividends. The standards still varied hugely among nations, but pioneers like China were finding their status challenged. The growing interest in the game had been fed by the World Cup and Olympic tournaments and for the 2007 finals 115 nations entered. It was no longer good enough to rely on talented individuals. Women's football was being professionalised at a rapid pace and the results were there to see in the 2007 finals.

2007 Overview

CHINA 2007

FIFA WOMEN'S WORLD CUP CHINA 2007

Story of the qualifiers

Familiar faces

This was the only World Cup apart from the first in 1991 where there were no newcomers present. 2006 had seen Africa, Asia and the Americas stage their continental championships, all of which served as qualifiers for the 2007 World Cup. Nigeria beat Ghana in the African Final, with both qualifying at the expense of Cameroon and South Africa, as had been the case four years earlier. There was a major shift in the dynamic of qualifying from Asia with Australia's move from Oceania to Asia. The Australians hosted the AFC Women's Asian Cup and reached the Final, where they lost on penalties to the already qualified China. Third-placed North Korea also qualified, as did fourth-placed Japan, who beat Mexico 3-2 on aggregate in a play-off. The Mexicans had finished third in the Concacaf Women's Gold Cup, a tournament won by the USA who beat Canada 2-1 with the 35-year-old Kristine Lilly scoring a 120th-minute winning penalty. In South America, Argentina caused a major sensation when they beat Brazil into second place, the only time the Brazilians have not won the title. In Oceania, without Australia, New Zealand made easy work of winning the 2007 OFC Women's Championship, beating Papua New Guinea 7-0 in the decisive match. There was a major upgrade to the European qualifying tournament where the elite division was expanded from 16 to 25 nations to take into account the rise in standards of the middle-ranked nations. That meant five groups of five teams with just the winners qualifying: Norway, Sweden, Denmark, Germany and England. Despite once again being unable to beat their great rivals, England gained revenge for their 2003 elimination by beating the French into second place in their group.

▲ The official 2007 World Cup pennant.
FIFA Museum Collection

Golden Ball

Marta BRA

Silver Ball: Birgit Prinz GER
Bronze Ball: Cristiane BRA

Group stage

GROUP A	GROUP B	GROUP C	GROUP D
GER 11-0 ARG	USA 2-2 PRK	GHA 1-4 AUS	NZL 0-5 BRA
JPN 2-2 ENG	NGA 1-1 SWE	NOR 2-1 CAN	CHN 3-2 DEN
ARG 0-1 JPN	SWE 0-2 USA	CAN 4-0 GHA	DEN 2-0 NZL
ENG 0-0 GER	PRK 2-0 NGA	AUS 1-1 NOR	BRA 4-0 CHN
GER 2-0 JPN	NGA 0-1 USA	NOR 7-2 GHA	CHN 2-0 NZL
ENG 6-1 ARG	PRK 1-2 SWE	AUS 2-2 CAN	BRA 1-0 DEN

	W	D	L	+	–	PTS
GER	2	1	0	13	0	7
ENG	1	2	0	8	3	5
JPN	1	1	1	3	4	4
ARG	0	0	3	1	18	0

	W	D	L	+	–	PTS
USA	2	1	0	5	2	7
PRK	1	1	1	5	4	4
SWE	1	1	1	3	4	4
NGA	0	1	2	1	4	1

	W	D	L	+	–	PTS
NOR	2	1	0	10	4	7
AUS	1	2	0	7	4	5
CAN	1	1	1	7	4	4
GHA	0	0	3	3	15	0

	W	D	L	+	–	PTS
BRA	3	0	0	10	0	9
CHN	2	0	1	5	6	6
DEN	1	0	2	4	4	3
NZL	0	0	3	0	9	0

Knockout stages

QUARTER-FINAL	QUARTER-FINAL	QUARTER-FINAL	QUARTER-FINAL
GER 3-0 PRK	USA 3-0 ENG	NOR 1-0 CHN	BRA 3-2 AUS

SEMI-FINAL	SEMI-FINAL
GER 3-0 NOR	USA 0-4 BRA

MATCH FOR THIRD PLACE
NOR 1-4 USA

FINAL
GER 2-0 BRA

Overview 2007

16 TEAMS

GERMANY WINNERS

BRA SECOND — USA THIRD

1 190 971 SPECTATORS **37 218** AVERAGE PER MATCH

HUA MULAN OFFICIAL MASCOT

OFFICIAL LOGO

32 MATCHES PLAYED

77 YELLOW CARDS

2 RED CARDS

111 GOALS

3.47 AVERAGE GOALS PER MATCH

TEAMGEIST BLUE OFFICIAL MATCH BALL

Host cities and stadiums

Beyond Guangzhou

China may have already hosted two international tournaments, but this was the first time that any matches had been staged beyond Guangzhou and the province of Guangdong. In the build-up to the 2008 Beijing Olympics, there was no place for the capital Beijing in the line-up, so the stage was left to China's biggest city Shanghai to stage both the opening ceremony and the Final.

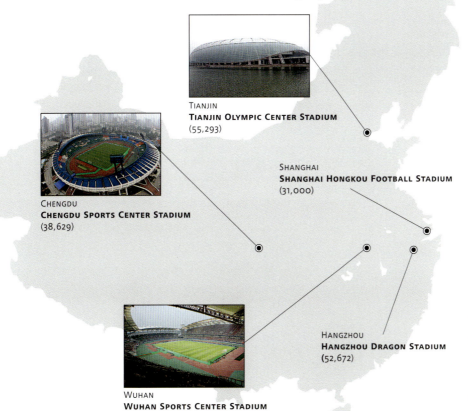

TIANJIN
TIANJIN OLYMPIC CENTER STADIUM
(55,293)

CHENGDU
CHENGDU SPORTS CENTER STADIUM
(38,629)

SHANGHAI
SHANGHAI HONGKOU FOOTBALL STADIUM
(31,000)

HANGZHOU
HANGZHOU DRAGON STADIUM
(52,672)

WUHAN
WUHAN SPORTS CENTER STADIUM
(52,357)

×7

Golden Boot

Marta BRA

Silver Boot: Abby Wambach USA ×6
Bronze Boot: Ragnhild Gulbrandsen SWE ×6

127

2007 Group stage

Shanghai Hongkou Football Stadium, Shanghai
10.09.2007, 20:00, **28,098**

GERMANY 🇩🇪 **11-0** 🇦🇷 **ARGENTINA**

Behringer (2) 12 24,
Garefrekes 17
Prinz (3) 29 45+1 59
Lingor (2) 51 90+1
Smisek (3) 57 70 79

Tammy Ogston AUS
Airlie Keen AUS & Sarah Ho AUS

GER • 1 Nadine **Angerer** - 2 Kerstin **Stegemann**, 13 Sandra **Minnert**, 17 Ariane **Hingst**, 6 Linda **Bresonik** - 14 Simone **Laudehr** ■ 60 (3 Saskia **Bartusiak** 74 ■ 86), 10 Renate **Lingor** - 18 Kerstin **Garefrekes** (11 Anja **Mittag** 84), 9 Birgit **Prinz** (c), 7 Melanie **Behringer** (20 Petra **Wimbersky** 68) - 8 Sandra **Smisek**. *Silvia Neid*
ARG • 12 Vanina **Correa** - 2 Eva **González** (c) ■ 56 - 3 Valeria **Cotelo**, 6 Celeste **Barbitta**, 4 Gabriela **Chávez** ■ 20 - 8 Clarisa **Huber** (15 Florencia **Mandrile** 74), 13 María **Quiñones** ■ 90+2, 17 Fabiana **Vallejos**, 11 Rosana **Gómez** ■ 16 (20 Mercedes **Pereyra** 66) - 18 María **Potassa**, 19 Analía **Almeida** (7 Ludmila **Manicler** 53). *Carlos Borrello*

Shanghai Hongkou Football Stadium, Shanghai
11.09.2007, 20:00, **27,146**

JAPAN 🇯🇵 **2-2** 🏴󠁧󠁢󠁥󠁮󠁧󠁿 **ENGLAND**

Miyama (2) 55 90+5   K Smith (2) 81 83

Kari Seitz USA
María Isabel Tovar MEX & Rita Muñoz MEX

JPN • 1 Miho **Fukumoto** - 3 Yukari **Kinga** (13 Kozue **Ando** 46), 2 Hiromi **Isozaki** (c) (17 Yuki **Nagasato** 86), 15 Azusa **Iwashimizu**, 20 Rumi **Utsugi** - 8 Tomoe **Sakai**, 7 Tomomi **Miyamoto** (6 Ayumi **Hara** 71), 16 Aya **Miyama** - 9 Eriko **Arakawa**, 10 Homare **Sawa**, 18 Shinobu **Ohno**. *Hiroshi Ohashi*
ENG • 1 Rachel **Brown** - 2 Alex **Scott** (20 Lindsay **Johnson** 89), 6 Mary **Phillip**, 5 Faye **White** (c), 3 Casey **Stoney** - 4 Katie **Chapman** ■ 23 - 11 Rachel **Yankey**, 10 Kelly **Smith** ■ 90+4, 7 Karen **Carney** - 9 Eniola **Aluko** (16 Jill **Scott** 74). *Hope Powell*

Shanghai Hongkou Football Stadium, Shanghai
14.09.2007, 17:00, **27,730**

ARGENTINA 🇦🇷 **0-1** 🇯🇵 **JAPAN**

                 Nagasato 90+1

Dagmar Damkova CZE
Tempa Ndah BEN & Souad Oulhaj MAR

ARG • 1 Romina **Ferro** - **González** (c) - Mandrile, 14 Catalina **Pérez**, Chávez - Huber (16 Andrea **Ojeda** 53), Quiñones (10 Emilia **Mendieta** 61), Vallejos, Pereyra - Potassa (Manicler 77), Almeida. *Borrello*
JPN • Fukumoto - Ando (Kinga 79), Isozaki (c) ■ 57, Iwashimizu, 4 Kyoko **Yano** (Utsugi 58) - Sakai, Miyamoto, Miyama - Nagasato, Sawa, Ohno (Arakawa 57). *Ohashi*

Shanghai Hongkou Football Stadium, Shanghai
14.09.2007, 20:00, **27,730**

ENGLAND 🏴󠁧󠁢󠁥󠁮󠁧󠁿 **0-0** 🇩🇪 **GERMANY**

Jenny Palmqvist SWE
Susanne Borg SWE & Hege Steinlund NOR

ENG • Brown - Phillip, White (c), 12 Anita **Asante**, Stoney - Chapman ■ 16, J Scott - A Scott, Williams ■ 55, Carney (Yankey 57) - K Smith. *Powell*
GER • Angerer - Stegemann, 5 Annike **Krahn** ■ 36, Hingst, Bresonik - Laudehr ■ 84, Lingor - Garefrekes, Prinz (c), Behringer (19 Fatmire **Bajramaj** 63 ■ 85) - Smisek. *Neid*

Hangzhou Dragon Stadium, Hangzhou
17.09.2007, 20:00, **39,817**

GERMANY 🇩🇪 **2-0** 🇯🇵 **JAPAN**

Prinz 21
Lingor 87p

Adriana Correa COL
Cristina Cini ITA & Rosa Canales ECU

GER • Angerer - Stegemann, Krahn, Hingst, Bresonik - Wimbersky, Lingor - Garefrekes ■ 82, Prinz (c), Behringer (Bajramaj 57) - Smisek (16 Martina **Müller** 78 ■ 88). *Neid*
JPN • Fukumoto - Kinga, Isozaki (c), Iwashimizu, Utsugi - Sakai ■ 16, 5 Miyuki **Yanagita**, Miyama (Arakawa 46) (Ohno 63), Hara - Nagasato (Miyamoto 76), 10 Sawa. *Ohashi*

Chengdu Sports Center Stadium, Chengdu
17.09.2007, 20:00, **30,730**

ENGLAND 🏴󠁧󠁢󠁥󠁮󠁧󠁿 **6-1** 🇦🇷 **ARGENTINA**

González OG 9, J Scott 10,   González 60
Williams 50p,
K Smith (2) 64 77
Exley 90p

Dianne Ferreira-James GUY
Cindy Mohammed TRI & Cynette Jeffery GUY

ENG • Brown - Phillip, White (c), Asante, Stoney - Williams ■ 61, J Scott - A Scott ■ 4 (15 Sue **Smith** 68), K Smith (19 Vicky **Exley** 80), Yankey - Aluko (17 Jody **Handley** 80). *Powell*
ARG • Ferro - González (c) ■ 42 - Mandrile, Pérez ■ 41 ■ 49 ■ 49, Chávez - Huber (Cotelo 52), Quiñones (Mendieta 76), Vallejos, Pereyra - Potassa, Almeida (9 Natalia **Gatti** 62). *Borrello*

Group A

	W	D	L	+	–	PTS
GER	2	1	0	13	0	7
ENG	1	2	0	8	3	5
JPN	1	1	1	3	4	4
ARG	0	0	3	1	18	0

▶ England returned for a second World Cup appearance, 12 years after their first.

11-0

Germany made history in their opening match against Argentina when they recorded the first double-figure score at the World Cup or Olympics.

▶ Germany's Sandra Smisek (8) scored a hat-trick against Argentina, as did Birgit Prinz, only the second time in World Cup history that two hat-tricks had been scored in one game.

England prevent a 100% tournament record for Germany

The sight of China legend Sun Wen rising skyward on a mechanical lift to place a silver ball atop a giant replica Women's World Cup trophy was a breathtaking moment in a dazzling opening ceremony in Shanghai that included fireworks, dance, music and song. The match that followed was no less spectacular, Sandra Smisek and captain Birgit Prinz hitting hat-tricks as Silvia Neid's reigning champions Germany secured a then competition record 11-0 win over an Argentina side shorn of captain Marisa Gerez and talismanic forward Mariela Coronel. England, meanwhile, had been absent from the world stage for 12 years and looked set to mark their return with a victory when Kelly Smith bagged two sublime goals in three minutes with either foot against Japan, kissing each boot in celebration. But Japan's own flair player and scorer of their opening goal, Aya Miyama, devastated Hope Powell's side with a free-kick leveller in the 95th minute. It took an injury-time winner from Yuki Nagasato for Japan to beat Argentina, who showed glimpses of the form that had seen them take Brazil's South American crown in qualifying. Germany were unbeaten in 16 encounters with England, including a 1995 World Cup quarter-final, with Neid wearing the captain's armband and Powell warming the bench, but England held their own here as the two sides played out the competition's first-ever goalless group match. The field was wide open, but the two old rivals would progress. England were knockout-bound after an eventful 6-1 win over Argentina that saw Eva González net for both teams, Catalina Pérez red-carded and postwoman Vicky Exley score from the spot. Germany were through too, as Prinz broke Michelle Akers' record of 12 Women's World Cup goals and Renate Lingor scored to seal victory over an ever-improving Japan.

Group stage 2007

Group B

	W	D	L	+	–	PTS
USA	2	1	0	5	2	7
PRK	1	1	1	5	4	4
SWE	1	1	1	3	4	4
NGA	0	1	2	1	4	1

◀ Sweden's Caroline Seger in an aerial dual with North Korea's Ri Un Gyong (12). Ri Kum Suk (10) and Nilla Fischer (18) look on.

Sweden suffer first group stage knockout

All four teams had been uneven group rivals in 2003, but with key veterans retiring and promising stars taking centre stage, every point was hard-fought in China. North Korea claimed one against the USA, with U-20 world champions Kil Son Hui and Kim Yong Ae both scoring while Abby Wambach, who had just bagged her 78th goal in USA colours, was off the pitch having a head wound stitched. Coach Greg Ryan had gambled with ten players for nine minutes, but Wambach eventually returned and Heather O'Reilly equalised soon after. Cynthia Uwak, one of Nigeria's seven U-20 quarter-finalists, vowed to "walk tall" at her Damallsvenskan club Falköping after levelling for the African champions against Thomas Dennerby's Sweden. Both sides were staring into the abyss after Wambach hit the 2003 silver medallists with two goals in Chengdu and Nigeria lost 2-0 to North Korea, whose captain Ri Kum Suk finally scored her first goal in her third World Cup. Sweden's stylish striker Lotta Schelin scored twice in a 2-1 thriller to beat North Korea, but the Asians progressed on goal difference behind the USA, Lori Chalupny's 54-second goal defeating Nigeria in a close-run match.

◀ America's match winner Lori Chalupny (17) is sent flying by Nigeria's Lilian Cole. This was the third successive World Cup that the two nations had been grouped together.

Chengdu Sports Center Stadium, Chengdu
11.09.2007, 17:00, **35,100**

USA 🇺🇸 **2-2** 🇰🇵 **KOREA DPR**

Wambach 50   Kil Son Hui 58
O'Reilly 69   Kim Yong Ae 62

Nicole Petignat SUI
Corinne Lagrange FRA & Karine Vives Solana FRA

USA • 18 Hope **Solo** - 3 Christie **Rampone** ■ 45, 15 Kate **Markgraf**, 4 Cat **Whitehill**, 14 Stephanie **Lopez** - 7 Shannon **Boxx**, 11 Carli **Lloyd**, 17 Lori **Chalupny** - 9 Heather **O'Reilly** (6 Natasha **Kai** 90+2), 20 Abby **Wambach**, 13 Kristine **Lilly** (c). *Greg Ryan*

PRK • 21 Jon Myong Hui - 5 Song Jong Sun, 15 Sonu Kyong Sun, 16 Kong Hye Ok, 3 Om Jong Ran - 2 Kim Kyong Hwa, 12 Ri Un Gyong, 8 Kil Son Hui - 10 Ri Kum Suk (c), 9 Ri Un Suk, 7 Ho Sun Hui (17 Kim Yong Ae 22) (19 Jong Pok Sim 90 ■ 90+1). *Kim Kwang Min*

Chengdu Sports Center Stadium, Chengdu
11.09.2007, 20:00, **35,100**

NIGERIA 🇳🇬 **1-1** 🇸🇪 **SWEDEN**

Uwak 82   Svensson 50

Niu Huijun CHN
Liu Hongjuan CHN & Fu Hongjue CHN

NGA • 1 Precious **Dede** - 14 Faith **Ikidi**, 16 Ulumma **Jerome**, 13 Christie **George** (c), 5 Onome **Ebi** - 11 Chi-Chi **Igbo** (7 Stella **Mbachu** 35), 15 Maureen **Mmadu** (2 Efioanwan **Ekpo** 59), 10 Rita **Chikwelu**, 18 Cynthia **Uwak** - 4 Perpetua **Nkwocha**, 8 Ifeanyichukwu **Chiejine**. *Ntiero Effiom*

SWE • 1 Hedvig **Lindahl** - 16 Anna **Paulson**, 4 Hanna **Marklund**, 3 Stina **Segerström**, 13 Frida **Östberg** - 15 Therese **Sjögran** ■ 12, 6 Sara **Thunebro**, 5 Caroline **Seger** - 8 Lotta **Schelin** (20 Linda **Forsberg** 83), 11 Victoria **Svensson** (c), 10 Hanna **Ljungberg** (14 Sara **Johansson** 69). *Thomas Dennerby*

Chengdu Sports Center Stadium, Chengdu
14.09.2007, 17:00, **35,600**

SWEDEN 🇸🇪 **0-2** 🇺🇸 **USA**

    Wambach (2) 34p 58

Gyöngyi Gaál HUN
María Luisa Villa Gutiérrez ESP & Cristina Cini ITA

SWE • Lindahl - Paulson, Marklund, Segerström ■ 34 (9 Therese **Lundin** 81), Östberg - Sjögran (18 Nilla **Fischer** 65), Forsberg, Seger ■ 90+3 - Schelin, Svensson (c), Ljungberg. *Dennerby*

USA • Solo - Rampone, Markgraf, Whitehill, Lopez - Lloyd (Boxx 46), 12 Leslie **Osborne**, Chalupny - 5 Lindsay **Tarpley** (O'Reilly 67), Wambach, Lilly (c). *Ryan*

Chengdu Sports Center Stadium, Chengdu
14.09.2007, 20:00, **35,600**

KOREA DPR 🇰🇵 **2-0** 🇳🇬 **NIGERIA**

Kim Kyong Hwa 17
Ri Kum Suk 21

Tammy Ogston AUS
Airlie Keen AUS & Sarah Ho AUS

PRK • Jon Myong Hui - Song Jong Sun, Sonu Kyong Sun, Kong Hye Ok, Om Jong Ran - Kim Kyong Hwa (Jong Pok Sim 77), Ri Un Gyong, Kil Son Hui - Ri Kum Suk (c) ■ 77, Ri Un Suk, Kim Yong Ae. *Kim Kwang Min*

NGA • Dede - Ikidi, Jerome ■ 52, George (c), Ebi (19 Lilian **Cole** 30) - Mbachu, Ekpo, Chikwelu (Mmadu 61), Uwak - Chiejine ■ 35 (Igbo 80), Nkwocha. *Effiom*

Shanghai Hongkou Football Stadium, Shanghai
18.09.2007, 20:00, **6,100**

NIGERIA 🇳🇬 **0-1** 🇺🇸 **USA**

    Chalupny 1 (54 secs)

Mayumi Oiwa JPN
Hisae Yoshizawa JPN & Liu Hsiu Mei TPE

NGA • Dede - Ikidi, Jerome, George (c), Cole ■ 14 - Mbachu, Ekpo, Chikwelu, Uwak (9 Ogonna **Chukwudi** 83) - Igbo (Chiejine 22), Nkwocha. *Effiom*

USA • Solo - Rampone (8 Tina **Ellertson** 77), Markgraf, Whitehill, Lopez - Boxx, Lloyd (Osborne 64), Chalupny - O'Reilly, Wambach, Lilly (c) (Tarpley 84). *Ryan*

Tianjin Olympic Center Stadium, Tianjin
18.09.2007, 20:00, **33,196**

KOREA DPR 🇰🇵 **1-2** 🇸🇪 **SWEDEN**

Ri Un Suk 22   Schelin (2) 4 54

Christine Beck GER
Irina Mirt ROU & Miriam Dräger GER

PRK • Jon Myong Hui ■ 88 - Song Jong Sun, Sonu Kyong Sun, Kong Hye Ok, Om Jong Ran - Kim Kyong Hwa (20 **Hong** Myong Gum 56), Ri Un Gyong, Kil Son Hui (6 **Kim** Ok Sim 85) - Ri Kum Suk (c), Ri Un Suk, Kim Yong Ae ■ 32 (Jong Pok Sim 60). *Kim Kwang Min*

SWE • Lindahl - Paulson (Johansson 69), Marklund, 2 Karolina **Westberg**, Östberg ■ 31 - Sjögran, Fischer, Seger - Schelin ■ 82, Svensson (c), Ljungberg (Thunebro 40) (Lundin 89). *Dennerby*

2007 Group stage

Hangzhou Dragon Stadium, Hangzhou
12.09.2007, 17:00, **30,752**

GHANA 1-4 AUSTRALIA

Amankwa 70   Walsh 15
              De Vanna (2) 57 81
              Garriock 69

Adriana Correa COL
Rosa Canales ECU & María Luisa Villa Gutiérrez ESP

GHA • 16 Memunatu **Sulemana** - 13 Yaa **Avoe** (20 Belinda **Kanda** 67), 12 Olivia **Amoako**, 2 Aminatu **Ibrahim**, 3 Mavis **Danso** - 15 Lydia **Ankrah**, 21 Memuna **Darku**, 6 Florence **Okoe**, 9 Anita **Amenuku** (17 Hamdya **Abass** 67) - 10 Adjoa **Bayor** (c), 18 Anita **Amankwa**. *Isaac Paha*

AUS • 1 Melissa **Barbieri** - 19 Clare **Polkinghorne** (13 Thea **Slatyer** 83), 2 Kate **McShea** ■ 87, 5 Cheryl **Salisbury** (c) ● 90, 4 Dianne **Alagich** - 15 Sally **Shipard**, 14 Collette **McCallum**, 10 Joanne **Peters** (3 Alicia **Ferguson** 62), 7 Heather **Garriock** - 9 Sarah **Walsh** ■ 53, 8 Caitlin **Munoz** (11 Lisa **De Vanna** 46). *Tom Sermanni SCO*

Hangzhou Dragon Stadium, Hangzhou
12.09.2007, 20:00, **30,752**

NORWAY 2-1 CANADA

R Gulbrandsen 52   Chapman 33
Stangeland Horpestad 81

Christine Beck GER
Irina Mirt ROU & Miriam Dräger GER

NOR • 1 Bente **Nordby** - 3 Gunhild **Følstad**, 7 Trine **Rønning**, 2 Ane **Stangeland Horpestad** (c), 5 Siri **Nordby** (6 Camilla **Huse** 46) - 21 Lene **Storløkken** (18 Marie **Knutsen** 76), 4 Ingvild **Stensland**, 8 Solveig **Gulbrandsen** - 11 Leni **Larsen Kaurin**, 16 Ragnhild **Gulbrandsen**, 10 Melissa **Wiik** (17 Lene **Mykjåland** 66). *Bjarne Berntsen*

CAN • 18 Erin **McLeod** - 2 Kristina **Kiss**, 10 Martina **Franko**, 11 Randee **Hermus**, 6 Tanya **Dennis** - 9 Candace **Chapman** (13 Amy **Walsh** 73), 19 Sophie **Schmidt**, 8 Diana **Matheson** - 15 Kara **Lang** (21 Jodi-Ann **Robinson** 83), 12 Christine **Sinclair** (c), 14 Melissa **Tancredi** (7 Rhian **Wilkinson** 46). *Even Pellerud NOR*

Hangzhou Dragon Stadium, Hangzhou
15.09.2007, 17:00, **33,835**

CANADA 4-0 GHANA

Sinclair (2) 16 62
Schmidt 55, Franko 77

Nicole Petignat SUI
Corinne Lagrange FRA & Karine Vives Solana FRA

CAN • McLeod - Kiss, Franko, Hermus, Dennis ■ 8 - Chapman, Schmidt, Matheson (5 Andrea **Neil** 84) - Lang (Wilkinson 63), Sinclair (c), 16 Katie **Thorlakson** (Robinson 45). *Pellerud NOR*

GHA • Sulemana - Avoe (Abass 35), Amoako ■ 78, Ibrahim, Danso - 14 Rumanatu **Tahiru**, Darku (Ankrah 77), Okoe, 11 Gloria **Foriwa** ■ 39 - Bayor (c) (7 Safia **Abdul** 71), Amankwa ■ 21. *Paha*

Hangzhou Dragon Stadium, Hangzhou
15.09.2007, 20:00, **33,835**

AUSTRALIA 1-1 NORWAY

De Vanna 83   R Gulbrandsen 5

Niu Huijun CHN
Liu Hongjuan CHN & Fu Hongjue CHN

AUS • Barbieri - 16 Lauren **Colthorpe** (Munoz 76), Slatyer, Salisbury (c), Alagich - Ferguson, McCallum, 17 Danielle **Small** (De Vanna 46), Garriock - 12 Kate **Gill** (Walsh 61), 20 Joanne **Burgess**. *Sermanni SCO*

NOR • B Nordby - Følstad, Rønning, Stangeland Horpestad (c), Huse - M Knutsen, Stensland, S Gulbrandsen (Storløkken 86) - Larsen Kaurin (14 Guro **Knutsen** 74), R Gulbrandsen, Wiik (Mykjåland 46). *Berntsen*

Hangzhou Dragon Stadium, Hangzhou
20.09.2007, 17:00, **43,817**

NORWAY 7-2 GHANA

Storløkken 4   Bayor 73, Okoe 80p
R Gulbrandsen (3) 39 59 62
Stangeland Horpestad 45p,
Herlovsen 56, Klaveness 69

Jennifer Bennett USA
Corinne Lagrange FRA & Karine Vives Solana FRA

NOR • B Nordby - S Nordby, 19 Marit Fiane **Christensen**, Stangeland Horpestad (c), Huse - Storløkken, Stensland, S Gulbrandsen (15 Madeleine **Giske** 46) - Larsen Kaurin (20 Lise **Klaveness** 61), R Gulbrandsen, Mykjåland (9 Isabell **Herlovsen** 46). *Berntsen*

GHA • 1 Gladys **Enti** (Sulemana 64) - Avoe, Amoako, Ibrahim ■ 15, Danso - Tahiru, 4 Doreen **Awuah** (Darku 58), Okoe, Amenuku (8 Sheila **Okai** 46 ■ 80) - Bayor (c), Amankwa. *Paha*

Chengdu Sports Center Stadium, Chengdu
20.09.2007, 17:00, **29,300**

AUSTRALIA 2-2 CANADA

McCallum 53   Tancredi 1 (32 secs)
Salisbury 90+2 Sinclair 85

Gyöngyi Gaál HUN
María Luisa Villa Gutiérrez ESP & Susanne Borg SWE

AUS • Barbieri - Colthorpe (De Vanna 46), McShea, Salisbury (c), Alagich - Shipard, McCallum ■ 90, Peters (Ferguson 76), Garriock - Walsh, Munoz (Burgess 62). *Sermanni SCO*

CAN • McLeod (20 Taryn **Swiatek** 79) - Wilkinson, Franko, Hermus ■ 89, Dennis - Chapman, Schmidt, Matheson - Lang (17 Brittany **Timko** 90+2), Sinclair (c), Tancredi (Robinson 68). *Pellerud NOR*

Group C

	W	D	L	+	-	PTS
NOR	2	1	0	10	4	7
AUS	1	2	0	7	4	5
CAN	1	1	1	7	4	4
GHA	0	0	3	3	15	0

Last-minute drama for Australia

Familiar faces dominated as returning Australia boss Tom Sermanni and Norway striker Ragnhild Gulbrandsen made World Cup comebacks in a thrilling group. Roared on by 30,000 spectators in Hangzhou, Australia finally won a Women's World Cup match, Heather Garriock scoring her third-ever finals goal in a 4-1 win over Ghana, with impressive teenager Anita Amankwa pulling one back for the Black Queens. Journalist Gulbrandsen, who had retired in 2005 through injury, scored on her return as Norway overcame their 1995 World Cup-winning coach Even Pellerud and his tight-knit Canada side, who had been in residency together since January. Canada kept pace with a 4-0 win over Ghana, captain Christine Sinclair netting twice to top her country's Women's World Cup scoring charts. With a second in two games, Gulbrandsen was flying, but so was Australia substitute Lisa De Vanna, who twisted and turned defenders inside out before hitting a crushing late equaliser. "Sensational game," enthused Sermanni, as was his team's thrilling clash with Canada. Chengdu erupted as 33-year-old captain Cheryl Salisbury's stoppage-time equaliser against the Canadians saw Australia progress along with Norway. The Norwegians crushed Ghana 7-2, with Gulbrandsen scoring the 500th World Cup goal on her way to a hat-trick.

▶ Ghana goalkeeper Memunatu Sulemana thwarts Australia's captain Cheryl Salisbury while Aminatu Ibrahim (2) looks on.

▶▶ Australia celebrate in style. A last-minute goal in their final match against Canada saw them through to the quarter-finals at the expense of the Canadians.

▶ Canada's Erin McLeod tips a Ghanaian effort over the bar in her side's 4-0 win over the Africans.

7

Norway's win against Ghana was the fifth time in four successive World Cups that the Norwegians had scored at least seven goals in a match.

Group stage 2007

Group D

	W	D	L	+	–	PTS
BRA	3	0	0	10	0	9
CHN	2	0	1	5	6	6
DEN	1	0	2	4	4	3
NZL	0	0	3	0	9	0

◀ Cristiane (11) celebrates her goal against New Zealand. It was the first of five goals she scored at her first World Cup, equalling the tally she scored at the 2004 Olympics.

Brazil stun the hosts

Brazil's new coach Jorge Barcellos brought 15 players with World Cup experience to China. With no World Cup outing for New Zealand in 16 years, boss John Herdman was limited to one, Wendi Henderson. With eight youth internationals in the squad, the Oceania champions were a team in the making and they had no answer to Brazil's Daniela, Cristiane, Renata Costa and two-goal Marta, losing a tough opener 5-0. China had fallen six places in the world ranking since 2003, but new coach Marika Domanski Lyfors had targeted a top-four finish here and "Daredevil" Song Xiaoli's 88th-minute winner kept them on track in a five-goal thriller with Denmark in their opener. Kenneth Heiner-Møller's side had been unsettled by an alleged spying incident at their training ground and hotel before that seventh consecutive finals defeat. They bounced back against New Zealand, trained nurse Cathrine Paaske Sørensen scoring her second in two games. Marta hit her fourth as she and Cristiane inflicted China's biggest Women's World Cup defeat in 22 matches with a 4-0 victory. The hosts recovered to beat New Zealand though, securing a knockout spot alongside Brazil, winners through an injury-time lob from Pretinha in Denmark's best, but last performance of the tournament.

4-0 China suffered the biggest defeat by a host nation when they lost to Brazil in Wuhan.

▼ Despite their defeat by Brazil, China's Bi Yan could still celebrate finishing second in the group.

▼ Denmark captain Katrine Pedersen scores from a free kick in the 2-0 victory over New Zealand. The Danes lost their two other matches to very late goals.

Wuhan Sports Center Stadium, Wuhan
12.09.2007, 17:00, **50,800**

NEW ZEALAND 0-5 **BRAZIL**

Daniela 10, Cristiane 54, Marta () 74 90+3
Renata Costa 86

⚑ Pannipar Kamnueng THA
🚩 Hisae Yoshizawa JPN & Liu Hsiu Mei TPE

NZL • 1 Jenny **Bindon** - 5 Abby **Erceg**, 15 Maia **Jackman**, 6 Rebecca **Smith** (c), 16 Emma **Humphries** (7 Zoe **Thompson** 72) - 4 Katie **Hoyle** (18 Priscilla **Duncan** 66) - 2 Ria **Percival** ■ 25, 8 Hayley **Moorwood**, 19 Emily **McColl**, 13 Ali **Riley** - 9 Wendi **Henderson** (17 Rebecca **Tegg** 46). John Herdman ENG

BRA • 1 **Andréia** - 3 **Aline** (c), 5 Renata **Costa**, 4 **Tânia** - 16 **Simone**, 8 **Formiga**, 20 **Ester**, 9 **Maycon** (6 **Rosana** 78) - 11 **Cristiane** (18 **Pretinha** 84), 7 **Daniela**, 10 **Marta**. Jorge Barcellos

Wuhan Sports Center Stadium, Wuhan
12.09.2007, 20:00, **50,800**

CHINA PR 3-2 **DENMARK**

Li Jie 30, Bi Yan 50   Eggers Nielsen 51
Song Xiaoli 88   Paaske Sørensen 87

⚑ Dianne Ferreira-James GUY
🚩 Cindy Mohammed TRI & Cynette Jeffery GUY

CHN • 18 **Han** Wenxia - 4 **Wang** Kun, 3 **Li** Jie (c) (16 **Liu** Yali 90+3), 11 **Pu** Wei, 15 **Zhou** Gaoping (19 **Zhang** Ying 68) - 6 **Xie** Caixia ■ 89, 8 **Pan** Lina, 7 **Bi** Yan, 12 **Qu** Feifei (5 **Song** Xiaoli 58) - 10 **Ma** Xiaoxu, 9 **Han** Duan. Marika Domanski Lyfors SWE

DEN • 1 Heidi **Johansen** - 2 Mia **Olsen**, 4 Gitte **Andersen**, 3 Katrine **Pedersen** (c), 5 Bettina **Falk** - 15 Mariann **Gajhede** (12 Stine **Dimun** 75), 10 Anne Dot **Eggers Nielsen** - 8 Julie **Rydahl Bukh**, 7 Cathrine **Paaske Sørensen** ■ 80, 13 Johanna **Rasmussen** (11 Merete **Pedersen** 75) - 9 Maiken **Pape** ■ 86. Kenneth Heiner-Møller

Wuhan Sports Center Stadium, Wuhan
15.09.2007, 17:00, **54,000**

DENMARK 2-0 **NEW ZEALAND**

K Pedersen 61
Paaske Sørensen 66

⚑ Mayumi Oiwa JPN
🚩 Hisae Yoshizawa JPN & Kim Kyoung Min KOR

DEN • Johansen - Olsen, Andersen, K Pedersen (c), Falk - Gajhede (Pape 46), Eggers Nielsen - Rydahl Bukh, Paaske Sørensen (17 Janne **Madsen** 86), Rasmussen (20 Camilla **Sand** 72) - M Pedersen. Heiner-Møller

NZL • Bindon ■ 90+2 - Erceg ■ 88, Jackman ■ 60, R Smith (c), 11 Marlies **Oostdam** - Duncan - Percival (Humphries 70), Moorwood (10 Annalie **Longo** 87), McColl, Riley - Henderson (Tegg 64). Herdman ENG

Wuhan Sports Center Stadium, Wuhan
15.09.2007, 20:00, **54,000**

BRAZIL 4-0 **CHINA PR**

Marta (2) 42 70
Cristiane (2) 47 48

⚑ Jennifer Bennett USA
🚩 Maria Isabel Tovar MEX & Rita Muñoz MEX

BRA • Andréia - Aline (c) ■ 41, Renata Costa ■ 61, Tânia - 2 **Elaine**, Formiga (Simone 89), Ester, Maycon - Cristiane (15 **Kátia** 85), Daniela ■ 10 (Rosana 79), Marta. Barcellos

CHN • Han Wenxia - Wang Kun, Li Jie, Pu Wei ■ 27, Liu Yali (Zhou Gaoping 57) - Xie Caixia (17 **Liu** Sa 67), Pan Lina (20 **Zhang** Tong 52 ■ 53), Bi Yan, Song Xiaoli - Ma Xiaoxu, Han Duan (c). Domanski Lyfors SWE

Tianjin Olympic Center Stadium, Tianjin
20.09.2007, 20:00, **55,832**

CHINA PR 2-0 **NEW ZEALAND**

Li Jie 57
Xie Caixia 79

⚑ Dagmar Damkova CZE
🚩 Souad Oulhaj MAR & Hege Steinlund NOR

CHN • 1 **Zhang** Yanru - Wang Kun, Li Jie, Pu Wei (c), Zhou Gaoping (Liu Yali 65 ■ 72) - Xie Caixia, Pan Lina (Zhang Tong 60), Bi Yan, 14 **Zhang** Ouying (Liu Sa 88) - Ma Xiaoxu, Han Duan. Domanski Lyfors SWE

NZL • Bindon - Erceg, Jackman, R Smith (c), Oostdam - Duncan ■ 56 - Percival (20 Merissa **Smith** 73), Moorwood ■ 25, McColl (14 Simone **Ferrara** 82), Riley - Henderson (Thompson 62). Herdman ENG

Hangzhou Dragon Stadium, Hangzhou
20.09.2007, 20:00, **43,817**

BRAZIL 1-0 **DENMARK**

Pretinha 90+1

⚑ Kari Seitz USA
🚩 Maria Isabel Tovar MEX & Rita Muñoz MEX

BRA • Andréia - Simone, 13 **Mônica** ■ 76, Tânia - Elaine, Formiga (c), Ester, Maycon - Cristiane (Pretinha 61), Daniela (Rosana 88), Marta. Barcellos

DEN • Johansen - Olsen, Andersen, K Pedersen (c) ■ 42, 18 Christina **Ørntoft** - Gajhede (M Pedersen 79), Eggers Nielsen - Rydahl Bukh (Rasmussen 65), Paaske Sørensen, Sand (Dimun 65) - Pape. Heiner-Møller

2007 Quarter-finals

Inexperienced Koreans undone by Germany

Wuhan Sports Center Stadium, Wuhan
22.09.2007, 17:00, **37,200**

GERMANY 3-0 KOREA DPR

Garefrekes 44
Lingor 67
Krahn 72

Tammy Ogston AUS
Sarah Ho AUS & Airlie Keen AUS

GER • Angerer - Stegemann, Krahn, Hingst, Bresonik (Minnert 77) - Laudehr, Lingor - Garefrekes, Prinz (c), Behringer - Smisek (Müller 74). *Neid*

PRK • Jon Myong Hui - Song Jong Sun ■ 51, Sonu Kyong Sun, Kong Hye Ok, Om Jong Ran - Hong Myong Gum (Jong Pok Sim 74), Ri Un Gyong, Kil Son Hui - Ri Kum Suk (c), Ri Un Suk, Kim Yong Ae (Kim Kyong Hwa 50). *Kim Kwang Min*

▲ Annike Krahn scored the third goal in Germany's 3-0 win over North Korea in Wuhan.

▲ Twelve years on from her first World Cup appearance, Germany's Birgit Prinz took the captain's armband at the 2007 finals in China.

A talented squad that featured six under-20 world champions, three under-16s and just four players with senior World Cup experience had at last delivered North Korea's first knockout spot in three finals. To make another historic leap, Kim Kwang Min's side would need to overturn the reigning world and European champions, whose defence was yet to concede in this tournament. Kim Yong Ae and captain Ri Kum Suk came close to testing Nadine Angerer's goal, but North Korea were always chasing the game after Kerstin Garefrekes had outmuscled their defence to curl in Germany's first. Renate Lingor finished a neat one-two with Sandra Smisek for their second. A fluky third off the thigh of U-19 Women's World Championship-winning skipper Annike Krahn was the icing on the cake for Germany, who celebrated as one with a circular can-can dance at full time.

England fall to second-half American onslaught

Tianjin Olympic Center Stadium, Tianjin
22.09.2007, 20:00, **29,586**

USA 3-0 ENGLAND

Wambach 48, Boxx 57, Lilly 60

Jenny Palmqvist SWE ▼ Susanne Borg SWE & Hege Steinlund NOR

USA • Solo - Rampone, Markgraf, Whitehill, Lopez - Boxx (Lloyd 82), Osborne, Chalupny - O'Reilly, Wambach (Kai 86), Lilly (c). *Ryan*

ENG • Brown - Phillip (18 Lianne **Sanderson** 80), White (c), Asante, Stoney - A Scott, Chapman, J Scott, Carney - K Smith, Aluko (Yankey 46). *Powell*

Last beaten by England in 1988 and yet to lose a Women's World Cup quarter-final, history was on the side of the Americans as they faced the English in Tianjin. Yet having held their opponents to a draw in the Four Nations Tournament in January, an England team packed with Arsenal's newly crowned UEFA Women's Cup champions were brimming with confidence. The two sides departed the first half having matched each other on the pitch and in the injury stakes, England skipper Faye White nursing a broken nose, USA defender Stephanie Lopez with a stapled head wound. A punishing 12-minute second-half goal rush would kill England off though, Abby Wambach marking her 100th appearance with a towering header, Shannon Boxx scoring with a long, low shot and 36-year-old captain Kristine Lilly capitalising on a mistake by keeper Rachel Brown to become the oldest scorer in Women's World Cup history until Formiga in 2015.

▶ Abby Wambach (20) opens the scoring for the USA in their 3-0 quarter-final victory over England.

▶▶ Thoughts of what might have been. England coach Hope Powell comforts Karen Carney.

Quarter-finals 2007

◀ Norway's Bente Nordby had to be at her best as Norway battled to preserve their slender lead against hosts China.

▲ Tears for the hosts. China's Wang Kun after the defeat at the hands of Norway.

◀ Leni Larsen Kaurin takes on China's Han Duan (9) in Norway's quarter-final victory in Wuhan.

China's quarter-final home jinx

Wuhan Sports Center Stadium, Wuhan
23.09.2007, 17:00, **52,000**

NORWAY 1-0 **CHINA PR**

Herlovsen 32

⚽ Gyöngyi Gaál HUN
🚩 María Luisa Villa Gutiérrez ESP & Cristina Cini ITA
NOR • B Nordby - Følstad ■ 59, Rønning ■ 85, Stangeland Horpestad (c), Huse - M Knutsen, Stensland, S Gulbrandsen (Storløkken 75) - Larsen Kaurin (Klaveness 64), R Gulbrandsen ■ 83, Herlovsen (Fiane Christensen 90+3). *Berntsen*
CHN • Zhang Yanru - Wang Kun ■ 69, Li Jie, Pu Wei, Liu Yali - Xie Caixia (Zhang Ouying 71), Pan Lina, Bi Yan (c), Zhang Tong (Liu Sa 75) - Ma Xiaoxu, Han Duan. *Domanski Lyfors SWE*

Bodies were put on the line, the woodwork rattled, the keepers tested time and again and the noisy crowd of 52,000 given plenty of reason to bang their drums and blow their whistles. A goal from 19-year-old Isabell Herlovsen settled it though, in her first start of the tournament and with her less favoured left foot. Two years earlier, a 16-year-old Herlovsen had scored as Norway eliminated Marika Domanski Lyfors' Sweden from Euro 2005. This time she helped end the 47-year-old's run with China. Domanski Lyfors had revitalised her new charges after being appointed as their first foreign coach in March. She and assistant Pia Sundhage had improved their fitness and increased the competition for places while teaching them Swedish football terms and playing fun motivational training games. A quarter-final berth had been their reward, but it was not the finale that the hosts or their coach had hoped for.

Australia test Brazil to the limit

Tianjin Olympic Center Stadium, Tianjin
23.09.2007, 20:00, **35,061**

BRAZIL 3-2 **AUSTRALIA**

Formiga 4   De Vanna 36
Marta 23p   Colthorpe 68
Cristiane 75

⚽ Christine Beck GER
🚩 Irina Mirt ROU & Miriam Dräger GER
BRA • Andréia - Aline (c), Renata Costa, Tânia - Elaine, Formiga (Simone 90+2), Ester, Maycon - Cristiane, Daniela, Marta. *Barcellos*
AUS • Barbieri - Colthorpe, Slatyer, Salisbury (c) (McShea 20), Alagich - Shipard (Munoz 78 ■ 85), McCallum, Peters ■ 63 (Burgess 81), Garriock - Walsh, De Vanna. *Sermanni SCO*

▶ Action from the Brazil v Australia quarter-final in Tianjin involving Heather Garriock (7), Formiga (8), Elaine (2) and Sally Shipard (15). Australia pulled back from 2-0 down but Cristiane scored a late winner.

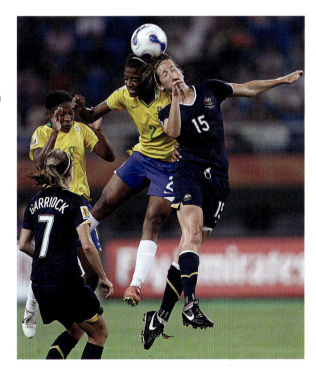

"We want to put a stamp on the World Cup," goalkeeper Melissa Barbieri had said ahead of China 2007, and with their fast passing game and last-gasp goals, Australia had done just that. Tom Sermanni was back for his second spell as head coach after managing in the USA's professional WUSA league, but he and his players were in unknown territory against Olympic silver medallists Brazil. One down after just four minutes to a Formiga thunderbolt from distance, they needed all of their "never-say-die" spirit when FIFA Women's World Player of the Year Marta made it 2-0 from the penalty spot. Live-wire striker Lisa De Vanna threw them a lifeline when she pounced on a poor backpass to become the first player to beat Andréia in China and Lauren Colthorpe became the second with a bullet header. But Wolfsburg striker Cristiane's sublime turn and shot won the game for Brazil.

2007 Semi-finals

▲ Norway keeper Bente Nordby can't prevent Kerstin Stegemann's shot making it 2-0 to Germany.

◀ Norway's Ragnhild Gulbrandsen (left) and Germany's Annike Krahn during the semi-final in Tianjin.

Norway succumb to Germany – again

Tianjin Olympic Center Stadium, Tianjin
26.09.2007, 20:00, **53,819**

GERMANY 🇩🇪 **3-0** 🇳🇴 **NORWAY**

Rønning OG 42, Stegemann 72, Müller 75

Dagmar Damkova CZE Irina Mirt ROU & Cristina Cini ITA

GER • Angerer - Stegemann, Krahn, Hingst, Bresonik (Minnert 81) - Laudehr, Lingor - Garefrekes, Prinz (c), Behringer (Bajramaj 40) - Smisek (Müller 65). *Neid*
NOR • B Nordby - Følstad (S Nordby 48), Rønning, Stangeland Horpestad (c), Huse - M Knutsen, Stensland, S Gulbrandsen (Storløkken 56) - Larsen Kaurin ■ 14, R Gulbrandsen, Herlovsen (Klaveness 46). *Berntsen*

Norway coach Bjarne Berntsen had led his side to a European Final in 2005, only to be thwarted by Germany, whereas Silvia Neid had captained Germany to the Women's World Cup Final in 1995, only to be denied by Norway. The two sides had drawn a friendly in Mainz just 27 days earlier, and now they were set to renew their old rivalry in Tianjin on the biggest stage of all. Norway's European finalist Solveig Gulbrandsen, back in action after the birth of her son, knew how tough it would be. "Germany is as difficult as it gets," she said. Norway edged the first half until Lady Luck came calling for Germany as defensive rock Trine Rønning accidentally headed Birgit Prinz's cross beyond Bente Nordby just before the break. "It was the crucial turning point," said Berntsen afterwards. Kerstin Stegemann's deflected goal after 72 minutes was the real energy sapper for Norway though, and it was game over when Martina Müller swooped on a poor backpass to fire in the 100th goal of the tournament three minutes later. "If we fail to defend the trophy now," said defender Ariane Hingst, "we'll only have ourselves to blame."

The USA in disarray

10
The number of matches in which Nicole Petignat refereed at the World Cup – a record. The USA v Brazil semi-final was her last.

▶ Leslie Osborne (12) and Formiga challenge for the ball in Brazil's historic 4-0 semi-final win over the USA. It was America's heaviest defeat at either the Olympics or World Cup.

Hangzhou Dragon Stadium, Hangzhou
27.09.2007, 20:00, **47,818**

USA 🇺🇸 **0-4** 🇧🇷 **BRAZIL**

Osborne OG 20, Marta (2) 27 79, Cristiane 56

Nicole Petignat SUI Karine Vives Solana FRA & Corinne Lagrange FRA

USA • 1 Briana **Scurry** - Rampone, Markgraf (2 Marian **Dalmy** 74), Whitehill, Lopez (Lloyd 46) - Boxx ■ 14 ■ 45+1 ■ 45+1, Osborne, Chalupny ■ 26 - O'Reilly (Ellertson 60), Wambach ■ 49, Lilly (c). *Ryan*
BRA • Andréia - Aline (c) ■ 28, Renata Costa ■ 45, Tânia - Elaine, Formiga, Ester, Maycon - Cristiane, Daniela, Marta. *Barcellos*

▼ Shannon Boxx is sent off just before half-time. By then the USA were 2-0 down to the Brazilians.

"Marta! Marta!" chanted the fans as a stadium packed with almost 48,000 spectators hailed the world-class striker and the part she had played in the biggest defeat in the USA's history. Brazil were out for revenge after losing the 2004 Olympic gold medal match to the Americans in extra time. Former NASL player Greg Ryan had taken charge since then, and even without the iconic players of previous campaigns, his side were unbeaten in 51 matches. Hope Solo had played her part, but Ryan selected 1999 World Cup winner Briana Scurry for this tie. "Bri has beaten Brazil the last two times we've played them," he said, but Brazil would not be beaten in Hangzhou. Ahead after Leslie Osborne turned Formiga's corner into her own net, they went in at the break two goals and one player up after Marta had skipped past two defenders to beat Scurry at the near post and midfielder Shannon Boxx had been red-carded. On their return, Brazil danced their way around their opponents, an unmarked Cristiane picking her spot for their third before Marta flicked a cute ball around Tina Ellertson, wrong-footed Cat Whitehill and blasted in the killer fourth. It was, quite simply, a Brazilian masterclass.

2007 Match for Third Place

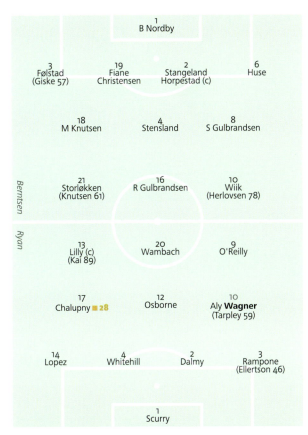

13 – lucky for some

From the 1988 International Women's Football Tournament through three Olympics to the match for third place at the 2007 World Cup, the USA played 50 matches. **KRISTINE LILLY PLAYED IN EVERY SINGLE ONE OF THEM!** That bears repeating … all 50 of them. There simply has been no one quite like her, and for every one of those games she wore the number 13 shirt. Unlucky for some, but not Kristine Lilly.

▶ Abby Wambach (20) scored twice in the 4-1 victory over Norway to help secure third place for the USA.

Wambach restores American pride

"This match is our chance to get back on the field and show our country and our fans how we can play soccer," declared veteran of five World Cups Kristine Lilly as the USA sought to put their humiliating loss to Brazil behind them. Preparations had been overshadowed by Hope Solo's public criticism of coach Greg Ryan's decision to drop her against Brazil and although the shot-stopper had apologised, it had been a distraction. Skipper Lilly sought to bring focus though, and Abby Wambach rose to the challenge with her fifth and sixth goals of the tournament. In 1991, a teenage Bente Nordby had watched from the bench as the USA beat her side to the inaugural title. Norway's first-choice keeper in four tournaments since, she was in the thick of the action in Shanghai as Wambach pounced with a back-heeled goal on the half-hour and a tap-in a mere 47 seconds after the re-start. Once Lori Chalupny and Heather O'Reilly had scored within a minute of one another, the tie was effectively over. Several World Cup careers would end here too, goalkeepers Nordby and Briana Scurry making their last finals appearances, and Ragnhild Gulbrandsen bowing out having scored her sixth goal of the tournament. Lilly, the world's most-capped footballer, bade the World Cup farewell too, earning deserved applause in the 89th minute having played in every one of the USA's 30 Women's World Cup matches, winning two gold medals and now, three bronze.

▼ By beating Norway in Shanghai, the USA maintained their record of finishing in the top three at the World Cup, a sequence that was broken only in 2023.

2007 World Cup Final

Shanghai Hongkou Football Stadium, Shanghai
30.09.2007, 20:00, **31,000**

GERMANY 2-0 **BRAZIL**

Prinz 52, Laudehr 86 (Marta penalty saved 64)

Tammy Ogston AUS · María Isabel Tovar MEX & Rita Muñoz MEX

▲ Birgit Prinz scored the opening goal of the 2007 World Cup Final. Here the striker takes on Brazil's Elaine.

Germany at the double

Marta had dazzled with her tricks and flicks, and Birgit Prinz had consigned Michelle Akers' World Cup goalscoring record to history. As Germany stood straight-lined and focused while waiting to enter the pitch in Shanghai and Brazil sprang on their heels and sang, the stage was set for a spectacular finale. Both sides had cause to feel confident. The cool and unflappable Germans had bagged 19 goals and conceded none on their way to a record third Final. Stylish and skilful Brazil had lit up the tournament in one of the most exciting semi-finals yet. A clash of styles lay ahead, but when the trophy was presented and the golden ticker tape rained down, only one team would be dancing with delight. "There's no way we can match the Brazilians player for player," coach Silvia Neid had said ahead of the tie. "What we have to do is give them as little space as possible." Brazil still found a way through though, Daniela forcing Nadine Angerer into action early on, and later unleashing a fine volley that crashed back off the post. But with Renate Lingor dictating Germany's play, the reigning champions came close too, Kerstin Garefrekes blasting into the side netting and Sandra Smisek nearly finishing off a neat move with a lofted shot that went over the bar. Goalless at the break, the teams flew into action on their return, and when Kerstin Stegemann launched a long pass into the box, Smisek laid the ball back to Prinz and the first woman to play in three Finals side-footed home. Then Brazil had a breakthrough, or so they thought, when Cristiane won a penalty after being felled in the box by Linda Bresonik. Tournament top scorer Marta stepped up and took the kick but watched in dismay as the agile Angerer saved it. Just over three minutes later, the Germany No.1 launched herself at Daniela's goal-bound free kick, touching it onto the post. Angerer had beaten Italy keeper Walter Zenga's 1990 World Cup record of playing 517 minutes without letting in a single goal. Brazil would concede once more, U-19 Women's World Championship winner Simone Laudehr with a perfectly timed header from Lingor's corner four minutes from time to see unbeaten Germany become the first team to win back-to-back Women's World Cup titles. "It was the perfect tournament," winning manager Neid would later recall. "Not a single goal against us, that will never happen again, it was sensational."

◀▲ Germany midfielder Simone Laudehr (14) takes on Brazil's Tânia and Maycon. Laudehr scored a late goal to seal the match for Germany.

◀◀ Marta's duel with Germany goalkeeper Nadine Angerer was one of the key features of the 2007 Final. Angerer's save from Marta's penalty meant that the keeper did not concede a single goal in the six matches Germany played at the tournament.

Final 2007

▲ Germany coach Silvia Neid had been Tina Theune-Meyer's assistant in the 2003 World Cup winning team.

▶ Germany's Birgit Prinz lifts the FIFA Women's World Cup Trophy.

3

Germany's Birgit Prinz was the first player to appear in three World Cup Finals – in 1995, 2003 and 2007. Team-mates Sandra Smisek and Sandra Minnert were in the squads for all three tournaments but did not play in all of the Finals.

> **" I just can't believe it. I have just won the World Cup and I am only 21. I can't believe I'm in the team – and I've scored a goal in a World Cup Final! "**
>
> SIMONE LAUDEHR

▶ The Germany team celebrate their historic triumph – the first team to successfully retain the World Cup.

◀ Marta sits disconsolately after losing the Final against Germany. It was her only appearance in a World Cup Final.

▲ "Brazil, we need support." After their World Cup Final defeat, the Brazilian players made a tearful plea to all Brazilians to get behind the team.

0

The number of goals conceded by Germany at the 2007 World Cup. No team has ever matched this feat at either the World Cup or the Olympics.

2008

Just eleven months after the 2007 World Cup in China, the world's best female players were back in the country for the 2008 Beijing Olympics. Brazil made it to their third Final in a row, but having lost the 2004 Olympic Final and then the 2007 World Cup Final, they were beaten once again. In a repeat of the 2004 gold medal match, they lost to the USA, Carli Lloyd scoring the only goal of the game to give the Americans their third Olympic title.

China puts on a show

▼ Jamaican athlete Usain Bolt was one of the stars of the Beijing Olympics.

Right from the spectacular opening ceremony with its synchronised drummers and extraordinary fireworks display, through to the amazing feats of Usain Bolt and Michael Phelps, these Olympics left a lasting impression. In a throwback to the great state-sponsored sporting showpieces of the past, the Chinese left nothing to chance. The pollution of Beijing was cleared for the Games, with emissions from factories and cars strictly controlled for the duration. China also topped the medal table for the first time in history, but it was two athletes from the Americas who stole the headlines. Phelps won eight golds in the pool, beating the record set in 1972 by fellow American Mark Spitz, while Jamaica's Usain Bolt smashed the world record in both the 100 and 200 metres. It was a Games for breaking records – more than 40 in total with just one women's event in the pool not seeing an Olympic or world record broken. In football, history repeated itself as Argentina's men matched the American women by winning successive golds, Lionel Messi inspiring his side to a 1-0 win over Nigeria in the Final.

2008 **Overview**

BEIJING 2008

WOMEN'S OLYMPIC FOOTBALL TOURNAMENT

Story of the qualifiers

England miss out again

As one of the three highest-ranked European teams at the 2007 World Cup, England should have by rights booked their place at the Beijing Olympics, and although there was talk of the English competing under the banner of Great Britain, the plan never got off the ground. Instead, a play-off was staged to see who would join Germany and Norway in Beijing. Sweden and Denmark were the two European teams that failed to make it out of their groups at the World Cup, and so they played off home and away. Both matches were won by the Swedes, 4-2 in Viborg and 3-1 at the Råsunda. In South America, Argentina were able to make the most of their 2006 continental title as they qualified directly for Beijing. That left Brazil facing a one-match play-off in Beijing against Ghana, who had finished second to Nigeria in an extensive qualifying competition played over 17 months. That was comfortably won 5-1 by the Brazilians, with Marta and Cristiane continuing their remarkable Olympic scoring feats with three of the goals between them. The 2007 Pacific Games were used for qualifying in Oceania, with the winners of that, Papua New Guinea, playing a one-off tie at home to New Zealand, which the Kiwis won 2-0. There were full-blown qualifying tournaments in both Concacaf and Asia, with the USA beating Canada on penalties in the Final of a tournament played in Mexico. With China having qualified automatically as hosts, there were two places up for grabs for Asia, which went to Japan and North Korea, who finished top of their groups in an eight-team final tournament played home and away.

▲ Beijing 2008 was the fourth time in 20 years that China had hosted a tournament for the world's best female players.

Overview 2008

12 TEAMS: ARG, BRA, CAN, CHN, GER, JPN, NGA, NOR, NZL, PRK, SWE, USA

USA WINNERS
BRA SECOND
GER THIRD

Top of the medal table

CHINA PR	48	22	30
UNITED STATES	36	39	37
RUSSIA	24	13	23
GREAT BRITAIN	19	13	18
GERMANY	16	11	14
AUSTRALIA	14	15	17

740 014 SPECTATORS
28 462 AVERAGE PER MATCH

26 MATCHES PLAYED
45 YELLOW CARDS
0 RED CARDS

66 GOALS
2.54 AVERAGE GOALS PER MATCH

TEAMGEIST2 MAGNUS MOENIA OFFICIAL MATCH BALL

Host cities and stadiums

16 and counting

The 2008 Olympics took the total number of stadiums in China used for women's world tournaments to 16. Seven were used in the greater Guangzhou metropolitan area during the 1988 International Women's Football Tournament and the 1991 World Cup. Five different cities were used during the 2007 World Cup with three more added during the 2008 Olympics: Qinhuangdao, Shenyang and host city Beijing, where the Final was played. The Tianjin Olympic Center Stadium was the only venue used in both 2007 and 2008 while the Shanghai Stadium was chosen over the Hongkou Stadium in Shanghai, which had hosted the Final in 2007.

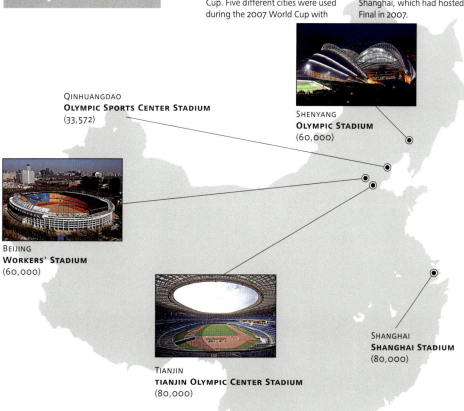

QINHUANGDAO
OLYMPIC SPORTS CENTER STADIUM
(33,572)

SHENYANG
OLYMPIC STADIUM
(60,000)

BEIJING
WORKERS' STADIUM
(60,000)

TIANJIN
TIANJIN OLYMPIC CENTER STADIUM
(80,000)

SHANGHAI
SHANGHAI STADIUM
(80,000)

×5

Top scorer

Cristiane BRA

Second Place: Angela Hucles USA ×4
Third Place: Marta BRA ×3

2008 **Fans**

Group stage 2008

Group E

◀ Chinese goalkeeper Zhang Yanru repels a Canadian attack in the 1-1 draw in Tianjin. China finished top of the group.

	W	D	L	+	-	PTS
CHN	2	1	0	5	2	7
SWE	2	0	1	4	3	6
CAN	1	1	1	4	4	4
ARG	0	0	3	1	5	0

Hosts China ease through

The People's Republic of China welcomed the world's elite to the Beijing Women's Olympic Football Tournament just 11 months after they had hosted the Women's World Cup. Shang Ruihua, who led China at the 1988 International Women's Football Tournament and at the first World Cup, was appointed head coach in April 2008 after a management shake-up with a mission to build team unity, enhance technical precision and reach the semi-finals. His players upset Sweden in their opening match with goals by attacking duo Xu Yuan and Han Duan. Olympic newcomers Argentina and Canada squared off as defender Candace Chapman's 27th-minute goal – the tournament's first – and Kara Lang's late header clinched a Canadian victory. Sweden made up for their opening defeat with a win over Argentina thanks to a Nilla Fischer goal, her first at the Olympics, while Canada skipper Christine Sinclair notched her own first Olympic goal in the team's draw with the hosts. China finished top of the group with a decisive win over Argentina thanks in part to an own goal by *La Albiceleste* midfielder Maria Quiñones. With the exception of this match, all group games were won by a single goal. Sweden finished second after a win over Canada, and the third-placed Canadians also progressed to the quarter-finals.

Olympic Center Stadium, Tianjin
6.08.2008, 17:00, **23,201**

ARGENTINA 1-2 **CANADA**
Manicler 85   Chapman 27
                       Lang 72

Christine Beck GER
María Luisa Villa Gutiérrez ESP & Inka Müller GER

ARG • 18 Vanina **Correa** - 6 Gabriela **Chávez**, 2 Eva **González**, 13 Maria **Quiñones** ▪ 71, 4 Florencia **Mandrile** (3 Yesica **Arrien** 90+1) - 11 Fabiana **Vallejos**, 10 Mariela **Coronel**, 5 Marisa **Gerez** (c), 15 Mercedes **Pereyra** (8 Emilia **Mendieta** 79) - 9 Maria **Potassa** (7 Ludmila **Manicler** 56), 16 Maria **Blanco**. *Carlos Borrello*

CAN • 18 Erin **McLeod** - 7 Rhian **Wilkinson**, 9 Candace **Chapman**, 10 Martina **Franko**, 3 Emily **Zurrer** - 6 Sophie **Schmidt**, 8 Diana **Matheson** (17 Brittany **Timko** 80), 4 Clare **Rustad** - 15 Kara **Lang**, 14 Melissa **Tancredi** (2 Jodi-Ann **Robinson** 42) (16 Jonelle **Filigno** 83), 12 Christine **Sinclair** (c). *Even Pellerud NOR*

Olympic Center Stadium, Tianjin
6.08.2008, 19:45, **37,902**

CHINA PR 2-1 **SWEDEN**
Xu Yuan 6   Schelin 38
Han Duan 72

Hong Eun Ah KOR
Sarah Ho AUS & Jacqueline Leleu AUS

CHN • 1 Zhang **Yanru** - 14 Liu **Huana**, 3 Li **Jie** (c), 5 Weng **Xinzhi**, 15 Zhou **Gaoping** - 11 Pu **Wei**, 7 Bi **Yan**, 6 Zhang **Na**, 4 Zhang **Ying** (16 Wang **Dandan** 57) - 9 Han **Duan** (12 Lou **Jiahui** 83 ▪ 88), 8 Xu **Yuan**. *Shang Ruihua*

SWE • 1 Hedvig **Lindahl** - 13 Frida **Östberg**, 7 Sara **Larsson**, 17 Charlotte **Rohlin** ▪ 87, 6 Sara **Thunebro** - 18 Nilla **Fischer** (9 Jessica **Landström** 76) - 14 Josefine **Öqvist** (16 Linda **Forsberg** 73), 5 Caroline **Seger**, 15 Therese **Sjögran** (10 Johanna **Almgren** 83) - 8 Lotta **Schelin**, 11 Victoria **Svensson** (c). *Thomas Dennerby*

Olympic Center Stadium, Tianjin
9.08.2008, 17:00, **38,293**

SWEDEN 1-0 **ARGENTINA**
Fischer 58

Dianne Ferreira-James GUY
Rita Muñoz MEX & Mayte Chávez MEX

SWE • Lindahl - 4 Anna **Paulson**, Larsson, Rohlin (3 Stina **Segerström** 90+1), Thunebro - Östberg, Fischer, Seger (Landström 80), Sjögran (Forsberg 71) - Schelin, Svensson (c). *Dennerby*

ARG • Correa - Chávez (Arrien 46), González, Quiñones, Mandrile - Vallejos, Gerez (c), Coronel, Pereyra (Mendieta 58) - Blanco (Potassa 62), Manicler. *Borrello*

Olympic Center Stadium, Tianjin
9.08.2008, 19:45, **52,600**

CANADA 1-1 **CHINA PR**
Sinclair 34   Xu Yuan 36

Dagmar Damková CZE
Irina Mirt ROU & Katarzyna Nadolska POL

CAN • McLeod - 11 Randee **Hermus** (Timko 63), Chapman, Franko, Zurrer ▪ 87 - Schmidt, Matheson (Robinson 74), Rustad - Wilkinson, Lang (Filigno 90), Sinclair (c). *Pellerud NOR*

CHN • Zhang Yanru ▪ 87 - Liu Huana (Wang Dandan 73), Li Jie (c), Weng Xinzhi, Zhou Gaoping - Pu Wei (17 Gu **Yasha** 46), Bi Yan, Zhang Na, Zhang Ying - Lou Jiahui (10 Liu **Sa** 88), Xu Yuan. *Shang Ruihua*

Olympic Sports Center Stadium, Qinhuangdao
12.08.2008, 19:45, **31,492**

CHINA PR 2-0 **ARGENTINA**
Quiñones OG 52
Gu Yasha 90

Nicole Petignat SUI
Cristina Cini ITA & Karine Vives Solana FRA

CHN • 18 Han **Wenxia** - Liu Huana, Li Jie (c), Weng Xinzhi, Zhou Gaoping - Pu Wei, Bi Yan, Zhang Na (Lou Jiahui 46), Zhang Ying (Gu Yasha 88) - Han Duan (Liu Sa 78), Xu Yuan. *Shang Ruihua*

ARG • Correa - Chávez, González ▪ 59, Quiñones - Vallejos (Mendieta 81), Gerez (c), Coronel, Mandrile - Manicler (Blanco 70), 14 Andrea **Ojeda** (Potassa 64), Pereyra. *Borrello*

◀ Lotta Schelin (left) celebrates with Therese Sjögran (15) and Victoria Svensson after the second of her two goals against Canada in the match that decided who finished second in the group. Sweden won 2-1 but the Canadians also qualified for the quarter-finals as one of the two best third-placed teams.

Workers' Stadium, Beijing
12.08.2008, 19:45, **51,112**

SWEDEN 2-1 **CANADA**
Schelin (2) 19 51   Tancredi 63

Pannipar Kamnueng THA
Widiya Shamsuri MAS & Ja Daw Kaw MYA

SWE • Lindahl - Östberg, Larsson, Rohlin, Thunebro (Paulson 86) - Forsberg, Fischer (Landström 27), Seger, Sjögran - Schelin, Svensson (c). *Dennerby*

CAN • McLeod - Wilkinson, Chapman, Franko, Zurrer (5 Robyn **Gayle** 81) - Rustad, Matheson, Schmidt (13 Amy **Walsh** 46), Lang - Tancredi, Sinclair (c) (Robinson 67). *Pellerud NOR*

143

2008 Group stage

Olympic Stadium, Shenyang
6.08.2008, 17:00, **20,703**

GERMANY 0-0 **BRAZIL**

🟡 Kari Seitz USA
🏳 Marlene Duffy USA & Veronica Perez USA

GER • 1 Nadine **Angerer** - 2 Kerstin **Stegemann**, 5 Annike **Krahn**, 17 Ariane **Hingst**, 6 Linda **Bresonik** - 18 Kerstin **Garefrekes**, 14 Simone **Laudehr**, 10 Renate **Lingor**, 7 Melanie **Behringer** (13 Célia **Okoyino da Mbabi** 73) - 9 Birgit **Prinz** (c), 8 Sandra **Smisek** (15 Fatmire **Bajramaj** 73). *Silvia Neid*

BRA • 1 **Andréia** - 2 **Simone**, 3 **Andréia Rosa**, 5 Renata **Costa**, 4 **Tânia** (c) ■ 31 - 6 **Maycon** - 8 **Formiga**, 7 **Daniela**, 18 **Rosana** - 11 **Cristiane** (14 **Pretinha** 81), 10 **Marta**. *Jorge Barcellos*

Olympic Stadium, Shenyang
6.08.2008, 19:45, **24,084**

KOREA DPR 1-0 **NIGERIA**
Kim Kyong Hwa 27

🟡 Shane De Silva TRI
🏳 Cindy Mohammed TRI & Milena López CRC

PRK • 1 **Jon** Myong Hui - 5 **Song** Jong Sun, 15 **Sonu** Kyong Sun, 16 **Kong** Hye Ok, 3 **Om** Jong Ran - 8 **Kil** Son Hui, 2 **Kim** Kyong Hwa (6 **Kim** Ok Sim 89), 11 **Ri** Un Gyong, 9 **Ri** Un Suk - 17 **Kim** Yong Ae (7 **Ho** Sun Hui 69), 10 **Ri** Kum Suk (c). *Kim Kwang Min*

NGA • 1 Precious **Dede** - 16 Ulumma **Jerome** - 11 Lilian **Cole** (5 Onome **Ebi** 46), 2 Efioanwan **Ekpo**, 13 Christie **George** (c), 14 Faith **Ikidi** - 7 Stella **Mbachu** (9 Sarah **Michael** 62), 12 Cynthia **Uwak**, 10 Rita **Chikwelu**, 4 Perpetua **Nkwocha** - 8 Ifeanyichukwu **Chiejine**. *Joseph Ladipo*

Olympic Stadium, Shenyang
9.08.2008, 17:00, **19,266**

NIGERIA 0-1 **GERMANY**
Stegemann 64

🟡 Jenny Palmqvist SWE
🏳 Helen Caro SWE & Hege Steinlund NOR

NGA • Dede - Ikidi, Jerome, George (c), Ebi ■ 33 - Uwak (Mbachu 70), Ekpo, Chikwelu, Chiejine (15 Tawa **Ishola** 85) - Michael, Nkwocha. *Ladipo*

GER • Angerer - Stegemann, Krahn, Hingst, Bresonik ■ 31 - Garefrekes, Laudehr (Okoyino da Mbabi 64), Lingor, Behringer - Prinz (c), Smisek (11 Anja **Mittag**, 62). *Neid*

Olympic Stadium, Shenyang
9.08.2008, 19:45, **19,616**

BRAZIL 2-1 **KOREA DPR**
Daniela 14   Ri Kum Suk 90+4
Marta 22

🟡 Niu Huijun CHN
🏳 Liu Hongjuan CHN & Liu Hsiu Mei TPE

BRA • Andréia - Renata Costa, 16 **Érika**, Tânia (c) - Simone, Formiga ■ 76, Maycon, Rosana (9 **Ester** 81) - Marta ■ 11, Daniela ■ 65 (13 **Francielle** 90+4), Cristiane (Pretinha 60). *Barcellos*

PRK • Jon Myong Hui - Song Jong Sun, Sonu Kyong Sun, Kong Hye Ok, Om Jong Ran - Kil Son Hui, Kim Kyong Hwa ■ 27 (Kim Ok Sim 86), Ri Un Gyong ■ 47, Ri Un Suk - Kim Yong Ae (Ho Sun Hui 59), Ri Kum Suk (c). *Kim Kwang Min*

Olympic Center Stadium, Tianjin
12.08.2008, 17:00, **12,387**

KOREA DPR 0-1 **GERMANY**
                   Mittag 86

🟡 Dianne Ferreira-James GUY
🏳 Rita Muñoz MEX & Mayte Chávez MEX

PRK • Jon Myong Hui ■ 83 - Song Jong Sun, Sonu Kyong Sun ■ 27, Kong Hye Ok, Om Jong Ran - Kil Son Hui ■ 15, Kim Kyong Hwa (Kim Ok Sim 64), Ri Un Gyong, Ri Un Suk - Kim Yong Ae (Ho Sun Hui 51), Ri Kum Suk (c). *Kim Kwang Min*

GER • Angerer - Stegemann, Krahn, Hingst, Bresonik - Garefrekes, Laudehr, Lingor, Behringer (Bajramaj 69) - Smisek (Mittag 63), Prinz (c). *Neid*

Workers' Stadium, Beijing
12.08.2008, 17:00, **51,112**

NIGERIA 1-3 **BRAZIL**
Nkwocha 19p   Cristiane (3) 33 35, 45+3

🟡 Hong Eun Ah KOR
🏳 Sarah Ho AUS & Jacqueline Leleu AUS

NGA • Dede - Ikidi, Jerome, George (c), Ebi - Uwak ■ 42, Ekpo ■ 54, Chikwelu (17 Edith **Eduviere** 85), Chiejine - Michael (Mbachu 70), Nkwocha. *Ladipo*

BRA • 12 **Bárbara** - Renata Costa, Érika, Tânia (c) - Ester - Simone, Maycon, Rosana (17 **Maurine** 78) - Cristiane, Daniela (Francielle 70), Marta. *Barcellos*

Group F

	W	D	L	+	-	PTS
BRA	2	1	0	5	2	7
GER	2	1	0	2	0	7
PRK	1	0	2	2	3	3
NGA	0	0	3	1	5	0

Cristiane dazzles for Brazil

Brazil, who had lost in the Final of both the 2004 Olympics and the 2007 World Cup, were drawn with the reigning world champions Germany, who were seeking the one title that had eluded them so far. This match brought together two of the world's best goalkeepers, Nadine Angerer and Andréia, and neither was beaten as the match finished goalless. Olympic debutants North Korea, the reigning Asian champions, defeated African champions Nigeria in a dominant performance led by veteran skipper Ri Kum Suk. The 29-year-old forward also scored the team's only goal in their loss to Brazil three days later. The Brazilians had almost not qualified for these Olympics after failing to win the South American Women's Football Championship for the first – and only – time, and they had to beat Ghana in an inter-continental play-off to make it to Beijing. But they were back in business against the Koreans with goals by Daniela and playmaker Marta. Nigeria and North Korea both failed to break through the Germans' solid defence, while Cristiane's hat-trick against Nigeria in Brazil's last group match sent her team into the quarter-finals alongside Germany.

▶ North Korea's Kim Yong Ae is closed down by Germany's Annike Krahn (5) and Kerstin Stegemann. The Koreans finished third but didn't qualify for the quarter-finals.

Perfect 3

Cristiane's hat-trick against Nigeria was the only one of the tournament. It was also a "perfect" hat-trick – one with the head, one with the left foot and one with the right, as well as being scored in the same half and without interruption!

▶ Brazil striker Cristiane is mobbed by Marta (10) and Daniela after scoring the second of her three goals against Nigeria – a spectacular overhead kick.

Group G

Group stage 2008

▶ Japan celebrate their extraordinary 5-1 victory over a Norwegian team that had earlier beaten the USA. Three years later they would be world champions.

	W	D	L	+	-	PTS
USA	2	0	1	5	2	6
NOR	2	0	1	4	5	6
JPN	1	1	1	7	4	4
NZL	0	1	2	2	7	1

Norway and the USA quick off the mark

The USA, gold medallists four years earlier in Athens, were without forward Abby Wambach, who had been injured in the build-up to the tournament. Few would have predicted that their first opponents, Norway, who were out to avenge their defeat to the Americans in the play-off for third place at the World Cup the year before, would be leading 2-0 just four minutes into the game between the two. It took Leni Larsen Kaurin just 61 seconds to open the scoring, which at that point was the fastest goal ever in women's Olympic football. Melissa Wiik added a second just two minutes later to inflict on the Americans only their second-ever defeat at the Olympics. The Norwegians had also been responsible for the first in the 2000 Final. In the group's other opening game, East Asian champions Japan came from behind to draw with New Zealand, Homare Sawa scoring a late equaliser. That stalemate made the Americans' path to the quarter-finals less complicated and they qualified after comfortable wins over both the Japanese and New Zealand. The most extraordinary result of the group, however, was Japan's 5-1 rout of Norway. That match signalled Japan's arrival at the top table and they joined the Norwegians in the quarter-finals.

40

The number of seconds it took Heather O'Reilly to score the USA's first goal against New Zealand. Leni Larsen Kaurin had scored after 61 seconds in Norway's opening match against the Americans, but O'Reilly beat her Olympic record just six days later! O'Reilly's record lasted until 2016.

▼ America's Carli Lloyd and Rebecca Smith (6) of New Zealand challenge for the ball.

Olympic Sports Center Stadium, Qinhuangdao
6.08.2008, 17:00, **10,270**

JAPAN 2-2 **NEW ZEALAND**

Miyama 72p   Yallop 37
Sawa 86   Hearn 56p

Deidre Mitchell RSA
Tempa Ndah BEN & Nomvula Masilela RSA

JPN • 1 Miho **Fukumoto** - 2 Yukari **Kinga**, 4 Azusa **Iwashimizu** ■ 56, 14 Kyoko **Yano**, 5 Miyuki **Yanagita** - 7 Kozue **Ando** (12 Karina **Maruyama** 82), 15 Mizuho **Sakaguchi** ■ 54, 10 Homare **Sawa** (c), 8 Aya **Miyama** - 11 Shinobu **Ohno** (9 Eriko **Arakawa** 79), 17 Yuki **Nagasato**. *Norio Sasaki*

NZL • 1 Jenny **Bindon** - 2 Ria **Percival**, 6 Rebecca **Smith**, 5 Abby **Erceg**, 17 Marlies **Oostdam** - 7 Ali **Riley**, 4 Katie **Hoyle** (10 Emily **McColl** 79), 8 Hayley **Moorwood** (c), 11 Kirsty **Yallop** - 9 Amber **Hearn** (13 Rebecca **Tegg** 87), 15 Emma **Kete** (16 Renee **Leota** 70). *John Herdman ENG*

Olympic Sports Center Stadium, Qinhuangdao
6.08.2008, 19:45, **17,673**

NORWAY 2-0 **USA**

Larsen Kaurin 2 (61 secs)
Wiik 4

Nicole Petignat SUI
Cristina Cini ITA & Karine Vives Solana FRA

NOR • 1 Erika **Skarbø** - 7 Trine **Rønning**, 12 Marit **Fiane Christensen**, 2 Ane **Stangeland Horpestad** (c), 3 Gunhild **Følstad** - 11 Leni **Larsen Kaurin** (14 Guro **Knutsen** 68), 6 Marie **Knutsen** (5 Siri **Nordby** 88), 4 Ingvild **Stensland**, 13 Lene **Storløkken**, 10 Melissa **Wiik** (17 Lene **Mykjåland** 69) - 8 Solveig **Gulbrandsen**. *Bjarne Berntsen*

USA • 1 Hope **Solo** - 2 Heather **Mitts**, 3 Christie **Rampone** (c), 15 Kate **Markgraf**, 17 Lori **Chalupny** (14 Stephanie **Cox** 15) (13 Tobin **Heath** 78) - 9 Heather **O'Reilly**, 7 Shannon **Boxx**, 11 Carli **Lloyd**, 5 Lindsay **Tarpley** (8 Amy **Rodriguez** 46) - 16 Angela **Hucles**, 6 Natasha **Kai**. *Pia Sundhage SWE*

Olympic Sports Center Stadium, Qinhuangdao
9.08.2008, 17:00, **16,912**

USA 1-0 **JAPAN**

Lloyd 27

Pannipar Kamnueng THA
Widiya Shamsuri MAS & Ja Daw Kaw MYA

USA • Solo - Mitts, Rampone (c), Markgraf, Cox (4 Rachel **Buehler** 83) - O'Reilly, Boxx, Lloyd, Tarpley (Heath 73) - Rodriguez (Kai 86), Hucles. *Sundhage SWE*

JPN • Fukumoto - Kinga, 3 Hiromi **Ikeda** (c) (Arakawa 82), Iwashimizu, Yanagita - Ando (Maruyama 62), Sawa ■ 74, Sakaguchi (13 Ayumi **Hara** 65), Miyama - Ohno, Nagasato. *Sasaki*

Olympic Sports Center Stadium, Qinhuangdao
9.08.2008, 19:45, **7,285**

NEW ZEALAND 0-1 **NORWAY**

Wiik 8

Estela Álvarez ARG
Marlene Leyton PER & Maria Rocco ARG

NZL • Bindon - Percival, Smith, Erceg, Oostdam (3 Anna **Green** 64) - Riley, Hoyle, Moorwood (c), Yallop - Hearn (Tegg 82), Kete (Leota 88). *Herdman ENG*

NOR • Skarbø - S Nordby, Fiane Christensen, Stangeland Horpestad (c), Følstad - Larsen Kaurin (G Knutsen 60), M Knutsen, Stensland, Storløkken (16 Elise **Thorsnes** 60), Wiik - S Gulbrandsen (9 Isabell **Herlovsen** 76). *Berntsen*

Shanghai Stadium, Shanghai
12.08.2008, 19:45, **16,872**

NORWAY 1-5 **JAPAN**

G Knutsen 27   Kinga 31, Følstad OG 51
               Ohno 52, Sawa 70, Hara 83

Shane De Silva TRI
Cindy Mohammed TRI & Milena López CRC

NOR • Skarbø - Rønning, Fiane Christensen, Stangeland Horpestad (c), Følstad - Larsen Kaurin, M Knutsen (G Knutsen 10), Stensland, Storløkken (Thorsnes 69), Mykjåland (Wiik 46) - S Gulbrandsen. *Berntsen*

JPN • Fukumoto - Kinga, Iwashimizu, Ikeda (c), Yano - Ando, Sawa, Sakaguchi (6 Tomoe **Kato** 87), Miyama - Nagasato (Hara 77), Ohno (Maruyama 84). *Sasaki*

Olympic Stadium, Shenyang
12.08.2008, 19:45, **12,453**

USA 4-0 **NEW ZEALAND**

O'Reilly 1 (40 secs),
Rodriguez 43,
Tarpley 56, Hucles 60

Dagmar Damková CZE
Irina Mirt ROU & Katarzyna Nadolska POL

USA • Solo - Mitts (Cox 62), Rampone (c), Buehler, Chalupny - O'Reilly (10 Aly **Wagner** 76), Boxx, Lloyd, Tarpley - Rodriguez (Kai 57), Hucles. *Sundhage SWE*

NZL • Bindon - Percival, Smith, Erceg, Oostdam ■ 46 (14 Kristy **Hill** 64) - Riley, Hoyle (Green 64), Moorwood (c), Yallop - Hearn ■ 55 (Tegg 74), Kete. *Herdman ENG*

2008 Quarter-finals

USA win four-hour classic

Shanghai Stadium, Shanghai
15.08.2008, 18:00, 26,129

USA 2-1 CANADA
AET

Hucles 12, Kai 101   Sinclair 30

Jenny Palmqvist SWE
Helen Caro SWE & Hege Steinlund NOR

USA • Solo - Mitts, Rampone (c), Markgraf, Chalupny - O'Reilly (Kai 91), Lloyd, Boxx, Tarpley (Heath 82) - Rodriguez (12 Lauren **Cheney** 109 ■ 112), Hucles. *Sundhage SWE*
CAN • McLeod (1 Karina **LeBlanc** 19) - Wilkinson, Chapman, Franko ■ 70, Zurrer - Schmidt, Rustad, Sinclair (c), Lang ■ 84 - Tancredi (Timko 46) (Filigno 90+2), Matheson. *Pellerud NOR*

The USA beat Canada thanks to an extra-time header by Natasha Kai in this epic four-hour North American derby that outlasted thunder, lightning and pouring rain. Despite the downpour, the USA took an early lead when Angela Hucles prodded a Heather O'Reilly header past goalkeeper Erin McLeod. McLeod was injured while trying to make the save and was replaced by Karina LeBlanc. The game was suspended in the 21st minute due to the heavy rain, resuming 100 minutes later. The break allowed Canada to regroup, and on the half-hour, captain Christine Sinclair equalised with a superb 25-yard drive that gave Hope Solo in the USA goal no chance. It remained deadlocked for the rest of normal time, with the heavy rain making the going tough. Then, 11 minutes into extra time, substitute Kai headed home a pinpoint cross from Shannon Boxx to send the USA into the semi-finals.

▶ Brazil midfielder Formiga in action with Norway's Leni Larsen Kaurin. This match was something of an end of an era for Norway, the former world and Olympic champions. This was their seventh quarter-final appearance at a global tournament but the eighth didn't come until 11 years later at the 2019 World Cup.

Marta sends Brazil into fourth consecutive Olympic semi-final

Olympic Center Stadium, Tianjin
15.08.2008, 18:00, 26,174

BRAZIL 2-1 NORWAY

Daniela 44, Marta 57   Nordby 83p

Kari Seitz USA
Marlene Duffy USA & Veronica Perez USA

BRA • Bárbara - Renata Costa, Érika, Tânia (c) - Simone, Ester, Daniela (Francielle 90+1), Formiga, Maycon - Cristiane, Marta. *Barcellos*
NOR • Skarbø - 15 Marita **Skammelsrud Lund** (S Nordby 63), Fiane Christensen, Stangeland Horpestad (c), Følstad - Larsen Kaurin (Herlovsen 73), S Gulbrandsen, Stensland, Storløkken (Rønning 84), Wiik - Thorsnes. *Berntsen*

Brazil's fast-paced, short-passing game prevailed over the aerial style favoured by Norway to send Jorge Barcellos's side into the semi-finals thanks to goals by Daniela and Marta. The Europeans were strong in the first half and tested Brazilian goalkeeper Bárbara in her first Olympic game, but they couldn't match the tempo set by her teammates. The Brazilians took the lead just before the break when Daniela unleashed one of her signature shots, a 30-yard drive that flew into the net beyond the reach of Erika Skarbø. Brazil maintained their momentum in the second half as Marta seized on indecision in the Norwegian defence following a long clearance by Tânia, her lightning speed taking Marit Fiane Christensen by surprise. Siri Nordby converted a penalty to put Norway back in the game and they could have equalised right at the end, but Solveig Gulbrandsen headed over from an Ingvild Stensland free kick.

◀ American midfielder Carli Lloyd and Canada's Candace Chapman cope as best as they can with the torrential downpour which temporarily called a halt to the quarter-final in Shanghai.

▶ Brazil's Daniela (7) in action with Norway's Ane Stangeland Horpestad (2). Along with Marta and Cristiane, Daniela was a key figure in Brazil's strike force and she scored a spectacular goal to open the scoring against Norway in the quarter-final in Tianjin.

◀ Sweden's Frida Östberg (13) and Germany's Melanie Behringer in action during the quarter-final in Shenyang. This was the sixth time in nine World Cups and Olympics that the two nations had met. The Swedes had won the first two, in 1991 and 1995, but this was the fourth victory in a row for Germany over their opponents.

Sweden fall to Germany – again

Olympic Stadium, Shenyang
15.08.2008, 21:00, **17,209**

SWEDEN 🇸🇪 **0-2** 🇩🇪 GERMANY
AET

Garefrekes 105, Laudehr 115

Dagmar Damková CZE
Irina Mirt ROU & Katarzyna Nadolska POL
SWE • Lindahl - Östberg, Larsson (Almgren 110), Rohlin, Thunebro - Forsberg (Paulson 67), Seger ■ 100, Svensson (c), Sjögran (19 Maria Aronsson 110) - Schelin, Landström ■ 56. *Dennerby*
GER • Angerer - Stegemann, Krahn, Hingst, Bresonik (4 Babett Peter 71) - Garefrekes, Laudehr, Lingor, Behringer - Mittag, Prinz (c) ■ 100. *Neid*

It took extra-time goals to send Germany into their third consecutive Olympic semi-final at the expense of Sweden in what was a re-match of the 2003 World Cup Final and the bronze medal match at the Athens Olympics. Germany dominated the early stages of the game, and Linda Bresonik hit the post from long range after eight minutes. Birgit Prinz then shot wide just after the half-hour with an open goal in front of her, but Sweden pressed more in the second half and Anna Paulson had a goal-bound shot tipped over by Nadine Angerer eight minutes before the 90 were up. In extra time, a looping Melanie Behringer header almost opened the scoring, but when the goal came it was simple, the tall Kerstin Garefrekes rising above the Swedish defence to head home from a corner. Hedvig Lindahl got a hand to it but couldn't stop it going in. Then, five minutes before the end, Simone Laudehr played a one-two with Birgit Prinz before firing home the second from a very tight angle.

◀ The changing of the guard in Asia. Having been the pre-eminent nation for so long, China saw their place taken by rivals Japan, for whom Homare Sawa (10) opened the scoring in this quarter-final in Qinhuangdao.

The hosts' quarter-final curse continues

Olympic Sports Center Stadium, Qinhuangdao
15.08.2008, 21.00, **28,459**

CHINA PR 🇨🇳 **0-2** 🇯🇵 JAPAN

Sawa 15, Nagasato 80

Christine Beck GER
María Luisa Villa Gutiérrez ESP & Inka Müller GER
CHN • Zhang Yanru - Liu Huana, Li Jie (c), Weng Xinzhi, Zhou Gaoping - Pu Wei, Zhang Na (Lou Jiahui 57), Bi Yan, Zhang Ying (Wang Dandan 55) - Xu Yuan, Han Duan. *Shang Ruihua*
JPN • Fukumoto - Kinga, Ikeda (c), Iwashimizu, Yano (Yanagita 54) - Ando, Sakaguchi, Sawa, Miyama - Ohno (Maruyama 86), Nagasato ■ 32 (Arakawa 87). *Sasaki*

Japan knocked out China in a closely contested East Asian derby thanks to goals by Homare Sawa and Yūki Nagasato as the Chinese quarter-final home jinx, which started at the 1991 World Cup and continued at the 2007 finals, struck for the third time here. Japan, buoyed by their extraordinary win over former world and Olympic champions Norway, started strongly and took the lead after 15 minutes thanks to a powerful Sawa header from an Aya Miyama corner. China missed opportunities to equalise, especially when Pu Wei, who came out of retirement for a third time to help guide Shang Ruihua's young team, almost scored with a bicycle kick in the 78th minute. Two minutes later, however, the Japanese secured the win when Shinobu Ohno broke from her own half. An exchange of passes with Nagasato split the Chinese defence, and she fired home to make it 2-0.

2008 Semi-finals

Germany suffer Brazilian blitz

Shanghai Stadium, Shanghai
18.08.2008, 18:00, **26,976**

BRAZIL 4-1 GERMANY

Formiga 43, Cristiane (2) 49 76, Marta 53 — Prinz 10

Hong Eun Ah KOR • Sarah Ho AUS & Liu Hongjuan CHN

BRA • Bárbara - Renata Costa ■ 21, Érika, Tânia (c) - Simone, Daniela (Francielle 76), Ester, Formiga ■ 90+4, Maycon - Cristiane (15 **Fabiana** 86), Marta ■ 61. Barcellos

GER • Angerer - Stegemann, Krahn, Hingst, Peter - Garefrekes, Laudehr ■ 40, Lingor, Behringer (Bajramaj 60) - Mittag (Okoyino da Mbabi 60), Prinz (c) ■ 88. Neid

▲ Formiga sees the way forward for Brazil. Her equaliser just before half-time unleashed a devastating second-half display by the Brazilians.

Brazil came from behind to end Germany's gold-medal hopes in a five-goal thriller. It sent the South Americans through to their second straight Olympic Final and condemned the Germans to a third successive semi-final defeat in the Olympics. Relying on the speed of their young stars Marta and Cristiane, the Brazilians exposed a German defence that was unusually out of sorts. The Germans began the match strongly and took the lead after ten minutes when Birgit Prinz benefited from a mistake by Érika to open the scoring. It was Formiga who hauled the Brazilians back into the match with a superbly worked goal just before half-time. Cristiane beat three defenders on the left and her cross was deftly flicked on by Marta before Formiga's powerful shot left Nadine Angerer with no chance. In the second half, it took Brazil just four minutes to edge ahead. From a German corner, Marta picked up the cleared ball and sprinted downfield before passing to Cristiane, who had the space to fire home. Marta was then rewarded for her hard work when she beat two German defenders before scoring from the tightest of angles, and it was all over when Cristiane scored her second after 76 minutes. A shell-shocked German team were pulled to pieces as she ran from inside her own half to score one of the all-time great goals.

First strike USA in growing rivalry with Japan

Workers' Stadium, Beijing
18.08.2008, 21:00, **50,937**

JAPAN 2-4 USA

Ohno 16, Arakawa 90+3 — Hucles (2) 41 81, Chalupny 44, O'Reilly 71

Nicole Petignat SUI • Cristina Cini ITA & Karine Vives Solana FRA

JPN • Fukumoto - Ando (Hara 56), Ikeda (c), Iwashimizu, Yano (Maruyama 73) - Kinga, Sakaguchi, Sawa, Miyama - Nagasato, Ohno (Arakawa 71). Sasaki

USA • Solo - Mitts ■ 50 (Cox 86), Rampone (c), Markgraf, Chalupny - O'Reilly ■ 40, Boxx, Lloyd, Tarpley (Kai 67) - Rodriguez (Cheney 83), Hucles. Sundhage SWE

▲ Head over heels. Cristiane celebrates her first goal against Germany. Her second goal was one of the greatest ever scored.

▼ USA forward Natasha Kai avoids a tackle by Japan's Azusa Iwashimizu during the semi-final in Beijing.

The USA fought their way past Japan to make it to a fourth straight Olympic Final, but they had to come from behind against a Japanese team rapidly growing in self-belief. Striker Shinobu Ohno opened the scoring in the 16th minute after the Americans failed to clear from a corner. Japan held on to their lead until just before half-time when they suffered a double sucker punch. After a superb run down the right wing, Heather O'Reilly sent in a perfect low cross which split the defence, leaving Angela Hucles free to score the equaliser. Lori Chalupny then scored an incredible solo goal three minutes later. Collecting the ball on the left wing, she cut inside and beat three defenders before unleashing a ferocious shot to give the USA a half-time lead. It was an important mental boost to take into the break for a team known for its emphasis on sports psychology. Midway through the second half, O'Reilly gave the Americans some breathing space with a speculative looping diagonal shot from the edge of the area, while Hucles got her second with nine minutes to go from a shot that was outside the area and from a seemingly impossible angle. There was a consolation injury-time goal for Eriko Arakawa, and in three years' time at the next World Cup, the Japanese would be more than a match for the Americans.

2008 Bronze Medal Match

Workers' Stadium, Beijing
21.08.2008, 18:00, **49,285**

GERMANY 2-0 **JAPAN**

Bajramaj (2) 69 87

Estela Álvarez ARG | Rita Muñoz MEX & Tempa Ndah BEN

Neid

- 1 Angerer
- 2 Stegemann
- 5 Krahn
- 17 Hingst
- 4 Peter
- 18 Garefrekes
- 14 Laudehr ■ 27 (Okoyino da Mbabi 64)
- 10 Lingor
- 7 Behringer (Bajramaj 59)
- 8 Smisek (16 Conny **Pohlers** 46)
- 9 Prinz (c)

Sasaki

- 17 Nagasato
- 11 Ohno (Maruyama 68)
- 8 Miyama
- 15 Sakaguchi
- 10 Sawa
- 13 Hara (Arakawa 75)
- 14 Yano (16 Rumi **Utsugi** 88)
- 4 Iwashimizu
- 3 Ikeda (c)
- 2 Kinga ■ 59
- 1 Fukumoto

The number of players who featured in all three of Germany's Olympic bronze medal-winning teams. Ariane Hingst, Birgit Prinz, Kerstin Stegemann and Renate Lingor played in all three bronze medal matches in 2000, 2004 and 2008, while Nadine Angerer was in the squad for all three but only played in 2008.

▲ An unlikely hero. Fatmire Bajramaj scores Germany's second goal against Japan. She had earlier scored Germany's first too, just ten minutes after coming on as a substitute.

Germany seal unique treble

Germany clinched the bronze medal with a brace of goals by substitute Fatmire Bajramaj to complete a remarkable treble of bronze medals at successive Olympic Football Tournaments. Japan coach Norio Sasaki knew his players were in for a tough match, but with Silvia Neid's team not at their best for much of the tournament and still smarting from their defeat to Brazil a few days earlier, the medal was there for the taking. For the first hour, it was an openly contested match with Japan having the upper hand. Midfielder Aya Miyama, in her first Olympic tournament, tested 29-year-old German goalkeeper Nadine Angerer in the 21st minute, who pulled off a great save, but in the second half Germany began to gain the upper hand. Neid brought on Bajramaj and the substitute changed the game. On 69 minutes, the 20-year-old Kosovo-born midfielder scored from a sharp angle from a rebound after Japan goalkeeper Miho Fukumoto failed to hold on to a Kerstin Garefrekes header. Prior to coming on, Bajramaj had played just 68 minutes in this tournament, and she got a second three minutes before the end. A clever feint in the box by Garefrekes bought her time to cross the ball to Bajramaj, who still had plenty to do. She beat a defender and fired past Miho Fukumoto in the Japan goal at the near post. The next time these two teams met in a major finals, it would be a very different story.

▶ The Germany team with their bronze medals. Beijing was the third consecutive Olympics at which the team finished third.

2008 Gold Medal Match

Workers' Stadium, Beijing
21.08.2008, 21:00, 51,612

BRAZIL 0-1 USA
AET

Lloyd 96

Dagmar Damková CZE • María Luisa Villa Gutiérrez ESP & Hege Steinlund NOR

12 Bárbara

5 Renata Costa   16 Érika ■ 107   4 Tânia (c)

2 Simone (Rosana 104 ■ 106)   7 Daniela (Fabiana 77)   9 Ester   8 Formiga (Franciélle 105+1)   6 Maycon

Barcellos

11 Cristiane   10 Marta

Sundhage SWE

8 Rodriguez (Cox 120)   16 Hucles

5 Tarpley (Cheney 71)   11 Lloyd   7 Boxx   9 O'Reilly (Kai 101 ■ 114)

17 Chalupny   15 Markgraf   3 Rampone (c)   2 Mitts ■ 37

1 Solo

Carli Lloyd breaks Brazilian hearts

Carli Lloyd's extra-time goal clinched the USA's third Olympic gold after a cagey game in which the defences of both teams had the upper hand. For Brazil, the defeat was a huge disappointment, having lost the 2004 Olympic Final to the Americans and the 2007 World Cup Final against Germany. A victory at any of the three Finals would have helped improve recognition of the game back home. Who can forget the banner held up by the players at the end of the 2007 World Cup Final, which read simply "We need support"? There had been some progress though. Playmaker Marta had at least become the first woman to have her feet imprinted in the Maracanã's Hall of Fame. Here in Beijing, at a packed Workers' Stadium, the two rivals tested each other out in the first half, neither side pushing too hard, although there were opportunities. Angela Hucles' 16th-minute corner landed on the bar, and Hope Solo saved well at the feet of Cristiane on the half-hour.

After half-time, the Brazilians took control and pressed for the goal, but Solo was in commanding form. On 53 minutes, Formiga held up the ball for Marta, who ran to the goal line and saw her cross well held by the American keeper. On 72 minutes, a rare mistake in the USA defence saw Marta sprint through but her fierce strike was brilliantly saved by Solo, whose right arm stayed firm against the power of the shot – a contender for the save of the tournament. As the Brazilians began to tire, the fitness and strength of the USA team saw them claw their way back into contention. Lloyd tried two long-range efforts that failed to trouble Bárbara in the Brazil goal, and with five minutes left, a Hucles shot from the edge of the box had Bárbara at full stretch to stop. The Brazilian keeper then pulled off a remarkable save when faced one-on-one with Amy Rodriguez, plucking the ball out of the air to stop what would have been a certain winner.

It was six minutes into extra time when the goal finally came. Lloyd was involved at the start of the move and she finished it off with a shot good enough to grace any final after a deft lay-off by Rodriguez. Lloyd's effort from just outside the penalty area flew past Bárbara like a rocket. Brazil pressed for an equaliser and Marta twice came close but it wasn't to be her day. Lloyd hit the post on a breakaway just before the end and Cristiane headed just wide right at the death. While the Americans celebrated a third gold, the Brazilians left the field in tears.

▼USA goalkeeper Hope Solo thwarts another Brazilian attack.

▼USA midfielder Heather O'Reilly evades Daniela while Cristiane (11) looks on during the Final at the Workers' Stadium, Beijing.

Gold medal match 2008

▲ Carli Lloyd's extra-time goal won gold for the USA.

A team effort

For the Americans, the Beijing Games were about redemption after a disappointing 2007 World Cup and the post-tournament fallout among the players. They came to China with a fresh slate and a new head coach in former Sweden superstar Pia Sundhage. The USA were also out to avenge their 4-0 semi-final thrashing at the hands of the Brazilians at that World Cup. However, they had to do it without star player Abby Wambach, who broke her left leg while playing an exhibition game against Brazil in July. Despite entering the tournament as underdogs, and losing their first game against Norway, the team pulled together. For midfielder Heather O'Reilly, this made the 2008 win one of the most rewarding ones. "It was a team effort because we were without our star," she said. "Beijing was a really meaningful team victory."

8

Eight members of the USA squad won gold in Athens and Beijing: Shannon Boxx, Angela Hucles, Kate Markgraf, Heather Mitts, Heather O'Reilly, Christie Rampone, Lindsay Tarpley and Aly Wagner. Of those, five played in both Finals: O'Reilly, Tarpley, Boxx, Markgraf and Rampone, with the last three playing every minute of both.

▶ Carli Lloyd is mobbed after scoring the only goal of the Final.

▲ Sweden's Pia Sundhage, who coached the USA team to gold in both Beijing and London.

The first

Pia Sundhage became the first foreigner to coach a team to the Olympic title. It has never been done at the World Cup.

◀ Beijing 2008 was the third Olympic gold won by the USA.

2011

Hosts Germany were favourites to complete a hat-trick of World Cup titles – but they suffered a shock 1-0 defeat by Japan in the quarter-finals. Captained by the tournament's top scorer Homare Sawa, Japan became the first Asian country to win the World Cup. In a dramatic Final in Frankfurt, they beat the USA on penalties. Japan scored two late equalisers, the second from a clever flick by Sawa in extra time.

Playing in the shadow of Fukushima

On 11 March 2011, Japan experienced an earthquake that registered a magnitude of 9.1. It was the fourth most powerful earthquake in history and caused the deaths of nearly 16,000 people. Many of the casualties and much of the destruction resulted from the devastating tsunami that followed it, which at 40 metres high in parts reached ten kilometres inland. Lying in its path was the Fukushima Daiichi Nuclear Power Plant at which three reactors suffered meltdown, images caught by television cameras. Two members of the Japan national team – Karina Maruyama and Aya Sameshima – had once worked at the plant, and before the New Zealand game and after the England match, the whole Japan team paraded a banner around the ground thanking "friends around the world" for supporting their nation during such a difficult time. No-one, however, could have expected that the team would go on to beat the hosts Germany in the quarter-finals and then defeat hot favourites the USA in the Final itself. The triumph of the *Nadeshiko* was a truly remarkable achievement and a rare moment of good news for a country desperately trying to clear up and get life back to normal.

▼The Japanese team parade a banner before the group match against New Zealand in Bochum.

2011 Overview

GERMANY 2011

FIFA WOMEN'S WORLD CUP GERMANY 2011™

Story of the qualifiers

China miss out

China were the big-name absentees from the 2011 finals in Germany. This was the first time that the hosts of four years earlier had missed out on qualifying for either of the two major women's tournaments. They lost to great rivals North Korea in the semi-finals of the 2010 AFC Women's Asian Cup, which once again was used to qualify Asian teams for the World Cup. With only three slots available, they then lost to Japan in the match for third place. Continental championships were used as qualifiers in the other confederations as well, apart from in Europe, and they produced few surprises, although there were first-time qualifications for Colombia from South America and Equatorial Guinea from Africa. In Europe, the system of only the top tier of strongest nations being eligible to qualify was dropped in favour of an open system. The eight group winners faced a play-off to determine the four spots available, which were won by England, France, Norway and Sweden. Italy then won a competition among the four losers but lost an intercontinental play-off against the USA. The Americans had surprisingly lost in the semi-finals of the Concacaf qualifiers to Mexico – their first-ever continental championship defeat – forcing them to play-off first against Costa Rica and then the Italians.

▶ Official World Cup pennant.
FIFA Museum Collection

Golden Ball

Homare Sawa JPN

Silver Ball: Abby Wambach USA
Bronze Ball: Hope Solo USA

Overview 2011

16 TEAMS

JAPAN WINNERS

USA SECOND SWE THIRD

KARLA KICK
OFFICIAL MASCOT

GERMANY 2011 FIFA WOMEN'S WORLD CUP
OFFICIAL LOGO

32 MATCHES PLAYED

63 YELLOW CARDS

4 RED CARDS

86 GOALS

2.69 AVERAGE GOALS PER MATCH

SPEEDCELL
OFFICIAL MATCH BALL

845 711 SPECTATORS   **26 428** AVERAGE PER MATCH

Host cities and stadiums

The World Cup returns to Europe

Germany 2011 was the first World Cup staged in Europe since 1995 and the third time that the world's best female players had gathered on the continent for a global tournament following on from Athens in 2004. This was also the first World Cup since 1995 in which stadiums hosted only one game on matchdays, with a record nine stadiums used in nine cities. Berlin and Frankfurt were the only venues that saw games at both the 2006 FIFA World Cup and the FIFA Women's World Cup 2011.

5

The number of games that finished with a winning margin of 3 goals or more – a sharp decline from previous tournaments. It showed that the gap in standards between countries was continuing to narrow.

BOCHUM
FIFA WOMEN'S WORLD CUP STADIUM
(20,452)

WOLFSBURG
ARENA IM ALLERPARK
(26,067)

BERLIN
OLYMPIASTADION
(73,680)

MÖNCHENGLADBACH
BORUSSIA-PARK
(45,867)

DRESDEN
RUDOLF-HARBIG-STADION
(25,598)

LEVERKUSEN
FIFA WOMEN'S WORLD CUP STADIUM
(29,870)

FRANKFURT
FIFA WOMEN'S WORLD CUP STADIUM
(48,817)

SINSHEIM
RHEIN-NECKAR-ARENA
(25,475)

AUGSBURG
FIFA WOMEN'S WORLD CUP STADIUM
(24,605)

×5

Golden Boot

Homare Sawa JPN

Silver Boot: Marta BRA × 4
Bronze Boot: Abby Wambach USA × 4

2011 **Group stage**

Olympiastadion, Berlin
26.06.2011, 18:00, **73,680**

GERMANY 2-1 CANADA

Garefrekes 10, Sinclair 82
Okoyino da Mbabi 42

Jacqui Melksham AUS
Allyson Flynn AUS & Sarah Ho AUS

GER - 1 Nadine **Angerer** - 10 Linda **Bresonik**, 5 Annike **Krahn**
■ 90, 3 Saskia **Bartusiak**, 4 Babett **Peter** - 18 Kerstin **Garefrekes**,
6 Simone **Laudehr** ■ 81, 14 Kim **Kulig**, 7 Melanie **Behringer**
(19 Fatmire **Bajramaj** 71) - 9 Birgit **Prinz** (c) (11 Alexandra **Popp**
56), 13 Célia **Okoyino da Mbabi** (8 Inka **Grings** 65). *Silvia Neid*

CAN - 18 Erin **McLeod** - 7 Rhian **Wilkinson**, 9 Candace **Chapman**,
2 Emily **Zurrer**, 20 Marie-Ève **Nault** (5 Robyn **Gayle** 46) - 8 Diana
Matheson, 13 Sophie **Schmidt**, 6 Kaylyn **Kyle** (3 Kelly **Parker** 46)
- 14 Melissa **Tancredi** (17 Brittany **Timko** 80), 12 Christine **Sinclair**
(c), 16 Jonelle **Filigno**. *Carolina Morace ITA*

Rhein-Neckar-Arena, Sinsheim
26.06.2011, 15:00, **25,475**

NIGERIA 0-1 FRANCE

Delie 56

Kari Seitz USA
Marlene Duffy USA & Veronica Perez USA

NGA - 1 Precious **Dede** (c) - 14 Faith **Ikidi** (15 Josephine
Chukwunonye 34), 3 Osinachi **Ohale**, 5 Onome **Ebi**, 6 Helen
Ukaonu - 7 Stella **Mbachu**, 11 Glory **Iroka**, 10 Rita **Chikwelu**,
8 Ebere **Orji** (19 Uchechi **Sunday** 78) - 4 Perpetua **Nkwocha**,
9 Desire **Oparanozie** (12 Sarah **Michael** 66). *Ngozi Uche*

FRA - 16 Bérangère **Sapowicz** - 2 Wendie **Renard** (11 Laure
Lepailleur 69), 4 Laura **Georges**, 5 Ophélie **Meilleroux**, 8 Sonia
Bompastor - 10 Camille **Abily**, 6 Sandrine **Soubeyrand** (c)
(9 Eugénie **Le Sommer** 46), 15 Élise **Bussaglia** - 17 Gaëtane **Thiney**
(12 Élodie **Thomis** 57), 18 Marie-Laure **Delie**, 14 Louisa **Nécib**.
Bruno Bini

FIFA Women's World Cup Stadium, Frankfurt
30.06.2011, 20:45, **48,817**

GERMANY 1-0 NIGERIA

Laudehr 54

Cha Sung Mi KOR
Widiya Shamsuri MAS & Kim Kyoung Min KOR

GER - Angerer - Bresonik, Krahn, Bartusiak, Peter - Garefrekes,
Laudehr, Kulig ■ 74, Behringer (Popp 31) - Prinz (c) (Grings 53),
Okoyino da Mbabi (Bajramaj 87). *Neid*

NGA - Dede (c) - Ikidi, Ohale ■ 51, Ebi, Ukaonu - Mbachu
(17 Francisca **Ordega** 85), Nkwocha, Chikwelu, Orji (20 Amenze
Aighewi 63) - Michael (Sunday 70), Oparanozie. *Uche*

FIFA Women's World Cup Stadium, Bochum
30.06.2011, 18:00, **16,591**

CANADA 0-4 FRANCE

Thiney (2) 24 60
Abily 66
Thomis 83

Etsuko Fukano JPN
Saori Takahashi JPN & Zhang Lingling CHN

CAN - McLeod - Timko (19 Chelsea **Stewart** 77), Chapman, Zurrer,
Wilkinson - Matheson ■ 52, Schmidt, Kyle (11 Desiree **Scott** 60) -
15 Christina **Julien** (Tancredi 60), Sinclair (c), Filigno. *Morace ITA*

FRA - Sapowicz - Lepailleur, Georges, 20 Sabrina **Viguier**,
Bompastor ■ 37 - Bussaglia, Soubeyrand (c) - Abily (Le Sommer 82),
Nécib, Thiney (3 Laure **Boulleau** 79) - Delie (Thomis 74). *Bini*

Borussia-Park, Mönchengladbach
5.07.2011, 20:45, **45,867**

FRANCE 2-4 GERMANY

Delie 56 Garefrekes 25
Georges 72 Grings (2) 32 68p
Okoyino da Mbabi 89

Kirsi Heikkinen FIN
Tonja Paavola FIN & Anu Jokela FIN

FRA - Sapowicz ■ 65 - Lepailleur, Georges ■ 41, Renard ■ 59,
Boulleau - Bussaglia ■ 40, Soubeyrand (c) - Le Sommer (1 Céline
Deville 68), Nécib (Abily 46), Thiney - Thomis (Delie 46). *Bini*

GER - Angerer - 2 Bianca **Schmidt**, Krahn (Popp 78), Bartusiak,
Peter - Laudehr (17 Ariane **Hingst** 46), 20 Lena **Goeßling** ■ 17 -
Garefrekes (c), Okoyino da Mbabi, Bajramaj ■ 82 - Grings. *Neid*

Rudolf-Harbig-Stadion, Dresden
5.07.2011, 20:45, **13,638**

CANADA 0-1 NIGERIA

Nkwocha 73

Finau Vulivuli FIJ
Jacqui Stephenson NZL & Lata Tuifutuna TGA

CAN - 1 Karina **LeBlanc** - Wilkinson, Chapman, Zurrer, Nault - Kyle
(Scott 78), Schmidt, Matheson - Tancredi (10 Jodi-Ann **Robinson**
84), Sinclair (c), Filigno (Julien 56). *Morace ITA*

NGA - Dede (c) - Ikidi, Ohale, Ebi ■ 59, Ukaonu - Mbachu (Ordega
72), Iroka, Chikwelu, Orji (13 Ogonna **Chukwudi** 54) - Oparanozie
(Sunday 84), Nkwocha. *Uche*

Group A

	W	D	L	+	-	PTS
GER	3	0	0	7	3	9
FRA	2	0	1	7	4	6
NGA	1	0	2	1	2	3
CAN	0	0	3	1	7	0

▶ Célia Okoyino da Mbabi celebrates her goal against France. Germany's 4-2 win at Borussia-Park in Mönchengladbach secured top spot for Germany and a quarter-final against Japan.

43/24

In her World Cup and Olympic career, Birgit Prinz played 43 games and scored 24 goals. Her appearance here against Nigeria was her last, and she left as the leading all-time World Cup goalscorer with 14. That total was matched by Marta later in the 2011 tournament and broken by the Brazilian four years later.

Germany lose captain Prinz to injury

A record European crowd of 73,680 packed into Berlin's iconic Olympiastadion to watch Germany kick off against Canada, but it wasn't the first match of the finals. Earlier in Sinsheim, over 25,000 had seen France beat Nigeria in a tight match enlivened by the rhythm of fans' trumpets and drums and settled by Marie-Laure Delie's 22nd goal in her 21st international. In Berlin, the 150th game in World Cup history was opened by flag-wielding Segway drivers, a giant mirrorball and a choreographed cast of thousands. It was an exuberant start and Germany were determined to make it a successful one. "I don't like to talk about defending the title, we want to win it," declared the 2010 FIFA Women's World Coach of the Year Silvia Neid. First they had to beat former Italy skipper Carolina Morace's Canada. A deafeningly noisy stadium was silenced when Christine Sinclair, battling on with a broken nose, scored a free kick to end keeper Nadine Angerer's unbeaten World Cup record on 622 minutes, but first-half goals from Kerstin Garefrekes and Célia Okoyino da Mbabi won it for the hosts. North American champions Canada had trained together in Rome since January, but they fell apart against France, Gaëtane Thiney scoring a brace on her 50th appearance. Like Morace, Nigeria boss Ngozi Uche had played against Germany in the 1991 World Cup and the former striker's veterans and teenagers frustrated the reigning champions for long periods in front of a sell-out crowd in Frankfurt, but Simone Laudehr's winning volley sent Germany through, with France joining the hosts. Inka Grings would help settle the battle for top spot, scoring twice in her first World Cup since 1999 as Germany beat ten-woman France 4-2. Meanwhile, Nigeria's 35-year-old Perpetua Nkwocha marked her third World Cup with the winning goal against Canada, who finished pointless for the first time in five finals.

▶ Simone Laudehr scores the only goal of the game for Germany against Nigeria. It was Nigeria's ninth game without a win at the World Cup, but they made amends by beating Canada in their final group game.

Mexico and New Zealand impress but England and Japan go through

They scored 50 goals without reply in qualifying, but a hard-tackling New Zealand side featuring 17-year-old striker Katie Bowen and 38-year-old keeper Jenny Bindon were still chasing a first finals point after Japan nicked the opener through Aya Miyama's immaculate free kick. Mexico, with 16-year-old Cecilia Santiago in goal, broke their finals duck when forward Mónica Ocampo unleashed an unstoppable equaliser against England. The ever-improving Mexicans had pulled off a shock win over the USA to reach their second finals, but they were well beaten by Japan in their next game, captain Homare Sawa hitting a hat-trick in her fifth World Cup. John Herdman's Oceania champions shed tears after England's Jill Scott equalised before teeing up Jess Clarke's winner to end their tournament. But they bowed out with a crowd-pleasing haka after Wolfsburg defender Rebecca Smith and teenager Hannah Wilkinson scored at the death against Mexico to finally take a point. It was a cruel blow for Leonardo Cuéllar's side, but a breakthrough tournament for both teams. Euro 2009 finalists England, meanwhile, pipped Japan to top spot with fine goals from Ellen White and Rachel Yankey, and a solid display from keeper Karen Bardsley.

◀ England's Jill Scott gets to grips with Mexico forward Stephany Mayor (21). Mónica Ocampo scored a spectacular equaliser to secure Mexico's first World Cup point.

Group B

	W	D	L	+	–	PTS
ENG	2	1	0	5	2	7
JPN	2	0	1	6	3	6
MEX	0	2	1	3	7	2
NZL	0	1	2	4	6	1

◀ Rebecca Smith heads a 90th-minute goal for New Zealand against Mexico. The Mexicans had led 2-0, but the Kiwis scored again moments later to equalise. It was their first-ever point at a World Cup.

FIFA Women's World Cup Stadium, Bochum
27.06.2011, 15:00, **12,538**

JAPAN 2-1 **NEW ZEALAND**

Nagasato 6　　　Hearn 12
Miyama 68

Kirsi Heikkinen FIN
Anu Jokela FIN & Tonja Paavola FIN

JPN • 21 Ayumi **Kaihori** - 2 Yukari **Kinga**, 3 Azusa **Iwashimizu**, 4 Saki **Kumagai**, 15 Aya **Sameshima** - 11 Shinobu **Ohno** (20 Mana **Iwabuchi** 55), 10 Homare **Sawa** (c), 6 Mizuho **Sakaguchi**, 8 Aya **Miyama** - 7 Kozue **Ando** (16 Asuna **Tanaka** 90+2), 17 Yūki **Nagasato** (18 Karina **Maruyama** 76). *Norio Sasaki*

NZL • 1 Jenny **Bindon** - 7 Ali **Riley**, 6 Rebecca **Smith** (c) ■ 67, 5 Abby **Erceg**, 3 Anna **Green** - 2 Ria **Percival** (16 Annalie **Longo** 76), 4 Katie **Hoyle**, 18 Katie **Bowen** ■ 45+1 (8 Hayley **Moorwood** 46) - 10 Sarah **Gregorius** (17 Hannah **Wilkinson** 62), 12 Betsy **Hassett**, 9 Amber **Hearn** ■ 77. *John Herdman ENG*

Arena im Allerpark, Wolfsburg
27.06.2011, 18:00, **18,702**

MEXICO 1-1 **ENGLAND**

Ocampo 33　　　Williams 21

Silvia Reyes PER
Mariana Corbo URU & Marlene Leyton PER

MEX • 20 Cecilia **Santiago** - 5 Natalie **Vinti**, 4 Alina **Garciamendez** ■ 87, 3 Rubí **Sandoval**, 15 Luz del Rosario **Saucedo** - 10 Dinora **Garza** (17 Teresa **Noyola** 85), 8 Guadalupe **Worbis**, 11 Nayeli **Rangel** - 21 Stephany **Mayor**, 9 Maribel **Domínguez** (c) (7 Juana **López** 76), 19 Mónica **Ocampo**. *Leonardo Cuéllar*

ENG • 1 Karen **Bardsley** - 2 Alex **Scott**, 5 Faye **White** (c) (15 Sophie **Bradley** 83), 6 Casey **Stoney** ■ 88, 3 Rachel **Unitt** - 4 Jill **Scott**, 8 Fara **Williams** - 12 Karen **Carney** (9 Ellen **White** 72), 10 Kelly **Smith**, 11 Rachel **Yankey** - 14 Eniola **Aluko**. *Hope Powell*

FIFA Women's World Cup Stadium, Leverkusen
1.07.2011, 15:00, **22,291**

JAPAN 4-0 **MEXICO**

Sawa (3) 13 39 80
Ohno 15

Christina Pedersen NOR
Hege Steinlund NOR & Lada Rojc CRO

JPN • Kaihori - Kinga, Iwashimizu, Kumagai, Sameshima - Ohno (9 Nahomi **Kawasumi** 69), Sakaguchi, Sawa (c) (13 Rumi **Utsugi** 83), Miyama - Ando (Iwabuchi 69), Nagasato. *Sasaki*

MEX • Santiago - Vinti, 6 Natalie **Garcia**, Garciamendez, Saucedo - Rangel (13 Liliana **Mercado** 46) - Mayor, Garza, 18 Veronica **Perez** (Noyola 79), Ocampo - Domínguez (c) (2 Kenti **Robles** 62). *Cuéllar*

Rudolf-Harbig-Stadion, Dresden
1.07.2011, 18:15, **19,110**

NEW ZEALAND 1-2 **ENGLAND**

Gregorius 18　　　J Scott 63, Clarke 81

Thérèse Neguel CMR
Tempa Ndah BEN & Lidwine Rakotozafinoro MAD

NZL • Bindon - Riley, R Smith (c), Erceg, Green - Percival (13 Rosie **White** 71), Hoyle, Bowen (Moorwood 46) - Gregorius (Wilkinson 90), Hassett, Hearn. *Herdman ENG*

ENG • Bardsley - A Scott, F White (c) (Bradley 86), Stoney, Unitt - J Scott, Williams - Aluko (Carney 46), Smith, Yankey (7 Jessica **Clarke** 65) - E White. *Powell*

FIFA Women's World Cup Stadium, Augsburg
5.07.2011, 18:15, **20,777**

ENGLAND 2-0 **JAPAN**

E White 15
Yankey 66

Carol Anne Chenard CAN
Marlene Duffy USA & Emperatriz Ayala SLV

ENG • Bardsley - A Scott, Bradley, Stoney (c), Unitt - J Scott, 18 Anita **Asante** - Carney, Smith (Aluko 62), Clarke (Yankey 46) - E White (17 Laura **Bassett** 90). *Powell*

JPN • Kaihori - Kinga, Iwashimizu, Kumagai, Sameshima - Ohno (Kawasumi 82), Sawa (c), Sakaguchi (Iwabuchi 75), Miyama - Ando (Maruyama 56), Nagasato. *Sasaki*

Rhein-Neckar-Arena, Sinsheim
5.07.2011, 18:15, **20,451**

NEW ZEALAND 2-2 **MEXICO**

R Smith 90　　　Mayor 2
Wilkinson 90+4　　　Domínguez 29

Jenny Palmqvist SWE
Helen Karo SWE & Anna Nyström SWE

NZL • Bindon - Riley, R Smith (c), Erceg, Green - Moorwood (11 Kirsty **Yallop** 60), Hoyle, Hassett (Percival 79) - Gregorius, White ■ 33 (Wilkinson 55), Hearn. *Herdman ENG*

MEX • Santiago - Robles (Saucedo 81), Garcia, Garciamendez, Vinti - Worbis, Rangel (Garza 46) - Mayor (16 Charlyn **Corral** 70), Perez, Ocampo - Domínguez (c) ■ 90. *Cuéllar*

2011 Group stage

Rudolf-Harbig-Stadion, Dresden
28.06.2011, 18:15, **21,859**

USA  **2-0** **KOREA DPR**

Cheney 54
Buehler 76

🏳 Bibiana Steinhaus GER
🚩 Marina Wozniak GER & Katrin Rafalski GER

USA • 1 Hope **Solo** - 11 Ali **Krieger**, 3 Christie **Rampone** (c), 19 Rachel **Buehler**, 6 Amy **LePeilbet** - 9 Heather **O'Reilly** (15 Megan **Rapinoe** 79), 10 Carli **Lloyd**, 7 Shannon **Boxx**, 12 Lauren **Cheney** - 20 Abby **Wambach**, 8 Amy **Rodriguez** (13 Alex **Morgan** 75). *Pia Sundhage SWE*

PRK • 1 Hong **Myong Hui** - 5 Song **Jung Sun**, 17 **Ri** Un Hyang, 16 **Jong** Pok Sim, 3 **Ho** Un Byol (20 **Kwon** Song Hwa 81) - 8 **Kim** Su Gyong, 10 **Jo** Yun Mi (c), 12 **Jon** Myong Hwa (13 **Kim** Un Ju 68), 11 **Ri** Ye Gyong - 9 **Ra** Un Sim, 7 **Yun** Hyon Hi (6 **Paek** Sol Hui 48). *Kim Kwang Min*

FIFA Women's World Cup Stadium, Leverkusen
28.06.2011, 15:00, **21,106**

COLOMBIA **0-1** **SWEDEN**

Landström 57

🏳 Carol Anne Chenard CAN
🚩 Emperatriz Ayala SLV & Cindy Mohammed TRI

COL • 12 Sandra **Sepúlveda** - 5 Nataly **Arias**, 14 Kelis **Peduzine**, 3 Natalia **Gaitán** (c), 8 Andrea **Peralta** (17 Ingrid **Vidal** 79) - 4 Diana **Ospina**, 6 Daniela **Montoya** (13 Yulieth **Domínguez** 66), 10 Yoreli **Rincón**, 9 Carmen **Rodallega** - 16 Lady **Andrade**, 7 Catalina **Usme** (18 Katerin **Castro** 59). *Ricardo Rozo*

SWE • 1 Hedvig **Lindahl** - 4 Annica **Svensson**, 7 Sara **Larsson**, 2 Charlotte **Rohlin**, 6 Sara **Thunebro** - 16 Linda **Forsberg** (10 Sofia **Jakobsson** 54), 5 Caroline **Seger** (c) 🟨 29 (18 Nilla **Fischer** 69), 17 Lisa **Dahlkvist**, 15 Therese **Sjögran** - 8 Lotta **Schelin**, 9 Jessica **Landström** (19 Madelaine **Edlund** 81). *Thomas Dennerby*

Rhein-Neckar-Arena, Sinsheim
2.07.2011, 18:00, **25,475**

USA **3-0** **COLOMBIA**

O'Reilly 12
Rapinoe 50, Lloyd 57

🏳 Dagmar Damková CZE
🚩 María Luisa Villa Gutiérrez ESP & Yolanda Parga ESP

USA • Solo - Krieger, Rampone (c), Buehler, LePeilbet (14 Stephanie **Cox** 56) - O'Reilly (17 Tobin **Heath** 62), Lloyd, 16 Lori **Lindsey**, Cheney - Wambach 🟨 84, Rodriguez (Rapinoe 46). *Sundhage SWE*

COL • Sepúlveda - Arias, Peduzine, Gaitán (c), 19 Fatima **Montaño** - Ospina, 11 Liana **Salazar** (Rincón 55), Domínguez, Rodallega - Castro, Usme (20 Orianica **Velásquez** 53). *Rozo*

FIFA Women's World Cup Stadium, Augsburg
2.07.2011, 14:00, **23,768**

KOREA DPR **0-1** **SWEDEN**

Dahlkvist 64

🏳 Estela Álvarez ARG
🚩 Maria Rocco ARG & Yoly Garcia VEN

PRK • Hong Myong Hui - Song Jong Sun, Ri Un Hyang, Jong Pok Sim, Ho Un Byol - Kim Su Gyong (Kim Un Ju 67), Jo Yun Mi (c), Jon Myong Hwa, Ri Ye Gyong (14 **Kim** Chung Sim 82) - Ra Un Sim, Yun Hyon Hi (19 **Choe** Mi Gyong 79). *Kim Kwang Min*

SWE • Lindahl - A Svensson, Larsson, Rohlin, Thunebro - Forsberg, Seger (c) 🟨 60, Dahlkvist, Sjögran (Fischer 86) - Schelin, Landström (14 Josefine **Öqvist** 76). *Dennerby*

Arena im Allerpark, Wolfsburg
6.07.2011, 20:45, **23,468**

SWEDEN **2-1** **USA**

Dahlkvist 16p   Wambach 67
LePeilbet OG 35

🏳 Etsuko Fukano JPN
🚩 Saori Takahashi JPN & Zhang Lingling CHN

SWE • Lindahl - A Svensson, Larsson, Rohlin, Thunebro - Forsberg, Fischer (c) 🟨 60 (3 Linda **Sembrant** 88), Dahlkvist (20 Marie **Hammarström** 77), Sjögran (11 Antonia **Göransson** 65) - Schelin, Öqvist. *Dennerby*

USA • Solo - Krieger, Rampone (c), Buehler, LePeilbet 🟨 14 (Cox 59) - Rapinoe (5 Kelley **O'Hara** 73), Boxx, Lloyd, Cheney - Rodriguez (Morgan 46), Wambach. *Sundhage SWE*

FIFA Women's World Cup Stadium, Bochum
6.07.2011, 20:45, **7,805**

KOREA DPR **0-0** **COLOMBIA**

🏳 Christina Pedersen NOR
🚩 Hege Steinlund NOR & Lada Rojc CRO

PRK • Hong Myong Hui - Paek Sol Hui, 15 **Yu** Jong Hui, Ri Un Hyang, Ho Un Byol - Kim Su Gyong (Kim Chung Sim 48), Kim Un Ju, Jon Myong Hwa, Ri Ye Gyong - Ra Un Sim (Yun Hyon Hi 56) (Choe Mi Gyong 76), Jo Yun Mi (c). *Kim Kwang Min*

COL • Sepúlveda - Arias, Peduzine, Gaitán (c), Montaño - Ospina, Montoya (Salazar 89), Domínguez, Rodallega - Castro (Vidal 88), Velásquez. *Rozo*

Group C

	W	D	L	+	–	PTS
🇸🇪 SWE	3	0	0	4	1	9
🇺🇸 USA	2	0	1	6	2	6
🇰🇵 PRK	0	1	2	0	3	1
🇨🇴 COL	0	1	2	0	4	1

▶ Colombia (in blue) prepare to make their World Cup debut against Sweden in Leverkusen. Midfielder Carmen Rodallega's cousin Hugo was an international for the Colombian men's team.

Sweden inflict first World Cup group defeat on USA

Only the third South American side to reach the finals, Colombia were out to impress in the "group of death" and a skilful team featuring 17-year-old under-20 star Yoreli Rincón contributed to a gripping opener against experienced Sweden. Skipper Natalia Gaitán, aged just 20, twice helped deny Lotta Schelin on the goal line, but a tap-in from Frankfurt striker Jessica Landström denied Ricardo Rozo's debutants, ranked 26 places below them. Only four World Cup veterans made North Korea's line-up to the USA's six, but as in 2007, the two sides served up an end-to-end opener, this one settled by finals debutants Lauren Cheney and Rachel Buehler. Quirky celebrations dominated as Sweden marked Lisa Dahlkvist's winner against North Korea with synchronised skipping, while Megan Rapinoe blared "Born in the USA" into a pitch-side microphone after scoring in a 3-0 win over Colombia. Sweden were on song against Swedish coach Pia Sundhage's world No.1 side though, beating the USA into second in a fast-paced thriller to win a World Cup group for the first-ever time. Colombia and North Korea bowed out without scoring, but after unleashing 33 shots between them, their encounter was certainly no bore draw.

0 The number of goals scored by North Korea and Colombia – the only nations that failed to score at these finals.

▶ Sweden's Lisa Dahlkvist scores the winner against North Korea. Her father Sven was a Swedish international footballer in the early 1980s.

Australia stun Norway to qualify

After seeing her side beat unknown quantities Equatorial Guinea, Norway's first female coach Eli Landsem declared: "I have never been involved in a game like that." With double-figure shots for both teams, crowd-pleasing touches from the debutants' elaborately coiffured captain Añonman and a late winner from Emilie Haavi, it had certainly been eventful. With Australia's 16-year-old Caitlin Foord shadowing five-time FIFA Women's World Player of the Year Marta, Rosana stepped up to deliver a tight win over the Asian champions. Marta enjoyed more freedom against Euro 2009 semi-finalists Norway as Brazil recorded a second three-goal finals win over the former champions. Brazil were through and super-sub Lisa De Vanna kept Australia in the hunt after a five-goal thriller that former African champions Equatorial Guinea almost nicked after two stylish goals from Jena striker Añonman. The world's 61st-ranked side pushed Brazil too, but Cristiane scored twice as the South Americans sailed into top spot without conceding. Norway rallied after losing keeper Ingrid Hjelmseth to injury against Australia, but they suffered a first-ever group-stage exit as two goals from W-League star of the year Kyah Simon saw Tom Sermanni's side progress.

◀ Equatorial Guinea made their World Cup debut in 2011. Here Ana Cristina (5) and Dorine challenge Australia's Emily van Egmond.

Group D

	W	D	L	+	–	PTS
BRA	3	0	0	7	0	9
AUS	2	0	1	5	4	6
NOR	1	0	2	2	5	3
EQG	0	0	3	2	7	0

3
Tom Sermanni became the first coach to take the same country to three World Cups. He had also coached Australia in 1995 and 2007.

Borussia-Park, Mönchengladbach
29.06.2011, 18:15, **27,258**

BRAZIL 1-0 AUSTRALIA

Rosana 54

Jenny Palmqvist SWE
Helen Karo SWE & Anna Nyström SWE

BRA • 1 Andréia - 4 Aline (c), 3 Daiane, 13 Érika - 14 Fabiana, 8 Formiga (15 Francielle 84), 7 Ester, 2 Maurine - 11 Cristiane, 6 Rosana, 10 Marta. *Kleiton Lima*

AUS • 1 Melissa Barbieri (c) - 9 Caitlin Foord, 10 Servet Uzunlar, 3 Kim Carroll, 8 Elise Kellond-Knight - 13 Tameka Butt (4 Clare Polkinghorne 86), 12 Emily van Egmond (15 Sally Shipard 61), 14 Collette McCallum, 7 Heather Garriock - 17 Kyah Simon (20 Samantha Kerr 79), 11 Lisa De Vanna. *Tom Sermanni SCO*

FIFA Women's World Cup Stadium, Augsburg
29.06.2011, 15:00, **12,928**

NORWAY 1-0 EQ. GUINEA

Haavi 84

Quetzalli Alvarado MEX
Rita Muñoz MEX & Mayte Chávez MEX

NOR • 1 Ingrid Hjelmseth - 15 Hedda Gardsjord, 3 Maren Mjelde ■ 63, 2 Nora Holstad Berge, 5 Marita Skammelsrud Lund - 4 Ingvild Stenslan (c), 7 Trine Rønning - 19 Emilie Haavi, 13 Madeleine Giske (17 Lene Mykjåland 46) (11 Leni Larsen Kaurin 70), 16 Elise Thorsnes ■ 90+2 - 9 Isabell Herlovsen (10 Cecilie Pedersen 62). *Eli Landsem*

EQG • 1 Miriam - 6 Vânia, 4 Carolina, 5 Ana Cristina, 2 Bruna, 3 Dulcia - 14 Jumária (15 Chinasa 52), 20 Christelle (21 Laetitia 46), 9 Dorine - 7 Diala (17 Adriana 65), 10 Añonman (c). *Marcello Frigerio ITA*

Arena im Allerpark, Wolfsburg
3.07.2011, 18:15, **26,067**

BRAZIL 3-0 NORWAY

Marta (2) 22 48
Rosana 46

Kari Seitz USA
Marlene Duffy USA & Veronica Perez USA

BRA • Andréia - Aline (c), Daiane ■ 19 (5 Renata Costa 85), Érika - Fabiana (Francielle 76), Formiga, Ester (19 Grazielle 89), Maurine - Cristiane, Rosana, Marta. *Lima*

NOR • Hjelmseth - Skammelsrud Lund, Mjelde, Holstad Berge, 18 Guro Knutsen Mienna - Stensland (c) (14 Gry Tofte Ims 67), Rønning - Larsen Kaurin (Thorsnes 46), Giske, Haavi (Pedersen 52) - Herlovsen. *Landsem*

FIFA Women's World Cup Stadium, Bochum
3.07.2011, 14:00, **15,640**

AUSTRALIA 3-2 EQ. GUINEA

Khamis 8, van Egmond 48   Añonman (2) 21 83
De Vanna 51

Gyöngyi Gaál HUN
Cristina Cini ITA & Natalie Aspinall ENG

AUS • 18 Lydia Williams - 16 Lauren Colthorpe, Uzunlar, Carroll, Kellond-Knight - Shipard (De Vanna 46 ■ 72), van Egmond, McCallum (c) (Polkinghorne 78) - Kerr (2 Teigen Allen 69), 19 Leena Khamis, Garriock. *Sermanni SCO*

EQG • Miriam - Bruna (Laetitia 83), Carolina, Dulcia - Vânia, Ana Cristina ■ 46, Jumária (12 Sinforosa 66 ■ 79), Dorine - Diala, Chinasa (Adriana 57), Añonman (c) ■ 41. *Frigerio ITA*

FIFA Women's World Cup Stadium, Frankfurt
6.07.2011, 18:00, **35,859**

EQ. GUINEA 0-3 BRAZIL

Érika 49
Cristiane (2) 54 90+3p

Bibiana Steinhaus GER
Marina Wozniak GER & Katrin Rafalski GER

EQG • Miriam - Bruna ■ 90+3, Laetitia, Carolina, Dulcia ■ 9 - Ana Cristina (Sinforosa 71), Jumária - Vânia, Añonman (c), Dorine - Diala ■ 60 (Adriana 86). *Frigerio ITA*

BRA • Andréia - Aline (c), Renata Costa ■ 77, Érika - Fabiana (18 Thaís Guedes 82), Formiga (9 Beatriz 90), Ester, Maurine - Cristiane, Rosana (Francielle 70 ■ 74), Marta. *Lima*

FIFA Women's World Cup Stadium, Leverkusen
6.07.2011, 18:00, **18,474**

AUSTRALIA 2-1 NORWAY

Simon (2) 57 87   Thorsnes 56

Estela Álvarez ARG
Maria Rocco ARG & Yoly García VEN

AUS • Barbieri (c) - Foord (6 Ellyse Perry 89), Carroll ■ 45+2, Uzunlar, Kellond-Knight - Kerr (5 Laura Alleway 80), McCallum, Polkinghorne, Garriock ■ 68 - De Vanna, Simon. *Sermanni SCO*

NOR • Hjelmseth (12 Erika Skarbo 46) - Gardsjord ■ 90+2, Rønning, Mjelde, Knutsen Mienna - Stensland (c), Ims (Herlovsen 81) - Haavi (6 Kristine Wigdahl Hegland 46), Mykjåland, Thorsnes - Pedersen. *Landsem*

◀ Kyah Simon (17 with hairband) scores the second of her two goals in Australia's 2-1 victory over Norway. Simon became the first indigenous Australian to score at a World Cup, with her goals ensuring a first-ever group-stage exit for Norway at either the World Cup or Olympics.

2011 Quarter-finals

Maruyama secures World Cup shock for Japan

ARENA IM ALLERPARK, WOLFSBURG
9.07.2011, 20:45, **26,067**

GERMANY 🇩🇪 **0-1** 🇯🇵 **JAPAN**
AET

Maruyama 108

👁 Quetzalli Alvarado MEX ⚑ Rita Muñoz MEX & Mayte Chávez MEX
GER • Angerer - Bresonik (Goeßling 65), Krahn, Bartusiak, Peter ■ 105+1 - Kulig (Schmidt 8), Lauderer - Garefrekes (c), Okoyino da Mbabi, Behringer - Grings (Popp 102). *Neid*
JPN • Kaihori - Kinga, Iwashimizu ■ 55, Kumagai ■ 115, Sameshima - Ohno (Iwabuchi 66) (Utsugi 116), Sawa (c) ■ 87, Sakaguchi ■ 72, Miyama - Ando, Nagasato (Maruyama 46). *Sasaki*

▶ Homare Sawa (10) and Yukari Kinga race to congratulate Karina Maruyama (18) after her goal against hosts Germany in Wolfsburg. It was the fourth time in six World Cups that the hosts had been knocked out in the quarter-finals.

Head coach Norio Sasaki inspired his players ahead of Japan's first quarter-final in 16 years by showing them pictures of the devastation that the recent earthquake and tsunami had wreaked upon their nation. "Within them, there were forward-looking images," said Aya Miyama, "so they became sources of strength." It worked, Japan silencing the crowd in Wolfsburg as a sublime extra-time winner from 2003 World Cup veteran Karina Maruyama condemned the hosts to a shock exit. Germany were last beaten in this competition in 1999 and Silvia Neid's side, who had worked with a sports psychologist since 2009, were building momentum on home soil. They had defeated Japan in the Beijing Olympics, but poor finishing, brave defending, Ayumi Kaihori's fine goalkeeping and Maruyama's super goal would deny them here. "We had the desire," said Neid afterwards, "but we could have played for all eternity today and still not scored."

600

Jill Scott's goal for England against France was the 600th scored at a World Cup.

▲ Boots used by Germany coach Silvia Neid during the 2011 World Cup.
FIFA Museum Collection

French 37-year hoodoo over England continues

FIFA Women's World Cup Stadium, Leverkusen
9.07.2011, 18:00, **26,395**

ENGLAND 🏴󠁧󠁢󠁥󠁮󠁧󠁿 **1-1** 🇫🇷 **FRANCE**
AET
3-4 PSO

J Scott 59   Bussaglia 88

Abily ✘ (saved) Smith ✓ Bussaglia ✓ Carney ✓ Thiney ✓ Stoney ✓ Bompastor ✓ Rafferty ✘ (missed) Le Sommer ✓ F White ✘ (missed)
👁 Jenny Palmqvist SWE ⚑ Anna Nyström SWE & Helen Karo SWE
ENG ■ Bardsley ■ 87 - A Scott (16 Steph **Houghton** 81), F White (c), Stoney, Unitt (20 Claire **Rafferty** 81) - Williams ■ 5, J Scott ■ 90+4 - Carney, Smith, Yankey (Asante 84) - E White ■ 77. *Powell*
FRA - Deville - Lepailleur, Georges, Viguier, Bompastor - Bussaglia, Soubeyrand (c) (Thomis 67) - Abily, Nécib (19 Sandrine **Brétigny** 79) (Le Sommer 106), Thiney - Delie. *Bini*

England had last beaten France in 1974, but it was a modern-day rivalry that spiced up this match in front of a raucous crowd of over 26,000 in Leverkusen. France had pipped England to a 2003 World Cup berth while the English had returned the favour in 2007. The talismanic Kelly Smith was England's only USA-based professional then. Now, Hope Powell had five in her squad, while the remainder played in The FA's new semi-professional Women's Super League, and they looked set for a famous victory after Everton's Jill Scott scored the 600th goal in World Cup history. Then, with two minutes remaining, Paris Saint-Germain's Elise Bussaglia let fly with a side-foot shot to send the match into extra time, then penalties. Having bravely stepped up, England skipper Faye White smacked her spot kick against the crossbar. English hearts were broken, but France were in the semis.

▶ The moment of triumph. England's Faye White misses her penalty and France are through to a first World Cup semi-final. France captain Sandrine Soubeyrand was the only player in the starting 22 who was alive when England last beat France – in 1974!

Sweden fly the flag for Scandinavia

FIFA Women's World Cup Stadium, Augsburg
10.07.2011, 13:00, **24,605**

SWEDEN 🇸🇪 **3-1** 🇦🇺 AUSTRALIA

Sjögran 11, Dahlkvist 16, Schelin 52   Perry 40

Silvia Reyes PER ▨ Mariana Corbo URU & Maria Rocco ARG

SWE • Lindahl - A Svensson (13 **Lina Nilsson** 90+2), Larsson, Rohlin, Thunebro - Forsberg (Fischer 67 ▪ 81), Seger (c), Dahlkvist, Sjögran ▪ 67 - Schelin, Öqvist (Edlund 83). *Dennerby*

AUS • Barbieri (c) - Perry (Butt 59), Uzunlar, Carroll, Kellond-Knight - Foord, van Egmond (Polkinghorne 58), McCallum (Shipard 79), Garriock ▪ 80 - Simon ▪ 23, De Vanna. *Sermanni SCO*

▲ Celebrations after Therese Sjögran gave Sweden the lead against Australia in the quarter-final in Augsburg. Sweden's win maintained Scandinavia's record of having at least one semi-finalist at every World Cup from 1991 to 2011. There were none four years later in 2015.

"Aussie! Aussie! Aussie!" chanted green-and-gold-clad fans in Augsburg as the youngest Australia squad in five finals sought to overcome a Sweden side that had forged an unbeaten path into the knockouts. Stalwarts Cheryl Salisbury, Joanne Peters and Dianne Alagich were among Australia's retirees since the last World Cup and the 2010 AFC Player of the Year Kate Gill was sidelined through injury. Encouragingly for Tom Sermanni, a squad featuring 19 players from Australia's three-year-old W-League, plus Sweden-based Heather Garriock and Lisa De Vanna of USA side magicJack, had all looked the part. They never gave up against Sweden, international cricketer Ellyse Perry hitting a blistering 25-yard stunner. But the Swedes scored at all the right times and a cool finish from their record caps holder Therese Sjögran, a searing header by Lisa Dahlkvist, and Lotta Schelin's audacious finish after a poor backpass ended Australia's campaign.

▼ Abby Wambach (20) scores a dramatic late equaliser for the USA against Brazil to take the quarter-final in Dresden to penalties.

▼▼ Ali Krieger scores the winning penalty against Brazil's Andréia to take the USA to a sixth consecutive World Cup semi-final.

So close, so far for Brazil

Rudolf-Harbig-Stadion, Dresden
10.07.2011, 17:30, **25,598**

BRAZIL 🇧🇷 **2-2** 🇺🇸 USA
AET
3-5 PSO

Marta (2) 68p 92   Daiane OG 2, Wambach 120+2

Boxx ⊛ Cristiane ⊛ Lloyd ⊛ Marta ⊛ Wambach ⊛ Daiane ✘ (saved) Rapinoe ⊛ Francielle ⊛ Krieger ⊛

Jacqui Melksham AUS ▨ Allyson Flynn AUS & Sarah Ho AUS

BRA • Andréia - Aline (c) ▪ 44, Daiane, Érika ▪ 117 - Fabiana, Formiga (Renata Costa 113), Ester, Maurine ▪ 112 - Cristiane, Rosana (Francielle 85), Marta ▪ 45. *Lima*

USA • Solo ▪ 67 - Krieger, Buehler ▪ 65, Rampone (c), LePeilbet - O'Reilly (Heath 108), Lloyd ▪ 29, Boxx ▪ 113, Cheney (Rapinoe 55 ▪ 90+1) - Wambach, Rodriguez (Morgan 72). *Sundhage SWE*

A red card, the competition's latest-ever goal and a retaken penalty were only a few of the ingredients that made this a classic. The USA may have beaten Brazil to Olympic gold in 2008, but they were desperate not to falter at the World Cup against the five-time South American champions as they had done in 2007. Gifted an own goal lead by Daiane, the USA had to dig deep when Rachel Buehler was sent off for a foul on Marta, and Hope Solo's save from Cristiane's subsequent penalty was scrubbed out for encroachment. Marta converted the retake and then hit a clever scooped goal in extra time to join Birgit Prinz as the Women's World Cup record scorer. But Abby Wambach's thumping 122nd-minute header took it to penalties, and when Solo triumphantly palmed away Daiane's attempt and Ali Krieger buried hers, the humiliating loss of four years earlier was avenged.

2011 Semi-finals

Historic win for Japan

FIFA Women's World Cup Stadium, Frankfurt
13.07.2011, 20:45, 45,434

JAPAN 3-1 SWEDEN

Kawasumi (2) 19 64, Sawa 60 — Öqvist 10

Carol Anne Chenard CAN — Rita Muñoz MEX & Mayte Chávez MEX

JPN • Kaihori - Kinga, Iwashimizu, Kumagai, Sameshima - Ohno (19 Megumi Takase 86), Sakaguchi, Sawa (c), Miyama (14 Megumi Kamionobe 89) - Ando, Kawasumi (Nagasato 74). *Sasaki*

SWE • Lindahl - A Svensson ■ 70, Larsson, Rohlin (c), Thunebro - Forsberg (Jakobsson 65), M Hammarström (Landström 69), Dahlkvist, Sjögran - Schelin, Öqvist (Göransson 75). *Dennerby*

▲ Homare Sawa gives Japan a second-half lead in the semi-final against Sweden in Frankfurt.

▼ Japan striker Nahomi Kawasumi (9) scored twice against Sweden. She has a photo of herself as a 12-year-old sitting on the lap of her hero Homare Sawa. Sawa scored the other goal in this semi-final!

Sweden had crashed out at the end of the group stage in 2007, but Thomas Dennerby had got his side back on track, and with an Olympic place in the bag, they were now training their sights on a second World Cup Final in eight years. In 1991's inaugural tournament, Sweden had trounced Japan 8-0. Such past glories would count for little in Frankfurt though, especially as the *Nadeshiko* had seen off Germany and were unbeaten against Sweden in their last four meetings, including their recent play-off for third place at the Algarve Cup. Still, a Sweden squad that sat just one place below Japan in the world rankings were hitting their stride in this tournament and they took the lead after ten minutes, Josefine Öqvist scoring in her first finals since taking 2003 by storm with a winning goal at this stage against Canada. Japan eased into the game though, equalising nine minutes later through Nahomi Kawasumi and constantly pressing and probing a Swedish side that had lost captain Caroline Seger to injury in the warm-up. They got their reward with two goals in four minutes, skipper Homare Sawa heading in before Kawasumi dispatched a long-range lob to secure Japan's historic place in the Final.

Late Wambach and Morgan goals take USA to first Final in 12 years

Borussia-Park, Mönchengladbach
13.07.2011, 18:00, 25,676

FRANCE 1-3 USA

Bompastor 55 — Cheney 9, Wambach 79, Morgan 82

Kirsi Heikkinen FIN — Tonja Paavola FIN & Anu Jokela FIN

FRA • Sapowicz - Lepailleur, Georges, Meilleroux, Bompastor - Bussaglia, Soubeyrand (c) (Thomis 78 ■ 90) - Abily, Nécib, Thiney - Delie (Le Sommer 46). *Bini*

USA • Solo - Krieger, 4 Becky **Sauerbrunn**, Rampone (c), LePeilbet - O'Reilly (Heath 87), Boxx, Lloyd (Rapinoe 65), Cheney - Wambach, Rodriguez (Morgan 56). *Sundhage SWE*

After coming third in their group in their only previous World Cup, Bruno Bini's France had already broken new ground by reaching the quarter-finals, and now they were set to tough it out in the semis against perennial medallists the USA. With a limited World Cup pedigree, France were outsiders before the tournament, but a squad dominated by Champions League winners from Olympique Lyonnais were not in Mönchengladbach just to take in the sights. The 25,676 spectators who came out to watch them on a rainy evening were hoping for a spectacle and they certainly got it. Lauren Cheney scored for the USA in the ninth minute, but France rallied with constant pressure that paid dividends in the second half when Sonia Bompastor launched a hopeful ball into the box that evaded not only onrushing team-mate Gaëtane Thiney, but Hope Solo too. After head coach Pia Sundhage threw on pacy attackers Alex Morgan and Megan Rapinoe, the USA reclaimed the initiative, and with 11 minutes remaining, Bompastor's former Washington Freedom team-mate Abby Wambach headed the USA back in front. Three minutes later, Rapinoe fed the ball through to Morgan, who chipped a shot over Bérangère Sapowicz for a killer third.

▲ Abby Wambach (20) gives the USA a 79th-minute lead against France in the semi-final at Borussia-Park. With this goal, Wambach equalled Michelle Akers' record of 12 World Cup goals for the USA.

Third top-three finish for Swedes in the World Cup

Rhein-Neckar-Arena, Sinsheim
16.07.2011, 17:30, **25,475**

SWEDEN 🇸🇪 **2-1** 🇫🇷 **FRANCE**

Schelin 29, M Hammarström 82   Thomis 56

Kari Seitz USA   Marlene Duffy USA & Veronica Perez USA

A truly sublime goal would settle only the second match for third place to feature two teams from Europe, and it was unleashed by the boot of one of the 29-year-old twins in Sweden's squad with just eight minutes remaining on the clock. World Cup debutant Marie Hammarström had warmed the bench with her goalkeeper sister Kristin for large parts of the campaign in Germany, but after coming on for Linda Forsberg and with Sweden down to ten after the sending-off of Josefine Öqvist, midfielder Hammarström produced the winner, bringing down a cleared corner with her left boot, controlling it with her right and then smashing it into the net with her left. "There was no way we were giving up because we really wanted that medal," she would say later.

Facing a side featuring seven of her Olympique Lyonnais team-mates as well as France's record caps holder Sandrine Soubeyrand, Lotta Schelin had opened the scoring after half an hour, racing on to Sara Larsson's pass from the halfway line to smack the ball into the net with the outside of her foot. In her bid to deny Schelin, keeper Bérangère Sapowicz hurt her ankle and was stretchered off, while Louisa Nécib, the player France manager Bruno Bini described as "an artist", also departed injured. Nécib's replacement and Schelin's club-mate Élodie Thomis would make her mark, firing in an equaliser from the edge of the box, but Hammarström's wonder goal would clinch Sweden's third World Cup medal.

37

At 37 years and 334 days, Sandrine Soubeyrand became the oldest outfield player at a World Cup or Olympics when she played for France against Sweden in the match for third place. She broke her own record at the London Olympics but was overtaken first by Christie Rampone (40) in 2015 and then by Formiga (41) in 2019.

2011 Match for Third Place

◀ Lotta Schelin (8) gives Sweden a first-half lead against France at the Rhein-Neckar-Arena.

◀ Sweden on their way to collect their medals.

▶ The Swedish team celebrate with their medals. This was the second time Sweden had finished third. With their second-place finish in 2003, they are ranked sixth overall in the World Cup medal table, the best record of any country not to have lifted the trophy.

2011 Final

▲ Alex Morgan (13) celebrates after giving the USA the lead in the Final against Japan in Frankfurt.

2011 World Cup Final

Japan – champions of the world!

FIFA Women's World Cup Stadium, Frankfurt
17.07.2011, 20:45, 48,817

JAPAN 2-2 **USA**
AET
3-1 PSO

Miyama 81, Sawa 117 — Morgan 69, Wambach 104

Boxx ✘ (saved) Miyama ✓ Lloyd ✘ (missed) Nagasato ✘ (saved) Heath ✘ (saved) Sakaguchi ✓ Wambach ✓ Kumagai ✓

Bibiana Steinhaus GER — Marina Wozniak GER & Katrin Rafalski GER

This was, quite simply, the best Final that the competition had yet produced. Twice Japan looked down and out against the USA, twice they fought back, and even when it came to the penalty shoot-out, the Asian side almost fluffed their lines. But Norio Sasaki's humble stars battled through all the drama and breathless moments to lift the trophy in front of almost 49,000 fans in Frankfurt.

Having garnered a reputation for singing to her players, USA coach Pia Sundhage serenaded the press before the Final with lines from Simon & Garfunkel's "Feelin' Groovy". The USA had felt happy enough under Sundhage in her three and a half years at the helm, winning Olympic gold and regaining their position as the top-ranked team in the world.

They had suffered defeats along the way, none more notable than the qualifying loss to Mexico that left them needing a play-off victory over Italy to reach this World Cup. "It was a humbling experience," said striker Abby Wambach. Japan had been tested too, having to overcome China in a play-off to claim their finals place and carrying on while their nation was reeling from a devastating natural disaster. But Sasaki believed his side had grown in confidence after their fourth-place finish at the Beijing Olympics and they certainly inspired their homeland with their run in this tournament.

Renowned for their technique and slick passing, Japan made an unusually rough start to the Final as the USA flew straight out of the blocks, but it was still goalless at the break. The two-time champions eventually took the lead through super-sub Alex Morgan, which was the signal for an extraordinary tit-for-tat exchange to start, Aya Miyama's goal pushing the game into extra time, Abby Wambach reclaiming the lead for the USA, Homare Sawa pulling her team back from the brink, Hope Solo denying Yūki Nagasato in the penalty shoot-out, Ayumi Kaihori keeping out Shannon Boxx and Tobin Heath, Carli Lloyd skying her spot kick. In the end, 1.FFC Frankfurt's new 20-year-old signing Saki Kumagai would dispatch the winner, but what a rollercoaster it had been.

"We came here for a medal but I could never have imagined winning it," said Japan's inspirational skipper Sawa afterwards. "When it became 2-1, I thought, 'Oh no' but we still had time and players around me were saying, 'We can still do it'." Do it they did, etching their names into World Cup history as the fourth nation to win the trophy and the first from Asia.

▼ Ayumi Kaihori saves Tobin Heath's penalty in the shoot-out victory over the USA.

Final 2011

◀ 2011 was the first Women's World Cup for which Panini produced a sticker album.
FIFA Museum Collection

▶ Armband worn by Japan captain Homare Sawa during the 2011 World Cup Final.
FIFA Museum Collection

> " It was a difficult moment for us because we were so close, but I think Japan, a country which has gone through so much over the past few months, almost needed the victory more than we did. The thought that their success will bring happiness and hope to the Japanese people is a consolation. "
>
> ABBY WAMBACH

◀ Head coach Norio Sasaki of Japan holds the FIFA Women's World Cup Trophy – the first man to coach a team to a world or Olympic title since 2000. Next to him is Homare Sawa with her Golden Boot, while Ayumi Kaihori holds Sawa's Golden Ball trophy.

▼ Homare Sawa lifts the FIFA Women's World Cup Trophy after Japan's penalty shoot-out victory over the USA in Frankfurt.

2012

The London Olympics was a truly British affair for football with the tournaments played in England, Scotland and Wales, and for the first time there was a Great Britain women's team. They lost in the quarter-finals to Canada who were then beaten by the USA in an epic semi-final. That meant a repeat of the previous year's World Cup Final in the gold medal match. In front of 80,203 at Wembley Stadium, the USA beat Japan 2-1 to claim gold for the third straight Olympics, and for the fourth time overall.

A full house

Women's boxing joined the line-up of sports for London 2012, which meant that there were women competing in every sport for the first time in the history of the Olympics. Britain's Nicola Adams won gold in the boxing flyweight division as Team GB finished third in the medal table, their best performance since the 1920 Games in Antwerp. This was also the first Olympics at which Brunei, Qatar and Saudi Arabia entered female athletes. USA swimmer Michael Phelps won a record 22nd Olympic medal as his country headed the medal table once again, with China finishing second. In the men's football tournament, a Brazilian gold medal remained as elusive as ever after they lost 2-1 in the Final at Wembley to Mexico in the first global Final staged at the stadium since the 1966 World Cup. It was Mexico's first Olympic football medal as was South Korea's bronze. They beat eternal rivals Japan 2-0 at Cardiff's Millennium Stadium.

▼ Boxer Nicola Adams with her gold medal.

2012 Overview

LONDON 2012

WOMEN'S OLYMPIC FOOTBALL TOURNAMENT

Story of the qualifiers

Germany's first absence

FIFA and the IOC were faced with the tricky question of what constitutes a host nation when London was awarded the 2012 Olympics. The four British football associations have historically been wary of joining together as Great Britain for fear of jeopardising their status as independent member associations of FIFA, and it was left to the British Olympic Committee to push for the entry of "Team GB" into the football tournaments. The idea did not, however, have the backing of the Irish, Scottish or Welsh football associations, but they stated they wouldn't stand in the way of players wishing to take part. Scotland's record goalscorer Julie Fleeting, along with others, ruled herself out of contention and it was an almost exclusively English team that took its place at the Games. Team GB were joined by the top two European nations from the 2011 World Cup, Sweden and France, which meant no place for Germany – the first time they had failed to qualify for an Olympics or World Cup. Also absent were China, who finished fourth in the final round of a qualifying tournament they hosted. Asia's two places went to world champions Japan and North Korea. There was also a surprise in Africa where Cameroon and South Africa secured a place in the finals with victories over Nigeria and Ethiopia respectively. New Zealand once again made light work of beating Papua New Guinea in the Final of the OFC qualifying tournament, while the USA and Canada secured their berths with victories over Costa Rica and Mexico at a tournament hosted in Vancouver. In South America the 2010 South American Women's Football Championship was used to determine the teams at both the 2011 World Cup and the 2012 Olympics. That meant a place for Colombia at both after they beat Argentina 1-0 to clinch second place behind Brazil.

▲ Japanese fans get behind their team, adding to the carnival atmosphere of the London Olympics.

Group stage

GROUP E	GROUP F	GROUP G
GBR 1-0 NZL	JPN 2-1 CAN	USA 4-2 FRA
CMR 0-5 BRA	SWE 4-1 RSA	COL 0-2 PRK
NZL 0-1 BRA	JPN 0-0 SWE	USA 3-0 COL
GBR 3-0 CMR	CAN 3-0 RSA	FRA 5-0 PRK
NZL 3-1 CMR	JPN 0-0 RSA	USA 1-0 PRK
GBR 1-0 BRA	CAN 2-2 SWE	FRA 1-0 COL

	W	D	L	+	–	PTS		W	D	L	+	–	PTS		W	D	L	+	–	PTS
GBR	3	0	0	5	0	9	SWE	1	2	0	6	3	5	USA	3	0	0	8	2	9
BRA	2	0	1	6	1	6	JPN	1	2	0	2	1	5	FRA	2	0	1	8	4	6
NZL	1	0	2	3	3	3	CAN	1	1	1	6	4	4	PRK	1	0	2	2	6	3
CMR	0	0	3	1	11	0	RSA	0	1	2	1	7	1	COL	0	0	3	0	6	0

Knockout stages

QUARTER-FINAL	QUARTER-FINAL	QUARTER-FINAL	QUARTER-FINAL
SWE 1-2 FRA	USA 2-0 NZL	BRA 0-2 JPN	GBR 0-2 CAN

SEMI-FINAL	SEMI-FINAL
FRA 1-2 JPN	CAN 3-4 AET USA

BRONZE MEDAL MATCH

CAN 1-0 FRA

GOLD MEDAL MATCH

USA 2-1 JPN

Overview 2012

	G	S	B
USA	46	28	29
CHINA PR	38	31	22
GREAT BRITAIN	29	17	19
RUSSIA	19	20	29
KOREA REPUBLIC	13	9	8
GERMANY	11	20	13

TOP OF THE MEDAL TABLE

12 TEAMS

USA WINNERS
JPN SECOND
CAN THIRD

660 986 SPECTATORS
25 423 AVERAGE PER MATCH

26 MATCHES PLAYED
43 YELLOW CARDS
1 RED CARDS

71 GOALS
2.73 AVERAGE GOALS PER MATCH

THE ALBERT OFFICIAL MATCH BALL

Host cities and stadiums
A first tri-hosted tournament

The 2012 Olympic Football Tournaments were the first FIFA championships to be co-hosted by three nations. In addition to the four stadiums in England, Wales hosted matches at the Millennium Stadium in Cardiff, while Scotland hosted matches at Hampden Park in Glasgow. All one country in the eyes of the IOC, but three different nations as far as FIFA is concerned.

GLASGOW
HAMPDEN PARK
(51,590)

NEWCASTLE
ST JAMES' PARK
(51,505)

MANCHESTER
OLD TRAFFORD
(74,040)

COVENTRY
CITY OF COVENTRY STADIUM
(32,570)

LONDON
WEMBLEY STADIUM
(89,683)

CARDIFF
MILLENNIUM STADIUM
(73,521)

×6

Top scorer
Christine Sinclair CAN

Second Place: Abby Wambach USA ×5
Third Place: Melissa Tancredi CAN ×4

2012 **Fans**

◀ Three in three games for Steph Houghton (3). Her first goal was against New Zealand in Cardiff with a long-range free kick. She celebrates with Kelly Smith.

Perfect start for Team GB

Great Britain hosted a global women's football tournament for the first time, and the land in which women had first played association football broke new ground by fielding a team that represented all four "home" nations for the first time. English players dominated, with just two Scots making the squad, while England coach Hope Powell led the team from the sidelines. Team GB, as they were referred to, opened the tournament on a hot summer's afternoon in Cardiff with a win over New Zealand thanks to 24-year-old defender Steph Houghton's free kick, and the newcomers never looked back. A 3-0 win over fellow Olympic first-timers Cameroon followed, with goals by skipper Casey Stoney, Jill Scott, and another from Houghton. In an electrifying atmosphere before a record-breaking crowd at Wembley, Houghton also delivered the winning goal in the first two minutes against Brazil to ensure top spot in the group. Brazil saw off Cameroon and New Zealand as their strike force of Marta and Cristiane continued their Olympic goalscoring form. The *Football Ferns*, despite opening with two losses, regrouped for a comfortable 3-1 win over Cameroon in their last match to secure third place and a spot in the quarter-finals. Cameroon, the gold medal winners at the 2011 All-Africa Games who defeated Nigeria to secure their Olympic berth, failed to win a point.

◀ Team GB on the attack in the group match against Brazil at Wembley.

Group E

	W	D	L	+	-	PTS
🇬🇧 GBR	3	0	0	5	0	9
🇧🇷 BRA	2	0	1	6	1	6
🇳🇿 NZL	1	0	2	3	3	3
🇨🇲 CMR	0	0	3	1	11	0

92

The match between Team GB and Brazil was watched by 70,584 at Wembley, a new record for a women's match in the UK. It broke a 92-year-old record set by Dick, Kerr's and St Helens for the 1920 Boxing Day match between the two at Goodison Park. The new record lasted just nine days before being broken in the Final.

Group stage 2012

Millennium Stadium, Cardiff
25.07.2012, 16:00, **24,445**

GREAT BRITAIN 🇬🇧 **1-0** 🇳🇿 **NEW ZEALAND**
Houghton 64

🚩 Kari Seitz USA
🚩 Veronica Perez USA & Marlene Duffy USA

GBR • 1 Karen **Bardsley** ENG - 2 Alex **Scott** ENG, 6 Casey **Stoney** ENG (c), 13 Ifeoma **Dieke** SCO, 3 Steph **Houghton** ENG - 14 Anita **Asante** ENG ■ 3, 4 Jill **Scott** ENG - 7 Karen **Carney** ENG (8 Fara **Williams** ENG 89), 12 Kim **Little** SCO (9 Ellen **White** ENG 46), 15 Eniola **Aluko** ENG - 10 Kelly **Smith** ENG (11 Rachel **Yankey** ENG 68). *Hope Powell ENG*

NZL • 1 Jenny **Bindon** - 2 Ria **Percival**, 6 Rebecca **Smith** (c), 5 Abby **Erceg**, 7 Ali **Riley** - 4 Katie **Hoyle** - 8 Hayley **Moorwood** (12 Betsy **Hassett** 59), 9 Amber **Hearn**, 11 Kirsty **Yallop** (16 Annalie **Longo** 74) - 17 Hannah **Wilkinson** ■ 43, 10 Sarah **Gregorius**. *Tony Readings ENG*

Millennium Stadium, Cardiff
25.07.2012, 18:45, **30,847**

CAMEROON 🇨🇲 **0-5** 🇧🇷 **BRAZIL**
Francielle 7,
Renata Costa 10,
Marta (2) 73p 88
Cristiane 80

🚩 Jenny Palmqvist SWE
🚩 Helen Karo SWE & Anna Nyström SWE

CMR • 1 Annette **Ngo Ndom** - 13 Claudine **Meffometou**, 2 Christine **Manie** ■ 6, 5 Augustine **Ejangue**, 10 Bebey **Beyene** - 8 Raissa **Feudjio** (6 Francine **Zouga** 64) - 16 Jeannette **Yango** ■ 61, 12 Françoise **Bella** (c) - 9 Madeleine **Ngono Mani**, 7 Gabrielle **Onguéné**, 3 Ajara **Nchout** (17 Gaëlle **Enganamouit** 71). *Carl Enow Ngachu*

BRA • 1 **Andréia** - 14 **Bruna**, 5 **Érika**, 16 **Renata Costa** - 2 **Fabiana**, 13 **Francielle** (3 **Daiane** 90+2), 7 **Ester**, 6 **Maurine** - 9 **Thaís Guedes** (11 **Cristiane** 46), 8 **Formiga** ■ 75 (17 **Grazielle** 81), 10 **Marta** (c). *Jorge Barcellos*

Millennium Stadium, Cardiff
28.07.2012, 14:30, **30,103**

NEW ZEALAND 🇳🇿 **0-1** 🇧🇷 **BRAZIL**
Cristiane 86

🚩 Bibiana Steinhaus GER
🚩 Marina Wozniak GER & Katrin Rafalski GER

NZL • Bindon - Percival, Smith (c), Erceg, Riley - Hoyle ■ 85 - Moorwood (Yallop 77), Hearn, Hassett (Longo 87) - Wilkinson ■ 75 (13 Rosie **White** 81), Gregorius. *Readings ENG*

BRA • Andréia ■ 90+3 - Bruna, Érika, Renata Costa - Fabiana (Daiane 88), Francielle (Thaís Guedes 58), Ester, Maurine - Cristiane, Formiga, Marta (c). *Barcellos*

Millennium Stadium, Cardiff
28.07.2012, 17:15, **31,141**

GREAT BRITAIN 🇬🇧 **3-0** 🇨🇲 **CAMEROON**
Stoney 18, J Scott 23
Houghton 82

🚩 Hong Eun Ah KOR
🚩 Sarah Ho AUS & Kim Kyoung Min KOR

GBR • Bardsley ENG - A Scott ENG, Bradley ENG, Stoney ENG (c), Dieke SCO (5 Sophie **Bradley** ENG 68), Houghton ENG - Asante ENG (F Williams ENG 60), J Scott ENG - Carney ENG, Little SCO, Aluko ENG - K Smith ENG (Yankey ENG 46). *Powell ENG*

CMR • Ngo Ndom - Meffometou, Manie ■ 17, Ejangue, Beyene (14 Bibi **Medoua** 33 ■ 36) - Yango (Nchout 62), Bella (c) - Zouga - Onguéné, Ngono Mani (Enganamouit 79), 11 Adrienne **Iven**. *Enow Ngachu*

City of Coventry Stadium, Coventry
31.07.2012, 19:45, **11,425**

NEW ZEALAND 🇳🇿 **3-1** 🇨🇲 **CAMEROON**
Smith 43, Sonkeng OG 49   Onguéné 75
Gregorius 62

🚩 Christina Pedersen NOR
🚩 Hege Steinlund NOR & Lada Rojc CRO

NZL • Bindon - Percival, Smith (c), Erceg, Riley - Hoyle - Hassett, Hearn, Longo (Yallop 82) - Gregorius (Moorwood 65), White. *Readings ENG*

CMR • Ngo Ndom - 4 Yvonne **Leuko**, 15 Ysis **Sonkeng**, Ejangue ■ 51, Medoua ■ 21 - Feudjio, Bella (c) (Yango 59 ■ 76) - Onguéné, Zouga (Enganamouit 78), Nchout (Ngono Mani 46) - Iven. *Enow Ngachu*

Wembley Stadium, London
31.07.2012, 19:45, **70,584**

GREAT BRITAIN 🇬🇧 **1-0** 🇧🇷 **BRAZIL**
Houghton 2
(K Smith penalty saved 56)

🚩 Carol Anne Chenard CAN
🚩 Marie Charbonneau CAN & Stacy Greyson JAM

GBR • Bardsley ENG - A Scott ENG, Bradley ENG, Stoney ENG (c), Houghton ENG - J Scott ENG, Asante ENG - Carney ENG (F Williams ENG 84), Little ENG, Aluko ENG (Yankey ENG 63) - K Smith ENG (E White ENG 84). *Powell ENG*

BRA • Andréia - Bruna ■ 32 (4 **Aline** 46 ■ 68), Érika, Renata Costa - Maurine (Daiane 46), Ester (Grazielle 72), Francielle ■ 56, 12 **Rosana** - Cristiane, Thaís Guedes, Marta (c). *Barcellos*

2012 Group stage

City of Coventry Stadium, Coventry
25.07.2012, 17:00, **14,119**

JAPAN 2-1 **CANADA**

Kawasumi 33, Miyama 44 — Tancredi 55

Kirsi Heikkinen FIN
Anu Jokela FIN & Tonja Paavola FIN

JPN • 1 Miho **Fukumoto** - 2 Yukari **Kinga**, 3 Azusa **Iwashimizu**, 4 Saki **Kumagai**, 5 Aya **Sameshima** - 8 Aya **Miyama** (c), 6 Mizuho **Sakaguchi**, 10 Homare **Sawa**, 9 Nahomi **Kawasumi** - 17 Yūki **Ōgimi**, 11 Shinobu **Ohno** (7 Kozue **Ando** 65). *Norio Sasaki*

CAN • 18 Erin **McLeod** - 7 Rhian **Wilkinson** (5 Robyn **Gayle** 71), 9 Candace **Chapman**, 4 Carmelina **Moscato**, 10 Lauren **Sesselmann** (3 Chelsea **Stewart** 71) - 11 Desiree **Scott** - 8 Diana **Matheson**, 13 Sophie **Schmidt**, 6 Kaylyn **Kyle** (15 Kelly **Parker** 76) - 14 Melissa **Tancredi**, 12 Christine **Sinclair** (c). *John Herdman ENG*

City of Coventry Stadium, Coventry
25.07.2012, 19:45, **18,290**

SWEDEN 4-1 **SOUTH AFRICA**

Fischer 7, Dahlkvist 20 — Modise 60
Schelin (2) 21 63

Salomé Di Iorio ARG
Mariana Corbo URU & Maria Rocco ARG

SWE • 1 Hedvig **Lindahl** - 13 Lina **Nilsson**, 3 Emma **Berglund**, 2 Linda **Sembrant**, 6 Sara **Thunebro** - 10 Sofia **Jakobsson**, 7 Lisa **Dahlkvist**, 5 Nilla **Fischer** (c) (14 Johanna **Almgren** 61), 12 Marie **Hammarström** (11 Antonia **Göransson** 84) - 15 Caroline **Seger**, 8 Lotta **Schelin** (9 Kosovare **Asllani** 73). *Thomas Dennerby*

RSA • 1 Roxanne **Barker** - 15 Refiloe **Jane**, 4 Amanda **Sister**, 5 Janine **van Wyk**, 3 Nothando **Vilakazi** ▮86 - 16 Mpumi **Nyandeni**, 8 Kylie **Louw**, 9 Amanda **Dlamini** (c), 12 Portia **Modise** - 11 Noko **Matlou** (10 Marry **Ntsweng** 62), 17 Andisiwe **Mgcoyi** (14 Sanah **Mollo** 80). *Joseph Mkhonza*

City of Coventry Stadium, Coventry
28.07.2012, 12:00, **14,160**

JAPAN 0-0 **SWEDEN**

Quetzalli Alvarado MEX
Mayte Chávez MEX & Shirley Perello HON

JPN • Fukumoto - Kinga, Iwashimizu, Kumagai, Sameshima - Miyama (c), Sakaguchi, Sawa (14 Asuna **Tanaka** 59), Kawasumi - Ōgimi (Ando 90+2), Ohno (16 Mana **Iwabuchi** 81). *Sasaki*

SWE • Lindahl - 4 Annica **Svensson**, Berglund, Sembrant, Thunebro (c) ▮22 - Jakobsson (Nilsson 78), Dahlkvist (Göransson 87), Seger, Hammarström - Almgren (Asllani 63), Schelin. *Dennerby*

City of Coventry Stadium, Coventry
28.07.2012, 14:45, **14,753**

CANADA 3-0 **SOUTH AFRICA**

Tancredi 7
Sinclair (2) 58 86

Christina Pedersen NOR
Hege Steinlund NOR & Lada Rojc CRO

CAN • 1 Karina **LeBlanc** - Wilkinson, Gayle (Stewart 68), Moscato, Sesselmann - Scott - Matheson, Schmidt, Kyle (16 Jonelle **Filigno** 74) - Tancredi (17 Brittany **Timko** 87), Sinclair (c). *Herdman ENG*

RSA • 18 Thokozile **Mndaweni** - 6 Zamandosi **Cele**, Sister, van Wyk, 13 Gabisile **Hlumbane** - Jane - Louw, Dlamini (c), Nyandeni - Mgcoyi (Mollo 69), Modise ▮53 (Matlou 83). *Mkhonza*

Millennium Stadium, Cardiff
31.07.2012, 14:30, **24,202**

JAPAN 0-0 **SOUTH AFRICA**

Thalia Mitsi GRE
María Luisa Villa Gutiérrez ESP & Yolanda Parga Rodríguez ESP

JPN • 18 Ayumi **Kaihori** - Kinga, Iwashimizu, Kumagai, 12 Kyoko **Yano** - 15 Megumi **Takase**, Tanaka, Miyama (c) (Sakaguchi 77), Iwabuchi (Kawasumi 58) - 13 Karina **Maruyama** (Ōgimi 90+3), Ando. *Sasaki*

RSA • Mndaweni - Hlumbane (Sister 61), van Wyk, Cele, Vilakazi - Louw (Ntsweng 90), Jane, Dlamini (c), Nyandeni - Modise, Matlou (Mollo 61). *Mkhonza*

St James' Park, Newcastle
31.07.2012, 14:30, **12,719**

CANADA 2-2 **SWEDEN**

Tancredi (2) 43 84 — Hammarström 14
Jakobsson 16

Hong Eun Ah KOR
Sarah Ho AUS & Kim Kyoung Min KOR

CAN • McLeod - Wilkinson, Moscato, Sesselmann, 20 Marie-Ève **Nault** (Stewart 86) - Matheson, Scott, Sinclair (c), Schmidt (Parker 88) - Filigno (Kyle 75), Tancredi. *Herdman ENG*

SWE • Lindahl - Nilsson ▮61, Berglund, Sembrant, Thunebro - Fischer (c) ▮29 (Dahlkvist 53), Seger - Jakobsson, Asllani (Almgren 63), Hammarström - Schelin. *Dennerby*

Group F

	W	D	L	+	-	PTS
SWE	1	2	0	6	3	5
JPN	1	2	0	2	1	5
CAN	1	1	1	6	4	4
RSA	0	1	2	1	7	1

▲ Swedish goalkeeper Hedvig Lindahl plucks the ball out of the air during the match against debutants South Africa in Coventry.

▲ South Africa's Marry Ntsweng and Japan's Nahomi Kawasumi share a moment during the 0-0 draw in Cardiff.

World champions ease through

A decision by world champions Japan to rest key players in their last group match against South Africa allowed Sweden to top the group. The Japanese had begun their Olympic campaign as favourites to add gold to the world title won the previous year in Germany, and they started with a 2-1 victory over Canada. In their next match, however, Norio Sasaki's side were frustrated by Sweden and held to a goalless draw. The Swedes, who had beaten South Africa in their opening game, led the group going into their last match, and Sasaki seemed content to let it stay that way in order to remain in Cardiff where their quarter-final would then be held.

Their 0-0 draw with the South Africans ensured just that. Two early goals meant that Sweden led for most of their final match against Canada, but two goals by Melissa Tancredi earned a draw for the Canadians, who joined the Swedes and Japanese in the quarter-finals. The North Americans had had a disappointing World Cup in Germany, but under new coach John Herdman they were focused on team-building, which paid off in their win over South Africa. The South Africans, twice denied an Olympic berth by rivals Nigeria, secured just the solitary point before heading home, although that point did come against the World Champions.

▼ Canada's Melissa Tancredi starts the fightback against Sweden with the first of her two goals. The Canadians had trailed to two early Swedish goals but the draw ensured they qualified as one of the two best third-placed teams.

◀ Colombia goalkeeper Sandra Sepúlveda denies USA striker Abby Wambach (14). However, Colombia lost all three group games and failed to score.

Clean sweep for defending champions USA

The USA and France dominated the only group from which just two teams qualified, with North Korea the only third-placed team not to make it through to the quarter-finals. The Americans were out to qualify for a fifth consecutive Final and to win a hat-trick of Olympic titles. Incredibly, they had yet to finish lower than third at any World Cup or Olympics and they got their campaign off to an excellent start by winning all three group games. Against France, who were making their Olympic debut, the USA found themselves 2-0 down after just 14 minutes, but they fought back to win 4-2 – the only time in the six Olympic tournaments that a team has come back to win from that position. The French finished in second place, despite an end to their 17-game winning streak which began after the 2011 third place play-off loss to Sweden. The North Koreans had started their campaign with a 2-0 win over Colombia, a match that, rather embarrassingly, had begun with the team being introduced with the South Korean flag. Sin Ui Gun and his players stormed off the pitch in fury, returning to play an hour later after being convinced the mistake had not been intentional.

◀ France defender Wendie Renard scores her side's fourth goal in the 5-0 victory over North Korea in Glasgow.

Group G

Group stage 2012

	W	D	L	+	–	PTS
USA	3	0	0	8	2	9
FRA	2	0	1	8	4	6
PRK	1	0	2	2	6	3
COL	0	0	3	0	6	0

Hampden Park, Glasgow
25.07.2012, 17:00, **18,090**

USA 4-2 FRANCE

Wambach 19, Morgan (2) 32 66, Lloyd 56 — Thiney 12, Delie 14

Sachiko Yamagishi JPN
Saori Takahashi JPN & Widiya Shamsuri MAS

USA • 1 Hope **Solo** - 6 Amy **LePeilbet**, 3 Christie **Rampone** (c), 16 Rachel **Buehler**, 5 Kelley **O'Hara** - 15 Megan **Rapinoe** (11 Sydney **Leroux** 84), 12 Lauren **Cheney**, 7 Shannon **Boxx** (10 Carli **Lloyd** 17), 17 Tobin **Heath** - 13 Alex **Morgan** (8 Amy **Rodriguez** 74), 14 Abby **Wambach**. *Pia Sundhage SWE*

FRA • 18 Sarah **Bouhaddi** - 7 Corine **Franco**, 5 Ophélie **Meilleroux** (c) (4 Laura **Georges** 46), 2 Wendie **Renard**, 8 Sonia **Bompastor** - 12 Élodie **Thomis**, 11 Marie-Laure **Delie**, 10 Camille **Abily** (6 Sandrine **Soubeyrand** 71), 15 Élise **Bussaglia**, 17 Gaëtane **Thiney** - 14 Louisa **Nécib** (9 Eugénie **Le Sommer** 46). *Bruno Bini*

Hampden Park, Glasgow
25.07.2012, 19:45, **18,900**

COLOMBIA 0-2 KOREA DPR

Kim Song Hui (2) 39 85

Carol Anne Chenard CAN
Marie Charbonneau CAN & Stacy Greyson JAM

COL • 18 Sandra **Sepúlveda** - 4 Natalia **Ariza** (5 Nataly **Arias** 46), 14 Kelis **Peduzine**, 3 Natalia **Gaitán** (c), 13 Yulieth **Domínguez** - 11 Liana **Salazar** (2 Tatiana **Ariza** 77), 10 Catalina **Usme**, 6 Daniela **Montoya** (15 Ingrid **Vidal** 46), 9 Carmen **Rodallega** - 7 Oriánica **Velásquez**, 16 Lady **Andrade**. *Ricardo Rozo*

PRK • 1 **Jo** Yun Mi - 3 **Kim** Myong Gum, 2 **Kim** Nam Hui, 4 **Ro** Chol Ok, 5 **Yun** Song Mi - 11 **Kim** Chung Sim (c) (12 **Kim** Un Hyang 40), 8 **Jon** Myong Hwa, 6 **Choe** Un Ju (20 **Choe** Yong Sim 88), 7 **Ri** Ye Gyong - 16 **Kim** Song Hui (9 **Choe** Mi Gyong 90+2), 10 **Yun** Hyon Hi ▪ 83. *Sin Ui Gun*

Hampden Park, Glasgow
28.07.2012, 17:00, **11,313**

USA 3-0 COLOMBIA

Rapinoe 33, Wambach 74, Lloyd 77

Thalia Mitsi GRE
María Luisa Villa Gutiérrez ESP & Yolanda Parga ESP

USA • **Solo** - 2 Heather **Mitts**, **Rampone** (c), **Buehler**, **O'Hara** - 9 Heather **O'Reilly** (**Heath** 67), **Lloyd**, **Cheney**, **Rapinoe** (**Rodriguez** 81) - **Morgan**, **Wambach** (**Leroux** 78). *Sundhage SWE*

COL • **Sepúlveda** - **Arias**, **Peduzine**, **Gaitán** (c), **Domínguez** - T **Ariza** (**Salazar** 71), **Usme**, **Andrade**, **Rodallega** (12 Ana **Montoya** 71) - **Velásquez**, **Vidal** (17 Melissa **Ortiz** 86). *Rozo*

Hampden Park, Glasgow
28.07.2012, 19:45, **11,743**

FRANCE 5-0 KOREA DPR

Georges 45, Thomis 70, Delie 71, Renard 81, Catala 87

Thérèse Neguel CMR
Tempa Ndah BEN & Lidwine Rakotozafinoro MAD

FRA • **Bouhaddi** - **Franco**, **Georges**, **Renard**, **Bompastor** ▪ 83 - **Bussaglia**, **Soubeyrand** (c) (**Abily** 62) - **Le Sommer** ▪ 54 (**Thomis** 62), **Nécib**, **Thiney** - **Delie** (13 Camille **Catala** 80). *Bini*

PRK • **Jo** Yun Mi - **Kim** Myong Gum (c), **Choe** Yong Sim, **Kim** Nam Hui, **Yun** Song Mi - **Kim** Un Hyang (**Kim** Chung Sim 59), **Jon** Myong Hwa (13 **O** Hui Sun 72), **Choe** Un Ju (**Kim** Song Hui 51), **Ri** Ye Gyong - **Choe** Mi Gyong, **Yun** Hyon Hi. *Sin Ui Gun*

Old Trafford, Manchester
31.07.2012, 17:15, **29,522**

USA 1-0 KOREA DPR

Wambach 25

Jenny Palmqvist SWE
Anna Nyström SWE & Helen Karo SWE

USA • **Solo** - **LePeilbet**, **Rampone** (c), **Buehler** (4 Becky **Sauerbrunn** 75), **O'Hara** - **O'Reilly**, **Cheney** ▪ 16 (**Rodriguez** 84), **Lloyd**, **Rapinoe** (**Heath** 46) - **Wambach**, **Morgan**. *Sundhage SWE*

PRK • 18 **O** Chang Ran - 14 **Pong** Son Hwa, **Choe** Yong Sim, **Kim** Nam Hui, **Kim** Myong Gum - **Jon** Myong Hwa - **Kim** Chung Sim (c) (**Kim** Un Hyang 80), **Choe** Un Ju, **Kim** Song Hui ▪ 42 (**Choe** Mi Gyong 63 ▪ 76 ▪ 81 ▪ 81), **Ri** Ye Gyong ▪ 13 - **Yun** Hyon Hi (21 **Kim** Su Gyong 31). *Sin Ui Gun*

St James' Park, Newcastle
31.07.2012, 17:15, **13,184**

FRANCE 1-0 COLOMBIA

Thomis 5

Quetzalli Alvarado MEX
Mayte Chávez MEX & Shirley Perello HON

FRA • **Bouhaddi** - **Franco** (16 Sabrina **Viguier** 84), **Georges**, **Renard**, **Bompastor** (3 Laure **Boulleau** 46) - **Abily**, **Soubeyrand** (c) (**Bussaglia** 55) - **Thomis**, **Nécib** ▪ 61, **Thiney** - **Delie**. *Bini*

COL • **Sepúlveda** - **Arias**, **Peduzine**, **Gaitán** (c), N **Ariza** - **Domínguez** ▪ 48, **Usme** (8 Yoreli **Rincón** 45+3), D **Montoya** ▪ 53, **Rodallega** - **Velásquez** (**Ortiz** 68), **Vidal** (T **Ariza** 81). *Rozo*

2012 Quarter-finals

▲ Sweden's Sara Thunebro tackles French playmaker Louisa Nécib. France's 2-1 victory made up in some measure for their defeat at the hands of the Swedes in the 2011 World Cup match for third place.

▲▶ Captain Nilla Fischer after Sweden's defeat by France in the quarter-final at Hampden Park, Glasgow. She had given her side an early lead.

French joy in Glasgow

Hampden Park, Glasgow
3.08.2012, 12:00, **12,869**

SWEDEN 1-2 **FRANCE**

Fischer 18   Georges 29, Renard 39

🎬 Kari Seitz USA
🚩 Marlene Duffy USA & Veronica Perez USA

SWE • Lindahl - A Svensson ■ 78 (16 Madelaine Edlund 82), Berglund, Sembrant, Thunebro - Jakobsson (Asllani 58), Dahlkvist, Fischer (c), Hammarström (Göransson 70) - Schelin, Seger. *Dennerby*

FRA • Bouhaddi - Franco ■ 21, Georges, Renard, Bompastor - Bussaglia, Soubeyrand (c) (Abily 71) - Thomis (Le Sommer 75), Nécib, Thiney (Catala 88) - Delie. *Bini*

France came back from behind thanks to two goals from defenders to upset Sweden, avenging their defeat to the Scandinavians in the 2011 World Cup play-off for third place. The Swedes took an early lead with an 18th-minute goal by midfielder Nilla Fischer, who deflected a Marie Hammarström corner off her neck and shoulder beyond France goalkeeper Sarah Bouhaddi. The French equaliser 11 minutes later also came from a corner, a header by Laura Georges, one of the first women to graduate from the country's famed elite football training centre at Clairefontaine. Then, with six minutes of the first half left, 22-year-old Wendie Renard scored the winner with a shot from inside the six-yard box. Sandrine Soubeyrand's deep free kick was headed back across the area by Georges and into the path of Renard off the back of Caroline Seger.

New Zealand make the USA work hard for victory

St James' Park, Newcastle
3.08.2012, 14:30, **10,441**

USA 2-0 **NEW ZEALAND**

Wambach 27, Leroux 87

🎬 Salomé Di Iorio ARG   🚩 Mariana Corbo URU & Maria Rocco ARG

USA • Solo - LePeilbet, Rampone (c), Buehler, O'Hara - Rapinoe (O'Reilly 71), Lloyd ■ 79, Cheney (Rodriguez 90+1), Heath - Morgan (Leroux 81), Wambach ■ 43. *Sundhage SWE*

NZL • Bindon - Percival, Smith (c), Erceg, Riley - Hoyle (Longo 90+5) - Hassett, Hearn, Yallop (Moorwood 57) - Wilkinson (White 77), Gregorius. *Readings ENG*

This was New Zealand's first appearance in the quarter-finals of either the World Cup or Olympics and against the Americans they were firm underdogs. Their only win against their opponents had come a quarter of a century previously in 1987. Coached by Englishman Tony Readings, they forced Pia Sundhage's players to work hard for their 2-0 victory. Just before the half-hour, 32-year-old Abby Wambach opened the scoring for the Americans, her fourth goal in as many games and matching her total from eight years earlier, after Alex Morgan ran on to a long clearance before threading the ball through a crowded box for Wambach to tap home. The USA dominated the second half but the *Ferns* held fast until just before the end when 22-year-old substitute Sydney Leroux picked up another long ball forward before firing through Jenny Bindon's legs to secure a place in the semi-finals.

▶ USA captain Christie Rampone (3) shakes hands with New Zealand's Rebecca Smith before the quarter-final at St James' Park, Newcastle. Smith grew up in the USA and had been a spectator at the Rose Bowl when the Americans won the 1999 World Cup.

Oh yes... for Ohno!

Millennium Stadium, Cardiff
3.08.2012, 17:00, 28,528

BRAZIL 0-2 **JAPAN**

Ogimi 27, Ohno 73

Kirsi Heikkinen FIN
Tonja Paavola FIN & Anu Jokela FIN

BRA • Andréia - Fabiana, Bruna ■ 70, Érika, Rosana (Ester 80) - Francielle, Formiga, Marta (c) ■ 49, Renata Costa (Grazielle 85) - Cristiane, Thaís Guedes. *Barcellos*

JPN • Fukumoto - Kinga, Iwashimizu, Kumagai, Sameshima - Miyama (c), Sakaguchi ■ 58, Sawa, Kawasumi - Ōgimi (Takase 89), Ohno (Ando 85). *Sasaki*

▶ Japan goalkeeper Miho Fukumoto thwarts another Brazilian attack during the quarter-final at the Millennium Stadium in Cardiff.

Defeat at the hands of Japan sealed Brazil's earliest-ever Olympic exit after they had reached at least the semi-finals at the first four tournaments. Remarkably, their 34-year-old midfielder Formiga was featuring in her fifth campaign, 16 years on from Atlanta. She couldn't, however, add to the two silver medals won in 2004 and 2008 as Brazil lost to the world champions in Cardiff. While Brazil tested Japan throughout the 90 minutes, they just couldn't break down their defence. The Japanese took the lead through a quickly taken Homare Sawa free kick just inside the Brazil half which caught the Brazilians off guard, striker Yūki Ōgimi latching onto a perfectly-weighted ball to score just before the half-hour mark. Japan wrapped up the win in the second half when Ōgimi's cross-field pass found her fellow striker Shinobu Ohno, who turned and wrong-footed Érika before lofting the ball over Andréia.

▶ No way through for Marta (10). Japan's 2-0 victory over Brazil meant that, for the first time, the South Americans failed to make it through to the Olympic semi-finals.

▼ Canada's Jonelle Filigno (white hair band) celebrates her early goal in the quarter-final against Team GB in Coventry.

▼ Canada's Christine Sinclair (12) in action during the quarter-final between Great Britain and Canada. She scored her third goal of the tournament against Team GB.

Canada end British dreams

City of Coventry Stadium, Coventry
3.08.2012, 19:30, 28,828

GREAT BRITAIN 0-2 **CANADA**

Filigno 12, Sinclair 26

Sachiko Yamagishi JPN
Saori Takahashi JPN & Widiya Shamsuri MAS

GBR • Bardsley ENG - A Scott ENG, Bradley ENG (Yankey ENG 84), Stoney ENG (c), Houghton ENG - Asante ENG, J Scott ENG - Carney ENG, Little SCO (17 Rachel **Williams** ENG 82), Aluko ENG - E White ENG (F Williams ENG 63). *Powell ENG*

CAN • McLeod - Wilkinson, Moscato, Sesselmann, Nault ■ 86 - Matheson, Scott, Schmidt (Parker 78) - Filigno (Kyle 61), Sinclair (c) (Timko 88), Tancredi. *Herdman ENG*

Two first-half goals by Canada within the space of 14 minutes brought the hosts' maiden Olympic run to an end at a packed stadium in Coventry. In a battle between two English coaches, it was John Herdman, just eleven months into the Canada job, who triumphed over Hope Powell. From a Sophie Schmidt corner, Jonelle Filigno opened the scoring with a powerful shot that curled its way past Team GB keeper Karen Bardsley. Great Britain were missing inspirational striker Kelly Smith but twice went close to equalising, first through a long-range shot by midfielder Jill Scott, and then through a Karen Carney header, but Canadian keeper Erin McLeod was up to the job. Then, after 26 minutes, captain Christine Sinclair scored a free kick from 25 metres out to extend her side's lead. It had been a unique adventure for Team GB but they would be absent four years later in Rio despite efforts to promote the idea of a British women's team coming together again for the Olympics in Rio.

2012 Semi-finals

Japan through to first Olympic Final

Wembley Stadium, London
6.08.2012, 17:00, **61,482**

FRANCE 1-2 JAPAN

Le Sommer 76　　Ōgimi 32, Sakaguchi 49
(Bussaglia penalty missed 79)

Quetzalli Alvarado MEX ■ Mayte Chávez MEX & Shirley Perello HON

FRA • Bouhaddi - Franco, Georges, Renard ■ 13, Bompastor - Bussaglia, Soubeyrand (c) (Abily 56) - Thomis, Nécib, Thiney (Le Sommer 58) - Delie. *Bini*

JPN • Fukumoto - Kinga, Iwashimizu, Kumagai, Sameshima - Miyama (c), Sakaguchi (Tanaka 84), Sawa, Kawasumi - Ōgimi, Ohno (Ando 74). *Sasaki*

Just four years after their breakout performance at the Beijing Olympics, Japan now had the chance to add an Olympic Final to their 2011 World Cup title. They managed to hold on to their lead in this semi-final despite a serious onslaught by the French at the end of the match in front of an impressive 61,482 fans at Wembley. Yūki Ōgimi opened the scoring just past the half-hour mark following a mistake by French goalkeeper Sarah Bouhaddi. She failed to gather the ball from a free kick and when it fell behind her, Ōgimi was part of a mêlée that saw it bundled over the line. Just four minutes into the second half, Japan doubled their lead from another deep free kick. This time it was more clear-cut as Mizuho Sakaguchi met Aya Miyama's kick with a superb header that gave Bouhaddi no chance. The French were left chasing the game, and with 14 minutes to go they pulled one back. Japan gave the ball away in midfield and Marie-Laure Delie broke down the right wing. She released the ball to Élodie Thomis, whose cross was put away by Eugénie Le Sommer. France had a golden opportunity to level things up just three minutes later when Le Sommer was brought down in the box but Élise Bussaglia put the spot kick just wide of the post.

▲▲ Yūki Ōgimi (17) celebrates scoring Japan's opening goal against France.

▲ Élise Bussaglia (15) after missing her penalty in the 2-1 semi-final defeat at the hands of Japan at Wembley. It was only the third unsuccessful penalty in Olympic history.

3 Christine Sinclair's hat-trick for Canada in the semi-final against the USA was the first time a player had scored three and ended up on the losing side at the Olympics, a feat later matched by Great Britain's Ellen White in 2020 and Zambia's Barbra Banda at both the 2020 and 2024 Games.

USA steal seven-goal thriller at the death

Old Trafford, Manchester
6.08.2012, 19:45, **26,630**

CANADA 3-4 USA
AET

Sinclair (3) 22 67 73　　Rapinoe (2) 54 70, Wambach 80p, Morgan 120+3

Christina Pedersen NOR ■ Hege Steinlund NOR & Lada Rojc CRO

CAN • McLeod - Wilkinson, Moscato, Sesselmann, Nault (Stewart 101) - Matheson, Scott ■ 60, Schmidt - Filigno (Kyle 67), Sinclair (c), Tancredi ■ 79. *Herdman ENG*

USA • Solo - LePeilbet (Leroux 76), Rampone (c), Buehler (Sauerbrunn 110), O'Hara - Rapinoe, Lloyd, Cheney (O'Reilly 101), Heath - Morgan, Wambach. *Sundhage SWE*

▼ Abby Wambach (14) scores from the penalty spot to draw the USA level at 3-3 in a dramatic semi-final against Canada at Old Trafford.

This was one of the all-time great matches, the USA coming from behind three times to beat rivals Canada in an epic North American derby. Canadian skipper Christine Sinclair scored a hat-trick, but it wasn't enough to deny the USA a fifth consecutive appearance in the Olympic Final. Sinclair opened the scoring in the 22nd minute with a superb goal, weaving through the American defence to power a shot past Hope Solo. It was a lead they held on to until nine minutes into the second half when Megan Rapinoe scored direct from an inswinging corner – the first time that had ever happened at the Olympics. Thirteen minutes later, Sinclair put Canada in front again, heading in Melissa Tancredi's inch-perfect cross. It was the start of a four-goal spree within 13 minutes as three minutes later, Rapinoe scored her second by firing home after a pin-point cross-field pass from Kelley O'Hara. Then came Sinclair's hat-trick – a header from a corner – her sixth goal, which saw her finish as the tournament's top scorer. Back came the Americans, again. This time their equaliser came from a penalty, scored by Abby Wambach after Marie-Ève Nault was adjudged to have handled the ball at a free kick taken inside the box. The match went into extra time, and the USA left it late to secure the victory. Two minutes and 22 seconds into injury time of the second period of extra time, substitute Heather O'Reilly crossed for Alex Morgan to head home. It was a game that few of those at Old Trafford will ever forget.

▼ USA striker Alex Morgan (13) scores a dramatic headed winner against Canada, three minutes into injury time of extra time. It secured a fifth consecutive appearance in the Olympic Final for the Americans.

2012 Bronze Medal Match

City of Coventry Stadium, Coventry
9.08.2012, 13:00, **12,465**

CANADA 🇨🇦 **1-0** 🇫🇷 **FRANCE**

Matheson 90+2

Jenny Palmqvist SWE / Anna Nyström SWE & Helen Karo SWE

Herdman ENG — Bini

Canada: 18 McLeod; 7 Wilkinson, 4 Moscato, 10 Sesselmann, 20 Nault (Chapman 83); 8 Matheson, 11 Scott, 13 Schmidt; 14 Tancredi (Timko 77), 16 Filigno (Kyle 55), 12 Sinclair (c)

France: 18 Bouhaddi; 8 Bompastor, 2 Renard, 4 Georges, 7 Franco; 6 Soubeyrand (c) (Abily 54 ▪ 90), 15 Bussaglia; 17 Thiney, 14 Nécib, 12 Thomis (Catala 90+2); 11 Delie (Le Sommer 60)

▼ Carmelina Moscato (4) and Candace Chapman celebrate winning Canada's first-ever Olympic football medal.

▼▶ Diana Matheson is mobbed by her teammates after scoring an injury-time winner against France.

▲ Action from the bronze medal match in Coventry.

Matheson injury-time winner secures first medal for Canada

After Canada's seven-goal epic with the USA in the semi-final, it was perhaps too much to expect more of the same and for the first half at least, this was a game of cat and mouse. Both had lost a semi-final before this tournament – Canada at the 2003 World Cup and France at the 2011 World Cup – and on each occasion both had gone on to lose the play-off for third place. This was a game that came alive in the second half. The first opportunity fell to France playmaker Louisa Nécib after 49 minutes. Her shot was deflected off Rhian Wilkinson, forcing Erin McLeod to make a fine save. Although France had returned from the break energised, Bruno Bini soon brought on playmakers Camille Abily and Eugénie Le Sommer to try to break the deadlock. On the hour, Élodie Thomis, a constant threat down the right, pulled the ball back from the goal line to Gaëtane Thiney, who rattled the post. From the clearance, the ball fell to Nécib whose shot forced a diving header from Carmelina Moscato. Moments later, Thomis hit the bar and there was barely time to catch your breath before Le Sommer shot just wide. Then, on 70 minutes, Desiree Scott cleared off the line for Canada from Corine Franco, who went close again seven minutes later but shot just over. As the clock ticked down, a Le Sommer header went agonisingly wide but somehow it remained scoreless after 90 minutes. Then, two minutes into injury time, came the sucker punch. A shot by Sophie Schmidt ricocheted off French captain Sonia Bompastor and fell to Diana Matheson, who slotted it home to win the game and the bronze medal for Canada.

2012 Gold Medal Match

▲▲ The USA and Japan walk onto the pitch before a record attendance for a match between national teams in Europe. This was the first appearance by Japan in an Olympic Final, but the USA had appeared in all of the first five.

▲ Carli Lloyd (10) heads the USA into an early lead in the 2012 Olympic Final at Wembley against Japan.

Lloyd secures remarkable hat-trick for the USA

Japan and the USA squared off for an Olympic Final at Wembley Stadium a year after the two had met in the Women's World Cup Final in Frankfurt. The Japanese were hoping to become only the third nation after the USA and Norway to win both the world and Olympic titles, but were denied by an American team which created history by winning a hat-trick of Olympic golds. The players were buoyed by the world's attention. The press was out in full force, as were more than 80,000 fans – an Olympic record and the highest for a match in Europe. And they were loud. "Not many people can say they've played at Wembley," recalls USA striker Carli Lloyd. 'I remember looking up at one point in the stands and seeing some 80,000 people there and it was amazing! That's something I'll remember forever." With just seven minutes on the clock, Lloyd sprinted down the field to stoop low and head home an Alex Morgan cross just as Abby Wambach was lining up a shot. It stayed at 1-0 until early in the second half but there were plenty of chances in between. Yūki Ōgimi, who had created so many opportunities for Japan throughout the tournament, went close twice within a minute. USA goalkeeper Hope Solo blocked her first chance and then tipped her second onto the crossbar. Just before the half-hour, Azusa Iwashimizu headed against her own post and then five minutes later Japan captain Aya Miyama hit the crossbar at the other end. In a game full of skill and creativity that delighted the crowd, Shinobu Ohno went close, but early in the second half the Americans increased their lead. Lloyd picked the ball up in the centre circle, ran 30 yards with it to the edge of the penalty area before unleashing an unstoppable shot – a goal fit to grace any Final. The Japanese, always full of invention, fought back – although their goal when it came was something of a scramble. Homare Sawa's first shot was blocked by USA captain Christie Rampone, but Kelley O'Hara knocked the ball onto Sawa and it fell in front of Ōgimi to tap home. No one deserved a goal more. Japan pressed for the remaining 27 minutes but couldn't break down a resolute American defence, Solo pulling off a great save from substitute Mana Iwabuchi with seven minutes left. The USA had a fourth Olympic title to celebrate, the last two of which had come under their Swedish coach Pia Sundhage, the only coach to win gold twice and the first foreigner to take a team to the summit in either the Olympics or World Cup.

Gold medal match 2012

4

The number of Americans who were part of all three Olympic gold medal-winning squads in 2004, 2008 and 2012. Two of them, Christie Rampone and Shannon Boxx, appeared in all three Finals while Heather O'Reilly appeared in the first two but was on the bench for the third. Heather Mitts appeared only in the 2008 Final.

◀ Underneath the arch. A record-breaking crowd for Europe watches the 2012 Olympic Final between the USA and Japan at Wembley.

Football comes home

Four years after David Beckham kicked off the countdown to London 2012 at the Beijing Olympics, a global women's football event landed for the first time in the country which had given the game to the world. USA veteran Heather O'Reilly recalled how special it was to play in some of football's most iconic stadiums. "As a footballer, from a football perspective, it was the coolest," she said of the memorable experience. "In England, there's an appreciation for the purest level of the game. You could sense from the supporters that they knew the game, that they knew football, and that obviously makes you excited as a player to partake in that." The fans' knowledge, historic arenas, record-breaking crowds and increased press attention, combined with the rise of social media – the London Games were the first covered in depth by Twitter and amplified by FIFA's official YouTube channel – meant that the women's football tournament was a landmark event that helped reach out to a new audience for the game.

▲ Japan acknowledge the crowd after winning silver.

Fair play?

The IOC provides all Olympic athletes with economy airline seats but it's up to the federations if they want to upgrade. As professionals, the Japanese men's football team – effectively an under-23 side – flew to London in business class while the women's team – the reigning world champions – were in economy. As Homare Sawa stated, "I guess it should have been the other way round. Even in terms of age, we are senior." Whatever the reasons behind it, or the rights and wrongs, it certainly sent out a poor message and was something that the international media quickly picked up on.

19

Olympic matches won by Christie Rampone – a record.

▶ The USA celebrate their unique Olympic hat-trick. It was their fourth gold in the five Olympic tournaments staged until then.

2015

The first World Cup played entirely on artificial turf was also the first with 24 teams. For the second time in a row, Japan and the USA met in the Final. This time the USA won – and how. When their captain Carli Lloyd scored from the halfway line, she completed the first hat-trick in a Final – and the USA led 4-0 after only 16 minutes. Their 5-2 win gave them the World Cup for a record third time.

Canada takes to the world's game

◄ Player of the tournament Carli Lloyd (10) celebrates the second of her three goals in the 2015 World Cup Final.

As with their neighbours down south, many Canadians have never historically been convinced by soccer and it is unlikely to ever replace ice hockey as the national sport. But, like in the USA, soccer is surely finding a solid niche in the sporting line-up of Canada and women are playing an important role in this transformation. The FIFA Women's World Cup 2015 was the sixth FIFA tournament to have been held in the country, following on from the 1976 Olympics, the 1987 U-16 World Cup, the 2002 U-19 Women's World Cup, the 2007 U-20 World Cup and the 2014 U-20 Women's World Cup. Only Germany has played host to more FIFA national team tournaments, and in 2026 Canada will host the FIFA World Cup along with the USA and Mexico. The MLS has three firmly established teams in Vancouver, Toronto and Montreal, and there are now more registered soccer players than in any other sport in Canada, including ice hockey. The challenge remains for soccer to engage the population as a spectator sport, but the encouraging crowds at the 2015 World Cup showed the potential. As with the American women's team, the Canadian women are the ones leading the charge. A consistent top-ten ranking, a bronze medal at the 2012 and 2016 Olympics and gold at Tokyo 2020 showed just what is possible.

2015 Overview

CANADA 2015

FIFA WOMEN'S WORLD CUP CANADA 2015™

Story of the qualifiers

The magnificent seven

The increase from 16 to 24 in the number of teams playing at the 2015 World Cup saw eight first-time qualifiers, matching the increased allocation. Three came from Europe – Spain, Switzerland and the Netherlands – two from Africa in the shape of Cameroon and Côte d'Ivoire, while Ecuador from South America, Costa Rica from Central America, and Thailand from Asia all also made their first appearance. The Dutch, Ivorians and Thais had all taken part in the 1988 International Women's Football Tournament, while Cameroon had played in the 2012 London Olympics. Equatorial Guinea and North Korea were the only absentees from the 2011 line-up, with the Koreans missing for the first time since 1995 following their ban for positive doping tests at the finals in Germany. The "Magnificent Seven" of Brazil, Germany, Japan, Nigeria, Norway, Sweden and the USA maintained their ever-present status at the World Cup.

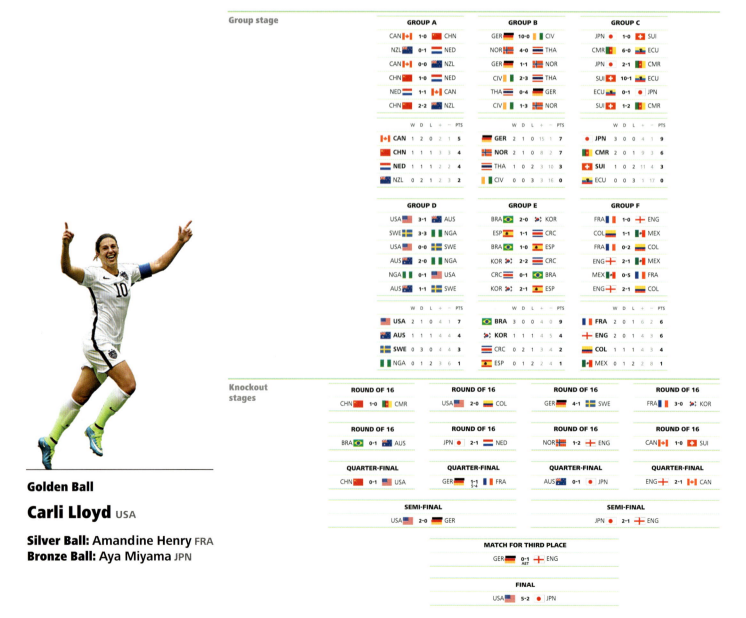

Golden Ball
Carli Lloyd USA

Silver Ball: Amandine Henry FRA
Bronze Ball: Aya Miyama JPN

Overview 2015

24 TEAMS
AUS BRA CAN CHN CIV CMR
COL CRC ECU ENG ESP FRA
GER JPN KOR MEX NED NGA
NOR NZL SUI SWE THA USA

USA
WINNERS

JPN
SECOND

ENG
THIRD

SHUÉME
OFFICIAL MASCOT

OFFICIAL LOGO

52
MATCHES PLAYED

110
YELLOW CARDS

3
RED CARDS

146
GOALS

2.81
AVERAGE GOALS PER MATCH

CONEXT15
OFFICIAL MATCH BALL

1 353 506
SPECTATORS

26 029
AVERAGE PER MATCH

Host cities and stadiums

Six of the best

Given the vast size of the country, just six stadiums were chosen for the 2015 World Cup, with each city hosting a group until the final round of group matches. The one notable absentee from the list was Toronto, Canada's biggest city, which in 2015 was hosting the Pan-American Games. Moncton, a city of just 71,000 in the Maritime provinces in the far east of the country, was the smallest of the six.

▲ The official 2015 World Cup pennant.
FIFA Museum Collection

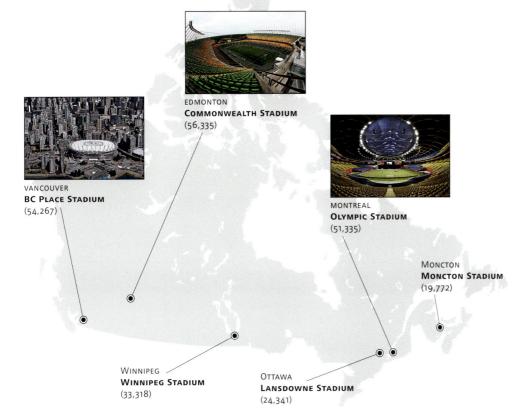

EDMONTON
COMMONWEALTH STADIUM
(56,335)

VANCOUVER
BC PLACE STADIUM
(54,267)

MONTREAL
OLYMPIC STADIUM
(51,335)

MONCTON
MONCTON STADIUM
(19,772)

WINNIPEG
WINNIPEG STADIUM
(33,318)

OTTAWA
LANSDOWNE STADIUM
(24,341)

×6

Golden Boot

Célia Šašić GER

Silver Boot: Carli Lloyd USA ×6
Bronze Boot: Anja Mittag GER ×5

2015 Group stage

Commonwealth Stadium, Edmonton
6.06.2015, 16:00, **53,058**

CANADA 🇨🇦 **1-0** 🇨🇳 **CHINA PR**

Sinclair 90+2p

🏳️ Kateryna Monzul UKR
🚩 Natalia Rachynska UKR & Sanja Rodak CRO

CAN • 1 Erin **McLeod** - 9 Josée **Bélanger**, 3 Kadeisha **Buchanan**, 10 Lauren **Sesselmann**, 15 Allysha **Chapman** - 14 Melissa **Tancredi** (19 Adriana **Leon**, 77), 11 Desiree **Scott** 🟨 22 (17 Jessie **Fleming** 71), 22 Ashley **Lawrence**, 16 Jonelle **Filigno** (6 Kaylyn **Kyle** 61) - 12 Christine **Sinclair** (c), 13 Sophie **Schmidt**. *John Herdman ENG*

CHN • 12 Wang **Fei** - 5 Wu **Haiyan** (c), 14 Zhao **Rong**, 6 Li **Dongna**, 2 Liu **Shanshan** - 19 Tan **Ruyin**, 23 Ren **Guixin** - 21 Wang **Lisi** (18 Han **Peng** 42), 10 Li **Ying** (20 Zhang **Rui** 62), 17 Gu **Yasha** (8 Ma **Jun** 87) - 9 Wang **Shanshan**. *Hao Wei*

Commonwealth Stadium, Edmonton
6.06.2015, 19:00, **53,058**

NEW ZEALAND 🇳🇿 **0-1** 🇳🇱 **NETHERLANDS**

Martens 33

🏳️ Quetzalli Alvarado MEX
🚩 Mayte Chávez MEX & Enedina Caudillo MEX

NZL • 1 Erin **Nayler** - 2 Ria **Percival**, 6 Rebekah **Stott**, 5 Abby **Erceg** (c), 7 Ali **Riley** - 16 Annalie **Longo**, 4 Katie **Duncan**, 14 Katie **Bowen** (12 Betsy **Hassett** 72) - 17 Hannah **Wilkinson**, 9 Amber **Hearn**, 10 Sarah **Gregorius** (8 Jasmine **Pereira** 67). *Tony Readings ENG*

NED • 1 Loes **Geurts** - 2 Desiree **van Lunteren**, 3 Stefanie **van der Gragt**, 4 Mandy **van den Berg** (c), 5 Petra **Hogewoning** - 8 Sherida **Spitse**, 10 Daniëlle **van de Donk** 🟨 32, 6 Anouk **Dekker** (17 Tessel **Middag** 84) - 7 Manon **Melis**, 9 Vivianne **Miedema** (22 Shanice **van de Sanden** 81), 11 Lieke **Martens** 🟨 64 (19 Kirsten **van de Ven** 90+2). *Roger Reijners*

Commonwealth Stadium, Edmonton
11.06.2015, 19:00, **35,544**

CANADA 🇨🇦 **0-0** 🇳🇿 **NEW ZEALAND**

(Hearn penalty missed 33)

🏳️ Bibiana Steinhaus GER
🚩 Katrin Rafalski GER & Marina Wozniak GER

CAN • McLeod - Bélanger, Buchanan, Sesselmann (4 Carmelina **Moscato** 68), Chapman 🟨 31 - Tancredi, Scott (Leon 73), Lawrence, Filigno (Kyle 63) - Sinclair (c), Schmidt. *Herdman ENG*

NZL • Nayler - Percival 🟨 52, Stott, Erceg (c), Riley - Longo, Duncan, Hassett (Bowen 77) - Wilkinson (Pereira 89), Hearn, Gregorius 🟨 71 (13 Rosie **White** 80). *Readings ENG*

Commonwealth Stadium, Edmonton
11.06.2015, 16:00, **35,544**

CHINA PR 🇨🇳 **1-0** 🇳🇱 **NETHERLANDS**

Wang Lisi 90+1

🏳️ Yeimy Martínez COL
🚩 Janette Arcanjo BRA & Liliana Bejarano BOL

CHN • Wang Fei - Wu Haiyan (c), Zhao Rong, Li Dongna, Liu Shanshan - Tan Ruyin, Ren Guixin (Ma Jun 71) - Wang Lisi, 13 Tang **Jiali** (16 Lou **Jiahui** 86), Han Peng - Wang Shanshan (11 Wang **Shuang** 57). *Hao Wei*

NED • 16 Sari **van Veenendaal** - Van Lunteren, Van der Gragt, Van den Berg (c), Hogewoning (15 Merel **van Dongen** 59) - Middag (Dekker 70), Van de Donk, Spitse - Melis, Miedema, Martens. *Reijners*

Olympic Stadium, Montreal
15.06.2015, 19:30, **45,420**

NETHERLANDS 🇳🇱 **1-1** 🇨🇦 **CANADA**

Van de Ven 87 · Lawrence 10

🏳️ Ri Hyang Ok PRK
🚩 Hong Kum Nyo PRK & Kim Kyoung Min KOR

NED • Geurts - Van Lunteren (13 Dominique **Janssen** 13), Van der Gragt 🟨 73, Van den Berg (c), Van Dongen - Dekker, Van de Donk (Van de Ven 72), Spitse - Melis, Miedema, Martens. *Reijners*

CAN • McLeod - Bélanger 🟨 72, Buchanan, Moscato, Chapman - Fleming (Scott 61), Kyle (Tancredi 61), Lawrence - Schmidt (7 Rhian **Wilkinson** 81), Sinclair, Leon. *Herdman ENG*

Winnipeg Stadium, Winnipeg
15.06.2015, 18:30, **26,191**

CHINA PR 🇨🇳 **2-2** 🇳🇿 **NEW ZEALAND**

Wang Lisi 41p · Stott 28
Wang Shanshan 60 · Wilkinson 64

🏳️ Katalin Kulcsár HUN
🚩 Katrin Rafalski GER & Marina Wozniak GER

CHN • Wang Fei - Wu Haiyan (c), Zhao Rong, Li Dongna, Liu Shanshan 🟨 75 - Tan Ruyin, Ren Guixin - Wang Lisi (Li Ying 90+3), Tang Jiali (Wang Shuang 72 🟨 86), Han Peng (Lou Jiahui 84) - Wang Shanshan. *Hao Wei*

NZL • Nayler - Percival, Stott, Erceg (c) 🟨 83, Riley - Hassett (Bowen 46), Duncan 🟨 86, Longo - Gregorius (White 46) (11 Kirsty **Yallop** 89), Hearn, Wilkinson. *Readings ENG*

Group A

	W	D	L	+	−	PTS
🇨🇦 CAN	1	2	0	2	1	5
🇨🇳 CHN	1	1	1	3	3	4
🇳🇱 NED	1	1	1	2	2	4
🇳🇿 NZL	0	2	1	2	3	2

▶ Dutch captain Mandy van den Berg shakes hands with New Zealand's Abby Erceg before the Netherlands' World Cup debut.

▶ Canada captain Christine Sinclair celebrates with coach John Herdman after her injury-time winner against China in the opening match of Canada 2015.

154

Christine Sinclair's winning goal against China was her 154th international goal and her eighth in World Cups. She scored a ninth in the quarter-finals and a 10th in 2019.

Sinclair to the rescue

It was 20 years to the day since Canada had debuted in the Women's World Cup with a 3-2 loss to England in front of 655 fans in Helsingborg. Now they were set to host the competition, kicking off at Edmonton's Commonwealth Stadium in front of more than 53,000 supporters. Canadian pop singers and dancing girl footballers had warmed up the fans in the sunshine, but the heat was on the Canucks against China. The Olympic bronze medallists were considered title contenders, but it took a 92nd-minute Christine Sinclair spot kick to beat a youthful Chinese side. "It was probably the most pressure-filled goal I've ever scored," said Sinclair, who celebrated by racing to the bench and hugging head coach John Herdman. A Lieke Martens wonder strike from 25 yards saw debutants Netherlands overcome Herdman's former team New Zealand, leaving the 2012 Olympic quarter-finalists still searching for a World Cup win. Tony Readings' side went close against Canada and their old boss, but a thrilling match that was halted for 30 minutes by a lightning storm ended goalless, both sides denied by the woodwork, including leading Kiwi scorer Amber Hearn from the penalty spot. China remained in contention with victory over the Netherlands, Wang Lisi slotting home in injury time after a delightful long-range pass from Tan Ruyin. And Hao Wei's team were into the round of 16 after a feisty draw with New Zealand, who departed bottom of the group for the fourth time. An 87th-minute equaliser from Netherlands super-sub Kirsten van de Ven cancelled out Ashley Lawrence's early goal for Canada, but a point was enough for the hosts to top the group, with the *Oranje Leeuwinnen* also through as one of the best third-placed teams.

Group stage 2015

◀ A steep learning curve. After heavy defeats in their World Cup debuts, Côte d'Ivoire and Thailand line up before their match in Ottawa. The Thais won a close game 3-2.

Tough for the debutants

The highest-scoring European side in qualification and the world's number-one ranked team Germany kicked off in Ottawa with the biggest win of the tournament. Célia Šašić and Anja Mittag bagged a hat-trick apiece in a 10-0 victory over a Côte d'Ivoire side ranked 66 places below them. Fellow newcomers Thailand were also undone by European opposition, Isabell Herlovsen scoring twice in a 4-0 win for Norway, overseen by Even Pellerud in his second spell as head coach. As a player, Silvia Neid lost a World Cup Final to Pellerud's Norway in 1995, but as Germany manager she had beaten her rival in the 2013 European Championship Final. It was honours even here as Maren Mjelde cancelled out Euro-title winning goalscorer Anja Mittag's sixth-minute opener. Thailand, led by their first female head coach, Nuengrutai Srathongvian, earned their first finals points after coming back from behind to beat Côte d'Ivoire, former futsal player Orathai Srimanee scoring twice in a 3-2 win. The debutants had entertained, but the Thais bowed out with a 4-0 loss to table-topping Germany, while Côte d'Ivoire returned home without a point after falling 3-1 to second-placed Norway, Ange N'Guessan scoring a late consolation.

Group B

	W	D	L	+	-	PTS
GER	2	1	0	15	1	7
NOR	2	1	0	8	2	7
THA	1	0	2	3	10	3
CIV	0	0	3	3	16	0

39 The 1-1 draw between Germany and Norway was the 39th time the two nations had played each other. The Germans have not faced any other opponents more times. This was the sixth draw, with the Germans leading 19 to 14 in wins.

◀ Norway celebrate in novel style – a selfie without a camera – following Isabell Herlovsen's second goal against Thailand.

Lansdowne Stadium, Ottawa
7.06.2015, 16:00, **20,953**

GERMANY 10-0 CÔTE D'IVOIRE
Šašić (3) 3 14 31,
Mittag (3) 29 35 64,
Laudehr 71, Däbritz 75
Behringer 79, Popp 85

Carol Anne Chenard CAN
Marie-Josée Charbonneau CAN & Suzanne Morisset CAN

GER • 1 Nadine **Angerer** (c) - 4 Leonie **Maier**, 5 Annike **Krahn**, 3 Saskia **Bartusiak**, 22 Tabea **Kemme** - 6 Simone **Laudehr** (19 Lena **Petermann** 73), 20 Lena **Goeßling**, 16 Melanie **Leupolz** (7 Melanie **Behringer** 17), 18 Alexandra **Popp** - 13 Célia **Šašić** (23 Sara **Däbritz** 46), 11 Anja **Mittag**. *Silvia Neid*

CIV • 16 Dominique **Thiamale** (c) ■ 40 - 22 Raymonde **Kacou**, 21 Sophie **Aguie** ■ 58, 2 Fatou **Coulibaly** ■ 70, 4 Nina **Kpaho** (13 Fernande **Tchetche** 38) - 6 Rita **Akaffou** ■ 36, 12 Ida **Guehai** - 14 Josée **Nahi** ■ 86, 7 Nadege **Essoh** (8 Ines **Nrehy** 51), 11 Rebecca **Elloh** ■ 66 (10 Ange **N'Guessan** 72) - 18 Binta **Diakité**. *Clémentine Touré*

Lansdowne Stadium, Ottawa
7.06.2015, 13:00, **20,953**

NORWAY 4-0 THAILAND
Rønning 15,
Herlovsen (2) 29 34,
Hegerberg 68
(Mjelde penalty saved 75)

Anna-Marie Keighley NZL
Sarah Walker NZL & Lata Kaumatule TGA

NOR • 1 Ingrid **Hjelmseth** - 6 Maren **Mjelde**, 7 Trine **Rønning** (c) (16 Elise **Thorsnes** 63), 11 Nora Holstad **Berge** (3 Marita **Skammelsrud Lund** 46), 13 Ingrid Moe **Wold** - 8 Solveig **Gulbrandsen** (20 Emilie **Haavi** 69), 4 Gry Tofte **Ims**, 17 Lene **Mykjåland** - 19 Kristine **Minde**, 9 Isabell **Herlovsen**, 21 Ada **Hegerberg**. *Even Pellerud*

THA • 1 Waraporn **Boonsing** - 9 Warunee **Phetwiset** ■ 51, 4 Duangnapa **Sritala** (c) ■ 75, 3 Natthakarn **Chinwong**, 10 Sunisa **Srangthaisong** - 6 Pikul **Khueanpet**, 7 Silawan **Intamee** - 12 Rattikan **Thongsombut**, 8 Naphat **Seesraum** (13 Orathai **Srimanee** 59), 17 Anootsara **Maijarern** (14 Thanatta **Chawong** 90) - 21 Kanjana **Sung-Ngoen**. *Nuengrutai Srathongvian*

Lansdowne Stadium, Ottawa
11.06.2015, 16:00, **18,987**

GERMANY 1-1 NORWAY
Mittag 6   Mjelde 61

Teodora Albon ROU
Petruța Iugulescu ROU & Mária Súkeníková SVK

GER • Angerer (c) - Maier, Krahn, Bartusiak ■ 59, Kemme - Goeßling, 10 Dzsenifer **Marozsán** - Laudehr (9 Lena **Lotzen** 66), Mittag (8 Pauline **Bremer** 80), Popp (Däbritz 70) - Šašić. *Neid*

NOR • Hjelmseth - Mjelde, Skammelsrud Lund, 2 Maria **Thorisdottir**, Wold - 14 Ingrid **Schjelderup**, Ims (S Gulbrandsen 46), Mykjåland - Minde (Thorsnes 60), Herlovsen (Haavi 90+2), Hegerberg. *Pellerud*

Lansdowne Stadium, Ottawa
11.06.2015, 19:00, **18,987**

CÔTE D'IVOIRE 2-3 THAILAND
N'Guessan 4, Nahi 88   Srimanee (2) 26 45+3
                         Chawong 75

Margaret Domka USA
Princess Brown JAM & Elizabeth Aguilar SLV

CIV • Thiamale (c) - Kacou, F Coulibaly, 3 Djelika **Coulibaly**, Tchetche - 15 Christine **Lohoues**, Guehai (9 Jessica **Aby** 81 ■ 90+4), Akaffou (Elloh 46) - N'Guessan, Nrehy, Diakité (Nahi 34). *Touré*

THA • Boonsing - Phetwiset, Sritala (c), Chinwong (2 Darut **Changplook** 90+7), Srangthaisong - Khueanpet, Intamee - Sung-Ngoen, Srimanee (Chawong 73), Maijarern - 23 Nisa **Romyen** (Thongsombut 43). *Srathongvian*

Winnipeg Stadium, Winnipeg
15.06.2015, 15:00, **26,191**

THAILAND 0-4 GERMANY
                Leupolz 24
                Petermann (2) 56 58
                Däbritz 73

Gladys Lengwe ZIM
Lidwine Rakotozafinoro MAD & Bernadettar Kwimbira MWI

THA • Boonsing - Phetwiset, Chinwong, Sritala (c), Srangthaisong - Khueanpet, Intamee - Thongsombut (Changplook 89), Srimanee (20 Wilaiporn **Boothduang** 79), Maijarern ■ 82 (11 Alisa **Rukpinij** 87) - Sung-Ngoen. *Srathongvian*

GER • Angerer (c) - 2 Bianca **Schmidt**, Krahn (17 Josephine **Henning** 61), 14 Babett **Peter**, 15 Jennifer **Cramer** - Behringer, Leupolz - Lotzen, Marozsán (Petermann 46), Däbritz - Šašić (Mittag 46). *Neid*

Moncton Stadium, Moncton
15.06.2015, 17:00, **7,147**

CÔTE D'IVOIRE 1-3 NORWAY
N'Guessan 71   Hegerberg (2) 6 62
                S Gulbrandsen 67

Salomé Di Iorio ARG
María Rocco ARG & Mariana de Almeida ARG

CIV • 23 Cynthia **Djohore** - 17 Nadège **Cissé** (Diakité 68) (Essoh 90+2), F Coulibaly (c) ■ 25, D Coulibaly, Tchetche - Lohoues (Akaffou 90+3), Guehai, Elloh - Nahi, Nrehy, N'Guessan. *Touré*

NOR • Hjelmseth (c) (12 Silje **Vesterbekkmo** 79) - Thorsnes, Skammelsrud Lund, Thorisdottir, Minde (Wold 46) - S Gulbrandsen, Schjelderup, Mykjåland - 5 Lisa-Marie **Utland** (Mjelde 64), Hegerberg, Haavi ■ 52. *Pellerud*

185

2015 Group stage

BC Place Stadium, Vancouver
8.06.2015, 19:00, **25,942**

JAPAN 1-0 **SWITZERLAND**

Miyama 29p

▸ Lucila Venegas MEX
▸ Kimberly Moreira CRC & Shirley Perello HON

JPN • 21 Erina **Yamane** - 19 Saori **Ariyoshi**, 3 Azusa **Iwashimizu**, 4 Saki **Kumagai**, 13 Rumi **Utsugi** - 11 Shinobu **Ohno** (9 Nahomi **Kawasumi** 90), 6 Mizuho **Sakaguchi**, 10 Homare **Sawa** (20 Yuri **Kawamura** 57), 8 Aya **Miyama** (c) - 17 Yūki **Ōgimi**, 7 Kozue **Ando** (15 Yuika **Sugasawa** 32). *Norio Sasaki*

SUI • 1 Gaëlle **Thalmann** ▪ 28 - 5 Noëlle **Maritz**, 15 Caroline **Abbé** (c) ▪ 90+3, 9 Lia **Wälti**, 4 Rachel **Rinast** - 16 Fabienne **Humm** (19 Eseosa **Aigbogun** 46), 7 Martina **Moser** (8 Cinzia **Zehnder** 81), 22 Vanessa **Bernauer**, 13 Ana-Maria **Crnogorčević** - 10 Ramona **Bachmann** ▪ 22, 11 Lara **Dickenmann**. *Martina Voss-Tecklenburg GER*

BC Place Stadium, Vancouver
8.06.2015, 16:00, **25,942**

CAMEROON 6-0 **ECUADOR**

Ngono Mani 34
Enganamouit (3)
36 73 90+4p
Manie 44p, Onguéné 79p

▸ Katalin Kulcsár HUN
▸ Natalie Aspinall ENG & Anna Nyström SWE

CMR • 1 Annette **Ngo Ndom** - 12 Claudine **Meffometou**, 13 Cathy **Bou Ndjouh**, 2 Christine **Manie** (c), 4 Yvonne **Leuko** - 8 Raissa **Feudjio**, 10 Jeannette **Yango** ▪ 38 - 17 Gaëlle **Enganamouit**, 20 Geneviève **Ngo Mbeleck** (6 Francine **Zouga** 61), 7 Gabrielle **Onguéné** (18 Henriette **Akaba** 83) - 9 Madeleine **Ngono Mani** (3 Ajara **Nchout** 74). *Carl Enow Ngachu*

ECU • 1 Shirley **Berruz** - 19 Kerlly **Real** ▪ 43, 3 Nancy **Aguilar**, 16 Ligia **Moreira** (c) ▪ 66, 6 Angie **Ponce** - 13 Madelin **Riera** - 5 Mayra **Olvera**, 20 Denise **Pesántes**, 21 Mabel **Velarde** (7 Ingrid **Rodríguez** 45 ▪ 45+2) - 10 Ámbar **Torres** (9 Giannina **Lattanzio** 54), 11 Mónica **Quinteros** (2 Katherine **Ortíz** 72 ▪ 70). *Vanessa Arauz*

BC Place Stadium, Vancouver
12.06.2015, 19:00, **31,441**

JAPAN 2-1 **CAMEROON**

Sameshima 6, Sugasawa 17   Nchout 90

▸ Pernilla Larsson SWE
▸ Anna Nyström SWE & Natalie Aspinall ENG

JPN • 18 Ayumi **Kaihori** - 2 Yukari **Kinga**, Iwashimizu, Kumagai, Utsugi - Kawasumi (Ohno 55), Sakaguchi (Sawa 64), Miyama (c), 5 Aya **Sameshima** - Ōgimi, Sugasawa (12 Megumi **Kamionobe** 85). *Sasaki*

CMR • Ngo Ndom - Meffometou, Bou Ndjouh, Manie (c), Leuko - Feudjio, Yango - Onguéné (5 Augustine **Ejangue** 72), Ngo Mbeleck ▪ 43 (Zouga 46), Enganamouit - Ngono Mani (Nchout 62). *Enow Ngachu*

BC Place Stadium, Vancouver
12.06.2015, 16:00, **31,441**

SWITZERLAND 10-1 **ECUADOR**

Ponce OG (2) 24 71   Ponce 64p
Aigbogun 45+2
Humm (3) 47 49 52,
Bachmann (3) 60p 61 81,
Moser 76

▸ Rita Gani MAS
▸ Widiya Shamsuri MAS & Sarah Ho AUS

SUI • Thalmann - Maritz (2 Nicole **Remund** 57), Abbé (c) (Zehnder 51), 14 Rahel **Kiwic** (6 Selina **Kuster** 72), Rinast - Aigbogun, Moser, Wälti, Crnogorčević - Humm, Bachmann. *Voss-Tecklenburg GER*

ECU • Berruz - Rodríguez, Ortíz (17 Alexandra **Salvador** 46), Aguilar (c), Ponce - Olvera, Pesántes ▪ 72 - Real, 15 Ana **Palacios** (18 Adriana **Barré** 69), Velarde (8 Erika **Vásquez** 79) - Quinteros. *Arauz*

Winnipeg Stadium, Winnipeg
16.06.2015, 16:00, **14,522**

ECUADOR 0-1 **JAPAN**

   Ōgimi 5

▸ Melissa Borjas HON
▸ Yolanda Parga ESP & Manuela Nicolosi FRA

ECU • Berruz - Rodríguez, Ortíz, Aguilar ▪ 52, Moreira (c), Ponce - Real, Pesántes, Olvera, Vásquez ▪ 39 (Riera 90) - Quinteros (14 Carina **Caicedo** 83). *Arauz*

JPN • 1 Miho **Fukumoto** - Ariyoshi, 23 Kana **Kitahara** (Kamionobe 46), Kawamura, Sameshima - Ohno 17 (22 Asano **Nagasato** 75), Sawa, 14 Asuna **Tanaka**, Miyama (c) - Ōgimi, Sugasawa (16 Mana **Iwabuchi** 80). *Sasaki*

Commonwealth Stadium, Edmonton
16.06.2015, 15:00, **10,177**

SWITZERLAND 1-2 **CAMEROON**

Crnogorčević 24   Onguéné 47
     Ngono Mani 62

▸ Claudia Umpiérrez URU
▸ Luciana Mascaraña URU & Loreto Toloza CHI

SUI • Thalmann - Maritz, Wälti ▪ 82, Kuster, Rinast - Bachmann, Moser (c), Kiwic (Bernauer 65), Dickenmann (Remund 80) - Humm (Aigbogun 69), Crnogorčević. *Voss-Tecklenburg GER*

CMR • Ngo Ndom - Ejangue, 11 Aurelle **Awona**, Manie (c), Meffometou ▪ 68 - Feudjio ▪ 19, Yango - Onguéné (Akaba 90+2), Zouga (19 Agathe **Ngani** 87), Nchout ▪ 35 (Ngono Mani 57) - Enganamouit ▪ 90+2. *Enow Ngachu*

Group C

	W	D	L	+	-	PTS
JPN	3	0	0	4	1	9
CMR	2	0	1	9	3	6
SUI	1	0	2	11	4	3
ECU	0	0	3	1	17	0

26

The age of Ecuador coach Vanessa Arauz, the youngest in World Cup history.

▸▸ Fabienne Humm wrote her name in the record books with the fastest hat-trick in World Cup and Olympic history in Switzerland's 10-1 win over Ecuador.

▸ Cameroon captain Christine Manie (2) celebrates her goal during her team's World Cup debut.

Just perfect

It took Switzerland's Fabienne Humm just 277 seconds to score her hat-trick at the beginning of the second half against Ecuador – the quickest hat-trick in World Cup or Olympic history. But it wasn't just that that made it so special. It was a perfect hat-trick – a goal with each foot and the head, uninterrupted and in one half.

▸ World champions Japan get their campaign underway with a 29th-minute penalty in a 1-0 victory over Switzerland in Vancouver. Homare Sawa set a new record in this match by playing in her sixth World Cup.

The *Indomitable Lionesses* roar

Japan got their World Cup defence off to a winning start against skilful debutants Switzerland. Captain Aya Miyama settled it from the spot, but the penalty came at a cost, midfielder Kozue Ando breaking her ankle as she collided with on-rushing goalkeeper Gaëlle Thalmann. The goals flew in as Cameroon's brightly coiffured striker Gaëlle Enganamouit hit a hat-trick the day before her 23rd birthday in a 6-0 win over Ecuador, who lost captain Ligia Moreira to a second-half red card. Worse was to come for La Tricolor and their 26-year-old coach Vanessa Arauz as they were thumped 10-1 by Switzerland, Fabienne Humm hitting the competition's fastest hat-trick in a blistering five-minute spell. Ecuador midfielder Angie Ponce also scored three, but two were into her own net. Japan became the first team to reach the knockouts after a 2-1 win over Cameroon, but they had to fight for their victory. A concluding win over Ecuador saw them top the group, but the South Americans ended their maiden finals with honour restored after restricting the champions to one goal. Surprise packages Cameroon took second with a 2-1 win over Switzerland, with both sides reaching the last 16.

Group stage 2015

Group D

◀ Carli Lloyd and Lotta Schelin shake hands before the USA-Sweden match in Winnipeg. This was the fifth time the two nations had faced each other at the group stage in seven World Cups.

Old foes reunited

A six-goal thriller opened this group as Nigeria levelled against Sweden with three minutes remaining, Ngozi Okobi weighing in with two assists and a coolly taken goal for the Super Falcons. Australia ramped up the drama against the USA in Winnipeg when skipper Lisa De Vanna equalised with her sixth goal in three World Cups, but a Megan Rapinoe brace proved key to an American victory. The Matildas bounced back, Kyah Simon scoring twice to beat nine-time African champions Nigeria. Meghan Klingenberg headed a Caroline Seger effort off the line and keeper Hedvig Lindahl athletically denied Carli Lloyd and Abby Wambach as the USA's gripping clash with former head coach Pia Sundhage's Sweden finished goalless. "I thought both teams left it all on the field," said USA boss Jill Ellis. Even so, the USA went on to overcome Nigeria, captain Wambach firing them into the knockouts in front of 52,193 spectators in Vancouver. Edwin Okon's side had arrived in Canada with high hopes and a squad that featured six of their 2014 U-20 Women's World Cup runners-up, but they fell at the first hurdle for the fourth time since 1999, while Australia and Sweden progressed after a 1-1 draw.

	W	D	L	+	-	PTS
USA	2	1	0	4	1	7
AUS	1	1	1	4	4	4
SWE	0	3	0	4	4	3
NGA	0	1	2	3	6	1

14
The USA's Abby Wambach scored her 14th World Cup goal in the group match against Nigeria, but in the round-of-16 match against Colombia she missed the opportunity to join Marta on a record 15 goals when she failed to convert a second-half penalty. Her 14 goals came in 25 games and she also scored 9 in 11 matches at the Olympics.

Winnipeg Stadium, Winnipeg
8.06.2015, 18:30, **31,148**
USA **3-1** AUSTRALIA
Rapinoe (2) 12 78, Press 61 — De Vanna 27
Claudia Umpiérrez URU
Luciana Mascaraña URU & Loreto Toloza CHI

USA • 1 Hope **Solo** - 11 Ali **Krieger**, 4 Becky **Sauerbrunn**, 19 Julie **Johnston**, 22 Meghan **Klingenberg** - 23 Christen **Press** (17 Tobin **Heath** 68), 12 Lauren **Holiday** ■ 56, 10 Carli **Lloyd**, 15 Megan **Rapinoe** ■ 64 (14 Morgan **Brian** 86) - 20 Abby **Wambach** (c), 2 Sydney **Leroux** (13 Alex **Morgan** 79). *Jill Ellis*

AUS • 18 Melissa **Barbieri** - 6 Servet **Uzunlar**, 5 Laura **Alleway** (3 Ashleigh **Sykes** 83), 7 Steph **Catley**, 9 Caitlin **Foord** - 19 Katrina **Gorry** (14 Alanna **Kennedy** 80), 8 Elise **Kellond-Knight**, 10 Emily **van Egmond** - 11 Lisa **De Vanna** (c), 22 Michelle **Heyman** (17 Kyah **Simon** 69), 20 Samantha **Kerr**. *Alen Stajcic*

Winnipeg Stadium, Winnipeg
8.06.2015, 15:00, **31,148**
SWEDEN **3-3** NIGERIA
Oparanozie OG 21, Fischer 31, Sembrant 60 — Okobi 50, Oshoala 53, Ordega 87
Ri Hyang Ok PRK
Hong Kum Nyo PRK & Kim Kyoung Min KOR

SWE • 1 Hedvig **Lindahl** - 23 Elin **Rubensson**, 5 Nilla **Fischer**, 4 Emma **Berglund** (14 Amanda **Ilestedt** 73), 16 Lina **Nilsson** - 9 Kosovare **Asllani** (22 Olivia **Schough** 46), 17 Caroline **Seger** (c), 7 Lisa **Dahlkvist** (3 Linda **Sembrant** 57), 15 Therese **Sjögran** - 8 Lotta **Schelin**, 10 Sofia **Jakobsson**. *Pia Sundhage*

NGA • 1 Precious **Dede** - 3 Osinachi **Ohale**, 6 Josephine **Chukwunonye**, 5 Onome **Ebi**, 23 Ngozi **Ebere** - 8 Asisat **Oshoala**, 14 Evelyn **Nwabuoku** (c), 12 Halimatu **Ayinde**, 13 Ngozi **Okobi** - 17 Francisca **Ordega**, 9 Desire **Oparanozie**. *Edwin Okon*

Winnipeg Stadium, Winnipeg
12.06.2015, 19:00, **32,716**
USA **0-0** SWEDEN
Sachiko Yamagishi JPN
Naomi Teshirogi JPN & Sarah Walker NZL

USA • Solo - Krieger, Johnston, Sauerbrunn, Klingenberg - Brian (8 Amy **Rodriguez** 58), Lloyd (c), Holiday, Rapinoe - Press (Wambach 67), Leroux (Morgan 78). *Ellis*

SWE • Lindahl - Rubensson, Ilestedt, Fischer, 18 Jessica **Samuelsson** - Jakobsson, Dahlkvist, Seger, Nilsson (Sembrant 70) - Sjögran (20 Emilia **Appelqvist** 75), Schelin (c). *Sundhage*

Winnipeg Stadium, Winnipeg
12.06.2015, 16:00, **32,716**
AUSTRALIA **2-0** NIGERIA
Simon (2) 29 68
Stéphanie Frappart FRA
Manuela Nicolosi FRA & Yolanda Parga ESP

AUS • 1 Lydia **Williams** - Foord, Alleway, Kennedy, Catley - Van Egmond, Kellond-Knight, Gorry (13 Tameka **Butt** 62) - De Vanna (c), Simon (Heyman 87), Kerr. *Stajcic*

NGA • Dede - Ohale (15 Ugo **Njoku** 52), Chukwunonye ■ 60, Ebi, Ebere - Oshoala (10 Courtney **Dike** 84), Nwabuoku (c) ■ 42, Ayinde, Okobi - Ordega, Oparanozie (4 Perpetua **Nkwocha** 54). *Okon*

BC Place Stadium, Vancouver
16.06.2015, 17:00, **52,193**
NIGERIA **0-1** USA
Wambach 45
Kateryna Monzul UKR
Natalia Rachynska UKR & Sanja Rodak CRO

NGA • Dede - 22 Sarah **Nnodim** ■ 38 ■ 69 ■ 69, Chukwunonye ■ 60, Ebi ■ 43, Ebere - Ordega (20 Cecilia **Nku** 77), Nwabuoku (c), Okobi ■ 68, 7 Esther **Sunday** (Ayinde 50) - Dike (Oparanozie 50), Oshoala. *Okon*

USA • Solo - Krieger, Johnston, Sauerbrunn, Klingenberg - Rapinoe (7 Shannon **Boxx** 74), Holiday, Lloyd, Heath (3 Christie **Rampone** 80) - Wambach (c), Morgan (Leroux 66). *Ellis*

Commonwealth Stadium, Edmonton
16.06.2015, 18:00, **10,177**
AUSTRALIA **1-1** SWEDEN
De Vanna 5 — Jakobsson 15
Lucila Venegas MEX
Mayte Chávez MEX & Enedina Caudillo MEX

AUS • Williams - Foord, Alleway, Kennedy, Catley - Gorry (Butt 85), Kellond-Knight, Van Egmond - De Vanna (c) (2 Larissa **Crummer** 63), Simon (Heyman 72), Kerr. *Stajcic*

SWE • Lindahl - Rubensson (6 Sara **Thunebro** 76), Ilestedt, Fischer, Samuelsson - Jakobsson, Dahlkvist, Seger, Nilsson (Asllani 74) - Sjögran, Schelin (c). *Sundhage*

◀ The USA's Abby Wambach heads the only goal of the game against Nigeria.

2015 Group stage

Olympic Stadium, Montreal
9.06.2015, 19:00, **10,175**

BRAZIL 🇧🇷 **2-0** 🇰🇷 **KOREA REPUBLIC**

Formiga 33, Marta 53p

🚩 Esther Staubli SUI
🚩 Ella De Vries BEL & Lucie Ratajová CZE

BRA • 1 **Luciana** - 2 **Fabiana**, 3 **Mônica**, 16 **Rafaelle** (14 **Géssica** 82), 6 **Tamires** - 20 **Formiga**, 5 **Andressinha** (18 **Raquel Fernandes** 81), 8 **Thaísa** - 10 **Marta** (c), 11 **Cristiane**, 9 **Andressa** (4 **Rafaela** 90+1). *Vadão*

KOR • 18 **Kim** Jung Mi - 20 **Kim** Hye Ri, 5 **Kim** Do Yeon, 4 **Shim** Seo Yeon, 2 **Lee** Eun Mi - 13 **Kwon** Hah Nul (22 **Lee** So Dam 77), 8 **Cho** So Hyun (c) ■ 52 - 16 **Kang** Yu Mi (15 **Park** Hee Young 90+1), 10 **Ji** So Yun, 7 **Jeon** Ga Eul - 12 **Yoo** Young A (11 **Jung** Seol Bin 67). *Yoon Duk Yeo*

Olympic Stadium, Montreal
9.06.2015, 16:00, **10,175**

SPAIN 🇪🇸 **1-1** 🇨🇷 **COSTA RICA**

Losada 13 — Rodríguez Cedeño 14

🚩 Salomé Di Iorio ARG
🚩 María Rocco ARG & Mariana de Almeida ARG

ESP • 1 **Ainhoa Tirapu** - 2 **Celia Jiménez** ■ 44 (5 **Ruth García** 62), 18 **Marta Torrejón**, 20 **Irene Paredes**, 3 **Leire Landa** - 14 **Vicky Losada**, 21 **Alexia Putellas** - 7 **Natalia Pablos**, 9 **Verónica Boquete** (c), 8 **Sonia Bermúdez** (12 **Marta Corredera** 72) - 10 **Jennifer Hermoso** (11 **Priscila Borja** 84). *Ignacio Quereda*

CRC • 1 **Dinnia Díaz** - 5 **Diana Sáenz**, 6 **Carol Sánchez**, 20 **Wendy Acosta**, 12 **Lixy Rodríguez** - 7 **Melissa Herrera** (2 **Gabriela Guillén** 88), 10 **Shirley Cruz** (c), 16 **Katherine Alvarado**, 11 **Raquel Rodríguez Cedeño**, 14 **María Barrantes** (17 **Karla Villalobos** 74) - 9 **Carolina Venegas** (15 **Cristin Granados** 80). *Amelia Valverde*

Olympic Stadium, Montreal
13.06.2015, 16:00, **28,623**

BRAZIL 🇧🇷 **1-0** 🇪🇸 **SPAIN**

Andressa Alves 44

🚩 Carol Anne Chenard CAN
🚩 Marie-Josée Charbonneau CAN & Suzanne Morisset CAN

BRA • Luciana - Fabiana (13 **Poliana** 77), Mônica, Rafaelle, Tamires - Thaísa (22 **Darlene** 60), Formiga, Andressinha - Marta (c), Cristiane (Raquel Fernandes 89 ■ 90+3), Andressa. *Vadão*

ESP • Tirapu - Jiménez, Torrejón, Paredes, Landa ■ 23 - Losada, 6 **Virginia Torrecilla** (Bermúdez 77), Boquete (c) - Corredera (Borja 70), Pablos (15 **Silvia Meseguer** 71), Putellas. *Quereda*

Olympic Stadium, Montreal
13.06.2015, 19:00, **28,623**

KOREA REPUBLIC 🇰🇷 **2-2** 🇨🇷 **COSTA RICA**

Ji So Yun 21p — Herrera 17
Jeon Ga Eul 25 — Villalobos 89

🚩 Carina Vitulano ITA
🚩 Michelle O'Neill IRL & Tonja Paavola FIN

KOR • Kim Jung Mi - Kim Hye Ri ■ 69 (3 **Lim** Seon Joo 84), 6 **Hwang** Bo Ram ■ 86, Shim Seo Yeon, Lee Eun Mi - Kwon Hah Nul, Cho So Hyun (c) - Kang Yu Mi (Jung Seol Bin 63), Ji So Yun, Jeon Ga Eul - Yoo Young A (23 **Lee** Geum Min 77 ■ 81). *Yoon Duk Yeo*

CRC • Díaz - Sáenz, C Sánchez, Acosta, Rodríguez - Herrera, Cruz (c), Alvarado, Rodríguez Cedeño, Barrantes (Villalobos 76) - Granados. *Valverde*

Moncton Stadium, Moncton
17.06.2015, 20:00, **9,543**

COSTA RICA 🇨🇷 **0-1** 🇧🇷 **BRAZIL**

— Raquel Fernandes 83

🚩 Thalia Mitsi GRE
🚩 Chrysoula Kouroumpylia GRE & Angela Kyriakou CYP

CRC • Díaz - Sáenz, C Sánchez, Acosta, Rodríguez - Cruz (c), Alvarado (19 **Fabiola Sánchez** 86), Rodríguez Cedeño - Herrera, Granados (Venegas 57), Barrantes (Villalobos 72). *Valverde*

BRA • Luciana - Poliana, Mônica (Géssica 66), Rafaelle, Tamires - Raquel Fernandes, 19 **Maurine** (c), Andressinha, 17 **Rosana** - 21 **Gabriela** (Rafaela 78), Darlene (7 **Beatriz** 59). *Vadão*

Lansdowne Stadium, Ottawa
17.06.2015, 19:00, **21,562**

KOREA REPUBLIC 🇰🇷 **2-1** 🇪🇸 **SPAIN**

Cho So Hyun 53 — Boquete 29
Kim Soo Yun 78

🚩 Anna-Marie Keighley NZL
🚩 Sarah Walker NZL & Allyson Flynn AUS

KOR • Kim Jung Mi - Kim Hye Ri (19 **Kim** Soo Yun 46), Shim Seo Yeon, Hwang Bo Ram ■ 69, Lee Eun Mi - Kwon Hah Nul, Cho So Hyun (c) - Kang Yu Mi (Park Hee Young 77), Ji So Yun, Jeon Ga Eul - 9 **Park** Eun Sun (Yoo Young A 59). *Yoon Duk Yeo*

ESP • Tirapu - Jiménez, Torrejón, Paredes, Landa - Corredera (19 **Erika Vázquez** 75), Losada (Meseguer 57), Torrecilla ■ 56, Boquete (c), Putellas - Pablos (Bermúdez 63). *Quereda*

Group E

	W	D	L	+	-	PTS
🇧🇷 BRA	3	0	0	4	0	9
🇰🇷 KOR	1	1	1	4	5	4
🇨🇷 CRC	0	2	1	3	4	2
🇪🇸 ESP	0	1	2	2	4	1

▶ History in the making. Brazil's Marta scores goal number 15 of her World Cup career.

Records tumble in Montreal

Spain and Costa Rica both made history by reaching their first Women's World Cup, but Vicky Losada's joy at scoring *La Roja*'s first goal lasted only 73 seconds as Raquel "Rocky" Rodríguez Cedeño swiftly replied with an equally historic tap-in for *Las Ticas*. Records were also set in Brazil's opener with South Korea, 37-year-old Formiga pouncing on a poor backpass to become the competition's oldest-ever goalscorer, and five-time FIFA Women's World Player of the Year Marta taking the highest-ever scorer crown after dispatching a penalty in a 2-0 win. Brazil were through to the knockouts after Andressa Alves scored a crucial goal in an even and exciting encounter with Euro 2013 quarter-finalists Spain, playing in only their third major tournament. Costa Rica took a point from South Korea, substitute Karla Villalobos rescuing the Concacaf runners-up in the dying minutes and although *Las Ticas* lost 1-0 to Brazil, their coach Amelia Valverde was proud of the way they "fought like warriors". Yoon Duk Yeo's South Korea would live to fight another day, half-time substitute Kim Soo Yun's cross flying into the net to secure a 2-1 win over Spain and a place in the round of 16.

15

Marta's penalty in Brazil's opening win over South Korea broke the World Cup scoring record she had shared with Birgit Prinz. Marta had scored her first goal in 2003 – with a penalty against South Korea!

6

The day after Japan's Homare Sawa appeared in her sixth World Cup, Brazil's Formiga joined her in that exclusive club.

▶ Raquel Rodríguez Cedeño scores Costa Rica's first World Cup goal, only moments after Vicky Losada had scored Spain's first World Cup goal. Both debutants failed to get past the group stage.

Three through in tight group

With faultless World Cup qualification campaigns under new managers, France and England arrived in Canada in buoyant mood. *Les Bleues* were the happier, though, after Eugénie Le Sommer's unstoppable shot maintained a 41-year unbeaten run against the *Lionesses*. A Mexico side bursting with former U-20 and U-17 World Cup quarter-finalists looked set for a first senior finals win in seven attempts after Veronica Perez gave them the lead against Colombia, but Daniela Montoya's super strike into the top corner levelled the match eight minutes from time. The South American side then pulled off a shock win over France, coolly taken goals from Lady Andrade and Catalina Usme and an inspired performance from keeper Sandra Sepúlveda avenging their 2012 Olympics loss to the French. England left it late to see off Mexico, Fran Kirby and Karen Carney scoring in a crucial 2-1 win, and they succeeded where France had faltered, winning an end-to-end match with Colombia to reach the round of 16. Even so, France topped the group with an emphatic 5-0 rout of Mexico, Marie-Laure Delie's 34th-second opener registering as the third fastest in the competition's history, while Colombia's four points secured their first knockout spot.

Group F

	W	D	L	+	−	PTS
FRA	2	0	1	6	2	6
ENG	2	0	1	4	3	6
COL	1	1	1	4	3	4
MEX	0	1	2	2	8	1

41
The number of years since the French had last lost against England, and they extended that run with a 1-0 victory in Moncton. The English finally ended the run at Euro 2017.

◀ Marie-Laure Delie scores for France after just 34 seconds against Mexico – the third-fastest goal in World Cup history. Only Lena Videkull (30 seconds) in 1991 and Melissa Tancredi (32 seconds) in 2007 have been quicker off the mark.

◀ Daniela Montoya, Yoreli Rincón (10), Isabella Echeverri (21) and Carolina Arbeláez (2) pose for a selfie after Colombia's victory over France.

◀◀ Lady Andrade celebrates her goal in Colombia's 2-0 victory over France.

Moncton Stadium, Moncton
9.06.2015, 14:00, **11,686**

FRANCE 1-0 **ENGLAND**
Le Sommer 29

Thalia Mitsi GRE
Chrysoula Kourompylia GRE & Angela Kyriakou CYP

FRA • 16 Karen Bouhaddi - 8 Jessica Houara, 4 Laura Georges, 2 Wendie Renard (c), 3 Laure Bouilleau - 12 Élodie Thomis (7 Kenza Dali 71), 6 Amandine Henry, 10 Camille Abily, 14 Louisa Nécib (11 Claire Lavogez 87) - 9 Eugénie Le Sommer (15 Élise Bussaglia 81), 17 Gaëtane Thiney. *Philippe Bergeröo*

ENG • 1 Karen Bardsley - 2 Alex Scott (22 Fran Kirby 68), 5 Steph Houghton (c), 6 Laura Bassett, 3 Claire Rafferty - 8 Jill Scott, 16 Katie Chapman ■ 65 (11 Jade Moore 76), 4 Fara Williams, 12 Lucy Bronze - 23 Ellen White (18 Toni Duggan 61), 9 Eniola Aluko. *Mark Sampson WAL*

Moncton Stadium, Moncton
9.06.2015, 17:00, **11,686**

COLOMBIA 1-1 **MEXICO**
Montoya 82   Perez 36

Thérèse Neguel CMR
Mana Dzodope TOG & Souad Oulhaj MAR

COL • 1 Stefany Castaño - 17 Carolina Arias, 13 Angela Clavijo, 14 Nataly Arias, 9 Oriánica Velásquez ■ 34 - 3 Natalia Gaitán (c) ■ 26, 6 Daniela Montoya ■ 55 - 4 Diana Ospina (18 Yisela Cuesta 88), 10 Yoreli Rincón, 16 Lady Andrade (15 Tatiana Ariza 77) - 11 Catalina Usme (7 Ingrid Vidal 78). *Fabián Taborda*

MEX • 1 Cecilia Santiago ■ 18 - 2 Kenti Robles, 3 Christina Murillo, 4 Alina Garciamendez, 5 Valeria Miranda - 7 Nayeli Rangel (c), 11 Mónica Ocampo (22 Fabiola Ibarra 87), 10 Stephany Mayor, 17 Veronica Perez - 9 Charlyn Corral, 19 Renae Cuéllar (6 Jennifer Ruiz 79). *Leonardo Cuéllar*

Moncton Stadium, Moncton
13.06.2015, 14:00, **13,138**

FRANCE 0-2 **COLOMBIA**
                       Andrade 19, Usme 90+3

Qin Liang CHN
Cui Yongmei CHN & Fang Yan CHN

FRA • Bouhaddi - Houara, Georges, Renard (c), Bouilleau - Dali (18 Marie-Laure Delie 77), Bussaglia (Henry 63), Abily, Nécib (Lavogez 63) - Le Sommer, Thiney. *Bergeröo*

COL • 12 Sandra Sepúlveda ■ 69 - C Arias, Clavijo, N Arias, Velásquez - Gaitán (c), Montoya - Ospina (21 Rincón (21 Isabella Echeverri 87), Andrade (T Ariza 90+1) - Vidal (Usme 55). *Taborda*

Moncton Stadium, Moncton
13.06.2015, 17:00, **13,138**

ENGLAND 2-1 **MEXICO**
Kirby 71, Carney 82   Ibarra 90+1

Anna-Marie Keighley NZL
Allyson Flynn AUS & Lata Kaumatule TGA

ENG • Bardsley - Bronze (A Scott 85), Houghton (c), Bassett, Rafferty (14 Alex Greenwood 53) - J Scott (10 Karen Carney 66 ■ 90+3), F Williams, Moore - Duggan, Aluko, Kirby. *Sampson WAL*

MEX • Santiago - Robles, 15 Bianca Sierra (Miranda 46), Garciamendez ■ 64, Ruiz - Rangel (c), Ocampo (Ibarra 89), Mayor, Perez - Corral, R Cuéllar (20 Maria Sánchez 77). *L Cuéllar*

Lansdowne Stadium, Ottawa
17.06.2015, 16:00, **21,562**

MEXICO 0-5 **FRANCE**
                       Delie 1 (34 secs), Ruiz OG 9
                       Le Sommer (2) 13 36
                       Henry 80

Sachiko Yamagishi JPN
Naomi Teshirogi JPN & Fang Yan CHN

MEX • Santiago - Robles, Garciamendez, 13 Greta Espinoza, Miranda ■ 62 - Rangel (c) (Murillo 83), Ruiz, Mayor (14 Arianna Romero 46), Ocampo - Corral (R Cuéllar 46), Perez ■ 87. *L Cuéllar*

FRA • Bouhaddi - Houara, Georges, Renard (c), Bouilleau (5 Sabrina Delannoy 78) - Thomis, Henry, Abily (Bussaglia 70), 22 Amel Majri - Delie, Le Sommer (Thiney 63). *Bergeröo*

Olympic Stadium, Montreal
17.06.2015, 16:00, **13,862**

ENGLAND 2-1 **COLOMBIA**
Carney 15, F Williams 38p   Andrade 90+4

Carol Anne Chenard CAN
Marie-Josée Charbonneau CAN & Suzanne Morisset CAN

ENG • Bardsley - A Scott ■ 65, Houghton (c), 15 Casey Stoney, Greenwood - 7 Jordan Nobbs, F Williams, Moore - Duggan (19 Jodie Taylor 81), Carney (20 Lianne Sanderson 56), Kirby (17 Jo Potter 66). *Sampson WAL*

COL • Sepúlveda ■ 85 - C Arias ■ 37, N Arias, Clavijo, Velásquez - Gaitán (c), Montoya - Usme ■ 36 (Vidal 58), Rincón (T Ariza 74), Andrade - Ospina (19 Leicy Santos 83). *Taborda*

2015 Round of 16

▲ China's Wang Shanshan (9) celebrates scoring the winning goal against Cameroon in Edmonton. It meant that the Chinese had made it to the quarter-finals in all six World Cups in which they had participated.

Indomitable Lionesses tamed by Steel Roses

Commonwealth Stadium, Edmonton
20.06.2015, 17:30, 15,958

CHINA PR 1-0 CAMEROON

Wang Shanshan 12

Bibiana Steinhaus GER
Katrin Rafalski GER & Marina Wozniak GER

CHN • Wang Fei - Wu Haiyan (c), Zhao Rong, Li Dongna, Liu Shanshan - Tan Ruyin, Ren Guixin - Wang Lisi (Lou Jiahui 72), Tang Jiali (Wang Shuang 40), Han Peng - Wang Shanshan (Gu Yasha 90+1). *Hao Wei*

CMR • Ngo Ndom - Meffometou ■ 90+3, Manie (c), Awona, Leuko - Yango, Feudjio - Onguéné, Zouga (Nchout 64), Enganamouit - Ngono Mani (Akaba 74). *Enow Ngachu*

Cheered on by enthusiastic fans wearing the green, red and yellow of their home nation, Cameroon were only the second African team in Women's World Cup history to reach the knockout stage. Echoes of the men's historic Italia '90 campaign resonated, but a team packed with overseas-based players would not overcome a Steel Roses side that had delivered a first Women's World Cup spot since 2007. Ajara Nchout, the first Cameroonian to play in the USA's professional NWSL, Gaëlle Enganamouit, who plied her trade in Sweden, and home-based striker Gabrielle Onguéné all went agonisingly close to scoring. Their keeper Annette Ngo Ndom played her part in a fast-flowing match too, acrobatically turning substitute Lou Jiahui's goalbound lob around the post. In the end, Wang Shanshan's instinctive 12th-minute side-foot from close range would settle it, but Carl Enow Ngachu's *Indomitable Lionesses* departed with a roar and not a whimper.

▶ Captain's armband worn by the USA's Carli Lloyd at Canada 2015.
FIFA Museum Collection

▶ Alex Morgan (pink hairband) celebrates with Ali Krieger (11) and Lauren Holiday after opening the scoring for the USA against Colombia in Edmonton.

Few problems for USA against the ten of Colombia

Commonwealth Stadium, Edmonton
22.06.2015, 18:00, 19,412

USA 2-0 COLOMBIA

Morgan 53, Lloyd 66p, (Wambach penalty missed 49)

Stéphanie Frappart FRA
Manuela Nicolosi FRA & Yolanda Parga ESP

USA • Solo - Krieger (16 Lori **Chalupny** 81), Sauerbrunn, Johnston, Klingenberg - Rapinoe ■ 41 (Press 75), Holiday ■ 17, Lloyd, Heath - Wambach (c) (Brian 69), Morgan. *Ellis*

COL • 22 Catalina **Pérez** ■ 47 - C Arias, N Arias, Clavijo ■ 65, Velásquez - Montoya (Santos 85), Gaitán (c) - Ospina, Rincón (Usme 72), Andrade - Vidal (Castaño 49). *Taborda*

Having beaten the odds to overcome France, Colombia now needed to pull off another shock win, this time over a team that were ranked 26 places ahead of them in the world. The youngest squad in the tournament would need to do so without first-choice keeper Sandra Sepúlveda, who was suspended. In her place came Catalina Pérez and the 20-year-old shot-stopper performed like a veteran, denying Tobin Heath, Alex Morgan and Abby Wambach with reflex saves in a tight but lively first half. It was still all to play for at the restart, but within minutes the young keeper was red carded after bringing down Morgan on the edge of the area and Colombia were down to ten. USA skipper Wambach missed the resulting penalty, but Morgan and Carli Lloyd wrapped up the match with a goal apiece. Colombia's run was over, but Fabián Taborda's team had impressed.

▶ Colombia threaten Hope Solo's goal during the first half, but after the break struggled to contain the Americans after their goalkeeper Catalina Pérez was sent off. Abby Wambach missed the resulting penalty and the chance to equal Marta's all-time World Cup scoring record, but the USA went on to win 2-0.

Round of 16 2015

France cruise past South Korea

Olympic Stadium, Montreal
21.06.2015, 16:00, **15,518**

FRANCE 3-0 KOREA REPUBLIC

Delie (2) 4 48, Thomis 8

Salomé Di Iorio ARG
María Rocco ARG & Mariana de Almeida ARG

FRA • Bouhaddi - Houara, Georges, Renard (c), Boulleau - Thomis, Henry, Abily (23 Kheira **Hamraoui** 77 ■ 80), Nécib - Delie (13 Kadidiatou **Diani** 84), Le Sommer (Thiney 74). Bergerôo

KOR • Kim Jung Mi - Kim Soo Yun, Shim Seo Yeon, Kim Do Yeon, Lee Eun Mi ■ 33 - Kwon Hah Nul (Lee So Dam 60), Cho So Hyun (c) - Kang Yu Mi (Park Hee Young 78), Lee Geum Min ■ 85, Jeon Ga Eul - Park Eun Sun (Yoo Young A 55). Yoon Duk Yeo

▲ A sense of déjà vu... Sweden and Germany prepare to play each other for the fourth time at a World Cup, but the two nations have also faced each other in four Olympic tournaments. The Swedes won in 1991 and 1995 but the Germans have been victorious in every match since.

South Korea had not appeared at the Women's World Cup since 2003, but in 2010 their youth sides had enjoyed remarkable success, the U-17s becoming world champions and the U-20s taking bronze. Seven of those players were in Yoon Duk Yeo's squad, among them talismanic No.10 Ji So Yun, but the Chelsea star was out after picking up a knock against France. After conceding twice in the first eight minutes, South Korea would miss her creativity and goalscoring prowess as they battled to get back on terms. Marie-Laure Delie and Élodie Thomis had beaten veteran keeper Kim Jung Mi to put France in the driving seat at Montreal's Olympic Stadium, and when Delie finished off a mazy dribble by fleet-footed Eugénie Le Sommer just after the break, the *Taeguk Ladies'* impressive run was over and Philippe Bergerôo's fast and determined side were quarter-final bound.

▶ French midfielder Élodie Thomis (12) makes it 2-0 after just eight minutes against South Korea in Montreal. Ten months earlier the French had beaten the South Koreans on penalties in the same stadium in the quarter-finals of the FIFA U-20 Women's World Cup.

Sweden's German jinx continues

Lansdowne Stadium, Ottawa
20.06.2015, 16:00, **22,486**

GERMANY 4-1 SWEDEN

Mittag 24, Šašić (2) 36p 78, Marozsán 88 | Sembrant 82

Ri Hyang Ok PRK
Hong Kum Nyo PRK & Widiya Shamsuri MAS

GER • Angerer (c) - Maier, Krahn, Bartusiak ■ 28, Kemme (Cramer 77) - Goeßling, Leupolz (Marozsán 46) - Laudehr, Mittag, Popp (Lotzen 89) - Šašić. Neid

SWE • Lindahl - Berglund (11 Jenny **Hjohlman** 80), Ilestedt ■ 35, Fischer, Samuelsson (Nilsson 46) - Rubensson (Asllani 67), Sembrant, Seger (c), Sjögran - Jakobsson, Schelin ■ 68. Sundhage

Pia Sundhage had scored in Sweden's first-ever meeting with Germany, the 1991 World Cup match for third place which the Swedes won and which Silvia Neid missed through injury. The two former captains also met as managers at Euro 2013, Neid's Germany eliminating Sundhage's Sweden in the semi-final in Gothenburg. Dzsenifer Marozsán had scored the goal that broke Swedish hearts then and the midfielder would grab one here too, but the player who inflicted the most damage as Germany overcame a Sweden side that had only just survived the "group of death" was one who was well known to the *Damallsvenskan* – FC Rosengård's Anja Mittag opened the scoring then won a penalty which Célia Šašić dispatched with aplomb. Šašić headed in her second with 12 minutes remaining, and although Linda Sembrant pulled a goal back and Sofia Jakobsson was denied by Nadine Angerer, half-time substitute Marozsán killed hopes of a revival with a late fourth.

▶ Anja Mittag consoles Sweden captain Caroline Seger after Germany's round-of-16 win in Ottawa. In an unusual arrangement Seger alternated the captaincy of Sweden with team-mate Lotta Schelin.

2015 Round of 16

Australia win knockout game at last

Moncton Stadium, Moncton
21.06.2015, 14:00, **12,054**

BRAZIL **0-1 AUSTRALIA**
Simon 80

Teodora Albon ROU
Petruța Iugulescu ROU & Mária Súkeníková SVK

BRA • Luciana - Fabiana ■ 14, Mônica, Rafaelle, Tamires (Raquel Fernandes 83) - Formiga, Thaísa (Beatriz 83) - Marta (c) ■ 81, Andressinha, Andressa - Cristiane. *Vadão*

AUS • Williams - Foord, Alleway, Kennedy, Catley - Butt (Gorry 72), Kellond-Knight, De Vanna (c), Van Egmond, Kerr - Heyman (Simon 64). *Stajcic*

Two players who had battled their way back from injury would be key as the Matildas became the first senior Australian team, men's or women's, to win a World Cup knockout match. These two sides had met before, but a five-goal thriller of a quarter-final in 2007 and a tight group game in 2011 had both ended in Brazil's favour. The *Matildas* would finally get the victory they craved after a tense, closely fought match in wet and windy Moncton. With goalkeeper Lydia Williams in inspired form on her return from a knee ligament injury, Australia kept Cristiane, Marta and Formiga at bay. Sam Kerr went close at the other end, but it was super-sub Kyah Simon, also back from a knee ligament injury, who scored the killer goal. "It's a huge moment for us," said coach Alen Stajcic. "Thinking about what might happen next is actually very exciting."

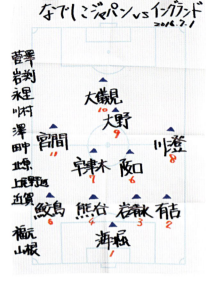

▶ Tactical plan written by Japan coach Norio Sasaki, the first man to have coached a World Cup-winning team since Tony DiCicco, who led the USA to the title in 1999.
FIFA Museum Collection

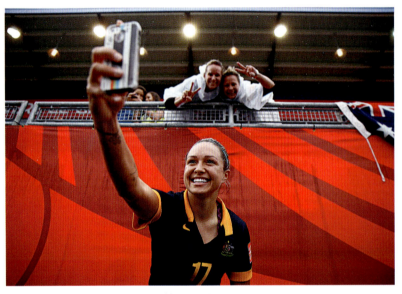

◀ Kyah Simon gets in on the selfie act. Her goal knocked out Brazil. It was her third of the tournament and fifth overall, two behind her captain Lisa De Vanna whose seven goals have come over three World Cups, including two in these finals.

◀ Saori Ariyoshi scores the opening goal of the game for Japan against the Netherlands. The Japanese kept a white bear wearing the number 7 shirt of Kozue Ando on the bench after she had broken her ankle in Japan's opening game and returned home.

Confident Japan ease through

BC Place Stadium, Vancouver
23.06.2015, 19:00, **28,717**

JAPAN  **2-1 NETHERLANDS**
Ariyoshi 10, Sakaguchi 78   Van de Ven 90+2

Lucila Venegas MEX
Mayte Chávez MEX & Enedina Caudillo MEX

JPN • Kaihori - Ariyoshi ■ 58, Iwashimizu, Kumagai, Sameshima - Kawasumi (Sawa 80), Sakaguchi, Utsugi, Miyama (c) - Ōgimi, Ohno (Iwabuchi 66). *Sasaki*

NED • Geurts - Van Lunteren, Van der Gragt, Van den Berg (c), Van Dongen (Middag 86) - Dekker, Van de Donk (Van de Ven 53), Spitse - Melis, Miedema, Martens. *Reijners*

The Netherlands had pulled through four crunch play-off matches to reach their maiden Women's World Cup and had survived a tough group to secure this historic knockout berth, but Roger Reijners' debutants were up against an almost irresistible Japan display in Vancouver. Saori Ariyoshi's daisycutter had given the reigning world champions an early lead, but Japan's second goal was a sumptuous effort featuring four players, a back-heel and neat feint then a curling Mizuho Sakaguchi shot that had many in the crowd of almost 29,000 up on their feet. The Netherlands went close to equalising from a Sherida Spitse corner, but keeper Ayumi Kaihori punched a deflection off Aya Sameshima clear and substitute Kirsten van de Ven's follow-up was kicked away by Sakaguchi. A mistake by Kaihori allowed Van de Ven to score in injury time and set up an edgy finish, but Japan held on.

Round of 16 2015

◀ Lucy Bronze celebrates scoring one of the goals of the tournament to secure victory for England over former world champions Norway in Ottawa. It was the first time that England had won a match in the knockout stages of a World Cup.

◀ Norway's Solveig Gulbrandsen (8 far left) had won gold at the Olympics in 2000. 15 years on she opened the scoring with a header here in this match. Her two children benefited from the Norwegian policy of allowing partners and children to stay at the team hotel.

Bronze to the rescue

Lansdowne Stadium, Ottawa
22.06.2015, 17:00, **19,829**

NORWAY 1-2 **ENGLAND**

S Gulbrandsen 54   Houghton 61, Bronze 76

Esther Staubli SUI
Ella De Vries BEL & Lucie Ratajová CZE

NOR • Hjelmseth - Mjelde, Rønning (c) (Thorisdottir 46), Skammelsrud Lund, Wold (Utland 87) - S Gulbrandsen, Mykjåland, Ims - Minde (Thorsnes 70), Herlovsen, Hegerberg. *Pellerud*

ENG • Bardsley - Bronze, Houghton (c), Bassett, Rafferty - F Williams - Moore, Carney, Chapman - Kirby (J Scott 54), Duggan (Taylor 63). *Sampson WAL*

Norway's 34-year-old midfielder Solveig Gulbrandsen had retired from international football in 2010, but she returned two years later to help steer Norway to the Final of Euro 2013. The mother-of-two gave Even Pellerud's side every chance of progressing here with her second goal of the tournament, a glancing header that ricocheted off the underside of the crossbar. Keeper Karen Bardsley had kept England in it up to that point, but parity was restored when captain Steph Houghton planted Fara Williams' looping corner into the net. Then came the winner, substitutes Jill Scott and Jodie Taylor combining to set up Lucy Bronze, who unleashed a powerful shot from 30 yards that Ingrid Hjelmseth got a hand to but could not keep out. England had finally won a Women's World Cup knockout match and manager Mark Sampson was already eyeing bigger things. "Make no mistake," he said, "this journey is not over."

Canadians edge spirited Swiss

BC Place Stadium, Vancouver
21.06.2015, 16:30, **53,855**

CANADA 1-0 **SWITZERLAND**

Bélanger 52

Anna-Marie Keighley NZL
Sarah Walker NZL & Allyson Flynn AUS

CAN • McLeod - Wilkinson (20 Marie-Ève **Nault** 88), Buchanan ▌74, Sesselmann, Chapman - Lawrence (Kyle 76), Scott, Schmidt - Tancredi (Filingo 69), Bélanger, Sinclair (c) - ▌13. *Herdman ENG*

SUI • Thalmann - Maritz, Abbé (c), Wälti, Kuster ▌46 (18 Vanessa **Bürki** 61) - Crnogorčević, Bernauer, Moser (Humm 72), Rinast (Kiwic 80) - Bachmann, Dickenmann. *Voss-Tecklenburg GER*

With a goalbound shot cleared off the line, heroics from Canada keeper Erin McLeod and her opposite number Gaëlle Thalmann, and a fizzing snapshot of a goal to settle it, a crowd of more than 53,000 were treated to a rousing knockout match in Vancouver. Switzerland boss Martina Voss-Tecklenburg was a veteran of three World Cups and had won the European Championship four times as a German national team player. The 1995 World Cup silver medallist's campaign with Switzerland ended here, however, Josée Bélanger thrilling the crowd with a 52nd-minute winner to keep the hosts in the competition. Taking heart, Voss-Tecklenburg insisted that her rookies had met all expectations while entertaining the fans and would learn from the experience. Canada's emotional coach John Herdman, meanwhile, admitted that the pressure to succeed was "immense" but the Englishman added: "Job done, we're moving on… England, Norway, let's do it!"

▼ Goalkeeper Erin McLeod punches away a Swiss attack during Canada's round-of-16 match in Vancouver. Canada's match winner Josée Bélanger had missed the 2011 finals and 2012 Olympics after a serious injury kept her out of the team for three years.

2015 Quarter-finals

◂ Carli Lloyd (centre) celebrates scoring her first goal at these finals from open play. She would go on to score four more to finish on six – the same as Germany's Célia Šašić. Both also had an assist but Lloyd missed out on the Golden Boot having played more minutes.

◂ Goalkeeper Wang Fei kissed both posts before the game, but couldn't prevent China exiting the World Cup at the quarter-final stage for the fourth time.

Germany win on penalties

Olympic Stadium, Montreal
26.06.2015, 16:00, 24,859

GERMANY 1-1 FRANCE
AET
5-4 PSO

Šašić 84p   Nécib 64

Behringer ⬤ Thiney ⬤ Laudehr ⬤ Abily ⬤ Peter ⬤ Nécib ⬤ Marozsán ⬤ Renard ⬤ Šašić ⬤ Lavogez ✘ (saved)

⚑ Carol Anne Chenard CAN
⚑ Marie-Josée Charbonneau CAN & Suzanne Morisset CAN

GER • Angerer (c) - Maier, Krahn, Peter, Kemme - Goeßling ▮ 68 (Behringer 79), Leupolz ▮ 91 - Laudehr, Mittag ▮ 37 (Marozsán 46 ▮ 68), Popp (Däbritz 70) - Šašić. *Neid*

FRA • Bouhaddi - Houara, Georges ▮ 57, Renard (c), Majri - Thomis (Lavogez 69), Henry, Abily, Nécib - Delie ▮ 55 (Hamraoui 101), Le Sommer (Thiney 91). *Bergerôo*

A penalty shoot-out victory had seen France crush English hopes at the quarter-final stage of the 2011 World Cup. This time, Les Bleues would suffer the agony of crashing out after penalties, veteran Germany keeper Nadine Angerer proving the difference between the two sides. France had pegged the European champions back in the first half and took the lead in the second through the excellent Louisa Nécib, but their precious advantage slipped through their fingers six minutes from time when Amel Majri was deemed to have handled Leonie Maier's cross in the area and Célia Šašić coolly converted the subsequent penalty. Substitute Gaëtane Thiney fired a great chance wide in extra time, but it would take penalties to settle it, Angerer launching herself at 21-year-old Claire Lavogez's spot kick and saving it with her knee to see Germany through and leave France pondering what might have been.

Lloyd makes it seven out of seven semi-finals for the USA

Lansdowne Stadium, Ottawa
26.06.2015, 19:30, 24,141

CHINA PR 0-1 USA

Lloyd 51

⚑ Carina Vitulano ITA
⚑ Michelle O'Neill IRL & Tonja Paavola FIN

CHN • Wang Fei - Wu Haiyan (c) ▮ 50, Zhao Rong, Li Dongna, Liu Shanshan - Tan Ruyin (3 Pang **Fengyue** 58), Ren Guixin - Wang Lisi, Lou Jiahui (Wang Shuang 35), Han Peng (Tang Jiali 74) - Wang Shanshan. *Hao Wei*

USA • Solo - Krieger, Johnston, Sauerbrunn, Klingenberg - 5 Kelley **O'Hara** (Press 61), Brian, Lloyd (c), Heath - Rodriguez (Wambach 86), Morgan (O'Reilly 81). *Ellis*

Keeper Wang Fei had watched the 1999 Final between the USA and China on television as a nine-year-old and had secretly set her sights on representing her country at a World Cup. Now aged 25, the Turbine Potsdam shot-stopper had achieved that much, playing through the pain of a shoulder injury against New Zealand and now preparing to face one of the tournament favourites. The only nation in Women's World Cup history to have reached the semi-finals in all six previous tournaments, the USA went into this crucial match without suspended stars Lauren Holiday and Megan Rapinoe, but they still dominated; Amy Rodriguez, Kelly O'Hara and Julie Johnston missing gilt-edged chances before captain Carli Lloyd headed the winning goal beyond Wang to make her mark on her 200th cap. China had given their all, but the USA were set for a seventh semi-final in seven tournaments played.

▴ Laura Georges (far left) looks on before the penalty shoot-out between France and Germany. Her World Cup career was about to come to an end having featured in every game France had ever played at the finals – in 2003, 2011 and here in Canada.

▾ Germany celebrate after Claire Lavogez misses her penalty. Célia Šašić (13) had scored a late second-half penalty to rescue the Germans. It was her sixth goal of the finals – enough to secure the Golden Boot as top scorer.

The hosts' quarter-final curse continues

BC Place Stadium, Vancouver
27.06.2015, 16:30, **54,027**

ENGLAND 2-1 CANADA

Taylor 11, Bronze 14   Sinclair 42

Claudia Umpiérrez URU
Luciana Mascaraña URU & Loreto Toloza CHI

ENG • Bardsley (13 Siobhan **Chamberlain** 52) - Bronze, Houghton (c), Bassett, Rafferty - Moore ■ 63, F Williams (E White 79), J Scott - Taylor, Chapman, Carney (Stoney 90+3). *Sampson WAL*

CAN • McLeod - Wilkinson (8 Diana **Matheson** 62), Buchanan, Sesselmann ■ 90+3, Chapman - Lawrence, Scott (Kyle 77), Schmidt - Tancredi (Leon 71), Bélanger, Sinclair (c). *Herdman ENG*

Canada coach John Herdman had called on the nation to propel his team to the title with their support, and Vancouver certainly responded, with an electric atmosphere to greet the hosts as they prepared to take on England. However, the sold-out crowd was silenced twice in the space of three minutes as Lioness striker Jodie Taylor opened the scoring with a tenacious solo goal before defender Lucy Bronze headed home a long-range free kick from Fara Williams. Taylor's Portland Thorns team-mate Christine Sinclair capitalised when Karen Bardsley spilt Ashley Lawrence's shot, the Canada skipper scoring her ninth World Cup goal in four finals, but while Bardsley would depart with an eye problem soon after the restart, her replacement Siobhan Chamberlain was barely troubled and the hosts were out. "It's not how we imagined it all to end," lamented Herdman afterwards. "We gave our best, but our best just wasn't quite good enough." It was the fifth time in seven World Cups that the host nation had lost in the quarter-finals.

▲ England's Lucy Bronze celebrates giving her side an early two-goal lead against host nation Canada. It was revenge of sorts as in the quarter-finals at the London Olympics, Canada had scored two early goals to knock out the largely English-based hosts Team GB.

Cup of tea anyone?

England midfielder Laura Bassett had made her England debut in 2003 and on away trips always made sure she had two things in her luggage – a kettle and a good supply of her favourite teabags!

◀ England's Jill Scott (8) congratulates Jodie Taylor on scoring the opening goal against Canada before a capacity crowd at BC Place in Vancouver.

Late Iwabuchi goal ends Aussie dreams

Commonwealth Stadium, Edmonton
27.06.2015, 14:00, **19,814**

AUSTRALIA 0-1 JAPAN

Iwabuchi 87

Kateryna Monzul UKR
Natalia Rachynska UKR & Sanja Rodak CRO

AUS • Williams - Foord, Alleway, Kennedy, Catley - Gorry (Heyman 76), Kellond-Knight, Van Egmond - De Vanna (c) (Crummer 67), Simon (Sykes 89), Kerr. *Stajcic*

JPN • Kaihori - Ariyoshi, Iwashimizu ■ 27, Kumagai, Sameshima - Kawasumi, Sakaguchi (Sawa 90), Utsugi, Miyama (c) - Ohno (Iwabuchi 72), Ōgimi. *Sasaki*

Rivals since Australia joined the Asian confederation in 2006, these two sides had most recently met in the Final of their World Cup qualifying competition, the 2014 AFC Women's Asian Cup. An Azusa Iwashimizu header had seen Japan take the continental title from Australia in Vietnam and a scrappy poacher's goal from substitute Mana Iwabuchi in the 87th minute would also end the *Matildas*' World Cup in the heat of Edmonton. Sam Kerr had tested Japan keeper Ayumi Kaihori with a solid side-foot shot, but Norio Sasaki's side, with their slick passing and boundless energy, dominated. Shinobu Ohno twice went close to scoring, skipper Aya Miyama's long-range strike was parried to safety by Lydia Williams, and Iwashimizu had a header blocked on the line. The *Matildas* were out, but they had impressed. "We recognise the growth of Australia in this World Cup," Sasaki said, "and my team will take confidence from this."

◀ In the AFC Women's Asian Cup Japan had beaten Australia in the Final to win the title for the first time. Here Mana Iwabuchi (16) inflicted more misery on the Aussies with a late winner.

2015 Semi-finals

▲ Kelley O'Hara (5) seals it for the USA as her late goal makes it 2-0 against Germany. This was the fourth meeting of these two nations in the seven World Cups, three in the semi-finals, and the third American victory. The USA also won an Olympic semi-final in 2004. Germany coach Silvia Neid had been involved in all of them, either as a player, assistant coach or here as the head coach.

A tale of two penalties

Olympic Stadium, Montreal
30.06.2015, 19:00, **51,176**

USA 🇺🇸 **2-0** **GERMANY** 🇩🇪

Lloyd 69p, O'Hara 84   (Šašić penalty missed 60)

Teodora Albon ROU   Petruța Iugulescu ROU & Mária Súkeníková SVK

USA • Solo - Krieger, Johnston ■ 59, Sauerbrunn ■ 38, Klingenberg - Heath (O'Hara 75), Holiday, Brian, Rapinoe (Wambach 80) - Lloyd (c), Morgan (Leroux 90+3). *Ellis*

GER • Angerer (c) - Maier ■ 34, Krahn ■ 67, Bartusiak, Kemme - Goeßling, Leupolz - Laudehr, Mittag (Marozsán 77), Popp - Šašić. *Neid*

More than 51,000 spectators turned out in Montreal to watch the top two ranked women's football nations go toe-to-toe for a coveted place in the Final. These rivals had met at this stage twice before, the USA emerging victorious in 1991, and Germany beating an American side featuring current players Christie Rampone, Shannon Boxx and Abby Wambach on their home turf in 2003. But Germany had not beaten the USA in a competitive game since, and with both sides vying to become the first to win the Women's World Cup three times, there was everything to play for. Nadine Angerer, on the substitutes bench in 2003, stood tall in the face of the USA, denying Julie Johnston and Alex Morgan with her feet in a goalless first half. Then came the drama, both sides awarded a penalty within the space of six minutes and while the tournament's leading scorer Célia Šašić missed hers, the irrepressible Carli Lloyd made no mistake. The USA captain then helped to finish the tie six minutes from time, squaring to substitute Kelley O'Hara who stuck out a leg to prod home her first for her country and end Germany's hopes of a dream finish.

◀ Headband worn by USA forward Alex Morgan during the finals.
FIFA Museum Collection

▶ Japan celebrate at the final whistle, moments after the winning goal. It meant a third successive Final against the USA after the 2011 World Cup and the 2012 Olympics.

Nightmare for Laura Bassett

Commonwealth Stadium, Edmonton
1.07.2015, 17:00, **31,467**

JAPAN 🇯🇵 **2-1** **ENGLAND** 🏴

Miyama 33p, Bassett OG 90+2   F Williams 40p

Anna-Marie Keighley NZL   Sarah Walker NZL & Allyson Flynn AUS

JPN • Kaihori - Ariyoshi, Iwashimizu, Kumagai, Sameshima - Kawasumi, Sakaguchi, Utsugi, Miyama (c) - Ohno (Iwabuchi 70), Ōgimi ■ 90. *Sasaki*
ENG • Bardsley - Bronze (A Scott 75), Houghton (c), Bassett, Rafferty ■ 31 - Moore, F Williams (Carney 86), Chapman - J Scott, Taylor (E White 60), Duggan. *Sampson WAL*

A crushing own goal in the dying moments would decide this match as Japan finally beat England in the finals at the third time of asking. Perennial quarter-finalist finishers, England were in unknown territory here, but Mark Sampson's blend of World Cup debutants and old hands had impressed so far, seeing off former champions Norway and hosts Canada on the road to Edmonton. They pushed Japan every step of the way in front of more than 31,000 spectators, Fara Williams calmly cancelling out Aya Miyama's 33rd-minute penalty with her own spot kick seven minutes later. Both sides flew at it at the restart, Toni Duggan hitting the crossbar, substitute Ellen White forcing Ayumi Kaihori into a flying save, and Jill Scott planting a header just wide of the post, while substitute Mana Iwabuchi and Mizuho Sakaguchi both had near misses. Extra time loomed but then the unthinkable happened. Nahomi Kawasumi sent the ball into the box for former Chelsea player Yūki Ōgimi to chase, Notts County skipper Laura Bassett attempted to intercept, but instead of clearing the ball, she accidentally sent it sailing into her own net. "Laura Bassett is devastated," said Sampson. "But without her, we wouldn't have been in this semi-final."

▲ That sinking feeling. England players can't quite believe it after an own goal deep into injury time saw their opponents Japan qualify for the Final.

Third place 2015

▲ The England players celebrate winning their first World Cup medal after beating Germany in the match for third place in Edmonton.

England break new ground

England needed to pick themselves up from their semi-final disappointment, and quickly, if they were to overcome Germany and win a historic bronze World Cup medal. But with 18 losses and two draws in 20 matches against eight-time European and two-time world champions Germany, the odds were not on England's side. Whatever happened, it would be the end of an era for Germany, veteran goalkeeper Nadine Angerer having already announced plans to retire at the end of the tournament and head coach Silvia Neid entering her final World Cup match too. Germany seized the initiative from the first whistle, striker Lena Petermann almost getting off the mark in the opening minute with a glancing header that Karen Bardsley managed to turn around the post. England captain Steph Houghton then kept her side in it with a goal-line clearance after Jo Potter nodded a Bianca Schmidt header goalwards, and stellar goalkeeping from Angerer and Bardsley kept the match goalless as it headed into extra time. England finally made the breakthrough in the 108th minute when substitute Lianne Sanderson was dragged down in the box by Tabea Kemme and 31-year-old midfielder Fara Williams stepped up to convert the penalty. The *Lionesses* had suffered a humbling 3-0 friendly loss to Germany at Wembley Stadium eight months earlier, but now, England and their Welsh head coach Mark Sampson had achieved the nation's second best-ever World Cup finish since the men's triumph on home soil back in 1966.

▼ Fara Williams (4) scores the only goal of the game against Germany. Her three goals in this tournament saw her become the first England player to score in three World Cups.

2015 Match for Third Place

Commonwealth Stadium, Edmonton
4.07.2015, 14:00, 21,483

GERMANY 0-1 **ENGLAND**
AET

F Williams 108p

Ri Hyang Ok PRK — Hong Kum Nyo PRK & Kim Kyoung Min KOR

◀ Ri Hyang Ok awarded the penalty that sealed third place for England, but she would have known exactly how the Germany players felt. She made history as the first former World Cup player to referee a match at the finals, having represented North Korea in 1999 and 2003. Liu Hsiu Mei of Chinese Taipei played at the 1991 World Cup and was also an assistant referee in 2003 and 2007.

▶ Shirt worn by England midfielder Fara Williams at the 2015 World Cup.
FIFA Museum Collection

2015 Final

Trebles all round!

A Carli Lloyd hat-trick secured a third world title for the USA in an extraordinary match. With four goals in a blistering 16-minute spell, the USA delivered the most dramatic opening moments of any Final in this competition's history. Captain Carli Lloyd was the architect of the Americans' lightning-fast start, Japan the victims, and if any of the 53,341 fans at BC Place had been late to take their seats, they might have missed the most spectacular goal of all. That came on the 16-minute mark when 32-year-old Lloyd saw Ayumi Kaihori off her line and unleashed a shot from the centre circle that flew over the keeper's flailing arms and into the net. Lloyd had scored both goals when the USA had beaten Japan in the 2012 Olympic Final, but this was something else. "I call her my beast and she is just a beast, unbelievable," said USA head coach Jill Ellis. Japan certainly looked incredulous when the first 14 minutes had yielded not just two goals for Lloyd but one for Lauren Holiday too, the midfielder showing great technique to volley a high defensive header straight into the opposition net. Two minutes later, Lloyd scored her wondergoal to complete the first-ever Women's World Cup Final hat-trick.

Japan were not about to give up, though, and Yūki Ōgimi pulled a goal back in the 27th minute, holding off Julie Johnston in the box to turn and shoot beyond Hope Solo. It was the first goal the USA had conceded in 540 World Cup minutes. Japan were fighting for every ball now and Norio Sasaki handed Homare Sawa her 205th cap shortly afterwards, sending the inspirational 2011 World Cup skipper on in place of defender Azusa Iwashimizu, then bringing striker Yuika Sugasawa on for midfielder Nahomi Kawasumi. A second goal was duly delivered just after the break, Johnston accidentally heading Japan captain Aya Miyama's free kick into her own net under pressure from Sawa. But the USA were determined not to allow Japan back into the Final as they had in 2011 and within two minutes, their three-goal lead was restored, Tobin Heath's side-foot finish in a crowded penalty area sealing the win. The penalty shoot-out loss of 2011, which saw both Lloyd and Heath miss a spot kick, had been put to bed and the USA had finally become the first nation to win a trio of Women's World Cups. "What we've done is remarkable," said Lloyd. "It's a historic performance."

▲ Carli Lloyd scores after just two minutes and 35 seconds – the quickest goal in a World Cup Final. The six previous Finals had seen just five first-half goals. That figure was matched in this Final alone.

2015 World Cup Final

BC Place Stadium, Vancouver
5.07.2015, 16:00, 53,341

USA 5-2 JAPAN

Lloyd (3) 3 5 16, Holiday 14, Heath 54 — Ogimi 27, Johnston OG 52

Kateryna Monzul UKR — Natalia Rachynska UKR & Yolanda Parga ESP

▼ Japan's Ayumi Kaihori can only get her fingertips to the ball as Carli Lloyd completes the first World Cup Final hat-trick. Her shot was from the halfway line.

Final 2015

9 When Christie Rampone came on for Megan Rapinoe in the second half, it completed a remarkable career. At 40 years and 11 days she set the mark as the oldest player in World Cup history up to that point, but there was so much more to celebrate. As Christie Pearce, she won a winners medal in 1999, the first of what would be a record haul of nine medals overall. Five of those were winners medals – two in the World Cup and three Olympic gold – another record. There was also one World Cup runners-up medal (2011), one Olympic silver (in 2000) and two World Cup third-place medals (in 2003 and 2007). All she is missing from her collection is an Olympic bronze!

▶ Kelley O'Hara celebrates with the fans after the USA's 5-2 victory over Japan in the Final.

▲ USA captain Carli Lloyd scores the second of her goals to put her team 2-0 up after just five minutes.

▼ That winning feeling... The USA are world champions for the third time. The most successful nation in women's football had gone 16 years without wining the title. In the meantime they had won three Olympic golds.

Turf wars

The Canada Women's World Cup was the first played on artificial turf, and a coalition of international players that included Abby Wambach, Marta, Nadine Angerer, Sam Kerr, Camille Abily and Ji So Yun stepped up to argue against playing on a surface they regarded as physically rough on players, from slide burns to lingering muscle and joint pain that doesn't occur when playing on grass. In October 2014, they filed a claim in a Canadian court, arguing that playing on turf was gender discrimination, as men's World Cup matches are only played on grass. It was a difficult situation, as Carli Lloyd noted. "Any time you're fighting for something, you have to get outside of your comfort zone and make other people uncomfortable," she said. The players dropped the suit in early 2015 when it became clear the tournament would progress on artificial turf, but their action helped move the needle on inequalities in women's football. "We definitely shook some things up," Lloyd said. "It definitely got the word out, and that helped."

3 Only three players have scored a hat-trick in the knockout rounds of the World Cup and Carli Lloyd's in the Final here was the first since 1991. Michelle Akers scored five in the quarter-finals of that first World Cup in China, while Carin Jennings scored three in the semi-finals that year. All of the other 17 World Cup hat-tricks have been scored during the group stage.

2016

Rio 2016 was the first time that the USA failed to make it to the Olympic Final after they were knocked out by Sweden on penalties in the quarter-finals. The Swedes then won another shoot-out in the semis against Brazil, ending Marta's hopes of a 'home' world title. The Brazilians missed out on a medal altogether when they lost the bronze medal match to Canada. The gold was won by Germany, who were appearing in their first Olympic Final. They beat Sweden 2-1 at the Maracanã to add the Olympic crown to their world titles of 2003 and 2007.

A first for South America

This was the first Olympic Games held in South America and it came two years after Brazil hosted the FIFA World Cup. The two events placed a huge strain on the country politically and economically but both were a success from a sporting perspective. Russia were banned from the athletics after allegations of state-sponsored doping, and it was the Americans who once again topped the medal table ahead of Great Britain in second place and China in third. Brazil finally won the gold medal that they wanted more than any other – in the men's football tournament. Neymar scored Brazil's goal in a 1-1 draw with Germany and then the winning penalty in the shoot-out to claim the Olympic title for the first time in their history. Elsewhere, Jamaica's Usain Bolt completed the treble treble, winning the 100m, 200m and 4x100m for the third Olympics running, although one of the relay titles was later stripped after team-mate Nesta Carter failed a drugs test in 2008. Katie Ledecky dominated in the pool winning four golds – the same number won by Simone Biles who shone in the gymnastics. There was redemption for Brazil's Rafaela Silva in the judo when, after having been disqualified for an illegal hold four years earlier, she won the host nation's first gold in Rio.

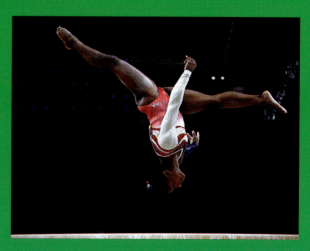

▼ The USA's Simone Biles won four golds in Rio.

2016 **Overview**

RIO 2016

WOMEN'S OLYMPIC FOOTBALL TOURNAMENT

Story of the qualifiers

No place for Japan

The most notable absentees from the Rio Olympics were former world champions and Olympic Finalists Japan. Their surprise elimination came despite hosting the final round of Asian qualifiers in Osaka where they lost to both Australia and China, who took the two slots available. In Africa, the early editions of the World Cup and Olympic qualifiers had been dominated by nations from west Africa, but for Rio both African slots went to nations in the south – Zimbabwe and South Africa. Zimbabwe beat Cameroon on away goals to qualify for their first global outing, while the South Africans knocked out Equatorial Guinea, who in the previous round had disposed of traditional giants Nigeria. In Oceania, New Zealand won their now-customary battle with Papua New Guinea to make it to Rio, while the USA and Canada emerged as the top two in a Concacaf qualifying tournament held in Texas. The route to Rio was less complex for Europe and South America. Once again, UEFA chose not to stage a qualifying tournament and nominated Germany and France who had been the second- and third-best European teams at the 2015 World Cup. They were joined by Sweden, who won a mini-tournament between the four teams that had been eliminated in the round of 16 in Canada. England had finished ahead of all three but there was little appetite to repeat the experiment of 2012 and enter a Team GB. There was only one South American slot on offer given Brazil's automatic qualification as hosts, and it went to Colombia who had finished as runners-up to Brazil in the 2014 *Copa América Femenina*, a tournament that also determined qualification for the 2015 World Cup.

▲ Germany's Olympic dreams came true in Rio.

Overview 2016

12 TEAMS

636 092 SPECTATORS

24 465 AVERAGE PER MATCH

GERMANY WINNERS

SWE SECOND

CAN THIRD

TOP OF THE MEDAL TABLE

USA	46	37	38
GREAT BRITAIN	27	23	17
CHINA PR	26	18	26
RUSSIA	19	17	20
GERMANY	17	10	15
JAPAN	12	8	21

26 MATCHES PLAYED

66 YELLOW CARDS

3 RED CARDS

66 GOALS

2.54 AVERAGE GOALS PER MATCH

ERREJOTA OFFICIAL MATCH BALL

Host cities and stadiums

The Maracanã makes history

Of the seven stadiums used during the football tournaments, Rio's Estádio Olímpico was the only one that had not been used two years earlier during the FIFA World Cup. And of those seven, the Maracanã was the only one to see action in the 1950 World Cup as well, making it the first to host four major global Finals – two in the FIFA World Cup and both Olympic Finals here.

MANAUS
ARENA DA AMAZÔNIA
(43,247)

SALVADOR
ARENA FONTE NOVA
(65,684)

BRASILIA
ESTÁDIO NACIONAL MANÉ GARRINCHA
(69,389)

RIO DE JANEIRO
ESTÁDIO OLÍMPICO
(49,905)

BELO HORIZONTE
MINEIRÃO
(52,660)

SÃO PAULO
ARENA CORINTHIANS
(62,276)

RIO DE JANEIRO
MARACANÃ
(71,655)

×5

Top scorer

Melanie Behringer GER

Second Place: Christine Sinclair CAN ×3
Third Place: Janine Beckie CAN ×3

2016 **Fans**

◂ China's Zhang Rui (15) in action against South Africa at the Estádio Olímpico in Rio.

Cristiane, the record-breaker

Brazil hoped that home advantage would bring them a first international title and help wipe away the memories of three defeats in World Cup and Olympic Finals. They opened their campaign with an impressive 3-0 win over China, a team they had not lost to since 1996, with Cristiane scoring the third. The 31-year-old striker then got another in the 5-1 victory over Sweden to take her combined total in the Olympics to 14, a record that will take some beating. Marta also chipped in with two against the Swedes, taking her Olympic total to 10. That win took Brazil into the quarter-finals, but then, remarkably, the goals dried up. That didn't matter in the 0-0 draw against South Africa, but it was to have serious consequences as the tournament progressed beyond the group stage. Despite their heavy defeat against Brazil, Sweden joined the hosts in the quarter-finals as one of the best third-placed teams, beating South Africa and then drawing with the Chinese, who finished in second place on goal difference. South Africa were fitter and stronger than in 2012 and they held Brazil to a draw, matching their record from 2012 where they had drawn with Japan.

◂ Brazil's Cristiane is congratulated after scoring a record 14th Olympic goal in the 5-1 victory over Sweden. Marta scored twice to take her Olympic total to 10. The outcome of the game would be very different when the two teams met again in the semi-finals.

Group E

Group stage 2016

	W	D	L	+	-	PTS
BRA	2	1	0	8	1	7
CHN	1	1	1	2	3	4
SWE	1	1	1	2	5	4
RSA	0	1	2	0	3	1

14/14

Rio 2016 was the 14th global tournament for women's football from the first in 1988. Brazil, Sweden and the USA were the only three teams present at all 14.

Estádio Olímpico, Rio de Janeiro
3.08.2016, 13:00, **13,439**

SWEDEN 1-0 **SOUTH AFRICA**
Fischer 76

Teodora Albon ROU
Petruța Iugulescu ROU & Mária Súkeníková SVK

SWE • 1 Hedvig **Lindahl** - 15 Jessica **Samuelsson**, 5 Nilla **Fischer**, 3 Linda **Sembrant**, 6 Magdalena **Eriksson** - 17 Caroline **Seger**, 7 Lisa **Dahlkvist** (16 Elin **Rubensson** 46), 9 Kosovare **Asllani** - 13 Fridolina **Rolfö** (12 Olivia **Schough** 76), 8 Lotta **Schelin** (c), 10 Sofia **Jakobsson** (11 Stina **Blackstenius** 69). *Pia Sundhage*

RSA • 1 Roxanne **Barker** - 2 Lebohang **Ramalepe** (14 Sanah **Mollo** 84), 5 Janine **van Wyk** (c), 4 Noko **Matlou**, 3 Nothando **Vilakazi** - 15 Refiloe **Jane**, 6 Mamello **Makhabane**, 7 Stephanie **Malherbe**, 12 Jermaine **Seoposenwe** - 9 Amanda **Dlamini** - 11 Shiwe **Nogwanya** (10 Linda **Motlhalo** 39). *Vera Pauw NED*

Estádio Olímpico, Rio de Janeiro
3.08.2016, 16:00, **27,618**

BRAZIL 3-0 **CHINA PR**
Mônica 36
Andressa 59
Cristiane 90

Carol Anne Chenard CAN
Marie-Josée Charbonneau CAN & Suzanne Morisset CAN

BRA • 1 **Bárbara** - 2 **Fabiana** (12 **Poliana** 85), 3 **Mônica**, 4 **Rafaelle**, 6 **Tamires** - 10 **Marta** (c) (7 **Debinha** 80), 8 **Formiga**, 5 **Thaísa** (17 **Andressinha** 58), 9 **Andressa** - 11 **Cristiane**, 16 **Beatriz**. *Vadão*

CHN • 1 **Zhao Lina** - 2 **Liu Shanshan**, 14 **Zhao Rong**, 6 **Li Dongna** (c), 5 **Wu Haiyan** ■ 22 - 8 **Tan Ruyin**, 13 **Pang Fengyue** - 10 **Yang Li**, 15 **Zhang Rui**, 12 **Wang Shuang** (17 **Gu Yasha** 79) - 11 **Wang Shanshan** (9 **Ma Xiaoxu** 64). *Bruno Bini FRA*

Estádio Olímpico, Rio de Janeiro
6.08.2016, 19:00, **25,000**

SOUTH AFRICA 0-2 **CHINA PR**
Gu Yasha 45+1
Tan Ruyin 87

Esther Staubli SUI
Lucie Ratajová CZE & Chrysoula Kourompylia GRE

RSA • Barker - Ramalepe, Van Wyk (c), Matlou ■ 72, Vilakazi - Makhabane (18 Mpumi **Nyandeni** 80), Malherbe - Motlhalo, Jane, 20 Thembi **Kgatlana** (Mollo 84) - Seoposenwe. *Pauw NED*

CHN • Zhao Lina - 4 **Gao Chen**, Zhao Rong (Wu Haiyan 29), Li Dongna (c), Liu Shanshan - Pang Fengyue - Wang Shuang, Tan Ruyin, Zhang Rui, Gu Yasha - Yang Li (Wang Shanshan 65). *Bini FRA*

Estádio Olímpico, Rio de Janeiro
6.08.2016, 22:00, **43,384**

BRAZIL 5-1 **SWEDEN**
Beatriz (2) 21 86   Schelin 89
Cristiane 24
Marta (2) 44p 80

Lucila Venegas MEX
Enedina Caudillo MEX & Mayte Chávez MEX

BRA • Bárbara - Fabiana (Poliana 83), Mônica, Rafaelle, Tamires - Formiga (Andressinha 56), Thaísa - Marta (c), Cristiane (Debinha 66), Beatriz, Andressa. *Vadão*

SWE • Lindahl - Rubensson, Fischer, 4 Emma **Berglund**, Eriksson ■ 44 (2 Jonna **Andersson** 46) - Seger (c), Dahlkvist, Asllani ■ 49 (14 Emilia **Appelqvist** 74) - Rolfö (Schough 64), Schelin, Jakobsson. *Sundhage*

Arena da Amazônia, Manaus
9.08.2016, 21:00, **38,415**

SOUTH AFRICA 0-0 **BRAZIL**

Stéphanie Frappart FRA
Manuela Nicolosi FRA & Yolanda Parga ESP

RSA • Barker - 17 Leandra **Smeda**, Matlou, Van Wyk (c), Vilakazi ■ 57 - Makhabane, Malherbe, Jane - Kgatlana (Dlamini 82), Motlhalo (Mollo 65), Seoposenwe. *Pauw NED*

BRA • 18 **Aline** - Poliana, 14 **Bruna** (c) ■ 40, Mônica, Tamires (Marta 46) - 13 **Érika**, Thaísa (Fabiana 82), Debinha - Andressa, 15 **Raquel Fernandes**, Andressinha ■ 44. *Vadão*

Estádio Nacional Mané Garrincha, Brasília
9.08.2016, 22:00, **7,648**

CHINA PR 0-0 **SWEDEN**

Olga Miranda PAR
Mariana de Almeida ARG & Yoleida Lara Cabarcas VEN

CHN • Zhao Lina - Gao Chen, Wu Haiyan, Li Dongna (c), Liu Shanshan - Pang Fengyue ■ 90+3 - Wang Shuang (Wang Shanshan 83), Tan Ruyin, Zhang Rui, Gu Yasha (7 **Li Ying** 89) - Yang Li. *Bini FRA*

SWE • Lindahl - Samuelsson, Fischer (Berglund 78), Sembrant, Eriksson - Seger, Dahlkvist (Asllani 62), Rubensson - Rolfö, Schelin (c), Schough. *Sundhage*

2016 Group stage

Arena Corinthians, São Paulo
3.08.2016, 15:00, **20,521**

CANADA 🇨🇦 **2-0** 🇦🇺 **AUSTRALIA**

Beckie 1 (20 secs)
Sinclair 78
(Beckie penalty saved 73)

👕 Stéphanie Frappart FRA
🚩 Manuela Nicolosi FRA & Yolanda Parga ESP

CAN • 1 Stephanie **Labbé** - 7 Rhian **Wilkinson** 🟨 22 (2 Allysha **Chapman** 46), 3 Kadeisha **Buchanan** 🟨 48, 4 Shelina **Zadorsky** 🟨 19, 10 Ashley **Lawrence**, 8 Diana **Matheson** (13 Sophie **Schmidt** 69), 11 Desiree **Scott**, 17 Jessie **Fleming** - 12 Christine **Sinclair** (c), 14 Melissa **Tancredi** (5 Rebecca **Quinn** 23), 16 Janine **Beckie**. *John Herdman ENG*

AUS • 1 Lydia **Williams** - 4 Clare **Polkinghorne** (c), 5 Laura **Alleway**, 14 Alanna **Kennedy**, 9 Caitlin **Foord** - 6 Chloe **Logarzo** (11 Lisa **De Vanna** 61), 3 Katrina **Gorry**, 8 Elise **Kellond-Knight**, 15 Samantha **Kerr** (7 Steph **Catley** 46) - 16 Michelle **Heyman** (17 Kyah **Simon** 71), 10 Emily **van Egmond**. *Alen Stajcic*

Arena Corinthians, São Paulo
3.08.2016, 18:00, **20,521**

ZIMBABWE 🇿🇼 **1-6** 🇩🇪 **GERMANY**

Basopo 50   Däbritz 22, Popp 36,
Behringer (2) 53 78
Leupolz 83, Chibanda OG 90
(Behringer penalty saved 78)

👕 Rita Gani MAS
🚩 Cui Yongmei CHN & Naomi Teshirogi JPN

ZIM • 16 Lindiwe **Magwede** - 14 Eunice **Chibanda**, 2 Lynett **Mutokuto**, 4 Nobuhle **Majika** 🟨 77, 3 Sheila **Makoto** 🟨 41 - 17 Kudakwashe **Basopo** (13 Erina **Jeke** 81), 5 Emmaculate **Msipa** (11 Daisy **Kaitano** 81), 6 Talent **Mandaza**, 7 Rudo **Neshamba** (c) (18 Felistas **Muzongondi** 46) - 12 Marjory **Nyaumwe** - 15 Rutendo **Makore** 🟨 90+1. *Shadreck Mlauzi*

GER • 1 Almuth **Schult** - 17 Isabel **Kerschowski** (12 Tabea **Kemme** 72), 5 Annike **Krahn**, 3 Saskia **Bartusiak** (c), 4 Leonie **Maier** - 10 Dzsenifer **Marozsán**, 7 Melanie **Behringer**, 13 Sara **Däbritz** - 11 Anja **Mittag** (8 Lena **Goeßling** 65), 9 Alexandra **Popp**, 6 Simone **Laudehr** (16 Melanie **Leupolz** 19). *Silvia Neid*

Arena Corinthians, São Paulo
6.08.2016, 15:00, **30,295**

CANADA 🇨🇦 **3-1** 🇿🇼 **ZIMBABWE**

Beckie (2) 7 35, Sinclair 19p   Chirandu 86

👕 Olga Miranda PAR
🚩 Mariana de Almeida ARG & Yoleida Lara Cabarcas VEN

CAN • 18 Sabrina **D'Angelo** - 9 Josée **Bélanger** 🟨 80, Buchanan 🟨 59, Quinn, Lawrence - Matheson (Chapman 63), Fleming 🟨 58 (15 Nichelle **Prince** 70), Schmidt, Beckie - Sinclair (c), Tancredi (6 Deanne **Rose** 61). *Herdman ENG*

ZIM • 1 Chido **Dzingirai** 🟨 18 - Chibanda, 8 Rejoice **Kapfumvuti**, Majika, Makoto - Basopo (Jeke 88), Msipa, Mandaza, Muzongondi (c) (10 Mavis **Chirandu** 68) - Makore (Kaitano 79), Nyaumwe. *Mlauzi*

Arena Corinthians, São Paulo
6.08.2016, 18:00, **37,475**

GERMANY 🇩🇪 **2-2** 🇦🇺 **AUSTRALIA**

Däbritz 45+1   Kerr 6
Bartusiak 88   Foord 45

👕 Anna-Marie Keighley NZL
🚩 Sarah Jones NZL & Lata Kaumatule TGA

GER • Schult - Kemme, Krahn (2 Josephine **Henning** 46 🟨 56), Bartusiak (c), Maier - Marozsán (Goeßling 70), Behringer, Däbritz - Leupolz, Popp 🟨 30, Mittag (Kerschowski 61). *Neid*

AUS • Williams - Polkinghorne, Alleway, Kennedy, Catley - Gorry, Kellond-Knight - Foord - De Vanna (c) (Heyman 67), Simon, Kerr (Logarzo 83). *Stajcic*

Arena Fonte Nova, Salvador
9.08.2016, 16:00, **5,115**

AUSTRALIA 🇦🇺 **6-1** 🇿🇼 **ZIMBABWE**

De Vanna 2   Msipa 90+1
Polkinghorne 15
Kennedy 37, Simon 50
Heyman (2) 55 66

👕 Esther Staubli SUI
🚩 Lucie Ratajová CZE & Chrysoula Kourompylia GRE

AUS • 18 Mackenzie **Arnold** - Logarzo 🟨 90+5, Polkinghorne (c), Kennedy, Catley - Kellond-Knight, Gorry (Heyman 52) - Van Egmond - De Vanna (2 Larissa **Crummer** 75), Simon, Foord (12 Ellie **Carpenter** 75). *Stajcic*

ZIM • Dzingirai (Magwede 58) - Chibanda, Mutokuto, Majika (c), Makoto 🟨 3 - Basopo, Mandaza, Msipa, Chirandu (Makore 46) - Kapfumvuti (Kaitano 75), Nyaumwe. *Mlauzi*

Estádio Nacional Mané Garrincha, Brasília
9.08.2016, 16:00, **8,187**

GERMANY 🇩🇪 **1-2** 🇨🇦 **CANADA**

Behringer 13p   Tancredi (2) 26 60

👕 Ri Hyang Ok PRK
🚩 Hong Kum Nyo PRK & Cui Yongmei CHN

GER • Schult - Henning (Krahn 46), 14 Babett **Peter**, Bartusiak (c), Kemme - Kerschowski (Leupolz 68), Goeßling, Behringer, 15 Mandy **Islacker** - Marozsán 🟨 59 (Popp 68), Mittag. *Neid*

CAN • Labbé - Wilkinson, Quinn, Zadorsky, Chapman - Scott - Bélanger, Fleming (Lawrence 46), Schmidt (Matheson 64), Rose (Prince 69 🟨 90) - Tancredi (c). *Herdman ENG*

Group F

	W	D	L	+	-	PTS
🇨🇦 CAN	3	0	0	7	2	9
🇩🇪 GER	1	1	1	9	5	4
🇦🇺 AUS	1	1	1	8	5	4
🇿🇼 ZIM	0	0	3	3	15	0

20

That's how many seconds it took for Canada's Janine Beckie to score against Australia – the quickest goal at any Olympics or World Cup.

Canada on song

Canada were the only team to win all three first-round matches, and their victory over Australia saw 21-year-old Janine Beckie scoring after just 20 seconds. That not only beat Heather O'Reilly's Olympic record of 40 seconds from 2008, but also Lena Videkull's quarter-of-a-century-old World Cup record which had stood at 29 seconds. Three days later, Canada beat Zimbabwe as veteran skipper Christine Sinclair scored her tenth goal at the Olympics, tying with Germany's Birgit Prinz and Brazil's Marta as the second highest on the all-time list. The Canadians then beat Germany for the first time ever to end a sensational group stage for them. The Germans, who had also arrived in Rio determined to capture gold, the only prize that had so far elluded them, opened with a 6-1 victory over Zimbabwe but then drew with Australia, a result which saw both teams through after the Australians beat Zimbabwe 6-1 in their final match. Zimbabwe had a difficult debut on the international stage but they won respect for the challenges they overcame to be in Rio. They had forfeited a qualification match due to a lack of travel funds, players worked in full-time jobs with limited training opportunities, while the coaching staff were replaced in September 2015.

▶ Melissa Tancredi (14) scored twice in Canada's 2-1 group victory over Germany. They would meet again in the semi-finals.

▶ Zimbabwe's Nobuhle Majika tackles Australia's Caitlin Foord (9). Zimbabwe scored a goal in all three of their games, but conceded 15, including six in this match in Salvador.

USA and France in control

The United States arrived in Rio as the reigning Olympic and world champions and were favourites for gold again, having retained 15 of the squad that won in Canada the previous year. They kicked off their campaign with a 2-0 win over New Zealand, Carli Lloyd carrying on from where she had left off in Canada by scoring the first goal. She scored again in the 1-0 win over France, but the victory owed as much to the skilled handiwork of goalkeeper Hope Solo, who was winning her 200th cap for the national team, the first international keeper to reach that milestone and the eleventh American to do so. In their final group match, the USA were denied a win over Colombia when Catalina Usme scored a last-minute equaliser for the South Americans. France were looking to improve on their fourth-place in London four years earlier and they finished in second place in the group after wins over both Colombia and New Zealand. New Zealand's 1-0 victory over Colombia was not enough to take them through to the quarter-finals as one of the best third-placed teams. Kiwi captain Abby Erceg was sent off in that match, a decision that was later overturned by FIFA.

Group G

	W	D	L	+	−	PTS
USA	2	1	0	5	2	7
FRA	2	0	1	7	1	6
NZL	1	0	2	1	5	3
COL	0	1	2	2	7	1

◀◀ The USA's Christen Press (12) and Colombia's Nataly Arias (14) fight for the ball during their group match in Manaus. The Colombians scored a last-minute equaliser to deny the USA a perfect group record.

▲ ◀ Alex Morgan (13) and Griedge Mbock Bathy (2) go head to head in the USA's 1-0 victory over France in Belo Horizonte. Carli Lloyd scored the winner.

13

The USA's win over France extended their run of consecutive Olympic victories to 13. The run came to an end in their next game, against Colombia.

◀ Amber Hearn celebrates scoring for New Zealand in their 1-0 win over Colombia. New Zealand were, however, the one third-placed team at Rio 2016 not to qualify for the quarter-finals.

Group stage 2016

Mineirão, Belo Horizonte
3.08.2016, 19:00, **10,059**

USA 2-0 NEW ZEALAND

Lloyd 9, Morgan 46

Kateryna Monzul UKR
Natalia Rachynska UKR & Sanja Rodak CRO

USA • 1 Hope **Solo** - 5 Kelley **O'Hara**, 8 Julie **Johnston**, 4 Becky **Sauerbrunn**, 7 Meghan **Klingenberg** - 2 Mallory **Pugh** (16 Crystal **Dunn** 51), 3 Allie **Long**, 14 Morgan **Brian** (9 Lindsey **Horan** 64), 17 Tobin **Heath** - 10 Carli **Lloyd** (c), 13 Alex **Morgan** (12 Christen **Press** 81). *Jill Ellis*

NZL • 1 Erin **Nayler** - 2 Ria **Percival** ■ 64, 6 Rebekah **Stott**, 5 Abby **Erceg** (c), 7 Ali **Riley** ■ 30 - 14 Katie **Bowen** (10 Sarah **Gregorius** 60), 16 Annalie **Longo**, 4 Katie **Duncan** (11 Kirsty **Yallop** 71), 12 Betsy **Hassett** ■ 18 - 17 Hannah **Wilkinson** (8 Jasmine **Pereira** 83), 9 Amber **Hearn**. *Tony Readings ENG*

Mineirão, Belo Horizonte
3.08.2016, 22:00, **6,874**

FRANCE 4-0 COLOMBIA

C Arias OG 2
Le Sommer 14
Abily 42, Majri 83

Ri Hyang Ok PRK
Hong Kum Nyo PRK & Allyson Flynn AUS

FRA • 16 Sarah **Bouhaddi** - 8 Jessica **Houara**, 2 Griedge **Mbock Bathy**, 3 Wendie **Renard** (c), 7 Amel **Majri** ■ 50 - 6 Amandine **Henry**, 15 Élise **Bussaglia** - 13 Kadidiatou **Diani** (12 Élodie **Thomis** 80), 10 Camille **Abily** (11 Claire **Lavogez** 72), 14 Louisa **Cadamuro** - 9 Eugénie **Le Sommer** (18 Marie-Laure **Delie** 74). *Philippe Bergeröo*

COL • 18 Sandra **Sepúlveda** - 17 Carolina **Arias**, 14 Nataly **Arias**, 13 Angela **Clavijo**, 9 Oriánica **Velásquez** - 4 Diana **Ospina** (7 Ingrid **Vidal** 67 ■ 71), 3 Natalia **Gaitán** (c), 6 Liana **Salazar**, 16 Lady **Andrade** (15 Tatiana **Ariza** 76) - 11 Catalina **Usme**, 10 Leicy **Santos** (8 Mildrey **Pineda** 89). *Fabián Taborda*

Mineirão, Belo Horizonte
6.08.2016, 17:00, **11,782**

USA 1-0 FRANCE

Lloyd 63

Claudia Umpiérrez URU
Loreto Toloza CHI & Neuza Back BRA

USA • Solo - O'Hara, 6 Whitney **Engen**, Sauerbrunn, Klingenberg (Press 90) - Dunn ■ 67 (11 Ali **Krieger** 70), Long, Brian, Heath - Lloyd (c) (Horan 82), Morgan. *Ellis*

FRA • Bouhaddi - Houara, Mbock Bathy ■ 80, Renard (c), Majri - Diani, Henry, Bussaglia, Cadamuro (Thomis 70) - Abily (17 Kheira **Hamraoui** 82) - Delie (Lavogez 86). *Bergeröo*

Mineirão, Belo Horizonte
6.08.2016, 20:00, **8,505**

COLOMBIA 0-1 NEW ZEALAND

Hearn 31

Gladys Lengwe ZIM
Bernadettar Kwimbira MWI & Souad Oulhaj MAR

COL • Sepúlveda - C Arias, N Arias, Clavijo, Velásquez - Andrade (T Ariza 73), Salazar ■ 21 (12 Nicole **Regnier** 89), Gaitán (c), Ospina (Vidal 79) - Santos, Usme. *Taborda*

NZL • Nayler - Percival, Stott, Erceg (c) ■ 88, Riley - Hassett, Longo, Duncan ■ 45, Gregorius (Bowen 57) - Wilkinson ■ 26 (13 Rosie **White** 62) (15 Meikayla **Moore** 90), Hearn. *Readings ENG*

■ Erceg's red card was overturned by the FIFA Disciplinary Committee

Arena da Amazônia, Manaus
9.08.2016, 18:00, **30,557**

COLOMBIA 2-2 USA

Usme (2) 26 90   Dunn 41, Pugh 60

Teodora Albon ROU
Petruța Iugulescu ROU & Mária Súkeníková SVK

COL • Sepúlveda - C Arias, N Arias, Clavijo, Velásquez (5 Isabella **Echeverri** 46) - Andrade (Ospina 62), Gaitán (c) ■ 88, Santos, Salazar ■ 72, T Ariza (Vidal 80) - Usme. *Taborda*

USA • Solo - Krieger ■ 86, Engen, Sauerbrunn, O'Hara - Brian (Long 65), Lloyd (c) (Morgan 46), Horan - Dunn, Press, 15 Megan **Rapinoe** (Pugh 33). *Ellis*

Arena Fonte Nova, Salvador
9.08.2016, 19:00, **7,530**

NEW ZEALAND 0-3 FRANCE

Le Sommer 38
Cadamuro (2) 63 90+1p

Lucila Venegas MEX
Mayte Chávez MEX & Enedina Caudillo MEX

NZL • Nayler - Percival, Stott, Erceg (c), Riley ■ 90+1 - Bowen (Pereira 78 ■ 83), Longo, Duncan, Hassett (Gregorius 60) - Wilkinson (White 71), Hearn. *Readings ENG*

FRA • Bouhaddi - Houara, 5 Sabrina **Delannoy**, Renard (c), 4 Sakina **Karchaoui** - Bussaglia (Abily 67), Henry (Hamraoui 72), Cadamuro - Thomis, Delie (Le Sommer 35), Lavogez. *Bergeröo*

2016 Quarter-finals

▲ An historic moment. Sweden celebrate their quarter-final penalty shoot-out win over the USA. It was the first time the Americans had failed to progress to the semi-finals of any Olympic or World Cup tournament. Rio 2016 was the first time they hadn't reached the Olympic Final.

◀ Lisa Dahlkvist scores the winning penalty for Sweden in their quarter-final shoot-out victory over defending champions the USA.

Sweden end the USA's remarkable run

Estádio Nacional Mané Garrincha, Brasilia
12.08.2016, 13:00, **13,892**

USA 🇺🇸 **1-1** 🇸🇪 **SWEDEN**
AET
3-4 PSO

Morgan 77   Blackstenius 61

Morgan ✘ (saved) Schelin ✓ Horan ✓ Asllani ✓ Lloyd ✓ Sembrant ✘ (saved) Brian ✓ Seger ✓ Press ✘ (missed - over bar) Dahlkvist ✓

Anna-Marie Keighley NZL ⎮ Sarah Jones NZL & Lata Kaumatule TGA

USA • Solo - O'Hara (Rapinoe 72) (Press 99), Johnston, Sauerbrunn, Klingenberg - Heath, Long (Dunn 65), Brian, Pugh (Horan 114) - Morgan, Lloyd (c) ■ 110. *Ellis*

SWE • Lindahl - Samuelsson (Berglund 119), Fischer, Sembrant, Rubensson (Eriksson 71) - Jakobsson (Schough 91), Asllani, Seger (c) ■ 78, Dahlkvist, Schelin ■ 57 - Rolfö (Blackstenius 18). *Sundhage*

This was a shock of seismic proportions. In their previous match, the USA had seen their run of 13 consecutive wins in the Olympics brought to a halt by a last-minute Colombian equaliser. Another draw here saw the Americans crash out on penalties. This was the first time the Americans had failed to reach the Final of the Olympics and the first time they had not made it through to at least the semi-finals at either the Olympics or the World Cup. Sweden were coached by Pia Sundhage, who had taken the Americans to their two most recent Olympic titles, and they opened the scoring on the hour when Lisa Dahlkvist fed a long ball through to Stina Blackstenius, who outran the opposition defence to score. Alex Morgan equalised 16 minutes later after the ball had inadvertently come off Swedish defender Jessica Samuelsson. In the shoot-out, both Morgan and substitute Christen Press missed their penalties, leaving Dahlkvist to land the killer blow for Sweden.

Behringer wins it for Germany

Arena Fonte Nova, Salvador
12.08.2016, 16:00, **9,642**

CHINA PR 🇨🇳 **0-1** 🇩🇪 **GERMANY**

(Wang Shuang penalty missed 84)   Behringer 76

Kateryna Monzul UKR ⎮ Natalia Rachynska UKR & Sanja Rodak CRO

CHN • Zhao Lina - Gao Chen, Wu Haiyan, Li Dongna (c), Liu Shanshan - Pang Fengyue (Ma Xiaoxu 79) - Wang Shuang, Tan Ruyin, Zhang Rui, Gu Yasha - Yang Li (Wang Shanshan 46 ■ 46 ■ 57 ■ 57). *Bini FRA*

GER • Schult - Maier ■ 83, Krahn, Bartusiak ■ 3, Kemme - Leupolz (19 Svenja Huth 69 ■ 86), Behringer, Däbritz, Mittag - Popp (Islacker 90), Marozsán (Goeßling 88). *Neid*

▲ Melanie Behringer scores the only goal of the game in Germany's quarter-final win over China in Salvador.

4 For the fourth tournament in a row, China's campaign ended at the quarter-final stage following on from the World Cups of 2007 and 2015, and the 2008 Olympics. They had also lost World Cup quarter-finals in 1991 and 2003.

▶ A dejected Wang Shuang after China's quarter-final defeat at the hands of Germany. She missed a late penalty that would have levelled the match.

Germany inched their way towards their Olympic dream with a hard-fought win over a determined Chinese team. China coach Bruno Bini had placed the emphasis on remaining strong defensively and the Germans struggled to find a way through. Leonie Maier, Dzsenifer Marozsán and Alexandra Popp all went close in the first half, and with the Germans continuing to press in the second, China held out until 14 minutes from the end. They were undone by a superb strike by Melanie Behringer, a 25-yard thunderbolt which gave six-foot-two Zhao Lina no chance in the Chinese goal. Forced to chase the game, China came out of their shell and were handed the lifeline of a penalty after Leonie Maier brought down Wang Shuang. The Chinese striker got up to take the penalty, but despite sending Almuth Schult the wrong way, her effort hit the post and their chance was gone.

Canada into semi-finals again

Arena Corinthians, São Paulo
12.08.2016, 19:00, **38,688**

CANADA 1-0 FRANCE
Schmidt 56

Claudia Umpiérrez URU
Loreto Toloza CHI & Neuza Back BRA

CAN • Labbé - Lawrence, Buchanan ■ 49, Zadorsky, Chapman (Bélanger 45+1 ■ 83) - Matheson (Rose 69), Scott, Schmidt ■ 57 (Quinn 81), Beckie - Fleming, Sinclair (c). *Herdman ENG*

FRA • Bouhaddi - Houara, Mbock Bathy, Renard (c), Karchaoui (Lavogez 84) - Henry ■ 85, Abily - Diani (Thomis 71), Bussaglia (Cadamuro 62), Majri - Le Sommer. *Bergerôo*

These two teams had met four years earlier in the bronze medal match at the London Olympics, and despite France having the upper hand in both games, the Canadians won again here, shattering French dreams of a first Olympic medal once again. Philippe Bergerôo's France side dominated much of the first half but failed to capitalise, notably when Wendie Renard glanced a header just wide moments before half-time. Canada fought back in the second half, and they took the lead 11 minutes in when Sophie Schmidt volleyed in Janine Beckie's cross. It was an advantage they kept hold of, making Canada the only team from the 2012 medal rounds to reach the 2016 semi-finals. Four days after this match, the two nations met in the basketball quarter-finals where the French gained some measure of revenge by beating the Canadians.

6

Rio 2016 was the sixth Olympics at which Brazilian midfielder Formiga had played, but it wouldn't be her last. The 38-year-old had taken part in the first tournament at the Atlanta Games in 1996, a span of 20 years.

▶ Sophie Schmidt (out of frame) scores Canada's winner in the quarter-final against France at the Arena Corinthians in São Paulo.

Brazil survive shoot-out drama

Mineirão, Belo Horizonte
12.08.2016, 22:00, **52,660**

BRAZIL 0-0 AUSTRALIA
AET
7-6 PSO

Andressa ✓ Kellond-Knight ✓ Andressinha ✓ Alleway ✓ Beatriz ✓ Van Egmond ✓ Rafaelle ✓ Polkinghorne ✓ Marta ✘ (saved) Gorry ✘ (saved) Debinha ✓ Heyman ✓ Mônica ✓ Logarzo ✓ Tamires ✓ Kennedy ✘ (saved)

Carol Anne Chenard CAN
Marie-Josée Charbonneau CAN & Suzanne Morisset CAN

BRA • Bárbara - Fabiana (Poliana 61), Mônica, Rafaelle, Tamires ■ 52 - Formiga, Thaísa (Andressinha 116) - Andressa ■ 90+2, Beatriz, Marta (c) ■ 77, Debinha. *Vadão*

AUS • Williams - Foord ■ 69, Alleway ■ 33, Kennedy ■ 81, Catley (Logarzo 20) - Gorry, Kellond-Knight - Van Egmond - De Vanna (c) (Polkinghorne 75), Simon (Heyman 60), Kerr (Crummer 105). *Stajcic*

Brazil failed to score for a second successive match, but they scraped past Australia after a nerve-wracking penalty shoot-out at a packed Estádio Mineirão in Belo Horizonte. The hosts outplayed their opponents for most of the game, gaining some redemption for their unexpected loss to Australia the previous year in the World Cup round of 16. There were missed opportunities during the game and the Australians had keeper Lydia Williams to thank for some fine goalkeeping. The best of the chances to break the deadlock fell near the end of regulation time to Chloe Logarzo, who rattled the crossbar with a fierce long-range shot, while Andressa could have sealed it right at the death but Williams made a fine goal line save to force extra time. In the shoot-out, Marta failed to score her penalty kick, but Katrina Gorry's was saved by Bárbara, as was Alanna Kennedy's, and Brazil were through to the semi-finals.

▲ Brazil players mob goalkeeper Bárbara after she had saved Alanna Kennedy's penalty to win the shoot-out against Australia.

▶ Brazil's Formiga (8) and Australia's Chloe Logarzo during the quarter-final between the two sides in Belo Horizonte.

Fourth time lucky for Germany

Mineirão, Belo Horizonte
16.08.2016, 16:00, **5,641**

CANADA 🇨🇦 **0-2** 🇩🇪 **GERMANY**

Behringer 21p, Däbritz 59

Ri Hyang Ok PRK   Hong Kum Nyo PRK & Allyson Flynn AUS

CAN • Labbé - Wilkinson (Matheson 60), Buchanan ■ 20, Zadorsky, Lawrence ■ 55 - Fleming, Scott (Rose 74), Schmidt - Beckie, Tancredi ■ 66 (Prince 85), Sinclair (c). *Herdman ENG*

GER • Schult - Maier, Krahn, Bartusiak (c), Kemme - Leupolz (Islacker 90+2), Behringer, Däbritz, Marozsán (Goeßling 46) - Mittag (Kerschowski 80), Popp. *Neid*

Germany dispatched the 2012 bronze medallists Canada with goals from Melanie Behringer and Sara Däbritz on the day that former FIFA President João Havelange died. Germany dominated the game from the start, constantly asking questions of the Canadians who had hoped to repeat their fine win over Silvia Neid's team during the group stage. It was the European champions who seemed to be more energised by their earlier defeat, however, and they took the lead in the 21st minute from a penalty awarded after Kadeisha Buchanan brought down Alexandra Popp just inside the area with the goal under no real threat. Behringer stepped up to coolly power the ball past Stephanie Labbé. Just before half-time, Buchanan almost made amends when her header from a corner was cleared off the line by Tabea Kemme. Ten minutes into the second half Janine Beckie came close to an equaliser for Canada, but Germany took control of the match when Däbritz made it 2-0 on the hour. Anja Mittag cleverly let a pass from Melanie Leupolz roll on to Däbritz whose low shot from the edge of the penalty area crept inside the post. After a rocky group stage and three previous Olympic semi-final defeats, the Germans could at last celebrate qualifying for their first Olympic Final.

▲▲ Melanie Behringer scored a first-half penalty to give Germany the lead over Canada. It was her fifth goal of the tournament in which she finished as top scorer.

▲ Big gloves to fill. Almuth Schult (in green) took over the No. 1 jersey from world champion Nadine Angerer. Here she battles with her opposite number Stephanie Labbé as the Canadians try to pull a goal back in the semi-final.

100

Germany skipper Saskia Bartusiak celebrated winning her 100th cap in the 2-0 semi-final victory over Canada.

Brazilian dreams shattered by Sweden

Maracanã, Rio de Janeiro
16.08.2016, 13:00, **70,454**

BRAZIL 🇧🇷 **0-0** 🇸🇪 **SWEDEN**
AET
3-4 PSO

Marta ⊙ Schelin ⊙ Cristiane ✘ (saved) Asllani ✘ (saved) Andressa ⊙ Seger ⊙ Rafaelle ⊙ Fischer ⊙ Andressinha ✘ (saved) Dahlkvist ⊙

Lucila Venegas MEX   Mayte Chávez MEX & Enedina Caudillo MEX

BRA • Bárbara - Poliana, Mônica, Rafaelle, Tamires - Formiga ■ 87, Thaísa (Andressinha 46) - Marta (c), Debinha (Cristiane 91), Beatriz ■ 65 (Raquel Fernandes 101), Andressa ■ 69. *Vadão*

SWE • Lindahl - Samuelsson (Berglund 120+1), Fischer, Sembrant, Rubensson - Appelqvist (Schough 104), Seger, Dahlkvist ■ 116, Asllani, Schelin (c) - Blackstenius (Jakobsson 61 ■ 76). *Sundhage*

▶ Brazilian goalkeeper Bárbara saved a penalty in the shoot-out against Sweden. Her opposite number Hedvig Lindahl saved two to send the Swedes through.

Just over 70,000 fans packed into the Maracanã – the biggest crowd ever to watch the Brazilian women's team play at home – to see an emotionally draining match in which the home nation's hopes of a first world title disappeared in a penalty shoot-out. With dogged determination and by riding their luck at times, Sweden held out for a goalless draw – the third match running in which Brazil had failed to score. Ten days earlier, they had put five past the Swedes and twice Debinha came close in the first half, the second with a header that Hedvig Lindahl tipped over the bar. Although Brazil dominated possession and Marta always posed a threat down the right, the chances were few and far between in the second half and extra time, and the game duly went to penalties. Cristiane, who came on in extra time and was making her first appearance since the group game against Sweden, saw her penalty saved by Lindahl and although Bárbara saved Kosovare Asllani's kick, Lindahl then stopped Andressinha's, leaving Lisa Dahlkvist to break Brazilian hearts. A distraught Marta, who had played so much of her career in Sweden, was consoled by the Swedish team who thought that perhaps her last shot at an international title had gone.

▶ Sofia Jakobsson (10) can hardly believe it as Sweden knock out hosts Brazil to reach the Final. In five matches, the Swedes had won just once.

2016 Bronze Medal Match

Arena Corinthians, São Paulo
19.08.2016, 13:00, **39,718**

BRAZIL 🇧🇷 **1-2** 🇨🇦 **CANADA**

Beatriz 79 — Rose 25, Sinclair 52

Teodora Albon ROU — Petruța Iugulescu ROU & Mária Súkeníková SVK

▲ Christine Sinclair (12) takes a free kick in the bronze medal match against hosts Brazil in São Paulo. She later scored what would be the winning goal for Canada.

> "We won a lot of fans during the Olympics. We filled the stadiums. That's the best prize."
> — MARTA

Hosts miss out on a medal as Canada win bronze again

The pursuit of gold for both the Brazilian women's and men's teams had become something of a national obsession, so it was with heavy hearts that Brazil took to the field for the bronze medal match against Canada. The men would finally win their gold the following day, but here the women could not secure bronze. Marta, contesting her fourth Olympiad, was, however, one of the Games' real heroines. Banners that read "Marta We Love You" graced stadiums to go alongside those dedicated to Neymar – a breakthrough for the women's game which had previously lacked popularity in Brazil. They faced a tough match against a Canadian team that flew out of the blocks. Christine Sinclair, who was earning her 250th cap, smacked a free kick against the crossbar before her team took the lead with a swift counter-attack. Ashley Lawrence sprinted down the left before crossing to 17-year-old Deanne Rose to score. Canada's second goal came seven minutes into the second half. Tamires was dispossessed in her own half by Jessie Fleming. She found Rose who this time turned provider. Her pass picked out Sinclair on the edge of the six-yard box, and the veteran striker fired home for her third goal of the tournament. Beatriz pulled one back with 11 minutes to go, after her control and turn in the box caught the Canadian defence out, but it was too little too late, and for the second Olympic Games running, Canada and their English coach John Herdman went home with bronze.

17

Canada's Deanne Rose became the youngest scorer in Olympic history at 17 years and 169 days with her goal against Brazil.

▶ Rio 2016 represented perhaps the best hope for Brazil's Cristiane (11), along with long-time team-mate Marta, to win that elusive title. But in the end, they couldn't even add a bronze to the Olympic silver and World Cup runners-up medals they had already won.

▼ Canada kiss their bronze medals at the 2016 Games. Six of the squad had also won bronze in 2012 – Diana Matheson, Sophie Schmidt, Desiree Scott, Christine Sinclair, Melissa Tancredi and Rhian Wilkinson.

2016 Gold Medal Match

Maracanã, Rio de Janeiro
19.08.2016, 17:30, **52,432**

SWEDEN 🇸🇪 **1-2** 🇩🇪 **GERMANY**

Blackstenius 67   Marozsán 48, Sembrant OG 62

Carol Anne Chenard CAN · Marie-Josée Charbonneau CAN & Suzanne Morisset CAN

▲ Germany's starting line-up for the Final. Back row (left to right): Annike Krahn, Saskia Bartusiak, Melanie Behringer, Dzsenifer Marozsán, Anja Mittag. Front row: Tabea Kemme, Melanie Leupolz, Leonie Maier, Almuth Schult, Sara Däbritz and Alexandra Popp.

A tale of two coaches

The Olympic Final was a showdown of two great coaches whose international careers had been a constant backdrop to the game for nearly four decades. Remarkably, however, this was only the third time they had directly faced each other at the World Cup or at the Olympics. The first time had been as players in the 1995 World Cup in Sweden. Neid earned 111 caps for Germany before a coaching career that included the 2007 world title, while Sundhage played 146 times for Sweden ahead of coaching the 2008 and 2012 Olympic gold medal-winning USA teams. Neid retired after Rio, and Sundhage stepped down as Sweden coach the following year.

> **We discovered our form from the quarter-finals onwards... it was clear that the team had arrived and wanted to win.**
>
> SILVIA NEID

▼ Sweden's Hedvig Lindahl saves a header from Germany's Tabea Kemme during the first half of the Final at the Maracanã.

▼ Germany celebrate going 2-0 ahead after an own goal by Sweden's Linda Sembrant. Stina Blackstenius pulled one back for the Swedes shortly after but it wasn't enough.

▲ The Maracanã was the setting for the 2016 Olympic Final. Germany added the Olympic title to the two world and eight European titles already won.

Clean sweep of titles for Germany

Sweden had won their opening match of this tournament against South Africa but had then failed to win any of their following four games. Yet here they were in the Final. In the first-ever all-European Olympic gold medal match, their opponents Germany were out to win the one title missing from their honours list. This was an old rivalry and a repeat of the 2003 World Cup Final, but the history between the coaches went back even further. Silvia Neid and Pia Sundhage had faced each other in the 1995 World Cup, and but for an injury to Neid, they would have been opponents in the 1991 World Cup play-off for third place too. Known for singing at press conferences to express her sentiments, Sundhage put reporters on notice with "the times, they are a-changing", before the game in her quest for a third consecutive Olympic title. For Neid, at stake was an Olympic gold to add to the world title she had coached Germany to in 2007.

Despite having scored just three goals in five games en route to the Final, the Swedes started brightly and Olivia Schough went close early on. The Germans worked their way into the game and threatened with a header from Melanie Leupolz and a shot from Anja Mittag, but all three goals came in the second half, the first of them just after the restart. What seemed like a harmless cross from Leupolz was not dealt with by the Swedish defence and Hungarian-born Dzsenifer Marozsán was left free to fire home from the edge of the box. Just past the hour, Germany were two up. Marozsán's free kick clattered the post and on the rebound Linda Sembrant's attempted clearance found the back of her own net. Sweden hit back quickly. Midfielder Kosovare Asllani, a role model within Sweden's immigrant community, fed Schough on the right and her inch-perfect centre was put away under pressure by substitute Stina Blackstenius. Sweden pressed for the equaliser but it was the Germans who came closest to scoring again when Hedvig Lindahl tipped another Marozsán free kick over the bar. At the end, Germany celebrated a first Olympic title and Sweden celebrated a first Olympic medal. The winners also bade farewell to Silvia Neid, a coach who had helped turn Germany's women into world-beaters in a 34-year career both on and off the pitch.

◀ Germany celebrate winning gold in Rio. They held up the shirt of Simone Laudehr who had sustained an ankle ligament injury in the group match against Zimbabwe. Her place in the squad was taken by Svenja Huth.

2019

France 2019 was a successful World Cup for Europe, who claimed a record seven quarter-final slots, but it was the USA who won the title for a fourth time. They beat five European teams, including the hosts in an epic quarter-final in Paris. In the Final, against the Netherlands in Lyon, player of the tournament Megan Rapinoe scored the first in her side's 2-0 win, with Rose Lavelle getting the second.

New horizons for women's football

▼ In France, fans enjoyed a spectacular World Cup.

"I think we are done with the questions like 'Are we worth it?', 'Should we have equal pay?' Everyone's done with that. Let's get to the next point of 'What's next?' How do we support women around the world? How can FIFA do that?" The clarion call of USA forward Megan Rapinoe summed up the mood of France 2019. This was a tournament of great skill and high drama watched by an ever-increasing audience of both women and men, in an ever-greater number of countries. Before the tournament kicked off, FIFA's Women's Football Division held a conference, featuring all of the key influencers in women's sport, where it presented its strategy for the future of the game. With five key goals to further develop women's football on and off the pitch, it was an ambitious statement of intent which aims to enhance the social impact of the game worldwide. Shortly after the tournament, the FIFA Council announced an increase in the number of teams at the 2023 World Cup from 24 to 32, in the belief that this would encourage more countries to create sustainable development programmes. In response, a record ten countries declared an interest in hosting the 2023 finals.

2019 Overview

FRANCE 2019

FIFA WOMEN'S WORLD CUP FRANCE 2019™

Story of the qualifiers

Four new nations join the party

The qualification of Chile, Jamaica, Scotland and South Africa took the total number of nations to have qualified for the World Cup to 36. Only the South Africans had any experience of global competition, having qualified for the Women's Olympic Football Tournament in 2012 and 2016. Continental championships were once again used as qualifying tournaments, with the exception of Europe. During the finals in France, the FIFA Council proposed to increase the number of teams at future finals to 32, reasoning that a place at the World Cup would give impetus to the development of the game beyond the traditional heartlands. This proposal was adopted after the finals, with the change coming into effect for the tournament in 2023.

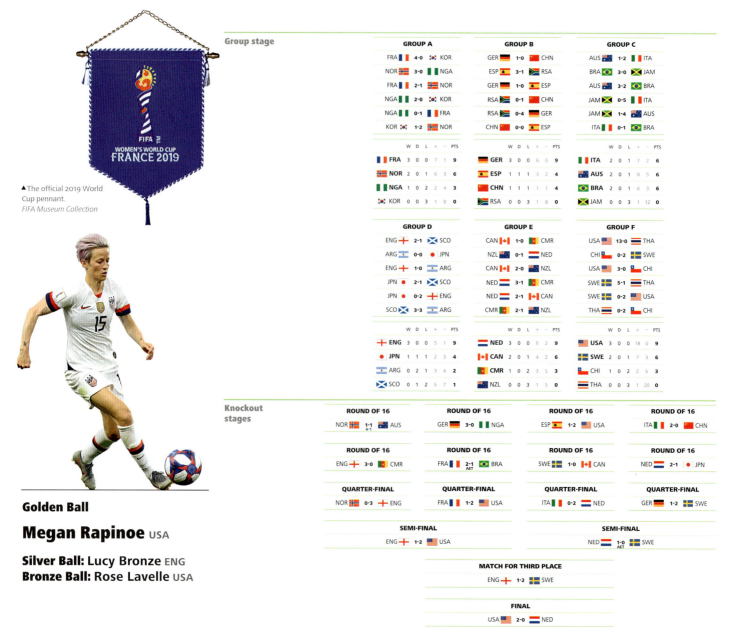

▲ The official 2019 World Cup pennant.
FIFA Museum Collection

Golden Ball
Megan Rapinoe USA

Silver Ball: Lucy Bronze ENG
Bronze Ball: Rose Lavelle USA

Overview 2019

24 TEAMS: ARG, AUS, BRA, CAN, CHI, CHN, CMR, ENG, ESP, FRA, GER, ITA, JAM, JPN, KOR, NED, NGA, NOR, NZL, RSA, SCO, SWE, THA, USA

USA WINNERS
NED SECOND
SWE THIRD

ETTIE OFFICIAL MASCOT

OFFICIAL LOGO

52 MATCHES PLAYED
124 YELLOW CARDS
4 RED CARDS

146 GOALS
2.81 AVERAGE GOALS PER MATCH

CONEXT19 OFFICIAL MATCH BALL

1 131 312 SPECTATORS
21 756 AVERAGE PER MATCH

Host cities and stadiums

From Paris to Lyon

The journey from the opening game in Paris to the Final in Lyon saw the 2019 World Cup played in nine stadiums, five clustered in the north and four in the south-east of the country. For the first time, one stadium – the Stade de Lyon – hosted both semi-finals and the Final. The tournament coincided with a heatwave which saw record temperatures throughout France, and this was a competition that the French public certainly warmed to. The finals captured the imagination of the country inside the stadiums while also dominating an ever-growing number of media outlets, helping to make the event a spectacular success.

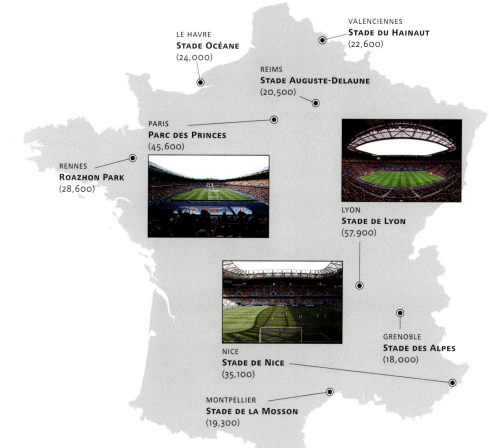

LE HAVRE — Stade Océane (24,000)
VALENCIENNES — Stade du Hainaut (22,600)
REIMS — Stade Auguste-Delaune (20,500)
PARIS — Parc des Princes (45,600)
RENNES — Roazhon Park (28,600)
LYON — Stade de Lyon (57,900)
GRENOBLE — Stade des Alpes (18,000)
NICE — Stade de Nice (35,100)
MONTPELLIER — Stade de la Mosson (19,300)

×6

Golden Boot

Megan Rapinoe USA

Silver Boot: Alex Morgan USA ×6
Bronze Boot: Ellen White ENG ×6

2019 Group stage

Parc des Princes, Paris
7.06.2019, 21:00, **45,261**

FRANCE 🇫🇷 **4-0** 🇰🇷 **KOREA REPUBLIC**

Le Sommer 9, Renard (2) 35
45+2, Henry 85

🚩 Claudia Umpiérrez URU
🚩 Luciana Mascaraña URU & Monica Amboya ECU
🚩 Mauro Vigliano ARG

FRA • 16 Sarah **Bouhaddi** - 4 Marion **Torrent**, 19 Griedge **Mbock Bathy**, 3 Wendie **Renard**, 10 Amel **Majri** (2 Ève **Périsset** 74) - 6 Amandine **Henry** (c), 15 Élise **Bussaglia**, 9 Eugénie **Le Sommer** - 20 Delphine **Cascarino** (13 Valérie **Gauvin** 70), 17 Gaëtane **Thiney** (8 Grace **Geyoro** 86), 11 Kadidiatou **Diani**. *Corinne Diacre*

KOR • 18 Kim Min **Jung** - 20 **Kim** Hye Ri, 4 **Hwang** Bo Ram, 5 **Kim** Do Yeon, 16 **Jang** Sel Gi - 15 **Lee** Young Ju (7 **Lee** Min A 69), 8 **Cho** So Hyun (c) - 12 **Kang** Yu Mi (23 **Kang** Chae Rim 52), 10 **Ji** So Yun, 17 **Lee** Geum Min - 11 **Jung** Seol Bin (13 **Yeo** Min Ji 86). *Yoon Deok Yeo*

Stade Auguste-Delaune, Reims
8.06.2019, 21:00, **11,058**

NORWAY 🇳🇴 **3-0** 🇳🇬 **NIGERIA**

Reiten 17, Utland 34,
Ohale OG 37

🚩 Kate Jacewicz AUS
🚩 Kathryn Nesbitt USA & Chantal Boudreau CAN
🚩 Danny Makkelie NED

NOR • 1 Ingrid **Hjelmseth** - 2 Ingrid Moe **Wold**, 6 Maren **Mjelde** (c), 3 Maria **Thorisdottir**, 17 Kristine **Minde** - 10 Caroline **Graham Hansen**, 8 Vilde Bøe **Risa** (18 Frida **Maanum** 84), 14 Ingrid Syrstad **Engen**, 16 Guro **Reiten** (20 Emilie **Haavi** 90+1) - 11 Lisa-Marie **Utland** (7 Elise **Thorsnes** 80), 9 Isabell **Herlovsen**. *Martin Sjögren SWE*

NGA • 1 Tochukwu **Oluehi** - 3 Osinachi **Ohale**, 14 Faith **Michael** (20 Chidinma **Okeke** 54), 5 Onome **Ebi**, 4 Ngozi **Ebere** - 18 Halimatu **Ayinde** (11 Chinaza **Uchendu** 51), 13 Ngozi **Okobi**, 10 Rita **Chikwelu** - 17 Francisca **Ordega** 🟨 45+1, 9 Desire **Oparanozie** (c) 🟨 13 (12 Uchenna **Kanu** 71), 8 Asisat **Oshoala**. *Thomas Dennerby SWE*

Stade des Alpes, Grenoble
12.06.2019, 15:00, **11,252**

NIGERIA 🇳🇬 **2-0** 🇰🇷 **KOREA REPUBLIC**

Kim Do Yeon OG 29,
Oshoala 75

🚩 Anastasia Pustovoitova RUS
🚩 Ekaterina Kurochkina RUS & Petruța Iugulescu ROU
🚩 Carlos del Cerro Grande ESP

NGA • 16 Chiamaka **Nnadozie** - Okeke, Ohale, Ebi, Ebere - Uchendu (Ayinde 65), Okobi, Chikwelu 🟨 61 - Oshoala (Kanu 83), Oparanozie (c), Ordega (7 Anam **Imo** 80). *Dennerby SWE*

KOR • Kim Min Jung - Kim Hye Ri, Hwang Bo Ram 🟨 71, Kim Do Yeon, Jang Sel Gi - Kang Chae Rim (19 **Lee** So Dam 76), Lee Min A (9 **Moon** Mi Ra 56), Cho So Hyun (c), Ji So Yun 🟨 49, Lee Geum Min - Jung Seol Bin (Yeo Min Ji 56). *Yoon Deok Yeo*

Stade de Nice, Nice
12.06.2019, 21:00, **34,872**

FRANCE 🇫🇷 **2-1** 🇳🇴 **NORWAY**

Gauvin 46, Le Sommer 72p   Renard OG 54

🚩 Bibiana Steinhaus GER
🚩 Katrin Rafalski GER & Chrysoula Kourompylia GRE
🚩 Felix Zwayer GER

FRA • Bouhaddi - Torrent, Mbock Bathy, Renard, Majri - Bussaglia, Thiney (14 Charlotte **Bilbault** 82), Henry (c) - Diani, Gauvin (Cascarino 85), Le Sommer 🟨 56. *Diacre*

NOR • Hjelmseth - Wold (5 Synne Skinnes **Hansen** 86), Mjelde (c), Thorisdottir, Minde - 21 Karina **Sævik** (Utland 76), Risa (Maanum 90+1), Engen 🟨 71, Reiten - Graham Hansen, Herlovsen. *Sjögren SWE*

Roazhon Park, Rennes
17.06.2019, 21:00, **28,267**

NIGERIA 🇳🇬 **0-1** 🇫🇷 **FRANCE**

                                    Renard 79p

🚩 Melissa Borjas HON
🚩 Shirley Perelló HON & Felisha Mariscal USA
🚩 Danny Makkelie NED

NGA • Nnadozie 🟨 77 - Okeke, Ebi, Ohale, Ebere 🟨 28 🟨 75 🟥 75 - Ayinde, Okobi, Chikwelu 🟨 90+5 - Ordega (6 Evelyn **Nwabuoku** 84), Oparanozie (c) (Kanu 90), Oshoala (Imo 85). *Dennerby SWE*

FRA • Bouhaddi - Périsset, Mbock Bathy, Renard, Majri - Bilbault, Thiney (Geyoro 89), Henry - Cascarino (Le Sommer 62) Gauvin 🟨 45+1 (Diani 62), 18 Viviane **Asseyi**. *Diacre*

Stade Auguste-Delaune, Reims
17.06.2019, 21:00, **13,034**

KOREA REPUBLIC 🇰🇷 **1-2** 🇳🇴 **NORWAY**

Yeo Min Ji 78   Graham Hansen 5p,
                         Herlovsen 50p

🚩 Marie-Soleil Beaudoin CAN
🚩 Princess Brown JAM & Stephanie-Dale Yee Sing JAM
🚩 Chris Beath AUS

KOR • Kim Min Jung - 2 **Lee** Eun Mi (3 **Jeong** Yeong A 79), 14 **Shin** Dam Yeong, Kim Do Yeon, Jang Sel Gi - Lee Geum Min, Cho So Hyun (c) 🟨 4, Kang Chae Rim (Lee Min A 66), Moon Mi Ra (Kang Yu Mi 82) - Yeo Min Ji 🟨 85, Ji So Yun. *Yoon Deok Yeo*

NOR • Hjelmseth - Wold, Mjelde (c), Thorisdottir, Minde - Graham Hansen (Maanum 54), Risa, Engen, Reiten - Utland (Sævik 46), Herlovsen (Thorsnes 69). *Sjögren SWE*

Group A

	W	D	L	+	-	PTS
🇫🇷 FRA	3	0	0	7	1	9
🇳🇴 NOR	2	0	1	6	3	6
🇳🇬 NGA	1	0	2	2	4	3
🇰🇷 KOR	0	0	3	1	8	0

▶ Wendie Renard heads home to give France a 2-0 lead in the opening match against South Korea. The hosts were one of five teams to emerge from the group stage with maximum points.

Hosts France power through

It was an unseasonably chilly night in Paris but the 'goosebump' moment of the eighth Women's World Cup opener was caused not by a gusty breeze. Rather, it came courtesy of the spine-tingling rendition of *La Marseillaise* that rang out around the Parc des Princes as France prepared to face Korea Republic. A full house had already witnessed an opening ceremony that featured 300 dancing 'players', acrobats and fireworks. Then came the biggest opening victory, 4-0, for a host nation in 28 years. A wall of noise greeted every goal, including one from Eugénie Le Sommer that would go down as the earliest of any Women's World Cup curtain-raiser, and a pearler from Griedge Mbock Bathy that was disallowed in the competition's first-ever VAR intervention. "We knew it was going to be a very emotional evening," said two-goal Wendie Renard later. Elsewhere, there was no room for sentiment as Martin Sjögren's Norway put three goals past a Nigeria side overseen by his old friend Thomas Dennerby. The African champions bounced back to beat South Korea 2-0, 18-year-old Chiamaka Nnadozie becoming the youngest shot-stopper to keep a Women's World Cup clean sheet over the course of a whole match. Ingrid Hjelmseth, the tournament's second oldest player at 39, could not deny Le Sommer, who dispatched a winning penalty awarded following a VAR review as France recovered from a Renard own goal to see off Norway. There was relief for Renard as the hosts edged Nigeria too, a VAR check for goalkeeper encroachment allowing the Lyon defender to successfully retake a penalty she had just missed. Dennerby was incensed, but Nigeria would still progress as one of the four best third-placed teams. Not so South Korea, who finally got off the scoring mark through 2010 U-17 World Cup-winning star Yeo Min Ji, but it was not enough in a 2-1 defeat to second-placed Norway.

39

Norway's goalkeeper Ingrid Hjemseth became the fourth oldest player in World Cup history when she played against Nigeria, behind America's Christie Rampone, Nigeria's Perpetua Nkwocha and Brazil's Meg. The following day, she dropped down to fifth after Formiga's appearance for Brazil against Jamaica.

5

Nigeria's Onome Ebi became the first African to play in five World Cups when she took to the field against Norway.

▶ Lisa-Marie Utland scores Norway's second goal against Nigeria. Their 3-0 win was the 14th World Cup match in which they had scored three or more goals, a total bettered only by Germany (20) and the USA (24).

Group stage 2019

◀ Spain's Jennifer Hermoso holds off a challenge from South Africa captain Janine van Wyk. The match marked South Africa's World Cup debut after having played in two Olympic tournaments.

◀ Germany take on China in the first match of Group B. This was the first time the Germans had come to a World Cup not as European champions, and before the match they had played 246 minutes without scoring a goal at the finals. That run was extended to 312 minutes before Giulia Gwinn's second-half winner.

Olympic champions Germany off to a perfect start

Martina Voss-Tecklenburg wore the No.7 shirt for Germany in 13 World Cup matches, including the 1995 semi-final victory over China, and the 51-year-old coach looked like she was still kicking every ball in a bruising opener with the Chinese that saw Dzsenifer Marozsán play on despite suffering a broken toe. Yang Li hit the post, but teenager Giulia Gwinn secured Germany's first World Cup victory since the last edition's round of 16. African player of 2018 Thembi Kgatlana hit a thunderbolt to get debutants South Africa off the scoring mark against Spain, but *La Roja* secured a maiden World Cup victory with Jennifer Hermoso bagging the competition's first-ever penalty brace. Spain bossed Germany too, but a poacher's goal from Paris Saint-Germain's new recruit Sara Däbritz won it for the Olympic champions. "One goal please!" chanted the fans as China faced South Africa, and Women's Asian Cup top scorer Li Ying duly delivered. It would end goalless between China and Spain, though, *La Roja* head coach Jorge Vilda unable to repeat the win he enjoyed against the same team on his debut in 2015. Both sides were through, but Germany took pole position with a 4-0 demolition of *Banyana Banyana*, who were applauded off the pitch by an appreciative crowd.

Group B

	W	D	L	+	-	PTS
GER	3	0	0	6	0	9
ESP	1	1	1	3	2	4
CHN	1	1	1	1	1	4
RSA	0	0	3	1	8	0

17 At 17, Lena Oberdorf became the youngest player to feature for Germany at the World Cup when she came on against China, beating Birgit Prinz's record by 52 days.

Roazhon Park, Rennes
8.06.2019, 15:00, **15,283**

GERMANY 1-0 CHINA PR
Gwinn 66

Marie-Soleil Beaudoin CAN
Princess Brown JAM & Stephanie-Dale Yee Sing JAM
Massimiliano Irrati ITA

GER • 1 Almuth **Schult** - 3 Kathrin **Hendrich**, 5 Marina **Hegering**, 23 Sara **Doorsoun**, 2 Carolin **Simon** (6 Lena **Oberdorf** 46 ■ 82) - 9 Svenja **Huth** (7 Lea **Schüller** 85), 10 Dzsenifer **Marozsán**, 18 Melanie **Leupolz** (20 Lina **Magull** 63), 13 Sara **Däbritz**, 15 Giulia **Gwinn** - 11 Alexandra **Popp** (c). *Martina Voss-Tecklenburg*

CHN • 12 Peng **Shimeng** - 6 Han **Peng**, 5 Wu **Haiyan** (c), 3 Lin **Yuping**, 2 Liu **Shanshan** ■ 50 - 4 Lou **Jiahui** (19 Tan **Ruyin** 33), 20 **Zhang** Rui, 21 **Yao** Wei (7 **Wang** Shuang 46 ■ 71), 17 Gu **Yasha** - 11 **Wang** Shanshan ■ 12, 9 **Yang** Li ■ 44 (15 **Song** Duan 69). *Jia Xiuquan*

Stade Océane, Le Havre
8.06.2019, 18:00, **12,044**

SPAIN 3-1 SOUTH AFRICA
Hermoso (2) 69p 82p, Kgatlana 25
L García 89

María Carvajal CHI
Leslie Vasquez CHI & Loreto Toloza CHI
Mauro Vigliano ARG

ESP • 13 Sandra **Paños** - 8 Marta **Torrejón** (c), 4 Irene **Paredes**, 16 María **León**, 7 Marta **Corredera** ■ 90+4 - 6 Vicky **Losada** (18 Aitana **Bonmatí** 46), 14 Virginia **Torrecilla**, 11 Alexia **Putellas** (22 Nahikari **García** 73) - 19 Amanda **Sampedro** (17 Lucia **García** 46), 10 Jennifer **Hermoso** - 9 Mariona **Caldentey**. *Jorge Vilda*

RSA • 16 Andile **Dlamini** - 2 Lebohang **Ramalepe**, 5 Janine van **Wyk** (c) ■ 68, 4 Noko **Matlou**, 3 Nothando **Vilakazi** ■ 59 ■ 81 ■ 81 - 19 Kholosa **Biyana** ■ 77, 15 Refiloe **Jane** - 9 Amanda **Mthandi** (12 Jermaine **Seoposenwe** 56), 10 Linda **Motlhalo** (21 Busisiwe **Ndimeni** 52), 11 Thembi **Kgatlana** - 8 Ode **Fulutudilu** (17 Leandra **Smeda** 77). *Desiree Ellis*

Stade du Hainaut, Valenciennes
12.06.2019, 18:00, **20,761**

GERMANY 1-0 SPAIN
Däbritz 42

Kateryna Monzul UKR
Maryna Striletska UKR & Oleksandra Ardasheva UKR
Danny Makkelie NED

GER • **Schult** - **Hendrich** (19 Klara **Bühl** 46), **Doorsoun**, **Hegering**, 17 Verena **Schweers** ■ 63 - **Gwinn**, **Däbritz**, 8 Lena **Goeßling** (**Leupolz** 80), **Oberdorf** (**Magull** 64) - **Huth**, **Popp** (c). *Voss-Tecklenburg*

ESP • **Paños** - **Torrejón** (c), **Paredes**, **León**, **Corredera** - 15 Silvia **Meseguer** (12 Patri **Guijarro** 66), **Torrecilla** - **Caldentey** (L **García** 59), **Hermoso**, **Putellas** (**Bonmatí** 77) - N **García**. *Vilda*

Parc des Princes, Paris
13.06.2019, 21:00, **20,011**

SOUTH AFRICA 0-1 CHINA PR
Li Ying 40

Katalin Kulcsár HUN
Katalin Török HUN & Sanja Rodak CRO
Chris Beath AUS

RSA • 20 Kaylin **Swart** - **Ramalepe**, 13 Bambanani **Mbane**, Van **Wyk** (c), **Matlou** ■ 83, 23 Sibulele **Holweni** (**Smeda** 72) - **Kgatlana**, **Biyana**, 6 Mamello **Makhabane**, **Jane** (**Motlhalo** 82) - **Fulutudilu** (**Seoposenwe** 60). *D Ellis*

CHN • Peng **Shimeng** - Han **Peng**, Wu **Haiyan** (c), Lin **Yuping**, Liu **Shanshan** - 10 **Li** Ying (**Yao** Wei 78), 13 **Wang** Yan (**Yang** Li 81), **Zhang** Rui, Gu **Yasha** (Lou **Jiahui** 65) - **Wang** Shanshan, **Wang** Shuang. *Jia Xiuquan*

Stade Océane, Le Havre
17.06.2019, 18:00, **11,814**

CHINA PR 0-0 SPAIN

Edina Alves Batista BRA
Neuza Back BRA & Tatiane Sacilotti BRA
Mauro Vigliano ARG

CHN • Peng **Shimeng** - Han **Peng**, Wu **Haiyan** (c), Lin **Yuping**, Liu **Shanshan** - **Wang** Shuang (16 **Li** Wen 55 ■ 63), **Zhang** Rui, **Wang** Yan, Gu **Yasha** (**Yao** Wei 87) - **Li** Ying, **Wang** Shanshan (**Yang** Li 46). *Jia Xiuquan*

ESP • **Paños** - **Corredera**, **Paredes** (c), **León**, 3 Leila **Ouahabi** - **Torrecilla**, **Guijarro**, L **García** (2 Celia **Jiménez** 86), **Hermoso**, **Caldentey** (21 Andrea **Falcón** 46) - N **García** (**Putellas** 67). *Vilda*

Stade de la Mosson, Montpellier
17.06.2019, 18:00, **15,502**

SOUTH AFRICA 0-4 GERMANY
Leupolz 14, Däbritz 29, Popp 40, Magull 58

Sandra Braz POR
Julia Magnusson SWE & Lisa Rashid ENG
Clément Turpin FRA

RSA • **Dlamini** - **Ramalepe** ■ 53, Van **Wyk**, **Matlou**, **Vilakazi** ■ 58 - **Biyana** (**Smeda** 89), **Jane**, **Makhabane** - **Mthandi** (**Kgatlana** 46), **Fulutudilu** (22 Rhoda **Mulaudzi** 46 ■ 66), **Ndimeni**. *D Ellis*

GER • **Schult** - **Gwinn**, **Doorsoun**, **Hegering**, **Schweers** (**Simon** 46) - **Huth** (16 Linda **Dallmann** 59), **Leupolz**, **Magull** ■ 54, **Däbritz** - **Popp** (c), **Bühl** (**Schüller** 66). *Voss-Tecklenburg*

2019 Group stage

Stade du Hainaut, Valenciennes
9.06.2019, 13:00, **15,380**

AUSTRALIA 1-2 **ITALY**

Kerr 22 — Bonansea (2) 56 90+5
(Kerr penalty saved 22)

Melissa Borjas HON
Shirley Perelló HON & Felisha Mariscal USA
Carlos del Cerro Grande ESP

AUS • 1 Lydia **Williams** - 21 Ellie **Carpenter**, 14 Alanna **Kennedy**, 4 Clare **Polkinghorne**, 7 Steph **Catley** - 16 Hayley **Raso** (19 Katrina **Gorry** 69), 13 Tameka **Yallop** (8 Elise **Kellond-Knight** 83), 10 Emily **van Egmond**, 6 Chloe **Logarzo** (11 Lisa **De Vanna** 61 ▮ 76) - 9 Caitlin **Foord**, 20 Sam **Kerr** (c). *Ante Milicic*

ITA • 1 Laura **Giuliani** - 2 Valentina **Bergamaschi** (19 Valentina **Giacinti** 77), 3 Sara **Gama** (c) ▮ 21, 5 Elena **Linari**, 7 Alia **Guagni** - 21 Valentina **Cernoia** ▮ 70, 23 Manuela **Giugliano**, 4 Aurora **Galli** (13 Elisa **Bartoli** 46) - 10 Cristiana **Girelli** ▮ 63, 18 Ilaria **Mauro** (9 Daniela **Sabatino** 58), 11 Barbara **Bonansea**. *Milena Bertolini*

Stade des Alpes, Grenoble
9.06.2019, 15:30, **17,668**

BRAZIL 3-0 **JAMAICA**

Cristiane (3) 15 50 64
(Andressa penalty saved 38)

Riem Hussein GER
Kylie Cockburn SCO & Mihaela Țepușă ROU
Bastian Dankert GER

BRA • 1 **Bárbara** - 13 **Letícia Santos**, 14 **Kathellen** (3 Daiane 76 ▮ 82), 21 **Mónica** (c), 6 **Tamires** - 7 **Andressa**, 8 **Formiga** ▮ 58, 5 **Thaísa**, 9 **Debinha** - 16 **Beatriz** (23 Geyse 65), 11 **Cristiane** (19 Ludmila 65). *Vadão*

JAM • 1 Sydney **Schneider** - 16 Dominique **Bond-Flasza**, 5 Konya **Plummer** (c), ▮ 17, 17 Allyson **Swaby**, 14 Deneisha **Blackwood** - 9 Marlo **Sweatman**, 4 Chantelle **Swaby** - 20 Cheyna **Matthews** (10 Jody **Brown** 62), 6 Havana **Solaun** (7 Chinyelu **Asher** 72) 18 Trudi **Carter** (15 Tiffany **Cameron** 79) - 11 Khadija **Shaw**. *Hue Menzies USA*

Stade de la Mosson, Montpellier
13.06.2019, 18:00, **17,032**

AUSTRALIA 3-2 **BRAZIL**

Foord 45, Logarzo 58, — Marta 27p, Cristiane 38
Mônica OG 66

Esther Staubli SUI
Sian Massey ENG & Susanne Küng SUI
Bastian Dankert GER

AUS • Williams - Carpenter, Kennedy, Catley, Kellond-Knight - Yallop, Van Egmond, Logarzo - 15 Emily **Gielnik** (Raso 72), Kerr (c), Foord (5 Karly **Roestbakken** 90+5). *Milicic*

BRA • Bárbara - Letícia Santos, Kathellen, Mónica, Tamires - Debinha, Formiga ▮ 14 (18 Luana 46 ▮ 87), Thaísa, Andressa ▮ 85 - Cristiane (Beatriz 75), 10 **Marta** (c) (Ludmila 46). *Vadão*

Stade Auguste-Delaune, Reims
14.06.2019, 18:00, **12,016**

JAMAICA 0-5 **ITALY**

Girelli (3) 12p 25 46,
Galli (2) 71 81

Anna-Marie Keighley NZL
Sarah Jones NZL & Maria Salamasina SAM
Danny Makkelie NED

JAM • Schneider ▮ 12 - 12 Sashana **Campbell**, Plummer (c), A Swaby, Blackwood - 21 Olufolasade **Adamolekun** (2 Lauren **Silver** 76), Solaun, C Swaby (Sweatman 46), Asher - Shaw ▮ 59, 22 Mireya **Grey** (Brown 66). *Menzies USA*

ITA • Giuliani - Guagni (17 Lisa **Boattin** 57), Gama (c), Linari, Bartoli - Bergamaschi (Galli 65) Giugliano, Cernoia - Sabatino, Girelli (Giacinti 72), Bonansea. *Bertolini*

Stade des Alpes, Grenoble
18.06.2019, 21:00, **17,402**

JAMAICA 1-4 **AUSTRALIA**

Solaun 49 — Kerr (4) 11 42 69 83

Katalin Kulcsár HUN
Katalin Török HUN & Sanja Rodak CRO
José María Sánchez ESP

JAM • 13 Nicole **McClure** - Campbell, Plummer (c) ▮ 71, A Swaby, Blackwood - C Swaby, Shaw, 19 Toriana **Patterson** - Grey (Brown 72), Matthews (Carter 59), Cameron (Solaun 46). *Menzies USA*

AUS • Williams - Carpenter, Kennedy, Catley, Roestbakken - Gielnik (Foord 59), Logarzo, Van Egmond ▮ 76, Gorry (3 Aivi **Luik** 87), De Vanna (Raso 63) - Kerr (c). *Milicic*

Stade du Hainaut, Valenciennes
18.06.2019, 21:00, **21,669**

ITALY 0-1 **BRAZIL**

— Marta 74p

Lucila Venegas MEX
Mayte Chávez MEX & Enedina Caudillo MEX
Carlos del Cerro Grande ESP

ITA • Giuliani - Guagni, Gama (c), Linari, Bartoli ▮ 15 (Boattin 71) - Galli, Giugliano, Cernoia - Giacinti (Bergamaschi 63), Girelli (Mauro 78), Bonansea. *Bertolini*

BRA • Bárbara - Letícia Santos ▮ 13 (2 Poliana 76), Kathellen ▮ 90+4, Mónica, Tamires - Marta (c) (Luana 84), 17 **Andressinha**, Thaísa, Debinha - Ludmila, Cristiane (Beatriz 65). *Vadão*

Group C

	W	D	L	+	−	PTS
ITA	2	0	1	7	2	6
AUS	2	0	1	8	5	6
BRA	2	0	1	6	3	6
JAM	0	0	3	1	12	0

Goal number 17 for Marta

Italy endured a rollercoaster of emotions in their first Women's World Cup match in two decades, twice celebrating goals against Australia only to have them both ruled out for offside. A 95th-minute winner from two-goal Barbara Bonansea would settle it for the Italians, though, the squad joyfully marking the moment by tossing the economics student into the air. Jamaica's Sydney Schneider, 19, pulled out all the stops to save an Andressa penalty, but Brazil still rolled back the years against the tournament's youngest team as 41-year-old Formiga became the competition's oldest-ever player and 34-year-old Cristiane the oldest to bag a hat-trick. Against Australia, Marta hit new heights as the first player to score in five World Cups, although the *Matildas* fought back to inflict Brazil's first group-stage loss in 24 years. Juventus forward Cristiana Girelli took just over half an hour to score Italy's first hat-trick in this competition since 1991 as Jamaica were felled 5-0. The debutants would depart with a maiden World Cup goal courtesy of substitute Havana Solaun against Australia, but Sam Kerr blitzed the *Reggae Girlz* with four, an Aussie World Cup record. Marta made history with her record-extending 17th World Cup goal, the only one of the game against Italy, but *Le Azzurre* still topped the group.

◀ Cristiane scores against Australia, a header that would later be voted as the goal of the tournament. In the previous match against Jamaica she had become the oldest player to score a World Cup hat-trick.

2 When they beat Brazil, Australia became only the second team in World Cup history to come from 2-0 down to win a match. In the other, Sweden beat Germany 3-2 in 1995.

41 At 41 years and 98 days, Formiga became the competition's oldest player when she appeared against Jamaica, surpassing the USA's Christie Rampone and also becoming the first player to take part in seven World Cups. When she made her debut 24 years previously, 150 players who appeared in France 2019 were yet to be born.

▼ Italy returned to the World Cup after an absence of 19 years and 347 days. With their passion and entertaining matches, the team captured the imagination of the public back home.

Group D

◀ Ellen White celebrates the second of her two goals against Japan. The 2-0 victory saw England gain maximum points in the group stage for the first time.

Scotland denied by last-gasp penalty

Hit for six by England on their major tournament debut at Euro 2017, Scotland were only narrowly defeated by the 'auld enemy' in their maiden World Cup match. Claire Emslie's late goal set up a tense finale after the Scots were rocked by an early VAR review for handball, but Nikita Parris's perfect penalty and Ellen White's left-foot curler saw England claim the spoils. Argentina surpassed expectations by qualifying for France 2019 after almost three years without a game or a coach, and they impressed again, frustrating Japan to secure a first-ever World Cup point and clean sheet. "A must-win," was six-time AFC women's coach of the year Asako Takakura's assessment of Japan's next match against Scotland and win they did, surviving two penalty shouts and a late Lana Clelland wonder-strike to win 2-1. Jodie Taylor's goal rescued England against Argentina after Vanina Correa pulled off a string of saves, including one to deny Parris from the spot. England No.1 Karen Bardsley was equally robust as an Ellen White double pipped Japan to top spot. Scotland were out, though, after letting slip a three-goal lead over Argentina, the killer equaliser coming in the 94th minute. Lee Alexander saved a penalty but after a VAR review it was retaken and Florencia Bonsegundo scored.

250 Japan against Scotland in Rennes was the 250th match in World Cup history.

15 Mariela Coronel's previous appearance for Argentina at the World Cup before coming on as a substitute against Japan had been 15 years and 256 days earlier at the 2003 finals against Germany. It was the second longest gap after New Zealand's Wendi Henderson (15 years and 295 days).

	W	D	L	+	-	PTS
ENG	3	0	0	5	1	9
JPN	1	1	1	2	3	4
ARG	0	2	1	3	4	2
SCO	0	1	2	5	7	1

Stade de Nice, Nice
9.06.2019, 18:00, 13,188

ENGLAND 2-1 SCOTLAND

Parris 14p, E White 40 — Emslie 79

Jana Adámková CZE
Lucie Ratajová CZE & Mária Súkeníková SVK
Felix Zwayer GER

ENG • 1 Karen **Bardsley** - 2 Lucy **Bronze**, 5 Steph **Houghton** (c), 6 Millie **Bright** (15 Abbie **McManus** 55), 3 Alex **Greenwood** - 8 Jill **Scott**, 4 Keira **Walsh**, 10 Fran **Kirby** (19 Georgia **Stanway** 82) - 7 Nikita **Parris**, 18 Ellen **White**, 22 Beth **Mead** (20 Karen **Carney** 71). *Phil Neville*.

SCO • 1 Lee **Alexander** - 15 Sophie **Howard** (14 Chloe **Arthur** 75), 4 Rachel **Corsie** (c), 5 Jenny **Beattie** ■ 43, 3 Nicola **Docherty** ■ 47 (2 Kirsty **Smith** 55) - 18 Claire **Emslie**, 16 Christie **Murray** (23 Lizzie **Arnot** 87), 9 Caroline **Weir**, 11 Lisa **Evans** - 8 Kim **Little** - 22 Erin **Cuthbert**. *Shelley Kerr*.

Parc des Princes, Paris
10.06.2019, 18:00, 25,055

ARGENTINA 0-0 JAPAN

Stéphanie Frappart FRA
Manuela Nicolosi FRA & Michelle O'Neill IRL
Clément Turpin FRA

ARG • 1 Vanina **Correa** - 13 Virginia **Gómez**, 2 Agustina **Barroso**, 6 Aldana **Cometti**, 3 Eliana **Stábile** - 11 Florencia **Bonsegundo** (19 Mariana **Larroquette** 77), 8 Ruth **Bravo** (5 Vanesa **Santana** 64), 16 Lorena **Benítez** (17 Mariela **Coronel** 79), 14 Miriam **Mayorga**, 10 Estefanía **Banini** (c) - 9 Sole **Jaimes**. *Carlos Borrello*.

JPN • 18 Ayaka **Yamashita** - 22 Risa **Shimizu** ■ 38, 4 Saki **Kumagai** (c), 12 Moeka **Minami**, 3 Aya **Sameshima** - 7 Emi **Nakajima** (19 Jun **Endo** 74), 6 Hina **Sugita** ■ 45+1, 17 Narumi **Miura**, 14 Yui **Hasegawa** - 9 Yuika **Sugasawa** (13 Saori **Takarada** 90), 20 Kumi **Yokoyama** (8 Mana **Iwabuchi** 57 ■ 85). *Asako Takakura*.

Roazhon Park, Rennes
14.06.2019, 15:00, 13,201

JAPAN 2-1 SCOTLAND

Iwabuchi 23, Sugasawa 37p — Clelland 88

Lidya Tafesse Abebe ETH
Mary Njoroge KEN & Queency Victoire MRI
Massimiliano Irrati ITA

JPN • Yamashita - Shimizu, Kumagai (c), 5 Nana **Ichise**, Sameshima ■ 19 - Nakajima, Miura, Sugita, Endo (11 Rikako **Kobayashi** 66) - Iwabuchi (Hasegawa 81), Sugasawa. *Takakura*.

SCO • Alexander - Smith, Corsie (c) ■ 36, Beattie, 7 Hayley **Lauder** - Evans (20 Fiona **Brown** 85), Little, Weir, Arnot (Emslie 60) - Cuthbert, 13 Jane **Ross** (19 Lana **Clelland** 76). *Kerr*.

Stade Océane, Le Havre
14.06.2019, 21:00, 20,294

ENGLAND 1-0 ARGENTINA

Taylor 62
(Parris penalty saved 28)

Qin Liang CHN
Fang Yan CHN & Kim Kyoung Min KOR
Felix Zwayer GER

ENG • 13 Carly **Telford** - Bronze, Houghton (c), McManus, Greenwood - J Scott, 16 Jade **Moore** ■ 45+2, Kirby (Carney 89) - Parris (17 Rachel **Daly** 87), 9 Jodie **Taylor**, Mead (Stanway 81). *Neville*.

ARG • Correa - 4 Adriana **Sachs**, Barroso ■ 69, Cometti ■ 39, Stábile - Bonsegundo, Bravo, Benítez (Santana 77), Mayorga, Banini (c) (Larroquette 68) - Jaimes (7 Yael **Oviedo** 90). *Borrello*.

Stade de Nice, Nice
19.06.2019, 21:00, 14,319

JAPAN 0-2 ENGLAND

E White (2) 14 84

Claudia Umpiérrez URU
Luciana Mascaraña URU & Monica Amboya ECU
Carlos del Cerro Grande ESP

JPN • Yamashita - Shimizu, Kumagai (c), Ichise, Sameshima - Kobayashi (Miura 62), Nakajima, Sugita, Endo (Takarada 85) - Iwabuchi, Yokoyama (Sugasawa 61). *Takakura*.

ENG • Bardsley - Bronze, Houghton (c), Bright, 12 Demi **Stokes** - J Scott, Walsh (Moore 72), Stanway (Carney 74) - Daly, E White, 11 Toni **Duggan** (Parris 83). *Neville*.

Parc des Princes, Paris
19.06.2019, 21:00, 28,205

SCOTLAND 3-3 ARGENTINA

Little 19, Beattie 49, Cuthbert 69 — Menéndez 74, Alexander OG 79, Bonsegundo 90+4p

Ri Hyang Ok PRK
Hong Kum Nyo PRK & Kim Kyoung Min KOR
Bastian Dankert GER

SCO • Alexander ■ 90+3 - Smith (Howard 86), Corsie (c), Beattie, Docherty - Little, 10 Leanne **Crichton**, Weir ■ 86 - Evans (Brown 86), Cuthbert ■ 85, Emslie. *Kerr*.

ARG • Correa - Bravo, Barroso, Cometti, Stábile - Larroquette ■ 75, Santana (Mayorga 82), Banini (c) (22 Milagros **Menéndez** 60), Benítez, Bonsegundo - Jaimes (20 Dalila **Ippólito** 70). *Borrello*.

◀ Scotland's Claire Emslie can't quite believe what has just happened. Argentina's injury-time equaliser meant the Scots failed to make it through to the round of 16.

2019 Group stage

Group E

Stade de la Mosson, Montpellier
10.06.2019, 21:00, **10,710**

CANADA 🇨🇦 **1-0** 🇨🇲 **CAMEROON**

Buchanan 45

🚩 Ri Hyang Ok PRK
🚩 Hong Kum Nyo PRK & Kim Kyoung Min KOR
④ Massimiliano Irrati ITA

CAN • 1 Stephanie **Labbé** - 10 Ashley **Lawrence**, 3 Kadeisha **Buchanan**, 4 Shelina **Zadorsky**, 2 Allysha **Chapman** - 15 Nichelle **Prince** (6 Deanne **Rose** 75), 11 Desiree **Scott**, 13 Sophie **Schmidt**, 16 Janine **Beckie** - 12 Christine **Sinclair** (c), 17 Jessie **Fleming**. *Kenneth Heiner-Møller DEN*

CMR • 1 Annette **Ngo Ndom** - 11 Aurelle **Awona**, 2 Christine **Manie** (c), 6 Estelle **Johnson** - 4 Yvonne **Leuko**, 8 Raïssa **Feudjio**, 10 Jeannette **Yango** (13 Charlène **Meyong** 82), 12 Claudine **Meffometou** - 3 Ajara **Nchout** (18 Henriette **Akaba** 67), 19 Marlyse **Ngo Ndoumbouk** 🟨 37 (17 Gaëlle **Enganamouit** 68 🟨 74), 7 Gabrielle **Aboudi Onguéné**. *Alain Djeumfa*

Stade Océane, Le Havre
11.06.2019, 15:00, **10,654**

NEW ZEALAND 🇳🇿 **0-1** 🇳🇱 **NETHERLANDS**

Roord 90+2

🚩 Edina Alves Batista BRA
🚩 Neuza Back BRA & Tatiane Sacilotti BRA
④ Carlos del Cerro Grande ESP

NZL • 1 Erin **Nayler** - 4 C.J. **Bott**, 6 Rebekah **Stott**, 8 Abby **Erceg**, 7 Ali **Riley** (c) - 12 Betsy **Hassett** (10 Annalie **Longo** 67), 2 Ria **Percival**, 14 Katie **Bowen**, 22 Olivia **Chance** - 11 Sarah **Gregorius** (19 Paige **Satchell** 73), 13 Rosie **White** (17 Hannah **Wilkinson** 73). *Tom Sermanni SCO*

NED • 1 Sari **van Veenendaal** (c) - 2 Desiree **van Lunteren**, 3 Stefanie **van der Gragt**, 20 Dominique **Bloodworth**, 5 Kika **van Es** (4 Merel **van Dongen** 70) - 14 Jackie **Groenen** (19 Jill **Roord** 75), 8 Sherida **Spitse** - 7 Shanice **van de Sanden** (21 Lineth **Beerensteyn** 86), 10 Daniëlle **van de Donk**, 11 Lieke **Martens** - 9 Vivianne **Miedema**. *Sarina Wiegman*

Stade du Hainaut, Valenciennes
15.06.2019, 15:00, **22,423**

NETHERLANDS 🇳🇱 **3-1** 🇨🇲 **CAMEROON**

Miedema (2) 41 85,   Aboudi Onguéné 43
Bloodworth 48

🚩 Casey Reibelt AUS
🚩 Lee Seul Gi KOR & Maiko Hagio JPN
④ Paolo Valeri ITA

NED • Van Veenendaal (c) - Van Lunteren, 6 Anouk **Dekker**, Bloodworth, Van Es (Van Dongen 86) - Groenen, Spitse, Van de Donk (Roord 71) - Van de Sanden (Beerensteyn 66), Miedema, Martens. *Wiegman*

CMR • Ngo Ndom - Meffometou, Manie (c) 🟨 14, Johnson, Leuko - Yango, 20 Genevieve **Ngo Mbeleck** 🟨 37 (Meyong 66), Feudjio 🟨 68 - 22 Michaela **Abam** (Nchout 60), Enganamouit (Akaba 75), Aboudi Onguéné. *Djeumfa*

Stade des Alpes, Grenoble
15.06.2019, 21:00, **14,856**

CANADA 🇨🇦 **2-0** 🇳🇿 **NEW ZEALAND**

Fleming 48, Prince 79

🚩 Yoshimi Yamashita JPN
🚩 Naomi Teshirogi JPN & Makoto Bozono JPN
④ José María Sánchez ESP

CAN • Labbé - 8 Jayde **Riviere** (A Chapman 75), Buchanan, Zadorsky, Lawrence - Prince (19 Adriana **Leon** 84), Scott, Schmidt, Beckie (5 Rebecca **Quinn** 83) - Sinclair (c), Fleming. *Heiner-Møller DEN*

NZL • Nayler - Bott (Longo 18), Stott, Erceg, Riley (c) - Chance, Percival, Bowen, Hassett (9 Emma **Kete** 85) - Gregorius (3 Anna **Green** 62), White. *Sermanni SCO*

Stade de la Mosson, Montpellier
20.06.2019, 18:00, **8,009**

CAMEROON 🇨🇲 **2-1** 🇳🇿 **NEW ZEALAND**

Nchout (2) 57 90+5   Awona OG 80

🚩 Kateryna Monzul UKR
🚩 Maryna Striletska UKR & Oleksandra Ardasheva UKR
④ Massimiliano Irrati ITA

CMR • Ngo Ndom - 5 Augustine **Ejangue**, Johnson - Feudjio, Nchout, Yango (14 Ninon **Abena** 84), Awona - Abam, Enganamouit (21 Alexandra **Takounda** 54 🟨 69), Aboudi Onguéné (c). *Djeumfa*

NZL • Nayler - Stott, Erceg, Green 🟨 68 (Hassett 68) - Bowen, Percival, 16 Katie **Duncan** (Wilkinson 68), Chance (Longo 88), Riley (c) - Gregorius, White. *Sermanni SCO*

Stade Auguste-Delaune, Reims
20.06.2019, 18:00, **19,277**

NETHERLANDS 🇳🇱 **2-1** 🇨🇦 **CANADA**

Dekker 54, Beerensteyn 75   Sinclair 60

🚩 Stéphanie Frappart FRA
🚩 Manuela Nicolosi FRA & Michelle O'Neill IRL
④ Felix Zwayer GER

NED • Van Veenendaal (c) - Van Lunteren, Dekker 🟨 23, Bloodworth, Van Dongen - Groenen, Spitse (Roord 70 🟨 90) - Van de Donk (13 Renate **Jansen** 87) - Van de Sanden, Miedema, Martens (Beerensteyn 70). *Wiegman*

CAN • Labbé - Lawrence, Buchanan 🟨 38, Zadorsky, A Chapman (Riviere 69) - Scott (Quinn 79 🟨 80), Fleming, Schmidt - Jordyn **Huitema**, Sinclair (c) (Leon 68), Beckie. *Heiner-Møller DEN*

	W	D	L	+	-	PTS
NED	3	0	0	6	2	9
CAN	2	0	1	4	2	6
CMR	1	0	2	3	5	3
NZL	0	0	3	1	5	0

▶ Ajara Nchout celebrates her injury-time winner against New Zealand, which saw Cameroon qualify for the round of 16 in dramatic style.

14

New Zealand's defeat at the hands of Cameroon was coach Tom Sermanni's 14th game as coach at a World Cup, joining Swede Marika Domanski Lyfors in third place on the all-time list. They would later be joined by USA coach Jill Ellis. Norway's Even Pellerud tops the list with 25 matches, followed by Germany's Silvia Neid with 17.

Dutch at the double

The heavens opened minutes before Lyon defender Kadeisha Buchanan dampened Cameroon's spirits by heading in a Janine Beckie corner to secure an opening-night win for Canada in Montpellier. The following day, a sea of orange-clad Netherlands fans basked in the Le Havre sunshine at the Stade Océane as Jill Roord's 92nd-minute header beat New Zealand, with Kiwi Olivia Chance denied by the woodwork, and Rosie White and Sarah Gregorius by the athleticism of keeper Sari van Veenendaal. The Dutch shot-stopper's Arsenal team-mate Vivianne Miedema honoured a bet with her brother by performing a forward roll after breaking the Dutch national goalscoring record in a 3-1 win over Cameroon. New Zealand full-back CJ Bott broke her wrist 14 minutes into a 2-0 defeat by Canada, and Tom Sermanni's Oceania champions would extend their unwanted record as the team with the longest winless streak in the competition after losing 2-1 to Cameroon. The West Africans reached the last 16 for the second consecutive tournament thanks to Ajara Nchout's stunning injury-time winner. In the tussle for top spot, Canada captain Christine Sinclair became the second player after Marta to score in five World Cups, but substitute Lineth Beerensteyn won it for the Dutch with the 100th goal of France 2019.

▶ Dutch defender Dominique Bloodworth restores her side's lead against Cameroon. The European champions, in only their second World Cup, gained maximum points in their three group matches.

Records tumble for the USA

Paris Saint-Germain keeper Christiane Endler was on fire as both she and Chile belied their World Cup debutant status in a storm-hit match against seasoned Sweden, who needed late goals from Kosovare Asllani and substitute Madelen Janogy to secure a first group-stage win since 2011. Coming in for injured No.1 Waraporn Boonsing, Thailand's Sukanya Chor Charoenying endured a chastening competition debut as she was beaten 13 times by the USA. The reigning champions would come under fire for celebrating each goal with equal enthusiasm, but coach Nuengrutai Srathongvian praised them for their hugs and kind words at full time. Thailand's tears turned to smiles against Sweden as Kanjana Sung-Ngoen hit her first World Cup goal in a 5-1 defeat. "This goal makes us happy," said Srathongvian. Chile would limit the USA to three goals in Paris, boos echoing around the Parc des Princes when Rocío Soto's dinked free kick was disallowed for offside. Lindsey Horan scored the earliest goal of the group stage as the USA survived their biggest test, beating Sweden 2-0 to avenge their 2016 Olympic quarter-final defeat and top the group. Chile came within a whisper of scoring the three unanswered goals they needed against Thailand to progress, but Francisca Lara hit a penalty against the crossbar in an agonising 2-0 win.

Group F

	W	D	L	+	−	PTS
USA	3	0	0	18	0	9
SWE	2	0	1	7	3	6
CHI	1	0	2	2	5	3
THA	0	0	3	1	20	0

10
Against Thailand, the USA scored a remarkable ten goals in the second half, including a spell of four in just 371 seconds.

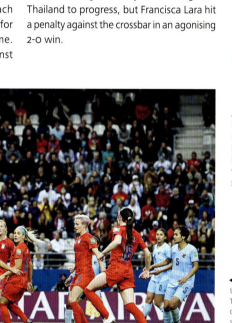

◀ Alex Morgan puts the USA 5-0 up against Thailand. It was the first of three goals in 177 seconds. With those three goals coming in less than three minutes, it was the fastest-ever triple strike at either the World Cup or Olympics.

◀ Chile goalkeeper Christiane Endler makes another save against the USA. She was one of a number of standout keepers during the tournament.

▲ Boots worn by USA striker Alex Morgan. She scored five goals in the match against Thailand, a feat matched only by compatriot Michelle Akers at the 1991 World Cup.
FIFA Museum Collection

29
The USA squad at France 2019 was the second oldest in the history of the World Cup – beaten only by the USA squad that won the title four years earlier in Canada.

Group stage 2019

Roazhon Park, Rennes
11.06.2019, 18:00, 15,875

CHILE 0-2 SWEDEN
Asllani 83, Janogy 90+4

🚩 Lucila Venegas MEX
🚩 Mayte Chávez MEX & Enedina Caudillo MEX
🚩 Chris Beath AUS

CHI • 1 Christiane **Endler** (c) - 15 Su Helen **Galaz**, 3 Carla **Guerrero** ■ 78, 18 Camila **Sáez**, 17 Javiera **Toro** - 8 Karen **Araya**, 10 Yanara **Aedo** (2 Rocío **Soto** 84), 4 Francisca **Lara** - 20 Daniela **Zamora**, 9 María José **Urrutia** (11 Yessenia **López** 59 ■ 90+6), 21 Rosario **Balmaceda**. *José Letelier*
SWE • 1 Hedvig **Lindahl** - 4 Hanna **Glas**, 5 Nilla **Fischer**, 3 Linda **Sembrant**, 6 Magdalena **Eriksson** ■ 67 - 23 Elin **Rubensson** (7 Madelen **Janogy** 81), 9 Kosovare **Asllani**, 17 Caroline **Seger** (c) - 10 Sofia **Jakobsson**, 11 Stina **Blackstenius** (19 Anna **Anvegård** 65), 18 Fridolina **Rolfö** (8 Lina **Hurtig** 65). *Peter Gerhardsson*

Stade Auguste-Delaune, Reims
11.06.2019, 21:00, 18,591

USA 13-0 THAILAND
Morgan (5) 12 53 74 81 87,
Lavelle (2) 20 56, Horan 32,
Mewis (2) 50 54, Rapinoe 79, Pugh 85, Lloyd 90+2

🚩 Laura Fortunato ARG
🚩 Mariana de Almeida ARG & Mary Blanco COL
🚩 Mauro Vigliano ARG

USA • 1 Alyssa **Naeher** - 5 Kelley **O'Hara**, 7 Abby **Dahlkemper**, 8 Julie **Ertz** (2 Mallory **Pugh** 69), 19 Crystal **Dunn** - 16 Rose **Lavelle** (10 Carli **Lloyd** 57), 9 Lindsey **Horan**, 3 Samantha **Mewis** - 17 Tobin **Heath** (23 Christen **Press** 57), 13 Alex **Morgan**, 15 Megan **Rapinoe** (c). *Jill Ellis*
THA • 18 Sukanya **Chor Charoenying** - 9 Warunee **Phetwiset** (13 Orathai **Srimanee** 71), 3 Natthakarn **Chinwong**, 2 Kanjanaporn **Saenkhun**, 10 Sunisa **Srangthaisong** - 21 Kanjana **Sung-Ngoen** (c), 20 Wilaiporn **Boothduang** (6 Pikul **Khueanpet** 35), 7 Silawan **Intamee**, 5 Ainon **Phancha**, 12 Rattikan **Thongsombut** (17 Taneekarn **Dangda** 65 ■ 72) - 8 Miranda **Nild**. *Nuengrutai Srathongvian*

Stade de Nice, Nice
16.06.2019, 15:00, 9,354

SWEDEN 5-1 THAILAND
Sembrant 6, Asllani 19, Sung-Ngoen 90+1
Rolfö 42, Hurtig 81,
Rubensson 90+6p

🚩 Salima Mukansanga RWA
🚩 Bernadettar Kwimbira MWI & Lidwine Rakotozafinoro MAD
🚩 Felix Zwayer GER

SWE • Lindahl - Glas, Fischer, Sembrant, Eriksson - Rubensson, Asllani, Seger (c) (22 Olivia **Schough** 69) - Rolfö (Janogy 46) Anvegård (20 Mimmi **Larsson** 77), Hurtig. *Gerhardsson*
THA • 1 Waraporn **Boonsing** - Phancha, Chinwong ■ 90+5, 19 Pitsamai **Sornsai**, Srangthaisong - Dangda ■ 45+1, Nild, Intamee (11 Sudarat **Chuchuem** 89), Khueanpet, Thongsombut (Srimanee 56) (15 Orapin **Waenngoen** 81) - Sung-Ngoen (c). *Strathongvian*

Parc des Princes, Paris
16.06.2019, 18:00, 45,594

USA 3-0 CHILE
Lloyd (2) 11 35, Ertz 26
(Lloyd penalty missed 81)

🚩 Riem Hussein GER
🚩 Kylie Cockburn SCO & Mihaela Țepușă ROU
🚩 Clément Turpin FRA

USA • Naeher - 11 Ali **Krieger**, Dahlkemper (14 Emily **Sonnett** 82), 4 Becky **Sauerbrunn**, 12 Tierna **Davidson** - 6 Morgan **Brian**, Ertz (22 Jessica **McDonald** 46), Horan ■ 23 (20 Allie **Long** 59 ■ 80) - Pugh, Lloyd (c), Press. *J Ellis*
CHI • Endler - Galaz ■ 90+4, Guerrero, Sáez, Toro - Araya, 6 Claudia **Soto** (López 46), Lara ■ 76 (14 Daniela **Pardo** 89) - Zamora, Urrutia (19 Yessenia **Huenteo** 68 ■ 80), Balmaceda. *Letelier*

Stade Océane, Le Havre
20.06.2019, 21:00, 22,418

SWEDEN 0-2 USA
Horan 3, Andersson OG 50

🚩 Anastasia Pustovoitova RUS
🚩 Ekaterina Kurochkina RUS & Petruța Iugulescu ROU
🚩 Danny Makkelie NED

SWE • Lindahl - 15 Nathalie **Björn**, 13 Amanda **Ilestedt**, Sembrant, 2 Jonna **Andersson** - Jakobsson ■ 87, 16 Julia **Zigiotti**, Seger (c) (Glas 63), Schough (Rolfö 56) - Asllani (Hurtig 79), Blackstenius. *Gerhardsson*
USA • Naeher - O'Hara ■ 59, Dahlkemper, Sauerbrunn, Dunn - Lavelle (Press 63), Horan, Mewis - Heath, Morgan (c) (Lloyd 46), Rapinoe (Pugh 83). *J Ellis*

Roazhon Park, Rennes
20.06.2019, 21:00, 13,567

THAILAND 0-2 CHILE
Boonsing OG 48, Urrutia 80
(Lara penalty missed 86)

🚩 Anna-Marie Keighley NZL
🚩 Sarah Jones NZL & Maria Salamasina SAM
🚩 Paolo Valeri ITA

THA • Boonsing ■ 85 - Phetwiset (Saenkhun 90+1), Chinwong, Sornsai ■ 59, Srangthaisong - Thongsombut (Waenngoen 58), Phancha, Nild, Khueanpet, Intamee (Chuchuen 73) - Sung-Ngoen (c). *Strathongvian*
CHI • Endler (c) - R Soto, Guerrero, Sáez, Lara - López, Araya (13 Javiera **Grez** 46) (7 María José **Rojas** 88), Aedo - Balmaceda, Urrutia, Zamora. *Letelier*

2019 Round of 16

▲ Grenoble's picturesque Stade des Alpes during the round-of-16 match between Germany and Nigeria.

▶ Kick-off ball for the round-of-16 match between Norway and Australia in Nice. As at Russia 2018, a different coloured version of the official ball was introduced after the group stage.
FIFA Museum Collection

Germany cruise through

Stade des Alpes, Grenoble
22.06.2019, 17:30, **17,988**

GERMANY 3-0 NIGERIA

Popp 20, Däbritz 27p, Schüller 82

Yoshimi Yamashita JPN • Naomi Teshirogi JPN & Makoto Bozono JPN • Carlos del Cerro Grande ESP
GER • Schult - Gwinn, Doorsoun, Hegering, Schweers (Simon 46) - Huth ■ 57, Leupolz (Bühl 46), Magull (Oberdorf 69), Däbritz - Popp (c) ■ 32, Schüller. *Voss-Tecklenburg*
NGA • Nnadozie - Okeke, Ebi, Ohale, Nwabuoku ■ 26 (15 Rasheedat **Ajibade** 46 ■ 82) - Ordega, Ayinde, Okobi, 19 Chinwendu **Ihezuo** (Uchendu 75) - Oparanozie (c) ■ 61, Kanu (22 Alice **Ogebe** 84). *Dennerby SWE*

An anxious three-day wait while the group stage reached its denouement had ended in joyful celebration for Nigeria as they pipped Chile to a place in the last 16 on goal difference. The only African side to feature in all eight Women's World Cups, it had still been 20 years since Nigeria last reached the knockouts. Now, even after playing no international fixtures in 2017, a largely professional *Super Falcons* squad based at clubs in Europe, the USA and China were ready to face world No.2 Germany.

Thomas Dennerby, head coach since 2018, insisted that Nigeria's world ranking of 38th belied their quality and they certainly gave the Olympic champions a run for their money but two goals in seven minutes would prove their undoing. Captain and centurion Alexandra Popp headed in the first, Sara Däbritz a cool second from the spot. Pacy teenage substitute Rasheedat Ajibade added spice to Nigeria's attack after the break, but Lea Schüller pounced on a defensive mistake to round off the scoring.

Australia out on penalties

Stade de Nice, Nice
22.06.2019, 21:00, **12,229**

NORWAY 1-1 AUSTRALIA
AET
4-1 PSO

Herlovsen 31   Kellond-Knight 83

Graham Hansen ⚽ Kerr ✘ (missed) Reiten ⚽ Gielnik ✘ (saved) Mjelde ⚽ Catley ⚽ Engen ⚽

Riem Hussein GER • Kylie Cockburn SCO & Mihaela Țepușă ROU • Felix Zwayer GER
NOR • Hjelmseth - Wold (Hansen 102), Mjelde (c), Thorisdottir, Minde ■ 53 - Sævik (Maanum 72), Risa ■ 105+2, Engen, Reiten - Herlovsen (Utland 77 ■ 96), Graham Hansen. *Sjögren SWE*
AUS • Williams - Carpenter (22 Amy **Harrison** 120+2), Kennedy ■ 104, Catley, Kellond-Knight (Polkinghorne 94) - Yallop, Van Egmond (Roestbakken 116), Logarzo - Raso (Gielnik 74), Kerr (c), Foord. *Milicic*

▼ Australia captain Sam Kerr misses a crucial penalty in the shoot-out against Norway.

"Only big players can miss penalties, because small ones don't take them," said coach Ante Milicic when asked about skipper Sam Kerr after Australia's shoot-out shocker against Norway. Kerr's unprecedented four-goal salvo against Jamaica had brought her team to this point on goal difference. Having inflicted Norway's only ever exit at the group stage in 2011, they were always going to face a bigger battle here. It looked like one that Martin Sjögren's side might win after Isabell Herlovsen scored her sixth goal in four World Cups, and a penalty against Maria Thorisdottir for handball was overturned by VAR. Yet Australia, whose shirts were adorned with their motto 'Never Say Die', came back with an outrageous Elise Kellond-Knight goal straight from a corner kick. Australia even held on in extra time after Alanna Kennedy's straight red for a foul on Lisa-Marie Utland, but the celebrations belonged to Norway after Kerr skied her spot kick and Ingrid Hjelmseth saved Emily Gielnik's.

▶ Former champions Norway celebrate reaching the World Cup quarter-finals for the first time since 2007 after their penalty shoot-out victory over Australia.

England keep their heads as Cameroon lose theirs in VAR spotlight

Stade du Hainaut, Valenciennes
23.06.2019, 17:30, **20,148**

ENGLAND 3-0 CAMEROON

Houghton 14, E White 45+4, Greenwood 58

Qin Liang CHN • Fang Yan CHN & Hong Kum Nyo PRK • Bastian Dankert GER

ENG • Bardsley - Bronze, Houghton (c), Bright, Greenwood - J Scott (23 Lucy **Staniforth** 78), Kirby, Walsh - Parris (14 Leah **Williamson** 84), E White (Taylor 64), Duggan. *Neville*

CMR • Ngo Ndom - Ejangue (15 Ysis **Sonkeng** 64), Awona, Johnson, Leuko ■ 4 - Nchout, Yango, Feudjio, Aboudi Onguéné (c) - Abam (Abena 68), Enganamouit (Takounda 53 ■ 90+10). *Djeumfa*

Cameroon had etched their names into the history books as the first team from their continent to progress from the group stage at two consecutive World Cups. Now the *Indomitable Lionesses* hoped to write a new chapter as the first African team to win a knockout match. They would make headlines of a different sort after losing to England, however. Behind to a precision Steph Houghton free kick after Annette Ngo Ndom had handled a backpass, Cameroon then felt so aggrieved by two VAR reviews that they held up play not once but twice while they vented their frustration. First, a VAR check allowed an Ellen White strike to stand when it had been flagged for offside, then the reverse happened and Ajara Nchout's searing shot was disallowed after another review. Alain Djeumfa's side would survive a VAR penalty review and another for a possible red card after a crunching tackle on Houghton, but they would not escape a third England goal and another second-round exit from the World Cup.

◀ England captain Steph Houghton opens the scoring against Cameroon with a perfectly placed free kick.

◀ Chinese referee Qin Liang explains to Cameroon captain Gabrielle Aboudi Onguéné why VAR had allowed Ellen White's goal to stand. In the second half, a Cameroon goal was disallowed for offside by the thinnest of margins.

▲ France captain Amandine Henry celebrates her winning goal against Brazil.

Amandine Henry sees France into the last eight

Stade Océane, Le Havre
23.06.2019, 21:00, **23,965**

FRANCE 2-1 BRAZIL
AET

Gauvin 52, Henry 107 — Thaísa 63

Marie-Soleil Beaudoin CAN • Princess Brown JAM & Stephanie-Dale Yee Sing JAM • Massimiliano Irrati ITA

FRA • Bouhaddi - Torrent (Périsset 109), Mbock Bathy, Renard ■ 36, Majri (7 Sakina **Karchaoui** 118) - Asseyi (Thiney 81), Henry (c), Bussaglia, Le Sommer - Diani, Gauvin (Cascarino 90+3). *Diacre*

BRA • Bárbara - Letícia Santos (Poliana 89), Kathellen ■ 101, Mónica, Tamires ■ 45+2 - Formiga ■ 70 (Andressinha 75), Thaísa - Ludmila (Beatriz 71 ■ 82), Cristiane (Geyse 96), Marta (c) - Debinha. *Vadão*

It had been 21 years since France's men overcame Brazil to lift the World Cup on home soil, but *Les Bleues* coach Corinne Diacre refused to see this clash through a historical lens. "It's not a legendary match from the past," she said, "it's a World Cup round-of-16 tie." Even so, it was one that her opposite number Vadão would justifiably describe as "incredible" after a dramatic 120 minutes. Valérie Gauvin scored an incisive opener in the second half having had an earlier effort ruled out, but Thaísa then bagged a swift equaliser after a VAR review helped overrule the assistant's flag for offside. Griedge Mbock Bathy made a crucial goal-line clearance to deny Debinha before France skipper Amandine Henry settled the tie with a superb winning volley. Seven players aged 30 or over were in Brazil's starting XI, and the talk afterwards was of "renewal" but these iconic veterans had set the standard for the generations to come.

Spain pay the penalty

Stade Auguste-Delaune, Reims
24.06.2019, 18:00, **19,633**

SPAIN 1-2 USA

Hermoso 9   Rapinoe (2) 7p 75p

Katalin Kulcsár HUN   Katalin Török HUN & Sanja Rodak CRO   Danny Makkelie NED

ESP • Paños - Corredera, Paredes (c) ■ 85, León, Ouahabi - Losada (N García 32), Torrecilla (Caldentey 83), Guijarro - L García, Hermoso, Putellas (Falcón 78). *Vilda*

USA • Naeher - O'Hara, Dahlkemper, Sauerbrunn, Dunn - Lavelle (Horan 89), Ertz, Mewis - Heath, Morgan (Lloyd 85), Rapinoe (c) ■ 37 (Press 90+7). *J Ellis*

Spain were the only European side to qualify for France with a 100 per cent record and they had already surpassed their previous run in the competition by securing this maiden knockout berth. In Reims, they would inflict the first World Cup goal in 317 minutes on the defending champions, Jennifer Hermoso pouncing on a defensive howler to score a mere two minutes after Megan Rapinoe had sent Sandra Paños the wrong way from the penalty spot. Spain maintained their composure when VAR confirmed the referee's call that Rose Lavelle had been fouled in the box, and while skipper Rapinoe's second penalty would prove decisive in this tight skirmish, the youngest coach in the tournament, Jorge Vilda, could not hide his pride. "If they've had to win through penalties then we've shown our worth and given them a run for their money," he said. "We are going to grow from this defeat and we've shown our potential for growth."

◀ The one that got away. Megan Rapinoe's shot is saved by Spain goalkeeper Sandra Paños. Rapinoe scored twice from the penalty spot to give the USA a 2-1 victory.

◀ Samantha Mewis of the USA in action against Spain during their round-of-16 match in Reims.

52

The number of players at the World Cup registered to clubs in Spain, the second most after the USA. Barcelona boasted the most players with 15, with ten in the Spain squad alone.

▲ Hedvig Lindahl is mobbed by her team-mates after saving a Janine Beckie penalty, becoming the first Swedish keeper to save a spot kick at the World Cup.

Lindahl saves the day for Sweden

Parc des Princes, Paris
24.06.2019, 21:00, **38,078**

SWEDEN 1-0 CANADA

Blackstenius 55   (Beckie penalty saved 69)

Kate Jacewicz AUS
Kathryn Nesbitt USA & Felisha Mariscal USA
José María Sánchez ESP

SWE • Lindahl - Glas, Fischer, Sembrant, Eriksson - Rubensson (Björn 79), Seger (c), Rolfö ■ 45 (Hurtig 89) - Jakobsson, Asllani ■ 68, Blackstenius (Anvegård 90+4). *Gerhardsson*

CAN • Labbé - Lawrence, Buchanan ■ 85, Zadorsky, A Chapman (Riviere 84) - Scott, Schmidt - Prince (Leon 64), Fleming, Beckie (Quinn 84) - Sinclair (c). *Heiner-Møller DEN*

Canada had twice gone toe-to-toe with Sweden in the 18 months since former Denmark manager Kenneth Heiner-Møller had taken over as head coach. Defeated at the Algarve Cup in 2018, the Canucks won a back-and-forth battle for bronze in a penalty shoot-out at the 2019 Algarve Cup. When VAR highlighted a Kosovare Asllani handball in the box in this match, a spot kick looked set to play a part here too. Behind after a wonderful Asllani pass was poked in by Stina Blackstenius, this was Canada's chance to level and history was on their side. In six attempts, no Swede had saved a Women's World Cup penalty, but that would change as Hedvig Lindahl dived full stretch to deny Janine Beckie. "An excellent save, too bad she pulled that out of the jersey today," said Heiner-Møller, adding that a youthful Canada would bounce back. "Just being at an event like this gives them a thicker skin, they know what it's about, which is a big thing for young players."

Le Azzurre enchant a nation

Stade de la Mosson, Montpellier
25.06.2019, 18:00, **17,492**

ITALY 🇮🇹 **2-0** 🇨🇳 **CHINA PR**

Giacinti 15, Galli 49

Edina Alves Batista BRA
Neuza Back BRA & Tatiane Sacilotti BRA
Mauro Vigliano ARG

ITA • Giuliani - Guagni, Gama (c), Linari, Bartoli - Bergamaschi (Mauro 63), Giugliano, Cernoia - Giacinti, Girelli (Galli 39), Bonansea (6 Martina **Rosucci** 71). *Bertolini*

CHN • Peng Shimeng - Han Peng, Wu Haiyan (c), Lin Yuping, Liu Shanshan - Wang Shuang, Zhang Rui, Wang Yan (Yao Wei 61), Gu Yasha (Yang Li 46) - Wang Shanshan (Song Duan 61), Li Ying. *Jia Xiuquan*

China's miserly defence had conceded just one goal on their way to maintaining a perfect record of always reaching the knockout stages of the World Cup, but they had scored just once on the road to this round-of-16 match, through Li Ying, and the *Steel Roses* needed to find their shooting boots. In contrast, Italy had won their group on goal difference and were buoyantly riding the crest of a hitherto unknown popularity wave back home. Before this tournament, the biggest television audience for a women's match in Italy had been 202,844, but record numbers of Italian viewers had lapped up *Le Azzurre*'s table-topping feats at France 2019. More than 4 million would tune in to watch this clash and they would not be disappointed. Wang Yan almost scored, but goals from Serie A top scorer Valentina Giacinti and impact substitute Aurora Galli were enough for Italy to end China's campaign and take their own to the next level.

▲ Valentina Giacinti celebrates giving Italy an early lead against China.

▶ Shanice van de Sanden (7) of European champions the Netherlands is challenged by Aya Sameshima (3) of Asian champions Japan.

▶ Vivianne Miedema's shot was adjudged by VAR to have hit the hand of Japanese defender Saki Kumagai. Lieke Martens scored from the resulting last-minute penalty to win the game for the Dutch.

23

By the end of the round of 16, 23 penalties had been awarded, surpassing the 22 awarded in the whole of the 2015 finals.

Last-gasp Netherlands

Roazhon Park, Rennes
25.06.2019, 21:00, **21,076**

NETHERLANDS 🇳🇱 **2-1** 🇯🇵 **JAPAN**

Martens (2) 17 90p — Hasegawa 43

Melissa Borjas HON — Shirley Perelló HON & Chantal Boudreau CAN — Chris Beath AUS

NED • Van Veenendaal (c) - Van Lunteren, Van der Gragt, Bloodworth, Van Dongen (Van Es 85) - Groenen, Spitse, Van de Donk (Roord 87) - Van de Sanden (Beerensteyn 68), Miedema, Martens. *Wiegman*

JPN • Yamashita - Shimizu, Kumagai (c) 88, Ichise, Sameshima - Nakajima (15 Yuka **Momiki** 72), Sugita, Miura, Hasegawa - Sugasawa, Iwabuchi (Takarada 90+1). *Takakura*

Both of these sides had rung the changes since meeting in the 2015 World Cup and both had new head coaches. Former Japan midfielder Asako Takakura had overseen a tactical and team revamp en route to her side retaining their Asian Cup crown and regaining the Asian Games title. Meanwhile, former Netherlands captain Sarina Wiegman had built momentum after leading her team to victory at the 2017 Euros on home soil, and then saw them boss a play-off battle with Denmark and Switzerland for a place at France 2019. Japan had beaten the Netherlands 2-1 at the same stage four years ago, but the roles were reversed here and in the cruellest way possible. Level at the break after a slick back-heel from Barcelona star Lieke Martens and a sumptuous Yui Hasegawa strike, Japan were kept at bay after the restart by a combination of the woodwork and Sari van Veenendaal. Then came a penalty shout at the death, Saki Kumagai penalised for handball, and up stepped Martens to exact revenge.

2019 Quarter-finals

▲ Jill Scott, England's most-capped player at the World Cup, scores an early goal to give her team the upper hand in the quarter-final against Norway in Le Havre.

◀ England celebrate their third goal against Norway, scored by Lucy Bronze.

Rapinoe power play trumps France

Parc des Princes, Paris
28.06.2019, 21:00, **45,595**

FRANCE 🇫🇷 **1-2** 🇺🇸 **USA**

Renard 81   Rapinoe (2) 5 65

Kateryna Monzul UKR Maryna Striletska UKR & Oleksandra Ardasheva UKR
Danny Makkelie NED

FRA • Bouhaddi - Torrent, Mbock Bathy ■ 4, Renard, Majri - Henry (c), Bussaglia ■ 90+4 - Diani, Thiney, Le Sommer (Asseyi 82) - Gauvin (Cascarino 76). *Diacre*

USA • Naeher - O'Hara, Dahlkemper, Sauerbrunn, Dunn - Lavelle (Horan 63), Ertz, Mewis (Lloyd 82) - Heath, Morgan (c), Rapinoe (Press 87). *J Ellis*

It was the warmest day ever recorded in France and the Parc des Princes was like a pressure cooker set to blow as over 45,000 screaming fans bedecked in red, white and blue urged on two of the tournament's hot favourites. The hosts versus the holders had always been a possibility since the draw was made in December, and France boss Corinne Diacre had spent the last six months observing the USA carefully. Both teams had their eye on the ultimate prize now, and according to Jill Ellis, this clash was nothing less than the "world game for women". Former Lyon midfielder Megan Rapinoe would be the woman of the moment, though, drawing first blood with a fizzing free kick through a sea of bodies and then stealing in unmarked to slot in a second. Wendie Renard threw France a late lifeline with another clinical header but the USA shored up their defence, survived a handball appeal against Kelley O'Hara and saw off their challengers.

England on song

Stade Océane, Le Havre
27.06.2019, 21:00, **21,111**

NORWAY 🇳🇴 **0-3** 🏴󠁧󠁢󠁥󠁮󠁧󠁿 **ENGLAND**

J Scott 3, E White 40, Bronze 57
(Parris penalty saved 83)

Lucila Venegas MEX Mayte Chávez MEX & Enedina Caudillo MEX
Massimiliano Irrati ITA

NOR • Hjelmseth - Wold (Hansen 85), Mjelde (c), Thorisdottir ■ 88, Minde - Sævik (Utland 64), Risa, Engen, Reiten (15 Amalie Vevle **Eikeland** 74) - Graham Hansen, Herlovsen. *Sjögren SWE*

ENG • Bardsley - Bronze, Houghton (c), Bright, Stokes - J Scott, Kirby (Stanway 74), Walsh - Parris (Daly 88), E White, Duggan (Mead 54). *Neville*

Having crashed out of Euro 2017 without a single goal or point to their name, Norway had rallied, retaining Swedish manager Martin Sjögren, signing an equal pay agreement, and then beating European champions the Netherlands to top spot in their World Cup qualifying group. Now a squad boasting a similar camaraderie to Norway's World Cup-winning class of 1995 were set to face a team that had eliminated them in the round of 16 four years earlier. "I still carry it with me," said Chelsea defender Maria Thorisdottir, recalling that 2-1 loss to England in Canada. A career-enhancing thunderbolt from Lucy Bronze had secured England's first-ever knockout win then, and the Lyon defender would unleash an almost identical shot here. Jill Scott had already stroked home the quickest goal of the tournament before Ellen White tapped in her fifth in four. Then Bronze walloped in the 900th Women's World Cup goal. Ingrid Hjelmseth would save a Nikita Parris penalty late on, but it mattered not.

▲ Megan Rapinoe (out of picture) gives the USA a fifth-minute lead in the quarter-final against hosts France. The Americans scored within the first 12 minutes of every game in France, apart from in the Final.

▶ The hosts are out. Delphine Cascarino (20) and Sakina Karchaoui (7) contemplate what might have been.

Yet another late show from the Dutch

Stade du Hainaut, Valenciennes
29.06.2019, 15:00, **22,600**

ITALY 🇮🇹 **0-2** 🇳🇱 **NETHERLANDS**

Miedema 70,
Van der Gragt 80

⚽ Claudia Umpiérrez URU
🚩 Luciana Mascaraña URU & Monica Amboya ECU
📋 Carlos del Cerro Grande ESP

ITA • Giuliani - Guagni 🟨 66, Gama (c), Linari 🟨 41, Bartoli (Boattin 46) - Galli, Bergamaschi (15 Annamaria **Serturini** 75), Giugliano, Cernoia 🟨 73 - Bonansea (Sabatino 55 🟨 79), Giacinti. *Bertolini*

NED • Van Veenendaal (c) - Van Lunteren, Van der Gragt (Dekker 87), Bloodworth, Van Dongen - Groenen, Spitse, Van de Donk - Van de Sanden (Beerensteyn 56), Miedema (Roord 87), Martens. *Wiegman*

▲ Stefanie van der Gragt makes it 2-0 to the Netherlands against Italy. Only two of the 11 Dutch goals in France were scored in the first half.

▲ ▶ Sofia Jakobsson (10) equalises for Sweden against Germany. It was the first time Germany had conceded a first-half goal at the World Cup since Sweden scored against them in the 2003 Final, 22 matches previously.

Redemption for Sweden

Roazhon Park, Rennes
29.06.2019, 18:30, **25,301**

GERMANY 🇩🇪 **1-2** 🇸🇪 **SWEDEN**

Magull 16 — Jakobsson 22, Blackstenius 48

⚽ Stéphanie Frappart FRA 🚩 Manuela Nicolosi FRA & Michelle O'Neill IRL 📋 José María Sánchez ESP

GER • Schult - Gwinn, Doorsoun, Hegering, Simon (4 Leonie **Maier** 43) - Huth, Popp (c), Däbritz, Dallmann (Marozsán 46) - Schüller (Oberdorf 69), Magull. *Voss-Tecklenburg*
SWE • Lindahl - Glas, Fischer (Ilestedt 66), Sembrant, Eriksson - Jakobsson, Rubensson (Björn 86), Seger (c), Rolfö 🟨 56 (Hurtig 90+5) - Asllani, Blackstenius. *Gerhardsson*

0

The number of Asian teams in the quarter-finals. This was the first World Cup not to feature an Asian team at this stage.

Italy's joy at advancing to the last 16 and then to the quarter-finals was writ large in France when the team merrily sang and danced the *Macarena* before leaving the pitches of Valenciennes and Montpellier. They had reached this tournament after a near-perfect qualification campaign under Milena Bertolini. Now her group, all but one of them amateurs in their domestic league, were set to battle with the champions of Europe for a historic place in the semi-finals. It remained goalless for 70 minutes, but then the Netherlands gained the edge in the sweltering late afternoon heat. Instructed to push up and keep possession by coach Sarina Wiegman, they were rewarded when two Sherida Spitse free kicks led to headed goals from English Women's Super League top scorer Vivianne Miedema and Barcelona defender Stefanie van der Gragt. *Le Azzurre* shed some tears, but they left to a rousing ovation from the fans having put Italy back on the World Cup map with their flair, tactical acumen and fair play.

As a player, Germany head coach Martina Voss-Tecklenburg was twice on the losing end of World Cup matches to Sweden. Since then, however, *Die Nationalelf* had claimed ten wins and a draw against the Swedes in the finals of the World Cup, European Championship and the Olympics. Peter Gerhardsson's players hoped to lay those tournament ghosts to rest in Rennes, but Lina Magull gave them an early setback with a delightfully executed half-volley that flew through the legs of Sweden keeper Hedvig Lindahl and into the net. That lead was quashed when Sofia Jakobsson pounced on a long pass out of defence to become the first player to beat Almuth Schult at France 2019, and although Germany threatened after Stina Blackstenius's close-range goal just after the break had given Sweden the lead, they could not find a reply. A 24-year-old major tournament undefeated streak had finally bitten the dust. Now Sweden were Lyon-bound.

▲ Gloves worn by Dutch goalkeeper Sari van Veenendaal. She won the Golden Glove award as the best goalkeeper of the tournament.
FIFA Museum Collection

▶ Sweden's Elin Rubensson and Germany's Sara Däbritz in action during the quarter-final in Rennes.

6 out of 8

France's loss maintained a sombre record for host nations at the World Cup. It was the sixth time in the first eight editions of the tournament that the hosts had been knocked out in the quarter-finals.

2019 Semi-finals

3

Alex Morgan became the third player to score in two World Cup semi-finals, following on from Bettina Wiegmann (1991 & 1995) and Josefine Öqvist (2003 & 2011).

▶ Anyone for tea? Alex Morgan celebrates her goal against England with the most talked-about celebration of France 2019.

▲ England thought they had equalised before Ellen White's goal was ruled out for the most marginal of offsides. Steph Houghton had the chance to level just before the end but her penalty was saved by Alyssa Naeher.

Lionesses out but with pride intact

Stade de Lyon, Lyon
2.07.2019, 21:00, **53,512**

ENGLAND 🏴󠁧󠁢󠁥󠁮󠁧󠁿 **1-2** 🇺🇸 USA

E White 19, Press 10, Morgan 31
(Houghton penalty saved 84)

⚽ Edina Alves Batista BRA 🚩 Neuza Back BRA & Tatiane Sacilotti BRA 📺 Carlos del Cerro Grande ESP

ENG • Telford - Bronze, Houghton (c), Bright ▪40 ▪86 ▪86, Stokes - J Scott, Walsh (Moore 71) - Daly (Stanway 89), Parris ▪90+5, Mead (Kirby 58), White. *Neville*

USA • Naeher - O'Hara (Krieger 87), Dahlkemper, Sauerbrunn ▪82, Dunn - Lavelle (Mewis 65) Ertz, Horan ▪46 - Heath (Lloyd 80), Morgan (c), Press. *J Ellis*

Former Manchester United defender Phil Neville declared that he had been waiting for this week since the day in January 2018 when, having never coached in the women's game, he was appointed the *Lionesses*' new manager. "The vision was to get to this point and then deliver," he said. With England having fallen in their last two major tournament semi-finals, "delivering" meant securing an historic place in the Final. Still undefeated in France and having drawn with the USA in March when they stole the Americans' own invitational SheBelieves Cup from under their noses, a side packed with professionals believed it possible. Self-belief had never been in short supply in the USA camp, though, and having reached an unrivalled eighth semi-final, they would go on to crush Neville's ambitions. Ellen White would again get on the scoresheet and Keira Walsh would come close, but powerful headed goals from Christen Press and Alex Morgan were key. As was a VAR-reviewed decision to rule out a potential leveller from White for being a toe's width offside and Alyssa Naeher's dive to deny a Steph Houghton penalty that could have forced extra time. A frenetic match had wowed a packed Stade de Lyon and a record 11.7m UK television viewers, but it was little consolation to England.

Groenen downs gallant Swedes

Stade de Lyon, Lyon
3.07.2019, 21:00, **48,452**

NETHERLANDS 🇳🇱 **1-0** 🇸🇪 SWEDEN
AET

Groenen 99

⚽ Marie-Soleil Beaudoin CAN 🚩 Princess Brown JAM & Stephanie-Dale Yee Sing JAM 📺 Massimiliano Irrati ITA

NED • Van Veenendaal (c) - Van Lunteren, Van der Gragt, Bloodworth, Van Dongen - Groenen, Spitse ▪85, Van de Donk ▪116 - Beerensteyn (Van de Sanden 71), Miedema, Martens (Roord 46). *Wiegman*

SWE • Lindahl - Glas, Fischer, Sembrant, Eriksson (Andersson 111) - Jakobsson, Rubensson (Zigiotti 79 ▪94), Seger (c), Hurtig (Janogy 79) - Blackstenius (M Larsson 111), Asllani. *Gerhardsson*

Two goalkeepers at the peak of their powers had more than played their part in the road to the final four for the Netherlands and Sweden. Familiar foes in the English Women's Super League until their departures in the run-up to the tournament, former Arsenal and Chelsea custodians Sari van Veenendaal and Hedvig Lindahl would be key here too, but it would be Lindahl's old Chelsea team-mate Jackie Groenen who would settle this battle in extra time. Buoyed by a momentous victory over Germany, Sweden were facing a more recent rival in the Netherlands, who had knocked them out of Euro 2017 at the quarter-final stage. That match had ended 2-0, but neither side was able to make inroads in 90 minutes at the Stade de Lyon after crucial saves by Van Veenendaal denied veteran Nilla Fischer, with Lindahl keeping out in-form forward Vivianne Miedema and lively substitute Shanice van de Sanden. Then, in the 99th minute, player of the match Groenen unleashed a long-range strike that Lindahl simply could not reach. The *Blågult* were out but still qualified for the Olympics, becoming the only European team to reach every edition, while the *Oranje Leeuwinnen* were heading for a second major Final on the trot.

3

The semi-final between the Netherlands and Sweden was only the third all-European semi-final. The previous two had been Sweden against Norway in 1991 and Germany against Norway in 2007.

▲▲ Jackie Groenen scores the only goal of a tense semi-final between the Netherlands and Sweden in Lyon.

▲ Sari van Veenendal saves a shot by Swedish striker Stina Blackstenius.

No-nonsense approach wins bronze for Sweden

Sweden had battled all the way to the World Cup Final in 2003, and although several of this current squad were schoolgirls then, they were nonetheless inspired. "I started dreaming of putting on the Swedish shirt when I saw the World Cup in 2003," recalled 29-year-old Montpellier forward Sofia Jakobsson. With one silver and two bronze in their World Cup medal collection, Sweden understood the value of this match. As did 2015's third-placed team England. "We want that bronze medal," said midfielder Karen Carney ahead of the tie. When it came down to it, Sweden were straight out of the blocks, even though they had played extra time three days earlier, and both Kosovare Asllani and Jakobsson punished two spells of poor defending from England. The *Lionesses* would come back, Fran Kirby cutting inside to curl a left-footed shot beyond former Chelsea team-mate Hedvig Lindahl, the ball flying in off the post. Two minutes later, Ellen White thought she had equalised but just as against the USA four days previously, her goal was ruled out after a VAR review. Despite having netted six goals, White would not take the golden boot. Nor would England win a medal, Nilla Fischer denying Lucy Bronze on the line as Sweden toughed it out to the very end. In a moment of emotion, Phil Neville called it a "nonsense game", but coach Peter Gerhardsson knew what it meant: "It's a huge difference between winning a bronze medal and ending up fourth. I thought it was very important to win this match."

2019 Match for Third Place

Stade de Nice, Nice
6.07.2019, 17:00, **20,316**

ENGLAND 1-2 SWEDEN

Kirby 31 — Asllani 11, Jakobsson 22

Anastasia Pustovoitova RUS — Ekaterina Kurochkina RUS & Petruța Iugulescu ROU
Felix Zwayer GER

England: 13 Telford; 2 Bronze, 5 Houghton (c), 15 McManus (Daly 83), 3 Greenwood; 8 J Scott, 16 Moore 90+4; 7 Parris (Carney 74), 10 Kirby, 22 Mead (Taylor 50); 18 E White. Neville.

Sweden: 1 Lindahl 85; 6 Eriksson, 3 Sembrant, 5 Fischer, 4 Glas; 17 Seger (c), 15 Björn (Ilestedt 72); 18 Rolfö (Hurtig 27), 9 Asllani (Zigiotti 46), 10 Jakobsson; 11 Blackstenius. Gerhardsson.

◀ Kosovare Asllani gives Sweden the perfect start in the match for third place against England.

▲ Sweden celebrate winning bronze in France. Their qualification for the Tokyo Olympics maintained their one hundred per cent qualification record for both the World Cup and Olympics, matched only by the USA and Brazil.

So near, yet so far

The race for the Golden Boot proved to be the tightest in World Cup history, with three players finishing on six goals. England's Ellen White finished with the bronze boot behind Megan Rapinoe and Alex Morgan due to having fewer assists. White actually celebrated scoring a goal eight times in the six games she played, all from open play, but had two overturned after VAR reviews. And what important goals they would have been. Her 'equaliser' in the semi-final against the USA was ruled offside by the tightest of margins, while another 'equaliser', against Sweden in the match for third place, was chalked off for handball. In previous World Cups, neither goal would have been controversial had they stood.

▶ Ellen White followed each of her goals in France with a goggle celebration, a nod to 1.FC Köln's French striker Anthony Modeste, who celebrates his goals in the same manner. White is a big fan of the Bundesliga and supports Köln.

2019 Final

Record-breakers USA world champions for the fourth time

▲ The European champions take to the field against the reigning world champions. The USA made history as the first team to appear in three successive Finals

▼ ▶ Megan Rapinoe puts the USA 1-0 up in the Final. It was her third penalty of the tournament and it won her the Golden Boot as top scorer.

They had struck iconic poses, scored killer goals and come through dramatic knockout bouts against genuine heavyweight contenders. Now the last two teams standing were ready to do battle in 'La Grande Finale' in front of almost 58,000 of the tournament's most colourful and vocal fans. It was the first time that two female head coaches had contested the Final since 2003, and history would be made regardless of the winner. Either Jill Ellis would become the first coach to lead a side to back-to-back Final victories, or Sarina Wiegman the first to lead the Netherlands to a World Cup crown. Former P. E. teacher Wiegman was no stranger to the USA, facing them four times in a glittering career and playing alongside greats Mia Hamm and Kristine Lilly under Anson Dorrance at college in North Carolina. She had led the Netherlands to European glory a mere six months into her tenure but while contenders for the title, the *Oranje Leeuwinnen* were hardly favourites in only their second World Cup. Firmly the underdogs against the world No.1 having surpassed expectations by reaching the showcase Final, they were nonetheless as hungry for success as their rivals. "We're European champions," midfielder Sherida Spitse declared, "but we want more." The Americans wanted more too, Ellis having rebuilt the USA team since steering them to a first World Cup in 16 years before falling to an unprecedented Olympic exit. Greats such as Abby Wambach had retired, but a raft of youngsters had been nurtured and were playing their part in a squad featuring 12 World Cup winners. Neither team held back in a full-throttle start in glorious sunshine at the Stade de Lyon. Having ripped into every team so far and almost immediately reaped their reward with a goal, the USA would heap tremendous pressure on Sari van Veenendaal and her defence in the first half. But they were fortress-like, repelling shot after shot and it remained goalless at half-time. Then came the breakthrough, a foul on Alex Morgan given an on-field VAR review and a penalty awarded. Stepping up, captain Megan Rapinoe puffed out her cheeks, licked her lips and calmly slotted the ball beyond a static Van Veenendaal. A Rose Lavelle rocket finally took the pressure off and but for the keeper, Morgan and Crystal Dunn might well have extended the lead. Spitse and Jill Roord almost found a reply, but the USA had their fourth World Cup title in the bag.

2019 World Cup Final

Stade de Lyon, Lyon
7.07.2019, 17:00, 57,900

USA 2-0 NETHERLANDS

Rapinoe 61p, Lavelle 69

Stéphanie Frappart FRA — Manuela Nicolosi FRA & Michelle O'Neill IRL
Carlos del Cerro Grande ESP

Final 2019

▲ That winning feeling… Julie Ertz revels in the moment.

6

The number of women who have now played in three World Cup Finals. Birgit Prinz was the first, having appeared in 1995, 2003 and 2007, but Tobin Heath, Ali Krieger, Carli Lloyd, Alex Morgan and Megan Rapinoe joined her after appearing in 2011, 2015 and 2019.

On top of the world

▲ Megan Rapinoe's match-prepared shirt from the 2019 World Cup Final.
FIFA Museum Collection

Thriving rather than wilting under pressure, Megan Rapinoe was showered with gold after her team lifted the World Cup, winning not only the trophy for the top scorer, but the best player as well. It was just reward for a stellar campaign, but the 34-year-old midfielder made an impact off the field in France too. Sporting a shock of purple hair and a devil-may-care attitude, Rapinoe had spoken frankly about the role of gay women in her sport, criticised US President Donald Trump's administration and passionately advocated for equality and support for elite women players. Was USA head coach Jill Ellis ever worried how her co-captain would cope in the spotlight? "Megan was built for these moments, built to be a spokesperson for others," said Ellis shortly after her team's World Cup triumph. "She's incredibly eloquent, speaks from her heart and we need people like that in the game, to be honest, to call things for what they are."

> **We put on the most incredible show that you could ever ask for. We can't do anything more to impress more, to be better ambassadors, to take on more, to play better… It's time to move that conversation forward to the next step.**
>
> MEGAN RAPINOE

12/17

By winning the Final, the USA extended their record World Cup-winning run to 12 games, and took their unbeaten run to 17. They had equalled Norway's then-record run of ten consecutive wins with their quarter-final victory over France.

100

The penalty scored in the Final by Megan Rapinoe was the 100th awarded in the history of the World Cup and the 78th to have been scored. It was only the second awarded in a Final, with the previous one coming in 2007 when Nadine Angerer saved from Marta.

▶ The USA, world champions for a record-extending fourth time.

32

The number of players to have won two World Cups. Twelve Americans joined the list while Jill Ellis became the first coach to win it twice. In 14 games at the finals, she has won 13 matches and drawn one.

233

2020

Against an eerie backdrop of empty stadiums echoing to the shouts of players and coaches, the COVID-19-delayed Tokyo Olympics produced first-time champions in Canada and a gold medal for their evergreen star player Christine Sinclair. A Jessie Fleming penalty saw the Canadians knock out the USA in the semi-finals, while the Final was settled by a dramatic penalty shoot-out. Sweden's Caroline Seger missed a spot kick that would have given her side a first world title before Julia Grosso fired home the winner for Canada.

The COVID Olympics

▼ Japan celebrate beating the USA in the baseball Final at Yokohama's ballpark.

The global COVID-19 pandemic disrupted sport across the world, but nowhere was this more evident than at the Tokyo Olympics. Originally scheduled to take place in July and August 2020, they were eventually staged 12 months later, the first time the Olympics had been held in an odd-numbered year. With stringent COVID-19-related safeguards in place throughout Japan, the Games were contested at empty stadiums or with just a handful of socially distanced spectators. Bermuda, the Philippines and Qatar won their first-ever Olympic golds, while the USA topped the medal table, but the usual sight of athletes having a medal put around their necks was replaced by them picking up their prize from a tray and putting it on themselves. Still, for the vast majority, the spectacle of the Olympic Games is played out on television and Tokyo 2020 provided the usual drama and sporting heroics. Brazil retained their men's football title while Kenya's Eliud Kipchoge became only the third marathon runner to claim successive golds. Baseball made a return to the Games, with Japan beating the USA in the gold medal game, one of 27 golds won by the host nation, the most in their history and the first time that they had featured in the top three of the medal table since 1968.

2020 **Overview**

TOKYO 2020

WOMEN'S OLYMPIC FOOTBALL TOURNAMENT

Story of the qualifiers

The show must go on

Germany were the first Olympic champions since Norway in 2004 not to defend their crown. UEFA again used World Cup placings to fill its slots for Tokyo 2020. The Netherlands claimed a maiden Olympic berth as 2019 World Cup Finalists, while third-placed Sweden qualified for the seventh time. Having been nominated by all four British associations, England took the third European place for Team GB by finishing fourth in France. Africa supplied a debutant for the third straight edition. Zambia reached their first global tournament by edging out favourites Cameroon in the final CAF qualifying round. That left Cameroon needing to beat 2018 CONMEBOL *Copa América Femenina* runners-up Chile in a two-legged play-off. They met a mere three months before the Games began, with Chile advancing after a 2-1 win and goalless draw. Joining their fellow South Americans were two-time silver medallists Brazil, who qualified for their seventh Olympics as continental champions. New Zealand grabbed the sole Oceania place by winning the 2018 OFC Women's Nations Cup. Asian qualifying took longer to settle, hampered by COVID-19-enforced postponements, venue changes and quarantine rules. Australia were Tokyo-bound after back-to-back play-off victories over Vietnam. A year later, China took the second AFC ticket after a thrilling 4-3 aggregate win over South Korea. As hosts, former silver medallists Japan were assured of a fifth Olympic appearance. Four-time champions the USA and double bronze medallists Canada dominated Concacaf's qualifiers.

▲ Empty (or near empty) stadiums greeted the 12 teams that qualified for the Women's Olympic Football Tournament Tokyo 2020.

Group stage

GROUP E	GROUP F	GROUP G
GBR 2-0 CHI	CHN 0-5 BRA	SWE 3-0 USA
JPN 1-1 CAN	ZAM 3-10 NED	AUS 2-1 NZL
CHI 1-2 CAN	CHN 4-4 ZAM	SWE 4-2 AUS
JPN 0-1 GBR	NED 3-3 BRA	NZL 1-6 USA
CHI 0-1 JPN	NED 8-2 CHN	NZL 0-2 SWE
CAN 1-1 GBR	BRA 1-0 ZAM	USA 0-0 AUS

	W	D	L	+	−	PTS
GBR	2	1	0	4	1	7
CAN	1	2	0	4	3	5
JPN	1	1	1	2	2	4
CHI	0	0	3	1	5	0

	W	D	L	+	−	PTS
NED	2	1	0	21	8	7
BRA	2	1	0	9	3	7
ZAM	0	1	2	7	15	1
CHN	0	1	2	6	17	1

	W	D	L	+	−	PTS
SWE	3	0	0	9	2	9
USA	1	1	1	6	4	4
AUS	1	1	1	4	5	4
NZL	0	0	3	2	10	0

Knockout stages

QUARTER-FINAL	QUARTER-FINAL	QUARTER-FINAL	QUARTER-FINAL
CAN 0-0 (4-3) BRA	GBR 3-4 AET AUS	SWE 3-1 JPN	NED 2-2 (2-4) USA

SEMI-FINAL	SEMI-FINAL
USA 0-1 CAN	AUS 0-1 SWE

BRONZE MEDAL MATCH

AUS 3-4 USA

GOLD MEDAL MATCH

SWE 1-1 (2-3) CAN

Overview 2020

12 TEAMS: AUS, BRA, CAN, CHI, CHN, GBR, JPN, NED, NZL, SWE, USA, ZAM

DUE TO STRICT COVID-19 PROTOCOLS, MATCHES WERE PLAYED EITHER BEHIND CLOSED DOORS (BCD) OR WITH A VERY LIMITED NUMBER OF SOCIALLY DISTANCED SPECTATORS.

CANADA WINNERS
SWE SECOND
USA THIRD

TOP OF THE MEDAL TABLE

USA	39	41	33
CHINA PR	38	32	19
JAPAN	27	14	17
GREAT BRITAIN	22	20	22
ROC	20	28	23
AUSTRALIA	17	7	22

26 MATCHES PLAYED
42 YELLOW CARDS
3 RED CARDS

101 GOALS
3.88 AVERAGE GOALS PER MATCH
CONEXT 21 OFFICIAL MATCH BALL

Host cities and stadiums
The 2002 legacy

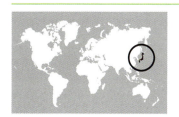

Five of the six stadiums used for the Women's Olympic Football Tournament had hosted matches during the 2002 FIFA World Cup.

International Stadium Yokohama was once again the setting for a major global Final – two, in fact, as it hosted both the women's and men's showpiece events.

The Final had been due to kick off at 11:00 at the Tokyo Stadium but was moved to 21:00 in Yokohama (the most suitable venue available at that time) owing to the intense heat.

SAPPORO — **SAPPORO DOME**
RIFU — **MIYAGI STADIUM**
SAITAMA — **SAITAMA STADIUM 2002**
KASHIMA — **IBARAKI KASHIMA STADIUM**
YOKOHAMA — **INTERNATIONAL STADIUM YOKOHAMA**
TOKYO — **TOKYO STADIUM**

× **10**

Top scorer

Vivianne Miedema NED

Second Place: Barbra Banda ZAM, Sam Kerr AUS & Ellen White GBR ×**6**

Group stage 2020

◀ Caroline Weir, in blue here against Chile, was one of two Scots in the Great Britain squad, while Sophie Ingle was the team's first-ever player from Wales.

The hosts' late show

A poacher's goal from 32-year-old Ellen White got this record high-scoring tournament off the mark. Debutants Chile battled, but after a White volley made it 2-0, Sapporo's empty stands reverberated to Team GB's cheers. Mana Iwabuchi's exquisite equaliser saved Japan's blushes against Canada, but the plaudits went to Christine Sinclair for a goal on her 300th international appearance and the injured Stephanie Labbé for saving Mina Tanaka's penalty before departing in agony. Keeper, captain and newly crowned French league champion Christiane Endler celebrated turning 30 the day before Chile's second-ever meeting with Canada. Janine Beckie's brace spoiled the party, but it was a nervy finish after Karen Araya bagged Chile's maiden Olympic goal. Hege Riise's Great Britain celebrated a knockout spot after a looping White header overcame Asako Takakura's Japan, a day shy of 25 years after the coaches faced off as players at Atlanta 1996. Having knocked Team GB out of London 2012, there was history between Canada and Great Britain too, but neither prevailed in Kashima and English coach Bev Priestman's *Canucks* were through. Japan joined them as one of the two best third-placed teams, a late Tanaka goal settling a winner-takes-all clash with Chile.

Group E

	W	D	L	+	-	PTS
GBR	2	1	0	4	1	7
CAN	1	2	0	4	3	5
JPN	1	1	1	2	2	4
CHI	0	0	3	1	5	0

187/300

Christine Sinclair had scored on her 200th cap and the 38-year-old hit the target against Japan on her 300th – her 187th international strike.

◀ Japan's Mina Tanaka reacts to having her penalty saved in the match against Canada.

Sapporo Dome, Sapporo
21.07.2021, 16:30, **BCD**

GREAT BRITAIN 2-0 **CHILE**
White (2) 18 72

Salima Mukansanga RWA
Bernadettar Kwimbira MWI & Mary Njoroge KEN
Abdulla Al Marri QAT

GBR • 1 Ellie **Roebuck** ENG - 2 Lucy **Bronze** ENG, 5 Steph **Houghton** (c) ENG, 14 Millie **Bright** ENG, 12 Rachel **Daly** ENG - 4 Keira **Walsh** ENG (6 Sophie **Ingle** WAL 69), 11 Caroline **Weir** SCO (18 Jill **Scott** ENG 90) - 17 Georgia **Stanway** ENG, 8 Kim **Little** SCO (20 Ella **Toone** ENG 90+2), 15 Lauren **Hemp** ENG (7 Nikita **Parris** ENG 69) - 9 Ellen **White** ENG. *Hege Riise NOR*

CHI • 1 Christiane **Endler** (c) - 6 Nayadet **López Opazo** (16 Rosario **Balmaceda** 81), 14 Daniela **Pardo**, 3 Carla **Guerrero**, 18 Camila **Sáez** - 15 Daniela **Zamora**, 8 Karen **Araya**, 11 Yessenia **López** (20 Francisca **Mardones** 70), 4 Francisca **Lara**, 10 Yanara **Aedo** (7 Yenny **Acuña** 78) - 9 María José **Urrutia**. *José Letelier*

Sapporo Dome, Sapporo
21.07.2021, 19:30, **BCD**

JAPAN 1-1 **CANADA**
Iwabuchi 83   Sinclair 6
(Tanaka penalty saved 53)

Edina Alves Batista BRA
Neuza Back BRA & Mónica Amboya ECU
Wagner Reway BRA

JPN • 1 Sakiko **Ikeda** - 2 Risa **Shimizu**, 4 Saki **Kumagai** (c), 5 Moeka **Minami**, 17 Nanami **Kitamura** - 13 Yuzuho **Shiokoshi** (12 Jun **Endo** 62), 8 Narumi **Miura**, 7 Emi **Nakajima** (6 Hina **Sugita** 76), 14 Yui **Hasegawa** (15 Yuka **Momiki** 89) - 9 Yuika **Sugasawa** (11 Mina **Tanaka** 46), 10 Mana **Iwabuchi**. *Asako Takakura*

CAN • 1 Stephanie **Labbé** 🟨 53 (18 Kailen **Sheridan** 58) - 10 Ashley **Lawrence**, 3 Kadeisha **Buchanan**, 4 Shelina **Zadorsky**, 2 Allysha **Chapman** - 11 Desiree **Scott**, 5 **Quinn** (6 Deanne **Rose** 72) - 15 Nichelle **Prince** (9 Adriana **Leon** 84), 17 Jessie **Fleming**, 16 Janine **Beckie** - 12 Christine **Sinclair** (c) (13 Évelyne **Viens** 83). *Bev Priestman ENG*

Sapporo Dome, Sapporo
24.07.2021, 16:30, **BCD**

CHILE 1-2 **CANADA**
Araya 57p   Beckie (2) 38 47
              (Beckie penalty missed 20)

Esther Staubli SUI
Katrin Rafalski GER & Susanne Küng SUI
Muhammad Taqi SGP

CHI • Endler (c) - Balmaceda, Pardo 🟨 19 (19 Javiera **Grez** 90+3), Guerrero, Sáez - Zamora, Araya, López 🟨 64 (Acuña 85), Lara, Aedo - Urrutia. *Letelier*

CAN • Sheridan - Lawrence, Buchanan, Zadorsky, 8 Jayde **Riviere** - Scott 🟨 79, 7 Julia **Grosso** (Quinn 61) - Beckie, Fleming, Prince (Rose 61) - Sinclair (c). *Priestman ENG*

Sapporo Dome, Sapporo
24.07.2021, 19:30, **BCD**

JAPAN 0-1 **GREAT BRITAIN**
                White 74

Anastasia Pustovoitova RUS
Ekaterina Kurochkina RUS & Sanja Rođak-Karšić CRO
Bibiana Steinhaus GER

JPN • 18 Ayaka **Yamashita** 🟨 79 - Shimizu, Kumagai (c), Minami, 16 Asato **Miyagawa** - Shiokoshi (Momiki 55), Nakajima (Iwabuchi 81), Sugita, Hasegawa - 20 Honoka **Hayashi** 🟨 30 (Miura 67), Tanaka (Endo 67). *Takakura*

GBR • Roebuck - Bronze, Houghton (c), 16 Leah **Williamson** ENG, 3 Demi **Stokes** ENG - Walsh, Ingle (Weir 59) - Parris (Daly 75), Little (Scott 88), Hemp (Stanway 88) - White. *Riise NOR*

Miyagi Stadium, Rifu
27.07.2021, 20:00, **1,326**

CHILE 0-1 **JAPAN**
                Tanaka 78

Melissa Borjas HON
Shirley Perelló HON & Mary Blanco COL
Paweł Raczkowski POL

CHI • Endler (c) - Pardo (Mardones 75), Guerrero, Sáez - Balmaceda (17 Javiera **Toro** 46), Araya, López (13 Fernanda **Pinilla** 83), Lara, Aedo (Acuña 83) - Urrutia, Zamora (Grez 55). *Letelier*

JPN • Yamashita - Shimizu, Kumagai (c) 🟨 90, 3 Saori **Takarada**, Kitamura - Hasegawa (21 Momoka **Kinoshita** 65), Miura 🟨 60 (Nakajima 83), Hayashi (Endo 54), Sugita - Iwabuchi, Sugasawa (Tanaka 46). *Takakura*

Ibaraki Kashima Stadium, Kashima
27.07.2021, 20:00, **BCD**

CANADA 1-1 **GREAT BRITAIN**
Leon 55   Prince OG 85

Kateryna Monzul UKR
Lucie Ratajová CZE & Maryna Striletska UKR
Mahmoud Mohamed Ashour EGY

CAN • Labbé - Riviere 🟨 24, 14 Vanessa **Gilles**, Buchanan (c), Lawrence (21 Gabrielle **Carle** 80) - 20 Sophie **Schmidt**, Quinn (Grosso 67) - Rose (19 Jordyn **Huitema** 46), Beckie (Fleming 46), Leon - Viens (Prince 54). *Priestman ENG*

GBR • Roebuck - Bronze, Williamson, Bright, Stokes - Ingle (c) (10 Fran **Kirby** ENG 77), Weir - Stanway, Scott (Little 63), Daly (White 63) - Parris. *Riise NOR*

2020 Group stage

Miyagi Stadium, Rifu
21.07.2021, 17:00, **1,645**

CHINA PR 0-5 **BRAZIL**

Marta (2) 9 73, Debinha 22, Andressa Alves 83p, Beatriz 89

🏁 Kateryna Monzul UKR
⚑ Lucie Ratajová CZE & Maryna Striletska UKR
📺 Guillermo Cuadra Fernández ESP

CHN • 12 Peng Shimeng - 17 Luo Guiping, 13 Yang Lina, 16 Wang Xiaoxue, 2 Li Mengwen - 7 Wang Shuang, 8 Wang Yan (18 Wurigumula 32), 4 Li Qingtong, 6 Zhang Xin (20 Xiao Yuyi 83) - 11 Wang Shanshan (c), 9 Miao Siwen (14 Liu Jing 83). *Jia Xiuquan*

BRA • 1 Bárbara - 13 Bruna Benites, 4 Rafaelle, 6 Tamires - 7 Duda (21 Andressa Alves 58), 8 Formiga (5 Julia 71), 17 Andressinha, 9 Debinha - 16 Beatriz, 10 Marta (12 Ludmila 82). *Pia Sundhage SWE*

Miyagi Stadium, Rifu
21.07.2021, 20:00, **1,822**

ZAMBIA 3-10 **NETHERLANDS**

B Banda (3) 19 82 83

Miedema (4) 9 14 29 60, Martens (2) 13 37, Van de Sanden 44, Roord 64, Beerensteyn 75, Pelova 80

🏁 Laura Fortunato ARG
⚑ Mariana de Almeida ARG & Mary Blanco COL
📺 Mauro Vigliano ARG

ZAM • 16 Hazel Nali - 8 Margaret Belemu (20 Esther Mukwasa 87), 5 Anita Mulenga (15 Agness Musesa 73), 3 Lushomo Mweemba, 4 Esther Siamfuko 🟨 66 - 14 Ireen Lungu, 6 Mary Wilombe - 12 Avell Chitundu, 10 Grace Chanda, 11 Barbra Banda (c) - 9 Hellen Mubanga (7 Ochumba Lubandji 72). *Bruce Mwape*

NED • 1 Sari van Veenendaal (c) - 17 Dominique Janssen, 3 Stefanie van der Gragt (2 Lynn Wilms 60), 4 Aniek Nouwen (15 Kika van Es 85 🟥 90), 5 Merel van Dongen - 10 Danielle van de Donk (13 Victoria Pelova 72), 14 Jackie Groenen, 6 Jill Roord - 7 Shanice van de Sanden (19 Renate Jansen 72), 9 Vivianne Miedema (18 Lineth Beerensteyn 60), 11 Lieke Martens. *Sarina Wiegman*

Miyagi Stadium, Rifu
24.07.2021, 17:00, **2,212**

CHINA PR 4-4 **ZAMBIA**

Wang Shuang (4) 6 21 23 83p

Kundananji 15, B Banda (3) 42p 46 68

🏁 Melissa Borjas HON
⚑ Shirley Perelló HON & Chantal Boudreau CAN
📺 Abdulkadir Bitigen TUR

CHN • Peng Shimeng - Li Mengwen, Li Qingtong 🟥 86, Wang Xiaoxue, Luo Guiping - Wang Shuang, Yang Lina, Miao Siwen (Liu Jing 65), Zhang Xin (Xiao Yuyi 65) - 15 Yang Man (Wurigumula 33), Wang Shanshan (c). *Jia Xiuquan*

ZAM • Nali - 17 Racheal Kundananji, Musesa, Mweemba 🟨 83, Siamfuko (Belemu 61) - Lungu, Wilombe (13 Martha Tembo 37) - Chitundu, Chanda, Lubandji (Mubanga 76) - B Banda. *Mwape*

Miyagi Stadium, Rifu
24.07.2021, 20:00, **2,621**

NETHERLANDS 3-3 **BRAZIL**

Miedema (2) 2 58, Janssen 79

Debinha 16, Marta 64p, Ludmila 67

🏁 Kate Jacewicz AUS
⚑ Kim Kyong Min KOR & Lee Seul Gi KOR
📺 Erick Miranda MEX

NED • Van Veenendaal (c) - Wilms, Van der Gragt 🟨 64, Nouwen, Janssen - Roord 🟨 72, Groenen, Van de Donk - Van de Sanden (Beerensteyn 66), Miedema (Pelova 88), Martens. *Wiegman*

BRA • Bárbara - Bruna Benites, Érika, Rafaelle, Tamires - Duda (Andressa Alves 46), Formiga (11 Angelina 46), Andressinha, Marta (c) (15 Geyse 74) - Beatriz (Ludmila 46 🟨 78), Debinha. *Sundhage SWE*

International Stadium Yokohama, Yokohama
27.07.2021, 20:30, **BCD**

NETHERLANDS 8-2 **CHINA PR**

Van de Sanden 11, Beerensteyn (2) 37 45+2, Martens (2) 46 70, Miedema (2) 65 76, Pelova 71

Wang Shanshan 28, Wang Yanwen 69

🏁 Salima Mukansanga RWA
⚑ Bernadettar Kwimbira MWI & Mary Njorge KEN
📺 Benoît Millot FRA

NED • Van Veenendaal (c) - Wilms (Van Es 46), Janssen, Nouwen (21 Anouk Dekker 76), Van Dongen - Roord (Pelova 46), Groenen, Van de Donk (Miedema 62) - Van de Sanden (Jansen 46), Beerensteyn, Martens. *Wiegman*

CHN • Peng Shimeng - Li Mengwen, 3 Lin Yuping 🟨 30, Wang Xiaoxue, Luo Guiping (19 Wang Ying 27 🟨 82) - Wang Shuang, Yang Lina, Wang Yan 🟨 44 (Liu Jing 59), Zhang Xin - Wang Shanshan (c), Xiao Yuyi (10 Wang Yanwen 59). *Jia Xiuquan*

Saitama Stadium 2002, Saitama
27.07.2021, 20:30, **BCD**

BRAZIL 1-0 **ZAMBIA**

Andressa Alves 19

🏁 Yoshimi Yamashita JPN
⚑ Naomi Teshirogi JPN & Makoto Bozono JPN
📺 Tiago Martins POR

BRA • Bárbara - 19 Letícia Santos, 2 Poliana (Bruna Benites 65), Rafaelle, 14 Jucinara - Andressa Alves (Debinha 81), Formiga (Julia 46), Angelina 🟨 78, Marta (c) (Duda 46) - Beatriz (20 Gio Queiroz 28), Ludmila (Geyse 65). *Sundhage SWE*

ZAM • Nali (22 Ngambo Musole 18) - Belemu, Musesa, Mweemba 🟨 14, Tembo - Chanda, Lungu - Chitundu (18 Vast Phiri 18 🟨 45+8), B Banda (c), Kundananji (19 Evarine Katongo 90+3) - Lubandji. *Mwape*

Group F

Dutch in flying form

	W	D	L	+	-	PTS
NED	2	1	0	21	8	7
BRA	2	1	0	9	3	7
ZAM	0	1	2	7	15	1
CHN	0	1	2	6	17	1

Records tumbled in a group that set these Games alight and those few fans allowed into the Miyagi Stadium witnessed an historic milestone when 35-year-old Marta put two past China to become the first player to score at five consecutive Olympics. Germany legend Birgit Prinz's 2004 record tally of four goals in one game was finally matched too, with Dutch striker Vivianne Miedema and Chinese playmaker Wang Shuang both netting quartets against first-timers Zambia. Miedema delivered her four in a women's Olympic record 10-3 scoreline, Wang in a 4-4 draw that included a disallowed goal, two penalties and a late red card for the Chinese. With three in both contests, Zambia's captain Barbra Banda – aged just 21 at the time – etched her name into Olympic history as the first woman to hit back-to-back hat-tricks and her team celebrated with a joyous "penguin dance" by the corner flag. A stylish Dominique Janssen equaliser capped a six-goal thriller between the Netherlands and Brazil. After a match-ending injury to first-choice goalkeeper Hazel Nali and an early red card, ten-player Zambia concluded their never-say-die debut with pride in rainy Saitama, beaten only by Brazilian Andressa Alves's free kick. They battled, but eight-time Asian champions China were no match for European title holders the Netherlands, an 8-2 defeat ending the former silver medallists' sixth Olympic campaign.

▶ Barbra Banda's shirt from Tokyo 2020, where she made history with back-to-back hat-tricks. *FIFA Museum Collection*

▶▶ Brazil captain Marta celebrates the opening goal against China. She scored twice more at the tournament to reach 13 Olympic goals, one behind compatriot Cristiane, the record holder.

43

Playing 25 years to the day since her Olympic debut, two-time silver medallist Formiga overtook compatriot Meg as the competition's oldest-ever player at the age of 43. The Brazilian also became the first athlete in a team sport to feature in seven editions.

▶ A jubilant Zambia perform their unique penguin dance after taking a 4-3 lead against China. They missed out on a win, however, when the Chinese equalised late on in the highest-scoring draw in women's Olympic history.

Group G

◀ Stina Blackstenius doubles Sweden's advantage in their 3-0 victory against the USA, bringing the Americans' record 15-match unbeaten run at the Olympics to a halt.

Sweden in fine form

Silver medallists at Rio 2016, Sweden signalled their intent in Tokyo with a blistering start, Stina Blackstenius and Lina Hurtig scoring in a 3-0 romp over the USA – the four-time champions' biggest loss on this stage yet. Australia laid their demons from three previous opening-day defeats to rest, old foes New Zealand beaten 2-1 as Tameka Yallop scored her first international goal in three years and Sam Kerr ended a five-game drought. Gabi Rennie gave the *Ferns* hope, netting with her first touch on her debut, but they were unable to salvage a point. On day two, Rennie's fellow U-17 World Cup 2018 bronze-medal winner, Anna Leat, battled to shut out the Americans on her Olympic bow. One of six veterans from their London 2012 quarter-final loss to the USA, Betsy Hassett scored late on to keep New Zealand in the chase. But with First Lady Jill Biden looking on and two own goals helping them along, American pride was restored as they won 6-1. Sweden were already through after a comeback against Australia, Hedvig Lindahl in flying form at her fifth Olympics to deny Kerr the chance of a hat-trick from the spot. A goalless stalemate saw the USA and Australia progress, but New Zealand finished pointless for the first time, Tom Sermanni's side rallying against Sweden but beaten by Anna Anvegård and Madelen Janogy's aerial power.

3
Sweden's 3-0 victory over the USA was only the third group game the Americans had lost at either the World Cup or the Olympics. The first came at the Beijing 2008 Olympics against Norway, while the second was against Sweden at the 2011 World Cup in Germany.

◀ Australia's Caitlin Foord battles for the ball with New Zealand's Daisy Cleverley (left) and Katie Bowen (right) in the first trans-Tasman encounter at the Olympics or World Cup.

	W	D	L	+	–	PTS
SWE	3	0	0	9	2	9
USA	1	1	1	6	4	4
AUS	1	1	1	4	5	4
NZL	0	0	3	2	10	0

Tokyo Stadium, Tokyo
21.07.2021, 17:30, **BCD**

SWEDEN 3-0 USA

Blackstenius (2) 25 54,
Hurtig 72

Yoshimi Yamashita JPN
Naomi Teshirogi JPN & Makoto Bozono JPN
Paweł Raczkowski POL

SWE • 1 Hedvig **Lindahl** - 4 Hanna **Glas**, 13 Amanda **Ilestedt**, 14 Nathalie **Björn**, 2 Jonna **Andersson** (20 Julia **Roddar** 88) - 16 Filippa **Angeldahl** (5 Hanna **Bennison** 75), 9 Kosovare **Asllani**, 17 Caroline **Seger** (c) - 10 Sofia **Jakobsson** (7 Madelen **Janogy** 75), 11 Stina **Blackstenius** (8 Lina **Hurtig** 63), 18 Fridolina **Rolfö** (15 Olivia **Schough** 63). *Peter Gerhardsson*

USA • 1 Alyssa **Naeher** - 5 Kelley **O'Hara**, 17 Abby **Dahlkemper**, 4 Becky **Sauerbrunn** (c), 2 Crystal **Dunn** (12 Tierna **Davidson** 80) - 16 Rose **Lavelle** (6 Kristie **Mewis** 80), 9 Lindsey **Horan**, 3 Samantha **Mewis** (8 Julie **Ertz** 46) - 11 Christen **Press**, 13 Alex **Morgan** (10 Carli **Lloyd** 46), 7 Tobin **Heath** (15 Megan **Rapinoe** 64). *Vlatko Andonovski*

Tokyo Stadium, Tokyo
21.07.2021, 20:30, **BCD**

AUSTRALIA 2-1 NEW ZEALAND

Yallop 20, Kerr 33 | Rennie 90+1

Lucila Venegas MEX
Mayte Chávez MEX & Enedina Caudillo MEX
Andrés Cunha URU

AUS • 1 Lydia **Williams** - 12 Ellie **Carpenter**, 4 Clare **Polkinghorne**, 7 Steph **Catley** - 16 Hayley **Raso** (14 Alanna **Kennedy** 83), 10 Emily **van Egmond**, 5 Aivi **Luik**, 13 Tameka **Yallop** (3 Kyra **Cooney-Cross** 75) - 17 Kyah **Simon** (11 Mary **Fowler** 75), 2 Sam **Kerr** (c), 9 Caitlin **Foord** (15 Emily **Gielnik** 90). *Tony Gustavsson SWE*

NZL • 1 Erin **Nayler** - 3 Anna **Green** (13 Paige **Satchell** 69), 8 Abby **Erceg**, 5 Meikayla **Moore** - 4 C.J. **Bott** ■ 71 (9 Gabi **Rennie** 88), 14 Katie **Bowen** ■ 81, 2 Ria **Percival**, 7 Ali **Riley** (c) - 12 Betsy **Hassett**, 17 Hannah **Wilkinson**, 11 Olivia **Chance** (15 Daisy **Cleverley** 68). *Tom Sermanni SCO*

Saitama Stadium 2002, Saitama
24.07.2021, 17:30, **BCD**

SWEDEN 4-2 AUSTRALIA

Rolfö (2) 20 62, Hurtig 51,
Blackstenius 81 | Kerr (2) 36 47
(Kerr penalty saved 69)

Edina Alves Batista BRA
Neuza Back BRA & Mónica Amboya ECU
Tiago Martins POR

SWE • Lindahl - Glas (Björn 46), Ilestedt, 6 Magdalena **Eriksson**, Andersson - Angeldahl (Bennison 78), Seger (c) - Jakobsson (Schough 78), Asllani, Rolfö (Janogy 87) - Hurtig (Blackstenius 59). *Gerhardsson*

AUS • 18 Teagan **Micah** - Carpenter, Polkinghorne, Luik (Kennedy 63) - Raso (Fowler 80), Van Egmond, Yallop (Cooney-Cross 63), Catley - Simon (Gielnik 86), Kerr (c), Foord. *Gustavsson SWE*

Saitama Stadium 2002, Saitama
24.07.2021, 20:30, **BCD**

NEW ZEALAND 1-6 USA

Hassett 72 | Lavelle 8, Horan 44, Erceg OG 62, Press 80, Morgan 87, Bott OG 90+3

Stéphanie Frappart FRA
Manuela Nicolosi FRA & Michelle O'Neill IRL
Marco Guida ITA

NZL • 18 Anna **Leat** - Bott, Moore, Erceg, Cleverley (Rennie 79) - Hassett (10 Annalie **Longo** 86), Percival, Bowen, Riley (c) - Wilkinson, Chance (Satchell 64). *Sermanni SCO*

USA • Naeher - 14 Emily **Sonnett**, Dahlkemper, Davidson, Dunn (20 Casey **Krueger** 83) - Lavelle (S Mewis 67), Ertz, Horan (19 Catarina **Macario** 83) - Heath, Lloyd (Morgan 73), Rapinoe (Press 67). *Andonovski*

Miyagi Stadium, Rifu
27.07.2021, 17:00, **884**

NEW ZEALAND 0-2 SWEDEN

Anvegård 17, Janogy 29

Laura Fortunato ARG
Mariana de Almeida ARG & Chantal Boudreau CAN
Mauro Vigliano ARG

NZL • Nayler - Bott, Moore, Erceg, Riley (c) - Cleverley (6 Claudia **Bunge** 88), Percival ■ 67 - Hassett, Bowen, 16 Emma **Rolston** (Satchell 60) - Wilkinson (Rennie 85). *Sermanni SCO*

SWE • 12 Jennifer **Falk** - Roddar, 3 Emma **Kullberg**, Eriksson (c) (Ilestedt 46), Andersson (Björn 46) - Janogy, Angeldahl (Seger 72), Bennison, Schough (Hurtig 65) - 19 Anna **Anvegård** (Asllani 86), 21 Rebecka **Blomqvist**. *Gerhardsson*

Ibaraki Kashima Stadium, Kashima
27.07.2021, 17:00, **BCD**

USA 0-0 AUSTRALIA

Anastasia Pustovoitova RUS
Ekaterina Kurochkina RUS & Sanja Rođak-Karšić CRO
Adil Zourak MAR

USA • Naeher - O'Hara, Sauerbrunn (c), Davidson, Dunn - Lavelle ■ 72 (K Mewis 88), Ertz, S Mewis (Horan 65) - Press (21 Lynn **Williams** 74), Morgan (Lloyd 74), Rapinoe ■ 38 (Heath 65). *Andonovski*

AUS • Micah - Carpenter, Kennedy, Polkinghorne - Yallop, Simon (Gielnik 84), 6 Chloe **Logarzo** (Cooney-Cross 62 ■ 69), Catley - Van Egmond, Kerr (c), Fowler. *Gustavsson SWE*

2020 Quarter-finals

▲ Goalkeeper Stephanie Labbé is mobbed by her Canada team-mates after her two saves in the shoot-out knock out Brazil.

◀ Brazil's Ludmila, in yellow, is challenged by Canada's Vanessa Gilles in the quarter-final between the two teams.

Brazil pay the penalty

Miyagi Stadium, Rifu
30.07.2021, 17:00, **3,403**

CANADA 0-0 **BRAZIL**
AET
4-3 PSO

Sinclair ✘ (saved) Marta ✔ Fleming ✔ Debinha ✔ Lawrence ✔ Érika ✔ Leon ✔ Andressa Alves ✘ (saved) Gilles ✔ Rafaelle ✘ (saved)

Stéphanie Frappart FRA   Manuela Nicolosi FRA & Michelle O'Neill IRL   Bibiana Steinhaus GER

CAN • Labbé - Lawrence ▌ 90+1, Gilles, Buchanan, Chapman (Riviere 109 ▌ 117) - Fleming, Scott, Quinn (Grosso 63) - Sinclair (c) - Beckie (Leon 105+2), Prince (Rose 63) (Huitema 114). *Priestman ENG*

BRA • Bárbara - Bruna Benites, Érika, Rafaelle, Tamires - Duda ▌ 59 (Andressa Alves 102), Formiga (Angelina 73), Andressinha, Marta (c) - Beatriz (Ludmila 59 ▌ 101), Debinha. *Sundhage SWE*

Two-time silver medallists Brazil were unbeaten in four outings against Canada during head coach Pia Sundhage's two-year tenure. Even so, memories of their pre-"Pia era" Olympic heartache at Canada's hands resonated in Miyagi, with both line-ups featuring six starters from the countries' bronze-medal battle of 2016. Yet, even with Brazil's leading goalscorer Marta and world-record striker Christine Sinclair leading the charge for a mammoth two hours, this time the two sides were in deadlock. A shoot-out inevitably followed and both captains stood up to be counted. Marta cleanly dispatched her spot kick, but Sinclair's had already been athletically batted away by Bárbara. Stephanie Labbé saved the day for Canada, though, the 34-year-old joyously mobbed by weeping team-mates after palming aside low shots from Andressa Alves and Rafaelle. Emotions ran high as Brazil huddled together too, inspirational leader Marta thumping her chest as she passionately consoled players who represented not just the best of Brazil's past, but their future as well.

Breakthrough for the *Matildas*

Ibaraki Kashima Stadium, Kashima
30.07.2021, 18:00, **BCD**

GREAT BRITAIN 3-4 **AUSTRALIA**
AET
White **(3)** 57 65 115   Kennedy 35, Kerr **(2)** 88 106, Fowler 103
(Weir penalty saved 102)

Salima Mukansanga RWA   Bernadettar Kwimbira MWI & Mary Njorge KEN   Benoît Millot FRA

GBR • Roebuck - Bronze ▌ 44 (Stanway 112 ▌ 120+1), Houghton (c), Williamson, Stokes (Bright 58) - Walsh (Ingle 97), Weir - Daly (Kirby 58), Little (Scott 80), Hemp (Parris 96) - White. *Riise NOR*

AUS • Micah - Carpenter, Kennedy, Luik (Gielnik 80) - Raso (Logarzo 88), Van Egmond, Yallop, Catley - Simon ▌ 71 (Fowler 80), Kerr (c) ▌ 26, Foord (Cooney-Cross 80) (Polkinghorne 108). *Gustavsson SWE*

These were unfamiliar global foes, but with eight *Matildas* and most of Team GB competing in England's Women's Super League, there was a familiarity to this clash. So, as the mercury nudged 29°C in Kashima and clubmates and domestic rivals went head-to-head, the 120 minutes that followed were electric. Norway great Hege Riise dug out her Sydney 2000 gold medal to inspire her charges ahead of these Games. Team GB responded with the meanest defence at Tokyo 2020 ahead of the knockout stage. Here, even Alanna Kennedy's breach of Ellie Roebuck's goalmouth was overcome with two trademark Ellen White goals. But WSL champion and top scorer Sam Kerr produced a devastating last-gasp equaliser. Draped in cooling vests to ready themselves for extra time, Team GB knew that they had to dig deep. But after W-League Goalkeeper of the Year Teagan Micah kept out Caroline Weir's penalty, the momentum fully shifted to Australia and teenage substitute Mary Fowler and Kerr swooped to put them in the driving seat, rendering White's third scant consolation for her side. At last the *Matildas* were through to a first semi-final.

▲ Australia's Alanna Kennedy opens the scoring in her side's 4-3 quarter-final victory over Great Britain.

3 Ellen White was the third player to end up on the losing side after scoring a hat-trick in women's Olympic football history after Christine Sinclair for Canada in 2012 and, earlier in this edition, Zambia's Barbra Banda.

▶ Having become Australia's leading Olympic goalscorer with three in the group stage, Sam Kerr celebrates after heading in what proved to be the winning goal in the quarter-finals against Great Britain.

Hosts Japan overpowered

Saitama Stadium 2002, Saitama
30.07.2021, 19:00, **BCD**

SWEDEN 3-1 JAPAN

Eriksson 7, Blackstenius 53, Asllani 68p — Tanaka 23

🧑‍⚖️ Lucila Venegas MEX
🚩 Mayte Chávez MEX & Enedina Caudillo MEX
📺 Mauro Vigliano ARG

SWE • Lindahl - Glas, Ilestedt 🟨 29, Björn, Eriksson - Angeldahl (Bennison 62), Seger - Jakobsson (Janogy 90), Asllani (Andersson 90), Rolfö (Schough 75) - Blackstenius (Hurtig 75). *Gerhardsson*

JPN • Yamashita - Shimizu, Kumagai, Minami, Miyagawa - Hasegawa (Kitamura 82), Nakajima (Hayashi 86), Miura 🟨 38 (Endo 72), Sugita - Iwabuchi, Tanaka. *Takakura*

▶ Amanda Ilestedt (No.13) and Hanna Glas (No.4) rejoice after the final whistle confirms Sweden's 3-1 quarter-final win against Japan.

Buoyed by their arrival in the Olympic Village and fully aware that the days of second chances were over, Japan had talked of leaving everything on the pitch against in-form Sweden – and they did. Asako Takakura's selection was strong in Saitama, with World Cup gold and Olympic silver medallists Saki Kumagai and Mana Iwabuchi, two-time Nadeshiko League player of the year Mina Tanaka and U-20 World Cup 2018 winners Moeka Minami and Asato Miyagawa starting. Sweden drew first blood when Magdalena Eriksson powerfully headed in Fridolina Rolfö's pinpoint cross, but an irresistible spell of possession yielded a Tanaka equaliser. The striker looked to have won a penalty minutes later too until referee Lucila Venegas overturned her initial decision following a VAR review. It was, perhaps, the springboard for Sweden, and Stina Blackstenius's left-footed finish and a cool-as-you-like Kosovare Asllani spot kick on her 152nd cap broke Japanese hearts on their home turf.

5.75

After scoring 23 times, the Netherlands boasted an average of 5.75 goals per match.

USA through by a whisker

International Stadium Yokohama, Yokohama
30.07.2021, 20:00, **BCD**

NETHERLANDS 2-2 USA
AET
2-4 PSO

Miedema (2) 18 54 — S Mewis 28, Williams 31
(Martens penalty saved 81)

Miedema ✖ (saved) Lavelle ✅ Janssen ✅ Morgan ✅ Van der Gragt ✅ Press ✅ Nouwen ✖ (saved) Rapinoe ✅

🧑‍⚖️ Kate Jacewicz AUS 🚩 Kim Kyong Min KOR & Lee Seul Gi KOR 📺 Abdulla Al Marri QAT

NED • Van Veenendaal (c) - Wilms, Van der Gragt, Nouwen, Janssen - Roord (Pelova 97), Groenen, Van de Donk 🟨 90+6 - Van de Sanden (Beerensteyn 63), Miedema, Martens. *Wiegman*

USA • Naeher - O'Hara 🟨 115, Dahlkemper, Sauerbrunn (c), Dunn - Horan 🟨 77, Ertz, S Mewis (Lavelle 57) - Heath (Rapinoe 64), Lloyd (Morgan 57), Williams (Press 57). *Andonovski*

Storms rumbled above Yokohama before this rematch of the 2019 World Cup Final, but it was merely a drum roll for the drama to come. So far, it was four-time champions the USA who had blown hot and cold, while debutants the Netherlands had breezed along. With 21 goals in three group matches, they had even smashed the USA's record of 16 over six games at London 2012. Already on eight, Vivianne Miedema marked her 100th cap with two more. The second strike, a long-range drive, cancelled out quick first-half goals from Sam Mewis and Lynn Williams. Then came Alyssa Naeher's turn to shine, the keeper guessing Lieke Martens' spot-kick intentions with nine minutes remaining. Hearts were in mouths in extra time as one Dutch and two USA efforts were ruled offside. After Naeher denied Miedema and Aniek Nouwen in the shoot-out, Megan Rapinoe dispatched the Netherlands and their departing head coach Sarina Wiegman.

▲ The USA's Lynn Williams is kept under close watch by Jackie Groenen and Aniek Nouwen in the quarter-finals against the Netherlands.

▶ Lieke Martens misses the chance to put the Netherlands 3-2 up when her penalty is saved by the USA's Alyssa Naeher.

2020 Semi-finals

Historic triumph for Canada

Ibaraki Kashima Stadium, Kashima
2.08.2021, 17:00, **BCD**

USA 🇺🇸 0-1 🇨🇦 CANADA

Fleming 75p

Kateryna Monzul UKR · Lucie Ratajová CZE & Maryna Striletska UKR · Paweł Raczkowski POL

USA • Naeher (18 Adrianna **Franch** 30) - O'Hara ■ 32 (S Mewis 80), Sauerbrunn, Davidson, Dunn - Lavelle, Ertz, Horan - Heath (Rapinoe 60), Morgan (Lloyd 61), Williams (Press 60). *Andonovski*

CAN • Labbé - Lawrence, Gilles, Buchanan, Chapman - Fleming, Scott, Quinn (Grosso 60) - Sinclair (c) (Huitema 87) - Beckie, Prince (Rose 60) (Leon 90). *Priestman ENG*

▲▲ Jessie Fleming converts the winning goal for Canada from the spot in their semi-final against the USA.

▲ Canada captain Christine Sinclair consoles Lindsey Horan after the Canadians beat the USA to qualify for the Final for the first time.

Head coach Bev Priestman called on Canada to "change the colour of the medal" at Tokyo 2020 after consecutive bronzes, and they knew that victory in Kashima would do exactly that. Their opponents had other ideas – and an historical edge. Unbeaten in 20 years against their North American rivals, among their 51 victories, the USA could count two extra-time Olympic classics. While those knockouts were epic, this 62nd meeting was more a question of who would blink first. Priestman started four of her six centurions, Vlatko Andonovski would play all ten of his over the 90 minutes and shot-stopper Stephanie Labbé had to look lively to deny Carli Lloyd, Julie Ertz and Lindsey Horan. By full time, the USA were on 60 per cent possession, with 13 shots to Canada's three, but ultimately Jessie Fleming's 75th-minute penalty kick made the difference. Seven-cap Adrianna Franch, on earlier for the injured Alyssa Naeher, had guessed the right way, but 23-year-old Fleming's shot was too powerful to be kept out. The USA still had bronze to chase, but this was their third goalless match at these Games, more than in their six previous campaigns combined. "We just didn't have it today," reflected Megan Rapinoe afterwards. "It's a bitter one to swallow."

Sweden into the Final – again

International Stadium Yokohama, Yokohama
2.08.2021, 20:00, **BCD**

AUSTRALIA 🇦🇺 0-1 🇸🇪 SWEDEN

Rolfö 46

Melissa Borjas HON · Shirley Perelló HON & Enedina Caudillo MEX · Nicolás Gallo COL

AUS • Micah - Carpenter ■ 90+6, Kennedy, Catley - Raso (Gielnik 84), Van Egmond, Logarzo (Cooney-Cross 69), Yallop (Polkinghorne 69) - Simon (Fowler 69), Kerr (c), Foord (21 Laura **Brock** 90+1). *Gustavsson SWE*

SWE • Lindahl - Glas, Ilestedt, Björn, Eriksson - Jakobsson (Andersson 90+1), Angeldahl (Bennison 73), Asllani, Seger (c), Rolfö - Blackstenius (Hurtig 90+4). *Gerhardsson*

This was becoming familiar territory for Sweden, who had now notched up three Olympic semi-finals in their history. By reaching their first, Australia were writing a new chapter in theirs. It was the kind of legacy Swede Tony Gustavsson had talked up when he was appointed *Matildas* head coach in September 2020, but had been hard to envisage from the outside looking in after an initial run of big-name friendly losses. Five weeks spent together before the Games had, though, bedded in four youngsters while reacquainting a tight group of veterans after a pandemic-induced 13 months apart. And while they stared down the barrel of a dismal record of two wins in 14 major tournament meetings with European sides before Tokyo 2020, their extra-time quarter-final thriller with Team GB had filled Australia with belief. Remarkably, Sweden had only ever won seven times across six previous Olympics, but with 12 goals in four victories at Tokyo 2020, Peter Gerhardsson's dynamic squad were flying. They were on cloud nine in Yokohama when Fridolina Rolfö pounced with an opportunistic finish and match-winning saves from Hedvig Lindahl edged them into the Final. It was agony for Australia, who had seen a Sam Kerr strike ruled out before the break, but afterwards the skipper rallied to focus on bronze, declaring: "Now is the time."

▶ Sweden's Fridolina Rolfö jumps for joy after scoring the only goal of the game against Australia.

5

For the fifth Olympics in a row, a Swede had led their team to the semi-finals, but this was the first time coaches with the same nationality had met in the final four.

▶ Magdalena Eriksson jostles with Kyah Simon, who became the first Indigenous *Matilda* to reach a century of caps when she faced Sweden in the semi-finals.

2020 Bronze Medal Match

Ibaraki Kashima Stadium, Kashima
5.08.2021, 17:00, **BCD**

AUSTRALIA 3-4 **USA**

Kerr 17, Foord 54, Gielnik 90   Rapinoe (2) 8 21, Lloyd (2) 45+1 51

Laura Fortunato ARG Mariana de Almeida ARG & Mary Blanco COL VAR Mauro Vigliano ARG

10/4

Carli Lloyd had scored the deciding goal in the gold medal game at the 2008 and 2012 Olympics and her brace in her 312th match for the USA clinched a first-ever bronze. She was the first USA player to score at four different Olympics, notching ten times overall – a record for the USA.

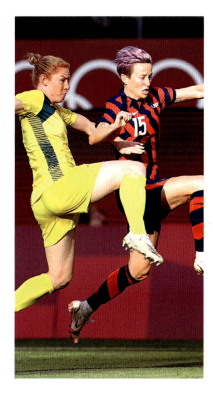

▶ Australia's Clare Polkinghorne (in yellow) battles for possession with Megan Rapinoe of the USA.

▲ Megan Rapinoe, out of the picture, scores direct from a corner. This *gol olimpico* was the first of seven goals as the USA beat Australia 4-3 to claim bronze and was the second time Rapinoe had scored straight from a corner at the Olympics, after doing so in the London 2012 semi-finals.

USA back on the podium

They boasted a trophy cabinet that included four Olympic gold medals and one silver, but the USA had never contested the battle for bronze before. It was an outcome few predicted for a squad rammed with 2019 World Cup winners in their first major tournament under Vlatko Andonovski. The USA's ninth head coach, the 44-year-old had been unbeaten since taking over in October 2019, but Tokyo 2020 standouts Sweden and Canada had changed that. Now they sought consolation against a nation led by Tony Gustavsson, a winner of Olympic gold and two World Cups while assistant coach with the USA. They had played out a goalless group-stage draw nine days earlier, but Australia skipper Sam Kerr knew another beast entirely awaited them in sunny Kashima. "The USA are a different kettle of fish when a medal is at stake," she said. "They have always shown up." They did, 36-year-old Megan Rapinoe producing a breathtaking *gol olímpico* straight from a corner and a thunderous volley either side of Kerr's neat leveller. Carli Lloyd's double on her 312th appearance was no less impressive, the 39-year-old dispatching a vicious left-footed shot and later seizing on Alanna Kennedy's hurried backpass to nutmeg Teagan Micah for the competition's 450th goal ever. The *Matildas*' motto was "Never say die" and Gustavsson's group were the epitome of that mentality as they swiftly replied through a Caitlin Foord header. Kerr was unlucky to smash hers into the upright, but substitute Emily Gielnik unleashed a long-range rocket to make it 4-3. It was too late. The USA claimed bronze, but they had been forced to fight for it.

▼ The USA took bronze at Tokyo 2020 to add to their four golds, won in 1996, 2004, 2008 and 2012, and the silver that they captured in 2000.

2020 Gold Medal Match

International Stadium Yokohama, Yokohama
Friday, 6.08.2021, 21:00, BCD

SWEDEN 1-1 CANADA
AET
2-3 PSO

Blackstenius 34   Fleming 67p

Asllani ✘ (hit post) Fleming ⚽ Björn ✘ Lawrence ✘ (saved) Schough ⚽ Gilles ✘ (hit crossbar) Anvegård ✘ (saved) Leon ✘ (saved) Seger ✘ (over crossbar) Rose ⚽ Andersson ✘ (saved) Grosso ⚽

Anastasia Pustovoitova RUS   Ekaterina Kurochkina RUS & Sanja Rođak-Karšić CRO   Bibiana Steinhaus GER

▲ Exactly 13 years to the day since making their respective Olympic debuts, Sweden skipper Caroline Seger and Canada captain Christine Sinclair came face to face in a fiercely competitive gold medal match. It was a 20th outing on the Olympic stage for both players.

▼ The No.12 shirt belonging to the all-time top scorer in international football, Christine Sinclair, who captained Canada to glory in Japan.
FIFA Museum Collection

Battle of the veterans

The respect that flowed between Caroline Seger and Christine Sinclair when the veteran skippers cheerily bumped fists in greeting in Yokohama was there for all to see. Room-mates during their title-winning spell at Western New York Flash ten years earlier, they were now icons in their own right. Seger, 36, was Europe's record appearance-maker; Sinclair, 38, the world's leading goalscorer. What both craved in the twilight of their international careers was a gold medal.

When the penalty shoot-out turned to sudden death in the Final, Sweden's captain was seconds away from realising her dream. But rather than test her Rosengård team-mate, Stephanie Labbé, Seger belted the ball skywards. Canada marched on to victory, but even amid the euphoria of a first major global title in 21 years, Sinclair did not forget her friend. "This will hurt her," she said. "But she can hold her head up high because she's an absolute legend."

> **When I started playing, we were losing to the US 9-0, so to be standing on top of the podium... I never thought it'd happen.**
> CHRISTINE SINCLAIR

▼ Jessie Fleming draws Canada level from the penalty spot midway through the second half.

Gold medal match 2020

▲ Canada's Stephanie Labbé makes her second save of the shoot-out, this time denying Jonna Andersson. Team-mate Julia Grosso then stepped up to score the winner.

Glory at last for Canada

Only three nations had won the Olympics since the first edition in 1996, but on the hottest night of the year so far, with no fans at International Stadium Yokohama to cheer on the achievement, new champions were crowned. Led out by iconic captains Christine Sinclair and Caroline Seger, the only unbeaten sides at Tokyo 2020 had both achieved podium finishes in Rio five years earlier, but only gold would do now. "We're not just happy reaching the Final this time," said defender Magdalena Eriksson, one of nine players in Sweden's Olympic squad to have won silver in Brazil. "It's got to be gold for us and we're not shy about saying that." Granted creative freedom on the pitch by Peter Gerhardsson, head coach since 2017, Sweden were thriving and with seven players contributing to 13 goals and a stingy defence conceding just three, they had sashayed into the Final. Canada had drawn three, but won when it mattered and, after a momentous victory over the USA, their manager for the past nine months and the youngest coach in the tournament, Bev Priestman, felt her group could deliver again. "We've come this far, so we want to come back home with gold," the 35-year-old insisted, little knowing it would take 120 energy-sapping minutes, nerves of steel and outstanding goalkeeping to achieve it. The half-time advantage lay with the *Blågult*, their record Olympic goalscorer, Stina Blackstenius, netting to make it two in as many gold medal matches and seven all told. Resolute Canada bit back when, following a lengthy VAR review, Amanda Ilestedt was penalised for clattering into Christine Sinclair and ice-cold Jessie Fleming repeated her semi-final heroics with a goal from the spot. Chances came and went, with Kadeisha Buchanan crucially blocking a last-gasp goal-bound shot from Kosovare Asllani. But with honours even in extra time, a shoot-out had to follow. The woodwork intervened, as did Hedvig Lindahl and Stephanie Labbé, both keepers at the top of their game. But after misses and saves, the first-ever shoot-out in an Olympic gold medal game was settled in sudden death by the left foot of second-half substitute, 20-year-old University of Texas midfielder Julia Grosso. It was harsh on dynamic Sweden, but after double bronze, Canada and their English coach had changed the colour of the medal and it glowed gold. "The past two years have been incredibly challenging for so many people around the world," said Labbé. "This is just a big props to all the hard work that this team has put in behind the scenes."

4

With victory over Sweden, Canada joined an elite group, becoming the fourth nation to win women's Olympic football gold after the USA, Norway and Germany.

◀ Canada celebrate their gold medal-winning heroics.

2023

A record 3.2 billion people watched the first World Cup in the southern hemisphere. The *Matildas*' semi-final against England became Australia's most-watched TV programme on record. Eight new teams debuted in an expanded 32-team tournament, with Morocco reaching the knockouts. Spain became the fifth nation to be crowned world champions with a 1-0 victory over England, thanks to the goal scored by Olga Carmona.

A celebration of Indigenous cultures

▼ The opening ceremony at Auckland/Tāmaki Makaurau's Eden Park.

For followers of rugby union, the haka performed by New Zealand's All Blacks had been a familiar pre-match ritual for decades, and the FIFA Women's World Cup 2023 built on that ceremonial tradition in both host countries. Each match was preceded by a welcome ceremony conducted by the Māori people for games in Aotearoa New Zealand and by the First Nations people for matches in Australia. The tournament also introduced a little-known lexicon to the wider world with the use of binational signage, traditional place names for host cities and training sites and the use of First Nations and Māori flags in the stadiums. Sarai Bareman, FIFA's Chief Women's Football Officer, who is of Samoan descent and was raised in Aotearoa New Zealand, said of the "Welcome to Country" that was performed when the teams emerged from the tunnel: "It is so special and so unique. How amazing is it that these two beautiful cultures are being shown to the entire globe?" The official tournament poster and those created for each venue were a further demonstration of the competition's Indigenous theme, with artists from both countries' communities contributing to their designs.

2023 Overview

AUSTRALIA & NEW ZEALAND 2023

FIFA WOMEN'S WORLD CUP AUSTRALIA & NEW ZEALAND 2023™

Story of the qualifiers

Eight more places on offer

The expansion of the competition to 32 teams saw eight nations welcomed onto the World Cup stage for the first time. The AFC Women's Asian Cup delivered the first five qualified sides, two of them debutants in the Philippines and Vietnam. An unprecedented four direct qualification spots were available through the CAF Women's Africa Cup of Nations, where runners-up Morocco and bronze medallists Zambia secured their maiden World Cup berths. The Republic of Ireland sealed their place at a first global finals after a hard-fought play-off win over Scotland. The last three names in the hat were decided by a ten-team intercontinental play-off tournament in New Zealand in February 2023. Portugal made it through, as did fellow newcomers Haiti and Panama, whose achievement brought the number of qualified Concacaf sides to six, the most of any World Cup to date.

◀ The official 2023 World Cup pennant.
FIFA Museum Collection

Golden Ball

Aitana Bonmatí ESP

Silver Ball: Jennifer Hermoso ESP
Bronze Ball: Amanda Ilestedt SWE

Group stage

GROUP A			GROUP B			GROUP C			GROUP D		
NZL	1-0	NOR	AUS	1-0	IRL	ESP	3-0	CRC	ENG	1-0	HAI
PHI	0-2	SUI	NGA	0-0	CAN	ZAM	0-5	JPN	DEN	1-0	CHN
NZL	0-1	PHI	CAN	2-1	IRL	JPN	2-0	CRC	ENG	1-0	DEN
SUI	0-0	NOR	AUS	2-3	NGA	ESP	5-0	ZAM	CHN	1-0	HAI
SUI	0-0	NZL	CAN	0-4	AUS	JPN	4-0	ESP	CHN	1-6	ENG
NOR	6-0	PHI	IRL	0-0	NGA	CRC	1-3	ZAM	HAI	0-2	DEN

	W	D	L	+	−	PTS		W	D	L	+	−	PTS		W	D	L	+	−	PTS		W	D	L	+	−	PTS
SUI	1	2	0	2	0	5	AUS	2	0	1	7	3	6	JPN	3	0	0	11	0	9	ENG	3	0	0	8	1	9
NOR	1	1	1	6	1	4	NGA	1	2	0	3	2	5	ESP	2	0	1	8	4	6	DEN	2	0	1	3	1	6
NZL	1	1	1	1	1	4	CAN	1	1	1	2	5	4	ZAM	1	0	2	3	11	3	CHN	1	0	2	2	7	3
PHI	1	0	2	1	8	3	IRL	0	1	2	1	3	1	CRC	0	0	3	1	8	0	HAI	0	0	3	0	4	0

GROUP E			GROUP F			GROUP G			GROUP H		
USA	3-0	VIE	FRA	0-0	JAM	SWE	2-1	RSA	GER	6-0	MAR
NED	1-0	POR	BRA	4-0	PAN	ITA	1-0	ARG	COL	2-0	KOR
USA	1-1	NED	FRA	2-1	BRA	ARG	2-2	RSA	KOR	0-1	MAR
POR	2-0	VIE	PAN	0-1	JAM	SWE	5-0	ITA	GER	1-2	COL
POR	0-0	USA	PAN	3-6	FRA	ARG	0-2	SWE	KOR	1-1	GER
VIE	0-7	NED	JAM	0-0	BRA	RSA	3-2	ITA	MAR	1-0	COL

	W	D	L	+	−	PTS		W	D	L	+	−	PTS		W	D	L	+	−	PTS		W	D	L	+	−	PTS
NED	2	1	0	9	1	7	FRA	2	1	0	8	4	7	SWE	3	0	0	9	1	9	COL	2	0	1	4	2	6
USA	1	2	0	4	1	5	JAM	1	2	0	1	0	5	RSA	1	1	1	6	6	4	MAR	2	0	1	2	6	6
POR	1	1	1	2	1	4	BRA	1	1	1	5	2	4	ITA	1	0	2	3	8	3	GER	1	1	1	8	3	4
VIE	0	0	3	0	12	0	PAN	0	0	3	3	11	0	ARG	0	1	2	2	5	1	KOR	0	1	2	1	4	1

Knockout stages

ROUND OF 16			ROUND OF 16			ROUND OF 16			ROUND OF 16		
SUI	1-5	ESP	JPN	3-1	NOR	NED	2-0	RSA	SWE	0-0 (5-4)	USA

ROUND OF 16			ROUND OF 16			ROUND OF 16			ROUND OF 16		
ENG	0-0 (4-2)	NGA	AUS	2-0	DEN	COL	1-0	JAM	FRA	4-0	MAR

QUARTER-FINAL			QUARTER-FINAL			QUARTER-FINAL			QUARTER-FINAL		
ESP	2-1 AET	NED	JPN	1-2	SWE	AUS	0-0 (7-6)	FRA	ENG	2-1	COL

SEMI-FINAL			SEMI-FINAL		
ESP	2-1	SWE	AUS	1-3	ENG

MATCH FOR THIRD PLACE		
SWE	2-0	AUS

FINAL		
ESP	1-0	ENG

Overview 2023

32 TEAMS: ARG, AUS, BRA, CAN, CHN, COL, CRC, DEN, ENG, ESP, FRA, GER, HAI, IRL, ITA, JAM, JPN, KOR, MAR, NED, NGA, NOR, NZL, PAN, PHI, POR, RSA, SUI, SWE, USA, VIE, ZAM

SPAIN WINNERS
ENG SECOND
SWE THIRD

1 978 274 SPECTATORS
30 911 AVERAGE PER MATCH

TAZUNI OFFICIAL MASCOT
OFFICIAL LOGO

64 MATCHES PLAYED
112 YELLOW CARDS
6 RED CARDS

164 GOALS
2.56 AVERAGE GOALS PER MATCH
OCEAUNZ OFFICIAL MATCH BALL

Host cities and stadiums

Two nations, ten stadiums

This was the first co-hosted FIFA Women's World Cup and it featured ten stadiums, four in New Zealand and six in Australia. Teams remained in the nation that hosted their group-stage matches, apart from four teams initially based in New Zealand who then switched to Australia for the round of 16, and the Final itself which took place in Sydney, Australia. There were capacity crowds at both Auckland and Dunedin in New Zealand, as well as at Stadium Australia in Sydney, along with Melbourne, Adelaide and Brisbane in Australia, while the tournament attracted just shy of two million spectators overall.

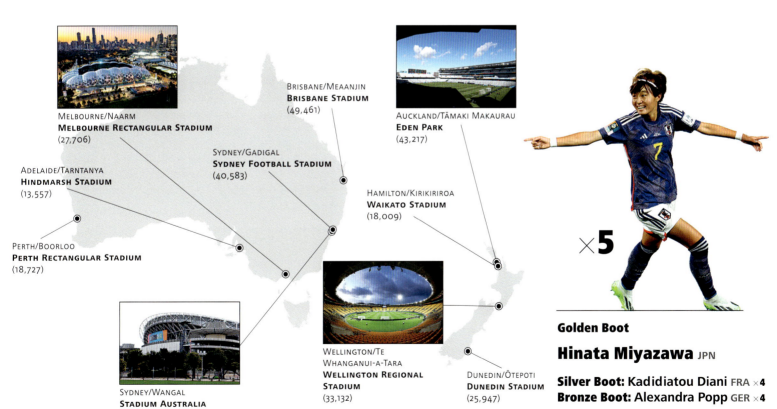

MELBOURNE/NAARM
MELBOURNE RECTANGULAR STADIUM
(27,706)

BRISBANE/MEAANJIN
BRISBANE STADIUM
(49,461)

AUCKLAND/TĀMAKI MAKAURAU
EDEN PARK
(43,217)

ADELAIDE/TARNTANYA
HINDMARSH STADIUM
(13,557)

SYDNEY/GADIGAL
SYDNEY FOOTBALL STADIUM
(40,583)

HAMILTON/KIRIKIRIROA
WAIKATO STADIUM
(18,009)

PERTH/BOORLOO
PERTH RECTANGULAR STADIUM
(18,727)

SYDNEY/WANGAL
STADIUM AUSTRALIA
(75,784)

WELLINGTON/TE WHANGANUI-A-TARA
WELLINGTON REGIONAL STADIUM
(33,132)

DUNEDIN/ŌTEPOTI
DUNEDIN STADIUM
(25,947)

×5

Golden Boot

Hinata Miyazawa JPN

Silver Boot: Kadidiatou Diani FRA ×4
Bronze Boot: Alexandra Popp GER ×4

2023 Group stage

Eden Park, Auckland/Tāmaki Makaurau
20.07.2023, 19:00, 42,137

NEW ZEALAND 1-0 **NORWAY**

Wilkinson 48
(Percival penalty missed 90 –
hit crossbar)

Yoshimi Yamashita JPN
Makoto Bozono JPN & Naomi Teshirogi JPN
Tatiana Guzmán NCA

NZL • 21 Victoria **Esson** - 4 C.J. **Bott**, 13 Rebekah **Stott** (3 Claudia **Bunge** 70), 14 Katie **Bowen**, 7 Ali **Riley** (c) - 12 Betsy **Hassett**, 2 Ria **Percival**, 6 Malia **Steinmetz**, 20 Indiah-Paige **Riley**, 17 Hannah **Wilkinson** (15 Paige **Satchell** 86), 16 Jacqui **Hand** (9 Gabi **Rennie** 90+4). *Jitka Klimková CZE*

NOR • 23 Aurora **Mikalsen** - 13 Thea **Bjelde** (2 Anja **Sønstevold** 90+3), 6 Maren **Mjelde** (c), 16 Mathilde **Harviken** 4 Tuva **Hansen** - 7 Ingrid Syrstad **Engen**, 18 Frida **Maanum** (8 Vilde **Bøe Risa** 74), 11 Guro **Reiten** - 10 Caroline **Graham Hansen**, 14 Ada **Hegerberg**, 17 Julie **Blakstad** (20 Emilie **Haavi** 56 ■ 85). *Hege Riise*

Dunedin Stadium, Dunedin/Ōtepoti
21.07.2023, 17:00, 13,711

PHILIPPINES 0-2 **SWITZERLAND**

Bachmann 45p, Piubel 64

Vincentia Amedome TOG
Carine Fomo CMR & Fanta Koné MLI
Drew Fischer CAN

PHI • 1 Olivia **McDaniel** - 17 Alicia **Barker**, 5 Hali **Long** (c), 3 Jessika **Cowart**, 16 Sofia **Harrison** ■ 38 - 20 Quinley **Quezada** (9 Isabella **Flanigan** 70), 4 Jaclyn **Sawicki**, 8 Sara **Eggesvik** (14 Meryll **Serrano** 70), 3 Angela **Beard** - 21 Katrina **Guillou**, 7 Sarina **Bolden** (10 Chandler **McDaniel** 81). *Alen Stajcic AUS*

SUI • 1 Gaëlle **Thalmann** - 19 Eseosa **Aigbogun**, 15 Luana **Bühler**, 2 Julia **Stierli**, 5 Noelle **Maritz** ■ 83 - 13 Lia **Wälti** (c) (16 Sandrine **Mauron** 75 - 17 Seraina **Piubel** (8 Nadine **Riesen** 90), 11 Coumba **Sow** - 6 Géraldine **Reuteler** (22 Meriame **Terchoun** 90) - 9 Ana-Maria **Crnogorčević**, 10 Ramona **Bachmann** ■ 23 (23 Alisha **Lehmann** 70). *Inka Grings GER*

Wellington Regional Stadium, Wellington/Te Whanganui-a-Tara
25.07.2023, 17:30, 32,357

NEW ZEALAND 0-1 **PHILIPPINES**

Bolden 24

Katia Itzel García MEX
Karen Díaz Medina MEX & Enedina Caudillo MEX
Abdulla Al Marri QAT

NZL - Esson - Bott, Stott, Bowen, A Riley - IP Riley (11 Olivia **Chance** 46), Steinmetz, Percival (18 Grace **Jale** 83), Hassett (10 Annalie **Longo** 46) - Hand, Wilkinson ■ 42. *Klimková CZE*

PHI - O McDaniel - Barker (19 Dominique **Randle** 70), Long (c), Cowart (12 Ryley **Bugay** 83), Beard ■ 49, Harrison - Quezada (6 Tahnai **Annis** 70), Sawicki, Eggesvik (Flanigan 63) - Guillou, Bolden (15 Carleigh **Frilles** 83). *Stajcic AUS*

Waikato Stadium, Hamilton/Kirikiriroa
25.07.2023, 20:00, 10,769

SWITZERLAND 0-0 **NORWAY**

Stéphanie Frappart FRA
Manuela Nicolosi FRA & Élodie Coppola FRA
Pol van Boekel NED

SUI - Thalmann - Aigbogun, Riesen, Stierli, Maritz - Wälti (c) - Sow, Reuteler (Mauron 78) - Piubel (Terchoun 88), Crnogorčević, Bachmann (14 Marion **Rey** 90+3). *Grings GER*

NOR - Mikalsen - Bjelde (19 Marit **Bratberg Lund** 88), Mjelde (c), Harviken, Hansen (Sønstevold 73) - Bøe Risa (Syrstad Engen 88) - Maanum, Reiten - 15 Amalie **Eikeland** (Graham Hansen 57), 22 Sophie **Román Haug** (9 Karina **Sævik** 73), Haavi. *Riise*

Dunedin Stadium, Dunedin/Ōtepoti
30.07.2023, 19:00, 25,947

SWITZERLAND 0-0 **NEW ZEALAND**

Tori Penso USA
Brooke Mayo USA & Mijensa Rensch SUR
Nicolás Gallo COL

SUI - Thalmann - Aigbogun, Maritz, Stierli, Riesen - Wälti (c) - Sow, Reuteler (Lehmann 71) - Piubel (18 Viola **Calligaris** 85), Crnogorčević (Terchoun 90+4), Bachmann (Mauron 85). *Grings GER*

NZL - Esson - Bott, Stott (Bunge 62), Bowen, A Riley (c) - Longo (Hassett 62), Percival (Jale 71), Steinmetz, Chance (IP Riley 46) - Hand, Wilkinson (Rennie 82). *Klimková CZE*

Eden Park, Auckland/Tāmaki Makaurau
30.07.2023, 19:00, 34,697

NORWAY 6-0 **PHILIPPINES**

Román Haug (3) 6 17 90+5,
Graham Hansen 31,
Barker OG 48, Reiten 53p

Marie-Soleil Beaudoin CAN
Chantal Boudreau CAN & Stephanie-Dale Yee Sing JAM
Drew Fischer CAN

NOR - Mikalsen - Bjelde (Sønstevold 68), Mjelde (c), Harviken (5 Guro **Bergsvand** 81), Hansen - Bøe Risa ■ 86 - Maanum (Syrstad Engen 68), Reiten - Graham Hansen (21 Anna **Jøsendal** 81), Román Haug, Haavi (Sævik 68). *Riise*

PHI - O McDaniel - Barker (Randle 57), Long (c), Cowart, Beard - Quezada (Serrano 81), Sawicki (Bugay 74), Eggesvik, Guillou ■ 54 - 9 Flanigan (Harrison 57 ■ 67), Bolden (C McDaniel 74). *Stajcic AUS*

Group A

	W	D	L	+	–	PTS
SUI	1	2	0	2	0	5
NOR	1	1	1	6	1	4
NZL	1	1	1	1	1	4
PHI	1	0	2	1	8	3

 New Zealand's Hannah Wilkinson in action against Norway. Her goal secured her team's first-ever World Cup win.

16

New Zealand finally won a Women's World Cup game at the 16th time of asking when they beat Norway 1-0 in the opening match. The *Football Ferns* graced the national stadium at Eden Park in Auckland for only the second time and briefly set a new record attendance for a football match in New Zealand in the process.

8

A record eight clean sheets were kept in Group A's six matches, the most in Women's World Cup history.

Goal difference undoes *Ferns*

A fountain of fireworks burst into the sky above Eden Park as a colourful opening ceremony kicked off the first Women's World Cup in the southern hemisphere. Featuring a traditional Māori *pao* or song, a haka, a vibrant "unity dance" and a rousing rendition of official tournament song *Do It Again*, it was a pitch-perfect curtain-raiser, but the showstopper was still to come. No New Zealand side had won a World Cup match before this night. But backed by the biggest football crowd their country had ever seen, Jitka Klimková's players overcame former champions Norway to change that. It was an end-to-end tussle, and although most-capped *Football Fern* Ria Percival missed a penalty, Hannah Wilkinson's cool second-half strike was enough. "We've been fighting for this for so long," sobbed skipper Ali Riley. "This is what dreams are made of." Captained by their only home-based player, Hali Long, the Philippines soon realised their own dreams. They lost their opener to Switzerland, Inka Grings's maiden victory as head coach secured by Ramona Bachmann's fourth-ever World Cup goal and Seraina Piubel's first. But they stunned New Zealand, who were undone by US-born Sarina Bolden's powerful header, a tight VAR-reviewed decision against Wilkinson and Olivia McDaniel's dynamic goalkeeping. Norway seemed in disarray when Caroline Graham Hansen questioned Hege Riise's team selection following their stalemate with Switzerland. But after the centurion's apology, they came together as one to block out a partisan crowd and hit ten-woman Philippines for six, with Graham Hansen belting in a super goal from range and Sophie Román Haug contributing three. The first Filipino World Cup side of any age or gender were out, but coach Alen Stajcic called for further investment, saying: "It's the starting point of a new history." Their goalless draw with Switzerland meant New Zealand were the first-ever hosts to exit at the group stage. But with her side having played in front of more than 100,000 fans over their three group games, Klimková remained positive. "We woke up the passion of football in New Zealand," she said. "And that is incredible for our future."

Seraina Piubel of Switzerland scores her team's second goal against the Philippines.

Group stage 2023

Group B

◀ Katrina Gorry of Australia controls the ball, despite the close attention of Ireland's Kyra Carusa.

◀ Kailen Sheridan of Canada punches the ball away from Nigeria's Ifeoma Onumonu in the goalless draw between the two sides in Melbourne.

	W	D	L	+	−	PTS
AUS	2	0	1	7	3	6
NGA	1	2	0	3	2	5
CAN	1	1	1	2	5	4
IRL	0	1	2	1	3	1

Australia pull off heroics

With the first co-hosted Women's World Cup already up and running, the baton was passed from Auckland to Sydney. Packed with a record 75,784 supporters, Stadium Australia was a riot of colour and noise, but a respectful hush fell as Dharug Elder Aunty Julie Jones delivered the "Welcome to Country" alongside the graceful Jannawi Dance Clan, and a momentous night was officially under way. A late calf injury to captain Sam Kerr had torn a superstar-sized hole in Australia's team sheet against the Republic of Ireland, and Vera Pauw's *Girls in Green* barely gave the *Matildas* a moment's rest. But Steph Catley and the fans in green and gold stepped up, the stand-in skipper's thunderous spot kick and a cacophony of cheers fuelling a slender victory. Although Canada and Nigeria arrived in Australia off the back of pay disputes with their respective football associations, the finals were now their focus. Chiamaka Nnadozie kept hers, the 22-year-old captain denying veteran skipper Christine Sinclair's penalty in Nigeria's first 0-0 draw in nine World Cups. A 3-2 thriller with Australia followed, winning goalscorer Asisat Oshoala the first African to net in three editions. Ireland's first goal on this stage was a stunner, inspirational leader Katie McCabe curling in a magnificent *gol olímpico* against Bev Priestman's Canada. The Olympic champions stunted the debutants' World Cup dreams, though, Julia Grosso's cross flying in off Megan Connolly and Adriana Leon poking home the winner. It had taken Ireland eight attempts to qualify for this global showpiece, and before facing Nigeria, Connolly insisted: "We want to prove to everyone we deserve to be here." They did just that by departing the competition with a clean sheet and a historic point. A goalless draw was enough for Nigeria to progress, but Canada fell to a first group-stage exit in 12 years after succumbing to a Hayley Raso-inspired thumping by Australia, leaving pragmatic Priestman to reflect: "These are the moments that make you."

18

Christine Sinclair wore the armband for Canada on this global stage for the 18th and final time. Sinclair had scored in five successive World Cups, but her saved spot kick against Nigeria saw her miss the chance to become the first player of any gender to score in six editions.

Stadium Australia, Sydney/Wangal
20.07.2023, 20:00, **75,784**

AUSTRALIA 🇦🇺 **1-0** 🇮🇪 **REPUBLIC OF IRELAND**

Catley 52p

⚽ Edina Alves Batista BRA
🚩 Neuza Back BRA & Leila Cruz BRA
📺 Diane Muniz BRA

AUS • 18 Mackenzie **Arnold** - 21 Ellie **Carpenter**, 15 Clare **Hunt**, 14 Alanna **Kennedy**, 7 Steph **Catley** (c) - 16 Hayley **Raso**, 19 Katrina **Gorry**, 23 Kyra **Cooney-Cross**, 5 Cortnee **Vine** (10 Emily **van Egmond** 75) - 9 Caitlin **Foord**, 11 Mary **Fowler** (4 Clare **Polkinghorne** 84). *Tony Gustavsson SWE*

IRL • 1 Courtney **Brosnan** - 5 Niamh **Fahey**, 4 Louise **Quinn**, 6 Megan **Connolly** - 14 Heather **Payne**, 10 Denise **O'Sullivan** 🟨 42, 8 Ruesha **Littlejohn**, 11 Katie **McCabe** (c) - 7 Sinead **Farrelly** (19 Abbie **Larkin** 63), 18 Kyra **Carusa** (22 Isibeal **Atkinson** 87), 20 Marissa **Sheva** (15 Lucy **Quinn** 63). *Vera Pauw NED*

Melbourne Rectangular Stadium, Melbourne/Naarm
21.07.2023, 12:30, **21,410**

NIGERIA 🇳🇬 **0-0** 🇨🇦 **CANADA**

(Sinclair penalty saved 50)

⚽ Lina Lehtovaara FIN
🚩 Chrysoula Kourompylia GRE & Karolin Kaivoja EST
📺 Pol van Boekel NED

NGA • 16 Chiamaka **Nnadozie** (c) - 22 Michelle **Alozie**, 14 Blessing **Demehin** 🟨 54, 2 Ashleigh **Plumptre**, 3 Osinachi **Ohale** - 10 Christy **Ucheibe**, 13 Deborah **Abiodun** 🟥 90+8 - 6 Ifeoma **Onumonu** (21 Esther **Okoronkwo** 85), 7 Toni **Payne**, 17 Francisca **Ordega** (12 Uchenna **Kanu** 73) - 8 Asisat **Oshoala** (19 Jennifer **Echegini** 90+1). *Randy Waldrum USA*

CAN • 1 Kailen **Sheridan** - 8 Jayde **Riviere** (2 Allysha **Chapman** 71), 3 Kadeisha **Buchanan**, 14 Vanessa **Gilles**, 10 Ashley **Lawrence** 🟨 74 - 5 **Quinn**, 7 Julia **Grosso** (15 Nichelle **Prince** 82) - 9 Jordyn **Huitema**, 12 Christine **Sinclair** (c) (13 Sophie **Schmidt** 71), 6 Deanne **Rose** (20 Cloé **Lacasse** 46) - 19 Adriana **Leon** (11 Évelyne **Viens** 64 🟨 90+9). *Bev Priestman ENG*

Perth Rectangular Stadium, Perth/Boorloo
26.07.2023, 20:00, **17,065**

CANADA 🇨🇦 **2-1** 🇮🇪 **REPUBLIC OF IRELAND**

Connolly OG 45+5, Leon 53 — McCabe 4

⚽ Laura Fortunato ARG
🚩 Mariana de Almeida ARG & Daiana Milone ARG
📺 Alejandro Hernández ESP

CAN • Sheridan - Riviere (Chapman 90+4), Buchanan 🟨 36 (4 Shelina **Zadorsky** 46), Gilles 🟨 61, Lawrence - Quinn - 17 Jessie **Fleming** (c), Grosso (Schmidt 46) - Huitema, Viens (Sinclair 46), Leon (Lacasse 59). *Priestman ENG*

IRL • Brosnan - Fahey, Louise Quinn, Connolly - 13 Áine **O'Gorman** (Sheva 59), O'Sullivan, Littlejohn (12 Lily **Agg** 65), McCabe (c) 🟨 90+8 - Lucy Quinn (Larkin 46), Carusa (9 Amber **Barrett** 65), Farrelly (Atkinson 65). *Pauw NED*

Brisbane Stadium, Brisbane/Meaanjin
27.07.2023, 20:00, **49,156**

AUSTRALIA 🇦🇺 **2-3** 🇳🇬 **NIGERIA**

Van Egmond 45+1, Kennedy 90+10 — Kanu 45+6, Ohale 65, Oshoala 72

⚽ Esther Staubli SUI
🚩 Katrin Rafalski GER & Susanne Küng SUI
📺 Marco Fritz GER

AUS • Arnold - Carpenter, Hunt, Kennedy, Catley (c) - Van Egmond - Gorry, Cooney-Cross, Vine (Polkinghorne 82), Foord 🟨 45+3, Raso (8 Alex **Chidiac** 85). *Gustavsson SWE*

NGA • Nnadozie (c) - Alozie 🟨 21, Ohale, Demehin, Plumptre (4 Glory **Ogbonna** 76) - Payne (5 Onome **Ebi** 90), 18 Halimatu **Ayinde** (Echegini 76), Ucheibe - Onumonu (Okoronkwo 63), Kanu (Oshoala 63 🟨 73), 15 Rasheedat **Ajibade**. *Waldrum USA*

Melbourne Rectangular Stadium, Melbourne/Naarm
31.07.2023, 20:00, **27,706**

CANADA 🇨🇦 **0-4** 🇦🇺 **AUSTRALIA**

Raso (2) 9 39, Fowler 58, Catley 90+4p

⚽ Stéphanie Frappart FRA
🚩 Manuela Nicolosi FRA & Élodie Coppola FRA
📺 Pol van Boekel NED

CAN • Sheridan - Riviere (Chapman 46), Buchanan, Gilles, Lawrence - Quinn (23 Olivia **Smith** 77) - Grosso (Schmidt 46), Fleming - Leon (Viens 64), Sinclair (c) (Lacasse 46), Huitema (Rose 46). *Priestman ENG*

AUS • Arnold 🟨 81 - Carpenter, Hunt, Kennedy, Catley (c) - Raso (Vine 75), Gorry (22 Charlotte **Grant** 90+6), Cooney-Cross, Van Egmond 🟨 68 (Polkinghorne 84) - Fowler, Foord. *Gustavsson SWE* 🟨 45+5

Brisbane Stadium, Brisbane/Meaanjin
31.07.2023, 20:00, **24,884**

REPUBLIC OF IRELAND 🇮🇪 **0-0** 🇳🇬 **NIGERIA**

⚽ Katia Itzel García MEX
🚩 Karen Díaz Medina MEX & Enedina Caudillo MEX
📺 Massimiliano Irrati ITA

IRL • Brosnan - Fahey (7 Diane **Caldwell** 90+5), Louise Quinn, Connolly - Payne (Sheva 83), Agg (Larkin 83), Littlejohn, McCabe (c) 🟨 68 - O'Sullivan, Carusa, Farrelly. *Pauw NED*

NGA • Nnadozie (c) - Alozie, Ohale, Demehin (Ebi 83), Plumptre - Ucheibe, Ayinde, Ajibade, Payne, Kanu (11 Gift **Monday** 67) - Oshoala (Onumonu 67). *Waldrum USA*

2023 Group stage

Wellington Regional Stadium, Wellington/Te Whanganui-a-Tara
21.07.2023, 19:30, **22,966**

SPAIN 🇪🇸 **3-0** 🇨🇷 **COSTA RICA**

Del Campo OG 21, Bonmatí
23, González 27
(Hermoso penalty saved 34)

👤 Casey Reibelt AUS
🚩 Ramina Tsoi KGZ & Xie Lijun CHN
📺 Marco Fritz GER

ESP • 1 Misa **Rodríguez** - 2 Ona **Batlle** (12 Oihane **Hernández** 88), 4 Irene **Paredes**, 5 Ivana **Andrés** (c), 19 Olga **Carmona** - 6 Aitana **Bonmatí**, 3 Teresa **Abelleira** (21 Claudia **Zornoza** 77) - 22 Athenea **del Castillo** (8 Mariona **Caldentey** 63), 10 Jennifer **Hermoso**, 18 Salma **Paralluelo** (11 Alexia **Putellas** 77) - 9 Esther **González** (17 Alba **Redondo** 63). *Jorge Vilda*

CRC • 23 Daniela **Solera** - 20 Fabiola **Villalobos**, 4 Mariana **Benavides**, 5 Valeria **del Campo** - 3 María Paula **Coto**, 16 Katherine **Alvarado** (c), 10 Gloriana **Villalobos** (19 Alexandra **Pinell** 73), 12 María Paula **Elizondo** (15 Cristín **Granados** 58) - 7 Melissa **Herrera**, 9 María Paula **Salas** (21 Sheika **Scott** 73), 14 Priscila **Chinchilla**. *Amelia Valverde*

Waikato Stadium, Hamilton/Kirikiriroa
22.07.2023, 19:00, **16,111**

ZAMBIA 🇿🇲 **0-5** 🇯🇵 **JAPAN**

Miyazawa (2) 43 62, Tanaka 55, Endo 71, Ueki 90+1 p

👤 Tess Olofsson SWE
🚩 Lucie Ratajová CZE & Polyxeni Iroдотou CYP
📺 Massimiliano Irrati ITA

ZAM • 1 Catherine **Musonda** 🟨 51 🟨 90+7 🟥 90+7 - 8 Margaret **Belemu**, 15 Agness **Musesa**, 5 Lushomo **Mweemba** (23 Vast **Phiri** 82), 14 Martha **Tembo** - 12 Evarine **Katongo**, 4 Susan **Banda**, 14 Ireen **Lungu** (7 Ochumba **Lubandji** 72), 17 Racheal **Kundananji** - 19 Siomala **Mapepa** (21 Avell **Chitundu** 72) (18 Eunice **Sakala** 90+9), 11 Barbra **Banda** (c). *Bruce Mwape*

JPN • 1 Ayaka **Yamashita** - 23 Rion **Ishikawa**, 4 Saki **Kumagai** (c), 3 Moeka **Minami** - 2 Risa **Shimizu**, 14 Yui **Hasegawa**, 10 Fuka **Nagano**, 7 Hinata **Miyazawa** (22 Remina **Chiba** 90+3), 13 Jun **Endō** (17 Kiko **Seike** 77) - 15 Aoba **Fujino** (8 Hikaru **Naomoto** 77), 11 Mina **Tanaka** (9 Riko **Ueki** 66). *Futoshi Ikeda*

Dunedin Stadium, Dunedin/Ōtepoti
26.07.2023, 17:00, **6,992**

JAPAN 🇯🇵 **2-0** 🇨🇷 **COSTA RICA**

Naomoto 25, Fujino 27

👤 Maria Sole Ferrieri Caputi ITA
🚩 Francesca Di Monte ITA & Mihaela Țepușă ROU
📺 Massimiliano Irrati ITA

JPN • Yamashita - 5 Shiori **Miyake**, Kumagai (c), Minami - Shimizu (19 Miyabi **Moriya** 90+1), 16 Honoka **Hayashi** (Nagano 74), Naomoto (Seike 74), Hasegawa, 6 Hina **Sugita** - Fujino (Miyazawa 59), Tanaka (Ueki 59). *Ikeda*

CRC • Solera - F Villalobos, Benavides, 2 Gabriela **Guillén** (G Villalobos 46) - Coto, Alvarado (c), Granados (11 Raquel **Rodríguez** 64), Elizondo - Herrera, Salas (Scott 76), Chinchilla 🟨 86. *Valverde*

Eden Park, Auckland/Tāmaki Makaurau
26.07.2023, 19:30, **20,983**

SPAIN 🇪🇸 **5-0** 🇿🇲 **ZAMBIA**

Abelleira 9, Hermoso (2) 13
70, Redondo (2) 69 85

👤 Oh Hyeon Jeong KOR
🚩 Lee Seul Gi KOR & Park Mi Suk KOR
📺 Muhammad Taqi SGP

ESP • Rodríguez - Batlle (Hernández 46), Paredes, Andrés (c), Carmona - Abelleira - Bonmatí (7 Irene **Guerrero** 61), Putellas (Redondo 46) - Paralluelo (15 Eva **Navarro** 46), Hermoso, Caldentey (Del Castillo 83). *Vilda*

ZAM • Sakala - Belemu, Musesa, Mweemba (Phiri 76), Tembo 🟨 90+10 - S Banda (6 Mary **Wilombe** 37) - Lungu, Katongo (Lubandji 76 🟨 90+1) - Kundananji, B Banda (c), Mapepa (Chitundu 37). *Mwape*

Wellington Regional Stadium, Wellington/Te Whanganui-a-Tara
31.07.2023, 19:00, **20,957**

JAPAN 🇯🇵 **4-0** 🇪🇸 **SPAIN**

Miyazawa (2) 12 40, Ueki
29, Tanaka 82

👤 Ekaterina Koroleva USA
🚩 Kathryn Nesbitt USA & Felisha Mariscal USA
📺 Drew Fischer CAN

JPN • Yamashita - 12 Hana **Takahashi**, Kumagai (c), Minami - Shimizu (Moriya 59), Hasegawa, Hayashi, Endō (Sugita 85) - Naomoto, Ueki (Tanaka 67), Miyazawa (Fujino 46). *Ikeda*

ESP • Rodríguez - Batlle, Paredes, 20 Rocío **Gálvez**, Carmona (c) 🟨 45+1 (Hernández 46) 🟨 89 - Abelleira (Zornoza 46) - Bonmatí, Putellas (Redondo 62) - Paralluelo (González 82), Hermoso, Caldentey (Navarro 62). *Vilda*

Waikato Stadium, Hamilton/Kirikiriroa
31.07.2023, 19:00, **8,117**

COSTA RICA 🇨🇷 **1-3** 🇿🇲 **ZAMBIA**

Herrera 47
Mweemba 3, *B Banda 31p, Kundananji 90+3

👤 Bouchra Karboubi MAR
🚩 Fatiha Jermoumi MAR & Soukaina Hamdi MAR
📺 Adil Zourak MAR

CRC • Solera - F Villalobos, Benavides 🟨 21, Del Campo 🟨 23 - Coto, G Villalobos (Salas 72), Alvarado (c) 🟨 6 (Pinell 90+1), Rodríguez - Herrera, Scott (13 Emilie **Valenciano** 85), Chinchilla. *Valverde*

ZAM • Musonda - Belemu, Musesa, Mweemba, Tembo 🟨 46 - S Banda - 20 Hellen **Chanda** (9 Hellen **Mubanga** 90+9), Katongo (Wilombe 74) - Chitundu (Mapepa 85), B Banda (c) 🟨 66, Kundananji. *Mwape*

* The 1,000th goal scored at the FIFA Women's World Cup finals

Group C

	W	D	L	+	-	PTS
🇯🇵 JPN	3	0	0	11	0	9
🇪🇸 ESP	2	0	1	8	4	6
🇿🇲 ZAM	1	0	2	3	11	3
🇨🇷 CRC	0	0	3	1	8	0

Pitch-perfect from Japan

With a raft of top players either dropped or making themselves unavailable after their call for a change in managerial methods had been rebuffed in late 2022, Spain's squad abounded with senior World Cup debutants. One of 11 to face Costa Rica, Esther González, forced an own goal and got herself on the scoresheet either side of Aitana Bonmatí's opportunistic strike. Daniela Solera's consolation on her 26th birthday was to stop veteran Jenni Hermoso's spot kick. Zambia, their COSAFA Women's Championship golden glove winner, Catherine Musonda, and two Mina Tanaka offsides frustrated Japan. But Hinata Miyazawa broke the deadlock, and after Musonda's stoppage-time red card, reigning WE League top scorer Riko Ueki completed an eventual rout.

"*Vamos Ticas*" banners and booming drums spurred on Amelia Valverde's Costa Rica against Japan, but first-half goals from Hikaru Naomoto and Aoba Fujino settled it. Spain put five past Zambia without reply to join Japan in the knockouts. But despite dominating possession, *La Roja* had no reply to clinical scorers Miyazawa, Ueki and Tanaka. Meanwhile, Costa Rica and Zambia played out a memorable farewell to their own campaigns, Lushomo Mweemba netting her country's maiden World Cup goal and Barbra Banda dispatching the competition's 1,000th since the first in 1991. Melissa Herrera became the first of *Las Ticas* to score in two editions, but Racheal Kundananji sealed a historic win for the first senior Zambian team at a World Cup.

1,000

Zambia captain Barbra Banda's goal against Costa Rica was the 1,000th in the competition's history; her boot and a signed ball from that day now sit on display in the FIFA Museum in Zurich.

▶ Player of the tournament Aitana Bonmatí scores Spain's second goal in their match against Costa Rica in Wellington.

▲ The boots worn by Barbra Banda when she scored the 1,000th goal in the history of the FIFA Women's World Cup.
FIFA Museum Collection

33 & 22

Racheal Kundananji, whose goal against Costa Rica put the finishing touches on a historic first World Cup win for Zambia, was the tournament's fastest player, reaching a top speed of 33.2km/h. With 22 stops, Costa Rica's Daniela Solera made the most saves.

▶ Barbra Banda of Zambia tackles Japan's Jun Endo during their group match in Hamilton.

Group D

A shot by England's Lucy Bronze is blocked by China's Yao Wei during the match in Adelaide.

England ease through

Haiti were the tournament's youngest team, and four teenagers made Nicolas Delépine's line-up against England. Georgia Stanway's coolly retaken penalty was ultimately enough to overcome the Caribbean side, but Mary Earps was key, superbly denying 19-year-old Melchie Dumornay and substitute Roseline Éloissaint. Led by Shui Qingxia, their nation's first female head coach and a 1996 Olympic silver medallist, China arrived at the finals having won their first continental title in 16 years. They were unbeaten in three against Denmark on this stage, but despite all their attacking endeavour, they succumbed to substitute Amalie Vangsgaard's last-gasp header. Vangsgaard walloped the upright in the Scandinavians' next outing, against England, but a Lauren James wonder strike decided a tight match marred by playmaker Keira Walsh's departure on a stretcher. A VAR-reviewed red card saw Zhang Rui leave the pitch on 29 minutes against Haiti, but ten-player China won a game dominated by penalty appeals thanks to a spot kick awarded following a VAR review, Wang Shuang scoring her first World Cup goal in three editions. The group hung in the balance, but after Sarina Wiegman had called for ruthlessness, a Lauren James brace helped propel England into the second round, their 6-1 win condemning China to a first-ever group-stage exit. Haiti's largely France and USA-based squad had entertained the crowds, but against Denmark the debutants were again unable to convert their chances, bowing out after Pernille Harder and Sanne Troelsgaard buried theirs to send the Danes into the knockouts for the first time since 1995.

	W	D	L	←	→	PTS
ENG	3	0	0	8	1	9
DEN	2	0	1	3	1	6
CHN	1	0	2	2	7	3
HAI	0	0	3	0	4	0

16
England's win over China meant that the *Lionesses* had now scored in a World Cup-record 16 consecutive matches, overtaking Norway's tally of 15 achieved between 1991 and 1999.

49
Haiti's women were starring in their first World Cup 49 years after their men had played in their first and only World Cup to date.

Defender Betina Petit-Frère of Haiti tackles Denmark's Amalie Vangsgaard during the match in Perth. Haiti conceded four goals at the finals, three of them penalties and the fourth coming in the tenth minute of injury time at the end of their final group game.

Brisbane Stadium, Brisbane/Meaanjin
22.07.2023, 19:30, **44,369**

ENGLAND 1-0 HAITI

Stanway 29p

Emikar Calderas Barrera VEN
Migdalia Rodríguez VEN & Mary Blanco Bolívar COL
Juan Soto VEN

ENG • 1 Mary **Earps** - 2 Lucy **Bronze**, 6 Millie **Bright** (c), 16 Jess **Carter**, 5 Alex **Greenwood** - 8 Georgia **Stanway** ■ 45+9, 4 Keira **Walsh**, 10 Ella **Toone** - 18 Chloe **Kelly**, 23 Alessia **Russo** (9 Rachel **Daly** 76), 11 Lauren **Hemp** ■ 51 (7 Lauren **James** 61). *Sarina Wiegman NED*
HAI • 1 Kerly **Théus** - 13 Betina **Petit-Frère**, 3 Jennyfer **Limage** (21 Ruthny **Mathurin** 31), 4 Tabita **Joseph**, 20 Kethna **Louis** - 7 Batcheba **Louis** (15 Darlina **Joseph** 90+3), 9 Sherly **Jeudy**, 19 Dayana **Pierre-Louis** ■ 19, 10 Nérilia **Mondésir** (c) - 22 Roselord **Borgella** (11 Roseline **Éloissaint** 78), 6 Melchie **Dumornay**. *Nicolas Delépine FRA*

Perth Rectangular Stadium, Perth/Boorloo
22.07.2023, 20:00, **16,989**

DENMARK 1-0 CHINA PR

Vangsgaard 90

Marie-Soleil Beaudoin CAN
Chantal Boudreau CAN & Stephanie-Dale Yee Sing JAM
Armando Villarreal USA

DEN • 1 Lene **Christensen** - 4 Rikke **Sevecke** ■ 40, 3 Stine **Ballisager**, 5 Simone **Boye**, 11 Katrine **Veje** - 2 Josefine **Hasbo**, 6 Karen **Holmgaard**, 12 Kathrine **Kühl** (20 Signe **Bruun** 62) - 19 Janni **Thomsen** (9 Amalie **Vangsgaard** 85), 10 Pernille **Harder** (c), 14 Nicoline **Sørensen** (17 Rikke Marie **Madsen** 72). *Lars Søndergaard*
CHN • 12 Xu **Huan** - 4 Li **Mengwen** (23 **Gao Chen** 85), 17 Wu **Chengshu** (21 **Gu Yasha** 90+1), 8 Yao **Wei**, 5 **Chen** Qiaozhu - 6 Zhang **Xin** (7 Wang **Shuang** 46), 13 **Yang Lina**, 10 **Zhang Rui**, 19 Zhang **Linyan** - 14 Lou **Jiahui** (9 **Shen Mengyu** 78), 11 Wang **Shanshan** (c). *Shui Qingxia*

Sydney Football Stadium, Sydney/Gadigal
28.07.2023, 18:30, **40,439**

ENGLAND 1-0 DENMARK

James 6

Tess Olofsson SWE
Lucie Ratajová CZE & Polyxeni Irodotou CYP
Tatiana Guzmán NCA

ENG • **Earps** - **Bronze**, **Bright** (c), **Greenwood**, **Daly** - **Toone** (**Hemp** 76), **Walsh** (17 Laura **Coombs** 38), **Stanway** - **James**, **Russo** (19 Bethany **England** 76), **Kelly**. *Wiegman NED*
DEN • **Christensen** - **Sevecke**, **Ballisager** (15 Frederikke **Thøgersen** 76), **Boye**, **Veje** - **Hasbo** (**Vangsgaard** 71), **Holmgaard** (7 Sanne **Troelsgaard** 87), **Kühl** - **Thomsen**, **Harder** (c), **Madsen** (**Sørensen** 76). *Søndergaard*

Hindmarsh Stadium, Adelaide/Tarntanya
28.07.2023, 20:30, **12,675**

CHINA PR 1-0 HAITI

Wang Shuang 74p

Marta Huerta de Aza ESP
Guadalupe Porras Ayuso ESP & Sanja Rođak-Karšić CRO
Alejandro Hernández ESP

CHN • 1 **Zhu Yu** - Li **Mengwen**, Wang **Shanshan** (c), Yao **Wei**, 15 **Chen** Qiaozhu - 16 Yao **Lingwei** (3 **Dou Jiaxing** 82), **Zhang Rui** ■ 29, Yang **Lina**, Zhang **Linyan** (18 **Tang Jiali** 88) - Wu **Chengshu** (Wang **Shuang** 46), Lou **Jiahui** (**Zhang Xin** 37). *Shui Qingxia*
HAI • **Théus** - **Petit-Frère**, **Mathurin** (2 Chelsea **Surpris** 81), T **Joseph**, K **Louis** - 5 Maudeline **Moryl** (**Dumornay** 46 ■ 63), **Jeudy** (17 Shwendesky **Joseph** 89), **Pierre-Louis** (8 Danielle **Étienne** 81) - B **Louis** (**Éloissaint** 64), **Borgella**, **Mondésir** (c). *Delépine FRA* ■ 90+13

Hindmarsh Stadium, Adelaide/Tarntanya
1.08.2023, 20:30, **13,497**

CHINA PR 1-6 ENGLAND

Wang Shuang 57p
Russo 4, Hemp 26, James (2) 41 65, Kelly 77, Daly 84

Casey Reibelt AUS
Ramina Tsoi KGZ & Heba Saadieh PLE
Juan Soto VEN

CHN • **Zhu Yu** - Li **Mengwen** (Wu **Haiyan** 75), Wang **Shanshan** (c), Yao **Wei**, **Chen** Qiaozhu - Wang **Shuang** (**Gu Yasha** 75), Yao **Lingwei** (**Dou Jiaxing** 90+3), Yang **Lina**, Zhang **Linyan** - Wu **Chengshu** (**Shen Mengyu** 90+3), Lou **Jiahui** (4 Wang **Linlin** 90+11). *Shui Qingxia*
ENG • **Earps** - **Carter**, **Bright** (c), **Greenwood** - **Bronze** ■ 56 (3 Niamh **Charles** 71), **Stanway** (**Coombs** 46), 20 Katie **Zelem**, **James** (**Toone** 81), **Daly** - **Hemp** (**Kelly** 71), **Russo** (**England** 71). *Wiegman NED*

Perth Rectangular Stadium, Perth/Boorloo
1.08.2023, 19:00, **17,897**

HAITI 0-2 DENMARK

Harder 21p, Troelsgaard 90+10

Oh Hyeon Jeong KOR
Park Mi Suk KOR & Makoto Bozono JPN
Muhammad Taqi SGP

HAI • **Théus** - **Petit-Frère** (**Mathurin** 87), T **Joseph**, K **Louis**, **Surpris** - B **Louis**, **Jeudy**, **Pierre-Louis** (**Borgella** 67), **Mondésir** (c) - **Dumornay**, **Éloissaint**. *Delépine FRA*
DEN • **Christensen** - **Thomsen**, **Sevecke**, **Boye**, **Veje** - **Madsen** (21 Mille **Gejl** 63), **Holmgaard** ■ 66 (**Troelsgaard** 80), **Kühl** (**Hasbo** 80) - **Sørensen** (**Bruun** 63), **Harder** (c) (18 Luna **Gevitz** 90+2), **Vangsgaard**. *Søndergaard*

2023 **Group stage**

Eden Park, Auckland/Tāmaki Makaurau
22.07.2023, 13:00, **41,107**

USA 🇺🇸 **3-0** 🇻🇳 VIETNAM

Smith (2) 14 45+7, Horan 77
(Morgan penalty saved 44)

🧑‍⚖️ Bouchra Karboubi MAR
🚩 Fatiha Jermoumi MAR & Soukaina Hamdi MAR
📺 Juan Martínez Munuera ESP

USA • 1 Alyssa **Naeher** - 23 Emily **Fox** (3 Sofia **Huerta** 84), 4 Naomi **Girma**, 8 Julie **Ertz**, 19 Crystal **Dunn** (5 Kelley **O'Hara** 84) - 9 Savannah **DeMelo** (16 Rose **Lavelle** 61), 10 Lindsey **Horan** (c) 🟨 **56** - 20 Trinity **Rodman** (7 Alyssa **Thompson** 76), 17 Andi **Sullivan**, 11 Sophia **Smith** - 13 Alex **Morgan** (15 Megan **Rapinoe** 61). *Vlatko Andonovski*

VIE • 14 Trần Thị Kim **Thanh** - 17 Trần Thị Thu **Thảo**, 2 Lương Thị Thu **Thương** (3 Chương Thị Kiều 61), 13 Lê Thị Diễm **My**, 4 Trần Thị **Thu**, 5 Hoàng Thị **Loan** - 10 Trần Thị Hải **Linh** (16 Dương Thị Vân 89), 11 Thái Thị **Thảo**, 23 Nguyễn Thị Bích **Thùy** (22 Nguyễn Thị Mỹ **Anh** 61), 7 Nguyễn Thị Tuyết **Dung** (21 Ngân Thị Vạn Sự 46) - 9 Huỳnh **Như** (c) 🟨 **76** (12 Phạm Hải **Yến** 76). *Mai Đức Chung*

Dunedin Stadium, Dunedin/Ōtepoti
23.07.2023, 19:30, **11,991**

NETHERLANDS 🇳🇱 **1-0** 🇵🇹 PORTUGAL

Van der Gragt 13

🧑‍⚖️ Kateryna Monzul UKR
🚩 Maryna Striletska UKR & Paulina Baranowska POL
📺 Drew Fischer CAN

NED • 1 Daphne **van Domselaar** - 8 Sherida **Spitse** (c), 3 Stefanie **van der Gragt**, 20 Dominique **Janssen** - 17 Victoria **Pelova** (18 Kerstin **Casparij** 90+4), 22 Esmee **Brugts**, 6 Jill **Roord**, 10 Daniëlle **van de Donk** 🟨 **78** (21 Damaris **Egurrola** 80) - 14 Jackie **Groenen** - 7 Lineth **Beerensteyn** (9 Katja **Snoeijs** 87), 11 Lieke **Martens**. *Andries Jonker*

POR • 1 Inês **Pereira** - 9 Ana **Borges**, 19 Diana **Gomes** 🟨 **84**, 15 Carole **Costa**, 2 Catarina **Amado** (3 Lúcia **Alves** 78) - 14 Dolores **Silva** (c) (20 Kika **Nazareth** 67) - 13 Fátima **Pinto**, 11 Tatiana **Pinto** - 8 Andreia **Norton** (6 Andreia **Jacinto** 78) - 10 Jéssica **Silva** 🟨 **56**, 16 Diana **Silva** (23 Telma **Encarnação** 78). *Francisco Neto*

Wellington Regional Stadium, Wellington/Te Whanganui-a-Tara
27.07.2023, 13:00, **27,312**

USA 🇺🇸 **1-1** 🇳🇱 NETHERLANDS

Horan 62   Roord 17

🧑‍⚖️ Yoshimi Yamashita JPN
🚩 Makoto Bozono JPN & Naomi Teshirogi JPN
📺 Juan Soto VEN

USA • Naeher - Fox, Girma, Ertz, Dunn - DeMelo (Lavelle 46) 🟨 **51**), Horan (c), Sullivan - Rodman, Morgan, Smith. *Andonovski*

NED • Van Domselaar - Spitse (c), Van der Gragt (4 Aniek **Nouwen** 46), Janssen - Pelova (Casparij 86), Roord (13 Renate **Jansen** 90+4), Groenen, Van de Donk, Brugts - Snoeijs (Egurrola 71), Martens. *Jonker*

Waikato Stadium, Hamilton/Kirikiriroa
27.07.2023, 19:30, **6,645**

PORTUGAL 🇵🇹 **2-0** 🇻🇳 VIETNAM

Encarnação 7, Nazareth 21

🧑‍⚖️ Salima Mukansanga RWA
🚩 Queency Victoire MRI & Mary Njoroge KEN
📺 Adil Zourak MAR

POR • 12 Patrícia **Morais** - Alves, 17 Ana **Seiça** (4 Silvia **Rebelo** 90), C Costa, 5 Joana **Marchão** - Nazareth (21 Ana **Capeta** 69), Jacinto (7 Ana **Rute** 90), T Pinto - Borges (c) 🟨 **86**, Encarnação (18 Carolina **Mendes** 75), J Silva (Norton 69). *Neto*

VIE • Trần Thị Kim Thanh - Trần Thị Thu Thảo, Lương Thị Thu Thương (Chương Thị Kiều 72), Lê Thị Diễm My, Trần Thị Thu, Hoàng Thị Loan - Nguyễn Thị Bích Thùy (Ngân Thị Vạn Sự 64), Dương Thị Vân - Trần Thị Hải Linh 64), Thái Thị Thảo, 19 Nguyễn Thị Thanh **Nhã** - Huỳnh Như (c) (Phạm Hải Yến (c) 72). *Mai Đức Chung*

Eden Park, Auckland/Tāmaki Makaurau
1.08.2023, 19:00, **42,958**

PORTUGAL 🇵🇹 **0-0** 🇺🇸 USA

🧑‍⚖️ Rebecca Welch ENG
🚩 Natalie Aspinall ENG & Anita Vad HUN
📺 Marco Fritz GER

POR • Pereira - T Pinto, Borges, C Costa 🟨 **56**, Gomes 🟨 **72**, Amado 🟨 **86** (Marchão 89) - Dolores Silva (c), Norton (Encarnação 81) - Nazareth (Jacinto 62) - J Silva, Diana Silva (Capeta 89). *Neto*

USA • Naeher - Fox, Girma 🟨 **81**, Ertz, Dunn (O'Hara 90+7) - Lavelle 🟨 **39**, Sullivan, Horan (c) (14 Emily **Sonnett** 84) - 6 Lynn **Williams** (Rodman 84), Morgan (Thompson 90+7), Smith 🟨 **52** (Rapinoe 61). *Andonovski*

Dunedin Stadium, Dunedin/Ōtepoti
1.08.2023, 19:00, **8,215**

VIETNAM 🇻🇳 **0-7** 🇳🇱 NETHERLANDS

Martens 8, Snoeijs 11, Brugts (2) 18 57, Roord (2) 23 83, Van de Donk 45

🧑‍⚖️ Ivana Martinčić CRO
🚩 Sanja Rodak-Karšić CRO & Karolin Kaivoja EST
📺 Carol Anne Chénard CAN

VIE • Trần Thị Kim Thanh (20 Khổng Thị Hằng 46) - Trần Thị Thu Thảo, Lương Thị Thu Thương (Chương Thị Kiều 28), Lê Thị Diễm My, Trần Thị Thu, Hoàng Thị Loan (Nguyễn Thị Mỹ Anh 28) - Nguyễn Thị Bích Thùy (Nguyễn Thị Tuyết Dung 60), Trần Thị Hải Linh, Dương Thị Vân 🟨 **83**, Nguyễn Thị Thanh Nhã - Phạm Hải Yến (c) (Huỳnh Như 60). *Mai Đức Chung*

NED • Van Domselaar - Spitse (c) (15 Caitlin **Dijkstra** 73), Van der Gragt, Janssen - Pelova (Casparij 46), Roord, Groenen (Egurrola 62), Van de Donk (19 Wieke **Kaptein** 46), Brugts (5 Merel **van Dongen** 80) - Snoeijs, Martens. *Jonker*

Group E

	W	D	L	+	-	PTS
🇳🇱 NED	2	1	0	9	1	7
🇺🇸 USA	1	2	0	4	1	5
🇵🇹 POR	1	1	1	2	1	4
🇻🇳 VIE	0	0	3	0	12	0

▶ Lindsey Horan (10) equalises for the USA in their 1-1 draw against the Netherlands in Wellington in a rematch of the 2019 Final. The draw brought to a halt a run of 13 consecutive victories for the *Stars and Stripes* at the FIFA Women's World Cup.

4

Four players in the USA squad had twin sisters: Aubrey Kingsbury, Alyssa Naeher, Megan Rapinoe and Emily Sonnett. For the first time, sisters would represent the USA at the World Cup, Samantha Mewis in 2019 and Kristie in 2023.

USA saved by the post

Pitted against the USA, Vietnam looked set for a baptism of fire. But the septuagenarian Mai Đức Chung insisted that his players were excited, not daunted. That much was evident on the pitch, their determined defence and keeper Trần Thị Kim Thanh only beaten by Sophia Smith's brace and Lindsey Horan's strong shot, with Alex Morgan denied from the spot. Like Vietnam, Portugal also faced 2019 Finalists on their debut, but while Francisco Neto's side finished a tactical encounter with the Netherlands strongly, they found no reply to Stefanie van der Gragt's header. The group's big guns had to settle for a point apiece when USA skipper Horan cancelled out Jill Roord's opener for the Netherlands. So, with Telma Encarnação and Kika Nazareth's goals having overcome Vietnam, Portugal knew that a first victory over the USA could see them progress at the expense of the *Stars and Stripes*. They came within a whisker of doing so at a packed Eden Park, the woodwork denying Ana Capeta an injury-time winner. "Please realise what Portugal has achieved," implored centurion Jéssica Silva afterwards. An emphatic 7-0 loss to the table-topping Netherlands was another learning curve for Vietnam, where hopes of establishing a professional league remained. "There is still much to do," said Chung. "But our inaugural participation in the World Cup can only mean good for Vietnamese football."

▶ Telma Encarnação (23) celebrates after scoring Portugal's first-ever World Cup goal in their 2-0 victory over Vietnam in Hamilton.

Unbeaten *Reggae Girlz* push on

Before these finals, Jamaica had criticised their football association for its "subpar" support, while an online fundraiser had collected money for backroom staff and players. Shrugging off their adversity and the goal threat of France's Kadidiatou Diani, they opened with a first-ever World Cup point, the downside being skipper Khadija Shaw's late red card. Backed by their football association, Ignacio Quintana's Panama had prepared for the finals with an unprecedented number of friendlies. But Brazil, featuring nine competition debutants, found their rhythm amid the fans' lively drumbeats, with Bia Zaneratto and three-goal Ary Borges on target. Centurions Eugénie Le Sommer and Wendie Renard stymied Pia Sundhage's Brazil, though, France motivated by coach Hervé Renard's pre-match cry of "Nothing's going to stop us!" Panama gave it everything. Out after losing to Jamaica by virtue of an Allyson Swaby header, they rocked France after 68 seconds, tearful skipper Marta Cox celebrating her stunning free kick with a skyward kiss in honour of her late mother. The battling newcomers scored twice more, but it ended 6-3 to *Les Bleues*, who were through as group winners. Jamaica joined them in the knockouts at the expense of a stunned Brazil, who paid the price for a goalless draw. It was the *Seleção*'s first early exit in 28 years and as their iconic forward Marta departed Melbourne, she issued a heartfelt plea for Brazil to back its women. "That's all I ask, to continue supporting," she said.

Group F

	W	D	L	+	-	PTS
FRA	2	1	0	8	4	7
JAM	1	2	0	1	0	5
BRA	1	1	1	5	2	4
PAN	0	0	3	3	11	0

◀ Panama keeper Yenith Bailey dives in vain as Léa Le Garrec of France scores her team's fourth goal just before half-time. The match in Sydney finished 6-3 in favour of the French, the highest-scoring game of the tournament.

3
Brazil coach Pia Sundhage became the first to lead three different nations at the World Cup, having taken the USA to the Final in 2011 and her homeland Sweden to the round of 16 in 2015. The game against Jamaica was her 13th on this stage.

68
Marta Cox's fine free kick opened Panama's World Cup account. Scored after 68 seconds, it was the fastest goal of the entire tournament.

◀ Jamaica celebrate after holding Brazil to a goalless stalemate in the final game of Group F. The result saw the *Reggae Girlz* progress to the round of 16 while the Brazilians exited at the group stage for the first time since 1995.

Sydney Football Stadium, Sydney/Gadigal
23.07.2023, 20:00, 39,045
FRANCE 0-0 JAMAICA

🏁 María Carvajal CHI
🚩 Leslie Vásquez CHI & Loreto Toloza CHI
📺 Nicolás Gallo COL

FRA • 16 Pauline **Peyraud-Magnin** - 2 Maëlle **Lakrar**, 20 Estelle **Cascarino**, 3 Wendie **Renard** (c), 7 Sakina **Karchaoui** - 6 Sandie **Toletti** - 8 Grace **Geyoro**, 10 Amel **Majri** (23 Vicki **Bêcho** 66) - 11 Kadidiatou **Diani**, 9 Eugénie **Le Sommer**, 12 Clara **Matéo** 🟨 14 (15 Kenza **Dali** 66). *Hervé Renard*
JAM • 13 Rebecca **Spencer** - 4 Chantelle **Swaby**, 17 Allyson **Swaby**, 3 Vyan **Sampson**, 19 Tierrny **Wiltshire** - 10 Jody **Brown**, 20 Atlanta **Primus** 🟨 24 (2 Solai **Washington** 70), 8 Drew **Spence**, 14 Deneisha **Blackwood** - 21 Cheyna **Matthews** (6 Havana **Solaun** 70), 11 Khadija **Shaw** (c) 🟨 37 🟨 90+2 🟥 90+2. *Lorne Donaldson*

Hindmarsh Stadium, Adelaide/Tarntanya
24.07.2023, 20:30, 13,142
BRAZIL 4-0 PANAMA
Ary Borges (3) 19 39 70,
Bia Zaneratto 48

🏁 Cheryl Foster WAL
🚩 Michelle O'Neill IRL & Franca Overtoom NED
📺 Massimiliano Irrati ITA

BRA • 12 **Letícia** - 2 **Antônia** (13 **Bruninha** 59), 14 **Lauren**, 4 **Rafaelle** (c), 6 **Tamires** - 17 **Ary Borges** (10 **Marta** 75), 21 **Kerolin**, 5 **Luana** (15 **Duda Sampaio** 75), 11 **Adriana** - 16 **Bia Zaneratto** (23 **Gabi Nunes** 59), 9 **Debinha** (18 **Geyse** 76). *Pia Sundhage SWE*
PAN • 12 Yenith **Bailey** - 4 Katherine **Castillo**, 5 Yomira **Pinzón**, 15 Rosario **Vargas** (14 Carmen **Montenegro** 83), 23 Carina **Baltrip-Reyes**, 2 Hilary **Jaén** (3 Wendy **Natis** 46) - 11 Natalia **Mills** (c) (7 Emily **Cedeño** 53), 20 Aldrith **Quintero** (6 Deysiré **Salazar** 65), 8 Schiandra **González**, 10 Marta **Cox** (19 Lineth **Cedeño** 79) - 9 Karla **Riley** (13 Riley **Tanner** 53). *Ignacio Quintana MEX*

Brisbane Stadium, Brisbane/Meaanjin
29.07.2023, 20:00, 49,378
FRANCE 2-1 BRAZIL
Le Sommer 17, Renard 83   Debinha 58

🏁 Kate Jacewicz AUS
🚩 Kim Kyoung Min KOR & Joanna Charaktis AUS
📺 Massimiliano Irrati ITA

FRA • **Peyraud-Magnin** - 22 Ève **Périsset**, **Lakrar**, **Renard** (c), **Karchaoui** 🟨 69 - **Toletti** 🟨 29 - **Geyoro**, **Dali** 🟨 11 (17 Léa **Le Garrec** 87) - **Diani**, **Le Sommer** (**Bêcho** 65), 13 Selma **Bacha**. *Renard* 🟨 98+8
BRA • **Letícia** - **Antônia** (19 **Mônica** 85), **Lauren**, **Rafaelle** (c), **Tamires** - **Ary Borges** (8 **Ana Vitória** 85), **Kerolin**, **Luana** 🟨 44, **Adriana** (**Bia Zaneratto** 80) - **Debinha** (**Marta** 85), **Geyse** (7 **Andressa** 61). *Sundhage SWE*

Perth Rectangular Stadium, Perth/Boorloo
29.07.2023, 20:30, 15,987
PANAMA 0-1 JAMAICA
                                A Swaby 56

🏁 Kateryna Monzul UKR
🚩 Maryna Strieletska UKR & Paulina Baranowska POL
📺 Juan Martínez Munuera ESP

PAN • **Bailey** - **Castillo**, **Natis**, **Baltrip-Reyes** (**Jaén** 87), **Pinzón**, **Salazar** 🟨 18 (**Quintero** 46) - E **Cedeño** 🟨 13, L **Cedeño** (**Riley** 65), **González** (**Montenegro** 78), **Cox** (c) - **Tanner**. *Quintana MEX*
JAM • **Spencer** - 15 Tiffany **Cameron** (**Wiltshire** 87), A **Swaby** (c), C **Swaby**, **Blackwood** 🟨 31 - **Sampson** - **Primus** (7 Peyton **McNamara** 87), **Spence** - **Brown** (**Washington** 80), 22 Kayla **McKenna** (9 Kameron **Simmonds** 80), 18 Trudi **Carter** (**Matthews** 65). *Donaldson*

Sydney Football Stadium, Sydney/Gadigal
2.08.2023, 20:00, 40,498
PANAMA 3-6 FRANCE
Cox 2 (68 secs), Pinzón 64p,   Lakrar 21, Diani (3) 28 37p
Cedeño 87   52p, Le Garrec 45+5, Bêcho
                                90+10

🏁 Laura Fortunato ARG
🚩 Mariana de Almeida ARG & Daiana Milone ARG
📺 Alejandro Hernández ESP

PAN • **Bailey** - E **Cedeño** (18 Erika **Hernández** 58), **Natis** (16 Rebeca **Espinosa** 62), **Pinzón**, **Baltrip-Reyes**, **Jaén** - **Montenegro** (**González** 58), **Salazar** (L **Cedeño** 46), **Quintero**, **Tanner** (**Mills** 81) - **Cox** (c). *Quintana MEX*
FRA • **Peyraud-Magnin** - **Périsset**, **Lakrar**, 5 **Élisa de Almeida**, **Cascarino** - **Bêcho**, **Le Garrec**, **Geyoro** (c) (**Majri** 46), **Bacha** (18 Viviane **Asseyi** 46) - **Matéo** - **Diani** (4 Laurina **Fazer** 60). *Renard*

Melbourne Rectangular Stadium, Melbourne/Naarm
2.08.2023, 20:00, 27,638
JAMAICA 0-0 BRAZIL

🏁 Esther Staubli SUI
🚩 Katrin Rafalski GER & Susanne Küng SUI
📺 Marco Fritz GER

JAM • **Spencer** - **Wiltshire**, A **Swaby**, C **Swaby**, **Blackwood** - **Sampson** - **Matthews** 🟨 30 (**Cameron** 46), **Primus**, **Spence**, **Brown** (**Washington** 85) - **Shaw** (c). *Donaldson*
BRA • **Letícia** - **Antônia** (**Geyse** 81), 3 **Kathellen**, **Rafaelle**, **Tamires** - **Ary Borges** (**Bia Zaneratto** 46), **Kerolin**, **Luana** (**Duda Sampaio** 81), **Adriana** - **Debinha**, **Marta** (c) (**Andressa** 81). *Sundhage SWE*

2023 Group stage

Wellington Regional Stadium, Wellington/Te Whanganui-a-Tara
23.07.2023, 17:00, **18,317**

SWEDEN 2-1 SOUTH AFRICA
Rolfö 65, Ilestedt 90 — Magaia 48

Ekaterina Koroleva USA
Kathryn Nesbitt USA & Felisha Mariscal USA
Carol Anne Chénard CAN

SWE • 1 Zećira **Mušović** - 14 Nathalie **Björn**, 13 Amanda **Ilestedt**, 6 Magdalena **Eriksson**, 2 Jonna **Andersson** - 16 Filippa **Angeldahl** (20 Hanna **Bennison** 67), 23 Elin **Rubensson** (17 Caroline **Seger** 81) - 19 Johanna **Kaneryd** (8 Lina **Hurtig** 88), 9 Kosovare **Asllani** (c), 18 Fridolina **Rolfö** (22 Olivia **Schough** 67) - 11 Stina **Blackstenius** (15 Rebecka **Blomqvist** 67). *Peter Gerhardsson*

RSA • 1 Kaylin **Swart** - 13 Bambanani **Mbane**, 2 Lebohang **Ramalepe**, 3 Bongeka **Gamede**, 18 Sibulele **Holweni** - 15 Refiloe **Jane** (c) ▪ 89, 19 Kholosa **Biyana** ▪ 74 - 12 Jermaine **Seoposenwe**, 10 Linda **Motlhalo** (22 Nomvula **Kgoale** 67), 11 Thembi **Kgatlana** - 8 Hildah **Magaia** (9 Gabriela **Salgado** 56). *Desiree Ellis*

Eden Park, Auckland/Tāmaki Makaurau
24.07.2023, 18:00, **30,889**

ITALY 1-0 ARGENTINA
Girelli 87

Melissa Borjas HON
Shirley Perelló HON & Sandra Ramírez MEX
Tatiana Guzmán NCA

ITA • 22 Francesca **Durante** - 4 Lucia **Di Guglielmo**, 5 Elena **Linari**, 23 Cecilia **Salvai**, 17 Lisa **Boattin** - 6 Manuela **Giugliano**, 16 Giulia **Dragoni** (10 Cristiana **Girelli** 83) - 8 Barbara **Bonansea** (c) ▪ 85, 18 Arianna **Caruso** ▪ 25 (20 Giada **Greggi** 58), 14 Chiara **Beccari** - 9 Valentina **Giacinti** (7 Sofia **Cantore** 74). *Milena Bertolini*

ARG • 1 Vanina **Correa** (c) - 13 Sophia **Braun**, 14 Miriam **Mayorga** ▪ 68, 6 Aldana **Cometti**, 3 Eliana **Stábile** ▪ 90+6 - 8 Daiana **Falfán** (10 Dalila **Ippólito** 90+2), 16 Lorena **Benítez** - 7 Romina **Núñez** (11 Yamila **Rodríguez** 77), 15 Florencia **Bonsegundo** ▪ 76, 22 Estefanía **Banini** - 19 Mariana **Larroquette** ▪ 12 (9 Paulina **Gramaglia** 90+2). *Germán Portanova*

Dunedin Stadium, Dunedin/Ōtepoti
28.07.2023, 12:00, **8,834**

ARGENTINA 2-2 SOUTH AFRICA
Braun 74, Núñez 79 — Motlhalo 30, Kgatlana 66

Anna-Marie Keighley NZL
Sarah Jones NZL & Maria Salamasina SAM
Abdulla Al Marri QAT

ARG • Correa (c) - Braun, Mayorga ▪ 45+1, Cometti, Stábile - Benítez (4 Julieta **Cruz** 46) - Gramaglia (Rodríguez 59), Falfán (Núñez 46), Bonsegundo, Banini - Larroquette (21 Érica **Lonigro** 69). *Portanova*

RSA • Swart - Ramalepe, Mbane, Gamede, 7 Karabo **Dhlamini** - Jane (c) (Biyana 25 ▪ 43) (14 Tiisetso **Makhubela** 54 ▪ 56), Motlhalo (Kgoale 83) - Seoposenwe, Magaia, 6 Noxolo **Cesane** (Holweni 54) - Kgatlana (17 Melinda **Kgadiete** 83). *Ellis*

Wellington Regional Stadium, Wellington/Te Whanganui-a-Tara
29.07.2023, 19:30, **29,143**

SWEDEN 5-0 ITALY
Ilestedt (2) 39 50, Rolfö 44, Blackstenius 45+1, Blomqvist 90+5

Cheryl Foster WAL
Michelle O'Neill IRL & Franca Overtoom NED
Pol van Boekel NED

SWE • Mušović - Björn, Ilestedt, Eriksson, Andersson - Angeldahl, Rubensson (Seger 75) - Kaneryd (10 Sofia **Jakobsson** 75), Asllani (c) (7 Madelen **Janogy** 62), Rolfö (Schough 62) - Blackstenius (Blomqvist 89). *Gerhardsson*

ITA • Durante - Di Guglielmo (19 Martina **Lenzini** 59), Linari, Salvai, Boattin - Giugliano, Caruso (21 Valentina **Cernoia** 71) - Bonansea (c) (15 Annamaria **Serturini** 59), Dragoni (Greggi 89), Beccari (Giacinti 75) - Cantore. *Bertolini*

Waikato Stadium, Hamilton/Kirikiriroa
2.08.2023, 19:00, **17,907**

ARGENTINA 0-2 SWEDEN
Blomqvist 66, Rubensson 90p

Salima Mukansanga RWA
Queency Victoire MRI & Mary Njoroge KEN
Adil Zourak MAR

ARG • Correa (c) - Braun, 17 Camila **Gómez Ares** ▪ 45+4 (Ippólito 71), Cometti, Stábile - 2 Adriana **Sachs**, Cruz (18 Gabriela **Chávez** 71) - Núñez, Banini, Bonsegundo (Falfán 41) (Rodríguez 79) - Larroquette (Lonigro 79). *Portanova*

SWE • 12 Jennifer **Falk** - 4 Stina **Lennartsson**, Ilestedt (3 Linda **Sembrant** 62), Eriksson, 5 Anna **Sandberg** - Bennison, Seger (c) (Rubensson 46) - Jakobsson (Kaneryd 76), Janogy (Blackstenius 90+3), Schough ▪ 20 (Hurtig 62) - Blomqvist. *Gerhardsson*

Wellington Regional Stadium, Wellington/Te Whanganui-a-Tara
2.08.2023, 19:00, **14,967**

SOUTH AFRICA 3-2 ITALY
Orsi OG 32, Magaia 67, Kgatlana 90+2 — Caruso (2) 11p 74

María Carvajal CHI
Leslie Vásquez CHI & Mónica Amboya ECU
Nicolás Gallo COL

RSA • Swart - Ramalepe (Makhubela 90+5), Mbane, Gamede, Dhlamini (Holweni 90+15) - 20 Robyn **Moodaly** (Kgoale 46), 4 Noko **Matlou**, Motlhalo, Magaia (23 Wendy **Shongwe** 90+5) - Seoposenwe, Kgatlana (c). *Ellis*

ITA • Durante - Di Guglielmo (13 Elisa **Bartoli** 64), Linari, 3 Benedetta **Orsi** (11 Benedetta **Glionna** 90+10), Boattin - Giugliano, Caruso (Greggi 83) - Beccari (Cantore 83), Dragoni, Bonansea (c) (Girelli 64) - Giacinti. *Bertolini*

Group G

	W	D	L	+	-	PTS
SWE	3	0	0	9	1	9
RSA	1	1	1	6	6	4
ITA	1	0	2	3	8	3
ARG	0	1	2	2	5	1

▶ Thembi Kgatlana of South Africa competes for the ball against Miriam Mayorga and Lorena Benítez of Argentina during their 2-2 draw in Dunedin. In the following game, Kgatlana scored an injury-time winner against Italy to take her side through to the round of 16.

39

Starting all three of their group matches, Argentina's Vanina Correa became the competition's oldest-ever goalkeeper at the age of 39 years and 353 days. The *Albiceleste* captain also became the only player to have featured in all four of her country's World Cup squads.

10

Sweden's 2-1 win over South Africa was the tenth match of this World Cup, and remarkably, it was the first to see both sides score.

▶ Defender Amanda Ilestedt jumps highest to head home Sweden's opening goal against Italy in Wellington. Despite scoring four goals at the tournament, Ilestedt missed out on the silver and bronze boot awards as a result of having provided fewer assists than Kadidiatou Diani and having played more minutes than Alexandra Popp, both of whom also scored four goals.

Banyana Banyana leave it late

Scoring exactly a year after her brace had secured South Africa's maiden continental title, Hildah Magaia put Sweden on the back foot in a wet and windy Wellington. Swedish pressure told, though, Fridolina Rolfö levelling and Amanda Ilestedt heading in a 90th-minute clincher. Argentina were also undone at the death, centurion Cristiana Girelli matching legend Carolina Morace's long-standing four-goal World Cup tally with a winning header after having just come on for Italy's only overseas-based player, 16-year-old Giulia Dragoni. Germán Portanova's players had battled back against Paraguay to clinch *Copa América* bronze and qualify for this World Cup, Argentina's fourth in two decades. They rekindled that fighting spirit against South Africa, Sophia Braun's dipping volley and substitute Romina Núñez's header cancelling out Linda Motlhalo and Thembi Kgatlana's earlier efforts. But having stunned Italy 5-0 – their biggest win on this stage since blitzing Japan 8-0 in 1991 – Sweden then sent Argentina home. Ahead through Rebecka Blomqvist's header, Elin Rubensson belted a powerful 90th-minute spot kick beyond the competition's oldest-ever goalkeeper, 39-year-old Vanina Correa, to seal pole position in the group for her nation. Milena Bertolini's Italy needed a point to pip South Africa to the knockouts. Their youngest World Cup side yet dared to dream after Arianna Caruso's dramatic late leveller, but Kgatlana's cool 92nd-minute strike saw Desiree Ellis's ecstatic *Banyana Banyana* prevail in their first-ever World Cup win.

Group H

◀ Morocco celebrate after their 1-0 victory over South Korea in Adelaide. A 1-0 win in their final group match against Colombia saw the North Africans finish second in the group, one of a record three African teams to make it through to the round of 16.

◀ Teenage sensation Linda Caicedo scores Colombia's first goal in their stunning 2-1 victory over Germany in Sydney. When the Germans could only draw with South Korea in their final match, it saw them exit at the group stage for the first time at the FIFA Women's World Cup.

Morocco make history in dramatic finale

Germany kick-started this campaign with a thumping 6-0 win over a Morocco side ranked 70 places below them. An Alexandra Popp double and two own goals helped put *Die Nationalelf* in a commanding position, while Klara Bühl's goal 22 seconds after the restart was the fastest second-half strike in the competition's history. Colombia's record scorer Catalina Usme got off the mark in the 300th Women's World Cup match, slotting a clinical penalty beyond South Korea keeper Yoon Young Geul. Linda Caicedo raised the bar though, the 18-year-old powering in her maiden goal on this stage. Morocco bounced back from their heavy defeat to Germany thanks to Ibtissam Jraïdi's glancing header, which was enough to beat Colin Bell's South Korea, ranked 17th in the world.

Caicedo, meanwhile, had Germany reeling when she jinked deceptively and curled in a *golazo*. Popp's late penalty almost rescued Martina Voss-Tecklenburg's side, but Germany fell to only their second group-stage loss ever, Manuela Vanegas's 97th-minute header rapturously received by a sea of yellow-clad fans. All four sides had been runners-up in their respective continental championships, but few expected that it would go down to the final day to separate them here. In yet another dramatic twist, Anissa Lahmari's goal in Morocco's narrow win over Colombia sent Germany and South Korea crashing out. Veterans Cho So Hyun and Alexandra Popp both found the net for their respective sides, but a frantic stalemate was ultimately not enough for either.

16

At 16 years and 26 days, speedy South Korea forward Casey Phair became the competition's youngest-ever player when she came off the bench against Colombia. Also brought on as a late substitute against Morocco, the US-raised high-school student led the line from the start against Germany.

	W	D	L	+	–	PTS
COL	2	0	1	4	2	6
MAR	2	0	1	2	6	6
GER	1	1	1	8	3	4
KOR	0	1	2	1	4	1

Melbourne Rectangular Stadium, Melbourne/Naarm
24.07.2023, 18:30, **27,256**

GERMANY 6-0 MOROCCO

Popp (2) 11 39, Bühl 46, Aït El Haj OG 54, Redouani OG 79, Schüller 90

🏁 Tori Penso USA
🚩 Brooke Mayo USA & Mijensa Rensch SUR
📺 Carol Anne Chénard CAN

GER • 1 Merle **Frohms** - 9 Svenja **Huth**, 3 Kathrin **Hendrich**, 23 Sara **Doorsoun**, 17 Felicitas **Rauch** (2 Chantal **Hagel** 89) - 18 Melanie **Leupolz** (14 Lena **Lattwein** 64), 13 Sara **Däbritz** - 22 Jule **Brand**, 20 Lina **Magull** (7 Lea **Schüller** 64), 19 Klara **Bühl** (16 Nicole **Anyomi** 64 ■ 79) - 11 Alexandra **Popp** (c) (10 Laura **Freigang** 82). *Martina Voss-Tecklenburg*

MAR • 1 Khadija **Er-Rmichi** - 17 Hanane **Aït El Haj**, 21 Yasmin **Mrabet** (5 Nesryne **El Chad** 82), 2 Zineb **Redouani** - 19 Sakina **Ouzraoui** (20 Sofia **Bouftini** 90+5), 6 Élodie **Nakkach** (10 Najat **Badri** 82), 4 Sarah **Kassi**, 11 Fatima **Tagnaout** - 7 Ghizlane **Chebbak** (c), 23 Rosella **Ayane** (9 Ibtissam **Jraïdi** 90+5), 16 Anissa **Lahmari** (8 Salma **Amani** 67. *Reynald Pedros FRA*

Sydney Football Stadium, Sydney/Gadigal
25.07.2023, 12:00, **24,323**

COLOMBIA 2-0 KOREA REPUBLIC

Usme 30p, Caicedo 39

🏁 Rebecca Welch ENG
🚩 Natalie Aspinall ENG & Anita Vad HUN
📺 Drew Fischer CAN

COL • 1 Catalina **Pérez** - 17 Carolina **Arias** ■ 45+6, 19 Jorelyn **Carabalí**, 3 Daniela **Arias**, 2 Manuela **Vanegas** ■ 10 - 5 Lorena **Bedoya Durango**, 6 Daniela **Montoya** (c) (4 Diana **Ospina García** 87) - 11 Catalina **Usme**, 10 Leicy **Santos** (8 Marcela **Restrepo** 76), 18 Linda **Caicedo** - 9 Mayra **Ramírez**. *Nelson Abadía*, with Angelo Marsiglia pitchside

KOR • 1 **Yoon** Young Geul - 20 **Kim** Hye Ri (c), 6 **Lim** Seon Joo ■ 45+7, 4 **Shim** Seo Yeon ■ 29 - 2 **Choo** Hyo Joo (12 **Moon** Mi Ra 87), 10 **Ji** So Yun, 8 **Cho** So Hyun (13 **Park** Eun Sun 68), 16 **Jang** Sel Gi - 11 **Choe** Yu Ri (19 **Casey Phair** 78), 9 **Lee** Geum Min, 7 **Son** Hwa Yeon (23 **Kang** Chae Rim 68). *Colin Bell ENG*

Hindmarsh Stadium, Adelaide/Tarntanya
30.07.2023, 14:00, **12,886**

KOREA REPUBLIC 0-1 MOROCCO

Jraïdi 6

🏁 Edina Alves Batista BRA
🚩 Neuza Back BRA & Leila Cruz BRA
📺 Daiane Muniz dos Santos BRA

KOR • 18 **Kim** Jung Mi - **Kim** Hye Ri (c), 1 **Hong** Hye Ji (Casey Phair 84), **Shim** Seo Yeon - **Choo** Hyo Joo (Moon Mi Ra 46), **Lee** Geum Min (15 **Chun** Ga Ram 88), **Ji** So Yun, **Cho** So Hyun, **Jang** Sel Gi - **Son** Hwa Yeon (**Choe** Yu Ri 46), **Park** Eun Sun (14 **Jeon** Eun Ha 69). *Bell ENG*

MAR • **Er-Rmichi** - **Aït El Haj**, 3 Nouhaila **Benzina** ■ 81, **El Chad**, **Redouani** - **Ouzraoui**, **Nakkach** (**Badri** 80), **Chebbak** (c), **Tagnaout** 80) - **Jraïdi** (**Ayane** 74), **Amani** (**Kassi** 69). *Pedros FRA*

Sydney Football Stadium, Sydney/Gadigal
30.07.2023, 19:30, **40,499**

GERMANY 1-2 COLOMBIA

Popp 89p   Caicedo 52, Vanegas 90+7

🏁 Melissa Borjas HON
🚩 Shirley Perelló HON & Sandra Ramírez MEX
📺 Armando Villarreal USA

GER • **Frohms** - **Huth**, **Hendrich**, **Doorsoun** (15 Sjoeke **Nüsken** 46), **Hagel** - **Däbritz**, 6 Lena **Oberdorf** ■ 57 - **Brand**, **Magull** (**Schüller** 67), **Bühl** (**Anyomi** 76) - **Popp** (c). *Voss-Tecklenburg*

COL • **Pérez** ■ 85, C **Arias**, **Carabalí** (20 Mónica **Ramos** 90+14), D **Arias**, **Vanegas** - 16 Lady **Andrade** (**Santos** 54), **Bedoya Durango** ■ 62, **Usme**, **Montoya** (c) (**Ospina García** 67 ■ 80) - **Ramírez**, **Caicedo** (**Restrepo** 90+6). *Abadía*, with Marsiglia pitchside

Brisbane Stadium, Brisbane/Meaanjin
3.08.2023, 20:00, **38,945**

KOREA REPUBLIC 1-1 GERMANY

Cho So Hyun 6   Popp 42

🏁 Anna-Marie Keighley NZL
🚩 Sarah Jones NZL & Maria Salamasina SAM
📺 Pol van Boekel NED

KOR • 18 **Kim** Jung Mi - **Kim** Hye Ri (c), **Chun** Ga Ram (**Park** Eun Sun 63), **Shim** Seo Yeon - **Choo** Hyo Joo, **Ji** So Yun, **Choe** Yu Ri, **Cho** So Hyun (**Kang** Chae Rim 90+10), **Jang** Sel Gi - **Phair** (**Moon** Mi Ra 86), 17 **Lee** Young Ju. *Bell ENG*

GER • **Frohms** - **Huth**, **Hendrich**, 5 Marina **Hegering** ■ 90+6, **Hagel** - **Däbritz** (**Lattwein** 64), **Oberdorf** - **Brand** (**Anyomi** 84), **Popp** (c), **Bühl** (8 Sydney **Lohmann** 64) - **Schüller**. *Voss-Tecklenburg*

Perth Rectangular Stadium, Perth/Boorloo
3.08.2023, 18:00, **17,342**

MOROCCO 1-0 COLOMBIA

Lahmari 45+4
(Chebbak penalty saved 45+4)

🏁 Maria Sole Ferrieri Caputi ITA
🚩 Francesca Di Monte ITA & Mihaela Țepușă ROU
📺 Carol Anne Chénard CAN

MAR • **Er-Rmichi** - **Aït El Haj**, **El Chad**, **Benzina**, **Redouani** - **Ouzraoui**, **Nakkach**, **Chebbak** (c) ■ 90+11, **Tagnaout** - **Lahmari** (**Amani** 71) - **Jraïdi** (**Ayane** 86). *Pedros FRA*

COL • **Pérez** - C **Arias** (**Restrepo** 90+1), **Carabalí**, D **Arias**, **Vanegas** ■ 51 - **Bedoya Durango** (21 Ivonne **Chacón** 86), **Montoya** (c) (**Ospina García** 59) - **Ramírez**, **Santos**, **Caicedo** - **Usme**. *Abadía*

2023 **Round of 16**

Spain into their stride

Eden Park, Auckland/Tāmaki Makaurau
5.08.2023, 17:00, **43,217**

SWITZERLAND 1-5 **SPAIN**

Codina OG 11 — Bonmatí (2) 5 36, Redondo 17, Codina 45, Hermoso 70

Cheryl Foster WAL — Michelle O'Neill IRL & Franca Overtoom NED — Marco Fritz GER

SUI • Thalmann - Aigbogun (Calligaris 46), Maritz, Stierli ■ 73, Riesen (3 Lara **Marti** 84) - Sow (Terchoun 46), Wälti (c), Reuteler (Mauron 46) - Piubel (20 Fabienne **Humm** 75), Crnogorčević, Bachmann. *Grings GER*
ESP • 23 Cata **Coll** - Batlle, Paredes, 14 Laia **Codina**, Hernández - Bonmatí (Guerrero 77), Abelleira (16 María **Pérez** 64), Hermoso (Putellas 77) - Paralluelo (Del Castillo 84), González (c) (Navarro 64), Redondo. *Vilda*

As a player, Switzerland boss Inka Grings was one of Germany's most prolific strikers. But with only two goals in an unbeaten group stage, her team had yet to find their shooting boots. Spain had already scored more than in their two previous World Cups combined, but like the Swiss, *La Roja* were seeking a first knockout win. Remarkably, of four new starters, 22-year-old keeper Cata Coll was making her senior international debut. But it was Switzerland's 37-year-old Spanish Liga F shot-stopper Gaëlle Thalmann, playing in a last World Cup before her retirement, who was the busier, as *Die Nati's* run of six first-half World Cup clean sheets was obliterated by Aitana Bonmatí's double either side of Alba Redondo's cute header. Defender Laia Codina made amends for a spectacular 45-yard own goal with a scrappy fourth before the break. Then, on 70 minutes, a sold-out Eden Park crowd were wowed as Jenni Hermoso topped off the highest-scoring round-of-16 match ever. "They sometimes played cat and mouse with us," said Swiss captain Lia Wälti. "We lost to an opponent who could go far in the tournament."

▲ Aitana Bonmatí (6) celebrates her second goal as Spain march on to their first-ever World Cup quarter-final.

Japan, last champions standing

Wellington Regional Stadium, Wellington/Te Whanganui-a-Tara
5.08.2023, 20:00, **33,042**

JAPAN 3-1 **NORWAY**

Syrstad Engen OG 15, Shimizu 50, Miyazawa 81 — Reiten 20

Edina Alves Batista BRA — Neuza Back BRA & Leila Cruz BRA — Diane Muniz BRA

JPN • Yamashita - Takahashi, Kumagai (c), Minami - Shimizu, Nagano, Hasegawa, Endō - Fujino, Tanaka (Ueki 72), Miyazawa. *Ikeda*
NOR • Mikalsen - Bjelde (3 Sara **Hørte** 88), Mjelde (c), Harviken, Hansen (Hegerberg 74) - Bøe Risa (Maanum 63), Syrstad Engen, Reiten - Graham Hansen, Román Haug, Haavi (Sævik 63). *Riise*

The only time these former champions and competition ever-presents had previously met on this stage was in 1999 when current Norway boss Hege Riise scored in a resounding 4-0 win. It was ten years, however, since the Scandinavians last overcame Japan, and Futoshi Ikeda's side raced into an early lead in Wellington when Ingrid Syrstad Engen accidentally diverted the ball beyond Aurora Mikalsen. Within minutes, her opposite number, Ayaka Yamashita, was beaten for the first time in these finals when Chelsea fans' favourite Guro Reiten rose highest to power home Vilde Bøe Risa's cross. It was Norway's 100th World Cup goal, but it would prove to be their last of the tournament. West Ham defender Risa Shimizu put Japan back on top, pouncing on a loose pass in the box to let fly a shot that deflected past Mikalsen. Riise threw on four substitutes, including the lively Karina Sævik and talismanic striker Ada Hegerberg, who was back from a group-stage groin injury, but when Hinata Miyazawa slotted home Japan's third and Yamashita clawed away Sævik's late header, it was all over for Riise and Norway.

▼ Japan keeper Ayaka Yamashita is beaten as Norway's Guro Reiten levels the score in the round-of-16 contest between the two former champions in Wellington.

▶ Japan's Hinata Miyazawa scores her side's third goal against Norway. It was her fifth goal of the tournament, enough to see her win the Golden Boot.

Round of 16 2023

Beerensteyn to the rescue

Sydney Football Stadium, Sydney/Gadigal
6.08.2023, 12:00, **40,233**

NETHERLANDS 🇳🇱 **2-0** 🇿🇦 **SOUTH AFRICA**

Roord 9, Beerensteyn 68

Yoshimi Yamashita JPN   Makoto Bozono JPN & Naomi Teshirogi JPN   Carol Anne Chénard CAN

NED • Van Domselaar - Spitse (c), Van der Gragt, Janssen - Groenen - Pelova (2 Lynn **Wilms** 88), Roord (Snoeijs 90+2), Van de Donk ■ 67 (Egurrola 75), Brugts (Casparij 88) - Beerensteyn, Martens (12 Jill **Baijings** 90+2). *Jonker*
RSA • Swart - Ramalepe, Mbane (Makhubela 42), Matlou, Dhlamini - Magaia (Cesane 90+2), Gamede - Biyana, Motlhalo (Kgadiete 90+2), Seoposenwe (Shongwe 30) - Kgatlana (c). *Ellis*

Donations had been needed to resolve a funding dispute with their federation before this World Cup, but South Africa had already proved their worth by reaching back-to-back editions. Now, the African champions faced the France 2019 runners-up. *Banyana Banyana* could have folded when Jill Roord nodded in her fourth goal of the tournament and striker Jermaine Seoposenwe and defender Bambanani Mbane suffered match-ending injuries. But fleet-footed US-based Thembi Kgatlana put the Netherlands and a 40,000-strong crowd on edge as she forced Daphne van Domselaar into a string of saves. The Dutch had only faced four shots on target in the entire group stage. They came up against seven here, but after Lieke Martens had a goal ruled out for offside, Lineth Beerensteyn settled it when the otherwise excellent Kaylin Swart fumbled her left-footed strike. Afterwards, Desiree Ellis hailed her players while calling for a fully professional league and more sponsorship. "I don't know how you can ignore something special like this," she said. "I don't know how you cannot assist in getting us to climb the ladder."

▲ Jill Roord gives the Netherlands the lead against South Africa in Sydney. With five goals in two World Cups, Jill Roord was now the Netherlands' all-time leading scorer in this competition.

USA, over and out

Melbourne Rectangular Stadium, Melbourne/Naarm
6.08.2023, 19:00, **27,706**

SWEDEN 🇸🇪 **0-0** 🇺🇸 **USA**
AET
5-4 PSO

Sullivan ✓, Rolfö ✓, Horan ✓, Rubensson ✓, Mewis ✓, Björn ✗ (over crossbar), Rapinoe ✗ (over crossbar), Blomqvist ✗ (saved), Smith ✗ (wide), Bennison ✓, Naeher ✓, Eriksson ✓, O'Hara ✗ (hit post), Hurtig

Stéphanie Frappart FRA
Manuela Nicolosi FRA & Élodie Coppola FRA
Massimiliano Irrati ITA

SWE • Mušović - Björn, Ilestedt, Eriksson, Andersson - Angeldahl (Bennison 97), Rubensson - Kaneryd (Jakobsson 81), Asllani (c) ■ 49 (Hurtig 81), Rolfö - Blackstenius (Blomqvist 112). *Gerhardsson*
USA • Naeher - Fox (O'Hara 120), Ertz ■ 119, Girma, Dunn - Sonnett (22 Kristie **Mewis** 120), Sullivan - Rodman (Williams 66), Horan (c), Smith - Morgan (Rapinoe 99). *Andonovski*

No nations have faced each other at the World Cup more times than Sweden and the USA, but this seventh encounter was their first in the knockout phase. The USA survived the group stage by the width of a post, but Vlatko Andonovski's blend of World Cup rookies and experienced heads seemed back to their best in Melbourne. Shot-stopper Zećira Mušović, however, was equal to every chance carved out by Lindsey Horan, Alex Morgan, Trinity Rodman and Lynn Williams throughout the 120 minutes. Only spot kicks remained, but after Megan Rapinoe missed hers and Sophia Smith skied a potential winner, the shoot-out rumbled on into sudden death. At 4-4 the USA were on the brink of their earliest World Cup exit ever, and Lina Hurtig sealed their fate with a shot that Alyssa Naeher was convinced she had saved, only for goal-line technology to determine otherwise. "Just not our day," shrugged Rapinoe, with hurt etched across her face at the close of a glittering career. "That's the cruel side of this beautiful game."

◀ Sweden's Lina Hurtig (8) celebrates scoring the winning penalty in the shoot-out against the USA.

▼ Sweden goalkeeper Zećira Mušović's water bottle with guidance for a penalty shoot-out. *FIFA Museum Collection*

◀ Dejected USA players reflect on their team's earliest-ever FIFA Women's World Cup exit.

2023 Round of 16

Kelly delivers from the spot

Brisbane Stadium, Brisbane/Meaanjin
7.08.2023, 17:30, **49,461**

ENGLAND 0-0 **NIGERIA**
AET
4-2 PSO

Stanway ✘ (wide), Oparanozie ✘ (wide), England ⚽, Alozie ✘ (over crossbar), Daly ⚽, Ajibade ⚽, Greenwood ⚽, Ucheibe ⚽, Kelly ⚽

Melissa Borjas HON · Shirley Perelló HON & Sandra Ramírez MEX · Armando Villarreal USA

ENG • Earps - Carter, Bright (c), Greenwood - Bronze, Stanway, Walsh (Zelem 120), Daly - James ■ 87 - Russo (Kelly 88), Hemp (England 106). *Wiegman NED*

NGA • Nnadozie (c) - Alozie, Ohale, Demehin, Plumptre - Ucheibe, Ayinde (Echegini 91) - Ajibade, Payne (9 Desire **Oparanozie** 114), Onumonu (Oshoala 58) - Kanu (Ordega 81). *Waldrum USA*

This was the first time Nigeria had headed into the World Cup without their continental crown. But Randy Waldrum's players had performed like champions, becoming the first African side to reach the knockouts for a third time. Former England youth player Ashleigh Plumptre signalled their intent here, bending the crossbar then forcing Mary Earps into a diving save. Nigeria survived a soft penalty shout, but Lauren James did not escape scrutiny, seeing red after a review for a stamp on defender Michelle Alozie. With the woodwork, Earps and Chiamaka Nnadozie prolonging the stalemate even in extra time, penalties decided it. And after one miss to Nigeria's two, Chloe Kelly's blistering strike finally saw England breathe a sigh of relief against a side that had outgunned the *Lionesses* by 18 shots to 12 and departed with three clean sheets in four matches. "I'm tired of people saying African teams are just strong and fast and count us out as being technical or tactical," declared Plumptre afterwards. "We made a statement here."

◂ England's Chloe Kelly (18) after scoring the winning penalty in the shoot-out against Nigeria. Her kick was measured at 110.79km/h, the fastest recorded at the finals. Mary Earps and Rachel Daly appreciate her efforts.

◂ Nigeria's Christy Ucheibe and England's Georgia Stanway (8) tussle for the ball during the match in Brisbane while Lucy Bronze (2) and Ashleigh Plumptre look on.

Hosts Australia march on

Stadium Australia, Sydney/Wangal
7.08.2023, 20:30, **75,784**

AUSTRALIA 2-0 **DENMARK**
Foord 29, Raso 70

Rebecca Welch ENG · Natalie Aspinall ENG & Anita Vad HUN · Nicolás Gallo COL

AUS • Arnold - Carpenter, Hunt, Kennedy, Catley (c) - Raso (20 Sam **Kerr** (c) 80), Gorry, Cooney-Cross, Foord (13 Tameka **Yallop** 90+5) - Fowler (Polkinghorne 90+1), Van Egmond (Vine 80). *Gustavsson SWE*

DEN • Christensen - Sevecke (Bruun 63), Ballisager, Boye, Veje - Thomsen ■ 67, Kühl (Hasbo 73), Holmgaard (Troelsgaard 82), Madsen (Gejl 63) - Vangsgaard (8 Emma **Snerle** 82), Harder (c). *Søndergaard*

16

Caitlin Foord and Emily van Egmond both made their 16th World Cup appearance in this match, overtaking the previous *Matildas* record of 15 held by Lisa De Vanna.

◂ Australia's Caitlin Foord (centre) opens the scoring against Denmark in front of a capacity crowd in the round-of-16 encounter in Sydney.

Denmark had inflicted a World Cup debut to forget on Australia in 1995. Yet, unlike the *Matildas*, the Danes had not appeared on this stage in 16 years, missing out on two editions by dint of disappointing play-off losses. Unassailable in qualifying, Lars Søndergaard's team had already surpassed Denmark's previous best with two group-stage victories. Now they faced an Australia side galvanised by their 12th player – the fans. All-time record scorer Pernille Harder played her usual game regardless, creating havoc with her movement and goal menace. But with deafening cheers greeting hometown heroine Caitlin Foord's every touch, the *Matildas* attacker seemed to grow in confidence, and when she dispatched Mary Fowler's perfect pass, Stadium Australia erupted. Denmark pushed on, even after Hayley Raso's second-half drive, and the late introduction of Sam Kerr to rapturous cheers. Yet while they exited with their pride intact, it was not the send-off they had envisaged for popular departing boss Søndergaard.

Colombia, last Americans standing

Melbourne Rectangular Stadium, Melbourne/Naarm
8.08.2023, 18:00, **27,706**

COLOMBIA 1-0 JAMAICA

Usme 51

Kate Jacewicz AUS
Kim Kyoung Min KOR & Joanna Charaktis AUS
Pol van Boekel NED

COL • Pérez - C Arias, Caralbalí, D Arias ■ 70, 15 Ana María **Guzmán** - Bedoya Durango, Ospina García - Caicedo, Santos (Montoya 87), Ramírez - Usme (c) (Restrepo 90+3). *Abadía*

JAM • Spencer - Wiltshire (Matthews 83), A Swaby, C Swaby ■ 41, Blackwood - Carter (Cameron 67), Sampson (McNamara 79), Spence ■ 45+1, Brown (Simmonds 83) - 12 Kalyssa **van Zanten** (Primus 46), Shaw (c). *Donaldson*

▶ Colombia goalkeeper Catalina Pérez outjumps Jamaica's Khadija "Bunny" Shaw (11) during their round-of-16 match in Melbourne.

Jamaica's 67-year-old boss Lorne Donaldson performed forward rolls to celebrate the *Reggae Girlz* unbeaten run to the last 16. Two days after Jamaican Independence Day, his players needed to showcase some moves of their own to stop attack-minded Colombia. Jamaica had yet to concede in this tournament, and keeper Becky Spencer seemed equally impassable here. Then, in the 51st minute, World Cup debutant Ana María Guzmán delivered an incisive long-range pass, which the Colombian professional league's record scorer, Catalina Usme, calmly collected before side-footing home. Jody Brown and Drew Spence both went close with headers, as did Leicy Santos at the other end, but Usme's goal ultimately decided the contest. Afterwards, Donaldson said his team had surpassed expectations. "Hopefully we all can come together now and figure something out," he added, "and start preparing for the future tomorrow."

▶ Colombia's Catalina Usme (11) celebrates scoring the only goal of the game against Jamaica as the South Americans booked their place in the quarter-finals for the first time.

5

France scored the most headed goals at the tournament, Eugénie Le Sommer bringing the total to five when, against the Moroccans, she notched her 92nd international goal.

France end Moroccan dreams

Hindmarsh Stadium, Adelaide/Tarntanya
8.08.2023, 20:30, **13,557**

FRANCE 4-0 MOROCCO

Diani 15, Dali 20, Le Sommer (2) 23 70

Tori Penso USA   Brooke Mayo USA & Mijensa Rensch SUR   Alejandro Hernández ESP

FRA • Peyraud-Magnin - Périsset (Cascarino 81), De Almeida, Renard (c), Karchaoui (14 Aïssatou **Tounkara** 90+1) - Dali, Geyoro, Toletti (Bècho 64), Bacha - Le Sommer (19 Naomie **Feller** 81) - Diani (Asseyi 90+1). *Renard*

MAR • Er-Rmichi - Aït El Haj ■ 57, El Chad, Benzina, Redouani - Ouzraoui, Nakkach (Kassi 64), Chebbak (c), Tagnaout (Bouftini 64) - Jraïdi, Lahmari (Ayane 64). *Pedros FRA*

▲ Kadidiatou Diani (centre) of France celebrates after opening the scoring against Morocco.

France had watched the last matches of Group H over dinner, fully expecting that they would be meeting Colombia or Germany in the next round. Instead, it would be Morocco, the first African team to win successive Women's World Cup matches and keep back-to-back clean sheets. Only Morocco captain Ghizlane Chebbak remained from the sides' sole previous meeting, a friendly in Casablanca in 2008, yet the two teams were no strangers to each other. The *Atlas Lionesses*' manager Reynald Pedros had led five players in *Les Bleues*' squad to Champions League glory at Lyon, four Morocco players had played for France in their youth, and France coach Hervé Renard had taken Morocco's men to the 2018 World Cup. Their kinship was soon set aside in Adelaide, though, France brutally clinical with three goals in eight first-half minutes from Kadidiatou Diani, Kenza Dali and Eugénie Le Sommer. Ibtissam Jraïdi came closest to a reply, but Le Sommer nodded in Vicki Bècho's cross to put the game to bed. The first Arab nation to feature in the competition had been knocked out, but they had written themselves into its history regardless.

2023 Quarter-finals

Paralluelo wins it for Spain

Wellington Regional Stadium, Wellington/Te Whanganui-a-Tara
11.08.2023, 13:00, **32,021**

SPAIN 2-1 NETHERLANDS
AET

Caldentey 81p, Paralluelo 111 Van der Gragt 90+1

Stéphanie Frappart FRA Manuela Nicolosi FRA & Élodie Coppola FRA Tatiana Guzmán NCA

ESP • Coll - Hernández ■ 35 (Carmona 91), Paredes, Codina (Andrés 77), Batlle - Bonmatí (Guerrero 87), Abelleira, Hermoso - Redondo (Paralluelo 71), González (Navarro 100), Caldentey (Putellas 100). *Vilda*

NED • Van Domselaar - Spitse (c) (Snoeijs 85), Van der Gragt (Casparij 106), Janssen - Pelova, Roord (Wilms 61), Groenen, Egurrola ■ 61 (Dijkstra 96), Brugts (Nouwen 89) - Beerensteyn, Martens. *Jonker*

Spain had yet to play outside New Zealand, but 2019 Finalists the Netherlands were returning to the country after their last-16 match in Sydney. The Dutch had overcome European opposition twice in the knockouts four years earlier, but of the current squad, only skipper Sherida Spitse had ever been on the winning side against Spain. In a sunny Wellington, the game went right to the wire. Both sides saw decisions go against them following VAR reviews, an Esther González goal judged to have been offside and a penalty shout for Lineth Beerensteyn ultimately turned down. The clock was ticking, but late substitute Salma Paralluelo helped put Spain in the ascendency when her cross was handled by Stefanie van der Gragt and Mariona Caldentey walloped the resulting penalty in off the upright. Former Barcelona defender Van der Gragt, in what would turn out to be her last international before retirement, joyously fired in a stoppage-time equaliser. Beerensteyn came agonisingly close for Andries Jonker's side in extra time, but U-20 World Cup champion Paralluelo hit the winner, surging into the box before powering the ball home.

▲ Spain's teenage sensation Salma Paralluelo celebrates scoring the winning goal against the Dutch in the quarter-final in Wellington.

◀ Jennifer Hermoso (10) of Spain controls the ball while closely marked by the Netherlands' double centurion Sherida Spitse.

Nadeshiko bow out

Eden Park, Auckland/Tāmaki Makaurau
11.08.2023, 19:30, **43,217**

JAPAN 1-2 SWEDEN

Hayashi 87, (Ueki penalty missed 76 – hit crossbar) Ilestedt 32, Angeldahl 51p

Esther Staubli SUI Katrin Rafalski GER & Susanne Küng SUI
Massimiliano Irrati ITA

JPN • Yamashita - Takahashi (20 Maika **Hamano** 90+2), Kumagai (c), Minami - Shimizu, Nagano (Hayashi 80), Hasegawa, Sugita (Endō 46) - Fujino, Tanaka (Ueki 52 ■ 79), Miyazawa (Seike 80). *Ikeda*

SWE • Mušović - Björn, Ilestedt, Eriksson, Andersson - Angeldahl, Rubensson (Bennison 84) - Kaneryd (Jakobsson 84), Asllani (c) (Janogy 73), Rolfö (Hurtig 73) - Blackstenius. *Gerhardsson*

Upon his appointment in 2021, Japan coach Futoshi Ikeda spoke of building a *Nadeshiko* side capable of reclaiming the World Cup title. But having already disposed of one former World Cup-winning side, Sweden had their sights set on eliminating another. Amanda Ilestedt set them on their way, tucking away a loose ball to become the first player to score four for Sweden in a single edition of the World Cup since 1991. With Japan's defence struggling, Ayaka Yamashita had to pull off flying saves to keep out Kosovare Asllani and Johanna Kaneryd. Filippa Angeldahl overcame Yamashita from the spot, though, the midfielder scoring the 150th goal of the tournament after a Fuka Nagano handball. Japan's luck remained in short supply, as substitute Riko Ueki was awarded but missed a penalty and Aoba Fujino's free kick was millimetres from crossing the line. Honoka Hayashi's walloping shot set up a gripping climax, but Sweden hung on by the skin of their teeth to put paid to the dreams of a distraught Japan.

▲ Amanda Ilestedt (13) of Sweden opens the scoring in the quarter-final against Japan in Auckland.

▶ Risa Shimizu of Japan tries to get past Jonna Andersson of Sweden.

Australia win epic shoot-out over France

▲ The moment of victory for Australia against France after the longest penalty shoot-out in World Cup history.

▲▶ Australia keeper Mackenzie Arnold saves Kenza Dali's spot kick, her third save of the shoot-out against France.

Brisbane Stadium, Brisbane/Meaanjin
12.08.2023, 17:00, 49,461

AUSTRALIA 0-0 **FRANCE**
AET
7-6 PSO

Bacha ✘ (saved), Foord ✔, Diani ✘ (saved), Catley ✘ (saved), Renard ✔, Kerr ✔, Le Sommer ✔, Fowler ✔, Périsset ✘ (saved), Arnold ✘ (hit post), Geyoro ✔, Gorry ✔, Karchaoui ✔, Yallop ✔, Lakrar ✔, Carpenter ✔, Dali ✘ (retaken then saved), Hunt ✘ (saved), Bècho ✘ (hit post), Vine ✔

⊕ María Carvajal CHI
⚑ Leslie Vásquez CHI & Mónica Amboya ECU
🎦 Nicolás Gallo COL

AUS • Arnold - Carpenter, Hunt, Kennedy, Catley (c) - Raso (Vine 104), Gorry ■ 92, Cooney-Cross (Yallop 116), Foord - Van Egmond (Kerr 55), Fowler. *Gustavsson SWE*
FRA • Peyraud-Magnin (1 Solène **Durand** 120+3) - Lakrar, Renard (c), De Almeida (Périsset 120+3), Karchaoui - Dali, Geyoro, Toletti (Bècho 64), Bacha - Le Sommer - Diani. *Renard*

Australia coach Tony Gustavsson declared, "We're going to embrace every second of it," before facing France in Brisbane. There were, perhaps, more seconds to this encounter than he might have expected, the *Matildas* and *Les Bleues* taking a mammoth battle beyond 120 minutes and into the longest penalty shoot-out in World Cup history. The shots had flown in from the start, but Mackenzie Arnold and Pauline Peyraud-Magnin were imperious throughout, while Élisa de Almeida bravely blocked a sure-fire Mary Fowler effort and Alanna Kennedy was relieved to see her own goal chalked off. With penalties looming, Hervé Renard boldly switched keepers, and unflappable tournament debutant Solène Durand saved twice. Despite missing a chance to net the winner, Arnold saved three and the woodwork denied France one more. Then, as a sold-out stadium held its collective breath, Cortnee Vine kept her cool and slotted the 20th spot kick home. A third consecutive last-eight exit induced a feeling of déjà vu for France, but Renard still wished Australia luck.

20

The number of years that had passed since a host nation had reached the semi-finals of the competition, the USA having finished third in 2003.

England rise to the challenge

Stadium Australia, Sydney/Wangal
12.08.2023, 20:30, 75,784

ENGLAND 2-1 **COLOMBIA**
Hemp 45+7, Russo 63   Santos 44

⊕ Ekaterina Koroleva USA ⚑ Kathryn Nesbitt USA & Felisha Mariscal USA 🎦 Carol Anne Chénard CAN
ENG • Earps - Carter, Bright (c), Greenwood - Bronze, Stanway, Walsh, Daly - Toone - Russo (Kelly 84), Hemp (England 90+3). *Wiegman NED*
COL • Pérez (13 Natalia **Giraldo** 67) - C Arias (Guzmán 10), Carabalí, D Arias, Vanegas - Santos, Ospina García (Chacón 78), Bedoya Durango - Ramírez, Usme (c), Caicedo. *Abadía*

With thousands of giddy *Matildas* fans taking their seats having just lived every moment of their side's epic encounter with France on the nearby fan park's big screen, the atmosphere inside a packed Stadium Australia was electric. Despite being ranked 25th in the world, Colombia were everyone's team on the night, and England were well aware of it. The last South American side to have made it to the same stage of the competition was Brazil in 2011, and a partisan crowd went wild when a dipping cross-cum-shot from Atlético Madrid's Leicy Santos gave Nelson Abadía's players the advantage. England were behind for the first time at the tournament, but within minutes, Lauren Hemp had capitalised on a defensive mix-up to prod home an equaliser. Both sides continued to threaten, but the *Lionesses*' comeback was complete just after the hour mark, Alessia Russo driving home the winner to break *Las Cafeteras* hearts. "The Colombians were incredible, not only the players but the fans," Russo said later. "That's what the World Cup is all about."

▶ England celebrate Alessia Russo's winner against Colombia. Their victory saw the *Lionesses* qualify for a third consecutive semi-final.

◀ Shirt worn by England's Alessia Russo in the quarter-final against Colombia. She scored the winning goal in the 2-1 victory.
FIFA Museum Collection

2 out of 10

Colombia became only the second of the ten South American nations to have reached the quarter-finals of the competition, Brazil having achieved the feat four times.

2023 Semi-finals

19

At 19 years and 275 days, Salma Paralluelo became the second-youngest player to have scored in a Women's World Cup semi-final, after Canada's 16-year-old Kara Lang in 2003.

▶ Action from the semi-final between Sweden and Spain in Auckland, the last of the 29 games played in New Zealand.

Swedish despair as Spain in wonderland

Eden Park, Auckland/Tāmaki Makaurau
15.08.2023, 20:00, **43,217**

SPAIN 2-1 SWEDEN

Paralluelo 81, Carmona 89 Blomqvist 88

Edina Alves Batista BRA ▪ Neuza Back BRA & Leila Cruz BRA ▪ Nicolás Gallo COL

ESP • Coll - Batlle, Paredes, Codina, Carmona (c) - Bonmatí, Abelleira, Putellas (Paralluelo 57) - Redondo (Navarro 73), Hermoso, Caldentey (González 90+5). *Vilda*

SWE • Mušović - Björn, Ilestedt, Eriksson, Andersson - Angeldahl, Rubensson (Hurtig 87) - Kaneryd (Schough 77), Asllani (c), Rolfö - Blackstenius (Blomqvist 77). *Gerhardsson*

A new name was destined for the trophy now that all the past winners were out. Before Sweden could advance their claim, there was a hoodoo to break. Semi-finalists at four World Cups, they had lost out at this stage on three occasions. And while they were unbeaten against Spain, the Swedes recognised the test ahead, believing this *La Roja* side to be on a technical par with Japan. "They'll make it difficult for us," admitted centurion Magdalena Eriksson, "but we're so ready." For Spain, even winning a World Cup knockout match had been a new experience. As preparation for this one, they strolled around Auckland's waterfront. This was their sixth and final game on Kiwi soil. It proved to be quite the goodbye, another full house at Eden Park treated to a furious finale. Speedy substitute Salma Paralluelo kicked it off, her 81st-minute shot through a sea of bodies surviving a VAR review. Sweden powered back, Rebecka Blomqvist barely off the bench before she banged in the equaliser. But a mere 95 seconds later, Olga Carmona's left-foot shot flew in off the crossbar to settle the tie. Spain had made history, but for Peter Gerhardsson's devastated Sweden, it was more of the same.

▲ Spain celebrate Olga Carmona's winning goal. Sweden had equalised just 95 seconds before Carmona's stunning strike from the edge of the box following a corner.

England end Australian odyssey

Stadium Australia, Sydney/Wangal
16.08.2023, 20:00, **75,784**

AUSTRALIA 1-3 ENGLAND

Kerr 63 Toone 36, Hemp 71, Russo 86

Tori Penso USA ▪ Brooke Mayo USA & Mijensa Rensch SUR ▪ Massimiliano Irrati ITA

AUS • Arnold - Carpenter, Hunt, Polkinghorne (Van Egmond 81), Catley - Raso (Vine 72), Gorry (Chidiac 88), Cooney-Cross, Foord - Kerr (c), Fowler. *Gustavsson SWE*

ENG • Earps - Carter, Bright (c), Greenwood ▪ - Bronze, Stanway, Walsh, Toone (Charles 90), Daly - Russo (Kelly 87 ▪ 90+5), Hemp. *Wiegman NED*

11

This match drew a record 11 million viewers in Australia, the first TV audience for a sports event to surpass the number that watched Cathy Freeman win Olympic gold at the very same stadium at Sydney 2000.

The only female coach left standing had taken her native Netherlands to the Final four years earlier. Now 53-year-old Sarina Wiegman sought to repeat the feat with England. "It's just very, very special to go so far in the tournament," she said, "but when you're there, you want to win it too." In a glittering 23 months with the *Lionesses* that had delivered a home European title, defeat by Australia had been the only blot in Wiegman's copybook. England failed to score then, but Ella Toone got them under way here with an emphatic opener. The noise was almost deafening when national heroine Sam Kerr unleashed a world-class leveller from 35 yards out. But Lauren Hemp bossed this match, silencing the crowd with a determined drive after a route-one ball out of defence from captain Millie Bright. Mary Earps pushed away a Cortnee Vine chance before Kerr shanked a glorious opportunity, and within 72 seconds, Hemp's tricksy reverse pass set up Alessia Russo for a cool finish. "That was probably the moment when I thought, 'We're going to be in a World Cup Final!'" purred Keira Walsh later. So it proved, leaving Tony Gustavsson to rally his shattered players for bronze with the following words: "We need to be strong now."

▲▲ England celebrate retaking the lead in the semi-final against Australia in Sydney.

▲ Hosts Australia and England were the two most popular attractions of the finals, drawing a total of 403,136 and 375,118 fans respectively to their games.

Sweden claim bronze... again!

Before this tournament, only the USA had gone beyond the last eight as hosts. As their campaign gathered spectacular momentum, Australia had rewritten that script. They had taken the public with them, millions watching their battles on television, thousands more making their support heard in stadiums and fan parks across the country. Talismanic captain Sam Kerr described the experience as the "most amazing four weeks of our careers". This was the last push. Head coach Tony Gustavsson was no stranger to medal success at the World Cup, having assisted the USA in two triumphs, but Sweden had departed the previous edition with bronze around their necks. Peter Gerhardsson's side had also beaten their countryman Gustavsson and Australia twice on the way to silver at Tokyo 2020. Two-time *Diamantbollen* winner Fridolina Rolfö scored in both of those games and was on target again here, stepping up on the half hour to score the 20th successful penalty of the tournament, after Clare Hunt was penalised for clipping Stina Blackstenius's heel. The momentum remained with Sweden and, after a neat interchange with Blackstenius, captain Kosovare Asllani's 62nd-minute drive saw her become the first player to score in two third-place play-offs. Hayley Raso and Kerr had come close, but Zećira Mušović kept both at bay. It was Gerhardsson's tenth World Cup win in 14 games and, as at France 2019, third place was his squad's consolation prize following their semi-final heartache. Australia, for their part, had succeeded in elevating women's football to unprecedented heights in the country. "The next thing now is investment," Gustavsson said, "the long-term investment to really make sure we benefit from this crossroad moment."

◀ Sweden goalkeeper Zećira Mušović thwarts another Australia attack during the match for third place in Brisbane.

2023 Match for Third Place

Brisbane Stadium, Brisbane/Meaanjin
19.08.2023, 18:00, 49,461

SWEDEN 2-0 AUSTRALIA

Rolfö 30p, Asllani 62

Cheryl Foster WAL   Michelle O'Neill IRL & Franca Overtoom NED   Marco Fritz GER

1 Mušović
14 Björn   13 Ilestedt   6 Eriksson   2 Andersson
16 Angeldahl   23 Rubensson ■ 89
19 Kaneryd (Sembrant 89)   9 Asllani (c) (Hurtig 67 ■ 90+4)   18 Rolfö
11 Blackstenius (Blomqvist 67)
Gerhardsson SWE

Gustavsson SWE
11 Fowler   20 Kerr (c)
9 Foord   23 Cooney-Cross   19 Gorry ■ 45+1 (Van Egmond 60)   16 Raso (5 Vine 60)
7 Catley   4 Polkinghorne (Chidiac 74)   15 Hunt   21 Carpenter (2 Courtney **Nevin** 74)
18 Arnold

Always the bridesmaid...

... and never the bride! Sweden settled for third place once again at the World Cup, but despite the disappointment of not gaining that elusive title, it demonstrated their position as one of the dominant forces in women's football on the global stage, stretching right back to the 1988 trial World Cup where they finished as runners-up. This was their eighth semi-final appearance at either the World Cup or Olympics, and from 1988 to 2023 they had been represented at every global tournament, a record shared only by the USA and Brazil. The Swedes were also the only nation to finish in the top three at Rio 2016, France 2019, Tokyo 2020 and here, with their fans hoping that one day their team will be standing on the winners podium and not next to it.

▶ Caitlin Foord's shirt from Australia's round-of-16 match against Denmark.
FIFA Museum Collection

▶ Déjà vu for Sweden: The *Blågult* finished third for a second consecutive edition and the fourth time overall, having done so in 1991, 2011 and 2019.

2023 Final

▲ Stadium Australia, Sydney, played host to five sell-out crowds, the last of those witnessing this historic FIFA Women's World Cup Final between Spain and England.

▼▶ Spain's Olga Carmona scores the only goal of the 2023 World Cup Final.

Spain cap meteoric rise with first title

Only four nations had lifted the Women's World Cup since 1991. Now, with the stands of Stadium Australia awash with the red and yellow of Spain and the red and white of England, a fifth name was set to be etched onto the hallowed trophy regardless of the victor.

Spain's arrival felt little short of phenomenal. *La Roja* had won once in their previous two World Cups. Here, a group featuring 18 competition debutants had set aside the internal strife that had denied them some stellar names to win five games. Chasing the all-important sixth victory, coach Jorge Vilda faced the architects of Spain's quarter-final exit from EURO 2022. "We knew last year we were on top," he reflected, "but what matters is the result."

Despite losing key players to retirement and injury since claiming their maiden European title, England were yet to be defeated in a competitive match under Sarina Wiegman. The *Lionesses* had paused a bonus dispute with The Football Association as they aimed to continue in that winning vein at this World Cup. From jet lag-reducing sunglasses and business-class travel, to a team base that included arcade games, arts and crafts, and a library, it seemed as though no stone had been left unturned to help them. Yet, having delivered in an unforgettable semi-final against Australia, England looked leggy in the face of Spain's possession game. Fittingly for a tournament packed with heroic goalkeeping, the Final brought out the best in England's Mary Earps, the Golden Glove winner athletically denying Alba Redondo, Mariona Caldentey and Ona Batlle and, after a lengthy VAR review, stopping a second-half Jenni Hermoso penalty. Of this World Cup's young revelations, Lauren Hemp hit the crossbar and Salma Paralluelo the post, while Cata Coll tipped away a late Lauren James shot. Ultimately, Olga Carmona's 29th-minute goal decided it. Scored following two incisive passes after Barcelona defender Lucy Bronze, in her 20th World Cup match, had lost possession in the middle of the park, the captain's strike drew comparisons with Andrés Iniesta's 2010 World Cup Final winner for Spain. That 23-year-old Carmona was unaware of the death of her father until after the match made her contribution all the more poignant. The first coach to steer two nations to the Final, Wiegman had to make do with silver once more. Her players were distraught, but the Dutchwoman remained gracious in defeat. "After all," she said, "I think Spain were just a little bit better than we were today."

2023 World Cup Final

Stadium Australia, Sydney/Wangal
20.08.2023, 20:00, 75,784

SPAIN 🇪🇸 1-0 🏴󠁧󠁢󠁥󠁮󠁧󠁿 ENGLAND

Carmona 29, (Hermoso penalty saved 70)

Tori Penso USA · Brooke Mayo USA & Kathryn Nesbitt USA · Tatiana Guzmán NCA

Spain (Vilda): 23 Coll; 2 Batlle, 4 Paredes, 14 Codina (Andrés 73), 19 Carmona (c); 6 Bonmatí, 3 Abelleira, 10 Hermoso; 17 Redondo (Hernández 60), 18 Paralluelo ▪ 78, 8 Caldentey (Putellas 90)

England (Wiegman NED): 1 Earps; 5 Greenwood, 6 Bright (c), 16 Carter; 9 Daly (Kelly 46), 10 Toone (England 87), 4 Walsh, 8 Stanway, 2 Bronze; 11 Hemp ▪ 55, 23 Russo (James 46)

Final 2023

27

Jenni Hermoso's penalty was the 27th awarded, beating the previous high of 26 set at France 2019. The only other player to have had a penalty saved in a Women's World Cup Final beyond shoot-outs was Brazil's Marta, who was denied by Germany's Nadine Angerer in 2007.

▲ England keeper Mary Earps, flanked by Millie Bright and Chloe Kelly, celebrates saving Jenni Hermoso's second-half penalty.

◀ Salma Paralluelo's Spain shirt from the 2023 World Cup Final against England. *FIFA Museum Collection*

La Roja triumph against the odds

In the run-up to the Final, goalscorer Olga Carmona recalled not being allowed to play the game as a child, while defender Irene Paredes described how many women players had felt that they had no place in their football-mad country. But Spain had taken this team to their hearts during this tournament and their triumph over England in Sydney made the front and back pages of the papers. The headlines would also be dominated in the days and months to follow by the behaviour of Spanish Football Association President Luis Rubiales during the trophy presentation and the kiss he gave Silver Ball winner Jenni Hermoso. FIFA responded with a disciplinary review, an immediate provisional suspension and, later, a three-year ban. Rubiales' unpresidential actions had marred *La Roja's* celebrations, but they should never be allowed to mask the team's immense achievement. Spain were now the first nation to hold the senior, U-20 and U-17 Women's World Cup titles simultaneously. History truly had been made.

9 and 10

Spain and England were the ninth and tenth teams to reach the Women's World Cup Final, and this was the first time since 1991 that the Final was contested by two teams who had never previously featured in the title match.

> **I have no words, I'm in shock. What we have done is remarkable, we have known how to suffer and enjoy.**
> AITANA BONMATÍ

3

Salma Paralluelo became the first player to win the Women's World Cup at all three levels (U-17, U-20 and senior), while Spain became the first country to hold all three of those titles at the same time.

▶ Spain celebrate winning the FIFA Women's World Cup 2023, just eight years after first qualifying for the finals in 2015.

3

Only three of the nine Women's World Cup Finals up to 2023 have been all-European affairs. Germany had been the last European team to be crowned champions, beating Brazil 2-0 in the 2007 Final to become the only nation to have won both the men's and women's World Cups. Spain now joined them.

2024

Notable for Sweden's first absence from a global finals, the Paris Olympics saw the USA claim gold for the fifth time. Sparking memories of the "triple-edged sword" of their World Cup-winning team of 1991, this time it was the "triple espresso" of Trinity Rodman, Sophia Smith and Mallory Swanson under newly appointed head coach Emma Hayes that helped power the *Stars and Stripes* to the title. In the quarter-finals, hosts France lost to Brazil, who then beat world champions Spain in an epic semi-final, but there was nothing Marta could do to stop the US juggernaut at the Parc des Princes in the gold medal match, with Swanson scoring the game's only goal.

The gender-parity Games

The Olympic Games returned to Paris 100 years after last being staged there and broke new ground with an opening ceremony that saw the athletes presented to the world on a flotilla of boats along the River Seine rather than in the stadium. The Olympic flame was also located away from the stadium, placed instead above the Grand Bassin Rond fountain in the Tuileries Garden, as the organisers made the most of the city's iconic locations. For the first time there was gender parity amongst the competitors, and there were first gold medals for Botswana, Dominica, Guatemala and Saint Lucia. Sweden's Armand "Mondo" Duplantis set the athletics competition alight with his extraordinary world record-breaking gold in the pole vault, while the swimming was dominated by France's Léon Marchand and the USA's Katie Ledecky. The USA overtook China PR at the head of the medal table in the final event of Paris 2024 when the women's basketball team edged their gold medal match against France. In the men's football tournament, Spain continued their magnificent summer by beating the hosts to gold, hot on the heels of their success at Euro 2024.

▼ Léon Marchand won four golds in the pool at Paris 2024.

2024 Overview

PARIS 2024

WOMEN'S OLYMPIC FOOTBALL TOURNAMENT

Story of the qualifiers

A first for Spain

Four-time gold medallists the USA secured their place at Paris 2024 well in advance of the tournament thanks to a 1-0 victory over Canada in the Concacaf W Championship Final in July 2022. Later that month, Brazil and Colombia were assured of CONMEBOL's two spots by reaching the *Copa América Femenina* Final, in which the Brazilians came out on top. Reigning champions Canada, meanwhile, took Concacaf's second ticket in September 2023 after back-to-back play-off wins over Jamaica. A high-scoring five-match winning streak in an eight-team Oceania qualifying tournament in Samoa saw New Zealand qualify next. As hosts, France were already guaranteed to appear, but in a historic first, UEFA's other two berths were settled by a newly introduced Nations League competition that included a league stage and finals. The Netherlands came close, but world champions Spain and previous gold medallists Germany made it through. Asian qualifying saw 25 nations vie for two Olympic spots. A bye to the second round followed by a table-topping run and then a 13-0 aggregate thumping of Uzbekistan saw Australia triumph. Japan made light work of their group stage too, but it took an edgy 2-1 second-leg win over North Korea to reach their sixth Olympics. In Africa, the deciding matches after four qualifying rounds were no less tense. Ultimately, Nigeria edged out South Africa after a 1-0 win in Abeokuta and a goalless draw in Pretoria. After losing 2-1 to Morocco at home, Zambia turned their fortunes around with a 2-0 extra-time return-leg victory that saw them qualify for a second Olympics on the bounce.

▲ Fans made a welcome return to the Olympic Football Tournaments after missing out in Tokyo.

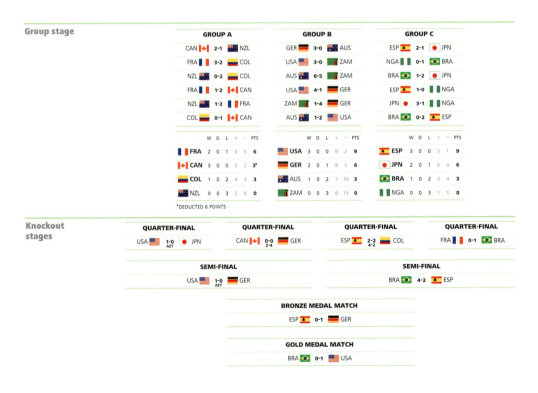

Group stage

GROUP A
CAN	2-1	NZL
FRA	3-2	COL
NZL	0-2	COL
FRA	1-2	CAN
NZL	1-2	FRA
COL	0-1	CAN

	W	D	L	+	−	PTS
FRA	2	0	1	6	5	6
CAN	3	0	0	5	2	3*
COL	1	0	2	4	4	3
NZL	0	0	3	2	6	0

*DEDUCTED 6 POINTS

GROUP B
GER	3-0	AUS
USA	3-0	ZAM
AUS	6-5	ZAM
USA	4-1	GER
ZAM	1-4	GER
AUS	1-2	USA

	W	D	L	+	−	PTS
USA	3	0	0	9	2	9
GER	2	0	1	8	5	6
AUS	1	0	2	7	10	3
ZAM	0	0	3	6	13	0

GROUP C
ESP	2-1	JPN
NGA	0-1	BRA
BRA	1-2	JPN
ESP	1-0	NGA
JPN	3-1	NGA
BRA	0-2	ESP

	W	D	L	+	−	PTS
ESP	3	0	0	5	1	9
JPN	2	0	1	6	4	6
BRA	1	0	2	2	4	3
NGA	0	0	3	1	5	0

Knockout stages

QUARTER-FINAL: USA 1-0 AET JPN
QUARTER-FINAL: CAN 0-0 (2-4) GER
QUARTER-FINAL: ESP 2-2 (4-2) COL
QUARTER-FINAL: FRA 0-1 BRA

SEMI-FINAL: USA 1-0 AET GER
SEMI-FINAL: BRA 4-2 ESP

BRONZE MEDAL MATCH: ESP 0-1 GER

GOLD MEDAL MATCH: BRA 0-1 USA

Overview 2024

	Gold	Silver	Bronze
USA	40	44	42
CHINA PR	40	27	24
JAPAN	20	12	13
AUSTRALIA	18	19	16
FRANCE	16	26	22
NETHERLANDS	15	7	12

TOP OF THE MEDAL TABLE

12 TEAMS — USA WINNERS — BRA SECOND — GER THIRD

398 704 SPECTATORS
15 335 AVERAGE PER MATCH

26 MATCHES PLAYED
54 YELLOW CARDS
3 RED CARDS

76 GOALS
2.92 AVERAGE GOALS PER MATCH

ÎLE-DE-FOOT 24 OFFICIAL MATCH BALL

Host cities and stadiums

A Final at last for the Parc des Princes

A total of seven stadiums were used for the 2024 Women's Olympic Football Tournament, with Paris staging three of the 26 games. All three were played at the Parc des Princes, including the gold medal match. Played the day after the men's Final, also at the Parc des Princes, it was the first time that the stadium had hosted a global football Final, after missing out in 1924, 1938, 1998 and 2019. Lyon, the venue for the 2019 World Cup Final, staged six matches, including the bronze medal match, while Marseille hosted five and Nantes four.

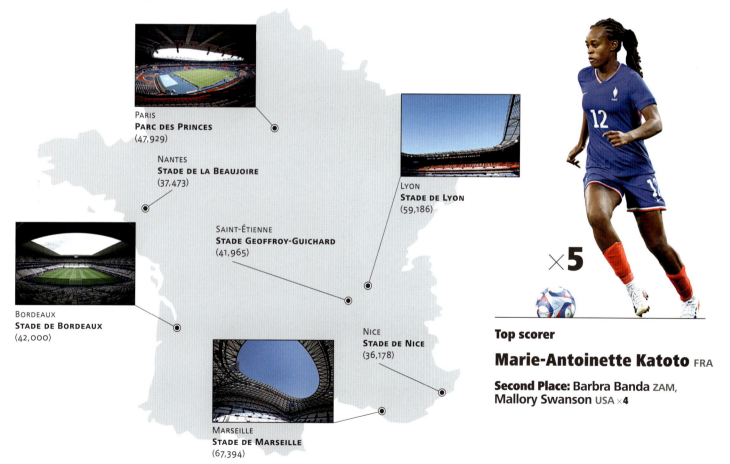

PARIS — PARC DES PRINCES (47,929)
NANTES — STADE DE LA BEAUJOIRE (37,473)
BORDEAUX — STADE DE BORDEAUX (42,000)
SAINT-ÉTIENNE — STADE GEOFFROY-GUICHARD (41,965)
LYON — STADE DE LYON (59,186)
NICE — STADE DE NICE (36,178)
MARSEILLE — STADE DE MARSEILLE (67,394)

×5

Top scorer

Marie-Antoinette Katoto FRA

Second Place: Barbra Banda ZAM, Mallory Swanson USA ×4

Group A

◀ Grace Geyoro (8) of France during their final group game against New Zealand, a match the hosts could not afford to lose. They won 2-1.

	W	D	L	+	–	PTS
FRA	2	0	1	6	5	6
CAN	3	0	0	5	2	3‡
COL	1	0	2	4	4	3
NZL	0	0	3	2	6	0

‡ Canada were deducted six points for using a drone to observe a New Zealand training session.

Canada defy the odds

With Canada under investigation after the sighting of a drone over New Zealand's training ground, head coach Bev Priestman opted to sit out their opener. Olympic debutant Mackenzie Barry added to the defending champions' woes with a strong turn and finish. But Cloé Lacasse levelled on her Games bow with a fierce shot, and *Serie A* top scorer Evelyne Viens drove home a late winner. Cruising against Colombia after a Marie-Antoinette Katoto double either side of a Kenza Dali rocket in the first half, France were relieved victors by full time. A confident spot kick from leading scorer Catalina Usme and clever dink by substitute Manuela Paví had revitalised their opponents, but a late red card for Mayra Ramírez stymied the comeback. By the time the hosts faced Canada, the *Canucks* had been docked six points by FIFA, with Priestman and two staff members handed year-long suspensions. The players rallied, battling back from a sublime Katoto shimmy and shot thanks to a Jessie Fleming toe-poke and last-gasp clincher from Vanessa Gilles. The Lyon defender then scored the only goal of the game against Colombia to see Canada progress against the odds. The South Americans also qualified thanks to a victory in their second outing, goals from Marcela Restrepo and Leicy Santos enough to overcome New Zealand, whose own hopes were ended by table-topping France and their prolific striker Katoto.

0
The second-half goal scored by Canada's Vanessa Gilles against Colombia ensured that, for the first time ever, there were no draws throughout the group stage of the women's competition.

◀ Vanessa Gilles, in white, heads home the only goal of the game in Canada's victory over Colombia. The Canadians won all three group games in France, extending their unbeaten run at the Olympics to ten, a total only ever bettered by the USA.

Group stage 2024

Stade Geoffroy-Guichard, Saint-Étienne
25.07.2024, 17:00, **2,674**

CANADA 2-1 NEW ZEALAND
Lacasse 45+4, Viens 79 — Barry 13

Tess Olofsson SWE
Almira Spahić SWE & Francesca Di Monte ITA
Rob Dieperink NED

CAN • 1 Kailen **Sheridan** - 12 Jade **Rose**, 14 Vanessa **Gilles**, 3 Kadeisha **Buchanan**, 10 Ashley **Lawrence** ■ 85, 5 **Quinn** (13 Simi **Awujo** 67), 17 Jessie **Fleming** (c), 2 Gabrielle **Carle** (4 Evelyne **Viens** 67), 11 Adriana **Leon** (20 Shelina **Zadorsky** 90+4), 15 Nichelle **Prince** (16 Janine **Beckie** 56), 6 Cloé **Lacasse** (9 Jordyn **Huitema** 56). *Andy Spence ENG*

NZL • 1 Anna **Leat** - 4 C.J. **Bott**, 14 Katie **Bowen** (c), 13 Rebekah **Stott**, 3 Mackenzie **Barry** (7 Michaela **Foster** 59 - 10 Indiah-Paige **Riley**), 2 Kate **Taylor** (9 Gabi **Rennie** 87), 6 Malia **Steinmetz** (8 Macey **Fraser** 59), 11 Katie **Kitching** - 17 Milly **Clegg** (16 Jacqui **Hand** 66), 18 Grace **Jale**. *Michael Mayne*

Stade de Lyon, Lyon
25.07.2024, 21:00, **29,208**

FRANCE 3-2 COLOMBIA
Katoto (2) 6 42, Dali 18 — Usme 54p, Paví 64

Tori Penso USA
Brooke Mayo USA & Kathryn Nesbitt USA
Tatiana Guzmán NCA

FRA • 16 Pauline **Peyraud-Magnin** - 2 Maëlle **Lakrar**, 18 Griedge **Mbock Bathy**, 3 Wendie **Renard** (c), 7 Sakina **Karchaoui** (13 Selma **Bacha** 72) - 15 Kenza **Dali**, 14 Sandie **Toletti**, 8 Grace **Geyoro** - 10 Delphine **Cascarino** (17 Sandy **Baltimore** 72), 12 Marie-Antoinette **Katoto** (9 Eugénie **Le Sommer** 90+5), 11 Kadidiatou **Diani** (6 Amandine **Henry** 90+1). *Hervé Renard*

COL • 12 Katherine **Tapia** - 17 Carolina **Arias** (5 Yirleidis **Quejada Minota** 83), 3 Daniela **Arias**, 16 Jorelyn **Carabalí**, 2 Manuela **Vanegas** - 8 Marcela **Restrepo**, 6 Daniela **Montoya** (c) (7 Manuela **Paví** 46), 10 Leicy **Santos**, 11 Catalina **Usme**, 18 Linda **Caicedo** - 9 Mayra **Ramírez** ■ 86. *Angelo Marsiglia* ■ 83

Stade de Lyon, Lyon
28.07.2024, 17:00, **5,212**

NEW ZEALAND 0-2 COLOMBIA
— Restrepo 27, Santos 72

Kim Yu Jeong KOR
Park Mi Suk KOR & Joanna Charaktis AUS
Khamis Al Marri QAT

NZL • Leat - Bott, Bowen (c), Stott, Barry (Foster 78) - Riley, Taylor (Rennie 78), Steinmetz (20 Annalie **Longo** 46), Kitching - Clegg (Jale 46), Hand (15 Ally **Green** 66). *Mayne*

COL • Tapia - C Arias (4 Daniela **Caracas** 86), D Arias, Carabalí, Vanegas - Paví, Restrepo, 13 Ilana **Izquierdo** (15 Liana **Salazar** 90), Caicedo (Quejada Minota 90) - Santos, Usme (c) (Montoya 78). *Marsiglia*

Stade Geoffroy-Guichard, Saint-Étienne
28.07.2024, 21:00, **17,555**

FRANCE 1-2 CANADA
Katoto 42 — Fleming 58, Gilles 90+12

Bouchra Karboubi MAR
Fatiha Jermoumi MAR & Diana Chikotesha ZAM
Ivan Bebek CRO

FRA • Peyraud-Magnin (1 Constance **Picaud** 63) - 5 Élisa de **Almeida**, Mbock Bathy, Renard (c) (Lakrar 72), Bacha - Dali, Toletti ■ 76, Geyoro - Cascarino (Karchaoui 63), Katoto, Diani (Henry 82). *Renard*

CAN • Sheridan - Rose, Gilles, Buchanan, Carle (Beckie 68) - Awujo (7 Julia **Grosso** 90), Quinn (Viens 67) - Lawrence ■ 45+2, Fleming (c), Huitema - Prince (Leon 46). *Spence ENG*

Stade de Lyon, Lyon
31.07.2024, 21:00, **21,946**

NEW ZEALAND 1-2 FRANCE
Taylor 43 — Katoto (2) 22 49

Edina Alves Batista BRA
Neuza Back BRA & Fabrini Bevilaqua Costa BRA
Daiane Muniz BRA

NZL • Leat - Bott, Stott (5 Meikayla **Moore** 54), Bowen (c), Foster (Barry 63) - Riley (Green 73 ■ 90+6), Taylor, Longo, Kitching (Clegg 54) - Jale, Hand (Steinmetz 74). *Mayne*

FRA • Peyraud-Magnin - De Almeida, Lakrar, Mbock Bathy (21 Ève **Périsset** 83), Bacha (Toletti 74) - Geyoro (Dali 63), Henry (c), Karchaoui - Cascarino (Le Sommer 83), Katoto (Diani 63), Baltimore. *Renard*

Stade de Nice, Nice
31.07.2024, 21:00, **5,388**

COLOMBIA 0-1 CANADA
— Gilles 61

Rebecca Welch ENG
Emily Carney ENG & Franca Overtoom NED
Paolo Valeri ITA

COL • Tapia - C Arias (c), D Arias, Carabalí, Vanegas - Quejada Minota ■ 19 (Montoya 78), Izquierdo, Restrepo, Caicedo ■ 90+3 - Paví ■ 6, Santos. *Marsiglia*

CAN • Sheridan - Rose, Gilles (Zadorsky 85), Buchanan - Beckie (Carle 85), Fleming (c), Grosso (Quinn 74), Lawrence - Leon ■ 45+3 (Viens 61), Huitema, Lacasse (Prince 46). *Spence ENG*

2024 Group stage

Group B

	W	D	L	+	-	PTS
USA	3	0	0	9	2	9
GER	2	0	1	8	5	6
AUS	1	0	2	7	10	3
ZAM	0	0	3	6	13	0

▶ Australia's Michelle Heyman is challenged by Rhoda Chileshe of Zambia. Heyman, who had come out of international retirement after a five-year hiatus, scored a 90th-minute winner to cap an extraordinary comeback for the *Matildas*.

Stade de Marseille, Marseille
25.07.2024, 19:00, **9,731**

GERMANY 3-0 AUSTRALIA

Hegering 24, Schüller 64, Brand 68

🧑‍⚖️ Katia Itzel García MEX
🚩 Sandra Ramírez MEX & Karen Díaz Medina MEX
📺 Carlos del Cerro Grande ESP

GER • 12 Ann-Katrin **Berger** - 15 Giulia **Gwinn**, 3 Kathrin **Hendrich**, 5 Marina **Hegering** (4 Bibiane **Schulze Solano** 73), 2 Sarai **Linder** - 16 Jule **Brand**, 11 Alexandra **Popp** (c), 6 Janina **Minge** 🟨45+1 (14 Elisa **Senß** 73), 17 Klara **Bühl** (18 Vivien **Endemann** 89) - 9 Sjoeke **Nüsken** (8 Sydney **Lohmann** 46), 7 Lea **Schüller**. *Horst* **Hrubesch**

AUS • 1 Mackenzie **Arnold** - 12 Ellie **Carpenter**, 14 Alanna **Kennedy**, 15 Clare **Hunt**, 7 Steph **Catley** (c) (3 Kaitlyn **Torpey** 77) - 16 Hayley **Raso** (10 Emily **van Egmond** 77), 6 Katrina **Gorry** (17 Clare **Wheeler** 59), 8 Kyra **Cooney-Cross**, 9 Caitlin **Foord** 🟨22 (2 Michelle **Heyman** 77) - 5 Cortnee **Vine** (19 Sharn **Freier** 59), 11 Mary **Fowler**. *Tony* **Gustavsson** SWE

Stade de Nice, Nice
25.07.2024, 21:00, **5,550**

USA 3-0 ZAMBIA

Rodman 17, Swanson (2) 24 25

🧑‍⚖️ Ramon Abatti BRA
🚩 Rafael da Silva Alves BRA & Guilherme Dias Camilo BRA
📺 Daiane Muniz BRA

USA • 1 Alyssa **Naeher** - 2 Emily **Fox**, 4 Naomi **Girma**, 12 Tierna **Davidson**, 7 Crystal **Dunn** - 10 Lindsey **Horan** (c) (14 Emily **Sonnett** 65), 17 Sam **Coffey** - 5 Trinity **Rodman** 🟨44 (6 Casey **Krueger** 65), 16 Rose **Lavelle** (3 Korbin **Albert** 46), 11 Sophia **Smith** (8 Lynn **Williams** 43) - 9 Mallory **Swanson** (13 Jenna **Nighswonger** 65). *Emma* **Hayes** ENG

ZAM • 18 Ngambo **Musole** - 4 Esther **Siamfuko**, 5 Pauline **Zulu** 🟨34, 3 Lushomo **Mweemba**, 13 Martha **Tembo** 🟨45 - 14 Prisca **Chilufya** (2 Aveli **Chitundu** 37), 15 Hellen **Chanda**, 10 Grace **Chanda** (16 Esther **Muchinga** 38), 17 Racheal **Kundananji** - 9 Kabange **Mupopo**, 11 Barbra **Banda** (c). *Bruce* **Mwape**

Stade de Nice, Nice
28.07.2024, 19:00, **4,441**

AUSTRALIA 6-5 ZAMBIA

Kennedy 7, Raso 35, Musole OG 58, Catley (2) 65 78p, Heyman 90
B Banda (3) 1 (40 secs) 33 45+2, Kundananji (2) 21 56

🧑‍⚖️ Emikar Calderas Barrera VEN
🚩 Migdalia Rodríguez VEN & Mary Blanco Bolívar COL
📺 Leodán González URU

AUS • **Arnold** - **Carpenter**, **Hunt**, **Kennedy** 🟨87, **Catley** (c) - **Gorry** (Torpey 57), **Cooney-Cross** - **Raso** (Heyman 57), **Van Egmond** (Wheeler 57), **Foord** - **Fowler**. *Gustavsson* SWE

ZAM • **Musole** - **Siamfuko**, **Muchinga** 🟨77, **Mweemba**, **Tembo** - 20 Racheal **Nachula** (Chilufya 83), 7 Misozi **Zulu** (6 Rhoda **Chileshe** 66), H **Chanda**, **Kundananji** - B **Banda** (c), **Mupopo** (Chitundu 83). *Mwape*

Stade de Marseille, Marseille
28.07.2024, 21:00, **12,845**

USA 4-1 GERMANY

Smith (2) 11 44, Swanson 26, Williams 89
Gwinn 22

🧑‍⚖️ Yael Falcón Pérez ARG
🚩 Maximiliano del Yesso ARG & Facundo Rodríguez ARG
📺 Tatiana Guzmán NCA

USA • **Naeher** - **Fox** (Krueger 90+2), **Girma**, **Davidson** (Sonnett 44), **Dunn** - **Horan** (c), **Coffey** 🟨22, **Lavelle** - **Rodman** (Nighswonger 90+2), **Swanson**, **Smith** (Williams 85). *Hayes* ENG

GER • **Berger** - **Gwinn**, **Hendrich** 🟨19, **Hegering**, 19 Felicitas **Rauch** - **Brand**, **Minge**, **Popp** (c) (Senß 77), **Bühl** - **Nüsken** (Lohmann 68), **Schüller**. *Hrubesch*

Stade Geoffroy-Guichard, Saint-Étienne
31.07.2024, 19:00, **2,642**

ZAMBIA 1-4 GERMANY

B Banda 49
Schüller (2) 10 61, Bühl 47, Senß 90+7

🧑‍⚖️ Yoshimi Yamashita JPN
🚩 Makoto Bozono JPN & Naomi Teshirogi JPN
📺 Ivan Bebek CRO

ZAM • **Musole** - Siamfuko, P Zulu, Mweemba, Tembo - Nachula (Chilufya 46), 8 Ochumba **Lubandji**, H **Chanda** 🟨35 (21 Mary **Wilombe** 65), **Kundananji** - B **Banda** (c), **Mupopo**. *Mwape*

GER • **Berger** - **Gwinn**, **Hendrich** (13 Sara **Doorsoun** 22), **Schulze Solano**, **Rauch** - **Brand** (Endemann 46), **Minge**, **Popp** (c) (Lohmann 69), **Bühl** - **Nüsken** (Senß 89) - **Schüller** (10 Laura **Freigang** 69). *Hrubesch*

Stade de Marseille, Marseille
31.07.2024, 19:00, **13,036**

AUSTRALIA 1-2 USA

Kennedy 90+1
Rodman 43, Albert 77

🧑‍⚖️ François Letexier FRA
🚩 Cyril Mugnier FRA & Mehdi Rahmouni FRA
📺 Jérôme Brisard FRA

AUS • **Arnold** - **Carpenter**, **Kennedy**, **Hunt**, **Catley** (c), **Torpey** (Heyman 59) - **Fowler**, **Gorry** (Van Egmond 59), **Cooney-Cross** (Wheeler 46), **Foord** - **Raso** (13 Tameka **Yallop** 85). *Gustavsson* SWE 🟨45

USA • **Naeher** - **Fox** (Krueger 65), **Girma**, **Sonnett**, **Dunn** (Nighswonger 46) - **Lavelle** (Albert 65 67), **Coffey** 🟨3, **Horan** (c) - **Rodman** (Williams 65), **Smith**, **Swanson** (20 Croix **Bethune** 80). *Hayes* ENG

3

Having netted six at Tokyo 2020 and a hat-trick against Australia at these Games, Barbra Banda became the first woman to score a trio of Olympic trebles.

2

By lining up against Australia, Zambia midfielder Racheal Nachula became a two-sport Olympian, having also competed in the women's 400m at Beijing 2008.

Goals galore

Germany hit their 50th goal at the Games when defender Marina Hegering powered in Giulia Gwinn's floated corner against Australia. Deprived of top scorer Sam Kerr through injury, the *Matildas* were well beaten once Lea Schüller dispatched another precise Gwinn corner and Jule Brand slotted home. A stylish turn and shot from Olympic debutant Trinity Rodman and Mallory Swanson's 70-second brace against Zambia handed the USA a dream start in their first competitive match under Emma Hayes. The tournament's lowest-ranked side deserved credit, though, withstanding teenager Pauline Zulu's dismissal and a USA onslaught to limit the scoring. In their next outing, Zambia captain Barbra Banda's record third Olympic hat-trick and a brace from fellow US-based professional Racheal Kundananji had Australia reeling. But from 5-2 down, the *Matildas* pulled off the competition's biggest winning comeback yet, levelling through an Ngambo Musole own goal and a Steph Catley double before 36-year-old Michelle Heyman's 90th-minute strike settled an 11-goal, 52-shot epic. Sophia Smith netted twice and claimed her maiden, and the USA's 80th, Olympic goal in a stunning 4-1 win over Germany. In a Schüller-inspired revival, the Germans bounced back to inflict that same, and somewhat harsh, scoreline on departing Zambia. Goal difference condemned Australia to a first early exit since Sydney 2000, Alanna Kennedy's late consolation not enough against a resurgent USA and neat goals from Rodman and Korbin Albert.

▶ The USA and Germany met for the first time in the group stage of a world tournament in this encounter in Marseille. Here, Lynn Williams celebrates scoring the last goal for the *Stars and Stripes* in a 4-1 victory.

Brazil squeeze through

Reigning Best FIFA Women's Player Aitana Bonmatí helped Spain find their feet on their Olympic debut. Behind to a stunning free kick from Japan's 20-year-old midfielder Aoba Fujino, she sidestepped Ayaka Yamashita to score *La Roja*'s maiden Olympic goal, before later setting up Mariona Caldentey for the winner. Quarter-finalists 20 years prior, Nigeria had not graced this stage since bowing out in the group stage in 2008, when they were beaten by Brazil in their final encounter. A new generation gave everything here. But now, as then, Marta was on the winning side, her sublime pass dispatched with aplomb by Gabi Nunes. Alexia Putellas was the next to break Nigeria's determined defence, taking Spain into the quarters with a late free kick after defender Osinachi Ohale had blocked her earlier goal-bound shot.

Brazil took the lead against Japan when Jheniffer powered home, although only after Lorena had saved Mina Tanaka's penalty. But Saki Kumagai levelled from the spot minutes after Marta's departure to a standing ovation on her 200th cap, and teenager Momoko Tanikawa nicked it at the death for the *Nadeshiko*. Brazil were floored by Spain, too, after losing an inconsolable Marta to her first-ever world tournament dismissal. Yet by limiting the world's number-one ranked side to Athenea del Castillo's second-half opener and another late Putellas wonder strike, the *Seleção* progressed on goal difference as one of the two best third-placed teams. The competition's 500th goal came courtesy of Nigeria's Paris Saint-Germain midfielder Jennifer Echegini, but it was not enough to overturn Japan's three.

◀◀ Aitana Bonmatí's shirt from Spain's group game against Japan. *FIFA Museum Collection*

◀ Nigeria's Rasheedat Ajibade (15) challenges Spain's Alexia Putellas. The Spaniard scored the only goal of the game to condemn the *Super Falcons* to a defeat in what was a disappointing tournament for the Africans.

200
The only veteran of Brazil's silver medal-winning campaigns of 2004 and 2008 to feature in the squad this time around, Marta became just the second *Seleção* player after Formiga to reach 200 caps when she faced Japan at her sixth Olympics.

◀ The only group game played in Paris was the match between Brazil and Japan, which drew a crowd of over 40,000 to the Parc des Princes.

Group C

Group stage 2024

	W	D	L	+	–	PTS
ESP	3	0	0	5	1	9
JPN	2	0	1	6	4	6
BRA	1	0	2	2	4	3
NGA	0	0	3	1	5	0

Stade de la Beaujoire, Nantes
25.07.2024, 17:00, **10,377**

SPAIN 2-1 JAPAN

Bonmatí 22, Caldentey 74 — Fujino 13

🏁 Bouchra Karboubi MAR
🚩 Fatiha Jermoumi MAR & Diana Chikotesha ZAM
📺 Jérôme Brisard FRA

ESP • 13 Cata **Coll** - 2 Ona **Batlle**, 4 Irene **Paredes** (c) ■ 42, 14 Laia **Aleixandri**, 18 Olga **Carmona** (5 Oihane **Hernández** 60) - 6 Aitana **Bonmatí**, 12 Patri **Guijarro** ■ 11 (3 Teresa **Abelleira** 82), 11 Alexia **Putellas** (10 Jennifer **Hermoso** 68) - 7 Athenea **del Castillo** (17 Lucía **García** 82), 9 Salma **Paralluelo**, 8 Mariona **Caldentey**. *Montserrat Tomé*

JPN • 1 Ayaka **Yamashita** - 3 Moeka **Minami**, 4 Saki **Kumagai** (c), 6 Toko **Koga** (20 Miyabi **Moriya** 90) - 2 Risa **Shimizu** (5 Hana **Takahashi** 69), 7 Hinata **Miyazawa**, 15 Aoba **Fujino**, 8 Kiko **Seike** (17 Maika **Hamano** 46) - 14 Yui **Hasegawa**, 11 Mina **Tanaka** (19 Remina **Chiba** 80), 10 Fuka **Nagano**. *Futoshi Ikeda*

Stade de Bordeaux, Bordeaux
25.07.2024, 19:00, **6,244**

NIGERIA 0-1 BRAZIL

— Gabi Nunes 37

🏁 Kim Yu Jeong KOR
🚩 Park Mi Suk KOR & Joanna Charaktis AUS
📺 Kate Jacewicz AUS

NGA • 16 Chiamaka **Nnadozie** - 2 Michelle **Alozie**, 3 Osinachi **Ohale**, 14 Blessing **Demehin**, 5 Chidinma **Okeke** (4 Nicole **Payne** 75) - 10 Christy **Ucheibe**, 13 Deborah **Abiodun** - 15 Rasheedat **Ajibade** (c), 7 Toni **Payne** (12 Uchenna **Kanu** 67), 11 Jennifer **Echegini** (18 Ifeoma **Onumonu** 67) - 17 Chinwendu **Ihezuo** (6 Esther **Okoronkwo** 46). *Randy Waldrum USA*

BRA • 1 **Lorena** - 2 **Antônia**, 3 **Tarciane**, 4 **Rafaelle**, 6 **Tamires** (13 **Yasmim** 36) - 14 **Ludmila** (11 **Jheniffer** 65), 8 **Vitória Yaya** ■ 22 (17 **Ana Vitória** 66), 5 **Duda Sampaio**, 10 **Marta** (c) - 16 **Gabi Nunes** (7 **Kerolin** 83), 18 **Gabi Portilho**. *Arthur Elias*

Parc des Princes, Paris
28.07.2024, 17:00, **40,918**

BRAZIL 1-2 JAPAN

Jheniffer 56 — Kumagai 90+2p, Tanikawa 90+6
(Tanaka penalty saved 45+3)

🏁 Rebecca Welch ENG
🚩 Emily Carney ENG & Franca Overtoom NED
📺 David Coote ENG

BRA • **Lorena** - 15 **Thaís**, 21 **Lauren** ■ 2 (**Tarciane** 46), **Rafaelle** - **Antônia**, 20 **Angelina** (**Duda Sampaio** 70), **Ana Vitória**, **Yasmim** - **Marta** (c) ■ 44 (**Kerolin** 85), **Gabi Nunes** (**Jheniffer** 46), 19 **Priscila** (**Ludmila** 46). *Elias*

JPN • **Yamashita** - **Koga** (**Seike** 70), **Takahashi**, **Kumagai** (c), **Minami** ■ 71, **Moriya** (12 **Momoko Tanikawa** 80) - **Miyazawa** (**Chiba** 80), **Hasegawa**, **Nagano** - **Tanaka**, **Hamano** (9 **Riko Ueki** 57). *Ikeda*

Stade de la Beaujoire, Nantes
28.07.2024, 19:00, **11,079**

SPAIN 1-0 NIGERIA

Putellas 85

🏁 Tori Penso USA
🚩 Brooke Mayo USA & Kathryn Nesbitt USA
📺 Paolo Valeri ITA

ESP • **Coll** - **Hernández** (**Carmona** 46), **Paredes** (c), **Aleixandri**, **Batlle** - **Abelleira** (**Guijarro** 59) - **García** (**Del Castillo** 46), **Bonmatí**, **Putellas**, **Caldentey** - **Paralluelo**. *Tomé*

NGA • **Nnadozie** - **Alozie** (N **Payne** 72), **Ohale**, **Demehin**, **Okeke** - **Ajibade** (c), **Abiodun**, **Ucheibe** (**Kanu** 85), T **Payne** - **Okoronkwo** (**Onumonu** 61), 8 Asisat **Oshoala** ■ 37 (**Ihezuo** 73). *Waldrum USA*

Stade de la Beaujoire, Nantes
31.07.2024, 17:00, **6,480**

JAPAN 3-1 NIGERIA

Hamano 22, Tanaka 32, Kitagawa 45+5 — Echegini 42

🏁 Emikar Calderas Barrera VEN
🚩 Migdalia Rodríguez VEN & Mary Blanco Bolívar COL
📺 Tatiana Guzmán NCA

JPN • **Yamashita** - **Moriya** (**Chiba** 80), **Takahashi**, **Kumagai** (c), 21 Rion **Ishikawa**, 13 Hikaru **Kitagawa** (**Miyazawa** 60) - **Hamano**, 16 Honoka **Hayashi**, **Hasegawa** (**Nagano** 60) - **Tanaka** (**Seike** 46), **Ueki** (**Tanikawa** 90+3). *Ikeda*

NGA • **Nnadozie** - **Alozie**, **Ohale** (**Kanu** 90+1), **Demehin** ■ 45+4, **Okeke** (N **Payne** 46) - **Ucheibe**, **Abiodun** (**Okoronkwo** 75) - T **Payne**, **Echegini**, **Ajibade** (c) - **Oshoala** (**Ihezuo** 60). *Waldrum USA*

Stade de Bordeaux, Bordeaux
31.07.2024, 17:00, **14,497**

BRAZIL 0-2 SPAIN

— Del Castillo 68, Putellas 90+17

🏁 Espen Eskås NOR
🚩 Jan Erik Engan NOR & Isaak Bashevkin NOR
📺 Rob Dieperink NED

BRA • **Lorena** - 9 **Adriana**, **Antônia**, **Lauren**, **Tarciane**, **Tamires** (**Yasmim** 61) - **Marta** (c) ■ 45+6, **Duda Sampaio** (**Ana Vitória** 61), **Vitória Yaya** (**Gabi Nunes** 87), **Ludmila** (**Gabi Portilho** 55) - **Kerolin** (**Jheniffer** 62). *Elias* ■ 81

ESP • **Coll** (1 Misa **Rodríguez** 75) - **Batlle**, 16 Laia **Codina**, **Aleixandri**, **Carmona** (c) - **Abelleira** - **Del Castillo**, **Guijarro** (**Putellas** 59), **Hermoso** (**Bonmatí** 59), 15 Eva **Navarro** (**Paralluelo** 46) - **García** (**Caldentey** 46). *Tomé* ■ 84

2024 Quarter-finals

◀ Defender Toko Koga (6) clears for Japan, despite the attentions of the USA's Sophia Smith.

◀ Trinity Rodman celebrates with team-mate Emily Fox (2) after scoring the only goal in the USA's victory over Japan.

Checkmate! USA edge tight contest

Parc des Princes, Paris
3.08.2024, 15:00, **43,004**

USA 🇺🇸 **1-0** 🇯🇵 **JAPAN**
AET

Rodman 105+2

Tess Olofsson SWE · Almira Spahić SWE & Francesca Di Monte ITA · Ivan Bebek CRO

USA • Naeher - Fox (Krueger 120+1), Girma, Sonnett ▪ 57, Dunn - Horan (c), Albert, Lavelle (Nighswonger 106) - Rodman, Smith, Swanson (Williams 91). *Hayes ENG*

JPN • Yamashita - Koga (Takahashi 91), Kumagai (c), Minami - Moriya, Nagano, Hasegawa (Hayashi 106), Kitagawa (Chiba 106) - Fujino (Miyazawa 81), Tanaka (Ueki 70), Seike (Hamano 46). *Ikeda*

Japan arrived in Paris aiming to end an unwelcome run of four past Games defeats to the USA. *Nadeshiko* captain Saki Kumagai was the only player from either side to have experienced the last of those – the gold medal match in 2012. It was, however, only four months since the majority of those lining up at the Parc des Princes had faced off in a slender 2-1 USA win at the SheBelieves Cup. Then, Kiko Seike had opened the scoring after 30 seconds. This time it took 107 minutes to deliver a goal in a tactical encounter, the USA facing extra time in a third successive Olympic quarter-final. In what USA captain Lindsey Horan would later describe as a "chess match", both sides sought openings. Alyssa Naeher blocked Mina Tanaka's best move. Ayaka Yamashita stood firm in a one-on-one with Sophia Smith. But this 41st meeting between the sides was finally settled when Trinity Rodman collected Crystal Dunn's lofted pass, jinked past Hikaru Kitagawa and curled in a wonderful left-foot strike.

15

By beating Japan, the USA qualified for their 15th semi-final in 17 global tournaments.

So near yet so far for Colombia

Stade de Lyon, Lyon
3.08.2024, 17:00, **10,355**

SPAIN 🇪🇸 **2-2** 🇨🇴 **COLOMBIA**
AET
4-2 PSO

Hermoso 79, Paredes 90+7 — Ramírez 12, Santos 52

Usme ✖ (saved), Caldentey ✓, Vanegas ✓, Navarro ✓, Salazar ✖ (over crossbar), Paralluelo ✓, Carabalí ✓, Bonmatí ✓

Katia Itzel García MEX · Sandra Ramírez MEX & Karen Díaz Medina MEX · Tatiana Guzmán NCA

ESP • Coll - Batlle, Paredes (c), Aleixandri ▪ 8 (Codina 78), Carmona (21 Alba **Redondo** 65) - Bonmatí, Guijarro (Abelleira 52), Putellas (Hermoso 65) - Del Castillo (Navarro 79), Paralluelo, Caldentey. *Tomé*

COL • Tapia - C Arias, D Arias ▪ 30, Carabalí, Vanegas - Usme (c), Restrepo (Quejada Minota 98) - Paví (Izquierdo 45+2), Santos (Salazar 86), Caicedo (Montoya 66) - Ramírez (Caracas 86). *Marsiglia*

▶ Spain celebrate beating Colombia on penalties after Aitana Bonmatí scored the winning spot kick.

▼ Irene Paredes equalises for Spain against Colombia deep into injury time, having trailed 2-0 with just 11 minutes of normal time to go.

Colombia had finished 11th in their two previous Olympics. So, having reached the quarters on goal difference as one of the two best third-placed teams, Angelo Marsiglia's players were already breaking new ground. Their momentous run looked set to continue when Mayra Ramírez and Leicy Santos put them into a commanding lead in this first-ever meeting with Spain. Yet while *La Roja* were the Games' only debutants, they were also world champions, and they summoned every ounce of the mentality that had helped them reach that pinnacle. Substitute Jenni Hermoso pulled them back from the brink mere moments after Cata Coll had crucially denied Ramírez a second. Captain Irene Paredes forced extra time with a 97th-minute equaliser, but after that ended in stalemate, only spot kicks would do. Coll was equal to Catalina Usme, and with the Colombian centurion's fellow Olympic veteran Liana Salazar having skied her chance, it fell to Aitana Bonmatí to decide it. It had taken a herculean effort, but Spain were through.

Berger performs heroics

Stade de Marseille, Marseille
3.08.2024, 19:00, **12,517**

CANADA 🇨🇦 **0-0** 🇩🇪 **GERMANY**
AET
2-4 PSO

Gwinn ✓, Quinn ✓, Minge ✓, Lawrence ✗ (saved),
Lohmann ✗ (over crossbar), Leon ✗ (saved), Rauch ✓, Beckie ✓,
Berger ✓

👁 Edina Alves Batista BRA
🚩 Neuza Back BRA & Fabrini Bevilaqua Costa BRA
📺 Daiane Muniz BRA

CAN • Sheridan - Rose, Gilles, Buchanan, Carle (Lacasse 57) - Awujo (Grosso 109), Quinn - Lawrence, Fleming (c) (Beckie 46), Huitema (Viens 57) - Prince (Leon 57). *Spence ENG*

GER • Berger - Gwinn ▌107, Hendrich, Hegering, Rauch ▌102 - Brand ▌79, Minge, Popp (c), Bühl (Endemann 65) (Senß 104) - Nüsken (Lohmann 65), Schüller (Freigang 114). *Hrubesch*

▶ Germany goalkeeper Ann-Katrin Berger scores the winning penalty against Canada having already saved two in the shoot-out.

73

Germany's coach, 73-year-old Horst Hrubesch, was the oldest in the competition's history and had led the men's U-23s to silver at Rio 2016.

With 41-year-old assistant coach Andy Spence taking the reins, defending champions Canada had won all three of their group-stage matches for only the second time in five appearances at the Olympics, which was quite a feat in the wake of a headline-grabbing drone spying scandal. Spence threw 13 gold medallists into the fray in Marseille. Only current captain Alexandra Popp remained from Germany's 2016 title triumph, though it was her fellow 33-year-old, goalkeeper Ann-Katrin Berger, who stole this show. It was a rollercoaster of a tie, as Klara Bühl and Lea Schüller tested keeper Kailen Sheridan, while Berger frustrated Evelyne Viens, Cloé Lacasse and Adriana Leon. Janine Beckie came agonisingly close to a last-gasp winner, and in extra time, Ashley Lawrence, Leon and Sydney Lohmann might have settled it too. But it took a shoot-out to separate the sides, and in just her 14th international, Berger lapped it up, denying Lawrence and Leon before sensationally dispatching the winning kick – the first penalty of her career.

Gabi Portilho knocks out hosts

Stade de la Beaujoire, Nantes
3.08.2024, 21:00, **32,280**

FRANCE 🇫🇷 **0-1** 🇧🇷 **BRAZIL**
(Karchaoui penalty saved 16)   Gabi Portilho 82

👁 Tori Penso USA   🚩 Brooke Mayo USA & Kathryn Nesbitt USA   📺 Rob Dieperink NED

FRA • Picaud - De Almeida (Dali 90+5), Mbock Bathy, Renard (c), Bacha - Geyoro, Toletti (Le Sommer 85), Karchaoui - Cascarino ▌90+10, Katoto ▌28, Baltimore (Diani 69 ▌90+4). *Renard* ▌28

BRA • Lorena - Thaís (Lauren 88), Tarciane, Rafaelle (c) (Tamires 54 ▌79) - Adriana, Duda Sampaio (Angelina 63 ▌90+9), Ana Vitória, Yasmim - Gabi Portilho ▌90+4, Jheniffer ▌1 (Ludmila 87) - Gabi Nunes (Kerolin 63 ▌79). *Elias*

Having reached their highest-ever FIFA ranking of world number two ahead of these Olympics, France eyed a podium finish on home soil. "It's everyone's dream," vice-captain Grace Geyoro declared. With head coach Hervé Renard set to depart at the end of the tournament, it would be the ideal farewell for him, too. They faced a nation that had never beaten France in 12 previous meetings, but they were still wary, Marie-Antoinette Katoto insisting beforehand: "Brazil is Brazil!" The *Seleção* wanted to win this one for suspended skipper Marta and were grateful to Lorena when, after a lengthy VAR review of Tarciane's tackle on Delphine Cascarino, the keeper palmed away Sakina Karchaoui's penalty kick. France knocked on the door again, Griedge Mbock Bathy's header ricocheting off the crossbar and Lorena tested by Cascarino and Selma Bacha. But with time running out, Gabi Portilho silenced the Nantes crowd, beating Élisa de Almeida and Mbock Bathy to an Adriana pass before unleashing a thunderous winning shot. A sixth Olympic semi-final awaited Brazil, but for the hosts it was adieu.

▲ Shirt worn by Adriana in Brazil's victory over hosts France. She wore the captain's armband in the Final.
FIFA Museum Collection

▶ Brazil's Gabi Portilho celebrates scoring the only goal of the game against France.

USA into sixth Olympic Final

Stade de Lyon, Lyon
6.08.2024, 18:00, **11,716**

USA 🇺🇸 **1-0** 🇩🇪 **GERMANY**
Smith 95
AET

Bouchra Karboubi MAR · Fatiha Jermoumi MAR & Diana Chikotesha ZAM · Ivan Bebek CRO

USA • Naeher - Fox, Girma, Davidson (Sonnett 46) - Rodman, Horan (c) (Albert 91), Coffey, Dunn (Nighswonger 91) - Swanson (Krueger 110), Smith, Lavelle (Williams 60). *Hayes ENG*
GER • Berger - Gwinn (c), Hendrich, Hegering ■ 44 (Schulze Solano 78), Rauch (Doorsoun 105) - Lohmann (Senß 91), Nüsken, Minge, Bühl - Brand ■ 108, 21 Nicole **Anyomi** (Freigang 69). *Hrubesch*

Before Paris 2024, the USA had not faced Germany at the Olympics in 20 years. Now the two most successful sides in women's football were meeting for the second time in ten days. Conscious of what her players still needed to give mentally and physically to see this one over the line, head coach Emma Hayes had inspired them with the story of ultrarunner Courtney Dauwalter and her approach to pain. Germany, meanwhile, were still smarting over their 4-1 loss to the *Stars and Stripes* in Marseille, and that seemed motivation enough. "We want to give it back," said defender Giulia Gwinn. Sidelined through illness and injury, key threats Alexandra Popp and Lea Schüller could only watch. But Germany still had attacking options, and Alyssa Naeher was forced into seven saves – the most she had made in a single match on any global stage. Ann-Katrin Berger and her defence were also steadfast, and the keeper's smart stop to deny Lindsey Horan's late flying header kept them in the game. Sophia Smith ended the deadlock, though, and was mobbed by her team-mates after beating the onrushing Berger in extra time. In a frantic finish, Laura Freigang might have equalised were it not for Naeher's foot, and Berger twice defied the lively Smith. But that 95th-minute effort proved enough, as captain for the day Gwinn later noted: "It was one goal too many, unfortunately."

▲▲ Germany's Jule Brand (16) and Crystal Dunn of the USA in action during the semi-final in Lyon.

▲ Sophia Smith scores the only goal of the game against Germany to secure the USA's sixth appearance in the gold medal match at the Olympics.

Brazil through in Marseille thriller

Stade de Marseille, Marseille
6.08.2024, 21:00, **14,201**

BRAZIL 🇧🇷 **4-2** 🇪🇸 **SPAIN**
Paredes OG 6, Gabi Portilho 45+4, Adriana 71, Kerolin 90+1 — Duda Sampaio OG 85, Paralluelo 90+12

Rebecca Welch ENG · Emily Carney ENG & Franca Overtoom NED · Jérôme Brisard FRA

BRA • Lorena - Thaís, Lauren (Kerolin 77), Tarciane - Ludmila (Adriana 56 ■ 90+5), Angelina c (Duda Sampaio 56), Vitória Yaya, Yasmim - Priscila (Gabi Nunes 77 ■ 90), Gabi Portilho, Jheniffer (Ana Vitória 69). *Elias*
ESP • Coll ■ 90 - Batlle, Paredes (c) (Aleixandri 51), Codina (Putellas 77), Carmona (Hernández 46) - Bonmatí, Abelleira ■ 45+4 (Guijarro 65), Hermoso - Navarro (del Castillo 46), Paralluelo, Caldentey. *Tomé*

After their sensational comeback against Colombia, Spain head coach Montserrat Tomé had compared her team's Olympic journey to stages in the Tour de France. "We have two more to go," she said. "We can and we will go for it." Yet while her charges had already overcome the *Seleção* in this tournament, the race was not yet over. "It's practically a new competition," insisted Brazil defender Lauren. Arthur Elias's side had their own mountain to climb, with injuries to Antônia, Rafaelle and Tamires, plus the suspension of star skipper Marta. But a day after celebrating their coach's 43rd birthday by presenting him with a cake adorned with the Olympic rings, Brazil then provided the icing and put a cherry on the top. They got a lucky break when a clearance from masked keeper Cata Coll deflected in off Irene Paredes. Defensive frailties saw an unfettered Gabi Portilho stroke in Yasmim's incisive pass too. Jenni Hermoso threatened with a thunderous second-half drive, but Portilho set up Adriana for the third. A late Duda Sampaio own goal offered Spain a glimmer of hope and Lorena acrobatically denied Alexia Putellas twice in the space of 20 seconds. But after Kerolin nutmegged Coll to make it 4-1, Salma Paralluelo's stoppage-time effort simply softened the score. "We played for Marta," said Lorena later, "and for all the girls who were injured."

▲ Kerolin (7) scores Brazil's fourth goal in their victory over world champions Spain.

ne This loss for 2023 victors Spain kept up a run that had seen the reigning World Cup champions never win the subsequent Olympics.

▶ Spain's Salma Paralluelo heads the ball towards the Brazilian goal where it was deflected by Duda Sampaio into her own net, reducing the Spanish arrears to 3-1 late on.

2024 Bronze Medal Match

Stade de Lyon, Lyon
9.08.2024, 15:00, **10,995**

SPAIN 0-1 GERMANY

(Putellas penalty saved 90+9)   Gwinn 65p

Katia Itzel García MEX   Sandra Ramírez MEX & Karen Díaz Medina MEX   Khamis Al Marri QAT

600

Goalkeeper Ann-Katrin Berger was the only Germany player to play all 600 of her team's minutes at this tournament. Only defender Ona Batlle had been ever-present for Spain's 570 minutes.

▼ Spain's Aitana Bonmatí (6) has her shot blocked in the bronze medal match against Germany.

▲ Giulia Gwinn scores the only goal of the bronze medal match from the penalty spot for Germany. Deep into added time, team-mate Ann-Katrin Berger saved a penalty taken by Spain's Alexia Putellas to secure bronze for the Germans.

A tale of two penalties

Brought in to steady the ship after their calamitous World Cup a year prior, 73-year-old interim coach Horst Hrubesch had not only secured Germany's return to the Olympics after having failed to qualify for Tokyo 2020, he had also brought them within touching distance of bronze. "A few months ago, many would not have thought we could do that," said Nia Künzer, the national team's sporting director and scorer of their 2003 World Cup-winning golden goal. Spain had gone for gold from the outset, and in this maiden Olympic campaign, under former World Cup-winning assistant Montserrat Tomé, they had outstripped all-comers in terms of completed passes, crosses, corners and attempts on target. After their defeat to Brazil, however, they had to refocus on what veteran striker Jenni Hermoso described as "a new final". They did their utmost to win it, but the woodwork, stalwart defending, a penalty queen and a keeper in the form of her career sent them home empty-handed. Teresa Abelleira and Aitana Bonmatí rattled the crossbar, Marina Hegering, Kathrin Hendrich and Sjoeke Nüsken helped nullify Spain's attack, and Giulia Gwinn won and calmly scored what turned out to be the deciding penalty – her sixth in a *Nationalelf* shirt. Finally, Ann-Katrin Berger saved Spain icon Alexia Putellas's firmly struck spot kick in the dying seconds to put the finishing touch on Germany's victory. It was Hrubesch's final match in charge, and through the tears, the tributes flowed. "We're delighted for Horst and the whole coaching team," said Hegering. "It's a great way to say goodbye."

▼ Paris 2024 was the fourth time Germany had won bronze at the Olympics, having done so at three consecutive Games between 2000 and 2008.

2024 Gold Medal Match

Parc des Princes, Paris
10.08.2024, 17:00, 43,813

BRAZIL 0-1 USA
Swanson 57

Tess Olofsson SWE — Almira Spahić SWE & Francesca Di Monte ITA — Ivan Bebek CRO

▲ Brazil and the USA line up for the gold medal match at the Parc des Princes. For the first time since the Olympics have featured both women's and men's football tournaments, and as a mark of respect, the women's Final was played the day after the men's Final.

Two decades of Marta

Two decades had passed since a teenage Marta sashayed her way onto this world stage, and the 38-year-old was still going strong at Paris 2024. "Queen Marta" may not have realised her dream of winning gold, but Brazil's iconic number ten chalked up her 200th appearance, became only the second player to feature in 30 Olympic matches and the first Brazilian footballer, male or female, to win three Olympic medals. However, as a player who has often used her voice to advocate for equality and investment in the women's game, Marta viewed this campaign not as a personal landmark but as a rallying cry for 2027 and Brazil's hosting of the Women's World Cup. "We accomplished what we set out to do: restore Brazilian pride and change the perception of women's football into something different, more competitive," she said. "We need that momentum to encourage the Brazilian people to have more faith in women's football."

> **Not only is she a credit to Brazil, but the generation that just played are all inspired greatly by her, as are many of us.**
> EMMA HAYES ON MARTA

▼ Marta watches from the sidelines before kick-off. She came on as a 61st-minute substitute.

▼ Match ball from the 2024 Olympic Final.
FIFA Museum Collection

Gold medal match 2024

Swanson strikes gold for the USA

As club coaches in their respective homelands, Arthur Elias and Emma Hayes had enjoyed trophy-laden careers. Now, in their first ever global tournament, they stood across the grass from one another in the searing heat of Paris having led two of the most talked-about national teams in the world to the brink of glory. In two decades, it was the third time that Brazil and the USA had faced off in the fight for gold. Victorious in both 2004 and four years later, the North Americans had the edge. But neither São Paulo-native Elias nor Londoner Hayes wanted to dwell on the past. Enlisted in the aftermath of shock early exits from the 2023 World Cup, the two were fully focused on the future. The tough calls had been made, Cristiane left out of a Brazil squad that included nine players aged 24 and under and Alex Morgan missing from a USA group with an average age of 26 – their youngest since Beijing 2008. Echoes of yesteryear still resonated in both camps, though. Brazil's samba style had returned under Elias. "We are happy, fearless, aggressive, yet looking for the win," two-time Olympic silver medallist Marta had said in the midst of a campaign that gave the *Seleção*'s entire roster a chance to shine. Hayes had only been in charge since May, but the talk among the USA's players throughout these Games was of a renewed sense of fun and focus. Their fear factor was coming back too. Reminiscent of their all-conquering 1991 World Cup "triple-edged sword" frontline, a "triple espresso" of 20-somethings – Trinity Rodman, Sophia Smith and Mallory Swanson – had scored or provided the assist for ten of the USA's 11 goals at the tournament to date. With 24-year-old Naomi Girma and evergreen veterans Alyssa Naeher and Crystal Dunn among those bossing the backline, they had conceded just twice. With a near-capacity Parc des Princes crowd on the edge of their seats and the coaches prowling their areas, Brazil's sixth different line-up set about an almost unchanged USA. Gabi Portilho tested Naeher's reflexes in the first half, while Ludmila had a goal ruled out for offside. But Swanson's 57th-minute side-foot shot on her 100th appearance was too good for Lorena, and nothing Brazil threw at the USA stuck, not even an Adriana free header in stoppage time that Naeher clawed out of the air. With just the one goal between them, the fairytale ending belonged to the USA and Hayes, but both teams departed with their heads held high.

◂▴ Brazil's Yasmim (13) holds off the USA's Trinity Rodman during the gold medal match in Paris.

▴ Mallory Swanson wheels away to celebrate after scoring the only goal of the game against Brazil. It was the third time the USA had beaten Brazil in the gold medal match at the Olympics.

9

With five Olympic golds and four World Cup titles, the USA have now won nine world titles, which is one more than everyone else combined.

7

USA players Tierna Davidson, Crystal Dunn, Lindsey Horan, Rose Lavelle, Alyssa Naeher, Emily Sonnett and Mallory Swanson had now all added an Olympic gold medal to the Women's World Cup crown that they secured at France 2019. Naeher was part of the triumphant 2015 squad too, but did not see any minutes.

◂ Team USA get a taste of gold again, 12 years after previously claiming the Olympic crown.

Records

Finals

International Women's Football Tournament

1988	China PR	NOR 🇳🇴	1-0	🇸🇪 SWE	Tianhe Stadium, Guangzhou	35,000
		Medalen 58			📺 Romualdo Arppi Filho BRA	

FIFA Women's World Cup

1991	China PR	USA 🇺🇸	2-1	🇳🇴 NOR	Tianhe Stadium, Guangzhou	63,000
		Akers-Stahl (2) 20 78		Medalen 29	📺 Vadim Zhuk BLR	
1995	Sweden	NOR 🇳🇴	2-0	🇩🇪 GER	Råsunda, Solna, Stockholm	17,158
		Riise 37, Pettersen 40			📺 Ingrid Jonsson SWE	
1999	USA	USA 🇺🇸	0-0 AET 5-4 PSO	🇨🇳 CHN	Rose Bowl, Pasadena, Los Angeles	90,185
					📺 Nicole Petignat SUI	
2003	USA	GER 🇩🇪	2-1 AET	🇸🇪 SWE	Home Depot Center, Carson, Los Angeles	26,137
		Meinert 46, Künzer 98 GG		Ljungberg 41	📺 Cristina Ionescu ROU	
2007	China PR	GER 🇩🇪	2-0	🇧🇷 BRA	Shanghai Hongkou Football Stadium, Shanghai	31,000
		Prinz 52, Laudehr 86			📺 Tammy Ogston AUS	
2011	Germany	JPN 🇯🇵	2-2 AET 3-1 PSO	🇺🇸 USA	FIFA World Cup Stadium, Frankfurt/Main	48,817
		Miyama 81, Sawa 117		Morgan 69, Wambach 104	📺 Bibiana Steinhaus GER	
2015	Canada	USA 🇺🇸	5-2	🇯🇵 JPN	BC Place Stadium, Vancouver	53,341
		Lloyd (3) 3 5 16 Holiday 14, Heath 54		Ōgimi 27, Johnston OG 52	📺 Kateryna Monzul UKR	
2019	France	USA 🇺🇸	2-0	🇳🇱 NED	Stade de Lyon, Lyon	57,900
		Rapinoe 61p, Lavelle 69			📺 Stéphanie Frappart FRA	
2023	Australia/New Zealand	ESP 🇪🇸	1-0	🏴󠁧󠁢󠁥󠁮󠁧󠁿 ENG	Stadium Australia, Sydney	75,784
		Carmona 29			📺 Tori Penso USA	

Women's Olympic Football Tournament

1996	Atlanta	USA 🇺🇸	2-1	🇨🇳 CHN	Sanford Stadium, Athens	76,489
		MacMillan 19, Milbrett 68		Sun Wen 32	📺 Bente Skogvang NOR	
2000	Sydney	NOR 🇳🇴	3-2 AET	🇺🇸 USA	Sydney Football Stadium, Sydney	22,848
		Espeseth 44, R Gulbrandsen 78, Mellgren 102 GG		Milbrett (2) 5, 90+2	📺 Sonia Denoncourt CAN	
2004	Athens	USA 🇺🇸	2-1 AET	🇧🇷 BRA	Karaiskaki, Athens	10,416
		Tarpley 39, Wambach 112		Pretinha 73	📺 Jenny Palmqvist SWE (Dianne Ferreira-James GUY 90)	
2008	Beijing	USA 🇺🇸	1-0 AET	🇧🇷 BRA	Workers' Stadium, Beijing	51,612
		Lloyd 96			📺 Dagmar Damková CZE	
2012	London	USA 🇺🇸	2-1	🇯🇵 JPN	Wembley Stadium, London	80,203
		Lloyd (2) 8 54		Ōgimi 63	📺 Bibiana Steinhaus GER	
2016	Rio de Janeiro	GER 🇩🇪	2-1	🇸🇪 SWE	Maracanã, Rio de Janeiro	52,432
		Marozsán 48, Sembrant OG 62		Blackstenius 67	📺 Carol Anne Chenard CAN	
2020	Tokyo	CAN 🇨🇦	1-1 3-2 PSO	🇸🇪 SWE	International Stadium Yokohama, Yokohama	BCD
		Fleming 67p		Blackstenius 34	📺 Anastasia Pustovoitova RUS	
2024	Paris	USA 🇺🇸	1-0	🇧🇷 BRA	Parc des Princes, Paris	43,813
		Swanson 57			📺 Tess Olofsson SWE	

Records

World Cup and Olympic Games winners

Team	Overall			FIFA Women's World Cup			Women's Olympic Football Tournament		
	1st	2nd	3rd	Winners	Runners-up	Third	Gold	Silver	Bronze
USA	9	2	4	4	1	3	5	1	1
GER	3	1	4	2	1		1		4
NOR	2	1	1	1	1		1		1
JPN	1	2		1	1			1	
CAN	1		2				1		2
ESP	1			1					
BRA		4	1		2	1		3	
SWE		3	4		1	4		2	
CHN		2			1			1	
ENG		1	1		1	1			
NED		1			1				

Multiple winners

Five titles
Christie Rampone 1999 2004 2008 2012 2015
Four titles
Shannon Boxx 2004 2008 2012 2015
Brandi Chastain 1991 1996 1999 2004
Joy Fawcett 1991 1996 1999 2004
Julie Foudy 1991 1996 1999 2004
Mia Hamm 1991 1996 1999 2004
Tobin Heath 2008 2012 2015 2019
Kristine Lilly 1991 1996 1999 2004
Carli Lloyd 2008 2012 2015 2019
Heather O'Reilly 2004 2008 2012 2015
Three titles
Michelle Akers 1991 1996 1999
Lauren Holiday 2008 2012 2015
Kate Markgraf 1999 2004 2008
Heather Mitts 2004 2008 2012
Alex Morgan 2012 2015 2019
Alyssa Naeher 2015 2019 2024
Kelley O'Hara 2012 2015 2019
Carla Overbeck 1991 1996 1999
Cindy Parlow 1996 1999 2004
Megan Rapinoe 2012 2015 2019
Amy Rodriguez 2008 2012 2015
Becky Sauerbrunn 2012 2015 2019
Briana Scurry 1996 1999 2004
Hope Solo 2008 2012 2015
Abby Wambach 2004 2012 2015

Top FIFA Women's World Cup appearances

30	Kristine Lilly	USA	1991-2007
27	Formiga	BRA	1995-2019
25	Abby Wambach	USA	2003-2015
25	Carli Lloyd	USA	2007-2019
24	Julie Foudy	USA	1991-2003
24	Birgit Prinz	GER	1995-2011
24	Homare Sawa	JPN	1995-2015
24	Christine Sinclair	CAN	2003-2023
23	Joy Fawcett	USA	1991-2003
23	Mia Hamm	USA	1991-2003
23	Marta	BRA	2003-2023
22	Hege Riise	NOR	1991-2003
22	Bettina Wiegmann	GER	1991-2003
22	Bente Nordby	NOR	1995-2007
22	Alex Morgan	USA	2011-2023
21	Cristiane	BRA	2003-2019
21	Jill Scott	ENG	2007-2019
21	Saki Kumagai	JPN	2011-2023
20	Sun Wen	CHN	1991-2003
20	Hedvig Lindahl	SWE	2007-2019
20	Caroline Seger	SWE	2007-2023
20	Eugénie Le Sommer	FRA	2011-2023
20	Megan Rapinoe	USA	2011-2023
20	Lucy Bronze	ENG	2015-2023

Top Women's Olympic Football Tournament appearances

33	Formiga	BRA	1996-2020
30	Marta	BRA	2004-2024
22	Christie Rampone	USA	2000-2012
22	Carli Lloyd	USA	2008-2020
20	Tânia	BRA	1996-2008
20	Cristiane	BRA	2004-2016
20	Caroline Seger	SWE	2008-2020
20	Christine Sinclair	CAN	2008-2020
19	Birgit Prinz	GER	1996-2008
19	Hedwig Lindahl	SWE	2004-2020
18	Pretinha	BRA	1996-2008
18	Kerstin Stegemann	GER	1996-2008
18	Tobin Heath	USA	2008-2020
17	Homare Sawa	JPN	1996-2012
17	Daniela	BRA	2000-2008
17	Andréia	BRA	2000-2012
17	Lotta Schelin	SWE	2004-2016
17	Sophie Schmidt	CAN	2008-2020

Top FIFA Women's World Cup and Women's Olympic Football Tournament combined appearances

60	Formiga	BRA	1995-2020
53	Marta	BRA	2003-2024
47	Carli Lloyd	USA	2007-2020
46	Kristine Lilly	USA	1991-2007
44	Christine Sinclair	CAN	2003-2023
43	Birgit Prinz	GER	1995-2011
41	Homare Sawa	JPN	1995-2015
41	Christie Rampone	USA	1999-2015
41	Cristiane	BRA	2003-2019
40	Julie Foudy	USA	1991-2004
40	Caroline Seger	SWE	2007-2023
39	Joy Fawcett	USA	1991-2004
39	Hedvig Lindahl	SWE	2004-2020
38	Mia Hamm	USA	1991-2004
38	Alex Morgan	USA	2011-2023
37	Tânia	BRA	1995-2008
36	Abby Wambach	USA	2003-2015
35	Sophie Schmidt	CAN	2007-2023
35	Saki Kumagai	JPN	2011-2024
34	Tobin Heath	USA	2008-2020
34	Megan Rapinoe	USA	2011-2023
33	Ariane Hingst	GER	1999-2011
33	Hope Solo	USA	2007-2016

Top FIFA Women's World Cup scorers

17	Marta	BRA
14	Birgit Prinz	GER
14	Abby Wambach	USA
12	Michelle Akers	USA
11	Cristiane	BRA
11	Sun Wen	CHN
11	Bettina Wiegmann	GER
10	Ann Kristin Aarønes	NOR
10	Carli Lloyd	USA
10	Heidi Mohr	GER
10	Christine Sinclair	CAN
9	Linda Medalen	NOR
9	Alex Morgan	USA
9	Megan Rapinoe	USA
9	Hege Riise	NOR
8	Kerstin Garefrekes	GER
8	Mia Hamm	USA
8	Kristine Lilly	USA
8	Liu Aling	CHN
8	Célia Šašić	GER
8	Marianne Pettersen	NOR
8	Homare Sawa	JPN
8	Eugénie Le Sommer	FRA

Top Women's Olympic Football Tournament scorers

14	Cristiane	BRA
13	Marta	BRA
12	Christine Sinclair	CAN
10	Birgit Prinz	GER
10	Barbra Banda	ZAM
10	Vivianne Miedema	NED
10	Carli Lloyd	USA
9	Abby Wambach	USA
8	Pretinha	BRA
7	Melissa Tancredi	CAN
7	Sam Kerr	AUS
7	Stina Blackstenius	SWE
6	Lotta Schelin	SWE
6	Ellen White	ENG
6	Alex Morgan	USA
5	Sun Wen	CHN
5	Mia Hamm	USA
5	Tiffeny Milbrett	USA
5	Janine Beckie	CAN
5	Melanie Behringer	GER
5	Megan Rapinoe	USA
5	Mallory Swanson	USA
5	Marie-Antoinette Katoto	FRA

Top Women's World Cup and Women's Olympic Football Tournament combined scorers

30	Marta	BRA
25	Cristiane	BRA
24	Birgit Prinz	GER
23	Abby Wambach	USA
22	Christine Sinclair	CAN
20	Carli Lloyd	USA
16	Sun Wen	CHN
15	Alex Morgan	USA
14	Ann Kristin Aarønes	NOR
14	Megan Rapinoe	USA
14	Bettina Wiegmann	GER
13	Michelle Akers	USA
13	Mia Hamm	USA
13	Sam Kerr	AUS
13	Linda Medalen	NOR
13	Vivianne Miedema	NED
13	Pretinha	BRA
13	Ellen White	ENG
12	Kristine Lilly	USA
12	Tiffeny Milbrett	USA
12	Marianne Pettersen	NOR

▲ The FIFA Museum in Zurich is home to the FIFA Women's World Cup Trophy.

www.fifamuseum.com

Opened in February 2016, the FIFA Museum sits in the heart of Zurich, opposite Enge station and a five-minute walk from the lake. With a mission to preserve, safeguard and celebrate the rich heritage of association football, it has more than 1,000 exhibits across three floors. The museum is divided into four main halls. **Planet Football** celebrates FIFA's 211 member associations through its rainbow of national team shirts and timeline of world football. The second hall is called **The Foundations**, which describes the early years of the game and how it became established across the world. **The FIFA World Cup Gallery** showcases every edition of the men's and women's World Cup, with historical artefacts and state-of-the-art interactive displays. It is also the home of the FIFA World Cup Trophy and the FIFA Women's World Cup Trophy, both of which are on permanent display at the entrance to the gallery. After watching an eight-minute film in our 180° cinema, glass lifts take you to the final hall, an area dedicated to highlighting football's influence on people around the world and revealing how the game inspires and entertains in equal measure. **The Virtual Pitch** allows visitors to discover the world of eFootball, while **Pinball** gives them the chance to test their own technical

skills. On the top floor, there is also a dedicated area for the FIFA Museum's temporary exhibitions.

The FIFA World Cup Gallery is the historic heart of the museum, and pride of place goes to the FIFA World Cup Trophy at the gallery entrance. From 1974 to 2016, Silvio Gazzaniga's masterpiece was kept securely locked in a Zurich bank vault between World Cup tournaments, but is now on permanent display at the museum when not on World Cup duty. It sits opposite the FIFA Women's World Cup Trophy in a gallery that also features the Wall of Champions, a display where World Cup winners can sign their name. For every edition of the World Cup, there is a showcase containing a specially commissioned poster telling the story of the tournament and featuring unique artefacts. From the 1930 exhibit displaying the silver medal awarded to Guillermo Stábile – the top scorer at the first-ever World Cup – to Kylian Mbappé and Lionel Messi's shirts from the 2018 and 2022 finals respectively, the story of every World Cup is told through objects, words, images and film. Interactive stations let you explore the history of the World Cup balls, posters and shirts. And there are games to play too: test your refereeing skills and see whether you can replicate some of the most famous goal celebrations in the **Soccer Dance** area. At the end of the gallery, there is a 180-degree cinema where visitors can watch short films featuring highlights from the men's and women's tournaments.

The FIFA Museum features a number of priceless exhibits from football's past, including all that remains of the Jules Rimet Trophy, created by Abel Lafleur for the first World Cup in 1930. A bigger lapis lazuli base, with room for more names, replaced the original in 1958, and now the original lapis lazuli base can be seen in **The Foundations**, along with the first book of minutes from the International Football Association Board meeting in 1886 and the draft Laws of the Game, handwritten by Sir Stanley Rous in 1934. The museum also contains one of the largest collections of football books, with over 10,000 in total, many of which are housed on-site in **The Library**, situated on the second floor, where researchers can also request access to view documents in the FIFA archives. On the final floor, visitors can explore a number of unique objects, from the smallest trophy ever made in world football to the museum's oldest football artefact – a 2,000-year-old sculpture of a Meso-American figure holding a ball. There are also 60 screens showing over 500 videos throughout the museum, including the giant 10 x 8m screen in **Planet Football**.

1. The Rainbow of national team shirts
2. The Foundations
3. The FIFA World Cup Trophy
4. and 5. The FIFA World Cup Gallery
6. The Galaxy of Balls

Picture credits

adidas: 67(ball), 77(ball), 91(ball), 115(ball), 127(ball), 141(ball), 169(ball), 183(ball), 203(ball), 217(ball)
Archivio La Stampa: 15bl
Bildbyran: 50, 51br, 51bl, 52bl, 53(Gävle), 53br, 54mr, 54bl, 54br, 55t, 56m, 56b, 57t, 57b, 58t, 58bl, 58br, 59t, 59m, 60m, 60b, 61t, 61b, 62t, 62b, 63t, 63bl, 63br, 66m
Moya Dodd's Private Collection: 29t, 31br
FIFA: 5(FIFA emblems), 7, 39(emblem), 39(mascot), 53(emblem), 77(emblem), 77(mascot), 99br, 101(emblem), 127(emblem), 127(mascot), 155(emblem), 155(mascot), 183(emblem), 183(mascot), 217(emblem), 217(mascot), 251(emblem), 251(mascot)
FIFA Museum: 2t, 3bl, 3br, 18ml, 21tr, 26m, 27(ball), 30t, 30b, 31tl, 31tr, 32tr, 32bl, 33tl, 38(trophy), 38tr, 38mr, 39(ball), 40b, 49tl, 49ml, 52(trophy), 52tr, 52mr, 53(mascot), 53(ball), 54mr, 63bl, 76(trophy), 76l, 76mr, 87tr, 100(trophy), 100tr, 100m, 100mr, 101(ball), 107m, 126(trophy), 126tr, 126mr, 140tr, 154(trophy), 154tr, 154mr, 155(ball), 160bl, 165tl, 165tr, 168tr, 182(trophy), 183(pennant), 190ml, 192t, 196ml, 197br, 202tr, 216-217, 216(trophy), 216(pennant), 223br, 224ml, 229bm, 233tr, 240t, 246bl, 250(medals), 250(pennant), 254bl, 261br, 265bl, 267bl, 269ml, 277ml, 279bl, 282bl, 286-287; /Bongarts: 116m; /International Sports Images: 84tl, 84ml, 88, 90bl, 92b, 93m, 94mr, 94br, 95tr, 95bl, 95br, 96tl, 96ml, 97t, 97m, 97bl; /LOC: 24, 25br, 27(emblem), 27(Guangzhou), 27(Panyu), 27(Jiangmen), 28b, 31bl, 33br, 34m, 35bl, 35br, 77(Chicago), 77(Los Angeles), 77(Washington DC); /Perry McIntyre Jr: 69b, 70b; /Mexsport: 116t, 119l, 119ml, 120mr, 120br; /Daniel Motz/MotzSports: 86b, 90m, 98, 102m, 102b, 103t, 103b, 108t, 108m, 108b, 109b, 110bl, 110br, 111t, 111bl; /Newsweek: 86m; /Norges Fotballforbund: 26(trophy), 34bl; /PAM/International Sports Images: 76bl, 80m, 81tr, 81b, 83tr, 83ml, 83bl, 84br, 100bl, 104b; /Pozzo Collection: 12(Turin); /Tony Quinn Photography: 71b, 73t, 73m, 73b; /Sideline Sports Photography: 112, 115(Cristiane), 117b, 118t, 118m, 118b, 120tl, 120ml, 121t, 121b, 122t, 122b, 123tl, 123tr, 123m, 123b; /Sport Archive: 16(Mexico City); /M. Stahlschmidt/Olympic Committee: 64; /Phil Stephens Photography: 36, 37br, 38bl, 39(Guangzhou), 39(Panyu), 39(Foshan), 39br, 40t, 40mr, 40br, 41t, 41b, 42t, 42b, 44tl, 44ml, 45tl, 45bl, 46tl, 46mr, 46br, 47tl, 47br, 48tl, 48br, 49tr, 49mr, 49b, 78t, 78bl, 79b, 87tl; /J. Brett Whitesell/International Sports Images: 77mc, 77mr, 78br, 79m, 80t, 82tr, 82mr, 82ml, 82bl, 84mr, 85tl, 85tr, 85b, 87br, 101bl, 104t, 104m, 105tl, 105tr, 105b, 109t, 111br; /J. Brett Whitesell/R. B. Sports Photography: 67br, 68t, 68b, 70t, 71t
Getty Images: /AFP: 69m, 119mr; /Aitor Alcalde/FIFA: 255b, 263bl; /Joe Allison/FIFA: 252b; / Naomi Baker/FIFA: 214, 227bl, 228br, 230mr, 231bl; /Scott Bales/Icon Sport Media: 146bl; / Scott Barbour/Allsport: 94tl; /Steve Bardens/FIFA: 203(Brasilia), 203br, 206m, 208tl, 208ml; / Lars Baron/Bongarts: 150br; /Lars Baron/FIFA: 6, 142t, 155(Augsburg), 156b, 157t, 158b, 161t, 162t, 164t, 165m, 183br, 185t, 185b, 189m, 191t, 191m, 193t, 193b, 194tl, 194ml, 197t, 199m; / Alexandra Beier/FIFA: 154bl, 159b, 161b; /Torsten Blackwood/AFP: 91(Sydney); /Bongarts: 53(Solna); /Shaun Botterill/FIFA: 237(Yokohama); /Sebastien Bozon/AFP: 271br; /Darrin Braybrook/Allsport: 91br; /Chris Brunskill/FIFA: 207tl; /Simon Bruty/Sports Illustrated: 96br, 138; /Alex Caparros/FIFA: 218t, 218bl, 223m, 225ml, 225bl, 226ml, 226bl, 229bl, 230br, 232br; / Tommy Cheng/AFP: 43t, 43b; /Chung Sung-Jun/FIFA: 202m, 206b, 208mr, 208br; /Robert Cianflone/Allsport: 92t; /Robert Cianflone/FIFA: 156t, 159b, 166, 169(Newcastle), 170t, 170b, 172b, 173t, 173b, 174b, 176tl, 178m, 179b 179m, 204b, 209t, 211t, 211bl, 211br, 222b; /Kevin Cox/FIFA: 155(Frankfurt), 160br, 162m, 165b, 183(Edmonton); /Kevin C. Cox/FIFA: 152; /Mark Dadswell/Allsport: 91(Canberra), 93b; /Dimitrou Dimitris/AFP: 117m; /Stephen Dunn: 101(Los Angeles); /Jonathan Elderfield: 77(Sissi); /Elsa/FIFA: 262tr, 262ml, 266br, 269tl; /Jonathan Ferrey: 101(Portland), 107t, 107bl; /Julian Finney: 140t; /Stuart Franklin/FIFA: 168mr, 172tl, 172tr, 175t, 175m, 177bl, 178t, 182bl, 183(Montreal), 188t, 188b, 191b, 194mr, 194br, 196t, 199t, 200, 203(Manaus), 203(Rio de Janeiro), 205t, 205b, 210mr, 210br, 212t, 212bl, 212br, 213t, 213b, 275b, 276t; /Robert Gauthier/Los Angeles Times: 113br; /Georgia/Collegiate Images: 67(Athens); /Goh Chai Hin/AFP: 148br; /Fiona Goodall/FIFA: 249bl, 251(Auckland), 264mr; /Louisa Gouliamaki/EuroFootball: 115(Athens); /Laurence Griffiths/FIFA: 153br, 155br, 158t, 201br; /Alex Grimm/FIFA: 237(Tokyo), 237(Miedema), 241t, 241b, 243bl, 243br, 263tr, 266tr, 270, 273(Paris), 277bl, 278tl, 278ml, 282tr, 283br, 283b; /Jeff Gross: 141br, 144b; /Stuart Hannagan: 115(Patras); /Masashi Hara/FIFA: 239t, 239b, 243tr, 244mr, 244br; /Tom Hauck: 107br; /Noriko Hayakusa: 147m; / Richard Heathcote: 227mr, 228tl, 230ml; /Scott Heavey: 167br; /Mike Hewitt/FIFA: 155(Berlin), 157b, 160t, 163bl, 164b, 183(Vancouver), 186ml, 186mr, 186b, 187b, 192b, 193bl, 195t, 195m, 196b, 198t, 198b, 199b; /Stephanie Himango/NBC/NBCU Photo Bank: 151bl; /Maja Hitij/FIFA: 254mr, 254br, 256t, 260mr, 260br, 264tl, 269b; /Hoang Dinh Nam/AFP: 143t, 146br, 150bl; / Hagen Hopkins/FIFA: 251(Wellington), 264ml; /Chris Hyde/FIFA: 265tr; /Walter Iooss Jr./Sports Illustrated: 67(Miami); /Catherine Ivill/FIFA: 217(Paris), 219m, 221b, 224mr, 227tr, 228ml, 230tl, 233tl; /Wang Jiang/VCG: 141(Shenyang); /Michael Kappeler/AFP: 149t, 149b, 151mr; /Teng Ke/VCG: 141(Beijing); /Eddie Keogh/FIFA: 277mr, 279br; /Matt King/FIFA: 4, 265br, 268tl, 268br; /Jan Kruger/FIFA: 252t, 256b, 264bl, 266ml; /Vincent Laforet: 75br; /Harriet Lander/FIFA: 273(Marseille), 274t, 276b, 279tr, 280mr, 280br, 281br, 282br, 283tl; /David Leeds/Allsport: 77ml; /Matthew Lewis/FIFA: 258t; /Tony Lewis/Allsport: 91(Melbourne); /Philip Littleton/AFP: 65br; /Liu Jin/AFP: 145t; /Alex Livesey/FIFA: 161m, 162b, 163m, 163br, 204t, 234, 236mr, 238t, 238b, 240t, 240br, 242tl, 242mr, 245br, 246br, 247tl, 247b; /Andy Lyons: 101(Columbus); /B. Marshall/Fox Photos: 11t; /Ronald Martinez: 67(Birmingham); /Joosep Martinson/FIFA: 217(Lyon), 217(Nice), 220b, 228mr, 231ml; /Marianna Massey/FIFA: 215br, 223bl, 226tr; /Hector Mata/AFP: 74, 87mr; /Jamie McDonald/FIFA: 169(London), 169br, 171b, 175bl, 175br, 176br, 177t, 177br; /Matt McNulty/FIFA: 273(ball), 273(Lyon), 273(Katoto), 275tr, 278mr, 278br, 280tl, 280ml, 281br, 281bl; /Mark Metcalfe/FIFA: 257ml, 259ml, 261tr; /Maddie Meyer/FIFA: 180, 181br, 184t, 184m, 190tl, 190mr, 190br, 195b, 196mr, 197mr, 197tr, 219t, 225tr, 231bl, 232tl, 233bm, 248, 251(Sydney); 253tl, 255t, 259tl, 262bl; /Pablo Morano/BSR Agency: 246tr; /Cathrin Mueller/FIFA: 217(Bordeaux); /Katelyn Mulcahy/FIFA: 251(Miyazawa), 258b; /Tim Nwachukwu/FIFA: 272mr, 273(Bordeaux), 274b; /Kiyoshi Ota/FIFA: 23ml; /Alex Pantling/FIFA: 250(Bonmati), 251(ball), 257bl, 261ml, 263mr, 266mr, 267br; /Peter Parks/AFP: 144m, 146t; /Doug Pensinger: 101(Philadelphia), 106br; /Hannah Peters/FIFA: 221t, 224br, 260tl; /Jerome Pollex/FIFA: 169(Manchester), 171t, 174tl, 174tr, 176br, 179b, 207tr, 207b, 209bl, 209br, 210tl, 210ml; / Popperfoto: 9b; /Adam Pretty/FIFA: 187b; /Ben Radford: 115(Prinz); /Matt Roberts/FIFA: 265tl, 267ml; /Clive Rose/FIFA: 189bl, 189br, 192m; /Martin Rose/FIFA: 237(Miyagi); /STR/AFP: 143b, 151br; /Ezra Shaw: 106t, 106bl, 114m; /Tim Shaw/FIFA: 251(Melbourne); /Johannes Simon/FIFA: 220m, 222t, 224tl; /Brian Snyder: 77(Sun Wen); /Cameron Spencer: 151tl; /Jamie Squire: 81tl; /Billy Stickland/Allsport: 89br; /Mackenzie Sweetnam/FIFA: 253ml, 261bl; /Bob Thomas: 55b, 72t, 72b; /Pedro Ugarte/AFP: 139bl, 148tl, 148mr; /VCG: 141(Tianjin); /Hector Vivas/FIFA: 237(ball), 237(Kashima), 242mr, 242br, 244ml, 244ml, 245mr, 245bl; /Koji Watanabe: 145b, 147t; /Sebastian Widmann/FIFA: 229tr, 229br
IOC: 5(Olympic emblems), 66(emblem), 90(emblem), 114(emblem), 140(emblem), 168(emblem), 202(emblem), 236(emblem), 236(medals), 272(emblem), 272(medals)
Imago: /ANE Edition: 115(Heraklion); /Stellan Danielsson: 53(Helsingborg); /Sven Simon: 16(Guadalajara); USA Today: 235br
Langton Collection: 8tr, 8bl
National Football Museum, Manchester: 12mr
Deborah Nichols' Private Collection: 29b
Official Programme: 13br, 16mr, 19bl
Offside Sports Photography: /Presse Sports: 10b, 17b
PA Images: /Ritzau: 20bl, 20br, 21ml, 21mr, 21bl, 21br
Private Collection: 12(trophy), 13tr, 14ml, 15tr, 15br, 16(trophy), 19tr, 21tl
Teamfoto: /Foto-net: 124, 125br, 126bl, 127(Tianjin), 127(Chengdu), 127(Wuhan), 127br, 128t, 128b, 129b, 130ml, 130mr, 130b, 131t, 131br, 132tl, 132tr, 132bl, 132br, 133tl, 133tr, 133ml, 133br, 134tl, 134ml, 134mr, 134bl, 135t, 135bl, 135br, 136tr, 136m, 136ml, 136bl, 137tl, 137tr, 137mr, 137bl, 137br, 142b

Every effort has been made to acknowledge correctly and contact the source and/or copyright holder of each picture. Any unintentional errors or omissions will be corrected in future editions of this book.